John Knox's
History of the Reformation
in Scotland

Volume One

John Knox's
History of the Reformation
in Scotland

Edited by
William Croft Dickinson D.Lit.

Volume One

PHILOSOPHICAL LIBRARY
NEW YORK

Published 1950 by the Philosophical Library Inc.
15 East 40th Street, New York, N.Y.

Copyright 1950
by
Thomas Nelson and Sons Ltd

Printed in Great Britain by
Thomas Nelson and Sons Ltd, Edinburgh and London

THIS BOOK IS DEDICATED
TO
MY WIFE

" I see the battle shall be great, for Sathan rageth
even to the uttermost ; and I am come (I praise
my God), even in the brunt of the battle."

" I have been fighting against Sathan, who is ever
ready to assault ; yea, I have fought against
spiritual wickedness in heavenly things and have
prevailed ! "

" What I have been to my country, albeit this
unthankful age will not know, yet the ages to
come will be compelled to bear witness to the
truth."

CONTENTS

VOLUME I

FOREWORD

It is really a loss to English and even to universal literature that Knox's hasty and strangely interesting, impressive, and peculiar Book, called the History of the Reformation in Scotland, *has not been rendered far more extensively legible to serious mankind at large. . . .*—CARLYLE.

WE are told that when one of the Edinburgh booksellers died in 1645, his stock included two hundred *Knoxes Histories*, valued at £317. Those would be copies of the edition brought out by David Buchanan in 1644, for the first (unfinished) edition by Vautrollier (1586–87) had been suppressed and seized.

Since then there have been many editions of *The History of the Reformation of Religion within the Realm of Scotland*, of which that by David Laing, published in 1846–48 for the Wodrow Society and the Bannatyne Club, and forming the first two volumes of his monumental edition of *The Works of John Knox*, is still the best. It was printed from the earliest of the manuscripts (the so-called ' MS. of 1566,' now in the Laing Collection in the library of the University of Edinburgh [1]), and was fortified by notes which only a scholar of David Laing's stature could provide.

Nevertheless, and despite two recent ' popular ' editions, Knox's book, full of life and dramatic power, remains largely unknown. Possibly the ' popular ' editions robbed the book of too much of its essential spirit ; possibly, for all save the student, the careful work of David Laing provided too many ' notes ' and too faithful a transcript of Knox's ' wild and erratic ' orthography.

The present edition strives to follow a middle course. Laing's transcript (corrected here and there from the manuscript) has formed the basis of the text, but the spelling has been modernized throughout.[2] Here, however, it should be noted that in the 1566 Manuscript we sometimes find the English present participle with its final *-ing*,

---

[1] See *infra*, xcv–cix

[2] Even Laing thought it necessary to simplify to some extent the orthography of the manuscript (*cf.* Laing's *Knox*, i, xliii, *note* 1, 15, *note* 2 ; ii, 5, *note* 8). Thus it is dangerous for philologists to rely upon Laing's printed text. Nor, apart from such simplifications, is Laing's text wholly accurate. Usually the inaccuracies in transcription do not affect the historical value of the text ; but in one or two instances, where important inaccuracies have been found, the necessary corrections have been made and an editorial note supplied.

sometimes the Scottish present participle with its final -*and* ; sometimes, in the past participle, we find the Scottish final -*it*, sometimes the English -*ed*. Similarly, in different parts of the manuscript, the same word may take a completely Scottish or a completely English form. We find, for example, *mo*, *mair*, and *more* ; *sic* and *such* ; *maun* and *must* ; *thir* and *these* ; *thai* and *those* ; *quhilk* and *which* ; *anys*, *ones*, and *once*. Moreover, when Knox writes himself, without the intermediary of a scribe (as in his familiar letters), he uses English forms and the ' Scotticisms ' are few and far between. His writing, under influences that are referred to in the Introduction, is English both in diction and in style. Thus the modernization of the spelling should call for no apology—though the modernization of the ' documents,' for the sake of uniformity, although more sparingly carried out, may be open to some criticism. This should be said, however, —and the exception is an important one—those vernacular words which still remain vernacular whatever their spelling may be, have been everywhere retained.

One other liberty has been taken with the text. Certain passages which are not the work of Knox (such as Frith's translation of Patrick Hamilton's treatise, or Foxe's account of the condemnation and martyrdom of George Wishart) and certain ' documents ' (such as the Confession of Faith and the Book of Discipline) have been lifted from the text and given in appendices. Valuable and interesting as they are, in the text they break the narrative ; and it is probable that had Knox been writing his *History* to-day he would have adopted some such rearrangement for himself.

Finally, the Fifth Book, by Knox's continuator,[1] has been included (as it was included by David Laing), not for its value, which is slight, but because it continues the story from 1564 to the deposition of Mary Queen of Scots in 1567.

In no respect does this claim to be a critical edition of one of our greatest ' Histories.' Yet as one of our greatest ' Histories ' Knox's book should be more widely read and understood. Thus the Introduction, sadly restricted for a theme so complicated, and perforce unable fully to take into account the international aspects of the Reformation movement, has been written for the general reader to provide a general background of the ' Movement,' the ' Man,' and the ' Book ' ; the notes appended to the text are mainly explanatory.[2]

[1] See *infra*, xciii–xcv

[2] Book V, not being the work of Knox, has been supplied with fewer explanatory notes than Books I–IV.

My indebtedness to the work of previous scholars is so apparent that acknowledgment would be superfluous. In particular I have taken full advantage of David Laing's notes and of a number of additional notes made by Hay Fleming in his own copy of Laing's edition now in the Hay Fleming Memorial Library at St. Andrews.

To avoid overburdening the text, biographical details have been provided in the Index.

It only remains for me to record the help I have received from willing friends. Dr. Gordon Donaldson and Miss Gladys Dickinson have read through all the proofs and have made many valuable suggestions. On certain points relating to the topography and antiquities of Edinburgh I have received the expert guidance of Dr. Marguerite Wood. The Index reflects the care and accuracy of Dr. J. C. Corson ; and the heavy task of correcting the proofs has been more than halved by the kind collaboration of Mr. James A. Smellie. Finally, Mr. Peter Morrison and the staff of Messrs. Thomas Nelson and Sons have amply proved that when there is full co-operation between the author and the publisher, the author alone is to blame for the faults of his book.

W. CROFT DICKINSON.

EDINBURGH
August 1947

INTRODUCTION

I

THE Scottish ' Reformation ' was not solely an ' uproar for religion.' It is true that the Roman Church, degenerate and corrupt, was despised and contemned, and that new questionings were being answered by a new faith ; but other factors were also at work—a ' murmuring ' of the people, the ' avarice ' of temporal lords, the ambitions of a noble house and, dominating all, the interplay of politics whereby a reformation in religion became a rebellion against the State.

The decay in the Roman Church is attested by its own historians. A Church whose servants had at one time sought ' religion and its increase ' was now ill-served. Its priests were ignorant and its prelates lax. Preaching was almost unknown. Successive Provincial Councils of the Scottish Church had passed enactments in which the clergy were enjoined to preach ' the word of God to the people '—for ' the little ones have asked for bread and there was none to break it unto them '—but the very necessity for re-enactment proved that the injunctions were of small effect. The sermon by Gavin Dunbar, " They say that we should preach : why not ? Better late thrive than never thrive. Have us still for your Bishop, and we shall provide better for the next time," [1] may be unfairly reported, but when, in 1552, in view of the ' urgent duty of preaching,' John Hamilton, Archbishop of St. Andrews, had prepared a Catechism *in the Scottish tongue*,[2] it was still deemed necessary to insist upon ' constant, frequent, and daily rehearsal of the lesson to be read ' lest the clergy should expose themselves to the ridicule of their hearers by stammering and stuttering in the mid-course of their reading.

Yet even if divine observance had become a mystery not wholly spiritual, ignorance alone might have been overcome had not greed

---

[1] *Infra*, i, 61. Double " quotes " are used to indicate Knox's own words.

[2] Although usually known as ' Archbishop Hamilton's Catechism,' the authorship has been ascribed by tradition to John Winram, Subprior of the Augustinian monastery at St. Andrews, who later joined the Reformers, and who had a large share in drafting the Confession of Faith and the [First] Book of Discipline. (But see the interesting query in A. F. Mitchell's facsimile edition of the *Catechism*, Intro., xvii)

and corruption followed hand in hand. The wealth and privileges of the Church were not slow to attract intruders moved by self-interest. Politics, faction, avarice and ambition all became factors in the appointment of men wholly unsuitable for holy office, while the needs of the Church and the people were forgotten and passed by. Revenues were 'devoured in luxury,' duties were 'forgotten,' and even the very buildings of the Church were allowed to fall into ruin and decay.[1] Therein popes and princes were alike to blame. The endeavours of the Councils to check the 'reservations' and 'provisions' of the popes [2] had been followed by a series of compromises in which, in face of a rising tide of nationalism, the popes began to share with kings the 'provision' to vacant benefices. And one such compromise had been made with Scotland when, by an Indult of 1487, King James III was granted the privilege of recommending, for appointment by the Pope, those persons who would be 'thankful to his Highness.' Admittedly the King could claim an interest in the promotion of men who, by virtue of their promotion, had voice in Council and in Parliament; but 'recommendation' soon gave way to nomination, and an interest in promotion soon became the interests of the royal policy or purse.[3] High office in the Church became a valuable part of the royal patronage, whereby rewards and favours could take the form of some rich living plenteously endowed by the piety of the past; and abbeys and priories became the gifts of God for younger sons, or for illegitimate sons of the royal house, even for illegitimate sons who were still in infancy. Whatever corruption in appointment there had been before, bishoprics and abbacies were now regarded solely for the revenues they would yield and not for the services they should perform—a position that was rendered doubly clear when, in 1543, after the death of James V, Parliament calmly decided that once a reasonable sustentation had been provided for the late King's illegitimate sons the surplus revenues of the abbeys and priories they enjoyed should be assigned to the finances of the Crown. In brief, in a poor country, with a poor soil and with a still primitive trade and commerce,

---

[1] *Cf. infra*, xviii

[2] Proceeding on the doctrine that every ecclesiastical benefice was in theory at the disposal of the Pope, successive popes had extended a system whereby they 'reserved' benefices to which they themselves would 'provide' upon a vacancy. Then, as corruption grew, so bargaining between rival candidates tended to make the Papal Curia little more than a money-market in which lucrative offices were bought and sold.

[3] See the excellent summary of the whole development in R. K. Hannay, *The Scottish Crown and the Papacy, 1424–1560* (Hist. Assoc. of Scot., Pamphlets, New Series, No. 6).

the Church had become the easiest, if not the only avenue to wealth.

Nor did the evil end there.   While a Church which enjoyed ' almost half the revenue of the whole kingdom ' [1] had thus become largely laicised in its higher ranks, laicism had been encouraged by earlier ' appropriations ' whereby the wealth of monasteries and cathedral seats had been increased at the expense of the local services to the local community.   More than half the parish churches within the realm had been ' assigned ' or ' appropriated ' to bishoprics or monasteries, when, after the lowest possible stipend had been paid to a vicar, the remaining revenues of the appropriated church went to swell the income of the monastery or the chapter, or, it might be, even to provide delicacies for the bishop's table.   Through pluralism, other churches had no priests at all, so that spiritual guidance was wholly lacking. [2]   Yet payments to the Church which once were voluntary were now demanded as of right [3] ;   when all too frequently an inordinate wealth was applied to the satisfaction of worldly desires. The sheep looked up and were not fed, for now the shepherds' only care was to find pasture for themselves.

Not unnaturally, wealth and ease of office soon bred corruption. ' The carnally promoted led carnal lives and suffered others to live carnally.'   The wealth originally bestowed upon the Church was indeed ' the offspring of a truly pious sentiment,' but piety, the mother, was smothered by ' luxury, the wanton daughter.'   The works of Dunbar and Lyndsay are eloquent of the ' corruption in morals and profane lewdness of life in churchmen of almost all ranks ' together with their ' crass ignorance '—and those are the very words of the clergy themselves when, in a Provincial Council of 1549, they sought the reasons for the fallen state of their Church.

---

[1] So wrote Cardinal Sermoneta to Pope Paul IV in 1556 (Pollen, *Papal Negotiations with Mary Queen of Scots*, Scot. Hist. Soc., 528) ; and it is to be noted that in national taxations in the period preceding the Reformation the clergy contributed one-half, the barons one-third, and the burghs one-sixth.   Dr. Donaldson's calculation for his edition of the Collectors' Accounts of the Thirds of the Benefices (shortly to be published by the Scottish History Society) is that ' the total annual revenues of the Church on the eve of the Reformation must have been substantially in excess of £300,000,' when the royal lands brought in only some £17,500.

[2] Apologists might argue that those within the service of the Church were many ; and that it was the *poverty* of individual ' livings ' (often through their ' assignment ' to monasteries or cathedral chapters) that led to pluralism.   There was also great inequality in ' livings.'   Probably the answer is twofold : not only was the Church too wealthy, but also it included too many within its ranks.

[3] Notably the mortuary dues which pressed heavily upon the poor. (See Hay Fleming, *Reformation in Scotland*, 157–159)

The statutes of 1549, with their denunciations of concubinage and of the promotion and dowering of the illegitimate children of spiritual men, are an official condemnation supporting contemporary unofficial comment [1]; but their repetition in 1559 proves that they were words and little more, while the private lives of the enactors gave the lie to their enactments. If the association of Cardinal Beaton with Marion Ogilvy was notorious,[2] so was the association of his successor, John Hamilton, with Lady Grizell Sempill; if Beaton had certainly eight illegitimate children, Hamilton's " holiness " was dismissed by Knox with the comment that the world knew how many wives and virgins he had enjoyed, " albeit not all," though " his bastard birds bear some witness." [3] Moreover, the recognition of abuse and the endeavours to reform came too late. No Scottish Provincial Council appears to have met between 1470 and 1536 ; no official attempt at reform from within appears to have been made until 1549 ; Hamilton's *Catechism* was not published until 1552 ; and the *Twopenny Faith* did not appear until the spring of 1559. In the words of Lord Hailes, ' When a house is in flames, it is vain to draw up regulations for the bridling of joists or the sweeping of chimneys.'

The Catholic historian Lesley, writing in the second half of the sixteenth century, was not slow to attribute this corruption in the Church to promotions made solely upon a royal supplication to the Pope : but the cancer, though undoubtedly hastened thereby, was not of recent or sudden growth ; its roots were many and all deep-seated in the past. As early as 1425 James I had charged the Benedictine and Augustinian houses to shake off their sloth, for everywhere monastic religion was in disgrace, abbots were dissolute and monks disorderly. Earlier still, a secretary to a Pope had written of ' ignorant and useless men,' of ' churches in ruins,' and of cardinals who ' devoured their revenues in luxury and neglected their duty.' [4] Or, to return to Scotland, in 1456 a chaplain at Linlithgow was required, upon appointment, to bind himself with sureties that he

---

[1] Though they by no means provide a full picture of the corruption and nepotism within the Church. They are silent, for example, in relation to the many financial transactions governing the fruits of benefices—' transactions which took place entirely without regard to the sacred functions pertaining to the offices concerned.' (*St. Andrews Formulare*, Stair Soc., ii, xvi)

[2] *Infra*, i, 76   [3] *Infra*, i, 59

[4] Nicolas de Clémanges, Secretary to Benedict XIII, quoted in A. R. MacEwen, *History of the Church in Scotland*, i, 302. And it should be stressed that the corruption in the Church was widespread throughout western Christendom : Scotland was neither exceptional nor alone.

would neither pawn the sacred books, plate, and vestments, nor maintain a ' continual concubine.' [1]

Exceptions there were, among both prelates and priests.[2] Men like Myln of Cambuskenneth, Elphinstone of Aberdeen, Crystall and Reid of Kinloss, were earnest in their endeavours for reform ; later still, some, like John Winram, went over to the Protestant cause and endowed it with their talents. In St. Andrews, Archbishop Forman (a good administrator, if nothing else) drew up new Synodal Constitutions and Ordinances. Some compromise, too, becomes apparent. Hamilton's *Catechism* significantly omits all reference to the Pope (and the Reformers had long held that the Pope was no Vicar of Christ on earth), while a moving passage on Faith [3] reads much like an echo of Luther's cry that, ' If a Christian has Faith, he has everything. . . . Faith unites Man to God,' and much like a justification of the tenets for which Patrick Hamilton had been burned.[4] But in view of Archbishop Hamilton's private life the people were not to be blamed if they had some regard to *works* as well as *faith* ; while the exceptional men had long been too few and their efforts too localized. Moreover, even those who recognized the corruption in their midst were still determined that the Church must be its own physician. Quintin Kennedy, alarmed by the ' pestilent preachers ' of the new faith, could recognize the evils and corruption in the Church—

> See we not daily, by experience, if a benefice be vacant the great men of the realm will have it for temporal reward. . . . And when they have got the benefice, if they have a brother, or a son,—yea, suppose he can neither sing nor say,—nourished in vice all his days, forthwith he shall be mounted on a mule, with a side-gown and a round bonnet, and then it is a question whether he or his mule knows best to do his office. Perchance Balaam's ass knew more than both of them ! . . . And not only such men have crept into the Kirk by means of some wicked great personages ; but thou mayest see daily, likewise by experience, a bairn and a babe, to whom scarcely would thou give

---

[1] P. Lorimer, *Life of Patrick Hamilton*, App. V, ii

[2] That scholarship was by no means lacking despite the general corruption and decay is manifest from the ' Bibliography ' in W. Forbes Leith, *Pre-Reformation Scholars in Scotland in the Sixteenth Century* (though that list is not wholly trustworthy) ; and that the Church could still take an interest in public works, in the development of agriculture, and in the social life of the people is clear from the accounts of Dunkeld during the episcopate of George Browne. (See *Rentale Dunkeldense, 1505–1517*, Scot. Hist. Soc.)

[3] *Hamilton's Catechism* (facsimile edn. by A. F. Mitchell), folios xciii–xciv

[4] *Infra*, Appendix I

a fair apple to keep, get perchance five thousand souls to guide. And all for avarice, ' the root of all vice,' that their parents may get the profit of the benefice. . . . The convent and place where God should be daily honoured and served goes clean to ruin . . . the poor simple people, so dearly bought by the blood and death of Jesus Christ our Saviour, miserably perish ; the Kirk is slandered ; God is dishonoured ; all heresies, wickedness and vice reign. . . .

but, even while remaining silent on the Pope and Rome, he could admit reform only by the appointed ministers and rulers of the Church. To Kennedy, reformation must be orderly ; no man may usurp authority ; authority pertains to the rulers and ministers of the Church, even though they may be ' vicious ' ; and a vicious life does not deprive the rulers of authority, for their authority is of God.[1]

Thus the people saw themselves under the spiritual rule of a wealthy Church whose worldly servants abused Christ's patrimony. The living Church was dying from slow corruption ; and men made no distinction between the Church and those who served it. So, in one respect, the Reformation movement was anti-clerical—a revolt of the people against the ' unhonesty and misrule of kirkmen both in wit, knowledge, and manners.' [2] And that revolt, gaining impetus from the discovery of printing, became more than anti-clerical ; it became anti-sacerdotal.

In the past the hold of the Church had been buttressed by fear, by ignorance and by need—a fear of the world to come, an ignorance of the way to salvation, and a need for the intercession of the Church. The Church was deemed to hold the keys of Heaven and of Hell, and thereby it could play upon men's minds by the alternations of fear and hope, of terror and of consolation. Men might be denied all access to the Word ; but men must still believe in the efficacy of the saints, their relics and their miracles. Yet now, a new spirit was in the air—a spirit of eager curiosity and a desire to know the truth in this as in all things else. Out of that spirit was born the art of printing, and printing gave it increase.

This new power in the hands of men was brought to Scotland

---

[1] See *Ane Compendius Tractive*, 1558 (in *Wodrow Soc. Misc.*, i, 122, 136–137, 151–152). The spelling has been modernized. In one place Knox himself admits that there may be " evil-livers" in the " true Kirk," but argues that their " life and conversation " is " no assured note, sign, or token of Christ's visible Kirk." (Laing's *Knox*, iv, 266–267)

[2] The words of the Scottish Parliament in 1541 when striving to secure the reform of abuses that had brought the Church into contempt. (*Acts Parl. Scot.*, ii, 370, *c.* 4)

in 1507 ; in 1508 Chepman and Myllar 'imprinted' their first book in the Southgate of Edinburgh ; and by 1543 'divers prentaris' were pouring forth a veritable flood of books, pamphlets and broadsides which were to give shape to doubts and questionings hitherto half-formed and dimly apperceived. In 1543 we hear of 'slanderous bills, writings, ballads, and books' daily written and printed to the defamation of all estates both spiritual and temporal. In 1549 the Provincial Council of the Church denounced the books of rhymes and popular songs containing infamous libels, calumnies and slanders defamatory of the Church and churchmen. In 1552 Parliament endeavoured to institute a censorship of the many ballads, songs, blasphemies and rhymes concerning the faith. But it was impossible to stop the flood. Unfortunately no contemporary copy of these early rhymes has come down to us, though Knox has preserved one of them in his *History*.[1] The sheets may well have been worn to shreds in passing from hand to hand. It may be assumed, however, that some of them found a place in the collection of *Gude and Godlie Ballatis* made by the brothers Wedderburn of Dundee,[2] and if so, we have there an indication of their nature. Most of the ballads in the Wedderburn collection are purely spiritual, setting forth 'with fond affection and winning simplicity the great truths of the Gospel' ; many are metrical versions of the Psalms ; while others again take popular songs, and give them a spiritual 'twist,' as in

> Johne, cum kis me now,
> Johne, cum kis me now ;
> Johne, cum kis me by and by
> And mak no moir adow.
> The Lord thy God I am,
>   That Johne dois thé call ;
> Johne representit man,
>   Be [3] grace celestiall.

Some few, however, are plain and outspoken lampoons on the Church and its priests,[4] of which the most famous is that beginning, 'The

---

[1] *Infra*, Appendix X

[2] These *Gude and Godlie Ballatis* are of varying date, but certain of them were undoubtedly in circulation in the fourth and fifth decades of the sixteenth century.

[3] *by*

[4] In Germany, likewise, the press had furthered the Reformation. A new literature had sprung up which flagellated Rome and the monastic orders in terms both rude and coarse. With virulent satire, however, went also Luther's hymns which became national songs, and of which *Ein feste Burg ist unser Gott* has been described as the *Marseillaise* of the Reformation in Germany. It is tempting to think that the Scottish

Paip, that pagane full of pryde,' and which contains among its verses :

> The blind Bischop he culd nocht preiche,
>> For playing with the lassis ;
> The syllie Freir behuffit to fleiche,[1]
>> For almous that he assis [2] ;
> The Curat his creid he culd nocht reid,
>> Schame fall the cumpanie :
> Hay trix, tryme go trix,
>> Under the grene wod tree.

And criticism and ridicule of this nature reached its height in Lyndsay's *Satyre of the Thrie Estatis* [3] which has been so often cited that one brief excerpt will suffice to indicate the outspokenness of its attack :

ABBOT

> Tuiching my office, I say to yow plainlie,
> My monks and I, we leif [4] richt easelie :
> There is na monks, from Carrick to Carraill,
> That fairs better, and drinks mair helsum aill.[5]
> My Prior is ane man of great devotioun :
> Thairfor, daylie, he gets ane double portioun.

SCRYBE

> My Lords, how have ye keipt your thrie vows ?

ABBOT

> Indeid richt weill, till I gat hame my bows.[6]
> In my Abbay, quhen I was sure professour,
> Then did I leife,[4] as did my predecessour.
> My paramours is baith als fat and fair,
> As ony wench, intill the toun of Air.

songs and ballads took their inspiration from Germany. Significantly, John Wedderburn had been in Germany and, according to Calderwood, ' translated manie of Luther's dytements into Scotish meeter, and the Psalmes of David ' (*History of the Kirk of Scotland*, i, 142–143). Moreover, the Wedderburns were ' of Dundee ' ; Dundee and Aberdeen were the main ports for trade with the Low Countries ; and both burghs were known to be centres from which Lutheran literature was disseminated.

[1] *behoved to flatter*   [2] *alms that he begs*

[3] Again it is difficult to say when the *Satyre* was written ; but we know that it was performed before James V, his Queen, and the Lords of Council, spiritual and temporal, on 6 January 1540.

[4] *live*   [5] *wholesome ale*   [6] *received my [papal] Bulls*

I send my sons to Pareis, to the scuillis,
I traist in God that thay sall be na fuillis.
And all my douchters, I have weill provydit,
Now, judge ye, gif my office be weill gydit.

SCRYBE

Maister Person, schaw us gif ye can preich ?

PERSON

Thocht [1] I preich not, I can play at the caiche [2] :
I wait [3] thair is nocht ane amang yow all,
Mair ferilie [4] can play at the fut-ball ;
And for the carts, the tabils, and the dyse,[5]
Above all persouns, I may beir the pryse.[6]

All this simply put into words what the people saw around them every day. It confirmed their homely proverbs : ' Priests and doos [7] mak foul houses ' ; or ' Nae penny, nae paternoster.' Opposed to it (for Lyndsay, while pouring scorn upon the Church, had no ' sermon of exhortation ') were the new devotional and spiritual songs, or, in prose, John Gau's rendering of *The Richt Vay to the Kingdom of Hevine*.

Yet inasmuch as the Word of God had been denied so was it the more desired. Men were yearning to know ' the unsearchable riches of Christ,' and the Gospel, when heard, fell like rain upon a thirsty land. The cry arose, ' Let us eagerly know the Gospel,' a cry to be quickly followed by another, ' Let us not only know, but live the Gospel.' But while knowledge had hitherto been limited by the fewness of the manuscript copies in the vulgar tongue,[8] now the art of printing came once more to meet a need that could scarce be satisfied. As early as 1525 Parliament had forbidden ' strangers ' to bring with them into the realm any Lutheran books or works ; in 1527 the Lords of Council deemed it necessary to extend the provisions of the Act to any of the King's own lieges who were ' assisters to ' Lutheran opinions ; and in that latter year there is evidence that copies of Tyndale's New Testament were reaching Scotland, probably in considerable numbers, through the eastern

---

[1] *Though*   [2] *catch-ball*   [3] *know*   [4] *wonderfully*
[5] *cards, tables for games or gaming, and dice*   [6] *bear the prize*   [7] *pigeons*
[8] See *The New Testament in Scots*, being Purvey's revision of Wycliffe's version turned into Scots by Murdoch Nisbet, *circa* 1520 (edited, T. G. Law, Scot. Text Soc.), and the review of that work in *Scottish Historical Review*, i, 260–273.

ports. A new belief in faith began to course through men's veins like new wine. Faith made 'God and Man friends'; it brought 'God and Man together.' [1] And for that new belief in faith, Patrick Hamilton was burned at St. Andrews in 1528. [2]

The martyrdom of Patrick Hamilton, young, noble, related to the King, and of blameless life, 'left the verity and truth of God more fixed and confirmed in the hearts of many than ever could after be plucked away.' To Knox, it was the first Act in the drama of the Scottish Reformation—for " the reek of Master Patrick Hamilton infected as many as it blew upon." [3] Now Knox begins to give us a tragic list of the Scottish martyrs ; now heresy-hunting becomes a preoccupation of the Church ; now, in the south-west, the parishioners of a certain town, prompted by their 'Lutheran' opinions and their reading of the New Testament, have decapitated a statue of the Blessed Virgin, while in the north-east, in Aberdeen, two men have been found guilty of 'hanging' an image of St. Francis.

But already there is more than an attack on the wealth and corruption of the Church. With the reading and the knowledge of the Word of God there arises a desire for a new Church, a Church pure and undefiled, a Church free from man-made ceremony and invention. The authority of the Pope, the " idolatry " of the Mass, the adoration of the Virgin and the invocation of Saints were all to be swept away. Such had been the articles of the ' Lollards of Kyle ' as early as 1494 [4]; such were the articles of John Knox in 1547. And where was the assurance of the Word of God for the ceremonies of the Roman Church, or for those works of man's invention— " pilgrimage, pardons, and other such baggage " ? [5]

But we are moving too fast. By 1545 ' heresy ' had become so prevalent that it was deemed ' doubtsome to punish by the law'; yet, in 1546, Master George Wishart, " that blessed martyr of God," was taken and burned. [6] Three months later, Cardinal Beaton, accused " of the shedding of the blood of that notable instrument of God," was surprised and killed in his castle at St. Andrews. And within a fortnight of his death the Privy Council found it necessary to pass an Act against the ' invasion ' and ' despoiling ' of abbeys and other religious houses.

The ' invasion ' of monastic houses and churches, and the ' away-taking ' of the ' jewels and ornaments of the kirk ' might be a ' purging of the churches of their monuments of idolatry,' but a movement

[1] See ' Patrick's Places ' (infra, Appendix I)   [2] Infra, i, 12–14   [3] Infra, i, 18
[4] Infra, i, 8–9   [5] Infra, i, 85, 87   [6] Infra, i, 67–74, and Appendix III

for reform could include more than those who condemned old
'baggage' or who had found a new faith.   It could include those
who had an eye to the wealth of a dying Church and an interest in
its death-bed property.   Already James V, good Catholic as he was,
had shown that the wealth of the Church might be tapped for
secular purposes [1]; already, too, the sons of noble houses, as prelates
or as commendators, [2] had tasted the fruits of spiritual office, and had
not denied a further taste to the members of their families. [3]   But
now there were some among the nobility who looked greedily upon
the lands which pious ancestors had too fondly given away for the
weal of their souls, and which now appeared to serve only the weal
of a bishop's children, or the fare of an abbot's table.   And upon
the admission that the Mass secured not remission of sins to the
quick and the dead, the lords were prompt to ask, " Why were the
Abbeys so richly endowed with our temporal lands ? " [4]   So, if some
of the nobility were moved by a new faith, others were moved by
old foundations and with calculating minds thought of the wealth
that might again be theirs.   Within the burghs, where the merchants
suffered from the trading privileges and exemptions granted to the
Church of old, [5] new economic ideas were stirring.   The burgess-
economists condemned the Church as a consumer of hard-won
wealth—a consumer but never a producer—and with that came
the wonder whether some redistribution of spiritual wealth for pro-
ductive purposes might not be advantageous to the commonwealth. [6]
To the poor, and they were many, there were neither doubts nor
difficulties : the wealth of the friaries consisted of endowments for

[1] Notably in the financial arrangements following the foundation of the College of
Justice. (See R. K. Hannay, *The College of Justice*, 51–58)
[2] That is, holding monastic houses *in commendam* (or, in trust), an arrangement under
which the commendator drew the bulk of the revenues while the spiritual office was
performed by another on his behalf.
[3] For example, when a Gordon was Bishop of Aberdeen there were many assedations
of church lands and revenues to members of the Gordon family ; when a Leslie was
Abbot of Lindores there were similar diversions of abbey lands to the Leslies.
[4] *Infra*, i, 353–354
[5] More than that, many of the clergy were ' not ashamed to busy themselves hiring
farms and estates ' or to occupy themselves ' in trafficking with cattle, fish, hides, and
the like.' (Pollen, *Papal Negotiations with Mary Queen of Scots*, Scot. Hist. Soc., 530)
[6] It is interesting to note that in Aberdeen, for example, when the ' uproar for religion '
came, the burgesses were careful to preserve the fabric of their church of St. Nicholas,
but ordained that the silver work and ornaments should be rouped, and the money applied
to the ' common weal and necessary adoes of this good town.' (*Extracts from the Council
Register of Aberdeen*, Spalding Club, i, 323, 329–331). Later, in 1562, it was agreed that the
proceeds should be applied, *inter alia*, to the renovation of the quay and the Brig of Don.
(*Ibid.*, i, 344)

the poor ; it was theirs of right ; and in the ' Beggars' Summonds ' they demanded early entry to an inheritance of which they had been falsely deprived whereby many of them had been left to perish and to die.[1] In the end, in every rank of society, ' every man . . . that could get anything pertaining to any kirkmen thought the same as well won gear.' [2]

In such a setting, the Reformation was a revolution : a rising of the people against the Church. Moreover the time was one of change. The bonds of mediaevalism were breaking : old values were being questioned, new ideas were in the air ; feudalism was dying, and a new ' money economy ' had been born ; power was passing to the many from the few. The burghs, independent self-governing communities which had long resisted the local lord, were now beginning to play a larger part in the affairs of the realm. To landward, the smaller barons, the ' lairds,' were gaining political consciousness. In 1557 the Queen Regent found that while ' les grands ' supported her policy, ' la noblesse ' sided with ' le peuple,' and, with them, formed ' la commune ' which opposed her ; and in 1558 Knox addressed the *Commonalty of Scotland* in a *Letter* separate from his *Appellation* to the *Nobility and the Estates*.[3] Later, and as a direct result of the impetus of the Reformation, an English agent could report in 1572, ' Methinks I see the noblemen's great credit decay . . . and the barons, boroughs and such-like take more upon them ' ; while in 1585, these self-same ' barons ' were willing to make a ' handsome contribution ' to James VI for the right to a vote and representation in Parliament—a right which, when it had been freely offered by James I in 1428, had been unaccepted and unexercised. The peasant class, the ' poor labourers of the soil,' though suffering under many a burden, had long evinced a virility unknown in other lands. In the *Complaynt of Scotlande* the poor labourer declares himself ' ane notabil membyr of ane realme,' and those were almost the exact words used by Knox when Mary, asking, " What have ye to do with my marriage ? Or what are ye within this Commonwealth ? " received the quick reply, " A subject born within the same, Madam. And albeit I neither be Earl, Lord, nor Baron within it, yet has God made me (how abject that ever

---

[1] *Infra*, Appendix V

[2] *Diurnal of Occurrents* (Bannatyne Club), 269

[3] His argument, running throughout that *Letter*, that, " in the hope of the life to come " God " hath made all equal " (Laing's *Knox*, iv, 526–534), is significant in the light of the later argument in the Book of Discipline.

I be in your eyes) a profitable member within the same." [1] As
one commentator has observed, ' Modern Democracy was born in
that answer.' The ' independence of the Scot ' had been nurtured
in a long struggle against the stronger England, and in a continuing
struggle against nature and the poverty of the land ; but now men
were becoming conscious of a new individuality and, with that, of
their equality before God.

In a time of change, and also in a time of rising prices due to
the influx of silver from the New World, nobles and commons alike
looked questioningly at the wealth of a Church which had declined
in devotion as it had increased in licentiousness. The Church was
fat with the wealth of the land, but, with a spiritual hold that was
failing fast, it could protect its wealth only with the secular support
of the State. Admittedly, through their influence in the councils of
the king the clergy might mould the policy of the state ; but already
the nobles, the ' born councillors ' of the realm, were becoming
distrustful of their fellow councillors. And how often, and for how
long had Scottish kings been able to assert an authority in opposition
to their nobility ? Yet, as Cardinal Beaton was quick to see, if the
Church was to maintain its hold, it was vital for it to secure the
continuance of the ' auld alliance ' with Roman Catholic France
and the continuance of the old antipathy to an England which,
under Henry VIII, had broken with Rome. The maintenance of
the old alliance and the safety of the old Kirk went together ; and
because of that, the rebellion against the Church became also a
rebellion against the State.

Thus, in the crisis of the struggle, the " Protestants of the Realm
of Scotland " took " the sword of just defence," not only for " Christ
Jesus his glorious Evangel," but also for " the liberty of this our
native country to remain free from the bondage and tyranny of
strangers." [2] And those ' strangers ' were the French. In pursuance
of old policies, Scotland had welcomed an army from France to aid
her in expelling an army from England ; and thereby a moral in
Æsop's Fables seemed likely to be proved.

The destructive invasions of Scotland by the Earl of Hertford
in 1544 and 1545 [3] were partly ' actions for breach of promise,' [4]
partly an ' English wooing ' to bully Scotland into marrying her

---

[1] *Infra*, ii, 83   [2] *Infra*, i, 146   [3] *Infra*, i, 56–59
[4] For, under Beaton's influence, Scotland had repudiated the Treaties of Greenwich
(1543) under which the infant Mary Queen of Scots was to marry Edward (later
Edward VI), the son of Henry VIII.

daughter to a suitor of England's choosing, and partly an attempt to persuade Scotland that peace with England was preferable to an alliance with France.[1] The death of Henry VIII in January 1547 saw no change in English policy. Hertford, now Duke of Somerset and ' Protector ' of England, continued the policy of rough ' wooing ' and, whatever may have been the chances of a new alignment between Scotland and England, the campaign of 1547, which concluded with the Battle of Pinkie,[2] literally drove Scotland into the arms of France. Following Pinkie, the English seized and fortified Haddington, to use it as a strategic base ; and also, following Pinkie, Scotland appealed to France for aid. The appeal was answered. The French troops came. But there were conditions. By the Treaty of Haddington (July, 1548) the child-queen Mary was to marry the Dauphin Francis, and Henry II, King of France, was to ' keep and defend ' the realm of Scotland in its liberties and laws. The old policy of the old alliance was buttressed by faction and by fear. So was ' everything put into the hands of the King of France '[3] ; so was Mary sent to France for her safety and her eventual marriage ; but also, in the words of Knox, " so was she sold to go to France, to the end that in her youth she should drink of that liquor [Roman Catholicism] that should remain with her all her lifetime, for a plague to this realm and for her final destruction." [4]

A combined Franco-Scottish army compelled the English to withdraw from Haddington ; in 1550 Scotland was included in the Treaty of Boulogne between England and France ; but, and more important still, Henry II of France had realized all his hopes. The English had wasted their strength in the Lothians of Scotland ; the French had regained Boulogne ; and, as early as December 1549, Henry had been speaking of ' maintaining the Kingdom of Scotland in the obedience of our son.'

By the Treaty of Boulogne the English forces vacated the Scottish strongpoints they still held ; but the French forces stayed on. Later, in 1554, the Queen-Mother, Mary of Guise, succeeded the Earl of Arran in the Regency of Scotland, and at once high offices were

---

[1] For with the consolidation of France under Louis XI and Louis XII, with the rise of the vast empire of Charles V, and with the virtual isolation of England, following the divorce of Catherine of Aragon, it was more than ever necessary for Henry VIII to be sure of his northern flank.

[2] *Infra*, i, 98–101

[3] The Queen-Mother's own words (Teulet, *Relations Politiques*, i, 179)

[4] *Infra*, i, 103

assigned to Frenchmen,[1] and Frenchmen possessed the Regent's ear. The French began to think themselves " more than masters in all parts of Scotland "[2]; and when, in 1558, the fifteen-year old Mary Queen of Scots, still absent in France, was married to the Dauphin, and the ancient crown of Scotland was sent to France to be placed on the Dauphin's head, it appeared as though French ascendancy was complete, and that the passing of time alone would bring Scotland to the status of a province of France.[3] Even the recent indulgence of Mary of Guise towards the Protestants brought thinking men to ask how far a French Queen Regent was simply seeking a united Scotland to further the political aims of an imperialistic France.

But if the Queen Regent ' neglected almost all the Scots nobility,' certain of the neglected nobility gravitated to the side of the Reformers. The Band, or Covenant, of 1557, " to maintain, set forward, and establish the most blessed word of God and his Congregation," was signed, among others, by the Earl of Argyll and his son, and by the Earls of Morton and Glencairn.[4] The Band, in its wording, was wholly religious ; but thereafter, as Knox admits, " the Lords and Barons professing Christ Jesus convened frequently in council," and their discussions touched the ' policy ' in addition to ' religion.'[5] However much the Reformers might declare that as for " the Policy, mind we to meddle no further than it hath Religion mixed with it,"[6] it had become hopelessly impossible to divorce religion from politics. Significantly the Reformers' first *Petition* to the Queen Regent prayed for a " public reformation as well in the religion as in the temporal government."[7]

Not merely was an old hatred of England already undermined by a new fear of French designs and policy, but, if England were to be Protestant, might not the Protestants of Scotland look to England for support ? Nor was the Queen Regent long left unaware that a ' band ' under the new name of a ' convenant ' was much like former baronial bands that had darkened the annals of Scottish kings. In July 1558, when, on the urgent demand of the clergy, she " summoned the preachers," the " Gentlemen of the West " assembled together and, pressing into the " very privy chamber where the Queen Regent and the bishops were," declared :

---

[1] And it is important to note that they were men of experience and distinction, well-trained in diplomacy and war.   [2] *Infra*, i, 104

[3] And had not the independence of Britanny been lost by the marriage of its heiress Anne to a King of France ?

[4] *Infra*, i, 136–137   [5] *Infra*, i, 137–138   [6] *Infra*, i, 6, 42   [7] *Infra*, i, 149

' Madam, we know that this is the malice and device of those jefwells [1] and of that bastard (meaning the Bishop of Saint Andrews) [2] that stand by you. We avow to God we shall make a day of it. They oppress us and our tenants for feeding of their idle bellies ; they trouble our preachers, and would murder them and us. Shall we suffer this any longer ? No, Madam. It shall not be.' *And therewith every man put on his steel bonnet.* [3]

But, for the Queen Regent also, politics and religion were inextricably interwoven. Compromise was imperative. France and Spain were at war. England, under Mary Tudor, now married to Philip II of Spain, had declared war on France. If Scotland were to be of help to France, it was vital to avoid internal disaffection. The " day of summons " was discharged, but therewith, and naturally so, " began the brethren universally to be further encouraged."

In this atmosphere of gathering storm, Mary Tudor died and was succeeded by Elizabeth. But Elizabeth was the daughter of Anne Boleyn of the bright eyes, and to the whole of Roman Catholic Europe Elizabeth was neither legitimate daughter of Henry VIII nor legitimate heir to the English throne. If the Roman Church could not recognize the divorce of Catherine of Aragon, Roman Catholic Europe was bound to recognize Mary Stewart, Queen of Scots and Dauphiness of France, as the rightful successor to the English crown. [4] Within two months of Elizabeth's accession, Francis and Mary, King and Queen of Scotland, and the future King and Queen of France, had assumed the title of King and Queen of England and Ireland. The policy of France was clear. England, as all men knew, was weak and unprepared. [5] If Scotland could be firmly secured, might not the fall of England follow ? For one brief

[1] *low-down rascals* (the bishops)

[2] John Hamilton, Archbishop of St. Andrews, was an illegitimate son of James, first Earl of Arran.

[3] *Infra*, i, 126. The italics are mine.

[4] Henry VIII had left three children—Mary Tudor, by Catherine of Aragon ; Edward VI, by Jane Seymour ; and Elizabeth by Anne Boleyn. Edward VI and Mary Tudor had reigned and died. Elizabeth's title rested on the validity of a Parliamentary enactment as compared with ' the divine right of inheritance ' under which Mary Stewart, legitimate descendant of the marriage of James IV with Margaret Tudor, the daughter of Henry VII, could claim the English throne. (See the Table, *infra*, ii, 352) But Elizabeth was the only living descendant of ' Bluff King Hal ' ; Mary Stewart was an alien, born of aliens ; and in England, to the people at large, Elizabeth's statutory title was all that stood between a reign of peace and ' wars of the roses which would also be wars of religion.'

[5] So weak, indeed, that Philip's envoy, the Count of Feria, hardly dared to think what would happen if a few French ships touched the shore.

period, an issue in Scotland became an issue for Western Europe. And at this very juncture the Queen Regent determined that the days of compromise and conciliation were over.

How far Mary of Guise was influenced by an increasing contempt of her authority, how far she was influenced by news, or instructions, reaching her from France, it seems impossible to say. The dates given by Knox are difficult to reconcile ; and it may well be that the Regent changed her policy, to conform with the ambitions of the House of Guise, once the Dauphin Francis had been assured of the Scottish ' matrimonial crown.' [1] But now, according to the *History*, " she began to spew forth and disclose the latent venom of her double heart," while " the Devil took more violent and strong possession in her than he had before." [2] An " intercession " on behalf of the Protestant preachers was received with the forthright answer that they should be " banished out of Scotland, albeit they preached as truly as ever did Saint Paul," [3] and the preachers continuing to preach, the more important of them were summoned to present themselves at Stirling, on 10 May 1559, there to " underlie the law." It was the eve of the ' uproar.' The " brethren " (Protestant lords and steel-bonneted lairds), taking the initiative into their own hands, assembled at Perth, though without armour, to support their preachers. Soon they were to call themselves " The Faithful Congregation of Christ Jesus in Scotland " [4] ; soon they were to enter upon " that same war which God commanded Israel to execute against the Canaanites." [5] A Church was to be overthrown ; an ' old alliance ' was to be dissolved ; and an ' earnest embracing ' of a new religion was to join Scotland and England more ' straitly together.' Above all, a new outlook on life, and on the things that are eternal, was to shape the Scottish character for long years to come.

And " in this meantime that the Preachers were summoned," John Knox returned to Scotland from his long absence abroad.[6]

II

Of Knox's early life we know almost nothing. The old accepted statements that he was born about 1505 and that he attended the University of Glasgow, where he sat under John Major, are now distrusted. More recent research would advocate 1514 for the year

[1] *Infra*, i, 140–141   [2] *Infra*, i, 158–159   [3] *Infra*, i, 159
[4] *Infra*, i, 165   [5] *Infra*, i, 172   [6] *Infra*, i, 159–161

of his birth, and the possibility of St. Andrews for his university.[1] But although his delight in dialectics and his love of disputation argue the ' schoolman,' he does not appear to have taken a degree. Ordained as a priest (presumably in his twenty-fifth year), he appears in the Haddington Protocol Books on 13 December 1540, as sir John Knox,[2] while as late as 27 March 1543 he was still acting as an apostolic notary.[3]

So much has been gleaned by the diligence of historians ; but Knox's own writings pass by these early years in silence [4] until, in 1546, JOHN KNOX enters the pages of his *History* as one who had awaited carefully upon George Wishart " from the time he came to Lothian," and who was then bearing before Wishart a " two-handed sword." [5] This is at once indicative of the man. Knox, the implacable opponent of the Roman Church, would have no one know his life until that time when it " pleased God to call him from the puddle of papistry " [6] ; but thereafter, the more fully " the simple truth be spoken without partiality " the greater the glory to God, that " posterity to come may be instructed how wondrously hath the light of Christ Jesus prevailed against darkness in this last and most corrupted age." [7]

[1] The date of Knox's birth can be calculated only from his age at death. He died in 1572, and his age at death was probably fifty-seven or fifty-eight. Knox's own reference to " our youth," in 1547 (*infra*, i, 88) may be a reference to his own age ; if so, he could hardly have been born in 1505 : and although his name does not occur in the registers of the University of St. Andrews, the registers at that time were not well kept and are by no means complete. The interested reader is referred to the contributions by Hay Fleming to *The Scotsman* (27 May 1904) and *The Bookman* (September 1905), and the article by Cowan in *The Athenaeum* (3 December 1904).

[2] ' Sir ' was the usual designation of a priest who had not obtained the university distinction of ' Master ' (*Magister*) ; it was derived from the Latin title *Dominus*. The date of this entry is also significant in relation to Knox's age.

[3] Laing's *Knox*, vi, xxi–xxii ; *Proc. Soc. Antiquaries of Scot.*, iii, 59–63 ; Fraser's *Earls of Haddington*, i, xl–xliii. Haddington was in the diocese of St. Andrews, which strengthens the argument that St. Andrews was his university. There was nothing particularly ' apostolic ' about the office of an apostolic notary. Notaries with authority to act *per mundum* could receive that authority either from the Pope (apostolic notaries) or from the Emperor (imperial notaries) ; but only apostolic notaries could act in ecclesiastical business.

[4] The lack of evidence indicates that he was of humble origin. Only once does he lift the veil when, in converse with Bothwell, he says that he has " a good mind " to the House of Hepburn, " For, my Lord, my grandfather, goodsire, and father, have served your Lordship's predecessors, and some of them have died under their standards " (*infra*, ii, 38, and *note*). See also the note in *Scottish Historical Review*, v, 370–71.

[5] *Infra*, i, 67–69. Possibly in imitation of St. Peter (John, xviii) ; but again bespeaking a young man of about thirty-two rather than a man of forty-one or forty-two.

[6] His words in his *Letter* to the Queen Regent. (Laing's *Knox*, iv, 439)

[7] *Infra*, i, 6

In 1546, however, the final struggle which was to end in the triumph of the " true Evangel " was still a long way off. Wishart, " that blessed martyr of God," caused the two-handed sword to be taken " from the said John Knox " and bade him return to his " bairns," [1] adding, significantly, " One is sufficient for a sacrifice." [2] That same night Wishart was taken—to be delivered to Cardinal Beaton and to martyrdom, which he suffered at St. Andrews on 1 March 1546 ; and three months later Beaton, " that bloody butcher," was surprised and killed in his own " Babylon," partly for the reason given by Knox—that he was " an obstinate enemy against Christ Jesus "—and partly for the baser motives of ' old enmity and feud.' [3]

A castle on the sea-coast of Fife was now held by men who had murdered a cardinal of the Church of Rome, who proclaimed them-selves the upholders of the " true Evangel," and who looked to England for their aid. Gradually their garrison grew in numbers as men, moved by varying motives, joined their band. And here, in the Easter of 1547, came John Knox with his " bairns," " wearied of removing from place to place by reason of the persecution that came upon him." [4] From these men Knox, with " grief and trouble " in his heart, unwilling to " run where God had not called him," received his call to be their preacher [5] ; to this strange company he delivered that sermon in the parish church of St. Andrews of which there were " divers bruits "—" Some said, ' Others sned [6] the branches of the Papistry, but he strikes at the root, to destroy the whole '. . . . Others said, ' Master George Wishart spake never so plainly, and yet he was burnt : even so will he be.' " [7] Almost immediately afterwards, however, in place of the expected succour from England, a French fleet anchored off the west sands of the bay. Ordnance was landed and placed on the tower of St. Salvator's and on the Abbey Kirk ; and some four weeks later the defenders of the castle, including their preacher, John Knox, had become prisoners in the French galleys. [8]

For nineteen months [9] Knox remained a prisoner. On this period, so clear a reverse to " Christ Jesus his Evangel," the *History* is again

---

[1] Knox was then acting as tutor to the two sons of Hugh Douglas of Longniddry and to the eldest son of John Cockburn of Ormiston (*infra*, i, 69, 82).

[2] *Infra*, i, 69   [3] *Infra*, i, 76–78   [4] *Infra*, i, 81–82   [5] *Infra*, i, 82–83
[6] *lop*   [7] *Infra*, i, 86   [8] *Infra*, i, 96–97
[9] " For one day of troubles, since my last arrival in Scotland, hath more pierced my heart than all the torments of the galleys did the space of 19 months." (Knox to Mrs. Anna Locke, 31 December 1559, in Laing's *Knox*, vi, 104)

silent—save for two incidents : the remarkable prophecy of a return to St. Andrews to preach,[1] and a " merry fact " which we must take as " advisedly " as we may.[2] Possibly the durance was not too severe. Communication between the Scotsmen in different prisons appears to have been permitted,[3] and despite later evidence of the effects on his health,[4] Knox still found opportunity, whilst at Rouen, " lying in irons, and sore troubled by corporal infirmity, in a galley named *Nostre Dame*," to revise (as far as the " incommodity of place would permit " !) a timely treatise on *Justification by Faith*, written by Henry Balnaves (another of the prisoners, then in the " old Palace of Rouen ") and to preface it with an Epistle from " John Knox the bound Servant of Jesus Christ." [5]

Released about February 1549, Knox found his way to England (then under the Protestant King, Edward VI),[6] where he was at first appointed to be a licensed preacher at Berwick—a town of " theft, debate, hatred and all iniquity," but one soon reduced to " great quietness " by his " weak labours " blessed by God. From Berwick he moved to Newcastle, where the Duke of Northumberland found him ' neither grateful nor pleasable,' but whence he was called " to London, and to the southern parts of England " to be one of the six chaplains to the King.[7] Now he has met Mrs. Elizabeth Bowes and her daughter Marjory, later to become his wife ; now the spirit and vigour of the man become increasingly evident —a zealot preaching every day of the week " if the wicked carcass will permit." But Knox has not yet found his work ; and the *History* dismisses these years in England in less than forty words.[8] He might have had the living of All-Hallows (Bread Street, London), or even

---

[1] *Infra*, 109. A prophecy fulfilled in June 1559, and recalled by Knox with the brief reference, " What torment I sustained in the galleys, and what were the sobs of my heart, is now no time to recite." (*Infra*, i, 182)

[2] *Infra*, i, 108   [3] *Infra*, i, 109

[4] " The pain of my head and stomach troubles me greatly ; daily I find my body decay, but the providence of my God shall not be frustrated " ; " I had lain Thursday at night, and Friday all day, sore troubled in the gravel " ; " My old malady troubles me sore, and nothing is more contrarious to my health than writing." (Letters of the period 1553–54, in Laing's *Knox*, iii, 351, 355, 364)

[5] Laing's *Knox*, iii, 5–28. See also *infra*, i, 107–108

[6] The Scottish prisoners had been released mainly through English intercessions.

[7] Undoubtedly Knox was the ' runnagate Scot ' who ' so much prevailed . . . at that time ' that he obtained the addition of the famous rubric in the revised or Second Book of Common Prayer that the act of kneeling at Communion meant no adoration of the bread or wine, " for that were idolatry, to be abhorred of all faithful Christians." (Laing's *Knox*, iii, 80 ; Hume Brown, *John Knox*, i, 127–132)

[8] *Infra*, i, 110. See also *infra*, ii, 15

the Bishopric of Rochester, but he refuses preferment,[1] for he has a "foresight of trouble to come . . . that the time would not be long that England would give me bread." [2] And with the accession of Mary Tudor in 1553 that trouble came. In company with others of the reformed faith, Knox fled to the Continent from the revival of Roman Catholic persecution.[3]

Now an exile, parted from all who were dear to him, and particularly from Marjory Bowes, " whom God hath offered unto me, and commanded me to love as my own flesh," all the exile's cares and anxieties fall to his lot. A letter which he writes from Dieppe, immediately after his flight, concludes, " Shortness of time, and multitude of cares, will not let me write at this present so plentifully as I would . . . I will not make you privy how rich I am, but off London I departed with less money than ten groats ; but God has since provided, and will provide." [4] *Jehovah jireh!* But the way was still long. With " sore troubled heart " and " whither God knoweth," he leaves Dieppe and finds his way to Geneva and Zurich ; thence, back to Dieppe again, probably in straitened circumstances, which pride will permit him to confess only in a brief apologetic postscript :

> My own estate I can not well declare ; but God shall guide the footsteps of him that is wilsome,[5] and will feed him in trouble, that never greatly solisted [6] for the world. If any collection might be made among the faithful, it were no shame for me to receive that which Paul refused not in the time of his trouble. But all I remit to his providence, that ever careth for his own.[7]

Now, too, his conscience asks him why he fled, and conscience has an insistent voice. Had he not " commonly " urged every man " to prepare himself for battle," and had he not fled the battle himself ? An *Exposition on the Sixth Psalm of David,* which he completed

---

[1] Laing's *Knox*, iii, 81*-86*. Knox was *not* inimical to an episcopal hierarchy (see Laing's *Knox*, vi, 619–622 ; also G. Donaldson, ' The Scottish Episcopate at the Reformation,' in *English Historical Review*, lx, 349–364) ; but it was to be one without " papistical rags " and ritual, and one with suitable checks from below as well as from above. There was certainly to be no apostolical succession.

[2] Although Knox later expressed a preference for pastoral work—he could have been " a great bishop " but chose rather to be " a painful preacher of the blessed Evangel " —it should be noted that he was by no means devoid of worldly wisdom. As a humble preacher in Edinburgh he drew a handsome stipend and was without the arduous duties of a superintendent ; and in Edinburgh he knew that he would receive, in times of difficulty, the ' following ' of his flocks

[3] Probably early in March 1554 (Laing's *Knox*, iii, 156)

[4] Laing's *Knox*, iii, 372   [5] *wandering wearily, uncertain of the course*

[6] *was never greatly solicitous*   [7] Laing's *Knox*, iii, 347–48

about this time, contains an open expression of his own reproach.
" Why did I flee ? " he writes. " Assuredly I can not tell ; but,"
rising to a stronger note, " of one thing I am sure, the fear of death
was not the chief cause of my fleeing. . . . My fleeing is no matter ;
by God's grace I may come to battle before that all the conflict be
ended." And, later, " Albeit that I have in the beginning of this
battle appeared to play the faint-hearted and feeble soldier (the
cause I remit to God), yet my prayer is, that I may be restored to
the battle again."

Soon work comes to relieve his conscience. He receives an
invitation to become one of the preachers to the English congregation
at Frankfurt-am-Main : an invitation which, in after years, he says
he accepted unwillingly, and certainly an invitation which, some six
months later, led to a quarrel over " unprofitable ceremonies."
Through that quarrel, and as one holding that all ceremonies
and " inventions " were a barrier between man and God, he was
compelled to leave that " superstitious and contentious company,"
and, returning to Geneva, was there elected as pastor to another
English congregation, and was to have ample opportunity to study
the government of a "perfect city" according to "the word of God."

From Geneva he pays a flying visit to Scotland in the " end of
the harvest," 1555,[1] when " the trumpet blew the old sound " again,
and he breaks forth, " O ! sweet were the death that should follow
such forty days in Edinburgh, as here I have had three." [2] Now
are laid the " small beginnings " of a Protestant Church in Scotland ; now, encouraged by the Queen Regent's toleration, Knox
addresses a *Letter* to her, praying her as a " Princess so honourable,
endued with wisdom and graces singularly," to " study how that
the true worshipping of God may be promoted, and the tyranny of
ungodly men repressed." [3] But Mary of Guise only passes his letter
to the Bishop of Glasgow with the " mockage ' Please you, my Lord,
to read a pasquil,' " [4] and, within a year, at a call from his old

---

[1] *Infra*, i, 118–119. Mainly, he says, at the urgency of Mrs. Bowes (Laing's *Knox*, iv, 217).

[2] Laing's *Knox*, iv, 218. It should be noted that, at this time, in view of the danger
to France from Spain (now allied to England by the marriage of Mary Tudor to Philip),
the Queen Regent was definitely following a policy of religious toleration, hoping for a
united Scotland as an ally to France. Hence Knox ran little danger in his visit.

[3] Laing's *Knox*, iv, 78, 83

[4] *Infra*, i, 123. *Pasquil*, a lampoon. Mary of Guise may well have wondered at the nature
of a letter which opened' with references to the Egyptian midwives, Nebuchadnezzar,
and Rahab the harlot ; but her words " coming to the ears of the said John " caused
him to rewrite his *Letter* with " additions " in which the " honourable Princess " is
addressed in more forthright terms. The two versions of the *Letter* are printed in Laing's
Knox, iv, 75–84, 429–460.

congregation, Knox has left the "brethren" in Scotland and is back in Geneva again—this time with Marjory Bowes, his wife,[1] and Elizabeth Bowes, his mother-in-law. In Edinburgh, he is "burnt in effigy at the Cross" and sentence of excommunication is passed against him; in Geneva, with a wife and mother-in-law, he is "now burdened with double cares" and with "daily troubles" in his "domestical charge," which, being unaccustomed, are therefore "the more fearful."

In some ways it is difficult to account for this return to Geneva and his desertion of his own country. Certainly he had a duty to his old congregation. But had he not also a duty to Scotland? The best interpretation we can offer is that, when the call came for his return to the Continent, Knox had reached the conclusion that in Scotland the time was not yet ripe for that complete reform which alone would satisfy his demand.

In May, 1557, however, came an invitation to return to Scotland once more, "where ye shall find all faithful that ye left behind you, not only glad to hear your doctrine, but will be ready to jeopard lives and goods in the forward setting of the glory of God."[2] The invitation reached him at an awkward time[3]; but, taking consultation with Calvin and other "godly ministers," he was told "he could not refuse that vocation unless he would declare himself rebellious unto his God and unmerciful to his country." With "reasonable expedition" he reached Dieppe on 24 October, only to find there "contrary letters"[4]; and, faint-hearted or wordly wise, he retraced his steps to the "perfect city." From Dieppe, indeed, angered and "confounded" by the letters which had awaited him, he could write to the Lords in words both "sharp and indiscreet"—

---

[1] The formal marriage probably took place in the spring of 1556 (Laing's *Knox*, vi, xxxiii–xxxiv), though J. F. Leishman (*A Son of Knox*, 5–6) has argued for a date as early as 1552. Marjory Bowes was the fifth daughter of Richard Bowes, captain of Norham Castle, and Elizabeth, daughter and co-heiress of Roger Aske of Aske. By her, Knox had two sons, Nathaniel and Eleazer, both of whom entered St. John's College, Cambridge, and (despite Knox's condemnation of the "mingle-mangle" of the English Church) became members of the Anglican communion. Both died in early manhood. (See Laing's *Knox*, vi, lxi–lxv; and Leishman, *op. cit.*, 3-19). It should be noted that Knox could write as sympathetically of England as of Scotland (*cf.* Laing's *Knox*, iii, 133), and that although he objected to the ceremonies of the Anglican Church and was 'severe in what he professed' and 'loath to remit anything,' it was Andrew Melville who sealed the isolation of Scottish presbyterianism

[2] *Infra*, i, 132

[3] Eustace Percy, *John Knox*, 248–249

[4] *Infra*, i, 133

I am not ignorant that fearful troubles shall ensue your enterprise
. . . but O joyful and comfortable are those troubles and adversities
which man sustaineth for [the] accomplishment of God's will, revealed
by his word ! For how terrible that ever they appear to the judgment
of the natural man, yet are they never able to devour nor utterly to
consume the sufferers. For the invisible and invincible power of God
sustaineth and preserveth, according to his promise, all such as with
simplicity do obey him . . . your subjects, yea, your brethren are
oppressed, their bodies and souls held in bondage : and God speaketh
to your consciences, (unless ye be dead with the blind world), that
you ought to hazard your own lives (be it against kings or emperors),
for their deliverance. For only for that cause are ye called Princes
of the people, and ye receive of your brethren honour, tribute, and
homage at God's commandment ; not by reason of your birth and
progeny (as the most part of men falsely do suppose), but by reason
of your office and duty, which is to vindicate and deliver your subjects
and brethren from all violence and oppression, to the uttermost of
your power.[1]

Yet back in Geneva he can wonder why again he should " flee
the battle," why God " permitted Sathan to put in my mind such
cogitations as did impede my journey"—cogitations which, in the light
of after events, included the strange query, " Shall Christ, the author
of peace, concord, and quietness, be preached where war is proclaimed, sedition engendered, and tumults appear to rise ? " Some
faint-heartedness there may have been, some shrinking from the
forwardness he preached to those in the forefront of the battle, some
desire for " the den of his own ease " ; but the final call has still to
come, and events were fast moving towards that call.

In Scotland, in December 1557, a number of the Protestant
nobility subscribed their " common band " to " maintain, set forward, and establish the most blessed word of God "[2] ; in April
1558 the aged Walter Myln was burned at St. Andrews[3] ; and in
September 1558 the " brethren " in Edinburgh overthrew the idol
of St. Giles, " dadding his head to the calsay." [4] In England, Elizabeth succeeded Mary Tudor in November 1558, and the Protestant
exiles began to return. In Europe, the Treaty of Cateau-Cambrésis
was finally concluded in April 1559 ; France and Spain were drawing together for the extirpation of heresy ; and if a heretic England
were to be assailed, France had need of Scotland on England's
northern flank. But by March 1559 Knox was again in Dieppe,

---

[1] *Infra*, i, 135   [2] *Infra*, i, 136–137   [3] *Infra*, i, 153   [4] *Infra*, i, 127–129

and on 2 May 1559 he had landed in Scotland. From Edinburgh the next day he writes for prayers that he " shrink not when the battle approacheth," but from Edinburgh, the day following, he is on his way north to " assist his brethren," and henceforth to assist them to the end.

III

These years of exile from 1554 to 1559, although again dismissed in the *History* in the briefest terms, are elsewhere represented in Knox's writings by a steady flow of ' Admonitions,' ' Comfortable Epistles,' and ' Letters of Wholesome Counsel ' addressed to the Protestants in England and Scotland in their afflictions. At times, in the sincerity of their ' counsel ' and in the simplicity of language in which that counsel is addressed, these writings reach a depth of beauty approaching that of the Epistles of St. Paul :

> I will use no threatenings, for my good hope is that ye shall walk as the sons of light in the midst of this wicked generation ; that ye shall be as stars in the night season, who yet are not changed into darkness ; that ye shall be as wheat amongst the cockle, and yet, that ye shall not change your nature which ye have received by grace through the fellowship and participation which we have with the Lord Jesus in his body and blood. And finally, that ye shall be of the number of the prudent virgins, daily renewing your lamps with oil, as they that patiently do abide the glorious apparition and coming of the Lord Jesus ; whose omnipotent Spirit rule and instruct, illuminate and comfort your hearts and minds in all assaults now and ever.[1]

But that mood is rare. Rather, let England repent ; let Scotland observe ! " As it was commanded to Ezekiel boldly to proclaim, so must I cry to you—That you shall perish in your iniquity." [2] God will " suddenly strike the Papists " ; his " vengeance shall fall upon them without provision," so that " altogether with a blast they shall be consumed . . . their palaces shall be a heap of stones, their congregations shall be desolate, and such as do depend upon their help shall fall into destruction." [3]

It is clear that these *Letters* were eagerly received and read, but for us they have a deeper significance. In them we can see the

[1] *A Letter of Wholesome Counsel addressed to his Brethren in Scotland,* 1556. (Laing's *Knox,* iv, 139–140). See also the closing passage of the *Letter to his Brethren in Scotland,* 1557. (Laing's *Knox,* iv, 275)
[2] *The Appellation to the Nobility and Estates of Scotland,* 1558. (Laing's *Knox,* iv, 519)
[3] *A Comfortable Epistle,* 1554. (Laing's *Knox,* iii, 244, 248)

purpose of the man gradually taking shape ; in them, step by step, we can see Knox formulating his philosophy of rebellion.[1] Although a Calvinist, and an admirer of that " great man," Knox is driven at last to a conclusion wholly at variance with Calvin's teaching that ' One cannot resist magistrates without resisting God ' ; but he arrives there with some stress on the ' just laws ' rather than the ' true religion,' and with some reliance on Calvin's doctrine of the ' lesser authorities,' on lords who might be obeyed before the King. Might not the ' lesser authorities,' the ' lords,' check or challenge the tyranny of a king ?   And in Scotland, might not profane history provide an answer to a question that was spiritual ?

At first, in the early days of exile, Knox can write of the " invincible justice of the everlasting God," and, asking the question, " Shall we go and slay all idolaters ? " can answer, " That were the office, dear Brethren, of every civil magistrate within his realm.   But of you is required only to avoid participation and company of their abominations as well in body as in soul." [2]   Yet, at that very time, he was already putting certain pertinent questions, first to Calvin, and then to Bullinger, including, significantly, one, " Whether obedience is to be rendered to a Magistrate who enforces idolatry and condemns true religion ; and whether the lords (*proceres*) up to now holding towns and fortresses in arms [the lesser authorities ?] are permitted to repel that ungodly violence from themselves and their friends ? "   But Bullinger was guarded—it was difficult to pronounce upon particular cases ; a full knowledge of the circumstances was essential ; there was need of much prayer and much wisdom ; there were the dangers of precipitancy and corrupt affections ; not knowing the whole circumstances it would be foolish of him to recommend or determine any specific course of action.[3]   Perhaps Knox strove to digest this answer for, a few weeks later, in his *Comfortable Epistle to the Afflicted Church of Christ*, he can still exhort the Brethren that they " presume not to be revengers " in their own cause, but that they " resign over vengeance " to God.[4]

By the summer of the same year (1554), however, he has progressed to the position that the " vengeance of God " may yet be executed by God's " instrument."   Now, in a *Faithful Admonition to*

---

[1] For a fuller treatment of this theme, the reader is referred to Eustace Percy, *John Knox*, 169–189, 255–273. We still await a critical analysis of Knox's political philosophy, showing the extent to which he draws upon other writers.

[2] *A Godly Letter to the Faithful in London, etc.*, 1554. (Laing's *Knox*, iii, 168, 194)

[3] Laing's *Knox*, iii, 221–226

[4] *Ibid.*, iii, 244

the Professors of God's Truth in England, which alternates between tenderness for the afflicted and invective against their oppressors, comes the prayer, " God, for his great mercy's sake, stir up some Phinehas, Elijah, or Jehu, that the blood of abominable idolaters may pacify God's wrath that it consume not the whole multitude." [1] More than that, his mind has begun to travel another course. In this same *Admonition* we find the significant passage—has not Mary Tudor shown herself " to be an open traitress to the Imperial Crown of England, contrary to the just laws of the Realm to bring in a stranger and make a proud Spaniard, King, to the shame, dishonour, and destruction of the nobility ; to the spoil from them and theirs of their honours, lands, possessions, chief offices and promotions ; to the utter decay of the treasures, commodities, navy, and fortifications of the Realm ; to the abasing of the yeomanry, to the slavery of the commonalty, to the overthrow of Christianity and God's true religion ; and, finally, to the utter subversion of the whole public estate and commonwealth of England " ? [2] Can resistance to a " traitress " be rebellion ?

But Knox has still to come to certainty. In 1556, in his *Letter to the Queen Regent*, the victory of God's people lies " in quietness, silence, and hope " [3] ; yet, in the augmented edition of that *Letter* (1558), only those men are acceptable to God, and faithful to their Princes, who resist to the death blasphemous laws and decrees against the religion approved by God's word ; nay more, " I answer with the prophet Isaiah, ' That all is not reputed before God sedition and conjuration, which the foolish multitude so esteemeth ' ; neither yet is every tumult and breach of public order contrary to God's commandment." [4] So, in the *Appellation to the Nobility and Estates of Scotland*, which was written about the same time as the augmented *Letter*, the final stage is reached with the assurance to be " noted " by the Lords, " That the punishment of such crimes, as are idolatry, blasphemy, and others that touch the Majesty of God, doth not appertain to kings and chief rulers only, but also to the whole body of that people, and to every member of the same, according to the vocation of every man, and according to that possibility and occasion which God doth minister to revenge the injury done against his glory, what time that impiety is manifestly known " ; for command is given to " the whole body of the people, yea, and every member

---

[1] *Ibid.*, iii, 309   [2] *Ibid.*, iii, 295

[3] *Ibid.*, iv, 75. Though it is to be noted that this passage does not occur in the original edition.   [4] *Ibid.*, iv, 441-442

of the same, according to their possibility," and then God wills
" that all creatures stoop, cover their faces and desist from reasoning,
when commandment is given to execute his judgment." [1] Here is
no call for a Phineas or Jehu ; here is no reliance upon the ' lesser
authorities ' or the ' lords.' Here judgment and its execution have
been given to *the people*.

Thus, when the people rise (obeying, if so it be, the ' lesser
authorities,' who are none other than the Protestant lords), they
may be called by God to suppress the wicked ruler and to overthrow
idolatry, or they may take arms against a traitorous Queen and seek
only the maintenance of the " just laws of the realm." Rebellion
can be doubly *constitutional* : for the defence of the earthly kingdom,
as well as for the defence of the kingdom of God.

Yet Knox was never wholly sure until the victory had been won ;
and although in the public proclamations of the Army of Christ
Jesus his Evangel—proclamations clearly drafted by Knox himself—
the appeal may be twofold :

> While strangers are brought in to suppress us, our commonwealth,
> and posterity, while idolatry is maintained, and Christ Jesus his true
> religion despised, while idle bellies and bloody tyrants, the bishops,
> are maintained, and Christ's true messengers persecuted ; while,
> finally, virtue is contemned and vice extolled, while that we, a great
> part of the nobility and commonalty of this realm, are most unjustly
> persecuted, what godly man can be offended that we shall seek refor-
> mation of these enormities (yea, even by force of arms, seeing that other-
> ways it is denied unto us) ? We are assured that neither God, neither
> nature, neither any just law, forbids us. God has made us councillors
> by birth of this realm ; nature binds us to love our own country ; and
> just laws command us to support our brethren unjustly persecuted.
> Yea, the oath that we have made, to be true to this commonwealth,
> compels us to hazard whatsoever God has given us, before that we
> see the miserable ruin of the same. If any think this is not religion
> which now we seek, we answer, That it is nothing else but the zeal
> of the true religion which moves us to this enterprise. For as the
> enemy does craftily foresee that idolatry can not be universally main-
> tained unless that we be utterly suppressed, so do we consider that
> the true religion (the purity whereof we only require) can not be
> universally erected unless strangers be removed and this poor realm
> purged of these pestilences which before have infected it [2]

[1] *Ibid.*, iv, 501–502. An argument again advanced by Knox in his ' reasoning ' with
Lethington (*infra*, ii, 120ff).

[2] *Infra*, i, 243

yet the stress is ever upon the " just laws of the realm." The
parallel to Mary Tudor and a " stranger and proud Spaniard, King,"
is now the Queen Regent and her proud French strangers who
would dispossess the true subjects of that which was theirs by right.[1]
This had been the burden of Knox's charge to the nobility as early
as October 1557 [2] ; now it is the Reformers' constant cry. " Thousands of strangers are laid here and there upon the necks of our
poor members of this commonwealth " [3] ; they have come " with
wives and bairns " ; they lay strong garrisons in our towns ; is not
this against " the ancient laws and liberties of our realm " ? [4] Are
not we (the Protestant nobility), " born councillors of this realm,
sworn to secure the profit of the same " ? [5] So, when the Queen
Regent is deposed, the Reformers' proclamation of her deposition is
based upon her " enterprised . . . overthrow of the liberty of their
native country," her inbringing of " strangers," and her alteration
of the " old law and consuetude " of the realm.[6] So, and perhaps
more significant still, we have the clue to Knox's persistence that
in the ' Appointment ' at the Links of Leith an article relating to
the withdrawal of the French forces was first granted and then
denied.[7]

IV

Immediately upon his arrival in Scotland Knox pressed on to
Dundee and Perth, anxious " to assist his brethren, and to give
confession of his faith with them." [8] At Perth, on 11 May 1559,
a sermon was preached " vehement against idolatry " ; a boy threw
a stone ; an image was broken ; and at once the " brethren " or
the " rascal multitude " [9] had purged Perth of " idolatry, [and] the
places and monuments thereof." [10] The revolution had begun. And
revolution it was bound to be. Too many long pent-up forces—
religious, social, economic, and political—had been released at one
and the same time. Nor could there be an armistice between the
Reformers and the Queen Regent. With the riot at Perth, Mary
of Guise had only the alternatives of crushing the Protestants or
abandoning her authority as the representative of the absent Mary
and of the interests of Roman Catholic France.

The Regent, however, was practically dependent upon her small

---

[1] *Cf. supra*, xxviii–xxix   [2] *Infra*, i, 134   [3] *Infra*, i, 222   [4] *Infra*, i, 224
[5] *Infra*, i, 199, 243, 254   [6] *Infra*, i, 251–255
[7] *Infra*, i, 202, 204–205, 216–218, 220-221, 226   [8] *Infra*, i, 161
[9] For Knox's accounts differ. See *infra*, i, 162, *note* 5   [10] *Infra*, i, 161–163

force of French troops, for, as their leader d'Oysel bitterly remarked, the Scots who were with them in the morning might be against them in the evening. There were initial truces and ' agreements '—local and of short duration ; there was marching and countermarching ; but, on 29 June 1559, the Army of Christ Jesus his Evangel, giving the French forces the slip, was able to occupy Edinburgh. Knox had preached at Perth on 11 May ; he had preached at St. Andrews (in fulfilment of his prophecy) on 11 June [1] ; and on 29 June he was preaching in St. Giles.

The Reformers, however, had their difficulties also ; and notably that their supporters could not long remain in the field in arms. During their first week in Edinburgh their forces had numbered some 5,000, but a fortnight later those forces had dwindled to little more than 1,500. The Regent, small though her regular force might be, was bound to gain by a waiting policy and prolonged negotiations. It was soon abundantly clear that the Congregation could hope to prevail only if they had the support of regular troops ; and regular troops could be sought only from Protestant England. Late in July 1559, the Lords of the Congregation appealed direct to England for aid, basing their appeal on the argument that France had " decreed no less the conquest of England than of Scotland." [2]

They had little need to stress their case. Henry II of France had died on 10 July, and Mary Queen of Scots was now Queen of France. Elizabeth and Cecil could well foresee the dangers of French dominion in Scotland ; but intervention in Scotland might result in an open war with France, for which England was far from ready. Moreover, to help rebellious subjects who were in arms against the lawful authority of their Prince was a two-edged weapon that might turn against an English Queen not too secure upon the English throne. And had not this self-same Knox, who now appealed to a Queen for aid, but lately written his *First Blast of the Trumpet against the Monstrous Regiment of Women*, which had opened with the proposition that, " To promote a Woman to bear rule, superiority, dominion, or empire above any realm, nation, or city is repugnant to nature, contumely to God, a thing most contrarious to his revealed will and ordinance, and finally, the subversion of good order, and of all equity and justice " ? Had he not argued that as for woman " it is no more possible that she being set aloft in authority above man shall resist the motions of pride, than it is able to the weak reed,

---

[1] *Infra*, i, 182, and *note* 4 ; see *supra*, xxxiv, and *note* 1   [2] *Infra*, i, 287

or to the turning weathercock, not to bow or turn at the vehemency of the inconstant wind " ? In vain Knox pled that his *Blast* had been blown against Mary Tudor and Mary of Guise ; in vain did he liken Elizabeth to the exceptional Deborah, that blessed mother in Israel, and declare his determination to justify her authority with tongue and pen.[1] Cecil appears to have been anxious to help, but Elizabeth was hard to move.

Knox, in fact, was too forthright to be a diplomat, as his letters to Elizabeth and Cecil clearly prove.[2] On his mission from the Lords to Berwick, in August 1559—a mission too open for England's liking at the time—Sir James Croft showed him the language of diplomacy : " I think it not expedient," he had said, when on tenterhooks to be rid of his unwelcome visitor, " that in such rarity of preachers ye . . . be any long time absent from the Lords." [3] Later still, Croft was to be " plain " with him : ' Ye are so open in your doings as you make men half afraid to deal with you, which is more than wisdom and policy doth require,' [4] and that, paradoxically, was part of a reply to the only ' diplomatic ' suggestion ever made by Knox—a reply to a suggestion, strangely coming from Knox, that England might send a thousand men or more to help the Congregation and, to avoid the danger of an open breach with France, England might declare her forces to be rebels once they had safely joined the Scots.[5]

Yet, although Elizabeth was slow to move English troops, when the young Arran, who had escaped from the clutches of the King of France,[6] arrived in England, she was quick to see the importance of his advent and quick to speed him north. With his son safely in Scotland, the old vacillating Arran, the " second person " in the realm and next in succession to the Crown, openly joined the Congregation and became its titular head. After all, if there were to be a revolution, the House of Hamilton might yet occupy the Scottish

---

[1] *Infra*, i, 291-294 [2] *Infra*, i, 282–287 ; 290-294 [3] *Infra*, i, 295 [4] Laing's *Knox*, vi, 92
[5] Laing's *Knox*, vi, 90. Knox had seen the same ' device ' adopted by the French (*infra*, i, 102) and was not over-perturbed by Croft's reply about ' honour and safety.' " Whether it may stand with wisdom," he writes, " to have such respect to that which some men do call honour, that in the meantime I shall see my friend perish, both to his destruction and mine, I refer to the judgment of the most honourable." (Laing's *Knox*, vi, 93). It should be noted, moreover, that Cecil had already suggested to Sadler that the Scots should be persuaded to devise such ways as they could for the English to help them while still remaining at peace with France. (*Sadler's State Papers and Letters*, i, 402–403)
[6] The serious illness of Mary in June 1559 had awakened Henry II of France to the danger of the Hamilton succession to the Scottish crown.

throne.[1] Had not the Reformers set a course which bound religion so closely to politics that the one could be changed only by a change in the other ? Knox might write " we mean neither sedition, neither yet rebellion against any just and lawful authority, but only the advancement of Christ's religion and the liberty of this poor realm "[2] ; but a manifesto to the Princes of Christendom rested the case of the Congregation almost entirely on France's intent and aim to conquer the Scottish realm.[3]

While England still delayed her help, the Queen Regent, in turn seeking the help of France, began to fortify Leith—a strategic centre and a port giving access to France. There were exchanges of letters and messengers between the Congregation in Edinburgh and the Regent in Leith. But the Regent could argue that she began her fortifications, and that she made her appeal to France, only after the Reformers had seized the capital and had made their appeal to England. To their demands that she should cease her fortifications, she could reply that the Reformers were in arms to pervert the people from their true obedience to the Crown, perhaps even to usurp the Crown. The futile exchanges came to an end. The Congregation, assuming a delegated authority they did not possess, and taking their stand solely on the Regent's tyranny and her sacrifice of Scotland to the policy of France, deposed Mary of Guise in the names of Francis and Mary [4] and prepared themselves for the attack on Leith. But their long delay and lack of resolution during the summer months had enabled their opponents to turn Leith into a fortress ; and the " country fellows " of the Army of the Congregation were unequal to their task. Moreover, scaling-ladders were made in St. Giles, which caused the preaching to be " neglected " and the preachers spared not to say " That they feared the success of that enterprise . . . because the beginning appeared to bring with it some contempt of God and of his Word " ;

[1] At the end of August 1559 Cecil had endorsed a memorandum of ' points for restoring the realm of Scotland to the ancient weal,' which included not only that France must not be allowed to make Scotland a footstool to look over England, *but also* that unless a Scotsman in blood were ruler, no accord could be looked for ; that the Hamiltons were next heirs ; and finally, if Mary were unwilling to break free from France, then was it apparent that God was pleased to transfer the rule of Scotland from her for the weal of that country. (*Calendar of Scottish Papers*, i, No. 537) It is impossible to understand the political background of this period without remembering that the Hamiltons were next in succession to the throne of Scotland. To illustrate the importance of their " nearness to the throne," a genealogical table is given below (*infra*, ii, 351)

[2] Knox to Sir Henry Percy, 1 July 1559. (Laing's *Knox*, vi, 36)
[3] Teulet, *Papiers d'État*, i, 414–428   [4] *Infra*, i, 251–255

there were spies in the camp who betrayed to the Regent the Reformers' very "counsel, purposes, and devices"; the Duke of Châtelherault (old Arran) was weak and "greatly troubled"; the paid soldiers mutinied for lack of their wages and, when a collection was made to meet their demands, "some were poor, and some were niggards and avaricious" so that "no sufficient sum could be obtained"; while, to crown all, a small sum sent secretly by Sadler and Croft from Berwick was intercepted by the way.[1] There were successful sallies by the French; "the courage of many was dejected"; and the Army of the Congregation began to break up. "Many fled away secretly, and those that did abide (a very few excepted) appeared destitute of counsel and manhood."[2] The siege of Leith was abandoned, and the Congregation "stayed not" till they came to Stirling—and the words read more like a flight than an orderly retreat.[3]

Then rose the real Knox, the Knox of whom Randolph was later to write, "I assure you the voice of one man is able in one hour to put more life in us than five hundred trumpets continually blustering in our ears."[4] Preaching from the 80th Psalm, he sought the reasons for their failure and the reasons why their God had deserted them:

> When we were a few number, in comparison of our enemies, when we had neither Earl nor Lord (a few excepted) to comfort us, we called upon God; we took him for our protector, defence, and only refuge. Amongst us was heard no bragging of multitude, of our strength, nor policy: we did only sob to God, to have respect to the equity of our cause, and to the cruel pursuit of the tyrantful enemy. But since that our number hath been thus multiplied, and chiefly since my Lord Duke's Grace[5] with his friends have been joined with us, there was nothing heard but, "This Lord will bring these many hundred spears; this man hath the credit to persuade this country; if this Earl be ours, no man in such a bounds will trouble us." And thus the best of us all, that before felt God's potent hand to be our defence, hath of late days put flesh to be our arm.

What then should be their course? Let them

> turn to the Eternal our God, (who beats down to death, to the intent that he may raise up again, to leave the remembrance of his wondrous deliverance, to the praise of his own name), which, if we do unfeignedly,

[1] *Infra*, i, 256ff   [2] *Infra*, i, 261   [3] *Infra*, i, 265
[4] Randolph to Cecil, 7 September 1561 (*Calendar of Scottish Papers*, i, No. 1017)
[5] The Duke of Châtelherault (old Arran)

I no more doubt that this our dolour, confusion, and fear shall be turned into joy, honour, and boldness than I doubt that God gave victory to the Israelites over the Benjamites, after that twice with ignominy they were repulsed and doung back. Yea, whatsoever shall become of us and of our mortal carcasses, I doubt not but that this cause (in despite of Sathan) shall prevail in the realm of Scotland. For, as it is the eternal truth of the eternal God, so shall it once [1] prevail, howsoever for a time it be impugned. [2]

No wonder that, the sermon ended, " the minds of men began wondrously to be erected." It may be true that the Army of the Congregation was dependent upon the support of the Protestant nobility, and upon the adherence of the small barons and burgesses who composed its ranks ; but it is equally true that Knox was the leader who stood firm when others faltered, and who could inspire others by the inspiration which he himself derived from his assurance in his cause. Yet, writing this part of his *History* about this very time, he concluded Book II with the humble prayer, " Look upon us, O Lord, in the multitude of thy mercies ; for we are brought even to the deep of the dungeon."

Now more than ever, was the aid of England essential ; now Maitland of Lethington (who had openly joined the Congregation after working for it in secret), took over the negotiations in place of Knox ; and now, at last, Elizabeth actively intervened. No longer did she content herself with vague promises and with the smuggling of niggardly sums across the Border from Berwick. Francis and Mary had assumed the English arms ; Mary had been publicly proclaimed in Paris as ' Queen of England, Scotland, and Ireland '; the Roman Catholic powers were making peace in preparation for their assault on heresy ; and the Pope had pronounced that princes guilty of heresy were *ipso facto* deprived of their temporal power. Elizabeth could answer the appeal from the Army of the Congregation and still satisfy herself that in so doing she was acting in her own defence. To fail to answer the appeal would be to give Roman Catholic France a northern base.

The Treaty of Berwick (February 1560) was a defensive alliance, but nothing more. Because the French intended to conquer Scotland and to unite it to the Crown of France, Elizabeth took Scotland beneath her protection and maintenance, to preserve the Scots in their freedoms and liberties, and to save them from conquest. To

[1] That is, *once and for all*
[2] *Infra*, i, 269–270

that end she would send help by sea and land. The Scots, in turn, were to send their help to England should Englai d be invaded by the French. But the Scots were not to withdraw their lawful obedience from their sovereigns if their liberties were not subverted. Nowhere in the Treaty was there any word of religion.[1] To Elizabeth, the Treaty, and its fulfilment, were political necessities ; and so far as religion was concerned, Knox was later to sum up the English Queen as " neither good Protestant nor yet resolute Papist." [2]

But the Treaty had already been anticipated, and England had anticipated France. Already, in the last week of January, an English fleet under Admiral Winter had anchored in the Forth (thus cutting the Queen Regent's communications with France); and now, towards the end of March, an English army crossed a friendly border to reinforce the Congregation in a second siege of Leith. The Regent, moreover, was a dying woman. Worn out by the difficulties of her task,[3] Mary of Guise had retired to the neutrality of the Castle of Edinburgh, and there, on the night of 10/11 June, she closed her " unhappy life." [4] Leith, though stoutly defended, could not hold out without relief; and that relief was never sent.[5] On 6 July 1560 the Treaty of Edinburgh brought the revolution to an end. Scotland was secured for the Scots and, for the first time in history, an English army left Scottish soil and left behind it Scottish gratitude. Yet English help had been far from disinterested and far from ' spiritual.' If English aid was necessary to secure the Scottish Reformation, equally England herself could never feel secure unless Scotland were firmly established in a new freedom from the old alliance and the old Kirk.

By the Treaty of Edinburgh (which was essentially a treaty between England and France), and by the ' Concessions ' to the Scots which accompanied it,[6] the Scots of their own accord professed their loyalty to Francis and Mary ; Elizabeth's right and title to the English throne were recognized ; Francis and Mary were to abstain from using and bearing the title and arms of King and Queen of England or Ireland ; the French and English forces

---

[1] *Infra*, i, 302–307   [2] *Infra*, i, 369

[3] Probably, as Pollen suggested, and quite apart from her political and ecclesiastical policy, the Queen Regent was too imbued with the French passion for *règlement* ever to have succeeded in unruly Scotland.   [4] *Infra*, i, 322

[5] Even as late as May 1560 the Papacy would not regard Scotland as ' schismatic ' (Pollen, *Papal Negotiations with Mary Queen of Scots*, 46) ; France and Spain were still in opposite camps (*ibid.*, 460–461) ; and, above all, England had command of the sea-routes.   [6] *Infra*, i, 323, *note 2*

were to be withdrawn from Scotland ; and henceforth no warlike preparations were to be made in England against the French or in France against the English. Again, to Elizabeth, the struggle had been solely political. Again, in the Treaty, the religious question was passed by. But to Knox and his fellow ministers, the whole struggle had been one for the " true religion," and they, well-knowing the risks inherent in delay, promptly strove to place a religious victory on firm foundations.

In the Parliament of August 1560, thronged by Protestant lairds, a *Confession of Faith* was approved ; the jurisdiction of the Pope was abolished ; the celebration of the Mass was forbidden ; and all doctrine and practice contrary to the *Confession* were utterly condemned.[1] And, " at the same time of Parliament," John Knox preached publicly from the Prophet Haggai on the building of the House of God.[2]

V

The *Confession of Faith*[3] was approved and engrossed in the Registers of Parliament, but its accompaniment, the *Book of Discipline*,[4] which would have laid the temporal foundations of the City of God on earth, was passed by. Faith was not followed by works.

The *Book of Discipline* was itself a ' Confession of Faith,' for it had been drafted between 29 April and 20 May 1560,[5] that is, even before the final victory of Christ Jesus his Evangel had been won. Yet much as it drew upon the Church Orders of Protestant congregations abroad,[6] it was a plan of work, an outstanding document proving abundantly that Knox and his fellow preachers could be as constructive in office as they had been destructive in opposition.

Opening with an " explication " of the " true doctrine " of the Evangel, it proceeds to examine the administration necessary for the Kirk and the finance necessary for that administration.

---

[1] *Infra*, i, 338–341. But see also *infra*, lvi, and *note* 3   [2] *Infra*, i, 335
[3] *Infra*, Appendix VI   [4] *Infra*, Appendix VIII   [5] *Infra*, ii, 280, 323
[6] Even as the *Confession of Faith* had drawn upon other Reformed Confessions. The continental parallels have frequently been noted (see, for example, A. F. Mitchell, *The Scottish Reformation*, 99–122, 144–183 ; Hume Brown, *John Knox*, ii, 122–151, and authorities there cited ; Janet G. MacGregor, *Scottish Presbyterian Polity*) ; but Dr. Donaldson has recently shown that the most striking parallel to the *Book of Discipline* is to be found in the Danish *Ordinatio Ecclesiastica* of 1537, which Cecil had actually recommended to the Scots as a model for the settlement of the property of the Roman Church and which was certainly well-known to the drafters of the Scottish *Book*. (See *Scottish Historical Review*, xxvii, 57–64)

" Strange " as the Lords might find it " at the first sight," [1] the
wealth of the Roman Church and the continuing payment of tithes
(henceforth to be "reasonably taken ") were to be dedicated to
the needs of the ministers of the Word and to those other purposes—
education and the relief of the poor—for which the Church had
formerly been so richly endowed.   In its system of church government, its insistence upon education, even with plans for educational
allowances and university bursaries for poor scholars (that men might
be of service to the Church or Commonwealth), and with its suggestions for the organization of poor relief, it reveals a concept of
society that, more rightly than any other, may be termed ' Christian
Socialism.'   By the *Book of Discipline* every class of society would
have been brought up to the service of Church and State, and the old
ascendancy of prelate and lord would have been swept away.   The
Book of Discipline would have raised a *people*.   Perhaps that, almost
as much as their desire for the lands and wealth of the Church, led
to the opposition of the nobility, so that the *Book* was passed by.
Certainly all was dependent upon the wealth of the old Church
being freed for the work of the new ; and in whose hands lay the
temporal lands and the revenues of the Church ?   Much was held
by the nobility as commendators or in feu ; some had been alienated
to the nobility in the hope of saving the rest ; and where the rest was
still in the enjoyment of the Roman clergy, not a few of the clergy
were related to noble houses.   Even if some of the Protestant lords
were wholly sincere, how could they hope to enforce such a transference of wealth against the rest, and against the country as a whole ?
In a land where the executive was notoriously weak, the strongest
of former kings might well have quailed before such a task ; and
where now, with the death of the Regent and the absence of the
Queen, could the executive authority be said to rest ?

Admittedly, the lands and revenues of the monastic foundations
were wholly omitted from the *Book* (doubtless because the Reformers
realized that what had been already largely seized was now largely
irrecoverable), but the financial proposals that were made still
failed to secure the approval of the nobility.   In the words of Knox,
avariciousness would not suffer this corrupt generation to approve
the policy of the godly ministers [2] : but the worldly-wise, like
Maitland of Lethington, saw far more than the complexities, nay
even the impracticability, of such a vast transference of wealth ;
they saw that to implement the " devout imaginations " of the

[1] *Infra*, ii, 323   [2] *Infra*, i, 374

ministers would be to split the Reformation party from top to bottom.
Too many, indeed, had already "greedily gripped to the possessions of the Kirk"; too many would find "their carnal liberty and
worldly commodity" somewhat impaired.[1] So men refused to
lay their hands to the building of the City of God, and the new
Church could not be financed from the wealth of the old. The
Reformers having won the war had lost the peace. The old Church
had been overthrown; but the new Church had no sure foundation.
And, as we shall see, with the return of Mary Queen of Scots the
struggle had to be fought anew.

Looking back we can now appreciate that the 'policy' of the
ministers was to be an organic whole; that each part was dependent
upon the fulfilment of the rest. The people were to be educated in
school, in college, and in university; and the ministers were to be
chosen by the people. But with the rejection of the 'policy,' a
possible 'balance' between the people and the ministers was lost.
The people were to reverence their ministers as the ambassadors of
the Lord, and to obey the commandments which they pronounced
from God's mouth and book "even as they would obey God himself"[2]; but the people remained largely uneducated, and thereby
the ministers gained a hold over their lives and thoughts which
would have been otherwise denied. Because of that, the ministers
became as infallible as former priests,[3] and later, 'new presbyter'
was to be seen as 'but old priest writ large.' Significantly, too, in
its opening statement of doctrine the *Book of Discipline* contained a
renunciation of all things for which no warrant could be found
within the Scriptures; but not all the ministers were to know the restraint that comes from the discipline of true education, whilst for all
men a new freedom had been gained—a freedom to read the Scriptures
and to have a direct contact with God unhindered by any "shaveling
priest." Now every man had "liberty to utter and declare his mind
and knowledge to the comfort and edification of the Church"[4];
and that new liberty was heady wine, dangerous to those without
restraint. Differing interpretations of the scriptural message soon
arose; and therewith arose the 'saints of God' who alone could
interpret God's will.[5] At first, when the young Queen Mary replied

---

[1] *Infra*, i, 343–344   [2] *Infra*, ii, 286

[3] And Knox, with his assurance, with his supreme confidence, with, in short, his
infallibility, had set no mean example.   [4] *Infra*, ii, 315

[5] Later, even Samuel Rutherford (though on a somewhat different argument) was
to assert that 'Practice in Scripture is a narrow rule of faith.' (*Lex Rex*, London, 1644,
364)

to Knox, " Ye interpret the Scriptures in one manner, and they [the Pope and the Cardinals] interpret in another. Whom shall I believe? And who shall be judge?" [1] the differences were still simple ; but ere long they were to grow complex.

The authority of the Word of God, moreover, might be strait and narrowing, particularly if the Books of the Hebrew Prophets were to be preferred to Christ's gospel of love,[2] and particularly in a country which had enjoyed no Renaissance and was unconscious of an ancient past bright with imaginary glory. With such a background, the new Church might be as uncompromising as the old. If the Roman Church had endeavoured to extirpate all heresy, now all doctrine for which no warrant could be found within the Word was to be " utterly suppressed as damnable to man's salvation." [3] Had one tyranny been overthrown only to be replaced by another ? In his ' reasoning ' with Lethington in 1564, Knox does not hesitate to say that it was the bounden duty " of the people of God " to arise and destroy idolatry, "sparing . . . neither man, woman, nor child." [4] Henceforth liberty of conscience was to be liberty to believe only as the ministers themselves believed. Admittedly the new order provides record of only two (and the two may be one) martyrdoms for the old faith. But we may still ask how far that was due to the initial insecurity of the new Church, or to the fact that those of the Roman faith, save perhaps in certain districts, refrained from open violation of the Protestant laws.

Finally, the concept of " the people of God " affirms the age-old belief in God as the defender of his "people"; a God who will punish the wicked ruler, even as he punished Pharaoh. The ruler must rule according to ' the law of God,' and that law is the law interpreted by the ministers. Naturally, out of this, arises a new covenant—a triangular ' band ' between God, the ruler, and the people.[5] If the ruler fails to rule according to the Word of God, so is the covenant broken, so may the people depose their ruler ; and again the ' judgment ' is to be the judgment of the ministers.

---

[1] *Infra*, ii, 18

[2] Later, Corbet accused the Covenanters—' All your testimonies are out of the Old Testament, but not one out of the New Testament.' (John Corbet, *The Ungirding of the Scottish Armour*, Dublin, 1639, 37)

[3] *Infra*, ii, 281   [4] *Infra*, ii, 120–121

[5] Such a covenant could be based upon the " infallible truth of God's word," for ' Jehoiada made a covenant between the Lord and the king and the people, that they should be the Lord's people ; between the king also and the people ' (II Kings, xi, 17) ; and Knox, in his ' reasoning ' with Lethington, advanced the example of Joash, " that the King and the people should be the people of the Lord " (*infra*, ii, 126).

Not unnaturally a young queen " stood as it were amazed " until at length she said, " Well, then, I perceive that my subjects shall obey you [Knox], and not me ; and shall do what they list, and not what I command. And so must I be subject to them, and not they to me." [1]

In the new City of God the ' policy ' of the Church was to be also the ' policy ' of the State ; but the worldlings rejected the ideal. Later, under Andrew Melville, a second ' Book of Discipline ' was to assert the independence (even the supremacy) of the ' policy ' of the Church ; but, like its predecessor, the second ' Book of Discipline ' was unacceptable to the temporal power. Whereas in England the Reformation had been achieved by agreement, and was a typical English compromise in which Church and State went hand in hand, in Scotland the Reformation had been a rebellion against both Church and State, and, ere long, the new Church was to become a rival government to the government of the State. Yet in their zeal to form a ' new rule ' for ' the people of God,' the Reformers failed to realize that the State rested on foundations far different from those of the Roman Church. So, in Scotland, came that long struggle between Church and State, a struggle between the ' Divine Right of Kings ' and the ' Divine Right of Presbyteries,' a conflict between government by the Council of the King and government by the counsel of God. That struggle was to endure for more than one hundred bitter years, and was to lead to many a tragic death on lonely moors and windswept hills.

But it would be unfair to see only the darker side. Out of the ' order ' of the new Church came the lay-elder, who, in the local kirk session (which was without its parallel in the local government of the State), could voice or formulate local opinion ; out of the ' order ' of the new Church came also the General Assembly, a democratic gathering far different from the Scottish Parliament in which the members had now no voice and which had become but the ' registrar of conclusions reached elsewhere.' In the General Assembly the *people*, for the first time, came into their own ; and because of that representation of the people in the General Assembly of the Church (which threatened to become more than a rival of the Scottish Parliament) an anxious king was later impelled to widen the representation of the people in the Estates of the Realm. Moreover, through the ministers and the new organization of the Church the people developed that critical appraisement of public affairs

[1] *Infra*, ii, 17

which was to become so marked a feature of Scottish history in succeeding years ; and whatever may be said against the hold obtained by the new ministers and the new Church, it must be remembered that, for the first time, the Church and its ministers awakened in the people a new concept of their place in the State. Later still, in the ' lean years ' following the Union of the Parliaments, the General Assembly of the Church, meeting annually in Edinburgh, was one of two solitary reminders and visible symbols that Scotland was still a nation and Edinburgh still a capital. All this was still to come ; much of it was the work of Melville ; but the first beginnings were of Knox and his fellow preachers.

Finally, the *Book of Discipline* had noted that " before God, there is no respect of persons." [1] That equality before God, branching out from a sturdy independence well-rooted in the past, gave to the Scot that sense of the ' divine right of manhood ' which has some-times been mistaken for pride. And perhaps more important still, the rejection of the financial proposals for maintaining the ' servants of God,' left the ministers as men ' poor amid the poor,' living upon the ' benevolence ' of others. As such, they became essentially *of* the people and *with* the people, each knowing the daily difficulties and constant troubles of his flock. Admittedly they were held in reverence ; admittedly their influence and authority might at times be absolute (and at times, alas, not always for good) ; but never were they to be a class apart, living as the ' proud prelates ' of an alien Church.

VI

Francis II, King of France and husband of Mary Queen of Scots, died on 5 December 1560—" suddenly stricken with an aposthume in that deaf ear that never would hear the truth of God " [2]—and in August 1561 Mary, not yet nineteen years old, returned to her own country. At her arrival,

The very face of heaven . . . did manifestly speak what comfort was brought unto this country with her, to wit, sorrow, dolour, dark-ness, and all impiety. For, in the memory of man, that day of the year was never seen a more dolorous face of the heaven than was at her

[1] *Infra*, ii, 320   [2] *Infra*, i, 347–349

arrival, which two days after did so continue. . . . The sun was not seen to shine two days before, nor two days after. That forewarning gave God unto us ; but alas, the most part were blind.[1]

Even before the return of the Queen, the General Assembly of the new Church had perceived that old " tyrants and dumb dogs " would again attempt to " erect their idolatry and take upon them to empire " in the land ; and again " the Barons and Gentlemen professing Christ Jesus within this realm " had declared themselves " fully determined to hazard life, and whatsoever we have received of our God in temporal things " in resistance to the Roman Antichrist.[2] And now Mary, a Roman Catholic, had returned to rule a, nominally, Protestant realm. The old Church had gone ; but the new Church was still to be built and the foundations so far laid were none too sure. The Acts of the Reformation Parliament of 1560, which had abolished Roman Catholicism and had confirmed the Protestant Confession of Faith, might be called in question. The composition of the Parliament had been unusual ; possibly it had exceeded its powers ; certainly the Acts still awaited a royal ratification they were never to receive.[3] True, there were Protestant ministers and a Protestant Kirk ; but the ministers were still few and for the most part living but ' a beggar's life,' while a lack of resolution, or perhaps an admission of the lack of power, had left the Roman clergy still in office and still drawing their revenues, or the greater part thereof. ' The General Assembly might meet twice a year ; but John Hamilton still went to Parliament as a reverend father in God and primate of Scotland.' If Mary was at first unsure of her strength in her own land, the Reformers were still unsure of their strength in victory. So, despite the bold words of the " Barons and Gentlemen professing Christ Jesus," compromise became the order of the day.[4]

It may be said, with some justice, that the politicians betrayed

[1] *Infra*, ii, 7. In view of the political situation, Mary's arrival, a week before she was expected, is significant. Elizabeth was still secretly supporting the Hamiltons ; and her refusal of a safe conduct to Mary, and her fleet at sea, may have been an attempt to force Mary to take the western route to Dumbarton, that is, to the Hamilton country.

[2] *Infra*, i, 361

[3] It is to be noted, and the point is important, that the last article of the Concessions at Edinburgh had stated that the Comissioners would not touch the question of religion, but remitted the same to be " decided by their Majesties " (*infra*, i, 330).

[4] Moreover, there was no longer a many-sided appeal, as in 1559, to hold together an ' Army of the Congregation.' After all, the French had been expelled and the nobility had tightened their grip on the monastic lands. Was the new faith in itself enough ?

the ministers ; but the politicians remembered that the protection and maintenance granted to Scotland by Elizabeth in the Treaty of Berwick was to endure only during the time of the marriage of Mary and Francis, and for one year thereafter ; and with the death of Francis II the ' one year thereafter ' expired in December 1561. If Mary were to assert her claim to the English throne, old enmities, so recently forgotten, would be renewed ; if the ' wars of Israel ' were to be fought again, would England again lend aid ? To the politicians, and above all to Lethington, compromise seemed essential. Perhaps Mary (who had constantly refused to ratify the Treaty of Edinburgh, recognizing Elizabeth's right and title to the English throne) might be persuaded to recognize Elizabeth as the lawful Queen of England, if Elizabeth could be persuaded to recognize Mary as her lawful successor. Perhaps thereby Mary might be ' won ' to the new alliance ; perhaps she might even be ' won ' to the new faith ; surely she could be ' won ' to ' sweet reasonableness ' in her dynastic claims and in her advocacy of the Church of her youth.[1] Only by an ' allurement ' of Mary towards friendship with England could the danger of a renewal of the old alliance be averted. And from such an ' allurement ' might not the union of Scotland and England be at last secured ?

But to Knox compromise was anathema. A week after Mary's return the English agent, Randolph, was writing that Knox ' thundereth out of the pulpit . . . he ruleth the roast, and of him all men stand in fear.' Yet, almost at once, this same Knox finds himself alone, desperately striving to defend the ' Evangel ' so lately won, and to defend it, not merely against the Queen, but against the desertion of former allies. He can find no agreement with the shifts and policies of Moray and of Lethington. He breaks with both ; and though the prophet may still thunder as of old, he finds less and less response and becomes a glowming and introspective monitor. Already, by October 1561, he "seeks for rest," "daily longing for an end of miseries," and fearing the one thing " more terrible

[1] Nor was this policy wholly without some indications of possible success. In view of Knox's constant attacks on Mary's uncles and his accounts of the determination of the house of Guise to repress all heresy, it should be noted that Charles de Guise, Cardinal of Lorraine, had ' flirted with Lutheranism,' had been denounced as ' damned and a heretic, or, to speak plainly, one of the protestants ' ; while it was even rumoured in Scotland, in February 1562, that he had advised Mary to embrace Anglicanism (*Calendar of Scottish Papers*, i, No. 1077 ; H. O. Evennett, *The Cardinal of Lorraine and the Council of Trent*). It is not possible to dismiss all this as solely ' political.' Mary apparently toyed with the advice tendered her ; but many of her motives and actions, in the years immediately following her return, defeat analysis.

than all others "—a return of the idolatry of the Mass.[1] The years become years of suspense—a kind of religious armistice—and out of that they become also years of contention and argument, of intrigue and plot.

We can now realize how hopeless were these political ambitions of Lethington ; how hopeless his fond idea that Mary might be ' won ' and Scotland and England ' more straitly joined together.' His scheme, ideal in its concept and desirous in itself, utterly failed to take account of the characters of the Queens. To Elizabeth, now more secure on her throne, a recognition of Mary's ultimate right might be an encouragement to the Roman Catholic powers to anticipate nature's course ; and Elizabeth had ever a ' complex ' against naming her successor and thereby ' wrapping herself in her own winding-sheet.' To Mary, young and impetuous, a child of the court of France, the scheme was distant and remote ; a lawful claimant was to be kept waiting for a succession which was hers by right. Nor was the initial conflict between the ministers and the politicians to be long delayed. On the first Sunday following her landing Mary heard Mass in her own chapel at Holyrood, and when men began to ask, " Shall that idol be suffered again ? " it was the Lord James, the warrior of the Army of the Congregation, who " took upon him to keep the chapel door " and to bar it against the " gentle-men of Fife " when they cried out that " The idolater priest should die the death." [2]

Perhaps there was " some enchantment whereby men were be-witched "[3]; certainly there was a desire to avoid precipitate action. But to Knox his duty was clear. In the Queen's Mass he saw only the thin end of a mighty wedge, and from his pulpit in St. Giles he ' inveighed ' as of old. To him one Mass was more fearful than if " ten thousand armed enemies were landed in any part of the realm, of purpose to suppress the whole religion. For . . . when we join hands with idolatry, it is no doubt but that both God's amicable presence and comfortable defence leaveth us, and what shall then become of us ? Alas, I fear that experience shall teach us, to the grief of many." [4]

For his sermon Knox was summoned to the first of his interviews with the Queen. He left it, to give his opinion of Mary " at the first, and ever since "—" If there be not in her a proud mind, a crafty wit, and an indurate heart against God and his truth, my

---

[1] Laing's *Knox*, vi, 129–131 (Knox to Mrs. Anna Locke, 2 October 1561)
[2] *Infra*, ii, 8   [3] *Infra*, ii, 12   [4] *Infra*, ii, 12

judgment faileth me." [1] Yet, some weeks later, Maitland was writing to Cecil still hoping a ' godly conjunction ' of the realms ; lamenting the ' vehemency ' of Knox and wishing he could deal ' more gently ' with the Queen, she ' being a young princess unpersuaded ' with whom ' much ' might be done in religion ; and finally commenting that for such hopes he himself was ' accounted to be too politic.' [2] Was not Lethington indeed too politic ? And did Knox need a prophet's vision to foresee that " The Devil, getting entry with his finger, will shoot forth his whole arm " ? [3] Writing to Cecil he damns all compromise with " Sathan "—

> Men delighting to swim betwix two waters, have often complained upon my severity ; fearing, as it seemed, that the same should trouble the quietness of brethren. But I do fear that that which men term lenity and dulceness doth bring upon themselves, and others, more fearful destruction than yet hath ensued the vehemency of any preacher within this Realm. That our Queen shall be allured by any such means as we yet use, is altogether contrary to my judgment ; for as I have spoken, so see I in experience, that by permission Sathan groweth bold. [4]

When the Lords continued to urge " That the Queen should have her religion free in her own chapel," Knox, with the principal ministers, was quick to retort, " That her liberty should be their thraldom ere it was long." [5] And when the Lords, striving to " please the Queen, and yet seem somewhat to satisfy the faithful," devised that the ministers might share with the Queen one-third of the revenues of the benefices of the Roman Church, the holders of the benefices still to enjoy the remaining two-thirds, " John Knox's judgment " was given without reserve : " I see two parts freely given to the Devil,[6] and the third must be divided betwix God and the Devil.[7] Well, bear witness to me that this day I say it, ere it be long the Devil shall have three parts of the Third ; and judge you then what God's portion shall be." [8] Yet Knox could not be unaware that if the ministers were to seek more than that now given, many a former Protestant lord would no longer " seek heaven rather than earth," but would turn to the party of the Queen, and would let greed take refuge in politics.

But might not the foundations of the Kirk be strengthened the better to resist assault ? Might not the old bonds of the Congrega-

---

[1] *Infra*, ii, 20   [2] *Calendar of Scottish Papers*, i, No. 1037   [3] *Infra*, ii, 23
[4] Knox to Cecil, 7 October 1561 (Laing's *Knox*, vi, 131)   [5] *Infra*, ii, 24
[6] The holders of the benefices, still retaining two-thirds of their revenues
[7] The remaining third, divided between the ministers and the Queen
[8] *Infra*, ii, 28, 29 ; for the Acts relating to the Thirds, see Appendix IX

tion be more firmly knit ? When Lethington doubted whether the General Assembly of the Kirk could be held without the knowledge and sanction of the Queen, Knox again was quick with his reply : " Take from us the freedom of Assemblies, and take from us the Evangel." What lay behind that answer we can only surmise. The struggle between the Assembly and the King was to come in the reign of Mary's son. But had Knox something more in mind than a gathering of the Church to guide and rule its work ? Was there some connecting thought that an Assembly of the Church might yet need to be a convocation of the now disbanded Army of Christ Jesus his Evangel ? And was not his letter of 8 October 1563, craving the " comfort and assistance " of " the Brethren," dangerously close to such a convocation of the lieges of the Queen ? [1]

Again politics and religion are to be inextricably interwoven. To Mary, the Church of Rome might be " the true Kirk of God " ; to Knox, it might be the Roman " harlot . . . altogether polluted with all kind of spiritual fornication ". [2] But what if Mary were to marry into the house of one of the Roman Catholic powers ? Could Protestantism in Scotland, and even in England, hope to survive ? [3] In Europe, the ' Wars of Religion ' had already begun ; and the Council of Trent, while calling the old Church to reform, had also called for a merciless repression of the Church that was heretic and new. Again an issue for Scotland became an issue for Western Europe ; and the question of Mary's marriage assumed an importance in Continental courts. Again the defence of the Kingdom of God became part and parcel with the defence of the Scottish realm. So, in his sermon of 1563 before " the most part of the nobility " at the time of the Parliament, Knox once more makes the double appeal :

> And now, my Lords, to put end to all, I hear of the Queen's marriage : Dukes, brethren to Emperors, and Kings strive all for the best game. But this, my Lords, will I say . . . whensoever the Nobility of Scotland professing the Lord Jesus, consents that an infidel (and all Papists are infidels) shall be head to your Sovereign, ye do so far as in ye lieth to banish Christ Jesus from this Realm ; ye bring God's vengeance upon the country, a plague upon yourselves, and perchance ye shall do small comfort to your Sovereign. [4]

---

[1] *Infra*, ii, 88–89   [2] *Infra*, ii, 17–18

[3] Already, in 1561, the Pope had been hoping for the marriage of Mary ' to some powerful Catholic prince, so as to be able to ensure the succession to the kingdom of England, which justly falls to her, after the present Queen Elizabeth.' (Pollen, *Papal Negotiations with Mary Queen of Scots*, Scot. Hist. Soc., 59–60)   [4] *Infra*, ii, 81

Had not the nobility God's cause in their own hands, to establish it as they pleased ?

> The Queen, say ye, will not agree with us. Ask ye of her that which by God's word ye may justly require, and if she will not agree with you in God, ye are not bound to agree with her in the Devil. Let her plainly understand so far of your minds ; and steal not from your former stoutness in God, and he shall prosper you in your enterprises.[1]

There follows another interview with Mary [2] ; there is a riot at Holyrood against the Mass ; two Edinburgh burgesses are summoned to " underlie the law " for invasion of the Queen's palace ; and Knox sends out his letter of 8 October 1563 to the Brethren. The ' Congregation ' must again gather for the " advancement of God's glory, the safety of their brethren and their own assurance, together with the preservation of the Kirk in these appearing dangers." [3] For that letter he is arraigned before the Privy Council, but the charge is allowed to rest. Already he is convinced that the war must be waged anew ; but these are only the preliminaries for position. The skies are heavy, but the storm has yet to break. And, in the end, Mary's own actions and character are to deprive the Roman Church of any chance of victorious recovery. Book IV of the *History*, (and the close of Knox's own writing,) ends with a long argument between Knox and Lethington on the rights of subjects to resist the idolatry of kings ; a note at the foot of the final folio, probably added in Knox's own hand, records and regrets his estrangement from Moray so that " in all that time . . . neither by word nor write was there any communication betwix them." [4]

And now Mary's reign moves swiftly to its climax and its close. Early in 1565 Henry, Lord Darnley, arrived in Scotland ; and in July 1565 Mary and Darnley were married. That marriage marked the end of compromise. To the Hamiltons, it meant the preferment of the Lennox-Stewarts and the ruin of their hopes of royalty [5] ; to Moray, it meant an end of influence and power ; and to Lethington it was an end to all his hopes of ' sweet reasonableness.' But to Knox the union of Mary and Darnley was a union of Roman Catholics and an open threat to the ' true religion.' Now all his warnings had been amply proved ; now " in the audience of many " he asked God's mercy " that he was not more vehement and upright in the suppressing of that idol in the beginning." [6] For now, with her marriage settled, Mary seized the opportunity to assert herself against the

[1] *Infra*, ii, 80–81　　[2] *Infra*, ii, 81–84　　[3] *Infra*, ii, 89　　[4] *Infra*, ii, 134
[5] See the Table, *infra*, ii, 351　　　　　　[6] *Infra*, ii, 13

preachers and the politicians alike. Too late Moray and Lethington, whose previous policies had fatally split the old Army of the Congregation, strove to bring that army together again. The Lords who gathered to demand the maintenance of the true religion *before* they would consent to the marriage, found themselves, *after* the marriage, driven in headlong rout in the Chase-about-Raid.

For a time a young Queen reigned supreme, only to discover that her marriage, from which she had expected so much, had been a grievous mistake. To Darnley she refused the crown-matrimonial ; to Riccio, " the poltroon Davie," she gave her confidence. And out of Darnley's jealousies and distrust a plot was hatched : Darnley was to have the crown-matrimonial ; the Protestant Lords, now in exile after the Chase-about-Raid, were to be restored ; the ' religion ' was to be fortified and maintained ; and last, but not least, Riccio's throat was to be cut. And cut it was. On 9 March 1566 Riccio was murdered ; and on the evening of the same day the exiled Protestant Lords rode into Edinburgh. But promptly the weak and unstable Darnley turned informer. Again two forces were in the field ; again Mary proved to be the stronger ; again she was able to assert herself much as she had done after the Chase-about-Raid ; and Knox, writing at this time the Preface to Book IV of his *History*, puts the question :

> From whence (alas) cometh this miserable dispersion of God's people . . . And what is the cause that now the just are compelled to keep silence ; good men are banished ; murderers, and such as are known unworthy of the common society (if just laws were put in due execution) bear the whole regiment and swing [1] within this Realm ?

To which he returns the answer :

> Because that suddenly the most part of us declined from the purity of God's word, and began to follow the world ; and so again to shake hands with the Devil and with idolatry. . . .

while the preachers who showed the dangers inherent in the Queen's Mass were " judged to be men of unquiet spirits." [2]

But Darnley was no longer despised by Mary ; now he was hated. And the counterpart to that hatred was the rise of Bothwell. Again a plot was hatched, a plot in which murder and marriage were to go together. On 10 February 1567 Darnley was ' blown up ' at Kirk o' Field ; and on 15 May Mary and Bothwell were married. For the third time in Mary's brief personal reign two forces were in the field ; but the hasty marriage with Bothwell had alienated too

---

[1] *rule and sway*   [2] *Infra*, ii, 4–5

many who would have otherwise supported the Queen.[1] On 15 June, exactly one month after her marriage to Bothwell, Mary surrendered at Carberry without a fight ; on 24 July she was constrained to demit her crown to her infant son and to appoint Moray as Regent of the realm ; and in December 1567 a Parliament, again attended by many Protestant lairds, re-enacted the anti-papal legislation of 1560 and re-affirmed the Confession of Faith.

Later, for a brief period, the ' Queen's men ' [2] and the ' King's men ' continued the strife. But, for a second time, an English army arrived to help a Scottish force besieging a Scottish stronghold. Edinburgh Castle, held in the name of Mary by Kirkcaldy of Grange (Knox's old companion and a gallant soldier too faithful to a doubtful cause), surrendered in 1573 even as Leith had surrendered in 1560. Kirkcaldy was hanged, lamenting with his latest breath his neglect of the counsels of Knox [3] ; an English army again withdrew across the Border ; and the child-king, James VI, could be regarded as reasonably secure on his mother's throne—though that did not mean that Protestantism also was secure. And, in the meantime, John Knox had died on the night of 24 November 1572.

In these final years of strain and stress the prophet plays a smaller part : religion has been almost lost in politics, and the Evangel of Christ has been forgotten in intrigue and plot. With the erection of Mary's Mass, Knox would have called the people to further battle for their God ; but those who should have led them in the fight had resorted to compromise, thereby slandering the Evangel, and exposing it to mockage.[4] The burgesses of Edinburgh might support him as of old ; but, even in Edinburgh, malicious tongues had grown busy with gossip over his second marriage—the marriage of a man of fifty to Margaret Stewart, the young seventeen-year-old daughter of Andrew, Lord Stewart of Ochiltree.[5]

---

[1] And not merely the Scottish nobility. On 2 July 1567 the Pope sent the message that as for Mary it was not ' his intention to have any further communication with her, unless indeed, in times to come he shall see some better sign of her life and religion than he has witnessed in the past.' (Pollen, *Papal Negotiations with Mary Queen of Scots*, 397, cxxviii–cxxxiii)

[2] Including, significantly, the old *politiques*, the Hamiltons

[3] Maitland of Lethington, who had supported the project for the marriage of Mary with the Duke of Norfolk, who had been warded by the Regent Moray, but who had escaped to the security of the castle, died soon after his capture—perhaps by his own hand—and so escaped the fate that befell Kirkcaldy.

[4] *Infra*, ii, 5, 65

[5] Marjory Bowes had died towards the end of November, or early in December 1560 (*infra*, i, 351), and Knox's second marriage took place in March 1564. By his second wife Knox had three daughters, Martha, Margaret, and Elizabeth.

Yet the voice of the prophet was not wholly stilled. Three weeks after the marriage of Mary and Darnley he preached in St. Giles from the twenty-sixth chapter of Isaiah. There, from the pulpit, with Darnley sitting before him, he did not spare to speak of the history of Ahab and Jezebel (a favourite theme)—

> But how did Ahab visit God again for his great benefit received ? Did he remove his idolatry ? Did he correct his idolatrous wife Jezebel ? No, we find no such thing ; but the one and the other we find to have continued and increased in former impiety. But what was the end hereof ? The last visitation of God was, that dogs licked the blood of the one, and did eat the flesh of the other.[1]

But his text also included the twentieth and twenty-first verses : ' Hide thyself as it were for a little moment, until the indignation be overpast. For, behold, the Lord cometh out of his place to punish the inhabitants of the earth for their iniquity.' Perhaps Moray and Lethington who had deserted him, but who were even now striving to recover the ground they had lost, might yet be able to do the work of the Lord. ' Hide thyself for a while,' said Isaiah ; and so, opening his sermon, he speaks of the necessity for present prudence and patience, and for a trust that assuredly God will render recompense—

> As the cunning mariner, being master, having his ship tossed with vehement tempest and winds contrarious, is compelled oft to traverse, lest that either by too much resisting to the violence of the waves his vessel might be overwhelmed ; or, by too much liberty granted, to be carried whither the fury of the tempest would, his ship should be driven upon the shore, and so make shipwreck. . . .[2]

Is this the Knox we knew ? The Knox to whom all temporizing was an abomination before the Lord ?

Soon, with the Protestant lords in exile after the Chase-about-Raid, he can do little save lament the affliction of the flock. He is sent from Edinburgh to visit the churches in the south and to stay there ' so long as occasion might suffer '—and that might well be read as a mission for his own safety. Later, with the murder of " that great abuser of this commonwealth, that poltroon and vile knave " Riccio,[3] he has again to seek refuge in the west. Then,

---

[1] Laing's *Knox*, vi, 256. See also *infra*, ii, 159
[2] Laing's *Knox*, vi, 234
[3] *Infra*, i, 112

on the very day it was learned that Darnley and Mary were together at Dunbar, with their forces rallying round them, he offered up his prayer—" Lord Jesus, receive my spirit, and put an end, at thy good pleasure, to this my miserable life ; for justice and truth are not to be found amongst the sons of men." [1] Then assurance left him, and the man who had boldly asked, " Why should the pleasing face of a gentlewoman effray me ? " [2] fled from that pleasing face ' west to Kyle.' During these days of exile, ' nursing his wrath ' and awaiting the greater wrath of the Lord, he continues work upon his *History*, adding here and revising there, and into his writing he pours all the wormwood and bitterness of his soul. [3] Back in Edinburgh again, in September 1566, he stays there only a few months, and during all the turmoil of 1567—the murder of Darnley, the marriage with Bothwell, and Mary's ultimate fall—he is absent in England, on a visit to his sons.

With the fall of Mary, however, once more the work of the Lord has prospered, and the prophet returns to his own land to ensure that this time the victory shall not be wasted when won. On 21 July 1567 Throckmorton reports that Knox was daily praying and exhorting the people against the Queen and Bothwell, threatening ' the great plague of God to this whole country and nation if she be spared from her condign punishment ' [4]; and that hatred of the Queen was to pursue her even after her flight to England in 1568. [5] On 29 July 1567 he preached at the coronation of the infant King, ' taking his text from the Book of Kings, when Joash was crowned very young.' He preached at the opening of the Parliament of December 1567. And, little more than two years later, he preached the funeral sermon of the Regent Moray (assassinated by a Hamilton), when he is said to have moved three thousand hearers to tears. ' Blessed are they that die in the Lord ' was his text ; and was not Moray doubly blessed as a lamb that had been lost and found again ?

In the autumn of 1570 he had a slight stroke ; and, at the end of that year, he entered into a bitter quarrel with his former com-

---

[1] Laing's *Knox*, vi, 483   [2] *Infra*, ii, 46   [3] *Infra*, xci–xcii
[4] *Calendar of Scottish Papers*, ii, No. 568
[5] Writing to Cecil, in January 1570 (but, we must remember, after the rebellion of the northern earls in England, a rebellion, *inter alia*, to release Mary from Tutbury) he does not hesitate to urge, " If ye strike not at the root, the branches that appear to be broken will bud again (and that more quickly than men can believe) with greater force than we would wish " ; adding, in a postscript, " More days than one would not suffice to express what I think." (Laing's *Knox*, vi, 568)

rade, Kirkcaldy, now holding Edinburgh Castle for the Queen.[1] In May 1571, because of that quarrel, he left Edinburgh [2] for the quietude of St. Andrews where he lodged in the Priory with his young wife, their three small daughters, and Richard Bannatyne his servant and secretary. At St. Andrews, James Melville, then a young student, heard him preach and teach—

> But of all the benefits I had that year was the coming of that most notable prophet and apostle of our nation, Mr. John Knox. . . . I heard him teach there the prophecy of Daniel [3] that summer and the winter following. I had my pen and my little book, and took away such things as I could comprehend. In the opening up of his text he was moderate the space of an half-hour ; but when he entered to application, he made me so to grew [4] and tremble, that I could not hold a pen to write. . . . Mr. Knox would sometimes come in and repose him in our College yard, and call us scholars unto him and bless us, and exhort us to know God and his work in our country, and stand by the good cause, to use our time well, and learn the good instructions and follow the good example of our masters. . . . I saw him every day of his doctrine go hulie and fear,[5] with a furring of martriks [6] about his neck, a staff in the one hand, and good godly Richard Bannatyne, his servant, holding up the other oxter,[7] from the Abbey to the parish kirk ; and, by the said Richard and another servant, lifted up to the pulpit, where he behoved to lean at his first entry ; but, ere he had done with his sermon, he was so active and vigorous that he was like to ding that pulpit in blads [8] and fly out of it.[9]

But the years have taken toll. On 26 May 1572, he dates a letter "Lying in Saint Andrews, half dead " ; on 12 July he writes, " I heartily salute and take my good-night [10] of all the faithful in both the Realms [11] . . . For as the world is weary of me, so am I of it " ; and, a week later, " out of bed, and

---

[1] Arising out of that quarrel, and Kirkcaldy's threatenings, the ' Brethren of the West ' wrote to Kirkcaldy in support of Knox, ' in whose protection and life . . . stands the prosperity and increase of God's Kirk,' of which Kirk God had made him ' both the first planter and also the chief waterer.' (Laing's *Knox*, vi, 584–585)

[2] ' Sore against his will, being compelled by the brethren of the Kirk and town ; because that his tarry would be an occasion of further trouble unto them, and an occasion of the shedding of their blood for his defence.'

[3] And from " the text written in Daniel, the seventh chapter " had been taken that sermon in St. Andrews, "which was the first that ever John Knox made in public" (*infra*, i, 84–86).   [4] *shudder*   [5] *carefully and slowly*   [6] *a fur of marten-skin*   [7] *armpit*, but here used in the sense of *taking his arm*   [8] *to break it in pieces*
[9] *Autobiography and Diary of Mr. James Melvill* (Wodrow Soc.), 26, 33. The spelling has been modernized.   [10] *farewell*   [11] Scotland and England

from my book, I come not but once in the week." Already he feels
the hand of death upon him ; and he must return to Edinburgh to
die. By slow stages he reaches Edinburgh towards the end of August
1572, and goes to his last house by the Netherbow.[1] On Sunday,
31 August, he is preaching in St. Giles again, but he is now so
feeble that ' scarce can he stand ' and his voice so weak that he
can be heard only by those immediately around him ; and, writing
to his chosen successor, James Lawson of Aberdeen, he adds the
postscript " Haste, lest ye come too late."

On 9 November he inducted his successor in St. Giles, but
on Tuesday 11 November he was ' stricken with a great host '[2]
which left him so weak that two days later he was compelled
to abandon ' his ordinary reading of the Bible.' That same day he
directed his wife to pay the servants their wages, paying one himself
on the morning after, and adding, with a touch of the old grim
humour, " Thou will never get no more of me in this life," and
therewith giving him twenty shillings above his due. On the
Saturday, two friends came in, not knowing how ill he was, and
for their sake he came to the table, and caused a hogshead of wine
to be broached in the cellar, willing one of them to send for it as
long as it lasted. A woman who called and began to praise his work,
was met with " Tongue ! tongue ! lady ; flesh of itself is over
proud, and needs no means to esteem itself." But now he was
failing rapidly. About five o'clock, on the afternoon of 24 November, he bade his wife " Go read where I cast my first anchor " ;
and so she read the seventeenth chapter of the Evangel of St. John.
The final comfort was in the elect of Christ. About eleven o'clock
he cried suddenly, " Now it is come ! " Those who were with him
gathered round the bed and asked him for a sign. ' He lifted up
his one hand, and incontinent thereafter rendered the spirit.'

Knox was buried in the churchyard of St. Giles. With the
growth of Edinburgh, and the removal of the old churchyard, the probable site of his grave is now marked by a plain **I. K. 1572** let into
the middle of the roadway, where men pass heedlessly over it.[3] A
contemporary diarist records his death with the words, ' John Knox,
minister, deceased in Edinburgh, who had, as was alleged, the most

[1] There is no proof that this was the house of James Mosman, the goldsmith, the
house now popularly known as ' John Knox's House.'
[2] A severe fit of *coughing*
[3] Though it should be remembered that the modern Parliament Square, to the
south of St. Giles, is raised ground, and that the old churchyard sloped steeply to the
Cowgate.

part of the wite of all the cummers [1] in Scotland since the slaughter of umquhile the Cardinal' [2]; but at his burial the Regent Morton is said to have spoken the words, ' Here lieth a man who neither feared nor flattered any flesh.' [3] The latter part of that ' testimony ' was certainly true.

VII

Knox's own conception of the part he felt called upon to play in the struggle for the " forward setting and maintenance of the Evangel of Christ " may be read in the Preface to his sermon of 19 August 1565—" considering myself rather called of my God to instruct the ignorant, comfort the sorrowful, confirm the weak, and rebuke the proud, by tongue and lively voice in these most corrupt days, than to compose books for the age to come." [4] And that is the Knox we visualize. Yet despite his own disclaimer, we find this same man, during the intensity of the struggle of 1559 to 1560, not only preaching and exhorting, but also acting as secretary to the Congregation, drafting their proclamations and manifestos, travelling to and fro on their affairs, and, finally, already writing his *History* as a justification of their cause.[5] This was the time when " in twenty-four hours I have not four free to natural rest," the time when watch was made for him, a price put upon his head, and he has " need of a good and an assured horse," and the time when his wife, helping with his writings, was so weary " that scarcely could she tell, upon the morrow, what she wrote at night." [6] So he writes in his private letters, and the *History* gives us the same picture of a man who is a stranger to all ease and hating ease in others ; a man constantly reaching forth unto those things which are before [7] and ever pressing ' toward the mark ' ; a man single in purpose, of a hard fibre, inflexible, tenacious, and, above all, of complete assurance that his cause and his interpretation of that cause is alone that which is right. The whole spirit of Knox pours itself into his writing, and the *History of the Reformation of Religion within the Realm of Scotland* is the history of both the man and the cause.

---

[1] the most part of the *blame* of all the *troubles*
[2] *Diurnal of Occurrents* (Bannatyne Club), 320
[3] Morton's words are variously reported.
[4] Laing's *Knox*, vi, 229
[5] See *infra*, lxxxviii–lxxxix
[6] Laing's *Knox*, vi, 88, 104
[7] The drafting of the Book of Discipline even before the victory had been won (*supra*, l) is an outstanding instance of his ' forward mindedness '.

The opening Preface, in which the " gentle reader " is warned not to expect a history of " all things that have occurred within this Realm during the time of this terrible conflict that has been betwix the saints of God and these bloody wolves who claim to themselves the title of clergy," is at once indicative of the central theme. To Knox, every issue is subordinate to the struggle between the Roman Church and the " Evangel of Christ "—a struggle, grim and merciless, in which " light and darkness strive within the realm " [1]; and in the *History*, first Knox and the Queen Regent, and then Knox and Mary Stewart tend to become the protagonists in that struggle. At first, there is a half-veiled attempt at anonymity, and some attempt to keep to a history of the movement itself ; but in Book IV, with the return of Mary Stewart, the *History* openly gives way to the story of a duel between Mary, ' troubled for the preservation of her silly Mass,' and Knox, convinced that Mary's Mass would give the Devil free rein to run forward in his course. To Knox, moreover, the spirit of that struggle is the spirit of a holy war—" Thus ceased not Sathan, by all means, to maintain his kingdom of darkness and to suppress the light of Christ's Evangel " [2]; or, on the other hand, " This was no small victory of Christ Jesus fighting against the conjured enemies of his verity." [3] In that war the arm of God is to be " evidently seen " : here a journey may be postponed to the disappointment of some hostile ambuscade [4]; there, the heart of a bitter opponent may be opportunely moved. At Cupar Muir " God did so multiply our number, that it appeared as [if] men had rained from the clouds," [5] while to a like divine dispensation must be attributed that miracle of the ordnance at Haddington, when " God so conducted " its fire that more than a hundred of the French fell at two shots only.[6] Yet to Knox this is but that same God of Israel who could raze the walls of Jericho and divide the waters of the Red Sea. The God who could punish the wickedness of man by flooding the face of the earth could still make manifest his displeasure with the masks and revels of the Court and the inordinate dancing of the Queen—

For upon the 20th day of January [1564] there fell wet in great abundance, which, in the falling, freezed so vehemently that the earth was but a sheet of ice. The fowls both great and small freezed, and might not fly : many died, and some were taken and laid beside

---

[1] *Infra*, i, 117   [2] *Infra*, i, 56   [3] *Infra*, i, 45   [4] *Infra*, i, 64
[5] *Infra*, i, 183. At the siege of Leith, it appeared as if God " had fed the army from above." (*Infra*, i, 317)   [6] *Infra*, i, 106

the fire, that their feathers might resolve. And in that same month the sea stood still, as was clearly observed, and neither ebbed nor flowed the space of twenty-four hours.[1]

The kingdom which has turned its heart to idolatry must endure the visitations of an angry God. When dearth and famine visit the land

> So did God, according to the threatening of his law, punish the idolatry of our wicked Queen, and our ingratitude that suffered her to defile the land with that abomination again, that God so potently had purged by the power of his word. For the riotous feasting and excessive banqueting, used in Court and country, wheresoever that wicked woman repaired, provoked God to strike the staff of bread and to give his malediction upon the fruits of the earth.[2]

Only by understanding this can we understand that injuction to the Queen Regent to " consider that ye fight not against man, but against the eternal God," [3] or realize the import of the Regent's cry, when news is brought to her of some small success in Fife, " Where is now John Knox's God ? My God is now stronger than his, yea, even in Fife." [4] Because of this, the victory of the English at Solway Moss was " the hand of God, fighting against pride for freedom of his . . . flock," [5] and Hertford's ruthless invasions were " a part of the punishment which God took upon the realm " [6] ; for we need only remember that at these times England was under a Protestant king, while Scotland was under a Roman faction, and that to Knox the Evangel was greater than the love of country or the love for friends.

Yet should the Protestant endeavour meet with the humiliation of defeat, we are reminded " that God gave victory to the Israelites over the Benjamites after that twice with ignominy they were repulsed " [7] ; or, if the victory is hardly won and of doubtful achievement, " God would not give the victory so suddenly, lest that man should glory in his own strength." [8] When the defenders of the Castle of St. Andrews bragged of the force and thickness of their walls, John Knox " was of another judgment " and prophesied that their walls " should be but egg-shells " ; when they vaunted " England will rescue us," he replied, " Ye shall not see them ;

---

[1] *Infra*, ii, 103   [2] *Infra*, ii, 70   [3] *Infra*, i, 246   [4] *Infra*, i, 277
[5] *Infra*, i, 38   [6] *Infra*, i, 58   [7] *Infra*, i, 270
[8] *Infra*, i, 312. Such interpretations of the issues of war—victory through the outstretched arm of the Lord ; defeat through too great a trust in the arm of the flesh— were later to reach their climax (and anti-climax) in the writings of the covenanting historians of the seventeenth century.

but ye shall be delivered in your enemy's hands, and shall be carried to a strange country." [1] Yet this same prophet in the hour of adversity, when he toiled with his companions in the French galleys, could still see the deliverance that was nigh—

> Whose answer was ever, from the day that they entered in the galleys, 'That God would deliver them from that bondage, to his glory, even in this life.' And lying betwix Dundee and Saint Andrews, the second time that the galleys returned to Scotland, the said John being so extremely sick that few hoped his life, the said Master James [Balfour] willed him to look to the land, and asked if he knew it? Who answered, " Yes : I know it well ; for I see the steeple of that place where God first in public opened my mouth to his glory, and I am fully persuaded, how weak that ever I now appear, that I shall not depart this life till that my tongue shall glorify his godly name in the same place." [2]

So spoke the prophets of Israel when their people groaned beneath the Babylonian yoke ; so had Wishart prophesied the approach of his own martyrdom, and the plague of Haddington by fire and sword and bondage [3] ; and was not Wishart Knox's master? Much of this prophecy may be *ex post facto*.[4] The prophecy of deliverance from the galleys was made in 1547 or 1548, but it was not committed to writing until about 1566 [5] ; the prophecy of " God's judgment " upon Mary of Guise [6] was likewise committed to writing some six years after the event, and it is more than likely that, even if the prophecy was made, Knox was well aware at the time of the seriousness of the Regent's disease. Yet, in *The First Blast of the Trumpet*, he had been more than successful with his prophecy of the early death of Mary Tudor,[7] and it is evident that a conviction of prophetic powers grew with the years.[8] In the Preface to his sermon of 1565 he does not hesitate to say, " I dare not deny (lest that in so doing I should be injurious to the giver), but that God hath revealed unto me secrets unknown to the world," [9] and that had long been part and parcel with his assurance in his cause, a cause whose members, as early as 1559, had claimed to be the

---

[1] *Infra*, i, 95-96　　　[2] *Infra*, i, 108-109. See *supra*, xxxiv, xliv　　　[3] *Infra*, i, 68
[4] The reader should consult the analysis of the times of writing (*infra*, lxxxviii-xciii).
[5] Knox himself admits that James Balfour denied he was ever in the galleys at all (*infra*, i, 97) ; elsewhere his " fully persuaded " becomes only an " assured hope " (*infra*, i, 182) ; and he certainly uses every endeavour to ensure fulfilment of the 'prophecy' (*infra*, i, 181-182).　　　[6] *Infra*, i, 319　　　[7] See Laing's *Knox*, iv, 420
[8] See *infra*, i, 123, 265　　　[9] Laing's *Knox*, vi, 229

elect of God.[1] There may, after all, be some significance in his " anchorage " in the seventeenth chapter of the Gospel according to St. John.[2]

Upon occasion, indeed, he might cover himself with a qualification that " if the result be happy, my judgment faileth me," but, more often, while the speaker was " nothing to be regarded," his words were " the infallible and eternal truth of God," a God who compelled him " to forespeak as well deliverance to the afflicted as destruction to certain inobedient." We need not wonder that in 1562 Randolph described him as being either ' of God's privy council ' or one who knew the very secrets of Mary's heart.[3] All this is in the character of the man, and Knox has been well likened to a Hebrew prophet in sixteenth-century Scotland. In 1559 he requires the Lords to lay his words before Mary of Guise " in the name of the eternal God, *as from my mouth*," and twice in the same passage he emphasizes " *in my name*." [4]

The temper of the *History* is the temper of the Psalmist that ' Bloody and deceitful men shall not live out half their days ' for ' Thou, O God, shalt bring them down into the pit of destruction ' ; and nowhere is this more evident than in the account of the assassination of Cardinal Beaton. There, when one or two of the conspirators would have cut down Beaton in the first fury of the moment, their hands were stayed by another who called them to remembrance that this was a " work and judgment of God," meet to be done with " greater gravity." The whole account, remarkable for its dramatic force, reveals an intensity of feeling born of religious fanaticism. " These things we write merrily," is Knox's final comment, " but," and there is a vast stress upon that word,

We would that the Reader should observe God's just judgments, and how that he can deprehend the worldy wise in their own wisdom, make their table to be a snare to trap their own feet, and their own presupposed strength to be their own destruction. *These are the works of our God*, whereby he would admonish the tyrants of this earth that in the end he will be revenged of their cruelty, what strength so ever they make in the contrary.[5]

[1] *Infra*, i, 170   [2] *Supra*, lxvii
[3] *Foreign Calendar, Elizabeth*, v, No. 1266. Knox's assurance must have led to a common saying that he was ' of God's secret council,' for in 1571 he felt impelled to make a formal denial. (Laing's *Knox*, vi, 592)
[4] *Infra*, i, 174. The italics are mine.
[5] *Infra*, i, 76-79. The italics are mine.

Or again, in a passage written in 1566 when Mary seemed about to triumph over the Protestant lords, her reign is to be seen as

> God's hand in his displeasure punishing our former ingratitude. Let men patiently abide, and turn unto their God, and then shall he either destroy that whore in her whoredom, or else he shall put it in the hearts of a multitude to take the same vengeance upon her that has been taken of Jezebel and Athaliah . . . for greater abomination was never in the nature of any woman than is in her, whereof we have but seen only the buds ; but we will after taste of the ripe fruit of her impiety, if God cut not her days short

with a marginal note, added on 15 June 1567 (the day that Mary surrendered herself to the Lords at Carberry Hill), *Perfice quod cepisti mi deus propter tui nominis gloriam.*[1] 'Blessed are the merciful' belongs to the New Testament and not to the books of wrath in the Old. Yet there is here something more than the wrath of God ; there is a narrow hate that diminishes the stature of the man and that chills us as we read.

In neither Mary Stewart nor her mother, Mary of Guise, could Knox find one redeeming virtue,[2] and twice he endeavours to slur their names with innuendos even more salacious than the outspokenness of this attack.[3] Was it because Mary of Guise remained unmoved by the prophet's threatenings, which to him were the threatenings of his God ? Was this that " spiritual hatred," that " perfect hatred which the Holy Ghost engendered in the hearts of God's elect " ?[4] Or was it that in her disregard the Regent had found the surest way to wound the prophet's pride ? For Mary Stewart, perhaps the former answer would suffice ; but Knox could never let such hatreds die, and even hatred of a less degree outruns his historical accuracy in more instances than one. Robert Reid, Bishop of Orkney, is described as dying " betwix his two coffers (some said upon them) : such was his god, the gold that therein was inclosed, that he could not depart therefrom, so long as memory would serve," with the concluding touch, that so he " departed this life ; whither, the great day of the Lord will declare "[5] ; but Reid was a liberal benefactor and an enlightened churchman, and from his bequest to found a college for the education of youth in Edinburgh sprang the present University. A nasty comment that

---

[1] 'Finish what thou hast begun, O my God, for the glory of thy name.' (*Infra*, i, 103)
[2] In the index, s.v. *Mary of Guise*, the reader will find collected Knox's many bitter comments upon the Queen Regent.
[3] *Infra*, i, 40, 322   [4] Laing's *Knox*, iii, 245   [5] *Infra*, i, 130

" shame " hastened the marriage of Mary Livingstone and John Sempill is not only unsavoury, but also untrue. [1]

In his hatreds, Knox was an adept at dismissing his opponents in the fewest words—John Sinclair, Bishop of Brechin, " blind of one eye in the body, but of both in his soul " [2]; Lord Sempill, " a man sold under sin, enemy to God, and to all godliness " [3] ; Lord Seton, " a man without God, without honesty, and oftentimes without reason " [4]; the Lady Erskine " a sweet morsel for the Devil's mouth." [5] The appointment of Mary of Guise as Queen Regent, in 1554, was " as seemly a sight (if men had eyes) as to put a saddle upon the back of an unruly cow." [6] Mary's own court was one of " scoupars, dancers, and dalliers with dames." [7] His adjectives, however, tend to become ' words of style,' so that " bloody " or " rotten " at once tells us he is speaking of a member of the Roman Church. These adjectives soon begin to pall, as also does his insistence upon certain Old Testament analogies—and notably that of Jezebel. Yet even when his analogy comes from the New Testament it still preserves its sting. The bishops who commit their victims to the secular arm are but following Pilate " who both did condemn, and also wash his hands " [8] ; and when the clergy, hoping to further their own ends, offer their money to the King, so " Sathan their father did to Christ Jesus if he would worship him." [9] At other times, however, the analogy may be more homely, as when the Queen Regent's burgh officials are as meet for office " as a souter [10] is to sail a ship in a stormy day " [11] ; and in such a homely phrase we can read part of Knox's appeal to the common man.

Here, too, we can see the keener play of satire and epigram. Oliver Sinclair in the rout of Solway Moss precedes Johnny Cope by a full two centuries, for " Stout Oliver was without stroke taken, fleeing full manfully." [12] The greed of James Beaton, Archbishop of St. Andrews, and also Abbot of Dunfermline, Arbroath, and Kilwinning, is dismissed with the trenchant line that " as he sought the world, it fled him not." [13] And this, again, is but part of a bolder

---

[1] Infra, ii, 102   [2] Infra, i, 112-113   [2] Infra, i, 174   [4] Infra, i, 192
[5] Infra, ii, 77. But Knox is less happy when he attempts an alliterative play upon words—" the carnal Cardinal " ; " his graceless Grace " ; " blasphemous Balfour " ; or " the bastard Bishop who yet was not execrated (consecrated they call it)." In one passage in his Admonition, however, he comes closer to real effect with " wily Winchester, dreaming Durham, and bloody Bonner," who " cannot cease nor assuage their furious fumes, for the Devil, their sire, stirreth, moveth, and carrieth them, even at his will." (Laing's Knox, iii, 285)
[6] Infra, i, 116. Another reading is sow   [7] Infra, ii, 102   [8] Infra, i, 7   [9] Infra, i, 31
[10] shoemaker   [11] Infra, i, 242   [12] Infra, i, 37   [13] Infra, i, 11

humour. Knox enjoyed the "merry bourd," even at his own expense.[1] Never is he happier than when describing to their ridicule some discomfiture of the priests. Then his prose becomes even more bold and vigorous, more 'unbuttoned.' The contest for precedence between the Archbishops of St. Andrews and Glasgow, in the bearing of their crosses, gives him full play, and after describing, half-seriously, half-humorously, the doubts and difficulties of the case, the account runs gloriously on—

> Rochets were rent, tippets were torn, crowns were knapped, and side gowns might have been seen wantonly wag from the one wall to the other. Many of them lacked beards, and that was the more pity ; and therefore could not bukkill other by the birse, as bold men would have done.[2]

Yet even that pales before his description of the tumult on St. Giles's Day, where the words themselves become the panting gasping tussle of men in hand-to-hand affray—

> for down goes the crosses, off goes the surplice, round caps corner with the crowns. The Grey Friars gaped, the Black Friars blew, the priests panted and fled ; and happy was he that first got [to] the house, for such a sudden fray came never amongst the generation of Antichrist within this realm before.[3]

So intensity is relieved by irony, by humour, and by anti-climax. The apt or striking phrase seems to come readily to his pen, and notably in biblical analogy. " God who plagued Pharaoh, repulsed Sennacherib, struck Herod with worms, and made the bellies of dogs the grave and sepulchre of despiteful Jezebel," [4] has a cumulative effect that reveals the master. His writing has all the vigour and vitality of the man, whilst at times it reaches unexpected heights. His letter to Elizabeth, in July 1559, concludes—

> But yet, if I should flatter your Grace, I were no friend, but a deceivable traitor. And therefore of conscience I am compelled to say, that neither the consent of people, the process of time, nor multitude of men, can establish a law which God shall approve ; but whatsoever He approveth by his eternal word, that shall be approved, and whatsoever He condemneth shall be condemned, though all men in earth would hazard the justification of the same. And therefore, Madam, the only way to retain and keep those benefits of God,

---

[1] See " The bishop's good mind toward John Knox " that if he preached he should be " saluted with a dozen of culverins whereof the most part should light upon his nose " (*infra*, i, 181).   [2] *Infra*, i, 73   [3] *Infra*, i, 128   [4] *Infra*, i, 227

abundantly poured now of late days upon you, and upon your realm, is unfeignedly to render unto God, to his mercy and undeserved grace, the whole glory of this your exaltation. Forget your birth, and all title which thereupon doth hang ; and consider deeply how, for fear of your life, ye did decline from God and bow to idolatry. Let it not appear a small offence in your eyes that ye have declined from Christ Jesus in the day of his battle. Neither yet would I that ye should esteem that mercy to be vulgar and common which ye have received : to wit, that God hath covered your former offence, hath preserved you when ye were most unthankful ; and, in the end, hath exalted and raised you up, not only from the dust, but also from the ports of death, to rule above his people for the comfort of his Kirk. It appertaineth to you, therefore, to ground the justice of your authority, not upon that law which from year to year doth change, but upon the eternal providence of Him who, contrary to nature, and without your deserving, hath thus exalted your head. If thus, in God's presence, ye humble yourself, as in my heart I glorify God for that rest granted to his afflicted flock within England, under you a weak instrument, so will I with tongue and pen justify your authority and regiment as the Holy Ghost hath justified the same in Deborah, that blessed Mother in Israel.[1]

And yet, having read the measured majesty of his prose, we pause to reflect that that was written at the very time when, as Knox himself well knew, English aid had become essential if the Army of the Congregation was to succeed in its struggle against the Queen Regent. Nor does our reflection end there. For, turning to the earlier part of this same letter, we find that Knox will withdraw " no point or proposition " of his *First Blast of the Trumpet* " till truth and verity do further appear." If he could never ' think it possible he might be mistaken,' we can also agree that he never " decked the matter for the pleasure of itching and delicate ears " ; if none could accuse him of speaking ' smooth things,' none could acquit him of ' speaking the truth unseasonably.' If it was the " office of a very friend to give true and faithful counsel," [2] Knox was ever ready to fulfil the part. The marriage of the Lord James was " public in the church of Edinburgh," yet even there the opportunity was taken for a timely warning to the bridegroom that " unto this day the Kirk of God hath received comfort by you, and by your labours ; in the which, if hereafter ye shall be found fainter than that ye were before, it will be said that your wife hath changed your

[1] *Infra*, i, 293-294   [2] *Infra*, i, 245

nature." [1] Awaiting, in an ante-chamber, the pleasure of an angry Queen, he can not forbear

> to forge talking of the ladies who were there sitting in all their gorgeous apparel ; which espied, he merrily said, " O fair Ladies, how pleasing were this life of yours, if it should ever abide, and then in the end that we might pass to heaven with all this gay gear. But fie upon that knave Death, that will come whether we will or not ! And when he has laid on his arrest, the foul worms will be busy with this flesh, be it never so fair and so tender ; and the silly [2] soul, I fear, shall be so feeble, that it can neither carry with it gold, garnishing, targetting, pearl, nor precious stones [3]

though we may find it hard to believe that " by such means procured he the company of women."

Not infrequently this " true and faithful counsel," or perhaps a challenge even more direct, came from the open pulpit as a ' special application ' of the text. In England, in his last sermon before Edward VI, the " ungodly councillors " of the King had been likened to Ahithophel, Shebna, and Judas ; in Scotland, Arran was contrasted with Jehoshaphat who came forth into the midst of his people and his soldiers and comforted them. [4] When such a preacher ' entered into application ' it is easy to understand why others ' as wise and learned as himself wished him to have held his peace.'

Yet for Knox there could be no conspiracy of silence, no " tempering of the tongue." The pulpit was his political platform, and throughout his life politics were inseparable from religion. Let the true religion be preached and observed, and the true politics would perforce follow. And from that arose the urgent need for *preachers* which lies at the very root of the Book of Discipline. In his *Letter to the Commonalty of Scotland* he had told the people that " although ye be but subjects, [ye] may lawfully require of your superiors . . . that they provide for you true Preachers " [5] ; and one of his last prayers was, " Lord, grant true pastors to thy Kirk." [6] Moreover, few could read, and the printed word was scarce. At St. Andrews the people, hearing his reply to Dean John Annan, had " cried with one consent, ' We cannot all read your writings, but we may all hear your preaching.' " [7] The pulpit reached the people. In England, the courtiers might absent themselves ; in Scotland, the Earl of Huntly might " pick his nails, pull down his bonnet over his eyes," and say, " When those knaves have railed their fill, then will they

---

[1] *Infra*, ii, 32   [2] *weak*   [3] *Infra*, ii, 84   [4] *Infra*, i, 278
[5] Laing's *Knox*, iv, 534   [6] *Ibid.*, vi, 624   [7] *Infra*, i, 84

hold their peace" [1] ; but Knox realized the power of the pulpit where to-day we speak of the ' power of the press.' John Knox was a preacher before all things else [2] ; and if, at all difficult times, " the principal comfort remained with the preachers," [3] the principal of the preachers was Knox.

> In your most extreme dangers I have been with you : St. Johnston, Cupar Muir and the Craigs of Edinburgh are yet recent in my heart ; yea, that dark and dolorous night wherein all ye, my Lords, with shame and fear left this town, is yet in my mind and God forbid that ever I forget it.[4]

Nor will the *History of the Reformation of Religion within the Realm of Scotland* allow " the posterities to come " to forget.

VIII

All this, and the spirit of it, is to be read in the *History*. Occasion-ally the language may seem coarse but, in the controversial writings of the time, Knox was not alone in his *virulentæ linguæ volubilitas*. The more brutal passages are different, but those, we must remember, were written in 1566, in the refuge of the west, when Mary seemed supreme and when all his hatred ran into his pen.[5] Those must have been the passages which Buchanan had in mind when, after Knox's death, he refers to the *History* as being in the hands of friends who were consulting together with a view to mitigating the acerbity of certain words and otherwise altering it ; while later, Archbishop Spottiswoode refused to recognize its ' scurrile discourses ' and ' ridiculous toys and malicious detractions ' as the work of Knox. Yet the historian himself had had opportunity to ' mitigate ' his language had he wished. Although he never saw his *History* in print,[6] there is evidence that he revised the manuscript [7] without revising its outspokenness.

Robust in style and rich in vocabulary, the language is essentially

---

[1] *Infra*, ii, 65

[2] Significantly, although Knox is mentioned only four times in Buchanan's *History*, upon each occasion he is delivering a sermon.

[3] *Infra*, i, 347

[4] *Infra*, ii, 80

[5] *Infra*, xci–xcii

[6] In a letter of February 1568 to Mr. John Wood, Knox seems to speak of withholding publication during his lifetime, " and then it shall be in the opinion of others whether it shall be suppressed or come to light." (Laing's *Knox*, vi, 558)

[7] *Infra*, xcv–cix

English.[1] So much does Knox write English, that his contemporary, Ninian Winzet, even accuses him of forgetting ' our auld plane Scottis quhilk zour mother lerit zou.' [2] This is very evident in the ' Admonitions,' ' Comfortable Epistles,' and ' Letters of Wholesome Counsel ' of the years of exile abroad ; but therein also lies the clue. Knox's work in England, his work with English congregations abroad, and, above all, his intimate knowledge of the English Bible, had a lasting influence on his idiom and his style. Our earliest manuscript of the *History*, although written by different scribes, appears to have been based on an earlier codex which was probably composed from notes or drafts written or dictated by Knox himself.[3] As such, it may be taken as representative of Knox's later style following his return to his native country. In the *History*, and particularly in the more dramatic parts, the ' auld plane ' Scots may intervene, but it does so only in a word or, at the most, in some happy phrase. It forms but a part of Knox's enjoyment in the richness of his vocabulary. If the language is English, it is English reinforced. If a homely Scottish word came easily to his pen, Knox wrote it down. French [4] and Latin were pressed into service as the need arose. If he were at a loss, he might even coin a word to suit his mood. So the reader will find ' placeboes ' (from the Latin *placebo*, ' I will please ') for the sixteenth-century ' yes-men ' of Church and Court ; he will hear of Bothwell being in the ' glondours ' of the Regent ; or he will roll his tongue round the ' dontybours ' who were the companions of the Queen.

In language and in style the *History* is a masterpiece, written by a man who could marshal words to meet his mood. Knox's belief in the cause for which he strove undoubtedly inspired his pen in the story of that cause and its vicissitudes. But the genius is deeper than that. Imaginative powers, a sense of dramatic values, and a sim-

---

[1] Otto Sprotte, *Zum Sprachgebrauch bei John Knox* (Berlin, 1906), provides a methodical (and almost statistical) analysis of Knox's language based on Laing's text (but see *supra*, xi, *note* 2). Sprotte notes, however, that although Knox writes English, he is apt to slip into the vernacular when recording direct speech ; and naturally so, for then he is writing ' by the ear ' and not ' by the eye.' Earlier, J. A. H. Murray had noted that in those passages where Knox is quoting or applying scriptural texts ' the language becomes entirely English ' (*The Dialect of the Southern Counties of Scotland*, 66) ; and again, naturally so, for all the printed versions of scriptural writings reached the people of Scotland in English form, and even the ' great Bible ' of Arbuthnot and Bassendyne was simply a reprint of the English Geneva version. (*Ibid.*, 66–67)

[2] *Certane Tractatis* (Maitland Club), 118 ; *idem* (Scot. Text Soc.), i, 138

[3] *Infra*, cvi–cix

[4] And sometimes with unusual meanings as, for example, *lardon* (*infra*, i, 366, *note* 1) and *marmouset* (*infra*, i, 127, *note* 4)

plicity of narrative all combine to form a living picture in the reader's mind. We are present in the times of which we read.

And what of it as ' history ' ? Later historians have tended to rely on Knox for their accounts of the ' uproar for religion.' Have they relied upon a trustworthy source ?

At first, the answer is an obvious one. In the *History*, as we have seen, the Roman Church is " Antichrist," its priests " that vermin of shavelings utterly corrupted " ; the Protestant martyrs are the " poor saints of God," the Protestant army " the Congregation of Christ Jesus his Evangel." How can we expect an objective account from a man who could never see good in any member of the Roman Church, [1] from a man who was one of the leaders of a revolution against both Church and State, and from a man who began his *History* in the very heat of the battle ?

Particularly does that apply to Book II, which is primarily a ' party pamphlet,' a piece of special pleading, a justification of the " Protestants of the Realm of Scotland . . . falsely accused of tumult and rebellion." There we have not merely a one-sided account with its sins of omission, but also, in at least two instances, what look like sins of commission as well. The evidence tends to show that Knox's account of the ' Appointment ' made at the Links of Leith was a ' coloured ' account to enable the Congregation still to lay stress upon the tyranny of the alien French ; and there, too, we find Knox denying, so far as he can, the negotiations with England. [2] These, and other points, are noted in their places in the text.

Yet in Book III Knox makes amends, and the negotiations with England are given without reserve. More than that, there and elsewhere he cites his documents in full. There he shows himself a good historian, basing much of his argument upon original sources and using those sources well. Moreover, whenever he can be checked we find that his transcripts are both faithful and accurate. [3] Indeed, the reader may now begin to think there are almost too

---

[1] *Supra*, lxix–lxxiv

[2] *Infra*, i, 194, *note* 2 ; 218, *note* 1. Andrew Lang was at some pains to show that in Book II Knox exceeded the limits of honest journalism, though Andrew Lang, in turn, somewhat over-stressed his case. (*Scottish Historical Review*, ii, 113–130. See also Andrew Lang, *John Knox and the Reformation*, *passim*)

[3] See, in particular, *infra*, i, 371, *note* 1, where he doubts his document but where the copy in the Public Record Office, London, proves his transcript to be correct. See also the comment made by the editor of the *Register of the Privy Council of Scotland* (i, xxxvi–xl) in relation to Knox's copy of Mary's Proclamation of 25 August 1561 (*infra*, ii, 9–10).

many documents ; but we must be grateful, for some of the documents here cited by Knox have since been lost. And, still on the
principle of giving ' full chapter and verse,' at the close of Book III
Knox registers for us *The Book of Discipline* to the end that "posterities
to come may judge as well what the worldlings refused, as what
policy the godly ministers required."

Thus, when he becomes the *historian*, and abandons the role of the
propagandist, Knox's ' history ' becomes more reasoned and trustworthy. We find him inviting the criticism of expert witnesses,[1]
and we find him seeking further sources of information. In September
1560 Randolph reports that in a conversation with Knox concerning
his *History*, he ' sayeth that he must have further help than is to
be had in this country, for more assured knowledge of things passed,
than he hath himself, or can come by here ' [2] ; while as late as
December 1571 Knox was in correspondence with the Clerk to the
Privy Council with regard to the availability and use of a number
of public documents.[3]

Certain minor inaccuracies and certain confusions in account
need not detain us. No book is without its errors ; and in one place
Knox himself admits that he strove " to express the verity " rather
than " scrupulously and exactly to appoint the times." [4] But we
must still be careful of the prophet's zeal. His eagerness to see the
' hand of God ' (or to see the discomfiture of Benhadad repeated in
his day and time) led to an account of Solway Moss—where " very
few more than three hundred " English put to flight " ten thousand
Scots "—which misled Froude and others ; while, on the other
hand, his eagerness to discredit the Roman Church led to
parallel exaggerations for which allowance must be made. Knox
stands up well to the tests of modern research, and his *History* is
vital for any study of his time ; but the critical reader must always
be on his guard and must always, where possible, seek the confirmation of other contemporary accounts.[5]

Finally, if we gain from a ' history ' written contemporaneously
by a man who knew the fears and hopes of those in the forefront
of the struggle, who heard their words and witnessed their deeds,
we also lose by the hatred that embittered his writing in 1566. The

---

[1] *Infra*, i, 348, *note* 7   [2] *Calendar of Scottish Papers*, i, No. 906
[3] Laing's *Knox*, vi, 606–612   [4] *Infra*, i, 55
[5] A good example of such a comparison of accounts is to be seen in *Two Missions
of Jacques de la Brosse* (Scot. Hist. Soc.), 56–179. There again Knox ' stands up well '
to the analysis. It is not possible to agree with Law Mathieson that ' Knox's book is
much more valuable as literature than as history.' (*Politics and Religion*, i, 107)

picture of Mary of Guise in 1566 is vastly different from the picture we would draw from his *Letter* of ten years earlier. In 1566 his bitterness suggests a distortion which, if there, can be corrected only by that biography of the Queen Regent which is long overdue.[1]

IX

Knox's supreme conviction that his cause was right and just led to the further conviction that the course he advocated was likewise that which was right. So religion and politics were bound together ; so Knox could not forbear to declaim both the cause and the course. By some he was hated, by some feared ; by some he was honoured and respected ; but by all he was recognized as a man whose " lively voice " was potent in the land. Knox, like St. Paul, had the power to shape men's minds. If, to Bishop Keith, he was a ' trumpeter of rebellion,' his own conception was that of a ' trumpeter of the Lord.' Those who would accuse him of intolerance must first be sure that they do not confuse tolerance with submission or apathy, and then ask themselves why, within their own times, the western democracies fought so fiercely against the national socialism of Germany. The Wars of Religion were much like our own recent wars, and the period of uneasy peace that followed the rise of Hitler might be compared with the religious armistice that followed the return of Mary. Both periods saw the appeasers for a time prevail. If Knox was for ever pouring forth the vials of God's wrath, was he not the Christian warrior combating the powers of darkness that compassed him around ? If his threatenings grew more fearful in defeat, was he not covering himself with the ' garments of the Lord's vengeance ' ? Those who would denounce the virulence and the implacability of his attack on Rome must not forget the spirit of the age in which he lived. War, waged in the name of God, was staining with blood the hands of men throughout Western Europe. The Massacre of St. Bartholomew's Day took place in the August preceding Knox's death.

We must remember that, apart from the brief twelve months of 1560–61, Knox spent his active life in opposition, fighting " the

---

[1] And it is more than probable that French sources, as yet untapped, would enable us to ' prove ' Knox's account in more places than one. It may well be that we draw our picture of the Queen Regent too much from Knox's words ; and it is probably not without significance, in more ways than one, that the name of Knox rarely occurs in those letters of Mary of Guise that have so far been printed.

Pope and his kingdom "—" the Whore of Babylon "—and the
" battle of the Lord " so occupied his life that only at rare intervals
could the sweet " peace of our Lord Jesus Christ " find place or
utterance. Yet although he governed his life and work upon the
rule that " If I had cast me to please men, I had not been the servant
of God," [1] there was still a strain of sympathy, patience, and kindness that was precluded in public by his own conception of his task.
We obtain a glimpse of this other Knox in the beauty of his treatise
on Prayer, [2] but it comes into full view when we turn to his ' familiar
letters.'

Of the fifty-six familiar letters which Laing has carefully gathered
together, no fewer than twenty-nine are addressed to Mrs. Bowes,
Knox's mother-in-law, while, of the remaining twenty-seven, nineteen
are to other women—to Mrs. Anna Locke and Mrs. Hickman, whose
hearts " were incensed and kindled with a special care over me " ;
to Mrs. Guthrie and Mrs. McGill ; even to certain ladies in Edinburgh who write to him concerning " the apparel of women," and
to whom he guardedly replies that it " is very difficult and dangerous
to appoint any certainty, lest in so doing we either restrain Christian
liberty, or else loose the bridle too far to the foolish fantasy of facile
flesh." [3]

No argument can be adduced from the survival of particular
letters, for we do not know the letters that have been lost. Nor
could Knox be expected to refer frequently to his " domestical
affairs " [4] ; certainly they could find no place in his *History*. But
these letters to the " women of his acquaintance " reveal a vastly
different Knox, a Knox ever ready to comfort weeping women, even

---

[1] Laing's *Knox*, iv, 49
[2] 1554. (Laing's *Knox*, iii, 83–105)
[3] Laing's *Knox*, iv, 225–26. But in the *History* (*infra*, ii, 78) the preachers " spoke
boldly " against the vanities of " foolish women " in their dress.
[4] Of Marjory Bowes, his first wife, he tells us strangely little. We have his first
letter to her, a sermon in miniature, ending with the shy (or is it pawky ?) sentence,
" I think this be the first letter that ever I wrote to you " (Laing's *Knox*, iii, 395), and
twice he refers to her, in letters, as his " left hand " or his helper in his writings : but
beyond that we learn nothing until a passing reference in the *History* speaks of his
" heaviness by reason of the late death of his dear bed-fellow " (*infra*, i, 351). Only
once does he refer to their sons, when he answers a weeping Queen, " Madam, in God's
presence I speak : I never delighted in the weeping of any of God's creatures ; yea,
I can scarcely well abide the tears of my own boys whom my own hand corrects "
(*infra*, ii, 83). His second wife, Margaret Stewart, is referred to only once throughout
all his writings and then, significantly, at the close of that humble prayer of March 1566
(*supra*, lxv; Laing's *Knox*, vi, 484). His brother, William Knox, is mentioned twice
in letters, and receives one mention in the *History* (*infra*, i, 214).

to weep with them. Although usually they are replies to doubts and difficulties " touching the interpretation of the Scriptures," one letter, to Mrs. Guthrie, opening, " Albeit I have no particular matter to write unto you, beloved sister, other than I have expressed in my other writings, yet I could not refrain to write these few lines to you in declaration of my remembrance of you," [1] shows Knox himself deliberately initiating the correspondence. And once he writes to Mrs. Locke from Geneva—

> Ye write that your desire is earnest to see me. Dear sister, if I should express the thirst and languor which I have had for your presence, I should appear to pass measure. . . . Yea, I weep and rejoice in remembrance of you ; but that would evanish by the comfort of your presence which, I assure you, is so dear to me, that if the charge of this little flock here, gathered together in Christ's name, did not impede me, my presence should prevent [2] my letter. [3]

Was that true ? Or was it mere hyperbole ?

The puzzle of these letters is beyond our purpose here. More are we concerned with the spirit they reveal. An occasional sentence or paragraph still shows the prophet of wrath ; but the unwonted gentleness and humility of

> The searching of the Scriptures for God's sweet promises, and for his mercies freely given unto miserable offenders (for his nature delighteth to show mercy where most misery reigneth), the collection and applying of God's mercies, I say, were unto me as the breaking and handling with my own hands of the most sweet and delectable unguents, whereof I could not but receive some comfort by their natural sweet odours [4]

is in the spirit of mercy. We leave the Knox who can write exhorting his brethren to pray :

> Repress the pride of these bloodthirsty tyrants ; consume them in thine anger according to the reproach which they have laid against thy holy name. Pour forth thy vengeance upon them, and let our eyes behold the blood of thy saints required of their hands. Delay not thy vengeance, O Lord ! But let death devour them in haste ; let the earth swallow them up ; and let them go down quick to the hells [5]

[1] Laing's *Knox*, iv, 246   [2] *come before*
[3] Laing's *Knox*, iv, 238   [4] Laing's *Knox*, iii, 338
[5] Laing's *Knox*, iii, 328

and pass to another Knox who writes :

> And thus I commit you to the protection of Him who by grace has called you from darkness to light ; by faith has purged your conscience and heart ; and of his free mercy shall glorify you, according to his promise made unto them that obediently receive the message of life in Christ Jesus our Lord.[1]

This Knox of the letters to his " dear sisters " is not the Knox we find in the pages of his *History*.

Is there here some strange dichotomy? When first he entered the castle of St. Andrews with his "bairns" he was reading in the Evangel of St. John[2] ; in St. John he took his last refuge.[3] For us his life opens and closes with Christ's message of intercession. But in all the years between he was engaged in the heat of battle or, in his hour of despair, he was calling the host to battle and finding none to answer his call. The tremendous question whether or not he was right in his conception of " the work of the Lord " can never be answered. If, indeed, he was moved by the message of peace, his life was spent as a messenger of wrath. Throughout that life, dedicated to " Christ Jesus his Evangel," the spirit of Christ is absent in all his public work. Never in public do we find an appreciation of the message of St. Paul—'Though I speak with the tongues of men and of angels, and have not charity, I am become as sounding brass or a tinkling cymbal.' Only at rare intervals, in the quietude of the chamber, is that spirit revealed.

But we must never forget that, throughout all his work in Scotland, Knox was ' in office ' only for those brief twelve months of 1560–61, and, even then, without the support which he regarded as God's due and his. Having cleared the land of the " rubbish " of Rome, he was denied the opportunity to lay firm the foundations of the Church of God. Moreover, even while the foundations of his Church were still hindered and delayed (by the avariciousness of men) the builder found himself ' out of office ' once more, and once more in opposition. Then, with the return of Mary, when those who had fought in the Army of Christ's Evangel forgot their God and turned to "mockage," anger burned deep within his soul, an anger accompanied by fear lest once more the light of truth should be suppressed. Could he, the prophet of the Lord, allow the land, so recently purged of sin, to be defiled again ?

Only by understanding all this can we understand the man.

---

[1] *Ibid.*, iii, 347   [2] *Infra*, i, 82   [3] *Supra*, lxvii

In all this, lies the supreme tragedy of his life. And the tragedy of his life lives after him. It has been his fate to be remembered largely as a destroyer of " idolatry " ; probably it was his hope to be remembered as the builder of a Church.

There was also Scotland's tragedy. The prophet had drawn ' the sword of the Lord's vengeance ' in a revolution against both Church and State. Succeeding years were to show that a revolution may change its course, but that the sword, once drawn, is not easily returned to the scabbard. Ere long, Scotland was to cry out with another prophet—' O thou sword of the Lord, how long will it be ere thou be quiet ? ' And what when the sword had at last been sheathed again ? Scotland, nourished in the creed of Knox—a creed, be it said, in many ways suited to a people faced with the stern realities of a life difficult, poor, and often dangerous,—was long to lack an appreciation of the ' things that are lovely,' and that, when ' of good report,' are also part of man's inheritance.

A DESCRIPTION OF JOHN KNOX [1]

In bodily stature he was rather below the normal height. His limbs were straight and well-proportioned ; his shoulders broad ; his fingers somewhat long. His head was of medium size, with black hair ; his appearance swarthy, yet not unpleasant. His countenance, which was grave and stern, though not harsh, bore a natural dignity and air of authority ; in anger his very frown became imperious. Under a rather narrow forehead his eyebrows rose in a dense ridge ; his cheeks were ruddy and somewhat full, so that it seemed as though his eyes receded into hollows. The eyes themselves were dark-blue, keen and animated. His face was somewhat long, with a long nose, a full mouth, and large lips of which the upper one was slightly the thicker. His beard was black, flecked with grey, thick, and falling down a hand and a half long.

[1] Being a somewhat free translation from the Latin of Sir Peter Young's reply to Beza, who had written for a picture of John Knox for inclusion in his *Icones*. Sir Peter Young's letter, of 13 November 1579, is printed by Hume Brown in his *John Knox*, ii, 322–324.

BIBLIOGRAPHICAL NOTE

The Writing of the History

Writing to Gregory Railton, on 23 October 1559, Knox refers to " our most just requests . . . together with our whole proceedings from the beginning of this matter, which we now are to set forth in manner of History." [1] This was undoubtedly a use of the ' historic present.' The general preface to the " gentle reader " states that order was taken " in the *beginning* of our enterprise " that " all our proceedings should be committed to register," [2] and internal evidence suggests that by the end of October 1559 Knox must have been well advanced with his work, which then consisted of the present Book II. About half-way through that book, for example, we find, in the body of the text, " where he yet remains, to wit, in the month of October, the year of God 1559 " [3] ; while the closing prayer, " Look upon us, O Lord, in the multitude of thy mercies ; for we are brought even to the deep of the dungeon " [4] reads as though it was written (and the Book completed), in the latter part of November 1559, following the " dark and dolorous " night of the retreat to Stirling.[5]

In Book II, its first form, the *History* was intended to be a justification of the action of the " Protestants of the Realm of Scotland " in taking " the sword of just defence " against those that most unjustly sought their destruction. This is made abundantly clear in the *Prefatio*—

> Lest that Sathan by our long silence shall take occasion to blaspheme, and to slander us the Protestants of the Realm of Scotland, as that our fact [6] tended rather to sedition and rebellion, than to reformation of manners and abuses in religion, we have thought expedient, so

---

[1] Laing's *Knox*, vi, 87   [2] *Infra*, i, 5. The italics are mine.
[3] *Infra*, i, 208   [4] *Infra*, i, 271
[5] Wider indications of the time of writing are to be seen in : " and we fear but over inward with her yet " (*infra*, i, 196), which must have been written before the death of the Queen Regent in June 1560 ; and in the use of the present tense in the *Prefatio*, " we are persecuted by France and their faction " (*infra*, i, 146), which indicates a time prior to the Treaty of Edinburgh in July 1560. The parenthesis, " as her accustomed manner was, and yet her daughter's is, ever to forge lies," (*infra*, i, 192), must have been added after Mary's return in August 1561.
[6] *action* (Fr. *fait*)

truly and briefly as we can, to commit to writing the causes moving us (us, we say, a great part of the nobility and barons of the realm) to take the sword of just defence against those that most unjustly seek our destruction. And in this our confession we shall faithfully declare what moved us to put our hands to the reformation of religion ; how we have proceeded in the same ; what we have asked and what presently [1] we require of the sacred authority [2] ; to the end that, our cause being known, as well our enemies as our brethren in all realms may understand how falsely we are accused of tumult and rebellion, and how unjustly we are persecuted by France and their faction : as also that our brethren, natural Scotsmen, of what religion so ever they be, may have occasion to examine themselves if they may, with safe conscience, oppose themselves to us, who seek nothing but Christ Jesus his glorious Evangel to be preached ; his holy sacraments to be truly ministered ; superstition, tyranny and idolatry to be suppressed in this realm ; and, finally, the liberty of this our native country to remain free from the bondage and tyranny of strangers. [3]

As such the Book is a piece of special pleading, a party-pamphlet rather than a history : and it was probably intended for immediate publication—to counteract the assertions of the Queen Regent and her French advisers that the Reformers meant " nothing but a rebellion " ; to state the case of the Congregation to their own countrymen ; and to seek the support of Protestants abroad, especially in England. As a party-pamphlet it is naturally one-sided in many of its statements : it glosses over the Reformers' negotiations with England while denouncing the Regent's reliance upon France ; and its account of the ' Appointment ' at the Links of Leith is open to grave suspicion. It was clearly written in haste amid Knox's many other tasks ; and, because of that, some of its misstatements and confusions can be attributed solely to the fact that its writer, who " then painfully travailed both by tongue and pen " [4] had little opportunity for correction or revision.

But Book II, although probably completed before the end of the year 1559, was not given to the world. Active intervention by England towards the close of January 1560, followed by the Treaty of Berwick in February 1560, rendered publication unnecessary ; and, for a time, Knox may have abandoned his writing. In a letter to Cecil, of 23 September 1560, Randolph reports, ' I have talked at large with Mr. Knox concerning his History. As much as is written thereof shall be sent to your Honour, at the coming

---

[1] now ; at present   [2] the authority of the state   [3] Infra, i, 146   [4] Infra, i, 5

of the Lords Ambassadors, by Mr. John Wood. He hath written only one Book. If you like that he shall continue the same, or add any more, he sayeth that he must have further help than is to be had in this country, for more assured knowledge of things passed, than he hath himself, or can come by here. It is a work not [to] be neglected, and greatly to be wished that it should be well handled.' [1] This clearly indicates a contemplated continuation of the work, and a possibility that such a continuation was already in hand. That continuation was the present Book III, carrying the story from " our dolorous departing from Edinburgh " to the return of Mary in August 1561, and referred to in the General Preface as the completion of Knox's task. [2]

Internal evidence for the time of writing Book III is scanty. A reference to the Master of Lindsay, " now Lord of Lindsay," [3] shows that that passage was written after December 1563, when the Master of Lindsay became Patrick, sixth Lord Lindsay of the Byres ; a reference to John Lesley as " now Abbot of Lindores " [4] indicates a time of writing between November 1565 and April 1566 [5] ; while on the next page the marginal identification " the lying Dean of Restalrig " was probably written before January 1566. [6] These are late dates ; but, as we shall see, Books II and III were revised by Knox in the spring and summer of 1566, and the references to Lesley and to Sinclair (Dean of Restalrig) may well be revisions made at that time. [7] One date, 20 October 1567, which occurs in the body of the text, [8] indicates a revision and rewriting even later still.

With the completion of Book III Knox felt " content, and never minded further to have travailed in that kind of writing." [9] But although, as so far written, the *History* was an answer to " divers bruits " and calumnies, an answer " committed to register " for " the posterity to come," yet, after consultation with " divers of the godly," it was deemed desirable " that faithful rehearsal should be made of such personages as God had made instruments of his glory by opposing of themselves to manifest abuses, superstition and idolatry." [10] Accordingly Knox again returned to his task, and an introductory

---

[1] Laing's *Knox*, vi, 121 ; *Calendar of Scottish Papers*, i, No. 906   [2] *Infra*, i, 5

[3] *Infra*, i, 279   [4] *Infra*, i, 353   [5] See Dowden, *Bishops of Scotland*, 231, *note* 2

[6] *Ibid.*, 192

[7] There are also the dates, 16 May 1566 (in the body of the text, *infra*, i, 319) and 20 May 1566 (added in the margin, *infra*, i, 317). Thus Hand C, transcribing this quire (see *infra*, c) may have been transcribing dates that were inserted by Knox following a revision of his original draft (see *infra*, cvi-cviii.)

[8] *Infra*, i, 356   [9] *Infra*, i, 5   [10] *Infra*, i, 5-6 ; 145

book, the present Book I, was written. Towards its end this introductory Book tends to overlap the story already told in Book II;
there is some repetition, and there are occasional discrepancies;
but in Book I the narrative runs more freely, and in Book I Knox's
style is at its best.

Although Knox probably began Book I soon after his completion
of Book III, it is clear from internal evidence that much of it was
written or revised in the spring and summer of 1566, during his
" retreat " in the west after the murder of Riccio. Part of it was
begun earlier, part of it may have been finished later; but to that
period of retreat must be assigned the more outspoken and scurrilous
passages.[1] Evidence of writing or revision in the spring and summer
of 1566 can be found in the marginal dates [2]; there are four cita-
tions of the year 1566 [3]; while two references, in the body of the
text, to Sinclair, Dean of Restalrig, Bishop of Brechin, and Lord
President of the College of Justice,[4] give limiting dates of November
1565 and April 1566.[5] The lament for the exile of Morton, Lindsay
and Ruthven [6] must have been written after 9 March 1566 (the
murder of Riccio) and before 30 December 1566 (when all three
are reported to have been relaxed from the horn) [7]; and although
the brutal marginal prayer, dated 15 June 1567,[8] is in the hand of
the text—thus indicating that that particular part of the present
manuscript was transcribed between 15 June 1567 (Carberry Hill)
and 13 May 1568 (Langside)—the text itself had clearly been first
written in April 1566 (as the marginal note informs us), when Mary
seemed to be supreme. A reference to " Harry, umquhile husband
to our Jezebel Mistress " [9] may indicate a revision after the murder
of Darnley in February 1567; certainly it supports the argument
of a transcription subsequent to June 1567.

During this period of " retreat " in the west Knox apparently
also revised Books II and III, and we have, for example, in Book III
the date 16 May 1566 in the body of the text, and 20 May 1566
added in the margin.[10]

The General Preface seems to contemplate a *History* comprising
only the present Books I, II, and III [11]; but now Knox began the
writing of a continuation, Book IV—a relation of warfare renewed,

---

[1] Outstandingly the denunciation of Mary and the marginal prayer (*infra*, i, 103)
[2] " Written the [   ] of April anno 1566 " (*infra*, i, 103) ; " 10 May, anno
1566 " (*infra*, i, 139)   [3] *Infra*, i, 30, 61 *bis*, 112   [4] *Infra*, i, 112, 131
[5] See Dowden, *Bishops of Scotland*, 191–92   [6] *Infra*, i, 112
[7] *Calendar of Scottish Papers*, ii, No. 458   [8] *Infra*, i, 103
[9] *Infra*, i, 59   [10] *Infra*, i, 317, 319. See also *supra*, xc, *note* 7   [11] *Infra*, i, 5–6

and taking the story from August 1561 to the end of June 1564. Books II and III had been the story of a " just defence " ending in victory and in the beginning of the building of the Temple of God ; so Book IV opens with the cry—

> For what was our force ? What was our number ? Yea, what wisdom or worldly policy was into us, to have brought to a good end so great an enterprise ? Our very enemies can bear witness. And yet in how great purity God did establish amongst us his true religion, as well in doctrine as in ceremonies ! To what confusion and fear were idolaters, adulterers, and all public transgressors of God's commandments within short time brought ! [1]

Yet what was now the position of the victors of 1560, now, in the year 1566, when the introduction to Book IV was written ?

> From whence (alas) cometh this miserable dispersion of God's people within this realm, this day, anno 1566, in May ? [2] And what is the cause that now the just are compelled to keep silence ; good men are banished ; murderers, and such as are known unworthy of the common society (if just laws were put in due execution) bear the whole regiment and swing [3] within this realm ? We answer, Because that suddenly the most part of us declined from the purity of God's word, and began to follow the world ; and so again to shake hands with the Devil, and with idolatry, as in this Fourth Book we will hear. [4]

Already, then, Knox has rearranged his *History* as Books I, II, and III ; and now he has applied himself to Book IV. The introduction gives us the date of its writing, and the late spring of 1566 is again indicated in the marginal rubric to the introduction's closing paragraph. [5] That the time of writing was subsequent to December 1565 is clear from the manner of the citation of that date in the body of the text. [6] The marginal rubric, " Let Papists judge this day. 1567," [7] is probably a later addition ; while the words " But unto this day, the 17 of December 1571," which form part of the

---

[1] *Infra*, ii, 3

[2] That is, after the flight of the Protestant Lords, and of Knox himself, following the murder of Riccio and Darnley's desertion to Mary.

[3] *rule and sway* [4] *Infra*, ii, 4 [5] *Infra*, ii, 6

[6] *Infra*, ii, 13. That the time of writing was subsequent to August 1565 is also clear from the citation of that date in the body of the text (*infra*, ii, 63). It is noticeable that the marginal dates ' Anno 1566 in May ' (*infra*, ii, 47) and ' 12 June 1566 ' (*infra*, ii, 61) are both in the text hand which is here Hand A. Accordingly both these dates may indicate the time of the writing of those parts of Book IV. (See *infra*, civ–cv)

[7] *Infra*, ii, 83

text,[1] indicate the time of writing of the concluding portion of the Book, which is probably an addition to the original codex.[2] As we have seen, Knox was still collecting record material as late as December 1571.[3]

Book IV may well account for Knox's unwillingness to publish his *History*.[4] After writing that Book, of which certainly the greater part was completed before the end of 1566, events were to move rapidly and were to culminate, in July and August 1567, with the abdication of Mary, the coronation of her infant son, and the appointment of Moray as Regent of the realm. But Book IV had inveighed against the apostasy of Moray and Lethington ; and now Moray had redeemed himself. Undoubtedly Knox was convinced that he had written only the truth, and that his account of Moray's defection was just ; but, in view of Moray's return to the " cause of God " and to high office therein, how could Knox publish the old and sorry tale of the years from 1561 to 1564 ? Pride may have kept him from destroying his story of those years in which " flesh and blood were preferred to God " ; the second victory of the Evangel undoubtedly kept him from publishing an indictment that was now out of place.

Book IV ends with the " disputation " between Knox and Lethington in June 1564 ; but the statement about Riccio, whose " end will require the description of the whole," [5] and the reference to George, Lord Gordon, who remained a prisoner in Dunbar " till the month of August, the year of God 1565, as we will after hear," [6] seem to imply that it was Knox's intention to continue with his task. No more of the *History*, however, has survived.[7] Book V was definitely not written by Knox.

Book V, continuing the story from July 1564 to July and August 1567, was published in 1644 by David Buchanan as the concluding part of his edition of the *History* ; but Buchanan's source for this Book is unknown. There are no manuscript copies, and Buchanan's published version is the only version that we have. The pedestrian style of the Book is evidence in itself that Book V never came from Knox's pen ; and in one place the writer half admits that the Book

---

[1] *Infra*, ii, 92 (in the manuscript, folio 359 *recto*). See *infra*, cv–cvi

[2] The hand (Hand C) that writes this, the last part of Book IV, is little more than a scrawl ; and it is probable that the original codex of the *History* ended on the present folio 358 *verso*. (See *infra* cix) Laing hazarded an opinion that this concluding portion might have been written by Richard Bannatyne from dictation. (Laing's *Knox*, i, xxx ; ii, 399, *note*)

[3] Laing's *Knox*, vi, 606–612   [4] *Supra*, lxxviii, *note* 6   [5] *Infra*, ii, 106   [6] *Infra*, ii, 63

[7] This is supported by Bannatyne's supplication to the General Assembly (*infra*, xciv).

was not the work of Knox.[1] The editor of the first accurate edition of the *History* (1732),[2] was of the opinion that while Book V might have been based upon papers left behind by Knox, its author was David Buchanan himself ; and certainly some of the phrases ring like Knox.   Moreover we know that in March 1573, Knox's servant and secretary, Richard Bannatyne, presented a supplication to the General Assembly that

> Where it is not unknown to your Wisdoms that he [John Knox] left to the kirk and town of Edinburgh his History, containing, in effect, the beginning and progress of Christ's true religion, now of God's great mercy established in this realm, wherein he hath continued, and perfectly ended, at the year of God 1564, so that, of things done since that time, nothing by him is put in that form and order as he hath done the former : Yet, nonetheless, there are certain scrolls, papers, and minutes of things left to me by him, to use at my pleasure, whereof a part was written and subscribed with his own hand, and another part by mine, at his command : Which, if they were collected and gathered together, would make sufficient declaration of the principal things which occurred since the ending of his former History, at the year foresaid, and so should serve for stuff and matter to any of understanding and ability in that kind of exercise, that would apply themselves to make an History, even to the day of his death.   But, forasmuch as the said scrolls are so intacked and mixed together, that if they should come to any hands not used nor accustomed with the same, as I have been, should altogether lose and perish ; and seeing also, that I am not able, upon my own costs and expenses, to apply myself, and spend my time to put them in order, which would consume a very long time, much less am I able to write them, and put them in register, as they require to be, without your Wisdoms make some provision for the same : Wherefore, I most humbly request your Wisdoms, that I may have some reasonable pension appointed to me by your Wisdoms' discretion, that thereby I may be more able to await and attend upon the same, lest that these things done by that servant of God, who was dear to you all, should perish and decay, which they shall do indeed, if they be not put in register, which I would do willingly, if your Wisdoms will provide, as said is."

In reply the Assembly ' appointed some learned men to assist the said Richard to put the said scrolls and papers in good form ; and allowed to him forty pounds . . . that he might the more easily

---

[1] ' Besides this supplication of the Assembly to the Nobility penned (as appeareth by the style) by John Knox ' (*infra*, ii, 196) ; though Knox uses similar phrases.

[2] Apparently the Rev. Matthew Crawford

wait upon that work.' [1] But there our evidence ends. We do not know whether or not Bannatyne was able to collect together and arrange these mixed and scattered scrolls ; we have no knowledge whether or not a series of ordered scrolls came into the hands of David Buchanan, or, if they did, what use he made of them and what was their final fate.

Knox's authorship of Books I-IV, however, admits of no doubt ; and evidence of his close attention to the form and content of his *History* is amply revealed in the earliest surviving manuscript—the ' Laing MS.' now preserved in the Library of the University of Edinburgh.

The ' Laing MS.' [2]

The early history of this manuscript is unknown, though an examination of its arrangement tempts us to identify it with the copy of the *History* left by Knox ' to the kirk and town of Edinburgh.' [3] ' Matt[hew] Reid Min[iste]r att Northberwick,' written in the top left-hand corner of folio I *recto*, proves it to be the same manuscript as that referred to by the editor [4] of the 1732 edition of the *History* where, in the preliminary ' Life of the Author,' he writes : ' There is also a complete MSS. Copy of the first four Books of this History belonging now to Mr. Gavin Hamilton, Bookseller in Edinburgh, which formerly belonged to the late Reverend Mr. Matthew Reid Minister of the Gospel at North Berwick.' [5] Later, the manuscript passed into the possession of the Rev. John Jamieson (the compiler of the *Etymological Dictionary of the Scottish Language*) ; at the sale of Jamieson's library, in 1839, it was purchased by David Laing (who has written ' D. Laing Edinburgh 1839 ' immediately below Matthew Reid's signature) [6] ; and by Laing it was bequeathed to Edinburgh University Library.

A note in Laing's handwriting, prefixed to the manuscript, runs :

[1] Calderwood, *History of the Kirk of Scotland* (Wodrow Soc.), iii, 276–277 ; Laing's *Knox*, vi, lix–lx
[2] Sometimes called the ' MS. of 1566.' This manuscript was used by David Laing for the text of his edition of the *History* (1846, 1848), and is now in the Laing Collection in the Library of the University of Edinburgh.
[3] *Supra*, xciv
[4] Apparently the Rev. Matthew Crawford
[5] *The Historie of the Reformatioun of Religioun within the Realm of Scotland* (Edinburgh, 1732), ' The Life of the Author,' lii
[6] See Laing's *Knox*, i, xxxi–xxxii

This Manuscript I consider to be peculiarly valuable and interesting from two circumstances. The first is that it presents the work in its most genuine and authentick form : being undoubtedly the most ancient copy that exists. The second, that it bears internal evidence of portions of it having been written in the year 1566, with occasional corrections between that date and 1571, and some of these at least appear to be made by *the Reformer* himself.

These statements will be considered later.

The manuscript contains the four Books of the *History*—that is, the whole of the *History* that can be attributed to the pen of Knox, including, in Book II, his recorded versions of the *Confession of Faith* and the *Book of Discipline*—together with two copies of the ' Beggars' Summons,' written on the last two folios which are odd leaves.

Excluding these two final leaves, the manuscript consists of 387 folios (each now measuring, with some slight variations, 28·4 cm. × 19·3 cm.), gathered in seventeen quires :

I	folios	1– 22	
II	folios	23– 44	
III	folios	45– 68	
IV	folios	69– 92	
V	folios	93–114	
VI	folios	115–136	
VII	folios	137–158	
VIII	folios	159–180	
IX	folios	181–204	(folio 203 bears the double number 203–204)
X	folios	205–228	
XI	folios	229–252	
XII	folios	253–272	
XIII	folios	273–294	
XIV	folios	295–309	(this quire includes three blank folios which are unnumbered)
XV	folios	310–333	
XVI	folios	334–358	(folio 354 is an inserted slip)
XVII	folios	359–387	

Originally the folios of certain quires were numbered by their writers in the top right-hand corner *recto*, but many of these original numbers have been clipped or completely cut away when the manuscript was trimmed for binding.[1] Certain other quires bear an

[1] The trimming was apparently done for an earlier binding and not for the present binding—a heavy blind-tooled black morocco with all edges gilt.

early, but not contemporary foliation in the top right-hand corner *recto*. A more modern numbering of the folios, in ink, in the top-centre *recto*, runs from 1 to 250, and a still later numbering, in pencil, in the top-centre *recto*, runs from 251 to 389. All references to the folios of the manuscript, in this note and in the footnotes to the text, are to these numberings in the *top-centre recto*.

In addition to the folio numbering, a pagination begins on folio 253 *recto*. Folio 253 *recto* is paged 252 (a discrepancy to be noted later), and the pagination, with certain omissions and inaccuracies (also to be noted later) runs to 515 (folio 387 *recto*).

As we shall see, a comparison of the original foliation (top right-hand corner *recto*) with the modern foliation (top-centre *recto*), together with the way in which new hands begin new quires, are of considerable importance in any attempted reconstruction of the writing of the manuscript.

In its present form, the manuscript is the work of no less than eight different scribes. The different hands appear as follows :

Hand A

This hand writes folios 1 to 114, that is, quires I to V. The same hand has numbered the folios 1–114 in the top right-hand corner *recto*, but the numbers (although very clear on certain folios —for example, folio 44) have mostly been cut away by an earlier binder.

On these folios 1–114 there are certain corrections and additions which appear to be in Knox's own hand :

folio 19 *recto* : *Mᶜaduell* first altered to *Mᶜakuell*, then scored through and *Makdwell* added in the margin.[1]

folio 20 *recto* : after *bischop of Murray* a caret, and the words *then being priour of Sanctandross* added in the margin.[2]

folio 32 *verso* : the marginal injunction [g]*et this name*. In the text a blank space had been left for the insertion of the name ; a rule appears to have been drawn under the blank space ; and the name *Hay* has been inserted later by Hand A.[3]

folio 34 *recto* : after *dumkelden* a caret, and *called* added in the margin.[4]

folio 35 *recto* : the marginal comment *the gouernour violated his fayth refused god and took absolutione of the dewill*.[5]

folio 41 *recto* : after *that now lyvith* a caret, and *anno 1566* added in the margin.[6]

[1] *Infra*, i, 23   [2] *Infra*, i, 24   [3] *Infra*, i, 44   [4] *Infra*, i, 47   [5] *Infra*, i, 50   [6] *Infra*, i, 61

folio 41 *verso* : after *that yitt lyveth* a caret, and *anno 1566* added in the margin.[1]

folio 64 *recto* : two words which look like *doe sned* scored through, a caret inserted, and *sned* added in the margin.[2]

folio 69 *verso* : the name *fekcam* added later in a space left by the scribe.[3]

folio 83 *recto* : the marginal rubric *Elezabeth Adamesoune & hir death*.[4]

folio 101 *recto* : the marginal injunction *heir intak in the beggars summonds warning the freres* added opposite the word *Amen*.[5]

thre scored through and *twa* added above the line.[6]

folio 111 *recto* : the marginal injunction (badly cut by the binder) *luk quhether it be best to tak in heir the beggars warning or in the place befoir appoynted* added opposite the word *advise*.[7]

folio 112 *verso* : a ϕ sign in the right-hand margin, opposite the word *Idolatrie*, and in the top margin, unfortunately badly cut by an earlier binder, the words *zealous brother . . . . upone the gaittes and portis of all the freires places, (few or none exceptit) within this realme in the moneth of Januar 1558 preceding that witsunday that they delodged, which is this etc. And so tak in heir the beggars warning*.[8]

After the words *counsall which* [9] the bottom half of folio 70 *verso* and a space of about twelve lines at the top of folio 71 *recto* have been left blank, presumably for the insertion of the letter there referred to. The letter, however, or a copy of it, was apparently unobtainable, and the text carries on with the words *which cuming to the handis*—thus showing no break.

This hand ends, at the foot of folio 114 *verso*, in the middle of the sentence *wold so/*[10] and is succeeded by Hand B.

Hand B

This hand, which starts the new quire (VI) with folio 115 *recto*, continues the broken sentence *wold so kendle that quhen some men . . .* and runs to the foot of folio 136 *verso*. There the hand ends in the middle of the sentence *nocht finallie/*[11] and is succeeded by Hand C.

Hand C

This hand, starting the new quire (VII) with folio 137 *recto*, continues the broken sentence *nocht finallie aggreit upoun . . .* and runs

---

[1] *Infra*, i, 61   [2] *Infra*, i, 86   [3] *Infra*, i, 97   [4] *Infra*, i, 119
[5] *Infra*, i, 139   [6] *Infra*, i, 139   [7] *Infra*, i, 159
[8] *Infra*, i, 161. Laing's note (Laing's *Knox*, i, 320) omits the words *few or none exceptit*.
[9] *Infra*, i, 98, line 21   [10] *Infra*, i, 166, line 4   [11] *Infra*, i, 206, line 8

to the foot of folio 158 *verso*. There the hand ends in the middle of the sentence *oure requeistis*/[1] and is succeeded by Hand A.

Laing thought that Hand C might be the hand of Knox's secretary, Richard Bannatyne.[2]

The scribe's numbering of the folios 137–158 (top right-hand corner *recto*), in his own hand and in the same ink, has escaped the binder's trimming. His numbering agrees with the more modern numbering (top-centre *recto*).

Hand A

This hand continues the broken sentence *requeastis, and with judgement to decerne* . . .[3] and writes the new quire (VIII) running from folio 159 to folio 180. At the foot of folio 180 *verso* it ends in the middle of the sentence *and dowghtaris*/[4] and is succeeded by Hand D.

Hand A, writing the eighth quire, concludes Book II of the *History* and opens Book III ; but there is no break in the manuscript, Book III beginning in the middle of folio 179 *recto*.

In this quire an early numbering of the folios (top right-hand corner *recto*), has escaped the binder's trimming, and this numbering, although not that of the scribe, agrees with the more modern numbering (top-centre *recto*).

Here again also, in Hand A, we have two corrections and additions which appear to be in Knox's own hand :

folio 165 *recto* : after *toun* a caret, and the words *of Sanct Johnestoun* added in the margin.[5]

folio 174 *verso* : *presence* scored through and *persoune* added in the margin.[6]

On folio 167 *recto*, after the words *day yeare and place foirsaidis*,[7] the bottom half of the page has been left blank for the insertion of the names of those who subscribed the Act of Suspension.

Hand D

This hand continues the broken sentence *dowghtaris gatt favouris* . . .[8] and writes the new quire (IX), running from folio 181 to folio 204. This is a quire of only twenty-three leaves, for folio 203 bears the double number 203–204 ; and this quire provides interesting

---

[1] *Infra*, i, 243, lines 33/34
[2] Laing's *Knox*, i, 411, *note*
[3] *Infra*, i, 243, lines 33/34
[4] *Infra*, i, 277, lines 22/23
[5] *Infra*, i, 252
[6] *Infra*, i, 265
[7] *Infra*, i, 255
[8] *Infra*, i, 277, line 23

evidence of the way in which the manuscript took its present form. Apparently the scribe soon realized that the material allotted to him would not take up his quire of twenty-four leaves. He had too much paper and too little text. Thus his hand grows larger and more open ; his lines grow shorter and the spacing between them grows wider. These desperate attempts to eke out his matter become very marked from folio 189 *verso* onwards. But all was in vain. Strive as he would, he had still one leaf too many. Folio 203 is accordingly given the double number 203–204, and, even then, its *verso* had to be left blank.

Hand D ends in the middle of the sentence *at glaskow the tent of*/[1] and is succeeded by

Hand C

This hand continues the broken sentence *tent of februar 1559,* and writes the new quire (X) running from folio 205 to 228. Again this scribe's numbering of the folios (top right-hand corner *recto*), in his own hand and in the same ink, has escaped the binder's trimming ; and his numbering agrees with the more modern numbering (top-centre *recto*).

Here Hand C also appears to have had a sufficiency of paper ; certain of his pages are written in a more open style with more generous margins. From time to time he makes experiments in his style of writing, and distinct changes in style are noticeable on folios 218 *verso* and 220 *verso*.

Hand C ends in the middle of the sentence *blissit societie quhilk we the memberis*/[2] and is succeeded by

Hand A

This hand, starting the new quire (XI) on folio 229 *recto*, continues the broken sentence *the membres have with . . .* and runs to the top of folio 249 *recto*. There, on the sixth line, the scribe writes the heading, *The electioun of the superintendis heirefter followed in this maner*,[3] and then leaves blank the rest of folio 249 *recto*, and the whole of the folios 249 *verso*, 250, 251, and 252, for the insertion of the method of election.[4] Folio 252 is the end of the quire.

Again an early numbering of the folios, identical with that of folios 159 to 180, has escaped the binder's trimming ; but it is to be noted that *per incuriam* the folio number 246 has been used twice—on folios 246 and 247—and that accordingly on folio 252

---

[1] *Infra*, i, 310, line 18
[3] *Infra*, i, 355, *note* 2
[2] In the *Confession of Faith*, cap. xi.
[4] See *infra*, Appendix VII

the number (which here unfortunately has been cut away by the binder) would have been the incorrect number, 251.

At the foot of folio 240 *verso* and the top of folio 241 *recto* the scribe left, as he thought, sufficient space for the later insertion of a copy of the Act abolishing the jurisdiction of the Pope,[1] but when he came to copy in the Act he found the blank space insufficient, and he was compelled to make the insertion in small and closely crowded writing.

Again, in Hand A, we find a number of corrections and additions which appear to be in Knox's own hand :

folio 242 *recto* : the names *M^r Jo^n winram* and *M^r Jo^n douglas* added in the margin, and the necessary corrections made in the text by the insertion of carets after *to* and *willok* and by scoring through the superflous words *the*.[2]

folio 243 *recto* : after *gordoun* a caret, and *byschop* added in the margin.[3]

folio 244 *recto* : after *saulles Seatoun* a caret, and *Mr Jo^n Sinklar dene of restarik* added in the margin.[4]

folio 245 *recto* : a long bracket, and *corrected be m^r george* added in the margin.[5]

folio 248 *recto* : after *abbote of londoris* a caret, and *and after wes made byschope of ross* added in the margin.[6]

On folios 245 *verso* and 246 *recto* the Latin verses and the translation are in a different hand, but the intermediary sentence—*The meanyng whairof Is that Charles*—is in hand A.[7]

Hand A ends with *heirefter followed in this maner*, and is followed by the blank folios as already noted.

Hand E

Starts the new quire (XII) on folio 253 *recto* with *As the servandis of God uprychtlie travellit*,[8] and writes the whole quire (one of twenty leaves only) ending, half-way down folio 272 *verso*, in the middle of a sentence and the middle of a word, with *In dekay and penuritie aucht suche proui*/[9]

There is a change of ink on folio 268 *verso* (line 4), and again a change of ink on folio 270 *recto* (line 13).

With this quire, and on folio 253 *recto*, a much later *pagination*

---

[1] *Infra*, i, 341
[2] *Infra*, i, 343
[3] *Infra*, i, 345
[4] *Infra*, i, 347
[5] *Infra*, i, 348
[6] *Infra*, i, 353
[7] *Infra*, i, 350
[8] *Infra*, i, 355
[9] In the Fifth Head of the Book of Discipline

begins. This pagination begins with the erroneous folio number 252 (the folio number 251 having been incorrectly given to folio 252, owing to the repetition of the number 246, as noted above) and folio 272 *verso* (the end of the quire) is page 290—the page number 285 having been repeated *per incuriam*. There are no original folio numbers for this quire.

Again this scribe had too much paper for his text, and more than half of folio 272 *verso* is blank.

On folio 253 *verso* the date *20 Octobris 1567* occurs in the body of the text and in the text hand,[1] having been inserted by the scribe in a space he had left for it at the end of the line. It is a reasonable assumption that there had been some earlier date, and that 20 October 1567 represents the date of the rewriting of this quire.[2]

Hand F

Starts the new quire (XIII) with folio 273 *recto*, continues the broken sentence *suche ~~prouidence~~ prouisioun be maid* . . .[3] and runs to the end of the quire on folio 294 *verso*.

The same early numbering of the folios in the top right-hand corner *recto* (as already noted for folios 159 to 180 and folios 229 to 249) has once more escaped the binder's trimming. It is to be noted, however, that this foliation runs from 275 to 296, whereas the later library foliation, in pencil, runs correctly, 273 to 294. Taken in conjunction with the facts that more than half of folio 272 *verso* is blank, and that Hand E's contribution ends in the middle of a word in the middle of the page, it would appear that the preceding quire (XII) was originally one of twenty-two leaves, reduced to twenty in the rewriting.

The pagination of this quire runs from 291 to 333—the page number 321 having been repeated *per incuriam*.

The comments, such as *The lordis aggreis with this heid of the resaving of the deaconis*,[4] or *Concludit be the lordis*,[5] are either, as in the first case, marginal and in the text hand or, as in the second case, part of the text itself. They are not additions. This would appear to indicate that the scribe had before him a copy of the *Book of Discipline* already furnished with these " conclusions " and " additions." One exception, however, and an important one, is to be noted. The paragraph *The lordis condiscendis that* . . . *quhair mansses ar of gret quantitie*[6] appears to have been added in the margin

---

[1] *Infra*, i, 356   [2] See *infra*, cviii   [3] *Infra*, In the Fifth Head of the Book of Discipline   [4] Folio 284 *recto* ; *infra*, ii, 303, *margin*
[5] Folio 283 *verso* ; *infra*, ii, 303   [6] Folio 285 *recto* ; *infra*, ii, 305

somewhat later by the same scribe—possibly following agreement
reached at a discussion then taking place. If that is so, this quire
must have been written in 1560–61 and was incorporated in the *History*
to save the labour of a further transcript of this part of the *Book of
Discipline*.[1] The hand, in the words of Laing, is a " kind of official
square hand " ; but the evidence of the " additions," interesting
as it is, seems hardly sufficient to warrant Laing's further statement
that this quire " was probably a portion of the copy [of the *Book of
Discipline*] laid before the Convention in January 1561." [2]

Hand F ends at the foot of folio 294 *verso* in the middle of the
sentence *that he enter not by disgressioun in explanyng* /[3] and is succeeded by

Hand G

This hand continues the broken sentence *Explanyng commoun
places* . . . and writes the new quire (XIV) running from folio 295
recto to 309 (and, in the pagination, 334 to 362). The *Book of
Discipline* ends on folio 300 *recto* ; the bottom half of 300 *recto* is
blank, as also is the whole of 300 *verso* (page 345). Thereafter
follow three blank folios which bear neither folio nor page numbers.
Book IV of the *History* then begins, in the same hand, on the next
folio, which is numbered 301 (paged 346), and Hand G continues
to folio 309 *recto* (paged 362). Folio 309 *verso*, which is blank, bears
no page number, and folio 310 *recto*, beginning the new quire with
Hand A, is paged 363.

This quire, including the blank folios which are unnumbered,
thus contains 18 leaves.

Again the writer had more paper than matter. His hand becomes
less cramped as he progresses, and the spaces between the lines
become wider. This is particularly noticeable from folio 306 *recto*
onwards. Even then, the matter cannot be spun out, and folio
309 *verso* is blank.

The marginal note on folio 307 *recto*, *When this was written thair
wes no appearance of Maries Empreasoment*,[4] which is in the same hand
and the same ink, seems to indicate that this quire was rewritten
some time after 16 June 1567, when Mary was sent as a prisoner
to Lochleven Castle, and sometime before 2 May 1568, when she
escaped from her gaolers[5] ; whilst the date " anno 1566 in May "
(folio 301 *verso*), coming in the body of the text, indicates an original
draft written at that time.

[1] See *infra*, cvii–cviii   [2] Laing's *Knox*, ii, 201, *note* 2
[3] In the Ninth Head of the Book of Discipline
[4] *Infra*, ii, 17   [5] But see *infra*, cviii

Hand G ends on folio 309 *recto* in the middle of the sentence *in the house of Mr James* / [1] and is succeeded by

Hand A

This hand, which starts the new quire (XV) on folio 310 *recto*, continues the broken sentence *of maister James Mackgill* . . . and runs to line 9 on folio 355 *recto*. A new quire (XVI) starts with folio 334. An inserted slip, between folios 353 and 355 is numbered as folio 354. The pagination runs from 363 to 451.

An earlier foliation (*not* by Hand A, and similar to that already noted for folios 159–180, 229–249, and 275–296) gives the folio numbers as 318 to 360 (folio 355 being inexplicably triplicated). Thus the fifteenth quire which begins with the (modern) folio number 310, begins, in this earlier foliation, with the folio number 318. These missing eight folios strengthen the contention that the twelfth quire was originally one of twenty-two leaves (instead of the present twenty),[2] and suggest that the fourteenth quire (now containing, with its blank folios, only eighteen leaves) was originally one of twenty-four leaves.

Again, in Hand A, we have a number of corrections and additions which appear to be in Knox's own hand :

folio 312 *recto* : after *one* and *ansured*, carets have been inserted, and *to wit Jo^n knox* is added in the margin, whilst *to wit Jone knox* has also been added above the line.[3]

folio 339 *verso* ; *keyth* scored through, a caret inserted, and *keir* added in the margin,[4]

folio 355 *recto* : a caret after *hir in the same*, the words *and that no one thing etc.* added in the margin, and, in the left-hand margin, the instruction *tak in this that Is sewed in this place quhar it is scraped out*. The passage 'scraped out' consists of lines 3, 4, and 5 on folio 355 *recto* which have been scored through and which ran *When suche thingis war schauin unto the quene Thei war but mocked at sche affirmyng that thei war devisit by maister Johne Wode and by the Lard of pettarrow as we sall after more planelie heare*. That 'that is sewed in' is an inserted slip written on one side only (now numbered folio 354) all in Knox's hand and bearing the passage running from *And that no one thing did him more regreat* down to *Idolatrie in hir chapell etc.*[5]

Hand A continues on folio 355 *recto* down to line 9, where it stops

---

[1] *Infra*, ii, 23, line 14   [2] *Supra*, cii   [3] *Infra*, ii, 27
[4] *Infra*, ii, 62, line 27   [5] *Infra*, ii, 86, *note* 3

in the middle of the sentence *the frenche menzea who rased up* / [1] and is succeeded by a new hand, Hand H.

On folio 341 *recto* the marginal rubric *Let the warlde judge nowe, 1571, for lethingtoun then was the father of all mischeif* [2] is not in the text hand, but is in a later hand that rubricates several passages in this part of the manuscript—for example, it is the hand of the preceding rubric, *the preacheouris raled upone of the courteouris*, [3] and of the later rubric, *Johne Knoxes discharge to the erle of Murray*. [4] The marginal dates May 1566 and 12 June 1566 [5] are, however, in Hand A, and may represent the actual time of writing of those parts of Book IV.

Hand H

This hand continues the broken sentence with the words *thair messe more publictlye* . . . in the ninth line of folio 355 *recto*, [6] and runs to the foot of folio 358 *verso*, where it ends with *The answer of* / [7] These folios are paged 451 to 458, and the earlier foliation is continued from 360 to 363. [8]

Hand C

Hand C now begins a new quire (XVII) at the top of folio 359 *recto*, where the words *Ressonyng betuix the maister of maxvell and Johne Knox* form a heading to the text, [9] and continues to the end of Book IV on folio 387 *recto*. [10] Folio 387 *verso* is blank. These folios are paged 459 to 515 ; the earlier foliation of quires XV and XVI is not continued on them.

As Laing observed, these concluding folios—twenty-nine leaves in all—are 'hastily written, more like a scroll copy from dictation, than an accurate transcript—many of the words are omitted or inaccurately written' [11] ; and if this hand is the hand of Richard Bannatyne these folios may be an example of part of the *History* in its first form.

On folio 359 *recto* the words *Bot into this day the 17 of december 1571* [12] form part of the text and show that these concluding folios must have been written at that time.

At the foot of folio 387 *recto*, and the close of Book IV, an added entry, probably in Knox's own hand, runs *In all that tyme the Erle*

---

[1] *Infra*, ii, 87, line 3
[2] *Infra*, ii, 65
[3] Folio 340 *verso* (*infra*, ii, 64)
[4] Folio 349 *verso* (*infra*, ii, 79)
[5] *Infra*, ii, 47, 61
[6] *Infra*, ii, 87
[7] *Infra*, ii, 91, line 1
[8] See *supra*, civ
[9] *Infra*, ii, 91, margin
[10] *Infra*, ii, 134
[11] Laing's *Knox*, ii, 399, *note* 2
[12] *Infra*, ii, 92

of Murray wes so formed [1] *to Johne Knox, that nowther be word nor write wes there ony communicatioun betwix thame.* [2]   Taken in conjunction with the date 17 December 1571 occurring in the text on folio 359 *recto*, this would seem to indicate that these concluding folios were written between 17 December 1571 and Knox's death in November 1572.

Following folio 387 are two separate leaves, each containing on its *recto* side a copy of the ' Beggars' Summons.' The first of these (folio 388) is in Hand H ; the second (folio 389) is in a new hand, Hand I.

From this analysis of the hands and of the make-up of the manuscript certain interesting points emerge.

In the first place it is possible that at one time there existed a manuscript of the *History*, from folio 1 to folio 355 *recto*, written throughout by Hand A. [3] Not only does Hand A write two hundred and one of these folios, but also it is noticeable that the openings of Book II and Book III both occur in the middle of folios, [4] without any break, and that in both cases the hand is Hand A. The blank spaces left for later insertions on folios 70 *verso* to 71 *recto*, 167 *recto*, and 249 to 252, as well as the way in which one such later insertion (on folios 240 *verso* to 241 *recto*) has been heavily crowded into the insufficient space left for it, also point to Hand A as representing the original codex.

Assuming such an original codex in Hand A, it would then appear to have been revised and corrected by Knox himself. Significantly in the present manuscript, the corrections and additions made by Knox occur only in those parts written by Hand A ; and of these, much the most interesting are those on folio 355 *recto* and the inserted slip now numbered folio 354. [5] Here, indeed, we may have a clue to the rewriting of certain quires by intermediary hands. In effect, certain sections of the manuscript, as written by Hand A, may have been so heavily corrected that rewriting was considered necessary, and the rewriting was then committed to various " scribes " or secretaries, perhaps to some of those of whose " fidelity " Knox upon one famous occasion asserted his " good opinion." [6]

---

[1] Probably for *fremmed*—that is, *foreign* or *strange*   [2] *Infra*, ii, 134

[3] David Laing would identify this hand with that of the writer of *The Kirkis Testimoniall to Mr. Ro*ᵗ*. Hammyltoun and Robert Campbell*, and suggests that Knox's amanuensis was perhaps John Gray, who was Scribe or Clerk to the Assembly from 1560 until his death in 1574. (See Laing's *Knox*, i, xxx and facsimile ; *Wodrow Soc. Miscellany*, i, 287–288 and facsimile)

[4] Folios 102 *verso* and 179 *recto* respectively   [5] See *supra*, civ

[6] *Infra*, ii, 94. Though Hand C is probably that of Richard Bannatyne.

This reconstruction of the ' make-up ' of the present manu-script gains support in many ways. The intermediary hands B, C, D, E, F, and G all write *complete quires* ; and, in view of the fact that their quires, with one exception, begin and end in the middle of a sentence (in one case even in the middle of a word [1]) it is clear that they were copying from *other quires*. Again, it is apparent that the material given to them to copy had been heavily corrected and revised. Hand D, for example, rewriting quire IX, progressively grows larger and larger, the lines grow shorter and shorter, and the spaces between the lines grow wider and wider. Even then, his revised material is insufficient to occupy his quire ; his twenty-four leaves are cut down to twenty-three (of which the *verso* of the last leaf is blank), and, in order that the original foliation may be preserved, his last leaf is given the double number 203–204.[2]

In the case of Hand E, an original quire (XII) of twenty-two leaves has apparently been rewritten as one of only twenty leaves [3] ; and this case raises a speculation more interesting still. Here it would appear that at some later stage of the *History* a manuscript of the *Book of Discipline*, carrying the comments and observations of " the Lords," came into Knox's hands and that he decided to incorporate the newly acquired manuscript into his *History*. But the insertion of the major part of the newly acquired manuscript in place of the original quire XIII (which was wholly occupied with another recension of the central portion of the *Book of Discipline*), necessitated the rewriting of quires XII and XIV, for those quires contained other material in addition to the beginning and the end, respectively, of the *Book of Discipline*. In the rewriting, however, it was found that the newly acquired and newly inserted quire XIII,[4] with probably other alterations made by Knox in those parts of his *History* contained in quires XII and XIV, had considerably reduced the material for those latter two quires. Quire XII was accordingly cut from twenty-two leaves to twenty leaves ; and in quire XIV, which now contains only eighteen leaves, Hand G was compelled to leave nearly four blank folios between the close of the *Book of Discipline* and the opening of Book IV of the *History*, and one final blank side (folio 309 *verso*) before connecting up again with Hand A on folio 310 *recto*. It is more than probable that the original version of these quires contained somewhat lengthier com-

---

[1] *Supra*, ci   [2] *Supra*, xcix-c   [3] *Supra*, cii

[4] See *supra*, cii–ciii, where it is suggested that this copy of the *Book of Discipline* acquired by Knox, and now represented by quire XIII (Hand F) was probably written in 1560–61.

ments, by Knox, on the 'conclusions' and 'additions' of 'the Lords.'

That these intermediary scribes were copying from other quires is also apparent in some of the mistakes they make. For example :

> folio 116 *recto* : *arme your selfis against us, ~~that be innocent and Just~~ your bretherin, and naturall countriemen ; yea against us that be innocent and Just. . . .*[1]

shows that the copyist's eye has been caught by the second *against us* ; and in all the intermediary hands we find repetitions scored through, omissions supplied in the margin, and misreadings corrected.

Certain indications of the time of the writing of the manuscript have already been noted. In particular, it would appear that the first five quires (*Hand A*) were transcribed between 15 June 1567 and 13 May 1568 [2] ; and there are indications that the quires written in hands other than Hand A were written about the same time. On folio 253 *verso*, for example, the date *20 Octobris 1567* occurs in the body of the text [3] in the rewriting of quire XII (Hand E), and on folio 307 *recto* [4] the marginal comment, in the hand of the text, *When this was written thair wes no appearance of Maries Empreasoment* [5] has already been noted [6] as indicating a date between 16 June 1567 and 2 May 1568. Taken now in conjunction with our analysis of the rewriting of quires XII and XIV, this marginal note may be ascribed to October 1567. A wider date is furnished by Hand D in the rewriting of quire IX. There, in his copy of the Treaty of Berwick, the scribe has inserted, after *the rycht honorable lord James Stewart*, a parenthetical explanation *now erle of Mwray* [7]—thus showing that this quire was rewritten before 21 January 1570, when the Regent Moray was assassinated.

How the original codex (Hand A) was compiled we have no means of knowing. It is possible that drafts were dictated by Knox to his secretaries—similar to the rough draft which now occupies folios 359 to 387—and that from these drafts, and perhaps also from notes written out by Knox himself, Hand A wrote a 'fair copy.' That Hand A was *copying* is clear from the many small corrections, omissions, and repetitions similar to those which occur in the intermediary hands.

---

[1] *Infra*, i, 167, lines 33–34   [2] *Supra*, xci   [3] *Infra*, i, 356. See also *supra*, cii
[4] Quire fourteen (Hand G)   [5] *Infra*, ii, 17   [6] *Supra*, ciii
[7] Folio 198 *verso* ; *infra*, i, 303, *note* 3

In the case of documents, it is evident that the copyist had either the original, or a copy of the original, in front of him. For example, the Assurance of 13 June 1559 is accompanied by the note, *The uther subscriptioun we culd nocht read, bot the simile is this*— [1] ; and at the close of the Act of the Secret Council of 27 January 1561 the scribe has made an attempt to write some of the signatures in facsimile.[2]

Finally, the concluding folios from 359 to 387 do not appear to form part of the original manuscript which, in its revised state, was probably completed before the end of 1567.[3] As already indicated, the date of the writing of these last folios may be assigned to a period including and immediately following 17 December 1571.[4] The marginal comment on folio 366 *verso*, *Prayit and written quhen she wes in grytest authoritie*,[5] which must apply to the autumn of 1565 or the early months of 1566, cannot mean that that prayer was written *in the manuscript* during that period. We have already noted that these final folios look much like a scroll copy from dictation ; probably Knox was dictating to his secretary from papers and drafts which he had before him ; and, when he came to dictate that prayer, he caused the marginal note to be inserted as an indication that he had so prayed and so written, not in 1571 when Mary was a refugee-prisoner in England, and when he was then dictating, but in 1565–66 when Mary was at the height of her power.

If we are right in assigning so late a date to these concluding folios, and if we are right in thinking that the final comment on the last folio, and at the end of Book IV, is in the hand of Knox,[6] then we have further proof that Knox, at the very close of his life, was still interesting himself in this abiding monument to his work.[7]

[1] Folio 126 *recto* ; *infra*, i, 186
[3] *Supra*, cviii
[5] *Infra*, ii, 103
[7] See also *supra*, lxxxi

[2] Folio 300 *recto* ; *infra*, ii, 324
[4] *Supra*, cv–cvi
[6] *Supra*, cv–cvi ; *infra*, ii, 134

THE HISTORY
OF THE
REFORMATION IN SCOTLAND

VOLUME ONE

THE FIRST BOOK
OF THE HISTORY OF THE REFORMATION OF RELIGION
WITHIN THE REALM OF SCOTLAND :
CONTAINING
THE MANNER AND BY WHAT PERSONS
THE LIGHT OF CHRIST'S EVANGEL
HATH BEEN MANIFESTED UNTO THIS REALM
AFTER THAT HORRIBLE
AND UNIVERSAL DEFECTION FROM THE TRUTH
WHICH HAS COME BY THE MEANS
OF THAT ROMAN
ANTICHRIST

THE PREFACE

TO THE GENTLE READER, GRACE AND PEACE FROM GOD
THE FATHER OF OUR LORD JESUS CHRIST, WITH THE
PERPETUAL INCREASE OF THE HOLY SPIRIT

IT is not unknown, Christian Reader, that the same cloud of ignorance that long hath darkened many realms under this accursed kingdom of that Roman Antichrist, hath also over-covered this poor realm ; that idolatry hath been maintained, the blood of innocents hath been shed, and Christ Jesus his eternal truth hath been abhorred, detested and blasphemed. But that same God that caused light to shine out of darkness, in the multitude of his mercies, hath of long time opened the eyes of some, even within this realm, to see the vanity of that which then was universally embraced for true religion ; and has given unto them strength to oppose themselves unto the same. And now, into these our last and most corrupt days, hath [God] made his truth so to triumph amongst us that, in despite of Sathan, hypocrisy is disclosed, and the true worshipping of God is manifested to all the inhabitants of this realm whose eyes Sathan blinds not, either by their filthy lusts or else by ambition and insatiable covetousness, which make them repugn to the power of God working by his word.

And because we are not ignorant what divers bruits were dispersed of us, the professors of Jesus Christ within this realm, in the beginning of our enterprise, order was taken that all our proceedings should be committed to register ; as that they were by such as then painfully travailed both by tongue and pen. And so was collected a just volume (as after will appear), containing things done from the fifty-eighth [1] year of God till the arrival of the Queen's Majesty forth of France, [2] with the which the Collector and Writer for that time was content, and never minded further to have travailed in that kind of writing. But, after invocation of the name of God, and after consultation with some faithful [brethren concerning that which] was thought by them expedient to advance God's glory, and

[1] That is, the year 1558
[2] Mary Queen of Scots arrived in Scotland from France on 19 August 1561. (*Infra*, ii, 7)

to edify this present generation and the posterity to come, it was concluded that faithful rehearsal should be made of such personages as God had made instruments of his glory, by opposing of themselves to manifest abuses, superstition and idolatry ; and, albeit there be no great number, yet are they more than the Collector would have looked for at the beginning, and therefore is the volume somewhat enlarged above his expectation. And yet, in the beginning, must we crave of all the gentle readers not to look of us such an History as shall express all things that have occurred within this realm during the time of this terrible conflict that has been betwix the saints of God and these bloody wolves who claim to themselves the title of clergy, and to have authority over the souls of men ; for, with the Policy,[1] mind we to meddle no further than it hath Religion mixed with it. And therefore, albeit that many things which were done be omitted yet, if we invent no lies, we think ourselves blameless in that behalf. Of one other [thing] we must forewarn the discreet readers, which is, that they be not offended that the simple truth be spoken without partiality ; for seeing that of men we neither hunt for reward, nor yet for vainglory, we little pass by the approbation of such as seldom judge well of God and of his works. Let not therefore the reader wonder, albeit that our style vary and speak diversely of men, according as they have declared themselves sometimes enemies and sometimes friends, sometimes fervent, sometimes cold, sometimes constant, and sometimes changeable in the cause of God and of his holy religion : for, in this our simplicity, we suppose that the Godly shall espy our purpose, which is, that God may be praised for his mercy shown, this present age may be admonished to be thankful for God's benefits offered, and the posterity to come may be instructed how wondrously hath the light of Christ Jesus prevailed against darkness in this last and most corrupted age.

[1] That is, political affairs ; the polity

HISTORIÆ INITIUM

In the scrolls of Glasgow [1] is found mention of one whose name is not expressed that, in the year of God 1422,[2] was burnt for heresy ; but what were his opinions, or by what order he was condemned, it appears not evidently. But our Chronicles make mention that, in the days of King James the First, about the year of God 1431,[3] was deprehended [4] in the University of Saint Andrews one named Paul Craw, a Bohemian, who was accused of heresy before such as then were called Doctors of Theology. His accusation consisted principally that he followed John Hus and Wycliffe in the opinion of the sacrament, who denied that the substance of bread and wine was changed by virtue of any words ; or that confession should be made to priests ; or yet prayers to saints departed. While that God gave unto him grace to resist them, and not to consent to their impiety, he was committed to the secular judge (for our bishops follow Pilate, who both did condemn and also wash his hands), who condemned him to the fire ; in the which he was consumed in the said city of Saint Andrews about the time afore written. And to declare themselves to be the generation of Sathan who, from the beginning, hath been enemy to the truth, and he that desireth the same to be hid from the knowledge of men, they put a ball of brass in his mouth to the end that he should not give confession of his faith to the people, neither yet that they should understand the defence which he had against their unjust accusation and condemnation.

But their fathers' practice did not greatly advance their kingdom of darkness, neither yet was it able utterly to extinguish the truth. For albeit that in the days of Kings James the Second and Third we find small question of religion moved within this realm, yet in the time of King James the Fourth, in the sixth year of his reign, and in the twenty-second year of his age, which was in the year of

[1] See *infra*, 8, *note* 2
[2] In the manuscript (folio 1 *verso*) the date has been inserted later in a space, of about two inches, which had been left blank. This martyrdom is not otherwise recorded : the reference can scarcely be to James Resby, who was burned at Perth in 1407.
[3] The date of Paul Craw's martyrdom was probably 1433.
[4] *apprehended*

God 1494,[1] were summoned before the King and his Great Council, by Robert Blacader, called Archbishop of Glasgow, the number of thirty persons, remaining some in Kyle-Stewart, some in King's-Kyle, and some in Cunningham ; amongst whom [were] George Campbell of Cessnock, Adam Reid of Barskimming, John Campbell of New Mylns, Andrew Shaw of Polkemmet, Helen Chalmers Lady Polkellie [and Marion] Chalmers Lady Stair. These were called the LOLLARDS OF KYLE. They were accused of the Articles following, as we have received them forth of the Register of Glasgow [2] :

I First, That images are not to be had, nor yet to be worshipped.

II That the relics of saints are not to be worshipped.

III That laws and ordinances of men vary from time to time, and that by [3] the Pope.

IV That is not lawful to fight, or to defend the faith. (We translate according to the barbarousness of their Latin and dictament.[4])

V That Christ gave power to Peter only, and not to his successors, to bind and loose within the Kirk.

VI That Christ ordained no priests to consecrate.

VII That after the consecration in the Mass, there remains bread ; and that there is not the natural body of Christ.

VIII That tithes ought not to be given to ecclesiastical men (as they were then called).

IX That Christ at his coming has taken away power from kings to judge.[5] (This article we doubt not to be the venomous accusation of the enemies, whose practice has ever been to make the doctrine of Jesus Christ suspect to kings and rulers, as that God thereby would depose them of their royal seats where, by the contrary, nothing confirms the power of magistrates more than does God's word.—But to the Articles.)

X That every faithful man or woman is a priest.

XI That the unction of kings ceased at the coming of Christ.

---

[1] From these details the date can be fixed as falling between 17 March and 10 June 1494.

[2] This " Register," and the " scrolls " referred to on p. 7, were probably the records of the Official—that is, the presiding officer or judge—of the ecclesiastical court of the Diocese of Glasgow. They are not now known to exist. (But see the criticism in *Juridical Review*, xlviii, 128)

[3] *without regard to*, or *despite*

[4] *phraseology*. The additions to Articles IV, VIII, IX, XIX, and XXXI, included within parentheses, are evidently comments by Knox himself.

[5] That is, in matters of religion, though Knox seems to confuse the issue.

xii That the Pope is not the successor of Peter, but where he said, " Go behind me, Sathan."

xiii That the Pope deceives the people by his Bulls and his Indulgences.

xiv That the Mass profiteth not the souls that are in purgatory.

xv That the Pope and the bishops deceive the people by their pardons.

xvi That Indulgences ought not to be granted to fight against the Saracens.

xvii That the Pope exalts himself against God, and above God.

xviii That the Pope can not remit the pains of purgatory.

xix That the blessings of the bishops (of dumb dogs they should have been styled) are of no value.

xx That the excommunication of the Kirk is not to be feared.

xxi That in to no case is it lawful to swear.

xxii That priests might have wives, according to the constitution of the law.

xxiii That true Christians receive the body of Jesus Christ every day.

xxiv That after matrimony be contracted, the Kirk may make no divorcement.

xxv That excommunication binds not.

xxvi That the Pope forgives not sins, but only God.

xxvii That faith should not be given to miracles.

xxviii That we should not pray to the glorious Virgin Mary, but to God only.

xxix That we are no more bound to pray in the Kirk than in other places.

xxx That we are not bound to believe all that the doctors of the Kirk have written.

xxxi That such as worship the Sacrament of the Kirk (we suppose they meant the Sacrament of the altar) commit idolatry.

xxxii That the Pope is the head of the Kirk of Antichrist.

xxxiii That the Pope and his ministers are murderers.

xxxiv That they which are called principals in the Church, are thieves and robbers.

By these Articles,[1] which God of his merciful providence caused the enemies of his truth to keep in their registers, may appear how mercifully God hath looked upon this realm, retaining within it

[1] A different version of the Articles is given in Spottiswoode's *History*, i, 120–121.

some spunk of his light, even in the time of greatest darkness. Neither yet ought any man to wonder, albeit that some things be obscurely, and some things scabrously [1] spoken ; but rather ought all faithful to magnify God's mercy who, without public doctrine, gave so great light.   And further, we ought to consider that, seeing that the enemies of Jesus Christ gathered the foresaid Articles, thereupon to accuse the persons foresaid, that they would deprave the meaning of God's servants so far as they could ; as we doubt not but they have done, in the heads of Excommunication, Swearing, and of Matrimony.   In the which it is no doubt but the servants of God did damn the abuse only, and not the right ordinance of God ; for who knows not, that excommunication in these days was altogether abused ; that swearing abounded without punishment, or remorse of conscience ; and that divorcements were made for such causes as worldly men had invented !—But to our History.

Albeit that the accusation of the Bishop and his complices was very grievous, yet God so assisted his servants, partly by inclining the King's heart to gentleness (for divers of them were his great familiars), and partly by giving bold and godly answers to their accusators, that the enemies in the end were frustrated of their purpose. For while the Bishop, in mocking, said to Adam Reid of Barskimming, " REID, Believe ye that God is in heaven ? " He answered, " Not as I do the Sacraments seven."   Whereat the Bishop thinking to have triumphed said, " SIR, Lo, he denies that God is in heaven." Whereat the King wondering, said, " Adam Reid, what say ye ? " The other answered, " Please your Grace to hear the end betwix the churl and me."   And therewith he turned to the Bishop, and said, " I neither think nor believe, as thou thinks, that God is in heaven ; but I am most assured that He is not only in the heaven, but also in the earth.   But thou and thy faction declare by your works that either ye think there is no God at all, or else that He is so shut up in the heaven that He regards not what is done into the earth ; for if thou firmly believed that God were in the heaven, thou should not make thyself cheek-mate [2] to the King, and altogether forget the charge that Jesus Christ the Son of God gave to his apostles, which was, to preach his Evangel, and not to play the proud prelates, as all the rabble of you do this day.   And now, Sir (said he to the King), judge ye whether the Bishop or I believe best that God is in heaven."   While the Bishop and his band could not well revenge themselves, and while many taunts were given them in their teeth,

[1] *rudely*   [2] That is, *boon companion*

the King, willing to put an end to further reasoning, said to the said Adam Reid, " Will thou burn thy bill ? " [1] He answered, " Sir, the Bishop and ye will." With these and the like scoffs the Bishop and his band were so dashed out of countenance, that the greatest part of the accusation was turned to laughter.[2]

After that diet,[3] we find almost no question for matters of religion, the space nigh of thirty years. For not long after, to wit in the year of God 1508, the said Bishop Blacader departed this life, going in his superstitious devotion to Jerusalem [4]; unto whom succeeded Mr. James Beaton, son to the Laird of Balfour, in Fife, who was more careful for the world than he was to preach Christ, or yet to advance any religion, but for the fashion only ; and as he sought the world, it fled him not, for it was well known that at once he was Archbishop of Saint Andrews, Abbot of Dunfermline, Arbroath, Kilwinning, and Chancellor of Scotland. For after the unhappy field of Flodden, in the which perished King James the Fourth, with the greatest part of the nobility of the realm, the said Beaton, with the rest of the Prelates, had the whole regiment [5] of the realm ; and by reason thereof, held and travailed to hold the truth of God in thraldom and bondage, till that it pleased God of his great mercy, in the year of God 1527, to raise up his servant, MASTER PATRICK HAMILTON, at whom our History doth begin. Of whose progeny, life and erudition, because men of fame and renown have in divers works written, we omit all curious repetition, sending such as would know further of him than we write to Francis Lambert,[6] John Firth,[7] and to that notable work, lately set forth by John Foxe, Englishman, of the Lives and Deaths of Martyrs within this isle in this our age.[8]

---

[1] To " burn one's bill," was an indication of recantation. According to Keith the accused burnt a faggot of dry sticks publicly, thereby signifying that he destroyed that by which he would himself have been destroyed. (*Hist. of Affairs of Church and State in Scotland*, Spottiswoode Soc., i, 16)

[2] Adam Reid presents something of a problem. Although Knox here turns his recantation into the form of a jest, it is clear, from other evidence, that he did not long adhere to Lollardy. (See *Juridical Review*, xlviii, 127)

[3] *After those proceedings*

[4] Blacader died on the way between Italy and the Holy Land, and therefore *intra fines Romanos*. Thus, technically, the Pope *provided* James Beaton to the vacant See of Glasgow. In the manuscript (folio 3 *verso*) the date is given, erroneously, as 1500. [5] *rule*

[6] Francis Lambert : *Exegeseos Francisci Lamberti Avenionensis in sanctam Divi Ioannis Apocalypsim, Libri VII.* [Quoted in Laing's *Knox*, i, 502–503]

[7] John Frith : *Dyvers Frutful Gatheringes of Scrypture concernyng Fayth and Workes.* (London, 1532 ?) [See below, Appendix I]

[8] John Foxe : *Actes and Monuments of these latter and perillous dayes . . . unto the tyme nowe present.* (London, 1563–64.) [The relevant extracts are quoted in Laing's *Knox*, i, 504–515.]

This servant of God, the said Master Patrick, being in his youth provided to reasonable honours and living (he was titular Abbot of Fearn), as one hating the world and the vanity thereof, left Scotland and passed to the schools in Germany ; for then the fame of the University of Wittenberg was greatly divulged in all countries, where, by God's providence, he became familiar with these lights and notable servants of Christ Jesus of that time, Martin Luther, Philip Melanchthon, and the said Francis Lambert,[1] and did so grow and advance in godly knowledge, joined with fervency and integrity of life, that he was in admiration with many. The zeal of God's glory did so eat him up that he could of no long continuance remain there, but returned to his country, where the bright beams of the true light which, by God's grace, was planted in his heart began most abundantly to burst forth, as well in public as in secret. For he was, besides his godly knowledge, well learned in philosophy : he abhorred sophistry, and would that the text of Aristotle should have been better understood and more used in the schools than then it was ; for sophistry had corrupted all as well in divinity as in humanity. In short process of time, the fame of his reasons and doctrine troubled the clergy, and came to the ears of Bishop James Beaton, of whom before we have made mention, who, being a conjured enemy to Christ Jesus, and one that long had had the whole regiment of this realm, bore impatiently that any trouble should be made to that kingdom of darkness whereof, within this realm, he was the head. And, therefore, he so travailed with the said Master Patrick that he got him to Saint Andrews where, after the conference of divers days, he had his freedom and liberty. The said Bishop and his bloody butchers, called doctors, seemed to approve his doctrine, and to grant that many things craved reformation in the ecclesiastical regiment. And amongst the rest, there was one that secretly con- sented with him almost in all things, named Friar Alexander Campbell, a man of good wit and learning, but yet corrupted by the world, as after we will hear. When the bishops and the clergy had fully understood the mind and judgment of the said Master Patrick, and fearing that by him their kingdom should be endamaged, they travailed with the King, who then was young, and altogether addicted to their commandment, that he should pass in pilgrimage

---

[1] Patrick Hamilton does not appear to have visited Luther and Melanchthon at Wittenberg, for the plague was then raging there. Instead, he proceeded to the new university of Marburg, and it was there that he came into contact with Francis Lambert. (See Alexander F. Mitchell, *The Scottish Reformation*, 26)

to Saint Duthus in Ross,[1] to the end that no intercession should be made for the life of the innocent servant of God, who, suspecting no such cruelty as in their hearts was concluded, remained still (a lamb amongst the wolves), till that upon a night he was intercepted in his chamber, and by the bishop's band was carried to the Castle, where that night he was kept ; and upon the morn, produced in judgment, he was condemned to die by fire for the testimony of God's truth. The Articles for the which he suffered were but of Pilgrimage, Purgatory, Prayer to Saints, and for the Dead, and such trifles [2] ; albeit that matters of greater importance had been in question, as his Treatise, which in the end we have added, may witness.[3] Now, that the condemnation of the said Mr. Patrick should have greater authority, they caused the same to be subscribed by all those of any estimation that with them were present, and to make their number great, they took the subscriptions of children, if they were of the nobility ; for the Earl of Cassillis,[4] which last deceased in France, then being but twelve or thirteen years of age, was compelled to subscribe his death, as [he] himself did confess. Immediately after dinner the fire was prepared before the Old College,[5] and he led to the place of execution. And yet men supposed that all was done but to give unto him a terror, and to have caused him to have recanted, and have become recreant to those bloody beasts. But God, for his own glory, for the comfort of his servant, and for manifestation of their beastly tyranny, had otherwise decreed ; for he so strengthened his faithful witness that neither the love of life, nor yet the fear of that cruel death, could move him a jot to swerve from the truth once professed. At the place of execution he gave to his servant, who had been chamber-child to him of a long time, his gown, his coat, bonnet, and such like garments, saying, " These will not profit in the fire ; they will profit thee. After this, of

[1] David Laing could find no evidence that James V passed in pilgrimage to the Shrine of St. Duthus at this time, as stated by Knox and by Spottiswoode (History, i, 126) ; but Lorimer has shown that James V was " in the north country " when an English messenger, sent from Greenwich on 13 February 1528, arrived in Edinburgh, and that on 30 March 1528 the King had just returned from " the north country, in the extreme parts of his realm." (P. Lorimer, Patrick Hamilton, 141, 266). See also Letters and Papers, Henry VIII, iv, pt. ii, Nos. 4115, 4084.

[2] But see Lorimer, Patrick Hamilton, 235 (7)   [3] See Appendix I

[4] See also Spottiswoode's History, i, 126. Gilbert Kennedy, third Earl of Cassillis, died at Dieppe 14 November 1558. (Infra, 130)

[5] St. Salvator's College, founded by Bishop Kennedy. It became known as the Old College to distinguish it from the later foundations of St. Leonard's and St. Mary's. The traditional place of Patrick Hamilton's martyrdom is marked by the letters PH let into the pavement just in front of the College archway.

me thou can receive no commodity, except the example of my death which, I pray thee, bear in mind ; for albeit it be bitter to the flesh, and fearful before men, yet is it the entrance unto eternal life, which none shall possess that denies Christ Jesus before this wicked generation."

The innocent servant of God being bound to the stake in the midst of some coals, some timber, and other matter appointed for the fire, a train of powder was made and set afire, which gave to the blessed martyr of God a glaise,[1] skrimpled [2] his left hand, and that side of his face, but neither kindled the wood, nor yet the coals. And so remained the appointed to death in torment, till that men ran to the Castle again for more powder, and for wood more able to take fire ; which at last being kindled, with loud voice he cried, " Lord Jesus, receive my spirit ! How long shall darkness overwhelm this realm ? And how long wilt thou suffer this tyranny of men ? " The fire was slow, and therefore was his torment the more. But most of all was he grieved by certain wicked men, amongst whom Campbell the Black Friar (of whom we spake before) [3] was principal, who continually cried, " Convert, heretic : call upon our Lady : say *Salve Regina*," etc. To whom he answered, " Depart, and trouble me not, ye messengers of Sathan." But while that the foresaid Friar still roared one thing in great vehemency, he said unto him, " Wicked man, thou knowest the contrary, and the contrary to me thou hast confessed : I appeal thee before the tribunal seat of Jesus Christ ! " After which and other words, which well could not be understood nor marked, both for the tumult, and [the] vehemency of the fire, the witness of Jesus Christ got victory, after long sufference, the last of February, in the year of God 1527.[4] The said Friar departed this life within few days after, in what estate we refer to the manifestation of the general day.[5] But it was plainly known that he died, in Glasgow, in a frenzy, and as one despaired.[6]

·   ·   ·   ·   ·   ·   ·

[1] *a short, sharp burst of heat*   [2] *scorched*
[3] *Supra*, 12. He is said to have been Prior of the Dominicans (or Black Friars) at St. Andrews.
[4] That is, 29 February 1528. At this time the year began on 25 March.
[5] *the Day of Judgment*
[6] Here Knox inserts " A Brief Treatise of Mr. Patrick Hamilton," translated into English by John Frith and called " Patrick's Places." This translation originally appeared under the title *Dyvers Frutful Gatheringes of Scrypture concernyng Fayth and Workes*. It is printed below as Appendix I.

When those cruel wolves had, as they supposed, clean devoured the prey, they find themselves in worse case than they were before ; for then within Saint Andrews, yea, almost within the whole realm (who heard of that fact), there was none found who began not to inquire : Wherefore was Master Patrick Hamilton burned ? And when his Articles were rehearsed, question was held if such Articles were [not] necessary to be believed under the pain of damnation.   And so within short space many began to call in doubt that which before they held for a certain verity, in so much that the University of Saint Andrews, and Saint Leonard's College principally, by the labours of Master Gavin Logie, and the novices of the Abbey, by the Sub-prior,[1] began to smell somewhat of the verity, and to espy the vanity of the received superstition.   Yea, within few years after, began both Black and Grey Friars publicly to preach against the pride and idle life of Bishops, and against the abuses of the whole ecclesiastical estate.   Amongst whom was one called Friar William Arth,[2] who, in a sermon preached in Dundee, spake somewhat more liberally against the licentious lives of the Bishops nor they could well bear.   He spake further against the abuse of cursing [3] and of miracles.   The Bishop of Brechin, having his placeboes [4] and jackmen [5] in the town, buffeted the Friar, and called him Heretic.   The Friar, impatient of the injury received, passed to Saint Andrews, and did communicate the heads of his sermon with Master John Mair,[6] whose word then was held as an oracle in matters of religion : and, being assured of him that such doctrine might well be defended, and that he would defend it, for it contained no heresy, there was a day appointed to the said Friar to make repetition of the same sermon ; and advertisement was given to all such as were offended at the former to be present. And so, in the parish kirk of Saint Andrews, upon the day appointed, appeared the said Friar, and had amongst his auditors Master John Mair, Master George Lockhart, the Abbot of Cambuskenneth,[7] Master Patrick Hepburn, the Prior of Saint Andrews, with all the Doctors and Masters of the Universities.   The theme of his sermon was, " Verity is the strongest of all things."   His discourse of Cursing was, " That if it were rightly used, it was the most fearful thing

---

[1] Probably John Winram
[2] Calderwood (*History*, i, 83) calls him " William Archbishop," but in sixteenth-century script *Arth* and *Arch* might be indistinguishable.   [3] *excommunication*
[4] " *Yes-men* " (from Latin, *placebo*, " I will please ")   [5] *liveried retainers*
[6] Better known as John Major   [7] Alexander Myln

upon the face of the earth ; for it was the very separation of man from God : but that it should not be used rashly and for every light cause, but only against open and incorrigible sinners. But now (said he) the avarice of priests, and the ignorance of their office, has caused it altogether to be vilipended ; for the priest (said he) whose duty and office is to pray for the people, stands up *Form and causes of the priests' old cursing* on Sunday, and cries, ' One has tynt [1] a spurtill.[2] There is a flail stolen from them beyond the burn. The goodwife of the other side of the gate has tynt a horn spoon. God's malison [3] and mine I give to them that knows of this gear, and restores it not.' " How the people mocked their cursing, he further told a merry tale : how, after a sermon that he had made at Dunfermline, he came to a house where gossips were drinking their Sunday's penny, and he, being dry, asked drink. " Yes, Father (said one of the gossips), ye shall have drink ; but ye must first resolve a doubt which is risen amongst us, to wit, What servant will serve a man best on least expenses." " The good Angel (said I), who is man's keeper, who makes great service without expenses." " Tush (said the gossip), we mean no so high matters : we mean, What honest man will do greatest service for least expenses ? " And while I was musing (said the Friar), what that should mean, he said, " I see, Father, that the greatest clerks are not the wisest men. Know ye not how the bishops and their officials serve us husbandmen ? Will they not give to us a Letter of Cursing for a plack,[4] to last for a year, to curse all that look over our dyke, and that keeps our corn better nor the sleeping boy, that will have three shillings of fee, a sark, and [a] pair of schone [5] in the year ? And therefore if their cursing do any thing, we hold the bishops best cheap servants [6] in that behalf that are within the realm." As concerning miracles, he declared what diligence the ancients took to try true miracles from false. " But now (said he), the greediness of priests not only receives false miracles, but also they cherish and fee knaves for that purpose, that their chapels may be the better renowned, and their offerand [7] may be augmented. And thereupon are many chapels founded, as that our Lady were mightier, and that she took more pleasure in one place than in another ; as of late days our Lady of Karsgreng has hopped from one green hillock to another. But honest men of Saint

---

[1] *lost*   [2] A large wooden stick used for stirring porridge   [3] *malediction ; curse*
[4] A small copper coin, originally worth four Scots pennies ; but the word was soon used, as here, to indicate a merely nominal payment .
[5] *shoes*   [6] *the best bargain in servants*   [7] receipts from *offerings*

Andrews (said he), if ye love your wives and your daughters, hold them at home, or else send them in honest company ; for if ye knew what miracles were kithed [1] there, ye would neither thank God nor our Lady." And thus he merrily taunted their trysts of whoredom and adultery used at such devotion.

Another article was judged more hard ; for he alleged the common law, That the Civil Magistrate might correct the Church-men, and deprive them of their benefices, for open vices. [2]

Another day, the same Friar made another sermon of the Abbot [of] Unreason,[3] unto whom and whose laws he compared the prelates of that age ; for they were subdued to no laws, no more than was the Abbot [of] Unreason. And amongst other things he told such a merry bourd.[4] " There was (said he) a prelate, or at least a prelate's peer, a true servant to the king of love, who, upon a night after supper, asked at his gentlemen, by the faith that they owed to the king of love, that they should truly declare how many sundry women every one of them had had, and how many of them were men's wives. One answered, He had lain with five, and two of them were married. The other answered, I have had seven, and three of them are married. It came at last to my Lord himself who, making it very nice for a little space, gave in the end a plain confession, and said, ' I am the youngest man, and yet have I had the round dozen ; and seven of them are men's wives.' Now (said the Friar), this god and king of love, to whom our prelates make homage, is the master devil of hell, from whom such works and fruits do proceed." This prelate was known by his proper tokens to have been Prior Patrick Hepburn, now Bishop of Moray, who to this day has continued in the profession that he once made to his god and king of love.

It was supposed, notwithstanding this kind of preaching, that this friar remained papist in his heart ; for the rest of the friars, fearing to lose the benediction of the bishops, to wit, their malt

---

[1] *practised*

[2] Whereas the Church of Rome had jealously refused to admit any secular jurisdiction over her priests until such time as she herself had stripped them of their priesthood and had degraded them to the status of laymen.

[3] The *Abbot of Unreason*, the *Abbot of Misrule*, the *Lord of Misrule*, the *Pope of Fools*, and so forth was elected annually to lead the people in their feast-day revels, when all lawful authority was turned into ridicule and the services of the Church were often burlesqued. (See A. J. Mill, *Mediaeval Plays in Scotland*, 16–19 ; and the examples given in Jamieson's *Scottish Dictionary*, s.v. *Abbot of Unressoun*.) In 1555 Parliament forbade any choosing of " Robert Hude nor Lytill Johne Abbot of unressoun Quenis of Maij nor utherwyse." (*Acts Parl. Scot.*, ii, 500, c. 40)

[4] *jest*

and their maill,[1] and their other appointed pension, caused the said friar to flee to England, where, for defence of the Pope and Papistry, he was cast in prison at King Harry's commandment. But so it pleaseth God to open up the mouth of Balaam's own ass, to cry out against the vicious lives of the clergy of that age. Short after this, new consultation was taken, that some should be burnt ; for men began very liberally to speak. A merry gentleman, named John Lindsay, familiar to Bishop James Beaton, standing by when consultation was had, said, " My Lord, if ye burn any more, except ye follow my counsel, ye will utterly destroy yourselves. If ye will burn them, let them be burnt in how [2] cellars ; for the reek of Master Patrick Hamilton has infected as many as it blew upon." Thus it pleased God, that they should be taunted in their own face. But here follows the most merry of all. Sandie Furrour, who had been imprisoned seven years in the Tower of London, sir [3] John Dingwall, according to the charity of churchmen, entertained his wife, and wasted the poor man's substance. For the which cause, at his returning, he spake more liberally of priests than they could bear, and so was he declared to be accused of heresy, and called to his answer to Saint Andrews. He leapt up merrily upon the scaffold and, casting a gawmound,[4] said, " Where are the rest of the players ? " Master Andrew Oliphant, offended therewith, said, " It shall be no play to you, Sir, before that ye depart." And so began to read his accusation. The first article whereof was, That he despised the Mass. His answer was, " I hear more Masses in eight days, than three Bishops there sitting says in a year." Accused secondly, Of contempt of the sacraments : " The priests (said he), were the most common contemners of sacraments, and especially of matrimony," and that he witnessed by any of the priests there present, and named the men's wives with whom they had meddled, and especially sir John Dingwall, who had seven years together abused his own wife, and consumed his substance ; and said, " Because I complained of such injuries, I am here summoned, and accused, as one that is worthy to be burnt. For God's sake (said he), will ye take wives of your own, that I and others, whose wives ye have

---

[1] *their food and their rents*   [2] *deep*

[3] The title *sir* here indicates that he was a priest ; it is derived from the Latin *dominus*. It is to be noted, however, that a priest who had taken a Master's degree at a university was invariably styled *Master*. Thus here, and elsewhere, the title *sir* is lower than that of *Master*. (See the admirable note in Laing's *Knox*, i, 555–557). To differentiate a priest from a knight, I have adopted *sir* for a priest, and *Sir* for a knight.

[4] *gambol*

abused, may be revenged upon you." Then Bishop Gavin Dunbar, named the Old Bishop of Aberdeen,[1] thinking to justify himself before the people, said, " Carl, thou shalt not know my wife." The said Alexander answered, " My Lord, ye are too old ; but, with the grace of God, I shall drink with your daughter or I depart." And thereat was smiling of the best, and loud laughter of some ; for the Bishop had a daughter married with Andrew Balfour in that same town. Then the Bishops bade, " Away with the carl." But he answered, " Nay ; I will not depart this hour ; for I have more to speak against the vices of priests than I can express this whole day." And so, after divers purposes, they commanded him to burn his bill. And he demanding the cause, they said, " Because ye have spoken these articles whereof ye are accused." His answer was, " The muckle devil bear them away that first and last said them." And so he took the bill and, chewing it, he after spat it in Mr. Andrew Oliphant's face, saying, " Now burn it or drown it, whether ye will : ye hear no more of me. But I must have some-what of every one of you to begin my pack again, which a priest and my wife, a priest's whore, has spent." And so every prelate and rich priest, glad to be quit of his evil, gave him somewhat ; and so departed he, for he understood nothing of religion.

But so fearful it was then to speak any thing against priests, that the least word spoken against them, yea, albeit it was spoken in a man's sleep, was judged heresy ; and that was practised upon Richard Carmichael, yet living in Fife,[2] who being young, and a singer in the Chapel Royal of Stirling, happened in his sleep to say, " The devil take away the priests, for they are a greedy pack." He, therefor accused by sir George Clapperton, Dean of the said Chapel, was compelled therefor to burn his bill.

But God short after raised up against them stronger champions. For Alexander Seton, a Black Friar, of good learning and estimation, began to tax the corrupt doctrine of the Papistry. For the space of a whole Lent, he taught the commandments of God only, ever beating in the ears of his auditors, That the law of God had of many years not been truly taught ; for men's traditions had obscured the purity of it. These were his accustomed propositions : First, Christ Jesus is the end and perfection of the law. 2. There is no sin where God's law is not violated. 3. To satisfy for sin lies not in man's power, but the remission thereof comes by unfeigned repen-

---

[1] To distinguish him from Gavin Dunbar, Archbishop of Glasgow
[2] That is, in the year 1566

tance, and by faith apprehending God the Father merciful in Christ Jesus, his son. While often times he puts his auditors in mind of these and the like heads, and makes no mention of purgatory, pardons, pilgrimage, prayer to saints, nor such trifles, the dumb doctors, and the rest of that forsworn rabble, began to suspect him ; and yet said they nothing publicly, till Lent was ended, and he passed to Dundee. And then, in his absence, one hired for that purpose openly damned the whole doctrine that before he had taught. Which coming to the ears of the said Friar Alexander, then being in Dundee, without delay he returned to Saint Andrews, caused immediately to jow the bell,[1] and to give signification that he would preach ; as that he did indeed. In the which sermon he affirmed (and that more plainly than at any other time) whatsoever in all his whole sermons he had taught before, the whole Lententide preceding ; adding that within Scotland there was no true bishop, if that bishops should be known by such notes and virtues as Saint Paul requires in bishops. This delation flew with wings to the Bishop's ears who, but [2] further delay, sent for the said Friar Alexander, and began grievously to complain, and sharply to accuse, that he had so slanderously spoken of the dignity of the bishops, as to say, " That it behoved a bishop to be a preacher, or else he was but a dumb dog, and fed not the flock, but fed his own belly." The man being witty, and minded of that which was his most assured defence, said, " My Lord, the reporters of such things are manifest liars." Whereat the Bishop rejoiced, and said, " Your answer pleases me well ; I never could think of you that ye would be so foolish as to affirm such things. Where are those knaves that have brought me this tale ? " Who, compearing, and affirming the same that they did before, he still replied, That they were liars. But while the witnesses were multiplied, and men were brought to attention, he turned him to the Bishop, and said, " My Lord, ye may see and consider what ears these asses have, who cannot discern betwix Paul, Isaiah, Zechariah, and Malachi and Friar Alexander Seton. In very deed, My Lord, I said that Paul says, ' It behoveth a Bishop to be a teacher ' : Isaiah sayeth, ' That they that feed not the flock are dumb dogs ' : And Zechariah sayeth, ' They are idle pastors ' : I, of my own head, affirmed nothing, but declared what the Spirit of God had before pronounced ; at whom, my Lord, if ye be not offended, justly ye can not be

---

[1] *to ring the bell* ; that is, to cause the bell-man ring the handbell throughout the burgh
[2] *without*

offended at me. And so yet again, my Lord, I say, that they are manifest liars that reported unto you, that I said, That ye and others that preach not are no bishops, but belly-gods."

Albeit after that the Bishop was highly offended, as well at the scoff and bitter mock, as at the bold liberty of that learned man ; yet durst he not hazard for that present to execute his malice conceived ; for not only feared he the learning and bold spirit of the man, but also the favour that he had as well of the people as of the Prince, King James the Fifth, of whom he had good credit ; for he was at that time his Confessor, and had exhorted him to the fear of God, to the meditation of God's law, and unto purity of life. But the said Bishop, with his complices, foreseeing what danger might come to their Estate if such familiarity should continue betwix the Prince and a man so learned, and so repugning to their affections, laboured by all means to make the said Friar Alexander odious unto the King's Grace, and easily found the means by the Grey Friars (who by their hypocrisy deceived many), to traduce the innocent as an heretic. This accusation was easily received and more easily believed of the carnal Prince, who altogether was given to the filthy lusts of the flesh, [and] abhorred all counsel that repugned thereto. And because he did remember what a terror the admonitions of the said Alexander were unto his corrupted conscience, without resistance he subscribed to their accusation, affirming that he knew more than they did in that matter ; for he understood well enough that he smelled of the new doctrine, by such things as he had shown to him under confession. And therefore he promised that he should follow the counsel of the bishops in punishing of him and of all others of that sect. These things understood by the said Alexander, as well by information of his friends and familiars as by the strange countenance of the King unto him, [he] provided the next way to avoid the fury of a blinded Prince : and so, in his habit, he departed the realm, and coming to Berwick, wrote back again to the King's grace his complaint and admonition, the very tenor and copy whereof follows.[1]

.   .   .   .

From the death of that constant witness of Jesus Christ, Master Patrick Hamilton, God disclosing the wickedness of the wicked, as before we have heard, there was one Forres of Linlithgow [2] taken

[1] Alexander Seton's letter to King James V is printed below as Appendix II.
[2] Henry Forrest of Linlithgow

who, after long imprisonment in the Sea Tower of Saint Andrews,[1] was adjudged to the fire by the said Bishop James Beaton, and his doctors, for none other crime but because he had a New Testament in English. Further of that history we have not, except that he died constantly, and with great patience, at Saint Andrews. After whose death, the flame of persecution ceased, till the death of Master Norman Gourlay, the space of ten years [2] or nearby ; not that those bloody beasts ceased by all means to suppress the light of God, and to trouble such as in any sort were suspected to abhor their corruption, but because the realm was troubled with intestine and civil wars, in the which much blood was shed ; first, at Melrose, betwix the Douglas and Buccleuch, in the year of God 1526, the nineteenth day of July [3] ; next, at Linlithgow, betwix the Hamiltons and the Earl of Lennox, where the said Earl, with many others, lost his life, the thirteenth day of September, the year foresaid [4] ; and last, betwix the King himself and the said Douglases, whom he banished the realm, and held them in exile during his whole days.[5] By reason of these, we say, and of other troubles, the bishops and their bloody bands could not find the time so favourable unto them as they required to execute their tyranny.

In this mid-time, so did the wisdom of God provide, that Harry the Eighth, King of England, did abolish from his realm the name and authority of the Pope of Rome and suppress the Abbeys and other places of Idolatry ; which gave esperance to divers realms that some godly reformation should thereof have ensued. And therefore from this our country did divers learned men, and others that lived in fear of persecution, repair to that realm ; where albeit they found not such purity as they wished (and therefore divers of them sought other countries), yet they escaped the tyranny of

[1] In the Sea Tower of the Castle ; probably in what is now known as the " Bottle Dungeon." (Similarly *infra*, 56, 78,)

[2] The chronology is here confused. Knox gives the date of Gourlay's martyrdom as 27 August, 1534 (*infra*, 25), and if Forrest had been burned " ten years " earlier his martyrdom would have taken place in 1524. Probably for " ten years " we should read " ten months," which would place Forrest's martyrdom in 1533—the date suggested by Keith (*Hist. of the Affairs of Church and State in Scotland*, i, 15)—but that would mean transposing Knox's accounts of the two immediately following conflicts, at Melrose and at Linlithgow.

[3] Archibald Douglas, 6th Earl of Angus, defeated Sir Walter Scott, the Laird of Buccleuch, near Melrose, 25 July 1526.

[4] Sir James Hamilton of Finnart and Archibald Douglas, 6th Earl of Angus, defeated and slew John Stewart, 3rd Earl of Lennox, near Linlithgow, 4 September 1526.

[5] Archibald Douglas, 6th Earl of Angus, George Douglas, his brother, and Archibald Douglas, their uncle, were forfeited by Parliament in September 1528.

merciless men, and were reserved to better times, that they might fructify within his Church, in divers places and parts, and in divers vocations. Alexander Seton [1] remained in England, and publicly (with great praise and comfort of many), taught the Evangel in all sincerity certain years. And albeit the craftiness of Winchester,[2] and of others, circumvened the said Alexander, that they caused him at Paul's Cross [3] to affirm certain things that repugned to his former true doctrine ; yet it is no doubt, but that as God potently had rung [4] with him in all his life, also in his death (which shortly after followed) he found the mercy of his God, whereupon he ever exhorted all men to depend. Alexander Alesius, Master John Fyfe, and that famous man Doctor Machabeus departed unto Dutch land,[5] where by God's providence they were distributed to several places. Macdowell,[6] for his singular prudence, besides his learning and godliness was elected borrow master in one of the Steads.[7] Alesius was appointed to the University of Lipsia [8] ; and so was Master John Fyfe where, for their honest behaviour and great erudition, they were held in admiration with all the godly. And in what honour, credit, and estimation Doctor Machabeus was with Christian King of Denmark [at] Copenhagen, famous men of divers nations can testify. Thus did God provide for his servants, and did frustrate the expectation of these bloody beasts who, by the death of one in whom the light of God did clearly shine, intended to have suppressed Christ's truth for ever within this realm. But the contrary had God decreed ; for his death was the cause (as said is) that many did awake from the deadly sleep of ignorance, and so did Jesus Christ, the only true Light, shine unto many, for the away-taking of one. And albeit that these notable men did never after (Master John Fyfe only excepted), comfort this country with their bodily presence [9] ; yet [God] made them fructify in his Church, and raised them up lights out of darkness, to the praise of his own mercy, and to the just condemnation of them that then ruled, to wit, of the King, council, and nobility, yea of the whole people, who suffered such notable personages, without crimes

---

[1] *Supra*, 21
[2] Stephen Gardiner, Bishop of Winchester
[3] St. Paul's Cross, London
[4] *reigned*
[5] That is, *Deutschland* (Germany)
[6] In the manuscript (folio 19 *recto*) originally *M°aduell*, which has been scored through and *Makdwell* added in the margin, probably in Knox's own hand.
[7] That is, burgomaster in one of the *stadts*, or towns
[8] *Leipzig*
[9] That is, they remained abroad. But there is no evidence to confirm the statement by Knox (and Calderwood) that John Fyfe returned to Scotland. (See Laing's *Knox*, i, 527)

committed, to be unjustly persecuted, and so exiled. Others were after even so entreated : but of them we shall speak in their own places.

No sooner got the bishops opportunity (which always they sought), but so soon renewed they the battle against Jesus Christ ; for the foresaid leprous Bishop,[1] in the year of God 1534, caused to be summoned sir William Kirk, Adam Dayes, Henry Cairnes [and] John Stewart, indwellers of Leith, with divers others, such as Master William Johnston [and] Master Henry Henderson, schoolmaster of Edinburgh, of whom some compeared in the Abbey Kirk of Holyroodhouse, and so abjured and publicly burnt their bills [2] : others compeared not, and therefore were exiled. But in judgment were produced two, to wit, David Stratoun, a gentleman, and Master Norman Gourlay, a man of reasonable erudition, of whom we must shortly speak. In Master Norman appeared knowledge, albeit joined with weakness. But in David Stratoun could only be espied, from the first, a haterent [3] against the pride and avariciousness of the priests ; for the cause of his delation was, he had made to himself a fish boat to go to the sea [and], the Bishop of Moray (then being Prior of Saint Andrews),[4] and his factors, urged him for the teind thereof. His answer was, if they would have teind of that which his servants won in the sea, it were but reason that they should come and receive it where he got the stock ; and so, as was constantly affirmed, he caused his servants cast the tenth fish in the sea again. Process of cursing was led against him, for non-payment of such teinds which, when he contemned, he was delated to answer for heresy. It troubled him vehemently ; and therefore he began to frequent the company of such as were godly ; for before he had been a man very stubborn, and one that despised all reading (chiefly of those things that were godly) ; but miraculously, as it were, he appeared to be changed ; for he delighted in nothing but in reading (albeit himself could not read), and was a vehement exhorter of all men to concord, to quietness, and to the contempt of the world. He frequented much the company of the Laird of Dun,[5] whom God in those days had marvellously illuminated. Upon a day, as the Laird of Lauriston,[6] that yet liveth, then being

---

[1] James Beaton, Archbishop of St. Andrews

[2] See *supra*, 11, note 1. For these trials for heresy, see the note in Pitcairn, *Criminal Trials*, i, 210*–211*.   [3] hatred

[4] In the manuscript (folio 20 *recto*) the words within parentheses have been added in the margin, probably in Knox's own hand.

[5] John Erskine of Dun   [6] Andrew Stratoun of Lauriston, Kincardineshire

a young man, was reading unto him upon the New Testament, in a certain quiet place in the fields, as God had appointed he chanced to read these sentences of our Master, Jesus Christ : " He that denies me before men, or is ashamed of me in the midst of this wicked generation, I will deny him in the presence of my Father, and before his angels." At which words, he suddenly being as one ravished, platt himself upon his knees, and extending both hands and visage constantly to the heaven a reasonable time, at length he burst forth in these words, " O Lord, I have been wicked, and justly may Thou extract thy grace from me. But, Lord, for thy mercy's sake let me never deny Thee, nor thy truth, for fear of death or corporal pain." The issue declared that his prayer was not vain : for when he, with the foresaid Master Norman, was produced in judgment in the Abbey of Holyroodhouse, the King himself (all clad in red) being present, great labours were made that the said David Stratoun should have recanted, and burnt his bill. But he ever standing at his defence, alleging that he had not offended, in the end was adjudged unto the fire ; and then, when that he perceived the danger, asked grace of the King (which he would willingly have granted unto him), the Bishops proudly answered, That the King's hands were bound in that case, and that he had no grace to give to such as by their law were condemned. And so was he, with the said Master Norman, after dinner, upon the twenty-seventh day of August, the year of God 1534 foresaid, led to a place besides the Rood of Greenside [1] ; and there those two were both hanged and burnt, according to the mercy of the Papistical Kirk. To that same diet were summoned, as before we have said, others, of whom some escaped in England and so for that present escaped the death.

This their tyranny notwithstanding, the knowledge of God did wondrously increase within this realm, partly by reading, partly by brotherly conference, which in those dangerous days was used to the comfort of many ; but chiefly by merchants and mariners who, frequenting other countries, heard the true doctrine affirmed, and the vanity of the papistical religion openly rebuked. Amongst whom were Dundee and Leith principals, against whom was made a very strait inquisition by David Beaton, cruel Cardinal ; and divers were compelled to abjure and burn their bills, some in Saint

[1] The Rood or Cross of Greenside was probably at the foot of the Calton Hill, Edinburgh, near the road to Leith. (Laing's *Knox*, i, 60, *note* 1.) The Rood Chapel is mentioned in 1525 when it was resigned in favour of the Carmelite Friars.

Andrews, and some at Edinburgh. About the same time Captain John Borthwick was burnt in figure, but by God's providence escaped their fury.[1] And this was done for a spectacle and triumph to Mary of Lorraine, lately arrived from France, as wife to James the Fifth, King of Scots. What plagues she brought with her, and how they yet continue, such as are not blind may manifestly see.

The rage of those bloody beasts proceeded so that the King's Court itself escaped not that danger ; for in it divers were suspected, and some accused. And yet ever still did some light burst out in the midst of darkness ; for the truth of Christ Jesus entered even in the cloisters, as well of friars, as of monks and canons. John Lyn, a Grey Friar, left his hypocritical habit, and the den of those murderers the Grey Friars. A Black Friar, called Friar Kyllour, set forth the History of Christ's Passion in form of a play,[2] which he both preached and practised openly in Stirling, the King himself being present, upon a Good Friday in the morning. In the which, all things were so lively expressed, that the very simple people understood and confessed that as the priests and obstinate Pharisees persuaded the people to refuse Christ Jesus, and caused Pilate to condemn him, so did the bishops and men called Religious blind the people, and persuade Princes and Judges to persecute such as profess Jesus Christ his blessed Evangel.

This plain speaking so inflamed the hearts of all that bore the beast's mark that they ceased not, till that the said Friar Kyllour, and with him Friar Beveridge, sir Duncan Simson, Robert Forster, a gentleman, and Dean Thomas Forret, Canon Regular and Vicar of Dollar, a man of upright life, who all together were cruelly murdered in one fire, the last day of February, in the year of [God] 1538.[3] This cruelty was used by the said. Cardinal, the

---

[1] Knox has here confused the order of events. Mary of Lorraine landed in Scotland in June 1538 ; and Sir John Borthwick, having made his escape to England, was condemned to be burned in effigy on 28 May 1540. (*Reg. St. Andrews Kirk Session*, Scot. Hist. Soc., i, 91–101.) The articles against Sir John Borthwick, printed in the *St. Andrews Kirk Session Register*, should be compared with those in the *St. Andrews Formulare* (see Herkless and Hannay, *Archbishops of St. Andrews*, iv, 225–226). Laing says that Beaton was not present at the condemnation (Laing's *Knox*, i, App. VIII), but the *Rentale Sancti Andree* shows that both Beaton and James V were in St. Andrews at the time, and were still there on 28 May 1540. (*Rentale Sancti Andree*, Scot. Hist. Soc., Intro., xxxvii ; Herkless and Hannay, *Archbishops of St. Andrews*, iv, 52)

[2] No copy of this play is known to have been preserved.

[3] That is, 28 February 1539. See also Calderwood's *History*, i, 125–129 ; Pitcairn, *Criminal Trials*, i, 211*–215*. In March 1539 Beaton's accounts bear a charge of £4, 10s. for making a great stand (*magna scala*) in the Church of Holyrood for the accusation of heretics in that month. (*Rentale Sancti Andree*, Scot. Hist. Soc., 64, 93)

Chancellor, Bishop of Glasgow, and the incestuous Bishop of Dunblane.[1]

After that this cruelty was used in Edinburgh, upon the Castle Hill, to the effect that the rest of the bishops might show themselves no less fervent to suppress the light of God than he of Saint Andrews was, were apprehended two in the Diocese of Glasgow. The one was named Jeronimus Russell, a Cordelier friar,[2] a young man of a meek nature, quick spirit, and good letters ; and one Kennedy, who passed not eighteen years of age, one of excellent engine [3] in Scottish poesy. To assist the Bishop of Glasgow in that cruel judgment, or at least to cause him dip his hands in the blood of the saints of God, were sent Master John Lauder, Master Andrew Oliphant, and Friar Maltman, sergeants of Sathan, apt for that purpose. The day appointed to their cruelty approached ; the two poor saints of God were presented before those bloody butchers ; grievous were the crimes that were laid to their charge. Kennedy at the first was faint, and gladly would have recanted. But while that place of repentance was denied unto him, the Spirit of God, which is the Spirit of all comfort, began to work into him, yea the inward comfort began to burst forth, as well in visage, as in tongue and word ; for his countenance began to be cheerful, and, with a joyful voice, upon his knees he said, " O eternal God ! how wondrous is that love and mercy that Thou bearest unto mankind, and unto me the most caitiff and miserable wretch above all others ; for, even now, when I would have denied Thee, and thy Son, our Lord Jesus Christ, my only Saviour, and so have cast myself in everlasting damnation, Thou, by thy own hand, has pulled me from the very bottom of hell, and makes me to feel that heavenly comfort which takes from me that ungodly fear, wherewith before I was oppressed. Now I defy death ; do what ye please : I praise my God I am ready." The godly and learned Jeronimus, railed upon by those godless tyrants, answered, " This is your hour and the power of darkness. Now sit ye as judges ; and we stand wrongfully accused, and more wrongfully to be condemned. But the day shall come when our innocence shall appear, and that ye shall see your own blindness, to your everlasting confusion. Go forward, and fulfil the measure of your iniquity." While that these servants of God thus

---

[1] That is, Cardinal Beaton ; Gavin Dunbar, Archbishop of Glasgow and Lord Chancellor ; and William Chisholm, Bishop of Dunblane. Foxe's account says " George Creichton, Bishop of Dunkeld." (Laing's *Knox*, i, 521)

[2] That is, a Franciscan or Grey Friar of the strict rule, who wore the knotted cord round his waist.   [3] *genius*

behaved themselves, ariseth a variance betwix the Bishop and the beasts [1] that came from the Cardinal ; for the Bishop said, " I think it better to spare these men, nor to put them to death." Whereat the idiot Doctors,[1] offended, said, " What will ye do, my Lord ? Will ye condemn all that my Lord Cardinal and the other Bishops and we have done ? If so ye do, ye show yourself enemy to the Kirk and us, and so we will repute you, be ye assured." At which words the faithless man, afraid, adjudged the innocents to die according to the desire of the wicked. The meek and gentle Jerome Russell comforted the other with many comfortable sentences, oft saying unto him, " Brother, fear not : more potent is He that is in us, than is he that is in the world. The pain that we shall suffer is short, and shall be light ; but our joy and consolation shall never have end. And therefore let us contend to enter in unto our Master and Saviour, by the same strait way, which He has trod before us. Death can not destroy us ; for it is destroyed already by Him for whose sake we suffer." With these and the like comfortable sentences, they passed to the place of execution ; and constantly triumphed over death and Sathan, even in the midst of the flaming fire.

And thus did those cruel beasts intend nothing but murder in all the quarters of this realm. For so far had that blinded and most vicious man, the Prince (most vicious, we shall call him, for he neither spared man's wife nor maiden, no more after his marriage than he did before)—so far, we say, had he given himself to obey the tyranny of those bloody beasts, that he had made a solemn vow, That none should be spared that was suspect of heresy, yea, although it were his own son. To press and push him forward in that his fury, he lacked not flatterers enough ; for many of his minions were pensioners to priests ; amongst whom, Oliver Sinclair, yet remaining enemy to God,[2] was the principal. And yet did not God cease to give to that blinded Prince documents [3] that some sudden plague was to fall upon him, in case he did not repent his wicked life ; and that his own mouth did confess. For after that Sir James Hamilton [4] was beheaded (justly or unjustly we dispute not), this vision came unto him, as to his familiars himself did declare : The said Sir James appeared unto him, having in his

---

[1] That is, Lauder, Oliphant, and Maltman   [2] That is, in 1566   [3] *admonitions*
[4] Sir James Hamilton of Finnart, natural son of James, first Earl of Arran, and for long a favourite of the King, was suddenly accused of treason, and after a summary trial was forfeited and executed (August 1540).

hands a drawn sword, by the which from the King he struck both the arms, saying to him these words, " Take that, while thou receive a final payment for all thy impiety." This vision, with sorrowful countenance, he showed on the morrow ; and shortly thereafter died his two sons, both within the space of twenty-four hours ; yea, some say, within the space of six hours.[1] In his own presence, George Steill, his greatest flatterer, and greatest enemy to God that was in his Court, dropped off his horse, and died without word that same day that, in open audience of many, the said George had refused his portion of Christ's kingdom if the prayers of the Virgin Mary should not bring him thereto. How terrible a vision the said Prince saw, lying in Linlithgow, that night that Thomas Scott, Justice-Clerk, died in Edinburgh, men of good credit can yet report. For, afraid at midnight, or after, he cried for torches, and raised all that lay beside him in the Palace, and told that Thomas Scott was dead ; for he had been at him with a company of devils, and had said unto him these words, " O woe to the day that ever I knew thee, or thy service ; for, for serving of thee against God, against his servants, and against justice, I am adjudged to endless torment." How terrible voices [2] the said Thomas Scott pronounced before his death, men of all estates heard ; and some that yet live can witness : his voice was ever, " *Justo Dei judicio condemnatus sum* " : that is, " I am condemned by God's just judgment." He was most oppressed for the delation and false accusation of such as professed Christ's Evangel as Master Thomas Marjoribanks, and Master Hew Rigg, then advocates, did confess to Master Henry Balnaves ; who,[3] from the said Thomas Scott, came to him,[4] as he and Master Thomas Bellenden were sitting in Saint Giles Kirk, and asked him forgiveness in the name of the said Thomas. None of these terrible forewarnings could either change or mollify the heart of the indurate, lecherous, and avaricious tyrant ; but still he does proceed from impiety to impiety. For, in the midst of these admonitions, he caused put hands on that notable man, Master George Buchanan, to whom, for his singular erudition and honest behaviour, was committed the charge to instruct some of his bastard children. But, by the merciful providence of God, he escaped (albeit with great difficulty) the rage of those that sought his blood, and remains

---

[1] James V's two sons, James and Arthur, both died in infancy in 1541 ; Arthur dying eight days after his birth, and James, about one year old, dying about *four weeks* afterwards.
[2] *what terrible cries*   [3] That is, Thomas Marjoribanks and Hew Rigg
[4] That is, Henry Balnaves

alive to this day, in the year of God 1566, to the glory of God, to the great honour of his nation, and unto the comfort of those that delight in letters and virtue. That singular work of David's Psalms in Latin metre and poesy,[1] besides many others, can witness the rare graces of God given to that man, which that tyrant,[2] by instigation of the Grey Friars,[3] and of his other flatterers, would altogether have devoured, if God had not provided remedy to his servant by escaping.[4]

This cruelty and persecution notwithstanding, those monsters and hypocrites, the Grey Friars, day by day came further in contempt; for not only did the learned espy their abominable hypocrisy, but also men, in whom no such graces nor gifts were thought to have been, began plainly to paint the same forth to the people; as the Rhyme, made by Alexander, Earl of Glencairn, yet alive, can witness.[5]

. . . .

When God had given unto that indurate Prince[6] sufficient documents[7] that his rebellion against his blessed Evangel should not prosperously succeed, he raises up against him war, as that he did against obstinate Saul, in the which he miserably perished, as we shall after hear.

The occasion of the war was this. Harry the Eighth, King of England, had a great desire to have spoken with our King; and in that point travailed so long, till that he got a full promise made to his Ambassador, Lord William Howard.[8] The place of meeting was appointed [at] York; which the King of England kept with

---

[1] *Psalmorum Davidis paraphrasis poetica, nunc primum edita; authore Georgio Buchanano* [Printed editions : ? 1564, 1566.]   [2] James V

[3] Buchanan's satires on the Franciscans, the *Somnium* (really a translation into Latin of Dunbar's *How Dunbar was desyrit to be ane Freir*), written about 1534, and the *Palinode* (offered as an ambiguous apology for the *Somnium*, but even more satirically insulting), written about 1537, had doubtless circulated in manuscript prior to his flight in 1539. His more celebrated satire, *Franciscanus* (according to his own account, written at the request of James V), was probably first drafted in 1538, but it was not completed until after his return to Scotland, probably in 1561. A printed edition appeared in 1566.

[4] Buchanan describes his own escape in 1539 : " Initio anni proximi, qui fuit 1539, Lutheranisme suspecti complures capti sunt . . . in his fuit Georgius Buchananus, qui sopitis custodibus, per cubiculi fenestrum evaserat." (*Rerum Scoticarum Historia*, lib. xiv)

[5] In the manuscript, ' as this Rhyme, which here we have inserted for the same purpose, made by ALEXANDER, EARL OF GLENCAIRN, yet alive, can witness.' This ' Rhyme ' is printed below, Appendix X.   [6] James V   [7] admonitions

[8] Knox appears to have confused the proposals made by Henry VIII for a meeting with James V in 1536, when Lord William Howard was Henry's ambassador (*Hamilton Papers*, i, Nos. 30, 31), with the later proposals made in 1541.

such solemnity and preparations as never for such a purpose was seen in England before. Great bruit[1] of that journey, and some preparation for the same was made in Scotland ; but in the end, by persuasion of the Cardinal David Beaton, and by others of his faction, that journey was stayed, and the King's promise falsified. Whereupon were sharp letters of reproach sent unto the King, and also unto his Council. King Harry, frustrated, returned to London, and after his indignation declared, began to fortify with men his frontiers foranent[2] Scotland. There were sent to the Borders Sir Robert Bowes, the Earl of Angus, and his brother, Sir George Douglas. Upon what other trifling questions (as for the debatable land and suchlike), the war broke up, we omit to write. The principal occasion was the falsifying of the promise before made. Our King perceiving that the war would rise, asked the Prelates and Kirkmen what support they would make to the sustaining of the same ; for rather would he yet satisfy the desire of his uncle, than he would hazard war, where he saw not his force able to resist. They promised mountains of gold (as Sathan their father did to Christ Jesus if he would worship him) ; for rather would they have gone to hell, or he should have met with King Harry : for then, thought they, farewell our kingdom ; and farewell, thought the Cardinal, his credit and glory in France. In the end, they promised fifty thousand crowns by [the] year, to be well paid, so long as the wars lasted ; and further, that their servants, and others that appertained unto them, and were exempted from common service, should none the less serve in time of necessity. These vain promises lifted up in pride the heart of the unhappy King : and so begins the war. The realm was quartered, and men were laid in Jedburgh and Kelso. All men (fools we mean) bragged of victory ; and in very deed the beginning gave us a fair show. For at the first warden raid, which was made at the Saint Bartholomew's day,[3] in the year of God 1542, was the Warden Sir Robert Bowes, his brother Richard Bowes, Captain of Norham, Sir William Malory, knight, a bastard son of the Earl of Angus, and James Douglas of Parkhead, then rebels, with a great number of borderers, soldiers, and gentlemen, taken.

The Raid was termed Haldane Rig.[4] The Earl of Angus and *Haldane* Sir George his brother did narrowly escape. Our papists and *Rig* priests, proud of this victory, encouraged the King, so that there

---

[1] *report ; talk*   [2] *directly opposite*   [3] 24 August
[4] Usually called Hadden Rig, about five miles north-east of Kelso

was nothing heard but, " All is ours. They are but heretics. If we be a thousand and they ten thousand, they dare not fight. France shall enter the one part, and we the other, and so shall England be conquered within a year." If any man was seen to smile at such vanity, he was no more but a traitor and a heretic. And yet by these means men had greater liberty than they had before as concerning their conscience ; for then ceased the persecution. The war continued till mid September ; and then was sent down the old Duke of Norfolk, with such an army as a hundred years before had not come in Scotland. They were in amassing their forces and setting forward of their preparations and munitions, which were exceeding great, till mid October, and after ; and then they marched from Berwick, and tended to the west, ever holding Tweed upon their one side, and never camped from that river the space of a mile during the whole time they continued in Scotland, which was ten or twelve days. Forays were run upon the day to Smailholm, Stichill, and such places near about, but many snappars[1] they got. Some corns they burnt, besides that which the great host consumed, but small butting[2] they carried away. The King assembled *Fala Raid* his force at Fala[3] (for he was advertised that they had promised to come to Edinburgh), and taking the musters all at one hour, two days before Allhallow Even,[4] there were found with him eighteen thousand able men. Upon the borders, that awaited upon the English army, were ten thousand men, with the Earl of Huntly, Lords Erskine, Seton, and Home. These were judged men enough to hazard battle, albeit the others were esteemed forty thousand. While the King lies at Fala, abiding upon the guns, and upon advertisement from the army, the Lords begin to remember how the King had been long abused by his flatterers, and principally by the pensioners of the priests. It was once[5] concluded, that they would make some new remembrance of Lauder-brig,[6] to see if that would, for a season, somewhat help the estate of their country. But, because the Lords could not agree amongst themselves upon the persons that deserved punishment (for every man favoured his friend), the whole escaped ; and the purpose was opened unto the

[1] *mishaps*

[2] *plunder*, or, perhaps, *household gear*. The *Oxford Dictionary* gives *butin* = plunder, or spoil ; but the French *butin* = plunder, or spoil, *or* household gear

[3] Fala Muir ; the plain to the west of Soutra Hill at the western end of the Lammermoors   [4] That is, on 29 October 1542   [5] *at one time*

[6] In 1482 James III's favourites had been seized by the nobles and hanged on Lauder Bridge—not far to the south of Fala Muir.

King, and by him to the courtiers who, after that, till that they came to Edinburgh, stood in no little fear. But that was suddenly forgot, as we shall after hear. While time is thus protracted the English army, for scarcity of victuals (as was bruited), retire them over Tweed upon the night, and so begin to skaill.[1] Whereof the King advertised, desires the Lords and barons to assist him, to follow them in England. Whose answer was, with one consent, " That to defend his person and realm, they would hazard life and whatsoever they had ; but to invade England, neither had they so just title as they desired ; neither yet could they be then able to do any thing to the hurt of England, considering that they had long before been absent from their houses, their provision was spent, their horse wearied, and that which was greatest of all, the time of year did utterly reclaim.[2] " This their answer seemed to satisfy the King ; for he in words praised their prudent foresight and wise counsel. But the mint [3] made to his courtiers, and that bold repulse of his desires given to him in his own face, so wounded his proud heart (for long had he roung [4] as himself listed), that he decreed a notable revenge which, no doubt, he had not failed to have executed, if God by his own hand had not cut the cords of his impiety. He returns to Edinburgh ; the nobility, barons, gentlemen, and commons to their own habitations : And this was the second and third days of November.

Without longer delay, at the Palace of Holyroodhouse, was a new Council convened, a Council, we mean, of his abusers ; wherein were accusations laid against the most part of the nobility. Some were heretics, some favourers of England, some friends to the Douglases, and so could there be none faithful to the King, in their opinion. The Cardinal and the priests cast faggots in the fire with all their force ; and finding the King wholly addicted to their devotion, delivered unto him a scroll, containing the names of such as they in their inquisition had convicted for heretics. For this was the order of justice which those holy fathers kept in condemning of innocent men : whosoever would delate any of heresy, he was heard ; no respect nor consideration had what mind the delator bore to the person delated ; whosoever were produced for witnesses were admitted, how suspicious and infamous that ever they were ; if two or three had proven any point, that by their law was held heresy, that was a heretic ; rested no more but a day

---

[1] disperse   [2] was utterly against it   [3] threat   [4] reigned

to be affixed to his condemnation, and to the execution of their corrupted sentence. What man could be innocent, where such judges were party, the world may this day consider. True it is, by false judgment and false witnesses have innocents been oppressed from the beginning. But this freedom to shed innocent blood got never the Devil but in the kingdom of Antichrist, " that the innocent should die, and neither know accusator nor yet the witnesses that testified against him." But how shall the Antichrist be known, if he shall not be contrary to God the Father, and his Son Christ Jesus, in law, life, and doctrine. But this we omit.

The same scroll had the Cardinal and prelates once presented unto the King before, what time he returned from the navigation about the Isles.[1] But then it was refused by the prudent and stout counsel of the Laird of Grange,[2] who opened clearly to the King the practice [3] of the Prelates, and the danger that thereof might ensue. Which considered by the King (for being out of his passion, he was tractable) [he] gave this answer in the Palace of Holyroodhouse to the Cardinal and prelates, after that they had uttered their malice, and shown what profit might arise to the Crown, if he would follow their

An answer worthy of a prince

counsel : " Pack you, jefwells [4] : get you to your charges, and reform your own lives, and be not instruments of discord betwix my nobility and me ; or else, I avow to God, I shall reform you, not as the King of Denmark by imprisonment does, neither yet as the King of England does, by hanging and heading ; but I shall reform you by sharp whingers,[5] if ever I hear such motion of you again." The Prelates, dashed and astonished with this answer, ceased for a season to tempt any further by rigour against the nobility. But now, being informed of all proceedings by their pensioners, Oliver Sinclair, [John] Ross, laird of Craigie, and others, who were to them faithful in all things, they conclude to hazard once again their former suit ; which was no sooner proposed but as soon it was accepted, with no small regret, made by the King's own mouth, that he had so long despised their counsel. " For (said he) now I plainly see your words to be true. The nobility neither desires my honour nor continuance ; for they would not ride a mile for my pleasure to follow my enemies. Will ye therefore find me the means how that

---

[1] In 1540. (See Gregory, *History of the Western Highlands and Isles of Scotland*, 2nd edition, 1881, 146–148)   [2] James Kirkcaldy of Grange   [3] *intrigues*

[4] *knaves*. This is apparently Knox's spelling of *jevel*, which is the Scottish form of the obsolete English *javel*, given in the *Oxford Dictionary* as meaning ' a low or worthless fellow, a rascal.' See also Jamieson's *Dictionary*, s.v. *jevel*

[5] *hangers* ; that is short swords, or daggers

I may have a Raid made in England, without their knowledge and *Solway Moss, how it began* consent, that may be known to be my own Raid, and I shall bind me to your counsel for ever?" There concurred together Ahab and his false prophets; there were gratulations and clapping of hands; there were promises of diligence, closeness, and felicity. Finally, conclusion was taken, that the west border of England, which was most empty of men and garrisons, should be invaded; the King's own banner should be there; Oliver,[1] the great minion, should be general lieutenant; but no man should be privy (except the Council that was there then present) of the enterprise till the very day and execution thereof. The bishops gladly took the charge of that Raid. Letters were sent to such as they would charge to meet the King, day and place appointed. The Cardinal, with the Earl of Arran,[2] were directed to go to Haddington, to make a show against the east border, when the others were in readiness to invade the west. And thus neither lacked counsel, practice, closeness, nor diligence, to set forward that enterprise : and so, amongst these consulters, there was no doubt of a good success; and so was the scroll thankfully received by the King himself, and put into his own pocket, where it remained to the day of his death, and then was found. In it were contained more than a hundred landed men, besides others of meaner degree, amongst whom was the Lord Hamilton himself, then second person of the realm, delated.

It was bruited that this Raid was devised by the Lord Maxwell; but the certainty thereof we have not. The night before the day appointed to the enterprise, the King was found at Lochmaben. To him comes companies from all quarters, as they were appointed, no man knowing of another (for no general proclamation passed, but privy letters), neither yet did the multitude know anything of the purpose till after midnight, when that the trumpet blew, and commanded all men to march forward, and to follow the King (who was constantly supposed to have been in the host). Guides were appointed to conduct them towards England, as both faithfully and closely they did. Upon the point of day they approached to the enemy's ground; and so passes the water without any great resistance made unto them. The foray goes forth, fire rises, herschip [3] might have been seen on every side. The unprovided [4] people were all together amazed; for bright day appearing, they saw an army of ten thousand men; their corns and houses upon every side send flames of fire

---

[1] That is, Oliver Sinclair
[2] James Hamilton, 2nd Earl of Arran
[3] *ravaging*
[4] That is, *unprepared*

10

unto the heaven. To them it was more than a wonder, that such
a multitude could have been assembled and convoyed, no knowledge
thereof coming to any of their Wardens. For support they looked
not ; and so at the first they were utterly despaired. And yet began
they to assemble together, ten in one company, twenty in another ;
and so, as the fray proceeded, their troops increased, but to no
number (for Carlisle, fearing to have been assaulted, suffered no
man to issue out of their yetts [1]) ; and so the greatest number
that ever appeared or approached, before the discomfiture, passed
not three or four hundred men ; and yet they made hot skirmishing,
as in their own ground, in such fates [2] they are most expert. About
ten hours, when fires were kindled and almost slaked on every
side, thought Oliver time to show his glory ; and so incontinent was
displayed the King's banner ; Oliver upon spears lifted up upon
men's shoulders, and there with sound of trumpet was he proclaimed
general lieutenant, and all men commanded to obey him as the King's
own person under all highest pains. There was present the Lord
Maxwell, Warden, to whom the regiment, [3] in absence of the King,
properly appertained : he heard and saw all, but thought more than
he spake. There were also present the Earls Glencairn and Cassillis,
with the Lord Fleming, and many other Lords, Barons, and gentlemen of Lothian, Fife, Angus, and Mearns. In this meantime did
the skirmishing grow hotter than it was before : shouts were heard
on every side. Some Scotsmen were stricken down ; some, not
knowing the ground, lared [4] and lost their horse. Some English
horse of purpose were let loose, to provoke greedy and imprudent
men to prick at them ; as many did, but found no advantage.
While such disorder rises more and more in the army, men cried in
every ear, " My Lord Lieutenant, what will ye do ? " Charge was
given, that all men should alight and go to array ; for they would
fight it. Others cried, " Against whom will ye fight ? Yon men
will fight not otherwise than ye see them do, if ye will stand here
while the morn." New purpose was taken, that the foot men (they
had with them certain bands of soldiers), should softly retire towards
Scotland, and the horsemen should take their horse again, and so
follow in order. Great was the noise and confusion that was heard,
while that every man calls his own sloghorne. [5] The day was near
spent, and that was the cause of the greatest fear. The Lord Maxwell,
perceiving what would be the end of such beginnings, stood upon

---

[1] *gates*   [2] *matters* (from French *faits*)   [3] *rule* ; direction of affairs
[4] *were bogged*   [5] *slogan, war cry*

his foot with his friends, who, being admonished to take his horse, and provide for himself, answered, " Nay, I will rather abide here the chance that it shall please God to send me, than to go home and there be hanged." And so he remained upon his foot, and was taken, while the multitude fled, and took the greater shame. The enemies, perceiving the disorder, increased in courage. Before they shouted ; but then they struck. They shot spears and dagged arrows, where the companies were thickest. Some reacuntars [1] were made, but nothing availed. The soldiers cast from them their pikes, culverins, and other weapons fencible ; the horsemen left their spears ; and so, without judgment, all men fled. The sea was filling, and so the water made great stop [2] ; but the fear was such as happy was he that might get a taker.[3] Such as passed the water and escaped that danger, not well acquainted with the ground, fell into the Sollen Moss.[4] The entry thereof was pleasing enough but, as they proceeded, all that took that way either lost their horse or else themselves and horse both. To be short, a greater fear and dis-comfiture, without cause, has seldom been seen. For it is said, That where the men were not sufficient to take the hands of prisoners, some ran to houses, and rendered themselves to women. Stout Oliver was without stroke taken, fleeing full manfully ; and so was his glory (stinking and foolish proudness we should call it) suddenly turned to confusion and shame. In that discomfiture were taken the two Earls foresaid, the Lords Fleming, Somerville, and many others barons and gentlemen, besides the great multitude of servants. Worldly men may think that all this came but by misorder and fortune (as they term it), but whosoever has the least spunk of the knowledge of God may as evidently see the work of his hand in this discomfiture, as ever was seen in any of the battles left to us in register by the Holy Ghost. For what more evident declaration have we that God fought against Benhadad, King of Aram, when he was discomfited at Samaria, than that we have that God fought 1. *Reg.* with his own arm against Scotland ? In this former discomfiture [20] there did two hundred and thirty persons in the skirmish, with seven thousand following them in the great battle, put to flight the said Benhadad with thirty kings in his company. But here there is, in this shameful discomfiture of Scotland, very few more than three hundred men, without knowledge of any back or battle to follow,[5]

---

[1] *rencontres* [2] *proved a great hindrance*
[3] That is, *one to take him prisoner* [4] Solway Moss
[5] *without knowledge of any supporting army*

put to flight ten thousand men without resistance made.[1]   There did every man reaconter his marrow,[2] till that the 230 slew such as matched them.   But here without slaughter the multitude fled. There had those of Samaria the prophet of God to comfort, to instruct, and to promise victory unto them.   But England, in that pursuit, had nothing, but as God secretly wrought by his providence in these men that knew nothing of his working, neither yet of the causes thereof, more than the wall that fell upon the rest of Benhadad's army knew what it did.   And therefore, yet again we say, that such as in that sudden dejection [3] beholds not the hand of God, fighting against pride for freedom of his own little flock, unjustly persecuted, does willingly and maliciously obscure the glory of God.   But the end thereof is yet more notable.

The certain knowledge of the discomfiture coming to the King's ears (who waited upon news at Lochmaben), he was stricken with a sudden fear and astonishment, so that scarcely could he speak, or hold purpose with any man.   The night constrained him to remain where he was, and so yead [4] to bed ; but rose without rest or quiet sleep.   His continual complaint was, " Oh, fled Oliver ! Is Oliver tane ? [5]   Oh, fled Oliver ! "   And these words in his melancholy, and as it were carried away in a trance, repeated he from time to time, to the very hour of his death.   Upon the morn, which was Saint Catherine's day,[6] returned he to Edinburgh, and so did the Cardinal from Haddington.   But the one being ashamed of the other, the bruit of their communication came not to public audience.   The King made inventory of his poise,[7] of all his jewels and other substance ; and thereafter, as ashamed to look any man in the face, secretly departed to Fife, and coming to the Hall-yards,[8] was humanely received of the Lady Grange, an ancient and godly matron (the Laird at his coming was absent).   In his company were only with him William Kirkcaldy, now Laird of Grange, and some others that waited upon his chamber.   The Lady at supper, perceiving him pensive, began to comfort him, and willed him to take the work of

---

[1] Although many of the details given by Knox are confirmed by the contemporary reports of the battle (cf. Hamilton Papers, i, pp. lxxxiii–lxxxvi, Nos. 240, 245, 256 (enclosure), 259 (enclosure)), it should be noted that in those reports the English themselves put the strength of their forces at two thousand or three thousand men, as compared with Knox's " very few more than three hundred."   For a defence of Oliver Sinclair, see Scottish Historical Review, ii, 372ff   [2] meet his match   [3] overthrow   [4] went
  [5] taken   [6] 25 November 1542   [7] hoarded treasure
  [8] Hallyards, a seat of Kirkcaldy of Grange in Auchtertool parish, Fife, less than two miles south-east of Lochgelly

God in good part. " My portion (said he), of this world is short, for I will not be with you fifteen days." His servants repairing unto him, asked, Where he would have provision made for his Yule which then approached ? He answered, with a disdainful smirk, " I can not tell : choose ye the place. But this I can tell you, or [1] Yule day ye will be masterless, and the realm without a King." Because of his displeasure, no man durst make contradiction unto him. So after that he had visited the Castle of Cairnie,[2] pertaining to the Earl of Crawford, where the said Earl's daughter, one of his whores, was, he returned to Falkland and took bed.[3] And albeit there appeared unto him no signs of death, yet he constantly affirmed, before such a day, " I shall be dead."

In this meantime was the Queen upon the point of her delivery in Linlithgow, who was delivered the eighth day of December, in the year of God 1542, of MARIE, that then was born, and *Reginæ* now does ring [4] for a plague to this realm, as the progress of *Nativitas* her whole life hath to this day declared. The certainty that a daughter was born unto him coming to his ears, he turned from such as spake with him, and said, " The devil go with it ! It will end as it began : it came from a woman ; and it will end in a woman." [5] After that he spake not many words that were sensible. But ever he harped upon his old song. " Fye, fled Oliver ! Is Oliver tane? All is lost." In this meantime, in his great extremity, comes the *Regis* Cardinal (an apt comforter for a desperate man). He cries in his ear, *exitus* " Take order, Sir, with your realm : who shall rule during the minority of your daughter ? Ye have known my service : what

---

[1] *ere*

[2] Lordscairnie, or Cairnie Castle, in Moonzie parish, Fife, about three and a half miles north-west of Cupar

[3] As Andrew Lang has pointed out, Knox is here very ungracious to James V and says nothing of the fact that between Solway Moss (24 November) and his death at Falkland (on 14 December) he spent nearly a week with his Queen at Linlithgow (*Scottish Hist. Review*, iii, 382). The story of the visit to Cairnie Castle is doubly salacious in that David, eighth Earl of Crawford had died there as recently as 27 or 28 November. On the other hand, it must be admitted that Lisle, writing on 12 December, says James returned from the West to Tantallon, where he had a mistress, " and, by report, he setteth not much store by the Queen." (*Letters and Papers, Henry VIII*, xvii, No. 1194)

[4] *reign*

[5] Thinking of Marjorie Bruce, through whom the Crown had come to the Stewarts. Pitscottie's version is more pleasing : " By this the post came out of Linlithgow showing to the King good tidings that the queen was delivered. The King inquired : ' whether it was man or woman.' The messenger said : ' it was a fair daughter.' The King answered and said : ' Adieu, fare well, it came with a lass, it will pass with a lass,' and so he recommended himself to the mercy of Almighty God and spake [but] a little then from that time forth, but turned his back unto his lords and his face unto the wall."

will ye have done? Shall there not be four Regents chosen? And shall not I be principal of them?" Whatsoever the King answered, documents were taken that so should be, as my Lord Cardinal thought expedient. As many affirm, a dead man's hand was made to subscribe a blank, that they might write above it what pleased them best.[1] This finished, the Cardinal posted to the Queen, lately before delivered, as said is. At the first sight of the Cardinal, she said, "Welcome, my Lord: Is not the King dead?" What moved her so to conjecture, divers men are of divers judgments. Many whisper, that of old his part was in the pot, and that the suspicion thereof caused him to be inhibited the Queen's company.[2] Howsoever it was before, it is plain that after the King's death, and during the Cardinal's life, whosoever guided the Court, he got his secret business sped of that gracious Lady, either by day or by night.[3] Howsoever the tidings liked her, she mended with as great expedition of that daughter as ever she did before of any son she bare. The time of her purification was sooner than the Levitical law appoints. But she was no Jewess, and therefore in that she offended not.

The noise of the death of King James divulged, who departed this life the thirteenth day of December, the year of God 1542 foresaid,[4] the hearts of men began to be disclosed. All men lamented that the realm was left without a male to succeed; yet some rejoiced that such an enemy to God's truth was taken away. He was called of some a good poor man's King: of others he was termed a murderer of the nobility, and one that had decreed their whole destruction. Some praised him for the repressing of theft and oppression; others

---

[1] These statements that "documents were taken that so should be, as my Lord Cardinal thought expedient," and that "a dead man's hand was made to subscribe a blank," have frequently been examined in the light of the other available evidence. See, in particular, Hay Fleming in *Contemporary Review*, lxxiv, 375ff (Sept. 1898), and Andrew Lang in *Scottish Hist. Review*, iii, 410ff. Sir David Lindsay recorded the contemporary popular opinion when he wrote: "Ane paper blank his Grace I gart subscryve." ("Tragedie of the Cardinall," line 121, in *Works*, edit. Laing, i, 143)

[2] For an analysis of this difficult passage, see *Scottish Hist. Review*, iii, 380–382. The "his" and "him" possibly apply to the King. There were contemporary reports that James V had died of poison, or of "an Italian posset"; but is there here more than a simple reference to James V's licentious living?

[3] Knox frequently makes similar insinuations against Mary of Lorraine (*cf. infra*, 75, 79). Sadler makes the same insinuation in 1543 (*Hamilton Papers*, ii, No. 55); but the general trend of the evidence is more in favour of Spottiswoode's eulogy. (*History*, i, 319–321)

[4] James V died at Falkland on 14 December. An analysis of the evidence is given in Dunbar, *Scottish Kings*, 2nd edition, 240–243, and Hay Fleming, *Mary Queen of Scots* (1898), 178, *note* 9.

dispraised him for the defouling of men's wives and virgins. And thus men spake even as affections led them. And yet none spake all together besides the truth ; for a part of all the foresaid was so manifest that, as the virtues could not be denied, so could not the vices by any craft be cloaked. The question of government was through this realm universally moved. The Cardinal proclaimed the King's last will,[1] and therein were expressed four Protectors, or Regents, of whom himself was the first and principal, and with him were joined the Earls Huntly, Argyle, and Moray. This was done the Monday at the Market Cross of Edinburgh.[2] But the Monday following, took the whole Regents remission for their usurpation ; for by the stout and wise counsel of the Laird of Grange, did the Earl of Arran, then second person to the Crown, cause assemble the nobility of the realm, and required the equity of their judgments in that his just suit to the government of this realm, during the minority of her to whom he was to succeed, failing of her and of her lawful succession.[3] His friends convened, the nobility assembled, the day of decision is appointed. The Cardinal and his faction oppone them to the government of one man, and especially to the regiment of any called Hamilton : " For who knows not (said the Cardinal), that the Hamiltons are cruel murderers, oppressors of innocents, proud, avaricious, double, and false ; and finally, the pestilence in this commonwealth." Whereto the said Earl answered, " Defraud me not of my right, and call me what ye please. Whatsoever my friends have been, yet unto this day, has no man cause to complain upon me, neither yet am I minded to flatter any of my friends in their evil doing ; but by God's grace [I] shall be as forward to correct their enormities, as any within the realm can reasonably require of me. And therefore, yet again, my Lords, in God's name I crave that ye do me no wrong, nor defraud me not of my just title before that ye have experience of my government." At these words, were all that feared God or loved honesty so moved, that with one voice they cried, " That petition is most just, and unless we will do against God, justice, and equity, it can not be denied." And, in despite of the Cardinal and his suborned faction, was he declared Governor, and with public proclamation so announced to the people. The King's

The cardinal's reasons against the Government of Hamiltons

---

[1] *Supra*, 40, and *note* 1

[2] But see the analysis of the evidence in relation to the Regents in Hay Fleming, *Mary Queen of Scots*, 180.

[3] James Hamilton, second Earl of Arran, was next in succession to the Crown after the infant Mary Queen of Scots—always assuming that the divorce between the first Earl of Arran and his first wife was valid. (See the fuller note, *infra*, 49, *note* 1)

Palace, treasure, jewels, garments, horse, and plate were delivered unto him by the officers that had the former charge ; and he honoured, feared, and obeyed more heartily than ever any King was before, so long as he abode at God. The cause of the great favour that was borne unto him was that it was bruited that he favoured God's word ; and because it was well known that he was one appointed to have been persecuted, as the scroll found in the King's pocket, after his death, did witness. These two things, together with an opinion that men had of his simplicity, bowed the hearts of many unto him in the beginning, who after, with dolour of hearts, were compelled to change their opinions. But hereof will after be spoken. The variety of matters that occurred we omit, such as the order taken for keeping of the young Queen ; of the provision for the Mother ; the home-calling of the Douglases ; and other such as appertain to an universal History of the time. For, as before we have said, we mind only to follow the progress of the Religion and of the matters that cannot be dissevered from the same.

The Governor established in government, godly men repaired unto him, exhorted him to call to mind for what end God had exalted him ; out of what danger he had delivered him ; and what expectation all men of honesty had of him. At their instant suiting, more than of his own motion, was Thomas Guilliame, a Black Friar, called to be preacher.[1] The man was of solid judgment, reasonable letters (as for that age), and of a prompt and good utterance : his doctrine was wholesome without great vehemency against super-stition. Preached also sometimes John Rough (who after, for the verity of Christ Jesus, suffered in England in the days of Marie of cursed memory [2]), albeit not so learned, yet more simple, and more vehement against all impiety. The doctrine of these two provoked against them, and against the Governor also, the hatterent [3] of all such as more favoured darkness than light, and their own bellies more than God. The Grey Friars (and amongst the rest Friar Scott, who before had given himself forth for the greatest professor of Christ Jesus within Scotland, and under that colour had disclosed, and so endangered many), these slaves of Sathan, we say, rowped [4] as they had been ravens, yea, rather they yelled and roared as devils in hell,

---

[1] According to Calderwood (*History*, i, 155–156), Thomas Guilliame was the " first man from whom Mr. Knox received any taste of the truth."

[2] That is, Mary Tudor   [3] *hatred*   [4] *croaked*

" Heresy ! heresy ! Guilliame and Rough will carry the Governor to the Devil." The Town of Edinburgh, for the most part, was drowned in superstition : Edward Hope, young William Adamson, Sibilla Lindsay, Patrick Lindsay, Francis Aikman ; and, in the Canongate, John Mackaw and Ryngzeane Brown, with few others, had the bruit of knowledge in those days. One Wilson, servant to the Bishop of Dunkeld, who neither knew the New Testament nor the Old,[1] made a despiteful railing ballad against the Preachers and against the Governor, for the which he narrowly escaped hanging. The Cardinal moved both heaven and hell to trouble the Governor, and to stay the preaching ; but yet was the battle stoutly fought for a season ; for he was taken, and was put first in Dalkeith, after in Seton.[2] But at length by budds [3] given to the said Lord Seton, and to the old Laird of Lethington, he was restored to St. Andrews,[4] from whence he wrought all mischief, as we shall after hear.

The Parliament approached, which was before the Pasche [5] ; there began question of the abolishing of certain tyrannical Acts, made before, at devotion of the Prelates, for maintaining of their kingdom of darkness, to wit, " That under pain of heresy, no man should read any part of the Scriptures in the English tongue, neither yet any tractate or exposition of any place of Scripture." [6] Such articles began to come in question we say, and men began to inquire if it was not as lawful to men that understood no Latin, to use the word of their salvation in the tongue they understood, as it was for Latin men to have it in Latin, [and] Greeks or Hebrews to have it in their tongues. It was answered, That the Kirk first had forbidden

---

[1] George Crichton, Bishop of Dunkeld, in an interview with Thomas Forret, Vicar of Dollar, is reported to have said : " I thank God, that I never knew what the Old and the New Testament were ! Therefore, Dean Thomas, I will know nothing but my portuise [breviary] and my pontifical." Of these words arose a proverb, which is common in Scotland, " Ye are like the Bishop of Dunkeld, that knew neither the New Law nor the Old Law." (Calderwood's *History*, i, 126–127)

[2] The *Rentale Sancti Andree* (138, 148) shows Beaton in prison at Dalkeith, Seton, and Blackness from 29 (28) January to 21 March 1543. He was at Dalkeith for a few days ; at Seton for the greater part of February ; and for the remainder of his captivity at Blackness. But he enjoyed the services of his own cook, and a bill for supplies amounting to over £380 does not suggest harsh treatment. (*Ibid.*, xlii)

[3] *bribes*   [4] *Cf. Diurnal of Occurrents*, 26–27

[5] *Easter.* The Parliament of 12 March 1543

[6] No such Act occurs in the records of Parliament. The nearest approach to Knox's statement is to be found in the Act of March 1541 which forbade the holding of congregations or conventicles in private houses for the discussion of the holy scripture "without thai be theologis apprevit be famouse universiteis or admittit therto be thame that hes lauchfull power." (*Acts Parl. Scot.*, ii, 370, c. 5)

all tongues but those three. But men demanded, when that inhibition was given ; and what council had ordained that, considering that in the days of Chrysostom he complains that the people used not the Psalms and other holy books in their own tongues ? And if ye will say they were Greeks and understood the Greek tongue, we answer that Christ Jesus commanded his word to be preached to all nations. Now, if it ought to be preached to all nations, it must be preached in the tongue they understand. Now, if it be lawful to preach it, and to hear it preached in all tongues, why shall it not be lawful to read it, and to hear it read in all tongues, to the end that the people may try the spirits,[1] according to the commandment of the Apostle ? Beaten with these and other reasons, they denied not but it may be read in the vulgar tongue, provided that the translation were true. It was demanded, what could be reprehended in it ? And when much searching was made, nothing could be found but that Love, say they, was put in the place of Charity. When the question was asked, What difference was betwix the one and the other, and if they understood the nature of the Greek term *Agape*, they were dumb. Reasoned for the party of the Seculars, the Lord Ruthven (father to him that prudently gave counsel to take just punishment upon that knave Davie,[2] for that he abused the unhappy King Harry [3] in more cases than one), a stout and discreet man in the cause of God, and Master Henry Balnaves, an old professor [4] : for the part of the Clergy, Hay, Dean of Restalrig,[5] and certain old bosses [6] with him.

[G]*et this name*

The conclusion was, the Commissioners of Burghs and a part of the Nobility required of the Parliament that it might be enacted, " That it should be lawful to every man to use the benefit of the translation which then they had of the Bible and New Testament, together with the benefit of other treatises containing wholesome doctrine, unto such time as the Prelates and Kirkmen should give and set forth unto them a translation more correct." The Clergy

---

[1] " *try the spirits* whether they are of God " (1 John, iv, 1)

[2] David Riccio. (See *infra*, 112)

[3] Henry (Lord Darnley), King of Scots, second husband of Mary Queen of Scots

[4] That is, a professor of Christ's Evangel—a Protestant. In his treatise on Justification by Faith Henry Balnaves later strongly urged the reading of the scriptures continually. (Laing's *Knox*, iii, 532–533, 538–539)

[5] In the manuscript (folio 32 *verso*) the name *Hay* appears to have been inserted later (in response to the marginal injunction which is probably in Knox's own hand), and a line under the name seems to indicate that a space had been left blank. No Dean of Restalrig of that name can be traced.

[6] Probably *old topers* : see the interesting note in Jamieson's *Dictionary*, s.v. *boss*

hereto long repugned ; but in the end, convicted by reasons and by multitude of votes in their contrary, they also condescended ; and so by Act of Parliament it was made free to all men and women to read the Scriptures in their own tongue, or in the English tongue [1] : and so were all Acts made in the contrary abolished.

This was no small victory of Christ Jesus, fighting against the conjured enemies of his verity ; no small comfort to such as before were held in such bondage that they durst not have read the Lord's Prayer, the Ten Commandments, nor articles of their faith, in the English tongue, but they should have been accused of heresy. Then might have been seen the Bible lying almost upon every gentleman's table. The New Testament was borne about in many men's hands. We grant that some (alas !) profaned that blessed word ; for some that, perchance, had never read ten sentences in it, had it most common in their hand ; they would chop their familiars on the cheek with it, and say, " This has lain hid under my bed-foot these ten years." Others would glory, " Oh ! how oft have I been in danger for this book : How secretly have I stolen from my wife at midnight to read upon it." And this was done of many to make court thereby ; for all men esteemed the Governor to have been the most fervent Protestant that was in Europe. Albeit, we say, that many abused that liberty granted of God miraculously, yet thereby did the know-ledge of God wondrously increase and God give his Holy Spirit to simple men in great abundance. Then were set forth works in our own tongue, besides those that came from England, that did disclose the pride, the craft, the tyranny, and abuses of that Roman Anti-christ.

The fame of our Governor was spread in divers countries, and many praised God for him. King Harry [2] sent unto him his ambas-sador, Mr. Sadler,[3] who lay in Edinburgh a great part of the summer. His commission and negotiation was to contract a perpetual amity betwix England and Scotland : the occasion whereof God had so offered, that to many men it appeared that from heaven He had declared his good pleasure in that behalf. For to King Harry, of Jane Seymour (after the death of Queen Katherine, and of all

---

[1] *Acts Parl. Scot.*, ii, 415, c. 12. Although the Act speaks of a translation " in English or Scots," no Scottish vernacular translation was ever published. The translations used in Scotland were those of Tyndale and Coverdale ; and the first Bible to be printed in Scotland (that of Arbuthnot and Bassendyne) appeared after the death of Knox and was, in effect, a reprint of the English Geneva version. (See the interesting comments in J. A. H. Murray, *The Dialect of the Southern Counties of Scotland*, 66–68)

[2] Henry VIII   [3] Sir Ralph Sadler

others that might have made his marriage suspect) [1] was given a
son, Edward the Sixth of blessed memory, older some years than our
Mistress, and unto us was left a Queen, as before we have heard.
This wonderful providence of God caused men of greatest judgment
to enter in disputation with themselves whether that, with good
conscience, any man might repugn to the desires of the King of
England, considering that thereby all occasion of war might be cut
off and great commodity might ensue to his realm. The offers of
King Harry were so large, and his demands so reasonable, that all
that loved quietness were content therewith. There were sent from
the Parliament to King Harry in commission, Sir William Hamilton,
Sir James Learmonth, and Master Henry Balnaves, who, long
remaining in England, so travailed that all things concerning the
marriage betwix Edward the Sixth and Marie Queen of Scots was
agreed upon, except the time of her deliverance to the custody of
Englishmen. Upon the final conclusion of the which head, were
added to the former Commissioners, William, Earl of Glencairn and
Sir George Douglas, to whom was given ample commission and good
instructions. In Scotland remained Master Sadler. Advertisements
passed frequently betwix [the realms], yea, the hands of our Lords
liberally were anointed, [2] besides other commodities promised, and
of some received ; for divers prisoners taken at Solway Moss were
sent home ransom free, upon promise of their fidelity, which, as it
was kept, the issue will witness. But in the end, so well were all ones
Note content (the Cardinal, the Queen, and the faction of France ever
Well excepted), that solemnly, in the Abbey of Holyroodhouse, was the
contract of marriage betwix the persons foresaid, together with all
the clauses and conditions requisite for the faithful observation
thereof, read in public audience, subscribed, sealed, approved and
allowed of the Governor for his part [and the] Nobility and Lords
for their parts ; and that nothing should lack that might fortify
the matter, was Christ's body sacred (as Papists term it), broken
betwix the said Governor and Master Sadler, Ambassador, and
received of them both as a sign and token of the unity of their minds,
inviolably to keep that contract, in all points, as they looked of

---

[1] Catherine of Aragon had died 8 January 1536 ; Anne Boleyn had been beheaded
on 19 May 1536 ; Henry VIII had married Jane Seymour on 30 May 1536 ; and
Edward VI was born on 12 October 1537. Edward VI was thus some five years older
than the infant Mary Stewart.

[2] A reference to the pensions granted to the Scottish lords by Henry VIII to secure
them to his interest.

Christ Jesus to be saved, and after to be reputed men worthy of credit before the world.

The Papists raged against the Governor, and against the Lords that consented and abode sure at [1] the contract foresaid. And they made a brag to depose the Governor, and to confound all, as after follows.[2] And without delay raised their forces, and came to Linlithgow, where the young Queen was kept. But, upon the returning of the said Ambassadors from England, pacification was made for that time ; for, by the judgment of eight persons for either party, chosen to judge, Whether that any thing was done by the said Ambassadors, in the contracting of that marriage, which to do they had not sufficient power from the Council and Parliament, it was found, That all things were done according to their commission, and that so they should stand : and so were the Seals of England and Scotland interchanged.[3] Master James Foulis, then Clerk of Register, received the Great Seal of England ; and Master Sadler received the Great Seal of Scotland. The heads of the contract we pass by. These things newly ratified, the merchants made frack [4] to sail, and to their traffic, which, by the trouble of wars, had some years been hindered. From Edinburgh were freighted 12 ships richly laden, according to the wares of Scotland. From other towns and ports departed others, who all arrived upon the coast of England, towards the south, to wit, in Yarmouth ; and without any great necessity entered not only within roads [5] but also within ports and places of commandment,[6] and where that ships might be arrested.[7] And because of the late contracted amity, and gentle entertainment that they found at the first, they made no great expedition.[8] But being, as they supposed, in security, in merriness they spend the time abiding upon the wind.

In this meantime, arrives from France to Scotland the Abbot of Paisley,[9] called bastard brother to the Governor (whom yet many esteemed son to the old Bishop of Dunkeld, called Crichton) and

The queen's marriage the second time ratified

---

[1] *stood by*

[2] In the manuscript (folio 33 *verso*) the whole of this sentence has been added in the margin, and the succeeding sentence 'And without . . . was kept ' has been scored through.

[3] That is, copies of the marriage-contract under the respective Great Seals of the two countries were interchanged.   [4] *ready*

[5] That is, roadsteads, or anchorages off the shore

[6] That is, places where they could be *commanded* (by shore-batteries, or by official action)

[7] According to sea-law a *ship* could be " arrested," quite apart from any diligence against its master and crew.   [8] *haste*

[9] He was the natural son of the first Earl of Arran (Herkless and Hannay, *Archbishops of St. Andrews*, v, 2–3). In the manuscript (folio 34 *recto*) there is a caret after *Dumkelden* and *called* has been added in the margin, probably in Knox's own hand.

with him Master David Panter (who after was made Bishop of Ross). The bruit of the learning of these two, and their honest life, and of their fervency and uprightness in religion was such that great esperance there was that their presence should have been comfortable to the Kirk of God.[1] For it was constantly affirmed of some that, without delay, the one and the other would occupy the pulpit and truly preach Jesus Christ. But few days disclosed their hypocrisy ; for what terrors, what promises, or what enchanting boxes [2] they brought from France, the common people knew not. But, short after, it was seen that Friar Guilliame was inhibited to preach, and so departed to England ; John Rough [departed] to Kyle (a receptacle of God's servants of old). The men of counsel, judgment, and godliness, that had travailed to promote the Governor, and that gave him faithful counsel in all doubtful matters, were either craftily conveyed from him, or else, by threatening to be hanged, were compelled to leave him. Of the one number, were the Laird of Grange foresaid, Master Henry Balnaves, Master Thomas Ballantyne, and Sir David Lindsay of the Mount ; men by whose labours he was promoted to honour, and by whose counsel he so used himself at the beginning, that the obedience given to him was nothing inferior to that obedience that any King of Scotland of many years had before him. Yea, in this it did surmount the common obedience, that it proceeded from love of those virtues that were supposed to have been in him. Of the number of those that were threatened, were Master Michael Durham, Master David Borthwick, David Forrest, and David Bothwell ; who counselled him to have in his company men fearing God, and not to foster wicked men in their iniquity, albeit they were called his friends, and were of his surname. This counsel understood by the foresaid Abbot, and by the Hamiltons (who then repaired to the Court as ravens to the carrion) in plain words it was said, " My Lord Governor nor his friends will never be at quietness till that a dozen of these knaves that abuse his Grace be hanged." These words were spoken in his own presence, and in the presence of some of them that had better deserved than so to have been entracted [3] : the speaker was allowed for his bold and plain speaking. And so the wicked counsel deprehended,[4] honest and godly men left the Court and him in the hands of such as by their

---

[1] There are indications that at one time John Hamilton was not wholly opposed to some reformation in religion. (Herkless and Hannay, *op. cit.*, v, 8–10 ; Spottiswoode, *History*, i, 372)

[2] *gifts*   [3] *detracted*   [4] *accepted, taken*

wicked counsel led him so far from God that he falsified his promise, dipped his hands in the blood of the Saints of God, and brought this commonwealth to the very point of utter ruin. And these were the first fruits of the Abbot of Paisley's godliness and learning : but hereafter we will hear more.

All honest and godly men banished from the Court, the Abbot and his council begin to lay before the inconstant Governor the dangers that might ensue the alteration and change of religion ; the power of the King of France ; the commodity that might come to him and his house by retaining the ancient league with France ; and the great danger that he brought upon himself if, in any jot, he suffered the authority of the Pope to be violated or called in doubt within this realm : considering that thereupon only stood the security of his right to the succession of the Crown of this realm ; for by God's word would not the divorcement of his father from Elizabeth Home, his first wife, be found lawful, and so would his second marriage be judged null, and he declared bastard.[1] Caiaphas spake prophecy, and yet wist not what he spake, for at that time there was no man, that truly feared God, that minded any such thing, but with their whole force would have fortified the title that God had given unto him, and would never have called in question things done in time of darkness. But this head we pass by, till God declare his will therein. One other practice was used ; for the Cardinal being set at liberty (as before we have heard),[2] ceased not to traffic with such of the nobility as he might draw to his faction, or corrupt by any means, to raise a party against the said Governor, and against such as stood fast at the contract of marriage and peace with England. And so assembled at Linlithgow, the said Cardinal, the Earls Argyll, Huntly, Bothwell, the Bishops and their bands ; and thereafter they passed to Stirling, and took with them both the Queens, the mother and the daughter, and threatened the deposition of the said Governor, as inobedient to their Holy Mother the Kirk (so term they that harlot

---

[1] James, first Earl of Arran, father of the " Governor," had married as his first wife Elizabeth Home, daughter of Alexander, second Lord Home. Sometime before November 1504 Arran raised an action of divorce against his wife, declaring that she had already been married to Thomas Hay, son of John, Lord Hay of Yester. A divorce was then pronounced, but, strangely, it was repeated in 1510. In 1516 the first Earl of Arran married as his second wife Janet Beaton, who was the mother of the second Earl of Arran, the " Governor," while Elizabeth Home was still alive. The whole circumstances of the divorce of the first Earl of Arran were peculiar, and are constantly commented upon by contemporaries ; for, if the divorce was invalid, then the second Earl of Arran was illegitimate, and accordingly could not be next in succession to the Crown—a position which in that event would devolve upon Matthew, fourth Earl of Lennox. (See *Scots Peerage*, iv, 358-360, 366-367)   [2] *Supra*, 43

of Babylon, Rome). The inconstant man, not thoroughly grounded upon God, left in his own default destitute of all good counsel, and having the wicked ever blowing in his ears, " What will ye do ! Ye will destroy yourself and your house for ever " :—The unhappy man (we say), beaten with these tentations, rendered himself to *The governor violated his faith, refused God, and took absolution of devil* [1] the appetites of the wicked ; for he quietly stole away from the Lords that were with him in the Palace of Holyroodhouse, passed to Stirling, subjected himself to the Cardinal and to his counsel, received absolution, renounced the profession of Christ Jesus his holy Evangel, and violated his oath that before he had made for observation of the contract and league with England.[2]

At that time was our Queen crowned,[3] and new promise made to France. The certainty hereof coming to King Harry,[4] our Scottish ships were stayed, the sails taken from their rayes, and the merchants and mariners were commanded to sure custody.[5] New commission was sent to Master Sadler (who then still remained in Scotland) to demand the causes of that sudden alteration and to travail, by all means possible, that the Governor might be called back to his former godly purpose, and that he would not do so foolishly and unhonestly, yea, so cruelly and unmercifully to the realm of Scotland ; that he would not only lose the commodities offered, and that were presently to be received, but that also he would expose it to the hazard of fire and sword, and other inconvenients that might ensue the war that was to follow upon the violation of his faith : but nothing could avail. The Devil kept fast the grip that he got, yea, even all the days of his government. For the Cardinal got his eldest son[6] in pledge, whom he kept in the Castle of Saint Andrews, while the day that God's hand punished his pride.[7]

---

[1] This marginal note is in Knox's own hand (folio 35 *recto*).

[2] This *volte-face* by Arran took place between 4 and 8 September 1543. On 8 September, Arran did penance for his apostasy in the Franciscan Church in Stirling—and the treaties of marriage and peace with England had been solemnly ratified by him in the Abbey Church of Holyrood as recently as the preceding 25 August ! (*Hamilton Papers*, ii, Nos. 5, 30)

[3] 9 September 1543   [4] Henry VIII

[5] Knox's interpretation is here incorrect. It was not Mary's coronation and " new promise " made to France that led to Henry VIII's arrest of the Scottish ships. (See *Hamilton Papers*, i, No. 451, p. 638)   [6] James, Lord Hamilton

[7] That is, until the murder of the Cardinal on 29 May 1546 (*infra*, 76–78). This is borne out by entries in the *Rentale Sancti Andree* (Scot. Hist. Soc.), 185, 198, 214 ; but the Governor's eldest son was thereafter held as a pledge by the " Castilians "—that is, the murderers of Beaton and those who subsequently joined them in the Castle of St. Andrews.

King Harry perceiving that all hope of the Governor's repentance was lost, called back his ambassador, and that with fearful threatenings, as Edinburgh after felt ; denounced war, made our ships prizes, and merchants and mariners lawful prisoners, which, to the burghs of Scotland, was no small hardship. But thereat did the Cardinal and priests laugh, and jestingly he said, " When we shall conquer England, the merchants shall be recompensed." The summer and the harvest pass over without any notable thing ; for the Cardinal and [the] Abbot of Paisley parted the prey amongst them : the abused Governor bare the name only.

In the beginning of the winter, came the Earl of Lennox [1] to Scotland, sent from France in haterent of the Governor, whom the King [2] (by the Cardinal's advice) promised to pronounce bastard, and so to make the said Earl Governor.[3] The Cardinal further put the said Earl in vain hope that the Queen Dowager should marry him. He brought with him some money, and more he after received from the hands of La Brosse.[4] But at length, perceiving himself frustrated of all expectation that he had, either by France, or yet by the promise of the Cardinal, he concluded to leave [the side of] France, and to seek the favours of England, and so began to draw a faction against the Governor [5] ; and in haterent of the other's inconstancy, many favoured him in the beginning; for there assembled at the Yule, in the town of Ayr, the Earls of Angus, Glencairn, Cassillis, the Lords Maxwell [and Somerville], the Laird of Drumlanrig [and] the Sheriff of Ayr,[6] with all the force that they, and the Lords that remained constant at the opinion of England, might make ; and after the Yule, they came to Leith. The Governor and Cardinal, with their forces, keep Edinburgh (for they were slackly pursued). Men excused the Earl of Lennox in that behalf, and laid the blame upon some that had no will of Stewart's regiment. Howsoever it was, such an appointment was made, that the said Earl of Lennox was disappointed of his purpose, and narrowly escaped ; and first got him to Glasgow, and after to Dumbarton. Sir George Douglas was delivered to be kept as pledge.[7] The Earl, his brother, was in the Lenten after, taken at the siege of Glasgow.[8] It was bruited that both the brethren, and others with them, had lost their

---

[1] Matthew, fourth Earl of Lennox   [2] Francis I of France
[3] See *supra*, 49, *note* 1   [4] Jacques de la Brosse
[5] See *Two Missions of Jacques de la Brosse* (Scot. Hist. Soc.), 19ff
[6] Sir Hugh Campbell of Loudoun
[7] In January 1544 (See *Hamilton Papers*, ii, No. 149). For his release, see *infra*, 57.
[8] On 3 April 1544 (*Hamilton Papers*, ii, Appendix No. V). For his release, see *infra*, 57.

heads if, by the providence of God, the English army had not arrived
the sooner.

After that the Cardinal had got the Governor wholly addict
to his devotion, and had obtained his intent above a part of his
enemies, he began to practise how that such as he feared, and
therefore deadly hated, should be set by the ears one against another
(for in that, thought the carnal man, stood his greatest security).
The Lord Ruthven he hated, by reason of his knowledge of God's
word : the Lord Gray he feared, because at that time he used the
company of such as professed godliness, and bare small favour to
the Cardinal.   Now, thus reasoned the worldly wise man, " If I
can put enmity betwix those two, I shall be rid of a great number of
unfriends ; for the most part of the country will either assist the one
or the other ; and so will they be otherwise occupied than to watch
for my displeasure."   He finds the means, without long process ;
for he labours with John Charteris [1] (a man of stout courage and
many friends) to accept the provostry of Saint Johnston, [2] which he
purchases to him by donation of the Governor, with a charge to the
said town to obey him as their lawful Provost.   Whereat, not only
the said Lord Ruthven, but also the town, being offended, gave a
negative answer, alleging, That such intrusion of men in office
was hurtful to their privilege and freedom ; which granted unto
them free election of their Provost from year to year, at a certain
time appointed, which they could not nor would not prevent. [3]
Hereat the said John, offended, said, " That he would occupy that
office by force, if they would not give it unto him of benevolence " ;
and so departed and communicated the matter with the Lord Gray,
with Norman Leslie, and with other his friends ; whom he easily
persuaded to assist him in that pursuit, because he appeared to have
the Governor's right, and had not only a charge to the town, as said
is, but also he purchased letters to besiege it, and to take it by strong
hand, if any resistance were made unto him.   Such letters, we say,
made many to favour his action.   The other made for defence, and
so the Master of Ruthven (the Lord that after departed in England) [4] took the maintenance of the town, having in his company
the Laird of Moncrieff, [5] and other friends adjacent.   The said
John made frack [6] for the pursuit ; and upon the Magdalene day, [7]

[1] John Charteris of Cuthilgurdy   [2] Perth   [3] *forgo*
[4] That is, Patrick, third Lord Ruthven, who fled to England after the murder of
Riccio (9 March 1566)   [5] William Moncrieff of that Ilk
     [6] *ready*   [7] 22 July

in the morning, anno 1543,[1] approached with his forces, the Lord Gray taking upon him the principal charge. It was appointed that Norman Leslie, with his friends, should have come by ship, with munition and ordnance, as they were in readiness. But because the tide served not so soon as they would, the other thinking himself of sufficient force for all that were in the town, entered in by the brig, where they found no resistance, till that the former part was entered a pretty space within the Fish Gate ; and then the said Master of Ruthven, with his company, stoutly recountered them, and so rudely repulsed the foremost, that such as were behind gave back. The place of the retreat was so strait, that men that durst not fight could not flee at their pleasure (for the most part of the Lord Gray's friends were upon the brig) ; and so the slaughter was great ; for there fell in the edge of the sword threescore men. The Cardinal had rather that the unhap had fallen on the other part ; but howsoever it was, he thought that such trouble was [to] his comfort and advantage.[2] The knowledge whereof came unto the ears of the party that had received the discomfiture, and was unto them no small grief ; for as many of them entered in that action for his pleasure, so thought they to have had his fortification and assistance, whereof finding themselves frustrated, they began to look more narrowly to themselves, and did not so much attend upon the Cardinal's devotion, as they had wont to do before : and so was a new jealousy engendered amongst them ; for whosoever would not play to him the good valet was reputed amongst his enemies. The Cardinal drew the Governor to Dundee ; for he understood that the Earl of Rothes and Master Henry Balnaves were with the Lord Gray in the Castle of Huntly.[3] The Governor sent and commanded the said Earl and Lord, with the foresaid Master Henry, to come unto him to Dundee, and appointed the next day, at ten hours before noon : which hour they decreed to keep ; and for that purpose assembled their folks at Balgavie,[4] or thereby. The Cardinal advertised of their number (they were more than three hundred men), thought it not good that they should join with the town, for he feared his own estate ; and so he persuaded the Governor to pass forth of Dundee before nine hours, and to take the straight way to Saint Johnston. Which per-

[1] This date should read 1544. (*Diurnal of Occurrents*, 34. But see also Hay Fleming in *Contemporary Review*, lxxiv, 386)

[2] For the subsequent proceedings before the Privy Council, to settle this dispute, see *Register of the Privy Council of Scotland*, i, 64, 68–70.

[3] In Longforgan parish, Perthshire, about seven miles west of Dundee

[4] Now Balgay, about two miles west of Dundee

ceived by the foresaid Lords, they began to fear that they were come to pursue them, and so put themselves in order and array, and marched forward of purpose to have bidden the uttermost. But the crafty fox foreseeing that in fighting stood not his security, ran to his last refuge, that is, to manifest treason ; and so consultation was taken how that the force of the others might be broken. And at the first, were sent the Laird of Grange and the Provost of Saint Andrews [1] (knowing nothing of treason) to ask " Why they molested my Lord Governor in his journey ? " Whereto they answered, " That they meant nothing less [2] ; for they came at his Grace's commandment, to have kept the hour in Dundee appointed by him, which because they saw prevented, and knowing the Cardinal to be their unfriend, they could not but suspect their unprovided [3] coming forth of the town ; and therefore they put themselves in order not to invade, but to defend in case they were invaded." This answer reported, was sent to them the Abbot of Paisley,[4] Master David Panter, the Lairds of Buccleuch [5] and Cowdenknowes,[6] to desire certain of the other company to talk with them ; which they easily obtained (for they suspected no treason). After long communication, it was demanded, If that the Earl and Lord and Master Henry foresaid, would not be content to talk with the Governor, provided that the Cardinal and his company were off the ground ? They answered, " That the Governor might command them in all things lawful, but they had no will to be in the Cardinal's mercy." Fair promises enough were made for their security. Then was the Cardinal and his band commanded to depart ; as that he did according to the purpose taken. The Governor remained and a certain with him ; to whom came without company the said Earl, Lord, and Master Henry. After many fair words given unto them all, to wit, " That he would have them agreed with the Cardinal ; and that he would have Master Henry Balnaves the worker and instrument thereof," he drew them forwards with him towards Saint Johnston, whither-to the Cardinal was ridden. They began to suspect (albeit it was too late), and therefore they desired to have returned to their folks, for putting order unto them. But it was answered, " They should send back from the town, but they must needs go forward with my Lord Governor." And so, partly by flattery and partly

---

[1] Sir James Learmonth of Dairsie   [2] *that was far from their intention*   [3] *unforeseen*
[4] In the manuscript (folio 37 *verso*) *the bischope of Sanctandross* has been underlined, in the text, for deletion, and *the abbot of Pasley* supplied in the margin.
[5] Sir Walter Scott of Buccleuch   [6] Sir John Home of Cowdenknowes

by force, they were compelled to obey. And how soon that ever they were within the town, they were apprehended,[1] and upon the morn sent all three to the Black Ness,[2] where they remained so long as that it pleased the Cardinal's graceless Grace, and that was till that the band of manrent and of service set some of them at liberty.[3] And thus the Cardinal with his craft prevailed on every side ; so that the Scottish proverb was true in him, " So long runs the fox, as he foot has."

Whether it was at this his journey, or at another, that that bloody butcher executed his cruelty upon the innocent persons in Saint Johnston, we cannot affirm ; neither yet therein study we to be curious ; but rather we travail to express the verity, wheresoever it was done, than scrupulously and exactly to appoint the times, which yet we omit not when the certainty occurs. The verity of that cruel fact is this. At Saint Paul's day,[4] before the first burning of Edinburgh,[5] came to Saint Johnston the Governor and Cardinal, and there, upon envious delation, were a great number of honest men and women called before the Cardinal, accused of heresy ; and albeit that they could be convicted of nothing but only of suspicion that they had eaten a goose upon Friday, four men were adjudged to be hanged, and a woman to be drowned ; which cruel and most unjust sentence was without mercy put in execution. The husband was hanged, and the wife, having a sucking babe upon her breast, was drowned.—" O Lord, the land is not yet purged from such beastly cruelty ; neither has thy just vengeance yet stricken all that were criminal of their blood : But the day approaches when that the punishment of that cruelty and of others will evidently appear." The names of the men that were hanged were James Hunter, William Lamb,[6] William Anderson, James Rannelt, burgesses of Saint Johnston. At that time were banished [7] sir Henry Elder, John Elder, Walter Piper, Laurence Pullar, with divers others, whose names came not to our knowledge. That sworn enemy to Christ Jesus, and unto all

[1] Rothes, Gray, and Balnaves were apprehended in November 1543. (*Hamilton Papers*, ii, Nos. 116, 117)   [2] Blackness Castle
[3] The bond of manrent between Cardinal Beaton and Patrick, fourth Lord Gray, is dated 22 October 1544. (*Spalding Club Misc.*, v, 295–296)   [4] 25 January
[5] Edinburgh was burned by the English troops under Hertford in May 1544 ; hence the date of these martyrdoms is January 1544.
[6] Calderwood, citing the Justiciary Records, gives the names as James Hunter, flesher ; Robert Lamb, merchant ; William Anderson, maltman ; James Ranoldsone, skinner ; and the name of the woman as Helene Stirk, spouse to James Ranoldsone. (*History*, i, 173–74.) But he also shows that the charge was more than one of " eating a goose upon Friday." (*Ibid.*, i, 171–175)
[7] Calderwood says, " were banished, or rather fled ". (*Ibid.*, i, 175)

in whom any spunk of true knowledge appeared, had about that same time in prison divers ; amongst whom was John Roger, a Black Friar, godly, learned, and one that had fruitfully preached Christ Jesus, to the comfort of many in Angus and Mearns, whom that bloody man caused murder in the ground of the Sea-tower of St. Andrews,[1] and then caused to cast him over the craig, sparsing a false bruit,[2] " That the said John, seeking to flee, had broken his own craig."

Thus ceased not Sathan, by all means, to maintain his kingdom of darkness, and to suppress the light of Christ's Evangel. But potent is he against whom they fought ; for when those wicked [men] were in greatest security, then began God to show his anger. For the third day of May, in the year of God 1544, without knowledge of any man in Scotland (we mean of such as should have had the care of the realm) was seen a great navy of ships arriving towards the Firth.[3] The posts came to the Governor and Cardinal (who both were in Edinburgh) what multitude of ships were seen, and what course they took. This was upon the Saturday before noon. Question was had, what should they mean ? Some said, It is no doubt but they are Englishmen, and we fear that they shall land. The Cardinal scripped[4] and said, " It is but the Island[5] fleet : they are come to make a show, and to put us in fear. I shall lodge all the men-of-war into my eye that shall land in Scotland." Still sits the Cardinal at his dinner, even as that there had been no danger appearing. Men convene to gaze upon the ships, some to the Castle Hill, some to the Crags, and other places eminent. But there was no question, " With what forces shall we resist, if we be invaded ? " Soon after six hours at night, were arrived and had cast anchor in the Road[6] of Leith, more than two hundred sails. Shortly thereafter the Admiral[7] shot a fleet boat which, from Granton crags to by-east Leith, sounded the deep, and so returned to her ship.

---

[1] See supra, 22, note 1. John Roger had been previously warned to cease from further preaching, but apparently had not obeyed the warning. (See Rentale Sancti Andree, Scot. Hist. Soc., 200)

[2] spreading a false rumour. The pun at the end of the sentence is on craig meaning rock, and craig meaning neck.

[3] But on 21 April letters had been sent out charging all men to be ready to meet the English ; on 24 April letters had been sent out charging the inhabitants of all towns on the south coast of the Forth to make trenches for resisting the English navy ; and on 1 May the host was summoned from the shires of Fife, Forfar, Kincardine, Stirling, Clackmannan, and Kinross to meet the Governor on the Burgh Muir of Edinburgh on 5 May. But these arrangements were too late. (See Accounts Lord High Treasurer, viii, 284ff.)   [4] made a mocking gesture   [5] ? Iceland   [6] Roadstead

[7] John Dudley, Lord Lisle, later Earl of Warwick, later Duke of Northumberland

Hereof were divers opinions. Men of judgment foresaw what it meant. But no credit was given to any that would say, " They mind to land." And so passed all man to his rest, as if those ships had been a guard for their defence.

Upon the point of day, upon Sunday the fourth of May, addressed they for landing, and ordered they their ships so that a galley or two laid their snouts [1] to the crags. The small ships, called pinnaces, and light horsemen approached as near as they could. The great ships discharged their soldiers in the smaller vessels, and they by boats, set upon dry land before ten hours ten thousand men, as was judged, and more. The Governor and Cardinal seeing then the thing that they could not, or at least they would not believe before, after that they had made a brag to fight, fled as fast as horse would carry them [2]; so that after, they approached not within twenty miles of the danger. The Earl of Angus and George Douglas were that night freed of ward (they were in Blackness). The said Sir George in merriness said, " I thank King Harry and my gentle masters of England."

The English army betwix twelve and one hour entered in Leith, found the tables covered, the dinners prepared, such abundance of wine and victuals, besides the other substance, that the like riches within the like bounds was not to be found, neither in Scotland nor England.[3] Upon the Monday the fifth of May, came to them from Berwick and the Border, two thousand horsemen, who, being somewhat reposed, the army upon the Wednesday marched towards the *The burning of* Town of Edinburgh, spoiled and burnt the same, and so did they the *Edinburgh* Palace of Holyroodhouse.[4] The horsemen took the house of Craigmillar,[5] and got great spoil therein ; for it being judged the strongest house near the town, other than the Castle of Edinburgh, all men sought to save their movables therein. But the stoutness of the Laird gave it over without shot of hackbut, and for his reward was

---

[1] *bows*

[2] Beaton had been present at the first engagement dressed in a " casacque de vellour jaulne fort descouppe plaine de taffetas blanc avec listes d'or que flocquoyent par les descoupeures," but was later reported to be " the first man that fled . . . like a valiant champion." (*Rentale Sancti Andree*, xliii–xliv, quoting *Letters and Papers of Henry VIII*, xix, 518, 533)

[3] Hertford reported that he found Leith " to be of good substance and riches, at the least £10,000, as we suppose, whereof there was great store of grain of all kinds." (*Hamilton Papers*, ii, No. 232)

[4] During this expedition under the Earl of Hertford, the town of Edinburgh was " utterly ruynate " and destroyed with fire, as also was " th' abbey called Holy Rode-house, and the pallice adjoynynge to the same." (See the contemporary account in Dalyell, *Fragments of Scotish History*, iii, 7)   [5] Craigmillar Castle

caused to march upon his foot to London. He is now [1] Captain of Dunbar and Provost of Edinburgh.[2]

The Englishmen seeing no resistance, hurled by force of men cannons up the calsay [3] to the Butter-trone, or above, and hazarded a shot at the fore-entry of the Castle. But that was to their own pains ; for they lying without trench or gabion, were exposed to the force of the whole ordnance of the said Castle, which shot, and that not all in vain ; for the wheel and extrye [4] of one of the English cannons were broken, and some of their men slain ; and so they left with small honour that enterprise, taken rather of rashness than of any advised counsel. When the most part of the day they had spoiled and burnt, towards the night they returned to Leith, and upon the morrow returned to Edinburgh, and executed the rest of God's judgments for that time. And so when they had consumed both the towns, they loaded the ships with spoil thereof, and they by land returned to Berwick, using the country for the most part at their own pleasure.

This was a part of the punishment which God took upon the realm for infidelity of the Governor, and for the violation of his solemn oath. But this was not the end ; for the realm was divided in two factions : the one favoured France ; the other the league lately contracted with England. The one did in nothing thoroughly credit the other ; so that the country was in extreme calamity ; for to the Englishmen were delivered divers strengths, such as Caerlaverock, Lochmaben and Langholm. The most part of the Borders were confederate with England. And albeit that first, at Ancrum Moor, in February, in the year of God 1544, was Sir Raif Evers,[5] with many other Englishmen, slain, and the year after were some of the said strengths recovered ; yet was it not without great loss and detriment to the commonwealth. For in the month of June, in the year of God 1545, Monsieur de Lorge,[6] with bands of men of war, came from France for a further destruction to Scotland ; for upon their brag [7] was an army raised. Forward go they towards Wark,[8] even in the midst of harvest. The Cardinal's banner was that day displayed, and all his feals [9] were charged to be under it. Many had before promised but, at the

---

[1] That is, in 1566   [2] Sir Simon Preston   [3] *causeway*   [4] *axle-tree*
[5] Sir Ralph Eure was defeated and slain by Archibald Douglas, sixth Earl of Angus, at Ancrum Moor in Roxburghshire, 27 February 1545.
[6] Jacques de Montgomery, Seigneur de Lorges
[7] Here used in the sense of *boastful incitement*
[8] Wark Castle, near Coldstream   [9] *vassals*

point, it was left so bare that with shame it was shut up in the pock [1] again, and they after a show returned with more shame to the realm than scathe to their enemies. The black book of Hamilton makes mention of great vassalage done at that time by the Governor and the French. But such as with their eyes saw the whole progress, knew that to be a lie, and does repute it amongst the venial sins of that race, which is to speak the best of themselves they can.

That winter following so nurtured the French men that they learned to eat (yea, to beg) cakes which at their entry they scorned. Without jesting, they were so miserably entreated that few returned to France again with their lives. The Cardinal had then almost fortified the Castle of Saint Andrews, which he made so strong, in his opinion, that he regarded neither England nor France. The Earl of Lennox, as said is, disappointed of all things in Scotland, passed to England, where he was received of King Harry in protection, who gave him to wife Lady Margaret Douglas, of whom was born Harry, umquhile [2] husband to our Jezebel Mistress. [3]

While the inconstant Governor was sometimes dejected and sometimes raised up again by the Abbot of Paisley, who before was called " chaster than any maiden," [the Abbot] began to show himself ; for after he had taken by craft the castle of Edinburghs and Dunbar, he took also possession of his eme's wife, [4] the Lady Stanehouse : the woman is and has been famous, and is called Lady Gilton. Her Ladyship was held always in property [5] ; but how many wives and virgins he has had since that time in common, the world knows, albeit not all, and his bastard birds [6] bear some witness. Such is the example of holiness that the flock may receive of the Papistical Bishops.

[1] bag [2] late

[3] Matthew Stewart, fourth Earl of Lennox, married in London, Margaret Douglas, only daughter and heiress of Archibald, sixth Earl of Angus and of Margaret Tudor, Queen-Dowager of James IV and sister of Henry VIII. Their eldest son was Henry, Lord Darnley, who was married to Mary Queen of Scots, 29 July 1565, and murdered February 1567.

[4] Lady Grisel Sempill was the eldest daughter of Robert, third Lord Sempill, and was the second wife of James Hamilton who had acquired the lands of Stanehouse by his first wife. She was divorced from James Hamilton before February 1546, and gained notoriety as the mistress of John Hamilton, Abbot of Paisley, and later Archbishop of St. Andrews. (See Herkless and Hannay, Archbishops of St. Andrews, v, 246, App. III.) Knox in his use of the word " eme " (kinsman) is more charitable than Pitscottie who speaks of Lord Sempill as " the bischopis goode father," that is, his father-in-law. (Chronicles, Scot. Text Soc., ii, 111)

[5] The sense seems to be that the Abbot of Paisley always held her to be his own private property.

[6] That is, his flock of bastards. (See Hay Fleming, The Reformation in Scotland, 51–52)

In the midst of all the calamities that came upon the realm after the defection of the Governor from Christ Jesus, came in Scotland that blessed martyr of God MASTER GEORGE WISHART, in company of the Commissioners before mentioned, in the year of God 1544 [1] ; a man of such graces as before him were never heard within this realm, yea, and are rare to be found yet in any man, notwithstanding this great light of God that since his days has shined unto us. He was not only singularly learned as well in godly knowledge as in all honest humane science, but also he was so clearly illuminated with the spirit of prophecy, that he saw not only things pertaining to himself, but also such things as some towns and the whole realm afterward felt, which he forespake not in secret, but in the audience of many, as in their own places shall be declared. The beginning of his doctrine was in Montrose. Therefrom he departed to Dundee where, with great admiration of all that heard him, he taught the Epistle to the Romans till that, by procurement of the Cardinal, Robert Myll, then one of the principal men in Dundee, and a man that of old had professed knowledge, and for the same had suffered trouble, gave, in the Queen's and Governor's name, inhibition to the said Master George that he should trouble their town no more ; for they would not suffer it. And this was said unto him, being in the public place ; which heard, he mused a pretty space, with his eyes bent unto the heaven, and thereafter looking sorrowfully to the speaker, and unto the people, he said, " God is witness, that I never minded your trouble, but your comfort. Yea, your trouble is more dolorous unto me than it is unto yourselves. But I am assured that to refuse God's Word, and to chase from you his messenger, shall not preserve you from trouble ; but it shall bring you into it. For God shall send unto you messengers who will not be afraid of horning, [2] nor yet for banishment. I have offered unto you the word of salvation, and with the hazard of my life I have remained amongst you. Now ye yourselves refuse me, and therefore must I leave my innocence to be declared by my God. If it be long prosperous with you, I am not led with the spirit of truth. But and if trouble unlooked for apprehend you, acknowledge the cause and turn to God, for he is merciful. But if ye turn not at the first, he shall visit you with fire and sword." These words pronounced, he came down from the

The words of Master George Wishart in Dundee

---

[1] But Knox here seems to contradict himself. The " commissioners " had returned to Scotland in 1543 (*supra*, 47), and *before* the " defection " of the Governor.

[2] Calderwood (*History*, i, 186) and Spottiswoode (*History*, i, 150) have *burning* for *horning* (that is, outlawry).

preaching place. In the kirk present was the Lord Marischal,[1] and divers noblemen, who would have had the said Master George to have remained, or else to have gone with him in the country. But for no request would he either tarry in the town or on that side of Tay any longer.[2] But with possible expedition passed to the westland, where he began to offer God's word, which was of many gladly received, till that the Bishop of Glasgow, Dunbar, by instigation of the Cardinal came with his gatherings to the town of Ayr, to make resistance to the said Master George, and did first occupy the kirk. The Earl of Glencairn being thereof advertised, repaired with his friends to the town with diligence, and so did divers gentlemen of Kyle (amongst whom was the Laird of Leiffnoris,[3] a man far different from him that now liveth, anno 1566,[4] in manners and religion), of whom to this day yet many live, and have declared themselves always zealous and bold in the cause of God, as after will be heard. When all were assembled, conclusion was taken that they would have the kirk ; whereto the said Master George utterly repugned, saying, " Let him alone ; his sermon will not much hurt : Let us go to the Market Cross " ; and so they did, where he made so notable a sermon, that the very enemies themselves were confounded. The Bishop preached to his jackmen, and to some old bosses of the town. The sum of all his sermon was : " They say that we should preach : why not ? Better late thrive than never thrive : have us still for your Bishop, and we shall provide better for the next time." This was the beginning and the end of the Bishop's sermon, who with haste departed the town, but returned not again to fulfil his promise. *The Bishop of Glasgow's preaching in Ayr*

The said Master George remained with the gentlemen in Kyle, till that he got sure knowledge of the estate of Dundee. He preached commonly at the kirk of Galston, and used much in the Barr.[5] He was required to come to the kirk of Mauchline, as that he did. But the Sheriff of Ayr[6] caused man the kirk, for preservation of a tabernacle that was there, beautiful to the eye. The persons that held the kirk were George Campbell of Mountgarswood, that yet liveth, anno 1566,[7] Mungo Campbell of Burnside, George Read in Daldilling

---

[1] William, fourth Earl Marischal

[2] But see the first Article against him (*infra*, ii, 236)

[3] Sir George Crawford of Leiffnoris, Ayrshire

[4] In the manuscript (folio 41 *recto*) this date has been supplied in the margin, and is probably in Knox's own hand.

[5] *much frequented the* [*House of*] *Barr*—just east of Galston, and the seat of John Lockhart of Barr   [6] Sir Hugh Campbell of Loudoun

[7] In the manuscript (folio 41 *verso*) this date has been supplied in the margin, and is probably in Knox's own hand.

[and] the Laird of Templeland. Some zealous of the parish, amongst whom Hew Campbell of Kinzeancleuch, offended that they should be debarred their parish kirk, concluded by force to enter. But the said Master George withdrew the said Hew, and said unto him, " Brother, Christ Jesus is as potent upon the fields as in the kirk ; and I find that he himself often preached in the desert, at the seaside, and other places judged profane, than that he did in the Temple of Jerusalem. It is the word of peace that God sends by me : the blood of no man shall be shed this day for the preaching of it." And so withdrawing the whole people, he came to a dyke in a moor edge, upon the south-west side of Mauchline, upon the which he ascended. The whole multitude stood and sat about him (God gave the day pleasing and hot). He continued in preaching more than three hours. In that sermon God wrought so wonderfully with him that one of the most wicked men that was in that country, named Laurence Rankin, laird of Shiel, was converted. The tears ran from his eyes in such abundance that all men wondered. His conversion was without hypocrisy, for his life and conversation witnessed it in all times to come.

While this faithful servant of God was thus occupied in Kyle, word rose that the plague of pestilence was risen in Dundee,[1] which began within four days after that the said Master George was inhibited preaching, and was so vehement that it almost passed credibility to hear what number departed every four and twenty hours. The certainty understood, the said Master George took his leave of Kyle, and that with the regret of many. But no request could make him to remain : his reason was, " They are now in trouble, and they need comfort. Perchance this hand of God will make them now to magnify and reverence that word which before (for the fear of men) they set at light price." Coming unto Dundee, the joy of the faithful was exceeding great. He delayed no time, but even upon the morrow gave signification that he would preach. And because the most part were either sick, or else were in company with those that were sick, he chose the head of the East Port of the town [2] for his preaching place ; and so the whole sat or stood

---

[1] Smyth's Chronicle records the raging of the pest in Edinburgh, Leith, Newbattle, Dundee, and Aberdeen under the date 24 June 1545 (*Recs. of the Monastery of Kinloss*, 11) ; and on 24 June 1545, because of the pest, the Session moved from Edinburgh to Linlithgow. (*Register of the Privy Council of Scotland*, i, 5)

[2] Usually the Cowgate Port is associated with Wishart's preaching, but Maxwell has advanced arguments in favour of the Port which stood in the Seagate. (*History of Old Dundee*, 220–222)

within, the sick and suspected without the Port. The text upon the which his first sermon was made, he took from the hundred and seventh Psalm ; the sentence thereof, " He sent his word and healed them " ; and therewith joined these words, " It is neither herb nor plaster, O Lord, but thy word healeth all." In the which sermon, he most comfortably did entreat the dignity and utility of God's word ; the punishment that comes for the contempt of the same ; the promptitude of God's mercy to such as truly turn to him ; yea, the great happiness of them whom God takes from this misery, even in his own gentle visitation, which the malice of man can neither eik nor pair.[1] By the which sermon he so raised up the hearts of all that heard him that they regarded not death, but judged them more happy that should depart than such as should remain behind ; considering that they knew not if they should have such a comforter with them at all times. He spared not to visit them that lay in the very extremity ; he comforted them as that he might in such a multitude ; he caused minister all things necessary to those that might use meat or drink ; and in that point was the town wondrous beneficial, for the poor were no more neglected than were the rich.

While he was spending his life to comfort the afflicted, the Devil ceased not to stir up his own son the Cardinal again, who corrupted by money a desperate priest named sir John Wigton,[2] to slay the said Master George, who looked not to himself in all things so circumspectly as worldly men would have wished. And upon a day, the sermon ended, and the people departing, no man suspecting danger, and therefore not heeding the said Master George, the priest that was corrupted stood waiting at the foot of the steps, his gown loose, and his whinger [3] drawn into his hand under his gown, the said Master George, as that he was most sharp of eye and judgment, marked him, and as he came near, he said, " My friend, what would ye do ? " And therewith he clapped his hand upon the priest's hand, wherein the whinger was, which he took from him. The priest, abashed, fell down at his feet and openly confessed the verity as it was. The noise rising, and coming to the ears of the sick, they cried, " Deliver the traitor to us, or else we will take him by force " ; and so they burst in at the yett.[4] But Master George took him in his arms, and said, " Whosoever troubles him shall trouble

---

[1] *increase nor impair*

[2] John Wigton, called *curatus* of Ballumby, had been a prisoner of Cardinal Beaton for some three years. (*Rentale Sancti Andree*, Scot. Hist. Soc., 130, 141, 200)

[3] *hanger*, that is a dagger or a short sword   [4] *gate*

me ; for he has hurt me in nothing, but he has done great comfort both to you and me, to wit, he has let us understand what we may fear in times to come. We will watch better." And so he appeased both the one part and the other, and saved the life of him that sought his.

When the plague was so ceased that almost there were none sick, he took his leave of them, and said, " That God had almost put end to that battle : he found himself called to another." The gentlemen of the West had written unto him, That he should meet them at Edinburgh [1] ; for they would require disputation of the Bishops, and that he should be publicly heard. Whereto he willingly agreed ; but first, he passed to Montrose, to salute the Kirk there ; where he remained occupied sometimes in preaching but most part in secret meditation, in the which he was so earnest that night and day he would continue in it. While he was so occupied with his God, the Cardinal drew a secret draft for his slaughter. He caused to write unto him a letter, as it had been from his most familiar friend, the Laird of Kinnear [2], " Desiring him with all possible diligence to come unto him, for he was stricken with a sudden sickness." In this meantime had the traitor provided three score men, with jacks and spears, to lie in wait within a mile and a half of the town of Montrose, for his despatch. The letter coming to his hand, he made haste at the first (for the boy had brought a horse), and so with some honest men he passes forth of the town. But suddenly he stayed and, musing a space, returned back ; whereat they wondering, he said, " I will not go : I am forbidden of God : I am assured there is treason. Let some of you (says he), go to yonder place, and tell me what ye find." Diligence made, they found the treason as it was ; which, being shown with expedition to Master George, he answered, " I know that I shall finish this my life in that bloodthirsty man's hands ; but it will not be of this manner."

The time approaching that he had appointed to meet the gentlemen at Edinburgh, he took his leave of Montrose and, sore against the judgment of the Laird of Dun, [3] he entered in his journey, and so returned to Dundee ; but remained not, but passed to the house of a faithful brother, named James Watson, who dwelt in Invergowrie, distant from the said town two miles, and that night (as information was given to us by William Spadin and John Watson, both men of good credit), before day a little he passed forth into a yard. The said William and John followed privily, and took heed what he did.

[1] See *infra*, 65   [2] John Kinnear of that Ilk   [3] John Erskine of Dun

When he had gone up and down into an alley a reasonable space, with many sobs and deep groans, he plat upon his knees, and sitting thereon his groans increased ; and from his knees he fell upon his face ; and then the persons forenamed heard weeping and, as it were an indigest sound, as it were of prayers, in the which he continued near an hour, and after began to be quiet ; and so arose and came in to his bed. They that awaited, prevented [1] him, as they had been ignorant, till that he came in ; and then began they to demand where he had been. But that night he would answer nothing. Upon the morrow, they urged him again ; and while that he dissembled, they said, " Master George, be plain with us ; for we heard your groans ; yea, we heard your bitter mourning, and saw you both upon your knees and upon your face." With dejected visage, he said, " I had rather ye had been in your beds, and it had been more profitable to you, for I was scarce well occupied." When they instantly urged him to let them know some comfort he said, " I will tell you, that I am assured that my travail is near an end ; and therefore call to God with me, that now I shrink not when the battle waxes most hot." And while that they wept and said, " That was small comfort unto them " ; he answered, " God shall send you comfort after me. This realm shall be illuminated with the light of Christ's Evangel, as clearly as ever was any realm since the days of the Apostles. The house of God shall be builded in to it. Yea, it shall not lack (whatsoever the enemy imagine in the contrary) the very cope stone " : meaning that it should once [2] be brought to the full perfection. " Neither (said he) shall this be long too : There shall not many suffer after me, till that the glory of God shall evidently appear, and shall once triumph in despite of Sathan. But, alas ! if the people shall after be unthankful, then fearful and terrible shall the plagues be that after shall follow." And with these words he marched forwards in his journey towards Saint Johnston ; and so to Fife, and then to Leith. Where arrived, and hearing no word of those that appointed to meet him (to wit, the Earl of Cassillis, and the gentlemen of Kyle and Cunningham) [he] kept himself secret a day or two. But beginning to wax sorrowful in spirit, and being demanded of the cause, of such as were not into his company of before, he said, " What differ I from a dead man, except that I eat and drink ? To this time God has used my labours to the instruction of others, and unto the disclosing of darkness ; and now I lurk as a man that

Prophecy spoken by Master George Wishart

---

[1] *went [in] before*   [2] *at one time*

were ashamed, and durst not show himself before men." By these and like words, they that heard him understood that his desire was to preach ; and therefore said, " Most comfortable it were unto us to hear you : but because we know the danger wherein ye stand, we dare not desire you." " But dare ye and others hear (said he), and then let my God provide for me, as best pleaseth him." Finally, it was concluded that the next Sunday he should preach in Leith ; as that he did, and took the text, " The Parable of the Sower that went forth to sow seed," (Matthew, 13.) And this was upon a fifteen days before Yule.[1] The sermon ended, the gentlemen of Lothian, who then were earnest professors of Christ Jesus, thought not expedient that he should remain in Leith, because that the Governor and Cardinal were shortly to come to Edinburgh ; and therefore they took him with them, and kept him sometimes in Brunstane, sometimes in Longniddry, and sometimes in Ormiston ; for those three [2] diligently awaited upon him. The Sunday following, he preached in the kirk of Inveresk, beside Musselburgh, both before and at afternoon, where there was a great confluence of people, amongst whom was Sir George Douglas who, after the sermon

The words of Sir George Douglas said publicly, " I know that my Lord Governor and my Lord Cardinal shall hear that I have been at this preaching (for they were then in Edinburgh). Say unto them that I will avow it, and will not only maintain the doctrine that I have heard, but also the person of the teacher to the uttermost of my power." Which words greatly rejoiced the people and the gentlemen then present.

One thing notable in that sermon we cannot pass by. Amongst others there came two Grey Friars and, standing in the entry of the kirk door, they made some whispering to such as came in. Which perceived, the preacher said to the people that stood nigh them, " I heartily pray you to make room to those two men : It may be that they be come to learn." And unto them he said, " Come near (for they stood in the very entry of the door), for I assure you ye shall hear the word of verity, which shall either seal in to you this same day your salvation, or condemnation." And so proceeded he in doctrine, supposing that they would have been quiet. But when he perceived them still to trouble the people that stood nigh them (for vehement was he against the false worshipping of God), he turned unto them the second time, and with an awful countenance

---

[1] It would thus be Sunday, 13 December 1545.

[2] That is, Alexander Crichton of Brunstane, Hugh Douglas of Longniddry, and John Cockburn of Ormiston

said, " O sergeants of Sathan, and deceivers of the souls of men, *Master* will ye neither hear God's truth, nor suffer others to hear it ? Depart *George Wishart's* and take this for your portion—God shall shortly confound and *threaten-* disclose your hypocrisy : Within this realm ye shall be abominable *Grey* unto men, and your places and habitations shall be desolate." This *Friars* sentence he pronounced with great vehemency, in the midst of the sermon ; and turning to the people, he said, " Yon wicked men have provoked the Spirit of God to anger." And so he returned to his matter, and proceeded to the end. That day's travail ended, he came to Longniddry ; and the two next Sundays preached in Tranent, with the like grace and like confluence of people. In all his sermons, after his departure from Angus, he forespake the shortness of the time that he had to travail, and of his death, the day whereof he said approached nigher than any would believe.

In the hinder end of those days that are called the Holy days of Yule,[1] passed he, by consent of the gentlemen, to Haddington, where it was supposed the greatest confluence of people should be, both by reason of the town and of the country adjacent. The first day before noon the auditure was reasonable, and yet nothing in comparison of that which used to be in that kirk. But the afternoon, and the next day following before noon, the auditure was so slender, that many wondered. The cause was judged to have been that the Earl Bothwell,[2] who in those bounds used to have great credit and obedience, by procurement of the Cardinal had given inhibition, as well unto the town as unto the country, that they should not hear him under the pain of his displeasure. The first night he lay within the town with David Forrest, now called the General,[3] a man that long has professed the truth, and upon whom many in that time depended. The second night, he lay in Lethington, the Laird [4] whereof was ever civil, albeit not persuaded in religion. The day following, before the said Master George passed to the sermon, there came to him a boy with a letter from the West land, which received and read, he called for JOHN KNOX,[5] who had awaited upon him carefully from the time he came to Lothian ; with whom he began to enter in purpose, " that he wearied of the world " : for he per-

[1] Christmas began on the Eve of the 24 December and the " Holy Days of Yule " continued until Twelfth Day, or Epiphany (6 January).

[2] Patrick Hepburn, third Earl of Bothwell

[3] David Forrest, at the time of writing, was Master or General of the Mint.

[4] Sir Richard Maitland of Lethington

[5] This is the first occasion on which Knox refers to himself.

ceived that men began to weary of God. The cause of his complaint was, the gentlemen of the West had written unto him that they could not keep diet at Edinburgh. The said John Knox wondering that he desired to keep any purpose before sermon (for that was never his accustomed use before), said, " Sir, the time of sermon approaches : I will leave you for the present to your meditation " ; and so took the bill containing the purpose foresaid, and left him. The said Master George paced up and down behind the high altar more than half an hour : his very countenance and visage declared the grief and alteration of his mind. At last he passed to the pulpit, but the auditure was small. He should have begun to have entreated the second table of the Law ; but thereof in that sermon he spake very little, but began on this manner ; " O Lord, how long shall it be that thy holy word shall be despised, and men shall not regard their own salvation. I have heard of thee, Haddington, that in thee would have been at a vain Clerk play [1] two or three thousand people ; and now to hear the messenger of the Eternal God, of all thy town nor parish can not be numbered a hundred persons. Sore and fearful shall the plagues be that shall ensue this thy contempt : with fire and sword thou shalt be plagued ; yea, thou Haddington, in special, strangers shall possess thee, and you, the present inhabitants shall either in bondage serve your enemies, or else ye shall be chased from your own habitations ; and that because ye have not known, nor will not know the time of God's merciful visitation." In such vehemency and threatening continued that servant of God near an hour and a half, in the which he declared all the plagues that ensued, as plainly as after our eyes saw them performed.[2] In the end he said, " I have forgotten myself and the matter that I should have entreated ; but let these my last words as concerning public preaching, remain in your minds, till that God send you new comfort." Thereafter he made a short paraphrase upon the Second Table, with an exhortation to patience, to the fear of God, and unto the works of mercy ; and so put end, as it were making his last testament, as the issue declared, that the spirit of truth and of true judgment were both in his heart and mouth. For that same night was he apprehended, before midnight, in the house of Ormiston, by the Earl Bothwell, made for money butcher to the Cardinal.

The manner of his taking was thus : departing from the town

---

[1] A play founded upon some subject taken from Scripture, and originally performed by clerks (that is, the clergy)

[2] For the fulfilment of the prophecy, see *infra*, 113

of Haddington, he took his good night, as it were for ever, of all his acquaintance, especially from Hew Douglas of Longniddry. John Knox pressing to have gone with the said Master George, he said, " Nay, return to your bairns,[1] and God bless you. One is sufficient for a sacrifice." And so he caused a two-handed sword (which commonly was carried with the said Master George) be taken from the said John Knox who, albeit unwillingly, obeyed, and returned with Hew Douglas of Longniddry. Master George having to accompany him, the Laird of Ormiston, John Sandilands of Calder, younger, the Laird of Brunstane, and others, with their servants, passed upon foot (for it was a vehement frost) to Ormiston. After supper he held comfortable purpose [2] of the death of God's chosen children, and merrily [3] said, " Methink that I desire earnestly to sleep " ; and therewith he said, " Will we sing a Psalm ? " And so he appointed the 51st Psalm, which was put in Scottish metre, and began thus :

> Have mercy on me now, good Lord,
> After thy great mercy, &c. [4] :

Which being ended, he passed to [his] chamber and, sooner than his common diet was, passed to bed with these words, " God grant quiet rest." Before midnight, the place was beset about that none could escape to make advertisement.[5] The Earl Bothwell came and called for the Laird,[6] and declared the purpose, and said, " that it was but vain to make him to hold his house ; for the Governor and the Cardinal with all their power were coming " (and indeed the Cardinal was at Elphinston,[7] not a mile distant from Ormiston) [8] ; " but and if he would deliver the man to him, he would promise *The Lord* upon his honour, that he should be safe, and that it should pass the *Bothwell's* power of the Cardinal to do him any harm or scathe." Allured *promise* with these words, and taking counsel with the said Master George (who at the first word said, " Open the yetts : the blessed will of my God be done ") they received in the Earl Bothwell himself, with

---

[1] See *infra*, 82 [2] *conversation* [3] That is, without any trace of sadness
[4] This forms the second verse of the 51st Psalm in the " Compendious Buik of Godlie Psalmes and Spirituall Sangis," known as " The Gude and Godlie Ballates." (See Laing's edn., 104) [5] *to make that known*—and so obtain succour
[6] John Cockburn of Ormiston [7] Elphinstone Tower
[8] The *Diurnal of Occurrents* (41) says that on 16 January 1546 " the governour and the cardinall, to the nomber of v[c] men, past to Ormestoun." Admittedly the *Diurnal* does not record the seizure of Wishart ; but, on the other hand, no mention is made of Bothwell.

some gentlemen with him, to whom Master George said, " I praise my God that so honourable a man as ye, my Lord, receives me this night, in the presence of these noble men ; for now, I am assured, that for your honour's sake, ye will suffer nothing to be done unto me besides the order of law. I am not ignorant, that their law [1] is nothing but corruption, and a cloak to shed the blood of the saints ; but yet I less fear to die openly, than secretly to be murdered." The said Earl Bothwell answered, " I shall not only preserve your body from all violence that shall be purposed against you without order of law, but also I promise, here in the presence of these gentlemen, that neither shall the Governor nor Cardinal have their will of you ; but I shall retain you in my own hands, and in my own place, till that either I shall make you free, or else restore you in the same place where I receive you." The Lairds foresaid [2] said, " My Lord if ye will do as ye have spoken, and as we think your Lordship will do, then do we here promise unto your Lordship that not only we ourselves shall serve you all the days of our life, but also we shall procure the whole professors [3] within Lothian to do the same. And upon either the preservation of this our brother, or upon his delivery again to our hands, we being reasonably advertised to receive him, that we, in the name and behalf of our friends, shall deliver to your Lordship, or to any sufficient man that shall deliver to us again this servant of God, our band of manrent in manner foresaid." As thus promise made in the presence of God, and hands stracked [4] upon both the parties for observation of the premises, the said Master George was delivered to the hands of the said Earl Bothwell who, immediately departing with him, came to Elphinston, where the Cardinal was ; who, knowing that Calder younger and Brunstane were with the Laird of Ormiston, sent back with expedition to apprehend them also. The noise of horsemen being heard,[5] the servants gave advertisement that more than departed, or that were there before, were returned ; and while that they dispute what should be the motive, the Cardinal's garrison had seized both the outer and the inner close. They called for the Laird and for the Laird of Calder who, presenting themselves, demanded what their commission was. " To bring you two," say they, " and the Laird of Brunstane to my Lord Governor." They were nothing content (as they had no cause)

---

[1] That is, the law of the Church
[2] That is, John Cockburn of Ormiston, John Sandilands of Calder, the younger, and Alexander Crichton of Brunstane
[3] That is, the professors of Christ's Evangel—the Protestants
[4] *clasped*   [5] At Ormiston

and yet they made fair countenance, and entreated the gentlemen to take a drink, and to bait their horse, till that they might put themselves in readiness to ride with them. In this meantime, Brunstane conveyed himself, first secretly, and then by speed of foot, to Ormiston wood, and from thence to Doundallon,[1] and so escaped that danger. The other two were put in the Castle of Edinburgh, where the one, to wit Calder younger, remained while his band of manrent to the Cardinal was the means of his deliverance, and the other, to wit Ormiston, freed himself by leaping of the wall of the Castle, betwix ten hours and eleven before noon ; and so breaking ward, he escaped prison, which he unjustly suffered.[2]

The servant of God, Master George Wishart, was carried first to Edinburgh ; thereafter brought back, for the fashion's sake,[3] to the house of Hailes [4] again, which was the principal place that then the Earl Bothwell [5] had in Lothian. But as gold and women have corrupted all worldly and fleshly men from the beginning, so did they him. For the Cardinal gave gold, and that largely,[6] and the Queen, with whom the said Earl was then in the glondours,[7] promised favours in all his lawful suits to women, if he would deliver the said Master George to be kept in the Castle of Edinburgh. He made some resistance at the first, by reason of his promise : but an effeminate man can not long withstand the assaults of a gracious *Ironice* Queen.[8] And so was the servant of God transported to Edinburgh Castle, where he remained not many days. For that bloody wolf the Cardinal, ever thirsting the blood of the servant of God, so travailed with the abused Governor, that he was content that God's

---

[1] Clearly Tantallon, then held by the Douglases. (See Sir George Douglas's declaration, *supra*, 66). The map in the Bodleian Library, reproduced in *National MSS. of Scotland* (pt. iii), and of date *circa* 1300, shows a castle on the same site called 'Dentaloune'.

[2] But certainly Crichton of Brunstane (and probably also Cockburn of Ormiston) was at this time in communication with Henry VIII, and involved in a plot to overthrow Cardinal Beaton. (See Tytler, *History of Scotland*, 1841, v, 333-334, 384-389)

[3] *as a matter of form*   [4] Hailes Castle

[5] Patrick Hepburn, third Earl of Bothwell

[6] But the Privy Council required Bothwell to deliver Wishart to the Governor. (*Letters and Papers of Henry VIII*, xxi, i, No. 88)

[7] This word is otherwise unknown to the lexicographers but would seem to mean *ill-humour*.

[8] It will be noticed that Knox is singularly restrained in relation to Bothwell's share in the apprehension of Master George Wishart ; but Knox admitted that he had " a good mind " to the House of Hepburn (*infra*, ii, 38). In a like way Buchanan was kind in his references to Darnley and to the House of Lennox.

servant should be delivered to the power of that tyrant. And so, small inversion being made, Pilate obeyed the petition of Caiaphas and of his fellows, and adjudged Christ to be crucified. The servant of God delivered to the hand of that proud and merciless tyrant, triumph was made by the priests. The godly lamented, and accused the foolishness of the Governor ; for by the retaining of the said Master George he might have caused Protestants and Papists (rather proud Romanists) to have served : the one to the end that the life of their preacher might have been saved ; the other for fear that he should have set him at liberty again, to the confusion of the Bishops. But where God is left (as he had plainly renounced him before) what can counsel or judgment avail ?

How the servant of God was entreated, and what he did from the day that he entered within the Sea-tower of Saint Andrews, which was in the end of January, in the year of God 1546,[1] unto the first of March the same year, when he suffered, we cannot certainly tell, except we understand that he wrote somewhat being in prison ; but that was suppressed by the enemies. The Cardinal delayed no time, but caused all Bishops, yea, all the clergy that had any pre-eminence, to be convocate to Saint Andrews against the penult of February, that consultation might be had in that question which, in his mind, was no less resolved than Christ's death was in the mind of Caiaphas ; but that the rest should bear the like burden with him, he would that they should before the world subscribe whatsoever he did.

In that day was wrought no less a wonder than was at the accusation and death of Jesus Christ, when that Pilate and Herod, who before were enemies, were made friends, by consenting of them both to Christ's condemnation ; [it] differs nothing, except that Pilate and Herod were brethren under their father the Devil, in the estate called Temporal, and these two, of whom we are to speak, were brethren (sons of the same father the Devil) in the estate Ecclesiastical. If we interlace merriness with earnest matters, pardon us, good Reader ; for the fact is so notable that it deserveth long memory.

The proud Cardinal and the glorious fool Dunbar

The Cardinal was known [to be] proud ; and Dunbar, Arch-bishop of Glasgow, was known a glorious [2] fool ; and yet, because sometimes he was called the King's Master,[3] he was Chancellor of

----

[1] Here the date is given as if the year had begun on 1 January. The change to the commencement of the year on 1 January took place in Scotland with 1 January 1600.

[2] *vainglorious*   [3] He had been tutor to James V.

Scotland. The Cardinal comes even this same year,[1] in the end of [the] harvest before, to Glasgow ; upon what purpose we omit. But while they remain together, the one in the town, the other in the Castle,[2] question rises for bearing of their crosses. The Cardinal alleged, by reason of his Cardinalship, and that he was *Legatus Natus,* and Primate within Scotland, in the kingdom of Antichrist, that he should have the pre-eminence, and that his cross should not only go before, but that also it only should be borne wheresoever he was. Good Gukstoun Glaikstour,[3] the foresaid Archbishop, lacked no reasons, as he thought, for maintenance of his glory : he was an Archbishop in his own diocese, and in his own Cathedral seat and Church, and therefore ought to give place to no man ; the power of the Cardinal was but begged from Rome, and appertained but to his own person, and not to his bishopric ; for it might be that his successor should not be Cardinal. But his [own] dignity was annexed with his office, and did appertain to all that ever should be Bishops of Glasgow. Howsoever these doubts were resolved by the doctors of divinity of both the Prelates, yet the decision was as ye shall hear. Coming forth (or going in, all is one) at the choir door of Glasgow Kirk, begins striving for state betwix the two cross-bearers, so that from glowming [4] they come to shouldering ; from shouldering, they go to buffets,[5] and from dry blows, by neffs and neffeling [6] ; and then for charity's sake they cry, *Dispersit dedit pauperibus,* and essays which of the crosses was finest metal, which staff was strongest, and which bearer could best defend his master's pre-eminence ; and that there should be no superiority in that behalf, to the ground go both the crosses. And then began no little fray, but yet a merry game ; for rochets were rent, tippets were torn, crowns were knapped,[7] and side gowns might have been seen wantonly wag from the one wall to the other. Many of them lacked beards, and that was the more pity ; and therefore could not bukkill other by the birse,[8] as bold men would have done. But fye on the jackmen that did not their duty ; for had the one part of them reacontered the other, then had all gone right. But the sanctuary, we suppose, saved

A question worthy of such two prelates

[1] Here " this same year " must refer to the year according to the old reckoning, for this ludicrous incident took place in June 1545 ; though " in the end of the harvest " seems impossible for June, and it may be that Knox has confused the 1545 incident with a similar affair in October 1543. (See Dowden, *Bishops of Scotland,* 345–347 ; Robertson, *Statuta Ecclesiae Scoticanae,* i, cxxx–cxxxii ; Herkless and Hannay, *Archbishops of St. Andrews,* iv, 171–174 ; D. E. Easson, *Gavin Dunbar,* 81ff)

[2] In his episcopal palace   [3] Good Mr. Trifling Folly   [4] *scowling*
[5] *buffeting*   [6] *fisticuffs*   [7] *cracked*
[8] *grapple with each other by the beard*

the lives of many. How merrily that ever this be written, it was bitter bourding [1] to the Cardinal and his court. It was more than irregularity ; yea, it might well have been judged lèse majesté to the son of perdition, the Pope's own person ; and yet the other in his folly, as proud as a peacock, would let the Cardinal know that he was a Bishop when the other was but Beaton, before he got Arbroath. [2] This enmity was judged mortal, and without all hope of reconciliation. [3]

But the blood of the innocent servant of God buried in oblivion all that bragging and boast. For the Archbishop of Glasgow was the first unto whom the Cardinal wrote, signifying unto him what was done, and earnestly craving of him that he would assist with his presence and counsel how that such an enemy unto their estate might be suppressed. And thereto was not the other slow, but kept time appointed, sat next to the Cardinal, voted and subscribed first in the rank, and lay over the East blockhouse [4] with the said Cardinal, till the Martyr of God was consumed by fire. For this we must note, that as all those beasts consented in heart to the slaughter of that innocent, so did they approve it with their presence, having the whole ordnance of the Castle of Saint Andrews bent towards the place of execution, [5] which was nigh to the said Castle, ready to have shot if any would have made defence or rescue to God's servant. [6]

·   ·   ·   ·   ·   ·   ·

After the death of this blessed martyr of God, began the people, in plain speaking, to damn [7] and detest the cruelty that was used. Yea, men of great birth, estimation, and honour, at open tables avowed, That the blood of the said Master George should be revenged, or else they should cost life for life. Amongst whom John Leslie, brother to the Earl of Rothes, was the chief ; for he, in all companies, spared not to say, " That same whinger (showing forth his dagger), and that same hand, should be priests to the Cardinal."

[1] *bitter jesting*

[2] That is, before he was made Abbot of Arbroath—his first high ecclesiastical preferment

[3] For the possible deeper significance of this incident see R. K. Hannay in *Rentale Sancti Andree* (Scot. Hist. Soc.), Intro., pp. xlvii–l

[4] This has now disappeared. (See the plan in *Royal Commission on Ancient and Historical Monuments : Fife, Kinross, and Clackmannan*, 251)   [5] *cf. infra*, ii, 244

[6] Here Knox inserts the " Accusation, Process and Answers " of George Wishart " as we have received the same from the Book of the Martyrs [*i.e.* Foxe's *Actes and Monuments*, London, 1563–64], which, word by word, we have here inserted, and that because the said book, for the great price thereof, is rare to be had." His account is printed below as Appendix III.   [7] *condemn*

These bruits came to the Cardinal's ears ; but he thought himself stout enough for all Scotland ; for in Babylon, that is in his new *The worldly strength of the Cardinal of Scotland* block-house,[1] he was sure, as he thought ; and upon the fields, he was able to match all his enemies. And to write the truth, the most part of the Nobility of Scotland had either given unto him their bands of manrent, or else were in confederacy and promised amity with him.[2] He only feared them in whose hands God did deliver him, and for them had he laid his nets so secretly (as that he made a full account) that their feet could not escape, as we shall after hear ; and something of his former practices we must recount.

After the Pasche he came to Edinburgh, to hold the seinze,[3] (as the Papists term their unhappy assembly of Baal's shaven sort). It was bruited that something was purposed against him, at that time, by the Earl of Angus and his friends, whom he mortally hated, and whose destruction he sought. But it failed, and so returned he to his strength, yea, to his God and only comfort, as well in heaven as in earth. And there he remained without all fear of death, promising unto himself no less pleasure nor did the rich man, of whom mention is made by our Master in the Evangel ; for he did not only rejoice and say, " Eat and be glad, my soul, for thou hast great riches laid up in store for many days " ; but also he said, " Tush, a fig for the feud, and a button for the bragging of all the *The bragging of the Cardinal a little before his death* heretics and their assistance in Scotland. Is not my Lord Governor mine ? Witness his eldest son there, pledge at my table ?[4] Have I not the Queen at my own devotion ?[5] (He meant of the mother to Mary that now mischievously reigns.) Is not France my friend, and I friend to France ? What danger should I fear ? " And thus, in vanity, the carnal Cardinal delighted himself a little before his death. But yet he had devised to have cut off such as he thought might cummer[6] him ; for he had appointed the whole gentlemen of Fife to have met him at Falkland, the Monday after that he was

[1] Beaton was engaged in strengthening his castle at St. Andrews from 1543 until his assassination in 1546. (*Rentale Sancti Andree*, Scot. Hist. Soc., 176, 194–195, 199, 222–224)
[2] See, for example, the charter to Archibald, Earl of Argyll, in *St. Andrews Formulare* (Stair Soc.), ii, No. 464
[3] *synod*, here used for a Provincial Council of the Church. A Provincial Council had been held in Edinburgh in January 1546 ; there is no record of a Provincial Council being held there after Easter in that year. Easter in 1546 was 25 April. This visit to Edinburgh shows that Beaton was no coward, and that he did not shut himself up in his " block-house." Actually he was in Edinburgh from 8 to 24 May, and attended a meeting of the Privy Council there. (Herkless and Hannay, *Archbishops of St. Andrews*, iv, 201). Is Knox confusing a meeting of the Privy Council with a meeting of the Provincial Council ? [4] *cf. supra*, 50 [5] *cf. supra*, 40 ; *infra*, 79 [6] *trouble*

*The
treason
of the
Cardinal*

slain upon the Saturday. His treasonable purpose was not under-
stood but by his secret council ; and it was this : That Norman
Leslie, Sheriff of Fife, and apparent heir to his father, the Earl of
Rothes, the said John Leslie, father-brother to Norman, the
Lairds of Grange, elder and younger [1], Sir James Learmonth of
Dairsie and Provost of Saint Andrews, and the faithful Laird of
Raith [2] should either have been slain, or else tane,[3] and after to have
been used at his pleasure. This enterprise was disclosed after his
slaughter, partly by letters and memorials found in his chamber,
but plainly affirmed by such as were of the council. Many purposes
were devised how that wicked man might have been taken away.
But all failed, till Friday, the 28 of May, Anno 1546, when the
foresaid Norman came at night to Saint Andrews ; William Kirkcaldy of Grange, younger, was in the town before, awaiting upon the
purpose ; last came John Leslie foresaid, who was most suspected.
What conclusion they took that night, it was not known but by the
issue which followed.

But early upon the Saturday, in the morning, the 29 of May,
were they in sundry companies in the Abbey kirk-yard, not far
distant from the Castle. First, the yetts being open, and the draw-
brig let down, for receiving of lime and stones, and other things
necessary for building (for Babylon was almost finished) [4]—first,
we say, essayed William Kirkcaldy of Grange, younger, and with him
six persons, and getting entrance, held purpose with the porter,

*How the
Cardinal
was occu-
pied the
night be-
fore that
in the
morning he
was slain*

" If My Lord was walking ? " [5] who answered, " No." (And so it
was indeed ; for he had been busy at his accounts with Mistress
Marion Ogilvy that night, who was espied to depart from him by
the privy postern that morning ; and therefore quietness, after [6] the
rules of physic, and a morning sleep was requisite for my Lord.)
While the said William and the porter talked, and his servants
made them to look the work and the workmen, approached Norman
Leslie with his company ; and because they were in no great
number, they easily got entrance. They address them to the midst
of the close, and immediately came John Leslie, somewhat rudely,
and four persons with him. The porter, fearing, would have drawn
the brig ; but the said John, being entered thereon, stayed, and
leapt in. And while the porter made him for defence, his head was
broken, the keys taken from him, and he cast in the fosse [7] ; and so

---

[1] James Kirkcaldy and William Kirkcaldy   [2] Sir John Melville of Raith
[3] *taken*   [4] See *supra*, 75, *note* 1   [5] *awake*   [6] *according to*
[7] the moat or ditch in front of the castle

the place was seized. The shout arises : the workmen, to the number of more than a hundred, ran off the walls, and were without hurt put forth at the wicket yett. The first thing that ever was done, William Kirkcaldy took the guard of the privy postern, fearing that the fox should have escaped. Then go the rest to the gentlemen's chambers, and without violence done to any man, they put more than fifty persons to the yett : The number that enterprised and did this, was but sixteen persons.[1] The Cardinal, awakened with the shouts, asked from his window, What meant that noise ? It was answered, That Norman Leslie had taken his Castle. Which understood, he ran to the postern ; but perceiving the passage to be kept without, he returned quickly to his chamber, took his two-handed sword, and gart [2] his chamber child cast kists,[3] and other impediments to the door. In this meantime came John Leslie unto it, and bids open. The Cardinal asking, " Who calls ? ", he answers, " My name is Leslie." He re-demands, " Is that Norman ? " The other says, " Nay ; my name is John." " I will have Norman," says the Cardinal, " for he is my friend." [4] " Content yourself with such as are here ; for other shall ye get none." There were with the said John, James Melville,[5] a man familiarly acquainted with Master George Wishart, and Peter Carmichael,[6] a stout gentleman. In this meantime, while they force at the door, the Cardinal hides a box of gold under coals that were laid in a secret corner. At length he asked, " Will ye save my life ? " The said John answered, " It may be that we will." " Nay," says the Cardinal, " Swear unto me by God's wounds, and I will open unto you." Then answered the said John. " It that was said, is unsaid " ; and so cried, " Fire, fire," (for the door was very stark) ; and so was brought a chimney [7] full of burning coals. Which perceived, the Cardinal or his chamber child, (it is uncertain), opened the door, and the Cardinal sat down in a chair and cried, " I am a priest ; I am a priest : ye will not slay me." The said John Leslie (according to his former vows) struck him first, once or twice, and so did the said Peter. But James Melville (a man of nature most gentle and most modest) perceiving them both in choler, withdrew them, and said, " This work and judgment of God (although it be secret) ought to be done with greater gravity " ; and presenting unto him the point of the sword, said, " Repent thee of thy former wicked life, but especially of the

The Cardinal's demand

The Cardinal's confession

---

[1] Spottiswoode says twelve (*History*, i, 164) ; the *Diurnal of Occurrents* (42) says eighteen
[2] *caused*   [3] *chests*   [4] See Leslie, *History* (Scot. Text Soc.), ii, 291–92
[5] James Melville of Carnbee   [6] Peter Carmichael of Balmedie   [7] *brazier*

The godly fact [1] and words of James Melville [2] shedding of the blood of that notable instrument of God, Master George Wishart, which albeit the flame of fire consumed before men, yet cries it a vengeance upon thee, and we from God are sent to revenge it : For here, before my God, I protest, that neither the hetterent [3] of thy person, the love of thy riches, nor the fear of any trouble thou could have done to me in particular, moved, nor moves me to strike thee ; but only because thou hast been, and remains an obstinate enemy against Christ Jesus and his holy Evangel." And so he struck him twice or thrice through with a stog sword [4] ;

The Cardinal's last words and so he fell, never word heard out of his mouth, but " I am a priest, I am a priest : fye, fye : all is gone."

While they were thus occupied with the Cardinal, the fray rises in the town. The Provost [5] assembles the community, and comes to the fosse's side, crying, " What have ye done with my Lord Cardinal ? Where is my Lord Cardinal ? Have ye slain my Lord Cardinal ? Let us see my Lord Cardinal." They that were within answered gently, " Best it were unto you to return to your own houses ; for the man ye call the Cardinal has received his reward, and in his own person will trouble the world no more." But then more enragedly, they cry, " We shall never depart till that we see him." And so was he brought to the east blockhouse head, and shown dead over the wall to the faithless multitude, which would not believe before it saw. How miserably lay David Beaton, careful Cardinal ! [6] And so they departed, without *Requiem æternam*, and *Requiescat in pace*, sung for his soul. Now, because the weather was hot (for it was in May, as ye have heard), and his funeral could not suddenly be prepared, it was thought best, to keep him from stinking, to give him great salt enough, a cope of lead, and a nook in the bottom of the Sea-Tower (a place where many of God's children had been imprisoned before) to await what exequies his brethren the Bishops would prepare for him.

[1] *act* or *deed* (from French *fait*)
[2] The marginal comment is in the hand of the text.
[3] *hatred*   [4] *a thrusting sword*
[5] Sir James Learmonth of Dairsie
[6] A letter, written by James Lyndesay on Sunday, 30 May, describes the assassination of Cardinal Beaton in detail ; and although his account differs slightly from that given by Knox, it supports Knox in many points. Lyndesay writes that the assassination took place between 5 a.m. and 6 a.m. on Saturday 29 ; and that when the Provost with three hundred or four hundred men came to the castle, Norman Leslie " speerit what they desirit to see," and forthwith, with a pair of sheets, hung the body of the dead cardinal over the wall by the arm and foot, " and bade the people see there their God." (*Letters and Papers of Henry VIII*, xxi, i, No. 948)

These things we write merrily. But we would that the Reader *Advertise-ment to the reader* should observe God's just judgments, and how that he can deprehend the worldly wise in their own wisdom, make their table to be a snare to trap their own feet, and their own presupposed strength to be their own destruction. These are the works of our God, whereby he would admonish the tyrants of this earth,[1] that in the end he will be revenged of their cruelty, what strength so ever they make in the contrary. But such is the blindness of man (as David speaks), " That the posterity does ever follow the footsteps of their wicked fathers, and principally in their impiety " ; for how little differs the cruelty of that bastard, that yet is called Bishop of Saint Andrews [2] from the cruelty of the former, we will after hear.

The death of this foresaid tyrant was dolorous to the priests, dolorous to the Governor, most dolorous to the Queen Dowager ; for in him perished faithfulness to France, and the comfort to all gentlewomen, and especially to wanton widows.[3] His death must be revenged. To the Court again repairs the Earl of Angus, and his brother Sir George. Labour is made for the Abbacy of Arbroath, and a grant was once [4] made of the same (in memory whereof George Douglas, bastard son to the said Earl, is yet called Postulate[5]). But it was more proper (think the Hamiltons) for the Governor's kitchen,[6] nor for reward to the Douglases. And yet in esperance thereof, the said Earl and George his brother were the first that voted that the Castle of Saint Andrews should be besieged. The *The Bishop of St. Andrews was glad, yet made himself to be angry at the slaughter of the Cardinal* Bishop,[7] to declare the zeal that he had to revenge the death of him that was his predecessor (and yet for his wish he would not have had him living again), still blew the coals. And first, he caused summon, then denounce accursed, and then last, rebels,[8] not only the first enterprisers, but all such also as after did accompany them. And last of all, the siege was concluded,[9] which began in the end of

[1] But Knox wrote far differently in an undated letter to Mrs. Bowes. (Laing's *Knox*, iii, 396–397)

[2] John Hamilton, bastard brother to the Governor, was translated to St. Andrews in succession to David Beaton in 1549.

[3] A continuation of the innuendo made before. (*Supra*, 40)   [4] *at one time*

[5] That is, the name of George Douglas had been put forward for the preferment. (*Reg. Privy Council of Scotland*, i, 57. But see the note in Laing's *Knox*, i, 180, and *Registrum Nigrum de Aberbrothoc*, Bannatyne Club, Preface, xiii)

[6] That is, for the revenues to go to the Governor and the upkeep of his establishment

[7] John Hamilton, though he had not yet been translated. (Similarly, *infra*, 82)

[8] Some overtures for their remission having proved abortive (*Acts Parl. Scot.*, ii, 470–472) those who had taken part in the assassination, and others who subsequently joined them, were pronounced guilty of high treason (*Ibid.*, ii, 477–479)

[9] the siege [of the castle, now held by the conspirators] *was determined upon*

August (for the 23 day thereof departed the soldiers from Edinburgh), and continued near to the end of January.[1] At what time,[2] because they[3] had no other hope of winning of it but by hunger; and thereof also they were despaired, for they within had broken through the east wall, and made a plain passage, by an iron yett to the sea, which greatly relieved the besieged, and abased the besiegers; for then they saw that they could not stop them of victuals, unless that they should be masters of the sea and that they clearly understood they could not be : for the English ships had once been there, and had brought William Kirkcaldy from London, and with much difficulty, (because the said yett was not then prepared), and some loss of men, had rendered him to the Castle again, and had taken with them to the Court of England John Leslie and Master Henry Balnaves,[4] for perfecting of all contracts betwix them and King Harry, who promised to take them in his protection, upon condition only, that they should keep the Governor's son, my Lord of Arran,[5] and stand friends to the contract of marriage, whereof before we have made mention. These things clearly understood (we say) by the Governor and his Council, the priests and the shaven sort, they conclude to make an Appointment,[6] to the end that, under truth, they might either get the Castle betrayed, or else some principal men of the company taken at unawares.[7] In the which head was the Abbot of Dunfermline[8] principal ; and for that purpose had the Laird of Montquhanie[9] (who was most familiar with those of the Castle) laboured at foot and hand, and proceeded so in his traffic, that from entrance upon daylight at his pleasure, he got licence to come upon the night whensoever it pleased him. But God had not

Upon what conditions King Harry took the castle of St. Andrews in his protection

[1] The first siege appears to have lasted from the beginning of September until the end of December 1546 (see *Acts Parl. Scot.*, ii, 590 *b*). The agreement bringing the first siege to an end was concluded on 17 December 1546. (Tytler, *History*, 1842, vi, 7, *note*)

[2] That is, at the end of January (? end December)

[3] That is, the Governor's besieging force

[4] The *Diurnal of Occurrents* (43) reports that William Kirkcaldy had passed to England, for supplies, on 26 October 1546, and that eight ships had come back with him from England ; further that on 20 November Henry Balnaves and John Leslie passed to England. Balnaves was again in England in April 1547, having arrived at Berwick by ship from St. Andrews. (Laing's *Knox*, iii, 419)

[5] James, Lord Hamilton, then about eight years old, who had been kept in the castle of St. Andrews by Beaton (*supra*, 50, 75), was there when Beaton was assassinated and the castle seized, and was now being held by the " Castilians " as a hostage who gave them a hold over the Governor.

[6] Negotiations for a truce had begun as early as December 1546. (*Reg. Privy Council of Scotland*, i, 57–58)   [7] *Cf. infra*, 241   [8] George Durie

[9] Sir Michael Balfour of Montquhanie, whose son was the famous Sir James Balfour of Pittendreich

appointed so many to be betrayed, albeit that he would that they should be punished, and that justly, as hereafter we will hear.

The heads of the coloured [1] appointment were :

1. That they should keep the Castle of Saint Andrews aye and while that the Governor and the authority of Scotland should get unto them a sufficient absolution from the Pope (Antichrist of Rome) for the slaughter of the Cardinal foresaid. [2]

2. That they should deliver pledges for delivery of that House, [3] how soon the foresaid absolution was delivered unto them.

3. That they, their friends, familiars, servants, and others to them pertaining, should never be pursued in the law, nor by the law, by the authority, for the slaughter foresaid. But that they should bruik [4] commodities spiritual or temporal, whatsoever they possessed before the said slaughter, even as if it had never been committed.

4. That they of the Castle should keep the Earl of Arran, [5] so long as their pledges were kept.—And suchlike Articles, liberal enough ; for they [6] never minded to keep word of them, as the issue did declare.

The Appointment made, all the godly were glad ; for some esperance they had, that thereby God's word should somewhat bud, [7] as indeed so it did. For John Rough (who soon after the Cardinal's slaughter entered within the Castle, and had continued with them the whole siege) began to preach in Saint Andrews ; and albeit he was not the most learned, yet was his doctrine without corruption, and therefore well liked of the people.

At the Pasche [8] after, came to the Castle of Saint Andrews *Anno* JOHN KNOX, who, wearied of removing from place to place, by *1547*

---

[1] *sham.* (See *infra*, 241)

[2] This had been suggested certainly as early as 9 August 1546 (*Acts Parl. Scot.*, ii, 470 a). But were the "Castilians" honest in their agreement? Tytler has shown that at this self-same time they wrote to Henry VIII (December 1546) asking him to write to the Emperor to intercede with the Pope " for the stopping and hindering of their absolution." (*History*, 1842, vi, 7-8.) Actually the "Castilians" were in a bad way but were out to gain time for English relief. The Governor, on the other hand, was concerned for the safety of his son, and therefore anxious to prevent the castle falling into English hands. (See *Reg. Privy Council of Scotland*, i, 58.) In fact neither side had any intention of keeping the agreement, and both sides were simply playing for time. (See Keith, *History*, i, 127)   [3] the castle   [4] *enjoy*

[5] See *supra*, 80, *note* 5. The *Diurnal of Occurrents* (43) dates the agreement 20 December (it was made on 17 December) and says the Governor gave [? left] his son in pledge in return for pledges from the " Castilians."

[6] That is, the Governor and his party   [7] *increase*

[8] Easter in 1547 was 10 April

reason of the persecution that came upon him by this Bishop of Saint Andrews,[1] was determined to have left Scotland, and to have visited the schools of Germany (of England then he had no pleasure, by reason that the Pope's name being suppressed, his laws and corruptions remained in full vigour).[2] But because he had the care of some gentlemen's children, whom certain years he had nourished in godliness,[3] their fathers solicited him to go to Saint Andrews, that himself might have the benefit of the Castle, and their children the benefit of his doctrine ; and so (we say) came he the time foresaid to the said place, and, having in his company Francis Douglas of Longniddry, George his brother,[4] and Alexander Cockburn, eldest son then to the Laird of Ormiston,[5] began to exercise them after his accustomed manner. Besides their grammar, and other humane authors, he read unto them a catechism, an account whereof he caused them [to] give publicly in the parish Kirk of Saint Andrews. He read moreover unto them the Evangel of John, proceeding where he left at his departing from Longniddry, where before his residence was ; and that lecture he read in the chapel, within the Castle, at a certain hour. They of the place, but especially Master Henry Balnaves[6] and John Rough, preacher, perceiving the manner of his doctrine, began earnestly to travail with him, that he would take the preaching place upon him. But he utterly refused, alleging " That he would not run where God had not called him " ; meaning, that he would do nothing without a lawful vocation.[7]

Whereupon they privily amongst themselves advising, having with them in council Sir David Lindsay of the Mount,[8] they concluded, that they would give a charge to the said John, and that publicly, by the mouth of their preacher. And so upon a certain

[1] This must refer to John Hamilton, though he had not yet been translated. (Similarly *supra*, 79) Knox was in the diocese of St. Andrews, and clearly it was the bishop's duty to lay hands on his heretical priest. (See also *infra*, 87, *note* 1)

[2] Although Henry VIII had broken with Rome and had ' defined the faith ' by the Six Articles and the ' King's Book,' the sacrament of the Mass had still been the keystone of his faith ; and to Knox the Mass was " at all times . . . idolatry and abomination before God."   [3] *Supra*, 69

[4] Francis Douglas and George Douglas, sons of Hugh Douglas of Longniddry

[5] John Cockburn of Ormiston

[6] This evidence is significant, for Balnaves, writing to Somerset from Berwick on the 18 April, says that he *left* the castle of St. Andrews on Saturday, that is, 16 April. (Laing's *Knox*, iii, 419–20)   [7] *calling*

[8] Sir David Lindsay of the Mount was not a " Castilian." The " council " may have taken place in the parish church of St. Andrews. (See *Works of Sir David Lyndsay*, edit. Laing, i, xxxix–xli)

day, a sermon [was] had of the election of ministers : What power the congregation (how small that ever it was, passing the number of two or three) had above any man, in whom they supposed and espied the gifts of God to be, and how dangerous it was to refuse, and not to hear the voice of such as desire to be instructed. These and other heads (we say), declared, the said John Rough, preacher, directed his words to the said John Knox, saying, " Brother, ye shall not be offended, albeit that I speak unto you that which I have in charge, even from all those that are here present, which is this : In the name of God, and of his Son Jesus Christ, and in the name of these that presently calls you by my mouth, I charge you, that ye refuse not this holy vocation, but that as ye tender [1] the glory of God, the increase of Christ his kingdom, the edification of your brethren, and the comfort of me, whom ye understand well enough to be oppressed by the multitude of labours, that ye take upon you the public office and charge of preaching, even as ye look to avoid God's heavy displeasure, and desire that he shall multiply his graces with you." And in the end he said to those that were present, " Was not this your charge to me ? And do ye not approve this vocation ? " They answered, " It was ; and we approve it." Whereat the said John, abashed, burst forth in most abundant tears, and withdrew himself to his chamber. His countenance and behaviour, from that day till the day that he was compelled to present himself to the public place of preaching, did sufficiently declare the grief and trouble of his heart ; for no man saw any sign of mirth of him, neither yet had he pleasure to accompany any man, many days together.

The first vocation by name of John Knox to preach

The necessity that caused him to enter in the public place, besides the vocation foresaid, was : Dean John Annand (a rotten Papist) had long troubled John Rough in his preaching. The said John Knox had fortified the doctrine of the preacher by his pen, and had beaten the said Dean John from all defences, that he was compelled to fly to his last refuge, that is, to the authority of the Church, " Which authority (said he), damned all Lutherans and heretics ; and therefore he needeth no further disputation." John Knox answered, " Before we hold ourselves, or that ye can prove us sufficiently convicted, we must define the Church, by the right notes given to us in God's Scriptures of the true Church. We must discern the immaculate spouse of Jesus Christ, from the mother of confusion, spiritual Babylon, lest that imprudently we embrace a

Dean John Annand

---

[1] *have regard to*

harlot instead of the chaste spouse ; yea, to speak it in plain words, lest that we submit ourselves to Sathan, thinking that we submit ourselves to Jesus Christ. For, as for your Roman Kirk, as it is now corrupted, and the authority thereof, wherein stands the hope of your victory, I no more doubt but that it is the synagogue of Sathan, and the head thereof, called the Pope, to be that man of sin, of whom the Apostle speaks, than that I doubt that Jesus Christ suffered by the procurement of the visible Kirk of Jerusalem. Yea, I offer myself, by word or writ, to prove the Roman Church this day further degenerate from the purity which was in the days of the Apostles, than was the Church of the Jews from the ordinance given by Moses, when they consented to the innocent death of Jesus Christ." These words were spoken in open audience, in the parish kirk of Saint Andrews, after that the said Dean John Annand had spoken what it pleaseth him, and had refused to dispute. The people hearing the offer, cried with one consent, " We cannot all read your writings, but we may all hear your preaching : Therefore we require you, in the name of God, that ye will let us hear the probation of that which ye have affirmed ; for if it be true, we have been miserably deceived."

The offer of John Knox first and last unto the Papists

And so the next Sunday was appointed to the said John to express his mind in the public preaching place. Which day approaching, the said John took the text written in Daniel, the seventh chapter, beginning thus : " And another king shall rise after them, and he shall be unlike unto the first, and he shall subdue three kings, and shall speak words against the Most High, and shall consume the saints of the Most High, and think that he may change times and laws, and they shall be given into his hands, until a time, and times, and dividing of times."

The first public sermon of John Knox made in the parish kirk of Saint Andrews

1. In the beginning of his sermon, he showed the great love of God towards his Church, whom it pleaseth to forewarn of dangers to come so many years before they come to pass. 2. He briefly entreated the estate of the Israelites, who then were in bondage in Babylon, for the most part ; and made a short discourse of the four Empires, the Babylonian, the Persian, that of the Greeks, and the fourth of the Romans ; in the destruction whereof, rose up that last Beast, which he affirmed to be the Roman Church : for to none other power that ever has yet been, do all the notes [of the Beast] that God has shown to the Prophet appertain, except to it alone ; and unto it they do so properly appertain, that such as are not more than blind, may clearly see them. 3. But before he

began to open the corruptions of the Papistry, he defined the true Kirk, showed the true notes of it, whereupon it was built, why it was the pillar of verity, and why it could not err, to wit, "Because it heard the voice of its own pastor, Jesus Christ, would not hear a stranger, neither yet would be carried about with every kind of doctrine."

Every one of these heads sufficiently declared, he entered to the contrary ; and upon the notes given in his text, he showed that the Spirit of God in the New Testament gave to this king other names, to wit, " the Man of Sin," " the Anti-christ," " the Whore of Babylon." He showed that this man of sin, or Antichrist, was not to be restrained to the person of any one man only, no more than by the fourth beast was to be understood the person of any one Emperor. But by such names the Spirit of God would forewarn his chosen of a body and a multitude, having a wicked head, which should not only be sinful himself, but that also should be occasion of sin to all that should be subject unto him (as Christ Jesus is cause of justice to all the members of his body) ; and is called the Antichrist, that is to say, one contrary to Christ, because that he is contrary to him in life, doctrine, laws, and subjects. And then began he to decipher [1] the lives of divers Popes, and the lives of all the shavelings for the most part ; their doctrine and laws he plainly proved to repugn directly to the doctrine and laws of God the Father, and of Christ Jesus his Son. This he proved by conferring [2] the doctrine of justification, expressed in the Scriptures, which teach that man is "justified by faith only " ; "that the blood of Jesus Christ purges us from all our sins " ; and the doctrine of the Papists, which attributeth justification to the works of the law, yea, to the works of man's invention, as pilgrimage, pardons, and other such baggage. That the papistical laws repugned to the laws of the Evangel, he proved by the laws made of observation of days, abstaining from meats, and from marriage, which Christ Jesus made free ; and the forbidding whereof, Saint Paul called " the doctrine of devils." In handling the notes of that Beast given in the text, he willed men to consider if these notes, " There shall one arise unlike to the other, having a mouth speaking great things and blasphemous," could be applied to any other but to the Pope and his kingdom. For " if these (said he) be not great words and blasphemous : ' the Successor of Peter,' ' the Vicar of Christ,' ' the Head of the Kirk,' ' most holy,' ' most blessed,' ' that can-

Contra dei spiritum ad Galatos ca. 2 versu 16, et 3, [11]

The great words which the Anti-Christ speaketh

---

[1] That is, *analyse*   [2] *comparing*

not err,' that 'may make right of wrong, and wrong of right,' that
' of nothing, may make somewhat,' and that ' hath all verity in the
shrine of his breast,' yea, 'that has power of all, and none power of
him,' nay, ' not to say that he does wrong, although he draw ten
thousand million of souls with himself to hell ' ; if these (said he)
and many other, able to be shown in his own Canon Law, be not
great and blasphemous words, and such as never mortal man spake
before, let the world judge.   And yet (said he) is there one most
evident of all, to wit, John, in his Revelation, says, ' That the
merchandise of that Babylonian harlot, amongst other things,
shall be the bodies and souls of men.'   Now, let the very Papists
themselves judge, if ever any before them took upon them power
to relax the pains of them that were in Purgatory, as they affirm
to the people that daily they do, by the merits of their Mass, and of
their other trifles."   In the end he said, " If any here (and there
were present Master John Mair,[1] the University, the Subprior,[2]
and many Canons, with some Friars of both the orders), that will
say, That I have alleged Scripture, doctor, or history, otherwise
than it is written, let them come unto me with sufficient witness,
and by conference I shall let them see, not only the original where
my testimonies are written, but I shall prove that the writers meant
as I have spoken."

Of this sermon, which was the first that ever John Knox made
in public, were there divers bruits.   Some said, " Others sned [3] the
branches of the Papistry, but he strikes at the root, to destroy the
whole."   Others said, " If the doctors, and *Magistri nostri*, defend
not now the Pope and his authority, which in their own presence
is so manifestly impugned, the Devil have my part of him, and
of his laws both."   Others said, " Master George Wishart spake
never so plainly, and yet he was burnt : even so will he be."   In
the end, others said, " The tyranny of the Cardinal made not his
cause the better, neither yet the suffering of God's servant made his
cause the worse.   And therefore we would counsel you and them,
to provide better defences than fire and sword ; for it may be that
else [4] ye will be disappointed : men now have other eyes than
they had then."   This answer gave the Laird of Nydie,[5] a man
fervent and upright in religion.

---

[1] John Major   [2] John Winram
[3] *lop*.   In the manuscript (folio 64 *recto*) the words *doe sned* in the text have been
scored through and *sned* added in the margin, possibly in Knox's own hand.
[4] *otherwise*   [5] James Forsyth of Nydie

The bastard Bishop, who yet was not execrated (consecrated [1] they call it), wrote to the Subprior of Saint Andrews, who (*sede vacante*) was Vicar General, "That he wondered that he suffered such heretical and schismatical doctrine to be taught, and not to oppose himself to the same." Upon this rebuke, was a convention of Grey Friars and Black fiends appointed, with the said Subprior Dean John Winram, in Saint Leonard's yards, whereunto was first called John Rough, and certain Articles read unto him ; and thereafter was John Knox called for. The cause of their convention, and why that they were called, was exponed [2] ; and the Articles were read, which were these :

I. No mortal man can be the head of the Church.

II. The Pope is an Antichrist, and so is no member of Christ's mystical body.

III. Man may neither make nor devise a religion that is acceptable to God : but man is bound to observe and keep the religion that from God is received, without chopping or changing thereof.

IV. The Sacraments of the New Testament ought to be ministered as they were instituted by Christ Jesus, and practised by his Apostles : nothing ought to be added unto them; nothing ought to be diminished from them.

V. The Mass is abominable idolatry, blasphemous to the death of Christ, and a profanation of the Lord's Supper.

VI. There is no Purgatory in the which the souls of men can either be pined [3] or purged after this life : but heaven rests to the faithful, and hell to the reprobate and unthankful.

VII. Praying for the dead is vain, and to the dead is idolatry.

VIII. There are no bishops, except they preach even by themselves, without any substitute.

IX. The teinds by God's law do not appertain of necessity to the kirk-men.

"The strangeness (said the Subprior) of these Articles, which are gathered forth of your doctrine, has moved us to call for you, to hear your own answers." John Knox said, "I, for my part, praise my God that I see so honourable, and apparently so modest and quiet an auditure. But because it is long since that I have

---

[1] John Hamilton, who was apparently not translated, from Dunkeld to St. Andrews, until 1549, despite a provision by the Pope, of 28 November 1547 (Dowden, *Bishops of Scotland*, 43, 89–90). But he had been consecrated as Bishop of Dunkeld in 1546. Knox is confusing his consecration with his translation.   [2] *explained*   [3] *punished*

heard that ye are one that is not ignorant of the truth, I must crave of you, in the name of God, yea, and I appeal your conscience before that Supreme Judge, that if ye think any Article there expressed contrarious unto the truth of God, that ye oppose yourself plainly unto it, and suffer not the people to be therewith deceived. But and if in your conscience ye know the doctrine to be true, then will I crave your patrociny [1] thereto ; that, by your authority, the people may be moved the rather to believe the truth, whereof many doubt by reason of our youth."

The Subprior answered, " I came not here as a judge, but only familiarly to talk ; and therefore, I will neither allow nor condemn ; but if ye list, I will reason. Why may not the Kirk (said he), for good causes, devise Ceremonies to decore [2] the Sacraments, and others [of] God's services ? "

John Knox

" Because the Kirk ought to do nothing but in faith, and ought not to go before ; but is bound to follow the voice of the true Pastor."

The Subprior

" It is in faith that the ceremonies are commanded, and they have proper significations to help our faith ; as the hards [3] in Baptism signify the roughness of the law, and the oil the softness of God's mercy ; and likewise, every one of the ceremonies has a godly signification, and therefore they both proceed from faith and are done into faith."

John Knox

" It is not enough that man invent a ceremony, and then give it a signification, according to his pleasure. For so might the ceremonies of the Gentiles, and this day the ceremonies of Mahomet, be maintained. But if that anything proceed from faith, it must have the word of God for the assurance ; for ye are not ignorant, ' That faith comes by hearing, and hearing by the word of God.' Now, if ye will prove that your ceremonies proceed from faith, and do please

---

[1] patronage : that is " your countenance "   [2] adorn

[3] Calderwood (History, i, 233) has " band," and later, " hurds " ; that is, a band of hardin, or coarse linen cloth—the hards or hurds being the coarser parts of flax or hemp separated in hackling (see Oxford Dictionary, s.v.). In December 1562, the sum of £28, 3s. 4d. was paid to " Robert Hendersone, chirugen, for expensis maid be him upoun spicis, vinagre, aquavitie, pulderis, odouris and hardis " together with his labours in the " handeling " of the Earl of Huntly's body [after Corrichie] that it should not putrefy. (Accs. Lord High Treas., xi, 226)

God, ye must prove that God in expressed words has commanded them : Or else shall ye never prove, That they proceed from faith, nor yet that they please God ; but that they are sin, and do displease him, according to the words of the Apostle, ' Whatsoever is not of faith is sin.' "

THE SUBPRIOR

" Will ye bind us so strait, that we may do nothing without the express word of God ? What and [1] I ask a drink ? Think ye that I sin ? And yet I have not God's word for me."

This answer gave he, as might appear, to shift over the argument upon the Friar, as that he did.

JOHN KNOX

" I would we should not jest in so grave a matter ; neither would I that ye should begin to elude the truth with sophistry ; and if ye do, I will defend me the best that I can. And first, to your drinking, I say, that if ye either eat or drink without assurance of God's word, that in so doing ye displease God, and ye sin into your very eating and drinking. For says not the Apostle, speaking even of meat and drink, ' That the creatures are sanctified unto man, even by the word and by prayer.' The word is this : ' All things are clean to the clean,' &c. Now, let me hear thus much of your ceremonies, and I shall give you the argument ; but I wonder that ye compare things profane and holy things so indiscreetly together. The question was not, nor is not of meat or drink, whereinto the kingdom of God consists not ; but the question is of God's true worshipping, without the which we can have no society with God. And here it is doubted if we may take the same freedom in the using of Christ's Sacraments, that we may do in eating and drinking. One meat I may eat, another I may refuse, and that without scruple of conscience. I may change one with another, even as oft as I please. Whether may we do the same in matters of religion ? May we cast away what we please, and retain what we please ? If I be well remembered, Moses, in the name of God, says to the people of Israel, ' All that the Lord thy God commands thee to do, that do thou to the Lord thy God : add nothing to it ; diminish nothing from it.' By this rule think I that the Kirk of Christ will measure God's religion, and not by that which seems good in their own eyes."

[1] if

The Subprior

" Forgive me : I spake it but in mowes,[1] and I was dry. And now, Father (said he to the Friar), follow the argument. Ye have heard what I have said, and what is answered unto me again."

Arbuckle, Grey-Friar

" I shall prove plainly that ceremonies are ordained by God."

John Knox

" Such as God has ordained we allow, and with reverence we use them. But the question is of those that God has not ordained, such as, in Baptism, are spittle, salt, candle, cuide [2] (except it be to keep the bairn from cold), hards, oil, and the rest of the Papistical inventions." [3]

Arbuckle

" I will even prove these that ye damn to be ordained of God."

John Knox

" The proof thereof I would gladly hear."

Arbuckle

" Says not Saint Paul, ' That another foundation than Jesus Christ may no man lay.' But upon this foundation some build gold, silver, and precious stones ; some hay, stubble, and wood. The gold, silver, and precious stones are the ceremonies of the Church, which do abide the fire, and consume not away. This place of Scripture is most plain," (says the foolish Fiend).

John Knox

" I praise my God, through Jesus Christ, for I find his promise sure, true, and stable. Christ Jesus bids us ' Not fear, when we shall be called before men, to give confession of his truth ' ; for he promises, ' that it shall be given unto us in that hour what we shall speak.' If I had sought the whole Scriptures, I could not have produced a place more proper for my purpose, nor more potent to confound you.

[1] *jest*   [2] the *chrisom*, or white face-cloth
[3] For the ritual of baptism, see *Catholic Encyclopedia*, s.v. *Baptism*, sec. xvi.

Now to your argument : The ceremonies of the Kirk (say ye) are gold, silver, and precious stones, because they are able to abide the fire ; but I would learn of you, what fire is it which your ceremonies do abide ? And in the meantime, till that ye be advised to answer, I will show my mind, and make an argument against yours, upon the same text. And first, I say, that I have heard this text adduced, for a proof of Purgatory ; but for defence of ceremonies, I never heard, nor yet read it. But omitting whether ye understand the mind of the Apostle or not, I make my argument, and say, That which may abide the fire, may abide the word of God : But your ceremonies may not abide the word of God : *Ergo*, They may not abide the fire ; and if they may not abide the fire then are they not gold, silver, nor precious stones. Now, if ye find any ambiguity in this term, 'Fire', which I interpret to be the word, find ye me another fire, by the which things builded upon Christ Jesus should be tried, than God and his word, which both in the Scriptures are called fire, and I shall correct my argument."

Arbuckle

" I stand not thereupon ; but I deny your Minor, to wit, that our ceremonies may not abide the trial of God's word."

John Knox

" I prove, that abides not the trial of God's word which God's word condemns : But God's word condemns your ceremonies : Therefore they do not abide the trial thereof. But as the thief abides the trial of the inquest, and thereby is condemned to be hanged, *" Optima* even so may your ceremonies abide the trial of God's word ; but not *collatio "* else. And now, in few words to make plain that wherein ye may seem to doubt, to wit, That God's word damns your ceremonies, it is evident ; for the plain and straight commandment of God is, ' Not that thing which appears good in thy eyes, shalt thou do to the *Deut.* 4 Lord thy God, but what the Lord thy God has commanded thee, that do thou : add nothing to it ; diminish nothing from it.' Now unless that ye be able to prove that God has commanded your ceremonies, this his former commandment will damn both you and them."

The Friar somewhat abashed what first to answer, while he wanders about in the mist, he falls in a foul mire ; for alleging that we may not be so bound to the word, he affirmed, " That the Apostles had not received the Holy Ghost, when they did write their Epistles ; but after, they received him, and then they did ordain the ceremonies." (Few would have thought that so learned a man would have given so foolish an answer ; and yet it is even as true as [that] he bare a grey cowl.) John Knox, hearing the answer, started, and said, " If that be true, I have long been in an error, and I think I shall die therein." The Subprior said to him, " Father, what say ye ? God forbid that ye affirm that ; for then farewell the ground of our faith." The Friar astonished, made the best shift that he could to correct his fall ; but it would not be. John Knox brought him oft again to the ground of the argument : but he would never answer directly, but ever fled to the authority of the Kirk. Whereto the said John answered oftener than once, " That the spouse of Christ had neither power nor authority against the word of God." Then said the Friar, " If so be, ye will leave us no Kirk." " Indeed (said the other), in David I read that there is a church of the malignants, for he says, *Odi ecclesiam malignantium.* That church ye may have, without the word, and doing many things directly fighting against the word of God. Of that church if ye will be, I can not impede you. But as for me, I will be of none other church except of that which hath Christ Jesus to be pastor, which hears his voice, and will not hear a stranger."

In this disputation many other things were merely scoffed over ; for the Friar, after his fall, could speak nothing to a purpose.

Friar Arbuckle's proof for Purgatory

For Purgatory he had no better proof, but the authority of Virgil in his sixth Æneid ; and the pains thereof to him was an evil wife.[1] How John Knox answered that, and many other things, himself did witness in a treatise that he wrote in the galleys, containing the sum of his doctrine, and confession of his faith, and sent it to his familiars in Scotland ; with his exhortation, that they should continue in the truth which they had professed, notwithstanding any worldly adversity that might ensue thereof.[2] Thus much of that disputation

The cause of the inserting of this disputation

have we inserted here, to the intent that men may see how that Sathan ever travails to obscure the light ; and yet how God by his power, working in his weak vessels, confounds his craft, and discloses his darkness.

[1] In mediæval literature a quarrelsome or nagging wife was frequently likened to the punishment of Purgatory.

[2] This exhortation appears in Knox's Epistle to " his best beloved Brethren of the Congregation of the Castle of St. Andrewes ", which he added to his revision of Balnaves's Treatise on Justification by Faith (also called " The Confession of Faith "), and which is doubtless the " Confession " to which he refers here. (See Laing's *Knox*, iii, 1–28, and particularly iii, 10)

After this, the Papists nor Friars had not great heart of further disputation or reasoning ; but invented another shift, which appeared to proceed from godliness ; and it was this : Every learned man in the Abbey, and in the University, should preach in the parish kirk his Sunday about. The Subprior began, followed the Official called Spittal,[1] (sermons penned to offend no man), followed all the rest in their ranks. And so John Knox smelled out the craft, and in his sermons, which he made upon the week days, he prayed to God that they should be as busy in preaching when there should be more mister [2] of it than there was then. "Always (said he) I praise God, that Christ Jesus is preached, and nothing is said publicly against the doctrine ye have heard. If in my absence they shall speak anything which in my presence they do not, I protest that ye suspend your judgment till that it please God ye hear me again." *The practice of Papists that their wickedness should not be disclosed*

The protestation of John Knox

God so assisted his weak soldier, and so blessed his labours, that not only all those of the Castle,[3] but also a great number of the town, openly professed, by participation of the Lord's Table, in the same purity that now it is ministered in the churches of Scotland, with that same doctrine that he had taught unto them. Amongst whom was he that now either rules or else misrules Scotland, to wit, Sir James Balfour (sometimes called Master James), the chief and principal Protestant that then was to be found in this realm. This we write, because we have heard that the said Master James alleges that he was never of this our religion ; but that he was brought up in Martin's [4] opinion of the Sacrament, and therefore he can not communicate with us. But his own conscience, and two hundred witnesses besides, know that he lies [5] ; and that he was one of the chief (if he had not been after copes) [6] that would have given his life, if men might credit his words, for defence of the doctrine that the said John Knox taught. But albeit that those that never were of us (as none of Montquhanie's [7] sons have shown *Master James Balfour once joined with the Church, and did profess all doctrine taught by John Knox*

---

[1] Mr. John Spittal   [2] *need*

[3] Calderwood wisely omits " all " which is over-written in the manuscript.

[4] That is, Martin Luther's

[5] Much later, Mary, in a remarkable proclamation before Langside, was to call him " that mensworne ethnik [heathen] " ; and any account of his life (even a brief summary such as that in Brunton and Haig, *Senators of the College of Justice*, 110–114), makes unpleasant reading. With justice he has been stigmatized as " the most corrupt man of his age."

[6] That is, if he had not been seeking a cope—as Official of Lothian. The meaning is rendered clear by the later passage " for then had not Master James Balfour been Official, neither yet borne a cope for pleasure of the Bishop." (*infra*, 108)

[7] Sir Michael Balfour of Montquhanie ; Sir James Balfour was his eldest son

themselves to be) depart from us, it is no great wonder; for it is proper and natural that the children follow the father; and let the godly liver of that race and progeny be shown [1]; for if in them be either fear of God, or love of virtue, further than the present commodity persuades them, men of judgment are deceived. But to return to our History.

The priests and bishops, enraged at these proceedings that were in Saint Andrews, ran now upon the Governor, now upon the Queen, now upon the whole Council, and there might have been heard complaints and cries, " What are we doing? Shall ye suffer this whole realm to be infected with pernicious doctrine? Fie upon you, and fie upon us." The Queen and Monsieur d'Oysel,[2] (who then was *a secretis mulierum* in the Court),[3] comforted them,

and willed them to be quiet, for they should see remedy or it was long. And so was proven in deed; for upon the penult day of June, appeared in the sight of the Castle of Saint Andrews twenty-one French galleys, with a skeife [of] an army,[4] the like whereof was never seen in that Firth before. This treasonable mean [5] had

the Governor, the Bishop, the Queen, and Monsieur d'Oysel, under the Appointment drawn.[6] But to excuse their treason, eight days before they had presented an absolution unto them, as sent from Rome, containing, after the aggravation of the crime, this clause, *Remittimus Irremissibile*, that is, We remit the crime that can not be remitted.[7] Which considered by the worst [8] of the company

that was in the Castle, answer was given, " That the Governor and Council of the Realm had promised unto them a sufficient and assured absolution, which that appeared not to be; and therefore could they not deliver the house, neither thought they that any reasonable man would require them so to do, considering that promise was not kept unto them." The next day, after that the

---

[1] That is, " [if he can be found] "

[2] Henri Cleutin, Seigneur d'Oysel et de Villeparisis et Saint-Aignan, the French ambassador in Scotland

[3] Compare the slur on the relations between the Queen Mother and D'Oysel (*infra*, 321)

[4] In the manuscript (folio 68 *verso*) the words " schair [?] men of " are deleted, and " skeife an " added above the line. The meaning seems to be a large force. (*Scare* and *skeife* may both mean a *section* or *division*)   [5] *design, intent*

[6] But equally the " Castilians " had been looking for an *English* fleet and army.

[7] That, according to Knox, would be 21 June; but an English spy, writing on 2 *April*, says that the Pope's absolution had arrived, that the " Castilians " had told the Governor that if " he keyp to thame, thai will keyp to him," but that in private they said they would sooner have a boll of wheat than all the Pope's remissions. (*Calendar of Scottish Papers*, i, No. 10.) The " Castilians " were then still confidently expecting aid from England.   [8] ? *maist*, that is, *most*

galleys arrived,[1] they summoned the house, which being denied, (because they knew them no magistrates in Scotland), they prepared for siege. And first they began to assault by sea, and shot two days. But thereof they neither got advantage nor honour ; for they danged the slates off houses, but neither slew man, nor did harm to any wall. But the Castle handled them so, that Sancta Barbara (the gunners' goddess) helped them nothing ; for they lost many of their rowers, men chained in the galleys, and some soldiers, both by sea and land. And further, a galley that approached nigher than the rest was so dung [2] with the cannon and other ordnance that she was stopped [3] under water and so almost drowned, and so had been, were [it] not that the rest gave her succour in time, and drew her first to the west sands, without the shot of the Castle, and thereafter to Dundee, where they remained, till that the Governor, who then was at the siege of Langhope,[4] came unto them, with the rest of the French faction. The siege by land was confirmed about the Castle of Saint Andrews, the xxiiij [5] day of July. The trenches were cast ; ordnance was planted upon the Abbey Kirk, and upon Saint Salvator's College (and yet was the steeple thereof burnt), which so annoyed the Castle, that neither could they keep their block-houses, the Sea-tower head, nor the west wall ; for in all these places were men slain by great ordnance, Yea, they mounted the ordnance so high upon the Abbey Kirk, that they might discover the ground of the close in divers places.[6] Moreover, within the Castle was the pest [7] (and divers therein died), which more effrayed some that was therein, than did the external force without. But John Knox was of another judgment, for he ever said, " That their corrupt life could not escape punishment of God " ; and that was his continual advertisement, from the time that he was called to preach.[8] When they triumphed of their victory (the first twenty days they had many prosperous chances) he lamented, and ever said, " They saw not what he saw." When they bragged of the force and thickness of their walls, he said, " They should be but egg-shells." When they vaunted, " England will rescue us,"

The gunners' goddess

The sentence of John Knox to the castle of St. Andrews before it was won

---

[1] Andrew Lang (*John Knox and the Reformation*, 27) has advanced evidence that the French galleys did not arrive until mid-July. [2] *struck* [3] *holed*

[4] Langholm, then held by the English [5] Laing's text reads, erroneously, xviiij

[6] That is, their cannon-balls could pass over the walls and land in the court of the castle [7] *plague*

[8] Knox's prophecy that God would punish the wickedness of those in the castle is also reported by Pitscottie (*Chronicles*, Scot. Text Soc., ii, 87) ; but Pitscottie may have been borrowing from Knox.

he said, " Ye shall not see them ; but ye shall be delivered in your enemy's hands, and shall be carried to a strange country."

Upon the penult of July [1] at night, was the ordnance planted for the battery ; xiiij cannons, whereof four were cannons royal, called double cannons, besides other pieces. The battery began at four hours in the morning,[2] and before ten hours of the day, the whole south quarter, betwix the fore-tower and the east block-house, was made assaultable. The lower transe [3] was condemned,[4] divers slain in it, and the east block-house was shot off from the rest of the place. Betwix ten hours and eleven, there fell a shower of rain, that continued near an hour, the like whereof had seldom been seen. It was so vehement, that no man might abide without a house. The cannons were left alone. Some within the Castle were of judgment, that men should have issued [forth] and put all in the hands of God. But because that William Kirkcaldy was
Prior of Capua communing [5] with the Prior of Capua,[6] who had the commission of that journey from the King of France, nothing was enterprised. And so was appointment made, and the Castle rendered, upon Saturday, the last of July.[7]

The heads of the Appointment were : " That the lives of all within the Castle should be saved, as well English as Scottish ; that they should be safely transported to France ; and in case that, upon conditions that by the King of France should be offered unto them, they could not be content to remain in service and
The castle of St. An-drews re-fused in their greatest extremity to appoint with the Governor freedom there, they should, upon the King of France's expenses be safely conveyed to what country they would require, other than Scotland." With the Governor they would have nothing ado, neither yet with any Scottish man ; for they had all traitorously betrayed them, " Which," said the Laird of Grange, elder,[8] a man simple, and of most stout courage, " I am assured God shall revenge it, or it be long."

The galleys, well furnished with the spoil of the Castle foresaid,[9] after certain days returned to France [10] ; and escaping a great danger (for upon the back of the sands they all shopped [11]), they

---

[1] Probably on the night of 29–30 July   [2] 4 a.m. on 30 July   [3] *close*
[4] *blocked up*   [5] *in conversation*   [6] Leon Strozzi, Prior of Capua
[7] In 1547 Saturday was 30 July   [8] Sir James Kirkcaldy of Grange
[9] The *Diurnal of Occurrents* (44) says the spoil was worth £100,000—mainly, no doubt, of Beaton's ingathering.
[10] The *Diurnal of Occurrents* (44) says that the galleys with six-score prisoners sailed back to France on 7 August.   [11] *struck*

arrived first at Fécamp,[1] and thereafter passed up the water of Sequane,[2] and lay before Rouen ; where the principal gentlemen, who looked for freedom, were dispersed and put in sundry prisons.[3] The rest were left in the galleys, and there miserably entreated, amongst whom the foresaid Master James Balfour was,[4] with his two brethren, David and Gilbert, men without God. Which we write, because that we hear that the said Master James, principal misguider now of Scotland, denies that he had anything to do with the Castle of Saint Andrews, or yet that ever he was in the galleys. Then was the joy of the Papists both of Scotland and France even in full perfection ; for this was their song of triumph :

Master James Balfour was fleyed [5] enough

Preasts content you now ; Preasts content you now ;
For Normond and his company has filled the galleys fow.[6]

The Pope wrote his letters to the King of France, and so did he to the Governor of Scotland, thanking them heartily for the taking pains to revenge the death of his kind creature, the Cardinal of Scotland, [and] desiring them to continue in their begun severity, that such things after should not be attempted. And so were all these that were deprehended in the Castle damned to perpetual prison ; and so judged the ungodly that after that in Scotland should Christ Jesus never have triumphed. One thing we cannot pass by : From Scotland was sent a famous clerk (laugh not, reader), Master John Hamilton of Milburn, with credit to the King of France, and unto the Cardinal of Lorraine (and yet he neither had French nor Latin, and some say his Scottish tongue was not very good).[7] The sum of all his negotiation was, That those of the Castle should be sharply handled. In which suit, he was heard with favour, and was dispatched from the Court of France with letters, and great credit, which that famous clerk forgot by the way ; for passing up to the craig of Dumbarton, before his letters were delivered, he broke his neck ; and so God took away a proud ignorant enemy. But now to our History.

These things against promises (but Princes have no fidelity further than for their own advantage) done at Rouen, the galleys departed to Nantes, in Bartainzie,[8] where upon the water of Loire they lay the whole winter.

Nulla fides regni sociis, etc.

---

[1] In the manuscript (folio 69 *verso*) *fekcam* has been added later (possibly in Knox's own hand) in a space left by the scribe.
[2] Seine   [3] *Cf. infra,* 107   [4] *Cf. infra,* 108–109   [5] *afraid*   [6] *full*
[7] A Hamilton, " more owlde than wise," left Scotland with d'Oysel on 23 November 1547. (*Calendar of Scottish Papers,* i, No. 92)   [8] Nantes, in Brittany

In Scotland, that summer, was nothing but mirth ; for all yead [1] with the priests even at their own pleasure. The Castle of Saint Andrews was razed to the ground, the block-houses thereof cast down, and the walls round about demolished. Whether this was to fulfil their law, which commands places where Cardinals are slain so to be used, or else for fear that England should have taken it, as after they did Broughty Craig, [2] we remit to the judgment of such as was of council.

This same year, in the beginning of September, entered in Scotland an army of ten thousand men from England, by land, and some ships with ordnance came by sea. The Governor and the *Pinkie* Bishop, hereof advertised, gathered together the forces of Scotland, *Cleuch* and assembled at Edinburgh. The Protector of England, [3] with the Earl of Warwick, [4] and their army, remained at Preston, and about Prestonpans [5] : for they had certain offers to have been proposed unto the Nobility of Scotland, concerning the promises before made by them, unto the which King Harry before his death gently required them to stand fast ; and if they so would do, of him nor of his realm they should have no trouble, but the help and the comfort that he could make them in all things lawful. And hereupon was there a letter directed to the Governor and Council [6] ; which coming to the hands of the Bishop of Saint Andrews, he thought it could not be for his advantage that it should be divulged, and therefore by his craft it was suppressed.

Upon the Friday, the [ix day] of September, the English army *The* marched towards Leith, and the Scottish army marched from *security of* Edinburgh to Inveresk. [7] The whole Scottish army was not assembled *the Scots-* and yet the skirmishing began ; for nothing was concluded but *men at* victory without stroke. The Protector, the Earl of Warwick, the *Pinkie* *Cleuch* Lord Grey, [8] and all the English Captains, were playing at the dice. No men were stouter than the priests and canons, with their shaven crowns and black jacks. The Earl of Warwick and the Lord Grey, who had the chief charge of the horsemen, perceiving the host to be molested with the Scottish prickers, [9] and knowing that the

---

[1] *went*   [2] Now Broughty-Ferry, about three miles east of Dundee
[3] Edward Seymour, Lord Hertford, Duke of Somerset
[4] John Dudley, Lord Lisle, Earl of Warwick, later Duke of Northumberland
[5] About eight miles east of Edinburgh
[6] In the manuscript half of folio 70 *verso* and nearly half of folio 71 *recto* have been left blank as if for the later insertion of this letter.
[7] Three-quarters of a mile south of Musselburgh
[8] William, Lord Grey de Wilton   [9] That is, light horsemen

multitude were neither under order nor obedience (for they were divided from the great army) sent forth certain troops of horsemen, and some of their Borderers, either to fight them, or else to put them out of their sight, so that they might not annoy the host. The skirmish grew hot, and at length the Scottishmen gave back, and fled without gane turn.[1] The chase continued far, both towards *Friday's chase* the east and towards the west ; in the which many were slain, and he that now is Lord Home [2] was taken, which was the occasion that the Castle of Home was after rendered to the Englishmen. The loss of these men neither moved the Governor, nor yet the Bishop, his bastard brother : They should revenge the matter well *Brags* enough upon the morn ; for they were hands enough [3] (no word of God) ; the English heretics had no faces ; they would not abide.

Upon the Saturday, the armies of both sides passed to array. The English army takes the mid part of Falside hill,[4] having their ordnance planted before them, and having their ships and two galleys brought as near the land as water would serve. The Scottish army stood first in a reasonable strength and good order, having betwix them and the English army the Water of Esk (otherwise called Musselburgh Water) ; but at length a charge was given in the Governor's behalf, with sound of trumpet, that all men should march forward, and go over the water. Some say that this was procured by the Abbot of Dunfermline [5] and Master Hew Rigg [6] for preservation of Carberry. Men of judgment liked not the journey ; for they thought it no wisdom to leave their strength. But commandment upon commandment, and charge upon charge, was given, which urged them so, that unwillingly they obeyed. The Earl of Angus,[7] being in the vanguard, had in his company the gentlemen of Fife, of Angus, Mearns, and the Westland, with many others that of love resorted to him, and especially those that were professors of the Evangel ; for they supposed that England would not have made great pursuit of him. He passed first through the water, and arrayed his host direct before the enemies. Followed the Earl of Huntly,[8] with his Northland men. Last came the Duke,[9] having in his company the Earl of Argyll,[10] with his own friends, and

---

[1] *again turning*
[2] Alexander, fifth Lord Home
[3] *they had men enough*
[4] About three miles south-east of Musselburgh
[5] George Durie
[6] Hugh Rigg of Carberry
[7] Archibald Douglas, sixth Earl of Angus
[8] George, fourth Earl of Huntly
[9] Arran, the Governor, but not yet Duke of Châtelherault
[10] Archibald, fourth Earl of Argyll

the body of the realm. The Englishmen perceiving the danger, and how that the Scottishmen intended to have taken the top of the hill, made haste to prevent the peril. The Lord Grey was commanded to give the charge with his men of arms, which he did, albeit the hazard was very unlikely ; for the Earl of Angus's host stood even as a wall, and received the first assaulters upon the points of their spears (which were longer than those of the Englishmen) so rudely that fifty horse and men of the first rank lay dead at once, without any hurt done to the Scottish army, except that the spears of the former two ranks were broken. Which discomfiture received, the rest of the horsemen fled ; yea, some passed beyond Falside hill. The Lord Grey himself was hurt in the mouth, and plainly denied to charge again ; for he said, " It was like as to run against a wall." The galleys and the ships, and so did the ordnance planted upon the mid hill, shot terribly. But the ordnance of the galleys, shooting alongst [1] the Scottish army, effrayed them wondrously. And while that every man labours to draw from the north, whence the danger appeared, they begin to reel, and with that were the English footmen marching forward, albeit that some of their horsemen were upon the flight. The Earl of Angus's army stood still, looking that either Huntly or the Duke should have recountered the next battle ; but they had decreed that the favourers of England, and the heretics (as the priests called them), and the Englishmen should part it [2] betwix them for the day.

The repulse of the horsemen of England

The fear rises, and at one instant they, which before were victors, and were not yet assaulted with any force (except with ordnance, as said is), cast from them their spears and fled. So that God's power was so evidently seen, that in one moment, yea, at one instant time, both the armies were fleeing. The shout came from the hill from those that hoped no victory upon the English part ; the shout rises, (we say), " They fly, they fly " ; but at the first it could not be believed, till at the last it was clearly seen that all had given back ; and then began a cruel slaughter (which was the greater by reason of the late displeasure of the men of arms). The chase and slaughter lasted till nigh Edinburgh upon the one part, and bewest Dalkeith, upon the other. The number of the slain upon the Scottish side were judged nigh ten thousand men. The Earl of Huntly was taken, and carried to London ; but he relieved himself, being surety for many ransoms, honestly or unhonestly we know

[1] That is, enfilading them
[2] *settle it*, in the sense of *sharing the fight*

not ; but, as the bruit passed, he used policy with England.[1] In that same battle was slain the Master of Erskine,[2] dearly beloved of the Queen, for whom she made great lamentation, and bare his death many days in mind. When the certainty of the discomfiture came, she was in Edinburgh abiding upon tidings ; but with expedition she posted that same night to Stirling, with Monsieur d'Oysel, who was as fleyed [3] as " a fox when his hole is smoked." And thus did God take the second revenge upon the perjured Governor, with such as assisted him to defend an unjust quarrel ; albeit that many innocents fell amongst the midst of the wicked. The English army came to Leith, and there taking order with their prisoners and spoil, they returned with this victory (which they looked not for) to England.

That winter following were great herschips [4] made upon all the Borders of Scotland. Broughty Craig was taken by the Englishmen, besieged by the Governor, but still kept ; and at it was slain Gavin, the best of the Hamiltons,[5] and the ordnance left. Whereupon the Englishmen, encouraged, began to fortify upon the hill above Broughty House, which was called the Fort of Broughty, and was very noisome to Dundee, which it burnt and laid waste ; and so did it the most part of Angus, which was not assured and under friendship with them.

That Lent following, was Haddington fortified by the English- 1548 men. The most part of Lothian, from Edinburgh east, was either assured or laid waste. Thus did God plague in every quarter ; but men were blind, and would not, nor could not, consider the cause. The Lairds Ormiston [6] and Brunstane [7] were banished,[8] and after forfeited, and so were all those of the Castle of Saint Andrews. The sure knowledge of the troubles of Scotland coming to France, there was prepared a navy and army. The navy was such as never was seen to come from France for the support of Scotland ; for besides the galleys, being twenty-two then in number,

---

[1] In the two agreements between the Protector Somerset and George, fourth Earl of Huntly, printed in *Spalding Club Miscellany*, iv, 144–150, the second definitely supports Knox's " bruit."

[2] Robert, Master of Erskine, eldest son of John, fifth Lord Erskine

[3] *frightened*   [4] *ravagings*

[5] Gavin Hamilton ; possibly Gavin Hamilton, natural son of Gavin Hamilton of Orbistoun

[6] John Cockburn of Ormiston   [7] Alexander Crichton of Brunstane

[8] They had certainly been working hand-in-glove with England. (See *Scottish Correspondence of Mary of Lorraine*, Scot. Hist. Soc., No. CL.)

they had threescore great ships, besides victuallers.[1] How soon
soever they took the plain seas, the Red Lion of Scotland was displayed, and they held as rebels unto France (such policy is no
falsity in Princes), for good peace stood betwix France and England,
and the King of France approved nothing that they did. The
chief men to whom the conducting of that army was committed,
were Monsieur d'Andelot,[2] Monsieur de Thermes,[3] and Pierre de
Strozzi.[4] In their journey they made some herschip upon the coast
of England ; but it was not great. They arrived in Scotland in
May, anno 1549.[5] The galleys did visit the fort of Broughty, but
did no more at that time. Preparations were made for the siege
of Haddington ; but it was another thing that they meant, as the
issue declared. The whole body of the realm assembled, the form

The Par- of a Parliament [6] was set to be held there, to wit, in the Abbey of
liament at
Hadding- Haddington. The principal head was the marriage of the Princess
ton
(by them before contracted to King Edward), to the King of France,[7]
and of her present delivery,[8] by reason of the danger that she stood
into by the invasion of our old enemies of England. Some were
corrupted with budds,[9] some deceived by flattering promises, and
some for fear were compelled to consent ; for the French soldiers
were the officers of arms in that Parliament. The Laird of Buccleuch,[10]
a bloody man, with many God's wounds, swore, " They that would
not consent should do war[11]". The Governor got the Duchy of
Châtelherault,[12] with the Order of the Cockle,[13] and a full discharge
of all intromissions with King James the Fifth's treasure and
substance whatsoever, with possession of the Castle of Dumbarton,

---

[1] *supply-ships*   [2] François de Coligny, Seigneur d'Andelot

[3] Paul de la Barthe, sieur de Termes. (See *Scot. Hist. Rev.*, xxvi, 158, *note* 7)

[4] Pierre Strozzi. (See Brantôme, *Œuvres Complètes, ed.* Lalanne, ii, 239–282)

[5] The year was 1548, but these leaders did not arrive until 1549. In the manuscript
(folio 73 *recto*) the date has been underlined (by Knox ?) as if for checking.

[6] But it appears to have been a duly constituted Parliament.

[7] To the Dauphin, Francis (later Francis II), son of Henry II, King of France

[8] *her immediate delivery* [to France]   [9] *bribes*

[10] Sir Walter Scott of Buccleuch, known as ' Wicked Wat '

[11] *should do worse*

[12] A formal grant of the Duchy of Châtelherault was made to James, second Earl of
Arran, and his heirs in February 1549 ; but the French King had bound himself to confer
the title of Duke on the Earl of Arran, with a Duchy in France, as early as January 1548
(Hay Fleming, *Mary Queen of Scots*, 193, *note* 83). Arran later received a full discharge
of all his ' intromissions ' when the regency was formally transferred to the Queen
Dowager in 1554. (See *Acts Parl. Scot.*, ii, 600–602)

[13] That is, the Order of St. Michael (see *La Grande Encyclopédie*, s.v. Michel (Saint), and
Keith, *History*, ii, 390, *note* 2). Brantôme, *Œuvres Complètes* (*ed.* Lalanne), v, 91–115,
gives a full account of the Order.

till that issue should be seen of the Queen's body. With these, and *The Duke's fact, and what appears to follow thereof* other conditions, stood he content to sell his Sovereign forth of his own hands, which in the end will be his destruction ; God thereby punishing his former wickedness (if speedy repentance prevent [1] not God's judgments, which we heartily wish). Huntly, Argyll, and Angus were likewise made Knights of the Cockle ; and for that and other good deed received, they sold also their part. Shortly, none was found to resist that unjust demand ; and so was she sold *Experience has taught and further will declare* to go to France, to the end that in her youth she should drink of that liquor that should remain with her all her lifetime, for a plague to this realm, and for her final destruction. And therefore, albeit that now a fire comes out from her, that consumes many, let no man wonder ; she is God's hand, in his displeasure punishing our *" Perfice quod cepisti mi deus propter tui nominis gloriam 15 Junij 1567 "* [2] former ingratitude. Let men patiently abide, and turn unto their God, and then shall he either destroy that whore in her whoredom, or else he shall put it in the hearts of a multitude to take the same vengeance upon her that has been taken of Jezebel and Athaliah, yea, and of others of whom profane histories make mention ; for greater abomination was never in the nature of any woman than is in her, *Written the [ ] of April* whereof we have but seen only the buds ; but we will after taste of the ripe fruit of her impiety, if God cut not her days short. But *Anno 1566* to return to our History.

This conclusion taken, that our Queen (but [3] further delay) should be delivered to France, the siege continues, great shooting, *The siege of Haddington Tuesday's chase* but no assaulting ; and yet they had fair occasion offered unto them. For the Englishmen approaching to the town, for the comforting of the besieged, with powder, victuals, and men, lost an army of six thousand men. Sir Robert Bowes so was taken, and the most part of the Borderers were either taken or slain. And so might the town justly have despaired of any further succour to have been looked for ; but yet it held good ; for the stout courage and prudent government of Sir James Wilford, general, did so encourage the whole captains and soldiers, that they determined to die upon their walls. But from the time that the French men had got the bone for

---

[1] *come before*

[2] " Finish what Thou hast begun, O my God, for the glory of Thy name, 15 June 1567." On 15 June 1567, one month after her marriage to Bothwell, Mary surrendered to the Confederate Lords at Carberry. This marginal note (folio 73 *verso*), written at the time (and subsequently scored through), is clearly added as a fulfilment of the prophecy contained in the text ; and the succeeding marginal note has been added to indicate when that prophecy was written. Both marginal notes are in the hand of the text, and not in the hand of Knox. [3] *without*

the which the dog barked, the pursuit of the town was slow. The siege was raised, and she [1] was conveyed by the West seas to France, with four galleys, and some ships; and so the Cardinal of Lorraine got her in his keeping, a morsel, [I] assure you, meet for his own mouth. [2]

We omit many things that occurred in this time; as the sitting down [3] of the ship called the *Cardinal* (the fairest ship in France) betwix Saint Colme's Inch [4] and Cramond, without any occasion, except negligence, for the day was fair, and the weather calm; but God would show that the country of Scotland can bear no Cardinals. In this time also was there a combat betwix the galleys and the English ships; they shot frackly [5] a while. An English ship took fire, or else the galleys had come short home and, as it was, they fled without mercy till that they were above Saint Colme's Inch. The Captains left the galleys, and took a fort made upon the Inch for their defence. But the English ships made no pursuit (except that they burnt the *Cardinal* where that she lay), and so the galleys and the galley men did both escape.

Order was taken, that next September, that some galleys should remain in Scotland, and that the rest should return to France [6]; as that they did, all except one that was taken by an English ship (by one English ship only, we say) as that they were passing betwix Dover and Calais.

That winter remained Monsieur de Arse [7] in Scotland, with the bands of French men. They fortified Inveresk, to stay that the English should not invade [8] Edinburgh and Leith. Some skirmishes there were betwix the one and the other, but no notable thing done, except that the French had almost taken Haddington; the occasion whereof was this.

The French men thinking themselves more than masters in all parts of Scotland, and in Edinburgh principally, thought that they could do no wrong to no Scottishman [9]; for a certain French man

---

[1] The child queen, Mary. She had been sent to Dumbarton in February 1548; she embarked at the end of July or early in August 1548; and she landed in France on 13 August 1548.   [2] *Cf.* the Lady Erskine, *infra*, ii, 77

[3] *settling down, stranding.* The *Cardinal*, of 500 tons burthen, was apparently lost in a storm which disabled the greater part of the French fleet. (See *Inventaire Chronologique*, Abbotsford Club, 93)

[4] Inchcolm   [5] *resolutely*   [6] *Cf. infra*, iii

[7] André de Montalembert, Seigneur d'Essé. In the manuscript (folio 74 *verso*) originally *monsieur de termes; termes* has been scored through and *de arse* added above the line. The forms *Darse, Darsye* and *Dersye*, for d'Essé, occur in *Accnts. Lord High Treasurer*, ix, 206–207, 240, 273.   [8] *prevent the English from invading*

[9] Even the Queen Dowager complained to France of the excesses of the French soldiers. (Teulet, *Papiers d'État*, i, 703; 12 November 1549)

delivered a culverin to George Tod, Scotsman, to be stocked,[1] who bringing it through the street, another French man claimed it, and would have reft it from the said George ; but he resisted, alleging that the French man did wrong. And so began parties to assemble, as well to the Scottishman, as to the French ; so that two of the French men were struck down, and the rest chased from the Cross to Niddry's Wynd head.[2] The Provost [3] being upon the street, apprehended two of the French, and was carrying them to the Tolbooth ; but from Monsieur de Essie's lodging and close issued forth French men, to the number of threescore persons, with drawn swords, and resisted the said Provost. But yet the town assembling repulsed them, till that they came to the Nether Bow ; and there Monsieur la Chapelle,[4] with the whole bands of French men enarmed, rencontered the said Provost, and repulsed him (for the town were without weapons, for the most part) and so made invasion upon all that they met. And first, in the throat of the Bow, were slain David Kirk and David Barbour (being at the Provost's back), and thereafter were slain the said Provost himself, being Laird of Stanehouse, and Captain of the Castle,[5] James Hamilton his son, William Chapman, a godly man, Master William Stewart, William Purves, and a woman, named Elizabeth Stewart ; and thereafter tarried within the town, by force, from five hours till after seven at night, and then retired to the Canongate as to their receptacle and refuge.

The slaughter of the captain of the castle of Edinburgh

The whole town, yea, the Governor and Nobility commoved at the unworthiness of this bold attempt, craved justice upon the malefactors, or else they would take justice of the whole. The Queen, crafty enough, Monsieur de Essie, and Monsieur d'Oysel, laboured for pacification, and did promise, " That unless the French men, by themselves alone, should do such an act as might recompense the wrong that they had done, that then they should not refuse, but that justice should be executed to the rigour." These fair words pleased our fools, and so were the French bands the next night directed to Haddington, to the which they approached a

---

[1] *to be given a new stock*   [2] *from the [Market] Cross to the head of Niddry's Wynd*

[3] See note 5, below

[4] Jacques de la Carbonières de la Chapelle-Biron. (See *Scot. Hist. Rev.*, xxvi, 166, *note* 4)

[5] James Hamilton of Stanehouse. He was not Provost of the burgh (as in Laing's *Knox*, i, 222 *note*), but captain or " Provost " of the castle. Leslie refers to him as " Provist of the Castel " (*History*, Scot. Text Soc., ii, 279). A number of writers have confused James Hamilton of Stanehouse with John, or James Hamilton of Samuelston and Clydesdale, an illegitimate son of the first Earl of Arran. The latter seems to have been Provost of the burgh for short intervals in 1544-45 and 1547.

little after midnight, so secretly, that they were never espied, till that the former were within the basse court, and the whole company in the churchyard, not two pair of boot lengths distant from the town. The soldiers, Englishmen, were all asleep, except the watch, the which was slender, and yet the shout arises, " Bows and bills : Bows and bills " ; which is signification of extreme defence, to avoid the present danger, in all towns of war. The afraid arise : weapons that first come to hand serve for the need. One, amongst many, comes to the east port, where lay two great pieces of ordnance, and where the enemies were known to be, and cried to his fellows that were at the yett [1] making defence, " Ware before " ; and so fires a great piece, and thereafter another, which God so conducted, that after them was no further pursuit made ; for the bullets redounded from the wall of the Friar Kirk,[2] to the wall of Saint Katherine's Chapel, which stood direct foiranent [3] it, and from the wall of the said Chapel to the said Kirk wall again, so oft, that there fell more than an hundred of the French at those two shots only. They shot oft, but the French retired with diligence, and returned to Edinburgh, without harm done, except the destruction of some drinking beer, which lay in the said Chapel and Kirk. And this was satisfaction more than enough, for the slaughter of the said Captain and Provost, and for the slaughter of such as were slain with him. This was the beginning of the French fruits.

Hadding-ton almost surprised by the French

This winter, in the time of Christmas, was the Castle of Home recovered from the English, by the negligence of the Captain named Dudley.[4]

The re-covery of the Castle of Home

This winter also did the Laird of Raith [5] most innocently suffer, and after was forfeited, because that he wrote a bill [6] to his son, John Melville,[7] who then was in England, which was alleged to have been found in the house of Ormiston ; but many suspected the paucks [8] and craft of Ringzen [9] Cockburn (now called Captain Ringzen), to whom the said letter was delivered. But howsoever it was, those cruel beasts, the Bishop of Saint Andrews [10] and Abbot of Dunfermline,[11] ceased not, till that the head of the said noble man was stricken from him ; especially because that he was known to

The death of the Laird of Raith

---

[1] *gate*   [2] The church of the Franciscan Friars   [3] *directly opposite*
[4] Edward Dudley   [5] Sir John Melville of Raith   [6] *letter*
[7] His natural son, John Melville (see Fraser's *Melvilles*, iii, 86–90, 102–108). It is doubtful if the Laird of Raith's communication was as innocent as Knox would have us believe. (See *Scottish Correspondence of Mary of Lorraine*, Scot. Hist. Soc., No. CLXXX)
[8] *cunning*   [9] Ninian   [10] John Hamilton
[11] George Durie

be one that unfeignedly favoured the truth of God's word, and was a great friend to those that were in the Castle of Saint Andrews ; of whose deliverance, and of God's wondrous working with them during the time of their bondage, we must now speak, lest that in suppressing of so notable a work of God, we might justly be accused of ingratitude.

And, first, the principals being put in several houses [1] as before *The entreatment* we have said, great labour was made to make them have a good *of those of* opinion of the Mass. But chiefly travail was taken upon Norman *the Castle of St.* Leslie, the Laird of Grange,[2] and the Laird of Pitmilly,[3] who were *Andrews* in the Castle of Shersburgh,[4] that they would come to the Mass *during their cap-* with the Captain : Who answered, " That the Captain had com- *tivity* mandment to keep their bodies, but he had no power to command their conscience." The Captain replied, " That he had power to command and to compel them to go where he yead." [5] They answered, " That to go to any lawful place with him, they would not refuse ; but to do anything that was against their conscience they would not, neither for him, nor yet for the King." The Captain said, " Will ye not go to the Mass ? " They answered, " No ; and if ye would compel us, yet will we displease you further ; for we will so use ourselves there, that all those that are present shall know that we despise it." These same answers (and somewhat sharper) William Kirkcaldy, Peter Carmichael, and such as were with them in Mont Saint Michael,[6] gave to their Captain ; for they said, " They would not only hear Mass every day, but that they would help to say it, provided that they might stick the priests, or else they would not." Master Henry Balnaves, who was in the Castle of Rouen,[7] was most sharply assaulted of all ; for because he was judged learned (as he was, and is, indeed), therefore learned men were appointed to travail with him, with whom he had many conflicts ; but God so ever assisted him, that they departed confounded, and he, by the power of God's Spirit, remained constant in the truth and profession of the same, without any wavering or declining to idolatry. In the prison he wrote a most profitable Treatise of Justification, and of the works and conversation of a

---

[1] *prisons (supra, 97)*   [2] James Kirkcaldy of Grange
[3] David Monypenny of Pitmilly (Laing's *Knox*, iii, 410)
[4] Cherbourg. They had reached Cherbourg from Rouen on 6 October 1547. (See the contemporary extract from the archives of the Tabellions de Cherbourg, printed in *Scot. Hist. Rev.*, iii, 506)   [5] *went*   [6] Mont St. Michel
[7] At Rouen Knox himself was " lying in irons and sore troubled by corporall infirmitie, in a galley named *Nostre Dame*." (Laing's *Knox*, iii, 8)

justified man [1] : but how it is suppressed, we know not.[2] Those
that were in the galleys were threatened with torments if they would
not give reverence to the Mass (for at certain times the Mass was
said in the galley, or else heard upon the shore, in presence of the
forsars[3]) ; but they could never make the poorest of that company
to give reverence to that idol. Yea, when upon the Saturday at
night, they sang their *Salve Regina*, the whole Scotsmen put on their
caps, their hoods, or such thing as they had to cover their heads ;
and when that others were compelled to kiss a painted brod,[4] (which
they called " Nostre Dame "), they were not pressed after once ;
Merry for this was the chance. Soon after the arrival at Nantes, their great
fact *Salve* was sung, and a glorious painted Lady was brought in to be
kissed and amongst others, was presented to one of the Scottishmen
then chained. He gently said, " Trouble me not ; such an idol is
accursed ; and therefore I will not touch it." The Patron and the
Arguesyn,[5] with two officers, having the chief charge of all such
matters, said, " Thou shalt handle it " ; and so they violently thrust
it to his face, and put it betwix his hands ; who seeing the extremity,
took the idol, and advisedly looking about, he cast it in the river,
and said, " Let our Lady now save herself : she is light enough ;
let her learn to swim." After that was no Scottish man urged with
that idolatry.

These are things that appear to be of no great importance ;
and yet if we do rightly consider, they express the same obedience
that God required of his people Israel, when that they should be
carried to Babylon ; for he gave charge unto them, that when they
Jere. 10 should see the Babylonians worship their gods of gold, silver, metal,
and wood, that they should say, " The gods that have not made the
heaven and the earth shall perish from the heaven, and out of the
earth." That confession gave that whole number, during the time of
their bondage : in the which, would God they had continued in
their freedom ; for then had not Master James Balfour been Official,[6]
neither yet borne a cope for pleasure of the Bishop. But to proceed.
The said Master James and John Knox being in one galley, and being
wondrous familiar with him, would often times ask his judgment,
" If he thought that ever they should be delivered ? " Whose
answer was ever, from the day that they entered in the galleys,

---

[1] This " Treatise on Justification " is printed in Laing's *Knox*, iii, 431–542. See also,
supra, 92, *note* 2
[2] The *Treatise* was first printed in Edinburgh in 1584. (Laing's *Knox*, iii, 4)
[3] *forsaires*, that is, *galley-slaves*   [4] *a painted board*, that is, *a picture*
[5] Lieutenant of the galley (French *Argousin*)   [6] He became Official of Lothian.

" That God would deliver them from that bondage, to his glory, even in this life." And lying betwix Dundee and Saint Andrews, the second time that the galleys returned to Scotland, the said John being *Quævis multa sint justorum mala* so extremely sick that few hoped his life, the said Master James willed him to look to the land, and asked if he knew it ? Who answered, " Yes : I know it well ; for I see the steeple of that place, where God first in public opened my mouth to his glory,[1] and I am fully per- suaded, how weak that ever I now appear, that I shall not depart this life, till that my tongue shall glorify his godly name in the same place." [2] This reported the said Master James in presence of many famous witnesses, many years before that ever the said John set his foot in Scotland, this last time to preach.

William Kirkcaldy, then of Grange, younger, Peter Carmichael, Robert and William Leslie, who were all together in Mont Saint Michael, wrote to the said John, asking his counsel, " If they might with safe conscience break their prison ? " Whose answer was, *John Knox's answer and coun- sel to the captives* " That if without the blood of any shed or spilt by them for their deliverance, they might set themselves at freedom, that they might safely take it : but to shed any man's blood for their freedom, thereto would he never consent." Adding further, " That he was assured that God would deliver them, and the rest of that company, even in the eyes of the world ; but not by such means as we had looked for, that was by the force of friends, or by their other labours." By such means he affirmed they should not be delivered, but that God would so work in the deliverance of them that the praise thereof should redound to his glory only. He willed, therefore, every one to take the occasion that God offered unto them, providing that they committed nothing against God's express commandment, for deliverance of themselves. He was the more earnest in giving his counsel, because that the old Laird of Grange,[3] and others, repugned to their purpose, fearing lest that the escaping of the others should be an occasion of their worse entreatment. Whereunto the said John answered, " That such fear proceeded not from God's Spirit, but only from a blind love of the self ; and therefore, that no good purpose was to be stayed for things that were in the hands and power of God." And added, " That in one instant God delivered all that company in the hands of unfaithful men, but so would he not relieve

---

[1] *Supra*, 84-86

[2] *Infra*, 182. Writing to Mrs. Anna Locke from St. Andrews on 31 December 1559, Knox refers to his torments in the galleys and concludes, " Then was I assuredlie perswaded that I sould not die till I had preached Christ Jesus, even where I now am." (Laing's *Knox*, vi, 104)   [3] James Kirkcaldy of Grange

them. But some would he deliver by one means, and at one time, and others must abide for a season upon his good pleasure." This counsel in the end embraced, upon the King's Even,[1] when French men commonly use to drink liberally, the foresaid four persons, having the help and conducting of a boy of the house, bound all those that were in the Castle, put them in sundry houses, locked the doors upon them, took the keys from the Captain, and departed, without harm done to the person of any, or without touching of any thing that appertained to the King, the Captain, or the house.

The escaping of William Kirkcaldy and his fellows forth of Mont Saint Michael

Great search was made through the whole country for them. But it was God's good pleasure so to conduct them, that they escaped the hands of the faithless, albeit it was with long travail, and great pain and poverty sustained ; for the French boy left them, and took with him the small poise [2] that they had ; and so neither having money, nor knowledge of the country, and further fearing that the boy should describe them (as that in very deed he did), they took purpose to divide themselves, to change their garments, and to go in sundry parts. The two brethren, William and Robert Leslie (who now are become, the said Robert especially, enemies to Christ Jesus and to all virtue) came to Rouen. William Kirkcaldy and Peter Carmichael, in beggar's garment, came to Conquet,[3] and by the space of twelve or thirteen weeks, they travelled as poor mariners, from port to port, till at length they got a French ship and landed in the West, and from thence came to England, where they met before them the said John Knox, who that same winter was delivered, and Alexander Clerk in his company.

The said John was first appointed preacher to Berwick, then to Newcastle ; last he was called to London, and to the south parts of England, where he remained to the death of King Edward the Sixth.[4] When he left England, then he passed to Geneva, and there remained at his private study till that he was called by the English congregation, that then was assembled at Frankfurt [5] to be preacher to them. Which vocation he obeyed (albeit unwillingly) at the commandment of that notable servant of God, JOHN CALVIN. At Frankfurt he remained, till that some of the learned (whose names we suppress), more given to unprofitable ceremonies than to sincerity of religion, began to quarrel with the said John ; and because they despaired to prevail before the Magistrate there, for

---

[1] That is, Epiphany. (See *infra*, ii, 231, *note* 8)   [2] *hoard of money*
[3] Le Conquet, Brittany   [4] 6 July 1553   [5] Frankfurt-am-Main

the establishing of their corruptions, they accused him of treason committed against the Emperor,[1] and against their Sovereign Queen Mary, that, in his ADMONITION TO ENGLAND,[2] he called the one little inferior to Nero, and the other more cruel than Jezebel.[3] The Magistrate perceiving their malice, and fearing that the said John should fall in the hands of his accusators, by one means or by other, gave advertisement secretly to him to depart their city; for they could not save him if he were required by the Emperor, or by the Queen of England in the Emperor's name; and so the said John returned to Geneva, from thence to Dieppe, and thereafter to Scotland, as we shall after hear.

The time and that winter that the galleys remained in Scotland,[4] were delivered Master James Balfour, his two brethren, David and Gilbert, John Auchinleck, John Sibbald, John Gray, William Guthrie, and Steven Bell. The gentlemen that remained in prisons were, by the procurement of the Queen Dowager to the Cardinal of Lorraine and to the King of France, set at liberty in the month of July, Anno 1550; who short thereafter were called to Scotland, their peace proclaimed,[5] and they themselves restored to their lands, in despite of their enemies. And that was done in hatterent [6] of the Duke,[7] because that then France began to thirst to have the regiment of Scotland in their own hands. Howsoever it was, God made the hearts of their enemies to set them at liberty and freedom. There rested [8] a number of common servants yet in the galleys, who were all delivered upon the contract of peace that was made betwix France and England after the taking of Boulogne [9]; and so was the whole company set at liberty, none perishing [10] (no not before the world), except James Melville, who departed from the misery of this life in the Castle of Brest in Bartainzea.[11]

---

[1] Charles V. His son, Philip [II] married Mary Tudor, July 1554.

[2] "A Faythfull Admonition made by Johnne Knox, unto the Professours of God's Truthe in England," written in 1554, is printed in Laing's Knox, iii, 257–330.

[3] See "A Brieff Discours off the Troubles begonne at Franckford" and the supporting documents printed in Laing's Knox, iv, 3–68.   [4] Cf. supra, 104

[5] That is, they were "restored to the King's peace" and were no longer "rebels and at the horn."   [6] hatred

[7] The Earl of Arran, Governor, and now Duke of Châtelherault   [8] remained

[9] Treaty of Boulogne, 1550

[10] This contradicts certain statements made, for example by Leslie and by Dempster, that all those concerned in the assassination of Cardinal Beaton died a violent death— though admittedly Norman Leslie died of his wounds at the Battle of Renti (1554), and Sir William Kirkcaldy of Grange, after his gallant defence of Edinburgh Castle, in the name of Mary Stewart, was publicly hanged at the Market Cross of Edinburgh (1573).

[11] Brest, in Brittany

This we write to let the posterities to come understand how potently God wrought in preserving and delivering of those that had but a small knowledge of his truth, and for the love of the same hazarded all ; that if that either we now in our days, having greater light, or our posterities that shall follow us, shall see a fearful dispersion of such as oppose themselves to impiety, or take upon them to punish the same, otherwise than laws of men will permit, if (we say) we or they shall see such left of men, yea, as it were, despised and punished of God, yet let us not damn the persons that punish vice (and that for just causes) ; nor yet despair, but that the same God that dejects (for causes unknown to us), will raise up again the persons dejected, to his glory and their comfort. And to let the world understand in plain terms what we mean, that *The slaughter of that villain Davy* [1] great abuser of this commonwealth, that poltroon and vile knave Davie, was justly punished, the ninth of March, in the year of God 1565, for abusing of the commonwealth, and for his other villany,[2] which we list not to express, by the counsel and hands of James Douglas, Earl of Morton,[3] Patrick Lord Lindsay,[4] and the Lord Ruthven,[5] with others assisters in their company, who all, for their just act, and most worthy of all praise, are now unworthily left of their brethren and suffer the bitterness of banishment and exile. But this is our hope in the mercies of our God, that this same blind generation, whether it will or not, shall be compelled to see that He will have respect to them that are unjustly pursued ; that He will pardon their former offences ; that He will restore them to the liberty of their country and commonwealth again ; and that He will punish (in despite of man), the head and the tail, that *The rulers of Mary, Anno 1566, and their prediction* now troubles the just and maintains impiety. The head is known : the tail has two branches ; the temporal Lords that maintain her abominations, and her flattering councillors, blasphemous Balfour, now called Clerk of Register,[6] Sinclair, Dean of Restalrig and Bishop of Brechin,[7] blind of one eye in the body, but of both in

---

[1] This marginal rubric (folio 79 *recto*) is in the hand of the text.

[2] David Riccio was assassinated 9 March 1566. At this time the year was reckoned as beginning on 25 March. In view of this comment by Knox, and of his attitude to Riccio's assassination, it is interesting to note that his young widow, Margaret Stewart of Ochiltree, later married one of the murderers, Sir Andrew Ker of Fawdonside, who was said to have held a pistol at Mary's breast at the time of the murder.

[3] James Douglas, fourth Earl of Morton   [4] Patrick, sixth Lord Lindsay of the Byres

[5] William, fourth Lord Ruthven, later first Earl of Gowrie

[6] Sir James Balfour of Pittendreich was appointed Lord Clerk-Register, immediately following the murder of Riccio, in place of Mr. James McGill, one of the conspirators.

[7] John Sinclair, Dean of Restalrig and Bishop of Brechin

and that we do unto them no wrong, although we search our own salvation where it is to be found, considering that they are but dumb dogs, and unsavoury salt, that has altogether lost the season." The Bishops hereat offended, said, "What prating is this? Let his accusation be read."

And then was begun, "False traitor, heretic, thou baptised thy own bairn : Thou said, there is no Purgatory : Thou said, that to pray to Saints and for the dead is idolatry and a vain superstition, &c. What says thou of these things?" He answered, "If I should be bound to answer, I would require an upright and indifferent judge." The Earl of Huntly disdainfully said, "Foolish man, wilt thou desire another judge nor my Lord Duke's Grace, great Governor of Scotland, and my Lords the Bishops, and the clergy here present?" Whereto he answered, "The Bishops can be no judges to me ; for they are open enemies to me and to the doctrine that I profess. And as for my Lord Duke, I cannot tell if he has the knowledge that should be in him that should judge and discern betwix lies and the truth, the inventions of men and the true worshipping of God. I desire God's word (and with that he produced the Bible) to be judge betwix the Bishops and me, and I am content that ye all hear, and if by this book, I shall be convict to have taught, spoken or done in matters of religion, any thing that repugns to God's will, I refuse not to die ; but if I cannot be convict (as I am assured by God's word I shall not) then I in God's name desire your assistance that malicious men execute not upon me unjust tyranny." The Earl of Huntly said, "What a babbling fool is this? Thou shalt get none other judges than those that sit here." Whereunto the said Adam answered, "The good will of God be done. But be ye assured, my Lord, with such measure as ye mete to others, with the same measure it shall be mete to you again. I know that I shall die, but be ye assured that my blood shall be required of your hands."

Alexander, Earl of Glencairn,[1] yet alive, said to the Bishop of Orkney,[2] and others that sat nigh him, "Take you yon, my Lords of the Clergy ; for here I protest, for my part, that I consent not to his death." And so, without fear, prepared the said Adam to answer. And first, to the baptising of his own child, he said, "It was and is as lawful to me, for lack of a true minister, to baptise my own child, as that it was to Abraham to circumcise his son Ishmael and his family. And as for Purgatory, praying to Saints,

Protestation of the Earl of Glencairn

---

[1] Alexander, fourth Earl of Glencairn ; "yet alive" in 1566   [2] Robert Reid

and for the dead, I have oft read (said he) both the New and Old Testaments, but I neither could find mention nor assurance of them ; and therefore I believe that they are but mere inventions of men, devised for covetousness sake." " Well (quod the Bishop) ye hear this, my Lords." " What says thou of the Mass ? " speirs [1] the Earl of Huntly. He answered, " I say, my Lord, as my master Jesus Christ says, ' That which is in greatest estimation before men, is abomination before God.' " Then all cried out, " Heresy ! heresy !" And so was the simple servant of God adjudged to the fire ; which he patiently sustained that same day, at afternoon, upon the Castle-hill. [2]

Lucæ [16]

And so began they again to pollute the land which God had lately plagued ; for yet their iniquity was not come to so full ripeness as that God would that they should be manifested to this whole realm (as this day they are) to be faggots prepared for the ever-lasting fire, and to be men whom neither plagues may correct, nor the light of God's word convert from their darkness and impiety.

The Peace, as said is, contracted, the Queen Dowager passed by sea to France, [3] with galleys that for that purpose were prepared, and took with her divers of the nobility of Scotland, to wit, the Earls Huntly, Glencairn, Marischal, [4] Cassillis, [5] the Lords Maxwell, [6] Fleming, [7] Sir George Douglas, together with all the King's sons, [8] and divers barons and gentlemen of ecclesiastical estate, the Bishop of Galloway, [9] and many others, with promises that they should be richly rewarded for their good service. What they received we cannot tell ; but few made ruse [10] at their returning. The Dowager had to practise somewhat with her brethren, the Duke of Guise, [11] and the Cardinal of Lorraine, [12] the weight whereof the Governor after felt : for shortly after her returning, was the Governor deposed of the government, (justly by God, but most unjustly by men), and she made Regent in the year of God 1554 [13] ; and a crown put upon her head, as seemly a sight (if men had eyes) as to put a saddle upon the back of an unruly cow. And so began she to practise practice

[1] *inquires*

[2] The cost of a scaffold (57s. 4d.) at " the time of the accusation of Wallace " was repaid in August 1550. (*Accounts Lord High Treasurer*, ix, 435)

[3] Probably on 7 September (Hay Fleming, *Mary Queen of Scots*, 199, *note* 7)

[4] William Keith, fourth Earl Marischal   [5] Gilbert, third Earl of Cassillis

[6] Robert, sixth Lord Maxwell   [7] James, fourth Lord Fleming

[8] That is, the illegitimate sons of James V   [9] Andrew Durie

[10] *boast*   [11] Francis, second Duke of Guise

[12] Charles de Guise, Cardinal of Lorraine

[13] Mary of Lorraine, the Queen Dowager, was made Regent of Scotland by Parliament, on the resignation of Arran, 12 April 1554.

upon practice how France might be advanced, her friends made rich, and she brought to immortal glory : for that was her common talk, " So that I may procure the wealth and honour of my friends, and a good fame unto myself, I regard not what God do after with me." And in very deed, in deep dissimulation, to bring her own purpose to effect, she passed the common sort of women, as we will after hear. But yet God, to whose Evangel she declared herself enemy, in the end frustrated her of all her devices.

Thus did light and darkness strive within the realm of Scotland ; the darkness ever before the world suppressing the light, from the death of that notable servant of God, Master Patrick Hamilton, unto the death of Edward the Sixth, that most godly and most *The death* virtuous King that hath been known to have reigned in England, or *and virtues of Edward* elsewhere, these many years bypast, who departed the misery of this *the Sixth* life the 6th of July, Anno, &c., 1553. The death of this Prince was lamented of all the godly within Europe ; for the graces given unto him of God, as well of nature as of erudition and godliness, passed the measure that accustomably useth to be given to other Princes in their greatest perfection, and yet exceeded he not sixteen years of age. What gravity above age, what wisdom passing all expectation of man, and what dexterity in answering in all things proponed, were into that excellent Prince, the Ambassadors of all countries (yea, some that were mortal enemies to him and to his realm, amongst whom the Queen Dowager of Scotland was not the least) could and did testify ; for the said Queen Dowager, returning from France through England, communed with him at length, and gave record when she came to this realm, " That she found more wisdom and solid judgment in young King Edward, than she would have looked for in any three Princes that were then in Europe." His liberality towards the godly and learned, that were in other realms persecuted, was such as Germans, Frenchmen, Italians, Scots, Spaniards, Poles, Greeks, and Hebrews born, can yet give sufficient document [1] ; for how honourably were Martin Bucer,[2] Peter Martyr,[3] Johannes Alasco,[4] Emmanuel,[5] Gualterus,[6] and many others, upon his

---

[1] *evidence* [2] Martin Bucer had fled to England from Strassburg in 1549.

[3] Pietro Martire Vermigli, known as Peter Martyr, had fled to England from Strassburg in 1547. [4] John à Lasco (Laski) had fled to England from Emden in 1548.

[5] Emmanuel Tremellius, the Hebrew scholar, had fled to England from Strassburg in 1547.

[6] Rodolph Gualter had visited England in 1537 (*Original Letters*, Parker Society, 124 and *note*), but I have been unable to trace any flight to England, from persecution, in the reign of Edward VI. Gualter was an honoured pastor in Zurich, and succeeded Bullinger as chief pastor there.

public stipends entertained, their patents can witness, and they themselves during their lives would never have denied.[1]

After the death of this most virtuous Prince, of whom the godless people of England (for the most part) were not worthy, Sathan intended nothing less than the light of Jesus Christ utterly to have been extinguished within the whole Isle of Britain ; for after him was raised up, in God's hot displeasure, that idolatress Jezebel, mischievous Mary, of the Spaniard's blood [2] ; a cruel persecutrix of God's people, as the acts of her unhappy reign can sufficiently witness. And in Scotland, that same time (as we have heard [3]) reigned that crafty practiser, Mary of Lorraine, then named Regent of Scotland ; who, bound to the devotion of her two brethren, the Duke of Guise, and Cardinal of Lorraine, did only abide the opportunity to cut the throats of all those in whom she suspected any knowledge of God to be within the realm of Scotland.[4] And so thought Sathan that his kingdom of darkness was in quietness and rest, as well in the one realm as in the other : but that provident eye of the Eternal our God, who continually watches for preservation of his Church, did so dispose all things that Sathan short after found himself far disappointed of his conclusion taken. For in that cruel persecution, used by that monster, Mary of England, were godly men dispersed in divers nations, of whom it pleased the goodness of our God to send some unto us for our comfort and instruction.

Who first after the death of King Edward began to preach in Scotland

And first came a simple man, WILLIAM HARLAW, whose erudition, although it excel not, yet for his zeal, and diligent plainness in doctrine, is he to this day worthy of praise, and remains a fruitful member within the Church of Scotland. After him came that notable man, JOHN WILLOCK, as one that had some commission to the Queen Regent from the Duchess of Emden.[5] But his principal purpose was to essay what God would work by him in his native country. These two did sometimes, in several companies, assemble the brethren who, by their exhortations, began greatly to be encouraged, and did show that they had an earnest thirst of godliness.

And last came JOHN KNOX, in the end of the harvest, in the year

---

[1] For the work of these reformers in England, see Constantin Hopf, *Martin Bucer and the English Reformation* (Oxford, 1946)

[2] Mary Tudor was the daughter of Henry VIII and Catherine of Aragon.

[3] *Supra,* 116

[4] This statement is too strong ; but Knox finds it impossible to be charitable towards Mary of Lorraine.

[5] John Willock had fled to Emden from England upon the accession of Mary Tudor. He visited Scotland on a trade mission from Anne, Duchess of Friesland. (See *Wodrow Miscellany*, i, 262–263)

of God 1555 ; who first being lodged in the house of that notable man of God, James Syme, began to exhort secretly in that same house ; whereunto repaired the Laird of Dun,[1] David Forrest, and some certain personages of the town, amongst whom was Elizabeth Adamson, then spouse to James Barron, burgess of Edin- *Elizabeth Adamson and her death*[2] burgh, who by reason that she had a troubled conscience, delighted much in the company of the said John, because that he, according to the grace given unto him, opened more fully the fountain of God's mercies than did the common sort of teachers that she had heard before (for she had heard none except Friars), and did with such greediness drink thereof, that at her death she did express the fruit of her hearing, to the great comfort of all those that repaired to her ; for albeit that she suffered most grievous torment in her body, yet out of her mouth was heard nothing but praising of God, except that sometimes she would lament the troubles of those that were troubled by her. Being sometimes demanded by her sisters, " What she thought of that pain which she then suffered in body, in respect of that wherewith sometimes she was troubled in spirit ? " she answered, " A thousand years of this torment, and ten times more joined unto it, is not to be compared to the quarter of an hour that I suffered in my spirit. I thank my God, through Jesus Christ, that has delivered me from that most fearful pain ; and welcome be this, even so long as it pleaseth his godly Majesty to exercise me there-with." A little before her departure, she desired her sisters, and some others that were beside her, to sing a psalm and, amongst others, she appointed the 103 Psalm beginning, " My soul praise thou the Lord always "[3] ; which ended, she said, " At the teaching of this Psalm began my troubled soul first effectually to taste of the mercy of my God, which now to me is more sweet and precious than [if] all the kingdoms of the earth were given to me to possess them a thousand years." The priests urged her with their ceremonies and superstitions ; to whom she answered, " Depart from me, ye ser-geants of Sathan ; for I have refused, and in your own presence do refuse, all your abominations. That which ye call your Sacrament and Christ's body (as ye have deceived us to believe in times past) is nothing but an idol, and has nothing to do with the right institution

[1] John Erskine of Dun

[2] This marginal rubric (folio 83 *recto*) is probably in Knox's own hand.

[3] These words form the commencement of Psalm 146, being one of seven metrical versions contributed by John Hopkins to the collection made by Thomas Sternhold in England and printed in 1551. (See Laing's edition of the *Gude and Godlie Ballates*, Edinburgh, 1868, Preface, xxx, xli–xlii)

of Jesus Christ; and therefore, in God's name, I command you not to trouble me." They departed, alleging, That she raved, and wist not what she said. And she short thereafter slept in the Lord Jesus, to no small comfort of those that saw her blessed departing. This we could not omit of this worthy woman, who gave so notable a confession, before that the great light of God's word did universally shine through this realm.

At the first coming of the said John Knox, he perceiving divers who had a zeal to godliness make small scruple to go to the Mass, or to communicate with the abused sacraments in the papistical manner, began as well in privy conference as in doctrine to show the impiety of the Mass, and how dangerous a thing it was to communicate in any sort with idolatry. Wherewith the conscience of some being effrayed, the matter began to be agitated from man to man, and so was the said John called to supper by the Laird of Dun, for that same purpose, where were convened David Forrest, Master Robert Lockhart, John Willock, and William Maitland of Lethington, younger, a man of good learning, and of sharp wit and reasoning. The question was proponed, and it was answered by the said John, " That no-wise it was lawful to a Christian to present himself to that idol." Nothing was omitted that might make for the temporiser, and yet was every head so fully answered, and especially one whereinto they thought their great defence stood, to wit, " That Paul at the commandment of James, and of the elders of Jerusalem, passed to the temple and feigned himself to pay his vow with others." [1] This, we say, and others, were so fully answered, that William Maitland concluded, saying, " I see perfectly, that our shifts will serve nothing before God, seeing that they stand us in so small stead before man." The answer of John Knox to the fact of Paul, and to the commandment of James, was, " That Paul's fact had nothing to do with their going to the Mass; for to pay vows was sometimes God's commandment, and was never idolatry : but their Mass, from the original, was and remained odious idolatry ; therefore the facts were most unlike. Secondly (said he), I greatly doubt whether either James's commandment or Paul's obedience proceeded from the Holy Ghost. We know their counsel tended to this, That Paul should show himself one that observed the very small points of the law, to the end that he might purchase to him the favours of the Jews, who were offended at him by reason of the bruits that were sparsed, [2] that he taught defection from Moses. Now, while

---

[1] *Acts*, xxi, 18–33   [2] *the rumours that were spread*

he obeyed their counsel, he fell into the most desperate danger that ever he sustained before, whereof it was evident that God approved not that means of reconciliation ; but rather that he plainly declared, ' That evil should not be done that good might come of it.' Evil it was to Paul to confirm those obstinate Jews in their superstition by his example ; worse it was to him to expose himself, and the doctrine which before he had taught, to slander and mockage ; and therefore (concluded the said John), the fact of Paul, and the sequel that thereof followed, appeared rather to fight against them that would go to the Mass, than to give unto them any assurance to follow his example, unless that they would that the like trouble should instantly apprehend them that apprehended him, for obeying worldly-wise counsel." After these and like reasonings, the Mass began to be abhorred of such as before used it for the fashion, and avoiding of slander (as then they termed it).

John Knox, at the request of the Laird of Dun, followed him to his place of Dun,[1] where he remained a month, daily exercised in doctrine, whereunto resorted the principal men of that country. After his returning, his residence was most in Calder,[2] where repaired unto him the Lord Erskine that now is,[3] the Earl of Argyll, then Lord of Lorne,[4] and Lord James, then Prior of Saint Andrews,[5] and now Earl of Moray ; where they heard and so approved his doctrine, that they wished it to have been public. That same winter he taught commonly in Edinburgh ; and after the Yule, by the conduct of the Laird of Barr,[6] and Robert Campbell of Kinzeancleuch, he came to Kyle, and taught in the Barr, in the house of the Carnell,[7] in the Kinzeancleuch, in the town of Ayr, and in the houses of Ochiltree,[8] and Gadgirth,[9] and in some of them ministered the Lord's Table. Before the Pasche, the Earl of Glencairn[10] sent for him to his place of Finlayston[11]; where, after doctrine, he likewise ministered the Lord's Table, whereof besides himself were partakers, his Lady, two of his sons, and certain of his friends. And so returned he to Calder, where divers from Edinburgh, and from the country about, convened, as well for the doctrine as for the right use of the Lord's Table,

---

[1] About midway between Montrose and Brechin   [2] Calder House, Mid-Calder
[3] John, sixth Lord Erskine, later Earl of Mar   [4] Archibald, fifth Earl of Argyll
[5] Lord James Stewart, natural son of James V, Prior of St. Andrews (*in commendam*), Earl of Moray (1563)
[6] John Lockhart of Barr   [7] Hugh Wallace of Carnell
[8] Andrew Stewart, second Lord Ochiltree, whose daughter, Margaret, was subsequently married to Knox as his second wife   [9] James Chalmers of Gadgirth
[10] Alexander, fourth Earl of Glencairn   [11] Finlayston, Renfrewshire

which before they had never practised. From thence he departed the second time to the Laird of Dun ; and teaching then in greater liberty, the gentlemen required that he should minister likewise unto them the Table of the Lord Jesus, whereof were partakers the most part of the gentlemen of the Mearns ; who, God be praised, to this day constantly do remain in the same doctrine which then they professed, to wit, that they refused all society with idolatry, and bound themselves, to the uttermost of their powers, to maintain the true preaching of the Evangel of Jesus Christ, as God should offer unto them preachers and opportunity.

The bruit hereof sparsed (for the Friars from all quarters flocked to the Bishops), the said John Knox was summond to compear in the Kirk of the Black Friars in Edinburgh, the 15 day of May [1556], which day the said John decreed to keep ; and for that purpose John Erskine of Dun, with divers other gentlemen, convened to the town of Edinburgh. But that diet held not ; for whether that the Bishops perceived informality in their own proceedings, or if they feared danger to ensue upon their extremity, it was unknown unto us.[1] But the Saturday before the day appointed, they cast their own summons [2] ; and the said John, the same day of the summons, taught in Edinburgh in a greater audience than ever before he had done in that town : The place was the Bishop of Dunkeld's [3] great lodging, where he continued in doctrine ten days, both before and after noon. The Earl of Glencairn allured the Earl Marischal,[4] who with Harry Drummond [5] (his councillor for that time) heard an exhortation (but it was upon the night), who were so well contented with it, that they both willed the said John to write unto the Queen Regent somewhat that might move her to hear the word of God. He obeyed their desire, and wrote that which after was imprinted, and is called " THE LETTER TO THE QUEEN DOWAGER " [6] ; which was delivered into her own hands

---

[1] In his " Letter to the Queen Dowager " Knox seems to indicate that he thought Mary of Lorraine had intervened on his behalf. (Laing's *Knox*, iv, 77)

[2] That is, they abandoned the charge. But Knox had scarcely returned to Geneva when he was condemned in his absence and burned in effigy. (See *infra*, 124). Hearing of that, he wrote and published his " Appellation . . . from the Cruell and most Injust Sentence pronounced against him " (Laing's *Knox*, iv, 465–520) which was accompanied by a " Letter to the Commonalty of Scotland." (*Ibid.*, iv, 523–538)

[3] Robert Crichton, Bishop of Dunkeld. Dr. Wood tells me that the Bishop's " great lodging " was probably on the north side of the High Street, a little to the west of Halkerston's Wynd—now lost through the cutting of Cockburn Street.

[4] William Keith, fourth Earl Marischal

[5] Possibly Henry Drummond of Riccarton

[6] Probably printed towards the close of 1556 (Laing's *Knox*, iv, 73–84)

by the said Alexander Earl of Glencairn. Which letter, when she had read, within a day or two she delivered it to that proud prelate, Beaton, Bishop of Glasgow,[1] and said in mockage, " Please you, my Lord, to read a pasquil." Which words coming to the ears of the said John, were the occasion that to his Letter he made his additions, as yet may be seen.[2] As concerning the threatenings pronounced against her own person, and the most principal of her friends, let their very flatterers see what hath failed of all that he *Nota* has written. And therefore it were expedient that her daughter, now mischievously reigning, should look to that which hath passed before, lest that in following the counsels of the wicked, she end more miserably than her crafty mother did.

While John Knox was thus occupied in Scotland, letters came unto him from the English Kirk that was assembled in Geneva (which was separated from that superstitious and contentious company that were at Frankfurt), commanding him in God's name, as he that was their chosen pastor, to repair unto them, for their comfort. Upon the which, the said John took his leave from us, almost in every congregation where before he had preached, and exhorted us to prayers, to reading of the Scriptures, and mutual conference, unto such time as God should give unto us greater liberty. And hereupon he sent before him to Dieppe, his mother in law Elizabeth Bowes, and his wife Marjory,[3] with no small dolour to their hearts, and unto many of us. He himself, by procurement and labours of Robert Campbell of Kinzeancleuch, remained behind in Scotland, and passed to the old Earl of Argyll,[4] who then was in the Castle of Campbell,[5] where he taught certain days. The Laird of Glenorchy,[6] (which yet liveth [7]) being one of his auditors, willed the said Earl of Argyll to retain him still ; but he, purposed upon his journey, would not at that time stay for no request, adding, " That if God so blessed those small beginnings,

---

[1] James Beaton, nephew of Cardinal Beaton

[2] Knox's " Letter to the Queen Dowager " was reprinted in 1558, " nowe augmented and explaned by the Author ". (Laing's *Knox*, iv, 423–460.) In this fuller version he comments upon the reception of his Letter by the Queen Regent and likens it to the burning of Jeremiah's prophecy by King Jehoiakim. (*Ibid.*, iv, 456–458)

[3] Knox was betrothed to Marjory Bowes as early as 1553, and in September of that year refers to her as " my Wyfe " (Laing's *Knox*, iii, 376) ; but the formal marriage did not take place until, probably, the spring of 1556 upon the occasion of his "flying visit" to Scotland from the Continent. (Laing's *Knox*, vi, xxxiii–xxxiv ; Hume Brown, *John Knox*, i, 191–193)

[4] Archibald, fourth Earl of Argyll   [5] Castle Campbell, Dollar, Clackmannanshire
[6] Colin Campbell of Glenorchy   [7] In 1566

that they continued in godliness, whensoever they pleased to command him, they should find him obedient " ; but said, " That once he must needs visit that little flock which the wickedness of men had compelled him to leave." And so in the month of July he left this realm, and passed to France, and so to Geneva. Immediately after, the Bishops summoned him, and for non-compearance, burnt him in effigy at the Cross of Edinburgh, in the year of God 1555 [1556] [1]. From the which unjust sentence the said John made his APPELLATION, and caused to print the same, and directed it to the Nobility and Commons of Scotland, as yet may be read. [2]

In the winter that the said John abode in Scotland, [3] appeared a comet, the course whereof was from the south and south-west, to the north and north-east. It was seen the months of November, December, and January. It was called " The fiery besom." Soon after died Christian, King of Denmark. And war rose betwix Scotland and England ; for the Commissioners of both realms, who almost the space of six months entreated upon the conditions of peace, and were upon a near point of conclusion [were disappointed]. The Queen Regent with her Council of the French faction decreed war at Newbattle, [4] without giving any advertisement to the Commissioners for the part of Scotland. [5] Such is the fidelity of Princes, guided by priests, whensoever they seek their own affections to be served.

War against England by the means of the Queen Regent

In the end of that next harvest, was seen upon the Borders of England and Scotland a strange fire, which descended from the heaven, and burnt divers corns in both the realms, but most in England. There was presented to the Queen Regent, by Robert Ormiston, a calf having two heads, whereat she scripped, [6] and said, " It was but a common thing." The war began in the end of the harvest, as said is, and conclusion was taken that Wark [7] should be

A calf with two heads

---

[1] Spottiswoode gives the correct date (*History*, i, 185) ; and Knox gives the correct year in his augmented "Letter to the Queen Dowager" (Laing's *Knox*, iv, 431), and in his " Appellation " (*ibid.*, iv, 467). See also *supra*, 122, *note* 2

[2] Reprinted in Laing's *Knox*, iv, 461-538

[3] The chronology is here confused. The comet, " the fiery besom," is dated by Spottiswoode, 1556 (*History*, i, 185), but by Leslie, correctly, 1558 (*History*, Scot. Text Soc., ii, 387) ; Christian II and Christian III, both died in 1559 ; and the Commissioners of Scotland and England made a joint proclamation of peace at Carlisle in July 1557. (*Cal. Scot. Papers*, i, No. 421)   [4] Newbattle, Midlothian

[5] Leslie says she commanded the Scots Commissioners to return from Carlisle in all haste, which they did on the swiftest horses they could find. (*History*, Scot. Text Soc., ii, 370)   [6] *scoffed*   [7] Wark Castle, on the Tweed, near Coldstream

besieged. The army and ordnance passed forward to Maxwell Heugh.[1] The Queen Regent remained in the Castle of Hume,[2] and thinking that all things were in assurance, Monsieur d'Oysel, then Lieutenant for France, gave charge that the cannons should be transported over the water of Tweed, which was done with expedition (for the French in such facts [3] are expert); but the nobility of Scotland nothing content of such proceedings, after consultation amongst themselves, passed to the palzeon [4] of Monsieur d'Oysel, and in his own face declared, "That in no wise would they invade England," and therefore commanded the ordnance to be retired; and that it was, without further delay.

The fact of the nobility of Scotland at Maxwell Heugh

This put an effray [5] in Monsieur d'Oysel's breath, and kindled such a fire in the Queen Regent's stomach, as was not well slakened till her breath failed. And thus was that enterprise frustrated. But yet war continued, during the which the Evangel of Jesus Christ began wondrously to flourish : for in Edinburgh began publicly to exhort, William Harlaw ; John Douglas, who had (being with the Earl of Argyll) preached in Leith, and sometimes exhorted in Edinburgh ; Paul Methven began publicly to preach in Dundee ; and so did divers others in Angus and the Mearns.

And last, at God's good pleasure, arrived John Willock the second time from Emden [6] ; whose return was so joyful to the brethren, that their zeal and godly courage daily increased. And albeit he contracted a dangerous sickness, yet he ceased not from labours, but taught and exhorted from his bed [7] : some of the nobility (of whom some are fallen back, amongst whom the Lord Seton [8] is chief) with many barons and gentlemen, were his auditors, and by him were godly instructed and wondrously comforted. They kept their conventions, and held councils with such gravity and closeness, that the enemies trembled. The images were stolen away in all parts of the country ; and in Edinburgh was that great idol called Saint Giles, first drowned in the North Loch, [9] [and] after burnt, which raised no small trouble in the town. For the Friars rowping like ravens [10] upon the Bishops, the Bishops ran upon the Queen, who to them was favourable enough, but that she thought it could not stand with her advantage to offend such a multitude

The second return of John Willock to Scotland

Lord Seton an Apostate

The abolishing of images and trouble therefor

---

[1] Maxwellheugh, Kelso   [2] Hume Castle, about five miles north of Kelso
[3] *matters*   [4] *pavilion*   [5] *fright*   [6] *Cf. supra,* 118, *note* 5
[7] *Cf. infra,* 148   [8] George, fifth Lord Seton
[9] The North Loch filled the low ground, where the railway now runs, between the Old Town and the New Town. But see *infra,* 129, *note* 2   [10] *croaking like ravens*

The
preachers
sum-
moned

as then took upon them the defence of the Evangel, and the name of Protestants. And yet consented she to summon the preachers ; whereat the Protestants neither offended, neither yet thereof effrayed, determined to keep the day of summons, as that they did.[1] Which perceived by the prelates and priests, they procured a proclamation

The prac-
tice of
prelates
and what
thereof
ensued

to be publicly made " That all men that were come to the town without commandment of the authority, should with all diligence repair to the Borders, and there remain xv days " : for the Bishop of Galloway,[2] in this manner of rhyme, said to the Queen, " MADAM,

> Becaus thei ar come without ordour,
> I red ye, send thame to the Bordour."

Now so had God provided, that the quarter of the West-land (in to the which were many faithful men) was that same day returned from the Border ; who, understanding the matter to proceed from the malice of the priests, assembled themselves together, and made passage to themselves till they came to the very privy chamber where the Queen Regent and the Bishops were. The Gentlemen began to complain upon their strange entertainment, considering that her Grace had found into them so faithful obedience in all things lawful. While that the Queen began to craft, a zealous and

The bold
words of
James
Chalmers
of Gad-
girth

a bold man, James Chalmers of Gadgirth, said, " Madam, we know that this is the malice and device of those jefwells[3] and of that bastard (meaning the Bishop of Saint Andrews [4]) that stand by you : We avow to God we shall make a day of it. They oppress us and our tenants for feeding of their idle bellies : they trouble our preachers, and would murder them and us. Shall we suffer this any longer ? No, Madam. It shall not be." And therewith every man put on his steel bonnet.[5] There was heard nothing of the Queen's part but " My joys, my hearts, what ails you ? Me means no evil to you nor to your preachers. The Bishops shall do you no wrong. Ye are all my loving subjects. Me knew nothing of this proclamation. The day of your preachers shall be discharged, and me will hear the controversy that is betwix the Bishops and you. They shall do you no wrong. My Lords," said she to the Bishops, " I forbid you either to trouble them or their preachers." And

---

[1] This was in July 1558 (see *Wodrow Miscellany*, i, 53). Pitscottie (*Chronicles*, Scot. Text Soc., ii, 137), and Buchanan (Aikman's edn., ii, 397) say 20 July 1558 ; Calderwood (*History*, i, 344) says 19 July.

[2] Andrew Durie   [3] *low-down rascals*, or *knaves* (see *supra* 34, *note* 4)

[4] John Hamilton was an illegitimate son of James, first Earl of Arran.

[5] Spottiswoode (*History*, i, 187) says " every man made to his weapon."

unto the gentlemen who were wondrously commoved, she turned again, and said, " O my hearts, should ye not love the Lord your God with all your heart [and] with all your mind, and should ye not *O crafty flatterer* love your neighbours as yourselves? " With these and the like fair words, she kept the Bishops from buffets at that time.

And so the day of summons being discharged, began the brethren universally to be further encouraged. But yet could the Bishops in no sort be quiet; for Saint Giles's day[1] approaching, *The command of* they gave charge to the Provost, Bailies, and Council of Edinburgh, *the bishops* either to get again the old Saint Giles, or else upon their expenses to make a new image. The Council answered, " That to them the *The answer of* charge appeared very unjust ; for they understood that God in *Edinburgh* some places had commanded idols and images to be destroyed , *burgh* but where he had commanded images to be set up, they had not read ; and desired the Bishop[2] to find a warrant for his commandment." Whereat the Bishop offended, admonished under pain of cursing ; which they prevented by a formal appellation ; appealing *Edinburgh appealed* from him, as from a partial and corrupt judge, unto the Pope's *pealed* holiness,[3] and so greater things shortly following, that passed in *from the sentence of* oblivion. Yet would not the priests and friars cease to have that *the Bishop* great solemnity and manifest abomination which they accustomably *of Saint Andrews* had upon Saint Giles's day, to wit, they would have that idol borne ; and therefore was all preparation necessary duly made. A marmoset[4] idol was borrowed from the Grey Friars (a silver piece of James Carmichael was laid in pledge) : It was fast fixed with iron nails upon a barrow, called their fertour.[5] There assembled priests, friars, canons, and rotten Papists, with tabors and trumpets, banners and bagpipes, and who was there to lead the ring, but the *Triumph* Queen Regent herself, with all her shavelings, for honour of that *for bearing of* feast. West about goes it, and comes down the High Street, and *stock Giles* down to the Canon Cross.[6] The Queen Regent dined that day in

---

[1] 1 September   [2] The Archbishop of St. Andrews

[3] According to the " Historie of the Estate of Scotland," the Archbishop of St. Andrews had caused his curate to " curse them as black as coal " (*Wodrow Misc.*, i, 54). In the burgh accounts for November 1558, £13 is paid to " David Symer for the commissioun upoun the appellatioun for upputting of the image of Sanct Geill." (R. Adam, *Edinburgh Records : The Burgh Accounts*, i, 278)

[4] *A small grotesque image* (Knox is here using a French term. See the interesting entry in Littré, *Dictionnaire de la Langue Française*, s.v. *marmouset*.)

[5] That is, a portable or stationary shrine, a reliquary (from Med. Latin *feretrum*)

[6] The Canon Cross was the market cross of the Canongate which stood in the roadway slightly to the east of the Canongate Tolbooth. Laing suggests the Girth Cross at the foot of the Canongate (*Knox*, i, 259, *note*), but that was always so named.

Sandy Carpentyne's house, betwix the Bows,[1] and so when the idol returned back again, she left it, and passed in to her dinner. The hearts of the brethren were wondrously inflamed and, seeing such abomination so manifestly maintained, were decreed to be revenged. They were divided in several companies, whereof not one knew of an other. There were some temporisers that day (amongst whom David Forrest, called the General,[2] was one) who, fearing the chance to be done as it fell, laboured to stay the brethren. But that could not be ; for immediately after that the Queen was entered in the lodging, some of those that were of the enterprise drew nigh to the idol, as willing to help to bear him, and getting the fertour upon their shoulders, began to shoulder, thinking that thereby the idol should have fallen. But that was provided and prevented by the iron nails, as we have said ; and so, began one to cry " Down with the idol ; down with it " ; and so without delay it was pulled down. Some brag made the priests' patrons at the first ; but when they saw the feebleness of their god (for one took him by the heels, and dadding[3] his head to the calsay,[4] left Dagon without head or hands, and said, " Fie upon thee, thou young Saint Giles, thy father would have tarried four such ") : this considered (we say), the priests and friars fled faster than they did at Pinkie Cleuch.[5] There might have been seen so sudden a fray as seldom has been seen amongst that sort of men within this realm ; for down goes the crosses, off goes the surplice, round caps corner with the crowns. The Grey Friars gaped, the Black Friars blew, the priests panted and fled ; and happy was he that first got the house ; for such a sudden fray came never amongst the generation of Antichrist within this realm before. By chance there lay upon a stair a merry Englishman, and seeing the discomfiture to be without blood, thought he would add some merriness to the matter, and so cried he over a stair, and said, " Fie upon you, whoresons, why have ye broken order ! Down the street ye passed in array and with great mirth. Why flee ye, villains, now, without order ? Turn and strike every one a stroke for the honour of his god. Fie cowards, fie, ye shall never be judged worthy of your wages again ! " But exhortations were

The down-casting of stock Giles, and dis-comfiture of Baal's Priests

A merry English-man

---

[1] Calderwood (*History*, i, 346) gives his name as Alexander Carpenter. He was made burgess and gild brother " in respect of the Queen's grace writings provided he dwell within this burgh " on 27 November 1556. He was therefore a person in whom the Regent took a particular interest.

[2] *Cf. supra*, 67, *note* 3

[3] *dashing*   [4] *causeway*   [5] See *supra*, 98–101

then unprofitable ; for after that Bell [1] had broken his neck, there was no comfort to his confused army. [2]

The Queen Regent laid up this amongst her other mementos, [3] till that she might have seen the time proper to have revenged it. Search was made for the doers, but none could be deprehended ; for the brethren assembled themselves in such sort, in companies, singing psalms, and praising God, that the proudest of the enemies were astonished.

This tragedy of Saint Giles was so terrible to some Papists, that Durie, sometimes called for his filthiness Abbot Stottikin, and then intitulate Bishop of Galloway, left his rhyming wherewith he was accustomed, and departed this life, even as that he lived : For *The death of the Bishop of Galloway and his last confession* the articles of his belief were, " I Refer : Decarte you : Ha, ha, the four Kings and all made [4] : The Devil go with it : It is but a varlet :

> Fra France we thought to have gottin a Rooby [5] ;
> And yit is he nothing but a cowhuby. [6] "

With such faith and such prayers, departed out of this life that *The vow of that marked beast Durie, Bishop of Galloway* enemy of God, who had vowed and plainly said, " That in despite of God, so long as they that then were prelates lived, should that word (called the Evangel) never be preached within this realm." After him followed that belly-god, Master David Panter, called Bishop of Ross, even with the like documents, [7] except that he departed *The death of David Panter* eating and drinking which, together with the rest that thereupon depends, was the pastime of his life.

The most part of the Lords that were in France at the Queen's marriage, [8] although that they got their congé from the Court, yet they forgot to return to Scotland. For whether it was by an Italian

---

[1] Possibly *Bel*, more probably *Baal*

[2] In a letter of January, 1559, Peter Martyr says the idol was thrown into the common sewer and that the Queen Regent and the nobility took refuge in the Castle. (*Foreign Cal., Elizabeth*, i, No. 212)

[3] things to be remembered   [4] These are references to calling at card games.

[5] A reference to Monsieur de Rubay, Keeper of the Great Seal during the regency of Mary of Lorraine. He was Yves de Rubay, Conseilleur du Roi et Maître de Requestes Ordinaires de son Hostel (see *Pièces Originales*, Bibliothèque Nationale, 2588). He is called Ynes de Rubbay in *Acts Parl. Scot.*, ii, 513a, and Sir Ives de Rubarye in *Cal. Scot. Papers*, i, No. 426.   [6] *cowboy* or *cowherd*, in the sense of a stupid fellow   [7] intimation

[8] James Beaton, Archbishop of Glasgow ; David Panter, Bishop of Ross ; Robert Reid, Bishop of Orkney ; George, Earl of Rothes ; Gilbert, Earl of Cassillis ; Lord James Stewart, Commendator of St. Andrews ; James, Lord Fleming ; George, Lord Seton ; and John Erskine of Dun received a Commission from Parliament (14 December 1557) to negotiate the marriage of Mary Stewart to the dauphin, Francis. (*Acts Parl. Scot.*, ii, 514)

posset, or by French figs, or by the potage of their potinger [1] (he was a French man), there departed from this life the Earl of Cassillis,[2] the Earl of Rothes,[3] Lord Fleming,[4] and the Bishop of Orkney,[5] whose end was even according to his life : For after that he was driven back by a contrarious wind, and forced to land again at *The death of the Bishop of Orkney, Reid* Dieppe, perceiving his sickness to increase, he caused make his bed betwix his two coffers (some said upon them) : such was his god, the gold that therein was inclosed, that he could not depart therefrom, so long as memory would serve him. The Lord James, then Prior of Saint Andrews, had (by all appearance) licked of the same bust [6] that despatched the rest, for thereof to this day his stomach doth testify : but God preserved him for a better purpose. This same Lord James, now Earl of Moray, and the said Bishop, were commonly at debate for matters of religion ; and therefore the said Lord, hearing of the Bishop's disease, came to visit him, and finding him not so well at a point as he thought he should have been, and as the honour of the country required, said unto him, " Fie, my Lord, how lie ye so ? Will ye not go to your chamber, and not lie here in this *Orkney's answer, and his friends whom* [7] common house ? " His answer was, " I am well where I am, my Lord, so long as I can tarry ; for I am near unto my friends (meaning his coffers and the gold therein). But, my Lord (said he), long have ye and I been in pley [8] for Purgatory : I think that I shall know or it be long whether there be such a place or not." While the other did exhort him to call to mind the promises of God, and the virtue of Christ's death, he answered, " Nay, my Lord, let me alone ; for ye and I never agreed in our life, and I think we shall not agree now at my death ; and therefore let me alone." The said Lord James *The Queen Regent's sentence of the death of her Papists. Insignia quidem elogium* [9] departed to his lodging, and the other short after departed this life ; whither, the great day of the Lord will declare.

When the word of the departing of so many patrons of the Papistry, and of the manner of their departing, came unto the Queen Regent, after astonishment and musing, she said, " What shall I say of such men ? They lived as beasts, and as beasts they die : God is not with them, neither with that which they enterprise." [10]

---

[1] *a drink supplied by their apothecary*   [2] Gilbert, third Earl of Cassillis
[3] George, fourth Earl of Rothes   [4] James, fourth Lord Fleming   [5] Robert Reid
[6] *had drunk from the same cup. Bust* or *buist* is a chest or *coffer* (as in " meal buist "), but Knox uses the word in relation to drinking more than once (*cf. infra*, ii, 21).
[7] That is, " and who were his friends "—namely, his coffers and his gold   [8] *debate*
[9] The last three words are scored through.
[10] It is wholly impossible to believe this statement. It accords with neither the character of the Queen Regent nor the character of the men thus maligned.

While these things were in doing in Scotland and France, that *Dean of* *Restalrig,* perfect hypocrite Master John Sinclair, then Dean of Restalrig, and *hypocrite,* now Lord President and Bishop of Brechin, began to preach in his *began to* *preach* Kirk of Restalrig ; and at the beginning held himself so indifferent, that many had opinion of him that he was not far from the kingdom of God. But his hypocrisy could not long be cloaked ; for when he understood that such as feared God began to have a good opinion of him, and that the Friars and others of that sect began to whisper, " That if he took not heed in time to himself, and unto his doctrine, he would be the destruction of the whole estate of the Kirk " ; this by him understood, he appointed a sermon, in the which he promised to give his judgment upon all such heads as then were in controversy in the matters of religion. The bruit hereof made his audience great at the first ; but that day he so handled himself, that after that, no godly man did credit him ; for not only gainsaid he the doctrine of Justification and of Prayer which before he had taught, but also he set up and maintained the Papistry to the uttermost prick [1] ; yea, Holy Water, Pilgrimage, Purgatory, and Pardons were of such virtue in his conceit, that without them he looked not to be saved.

In this meantime, the clergy made a brag that they would dispute. But Master David Panter, which then lived and lay at *Master* *David* Restalrig, dissuaded them therefrom, affirming, " That if ever they *Panter's* disputed, but where themselves were both judge and party, and *counsel to* *his for-* where that fire and sword should obey their decree, that then their *sworn* cause was wrecked for ever ; for their victory stood neither in God *brethren* *the* nor in his word, but in their own wills, and in the things concluded *bishops* by their own Councils (together with sword and fire), whereto (said he), these new start-up fellows will give no place. But they will call you to your account book, and that is to the Bible ; and by it ye will no more be found the men that ye are called, than the Devil will be approved to be God. And therefore, if ye love yourselves, enter never in disputation ; neither yet call ye the matter in question ; but defend your possession, or else all is lost." Caiaphas could not give a better counsel to his companions ; but yet God disappointed both them and him, as after we shall hear.

At this same time,[2] some of the Nobility directed their letters to call JOHN KNOX from Geneva, for their comfort, and for the comfort

---

[1] *point*

[2] For fuller details of these negotiations in 1557, and for the letters that were interchanged, see Laing's *Knox*, iv, 257–286.

of their brethren the preachers, and others that then courageously fought against the enemies of God's truth. The tenor of their letter is this :

Grace, Mercy, and Peace, for Salutation, &c.

The second vocation of John Knox by letters of the Lords

DEARLY BELOVED in the Lord, the faithful that are of your acquaintance in these parts (thanks be unto God) are steadfast in the belief whereinto ye left them, and have a godly thirst and desire, day by day, of your presence again ; which, if the Spirit of God will so move and permit time unto you, we will heartily desire you, in the name of the Lord, that ye will return again in these parts, where ye shall find all faithful that ye left behind you, not only glad to hear your doctrine, but will be ready to jeopard lives and goods in the forward setting of the glory of God, as he will permit time. And albeit the Magistrates in this country be as yet but in the state ye left them, yet, at the making hereof, we have no experience of any more cruelty to be used nor was before ; but rather we have belief that God will augment his flock, because we see daily the Friars, enemies to Christ's Evangel, in less estimation both with the Queen's Grace and the rest of the Nobility of our realm. This in few words is the mind of the faithful, being present, and others absent. The rest of our minds this faithful bearer will show you at length. Thus, fare ye well in the Lord.

Off Stirling, the tenth of March, Anno 1556.[1]

(This is the true copy of the bill, being subscribed by the names underwritten :

Sic subscribitur,
GLENCAIRN
LORNE (now ARGYLL)
ERSKINE[2]
JAMES STEWART)

These letters were delivered to the said John in Geneva, by the hands of James Syme, who now resteth with Christ, and of James Barron, that yet liveth,[3] in the month of May immediately thereafter. Which received, and advised upon, he took consultation as well

[1] That is, 10 March 1557

[2] This can scarcely be John, sixth Lord Erskine, later Earl of Mar, although he had listened to Knox, at Calder House, during the latter's recent visit to Scotland (*supra*, 121). Keith supposes it was Erskine of Dun. (*Affairs of Church and State*, i, 153, *note*)

[3] That is, in 1566

with his own church as with that notable servant of God, John Calvin, and with other godly ministers who, all with one consent, said, " That he could not refuse that vocation, unless he would declare himself rebellious unto his God, and unmerciful to his country." And so he returned answer, with promises to visit them with reasonable expedition, and so soon as he might put order to that dear flock that was committed to his charge. And so, in the end of the next September after, he departed from Geneva, and came to Dieppe, where there met him contrary letters ; as by this answer thereto we may understand :

> *The Spirit of wisdom, constancy, and strength be multiplied with you, by the favour of God our Father, and by the grace of our Lord Jesus Christ.*

ACCORDING to my promise, Right Honourable, I came to Dieppe, the xxiiij of October, of full mind, by the good will of God, with the first ships to have visited you. But because two letters, not very pleasing to the flesh, were there presented unto me, I was compelled to stay for a time. The one was directed to myself from a faithful brother, which made mention, that new consultation was appointed for final conclusion of the matter before purposed, and willed me therefore to abide in these parts, till the determination of the same. The other letter was directed from a gentleman to a friend, with charge to advertise me, that he had communed with all those that seemed most frack [1] and fervent in the matter, and that into none did he find such boldness and constancy as was requisite for such an enterprise ; but that some did (as he writeth) repent that ever any such thing was moved ; some were partly ashamed ; and others were able to deny that ever they did consent to any such purpose, if any trial or question should be taken thereof, &c. Which letters, when I had considered, I partly was confounded, and partly was pierced with anguish and sorrow. Confounded I was, that I had so far travailed in the matter, moving the same to the most godly and the most learned that this day we know to live in Europe, to the effect that I might have their judgments and grave counsels, for assurance as well of your consciences as of mine, in all enterprises : And then that nothing should succeed so long consultation cannot but redound either to your shame or mine ; for either it shall appear that I was marvellous vain, being so solicitous where no necessity required, or else that such as were my movers thereto lacked the

---

[1] *resolute*

ripeness of judgment in their first vocation. To some it may appear a small and light matter that I have cast off, and as it were abandoned, as well my particular care, as my public office and charge, leaving my house and poor family destitute of all head, save God only, and committing that small (but to Christ dearly beloved) flock, over the which I was appointed one of the ministers, to the charge of another. This, I say, to worldly men may appear a small matter, but to me it was, and yet is such, that more worldly substance than I will express could not have caused me willingly behold the eyes of so many grave men weep at once for my cause, as that I did, in taking of my last good night from them. To whom, if it please God that I return, and question be demanded : What was the impediment of my purposed journey ? judge you what I shall answer. The cause of my dolour and sorrow (God is witness) is for nothing pertaining either to my corporal contentment or worldly displeasure ; but it is for the grievous plagues and punishments of God, which assuredly shall apprehend not only you, but every inhabitant of that miserable realm and isle, except that the power of God, by the liberty of his Evangel, deliver you from bondage. I mean not only that perpetual fire and torment, prepared for the Devil, and for such as denying Christ Jesus and his known verity

The matri-monial crown was granted, and French bands were arrived

do follow the sons of wickedness to perdition (which most is to be feared), but also that thraldom and misery shall apprehend your own bodies, your children, subjects, and posterity, whom ye have betrayed (in conscience, I can except none that bear the name of Nobility), and presently do fight to betray them and your realm to the slavery of strangers. The war begun (although I acknowledge it to be the work of God) shall be your destruction, unless that, betime, remedy be provided. God open your eyes, that ye may espy and consider your own miserable estate. My words shall appear to some sharp and indiscreetly spoken ; but as charity ought to interpret all things to the best, so ought wise men to understand that a true friend cannot be a flatterer, especially when the questions of salvation, both of body and soul, are moved ; and that not of one nor of two, but as it were of a whole realm and nation. What are the sobs, and what is the affection [1] of my troubled heart, God shall one day declare. But this will I add to my former rigour and severity, to wit, if any persuade you, for fear of dangers that may follow, to faint in your former purpose, be he never esteemed so wise and friendly, let him be judged of you both foolish and your mortal

---

[1] *emotion*

enemy : foolish, for because he understandeth nothing of God's approved wisdom ; and enemy unto you, because he laboureth to separate you from God's favour ; provoking his vengeance and grievous plagues against you, because he would that ye should prefer your worldly rest to God's praise and glory, and the friendship of the wicked to the salvation of your brethren. I am not ignorant *Let the Papists themselves judge of what spirit those sentences could proceed* that fearful troubles shall ensue your enterprise (as in my former letters I did signify unto you) ; but O joyful and comfortable are those troubles and adversities, which man sustaineth for accomplishment of God's will, revealed by his word ! For how terrible that ever they appear to the judgment of the natural man, yet are they never able to devour nor utterly to consume the sufferers : For the invisible and invincible power of God sustaineth and preserveth, according to his promise, all such as with simplicity do obey him. The subtle craft of Pharaoh, many years joined with his bloody cruelty, was not able to destroy the male children of Israel ; neither were the waters of the Red Sea, much less the rage of Pharaoh, able to confound Moses and the company which he conducted ; and that because the one had God's promise that they should multiply, and the other had his commandment to enter into such dangers. I would your Wisdoms should consider that our God remaineth one, and is immutable ; and that the Church of Christ Jesus hath the same promise of protection and defence that Israel had of multiplication ; and further, that no less cause have ye to enter in your former enterprise, than Moses had to go to the presence of Pharaoh ; for your subjects, yea, your brethren are oppressed, their bodies and souls held in bondage : and God speaketh to your consciences *The duty of the nobility* (unless ye be dead with the blind world) that you ought to hazard your own lives (be it against kings or emperors) for their deliverance. For only for that cause are ye called Princes of the people, and ye receive of your brethren honour, tribute, and homage at God's commandment ; not by reason of your birth and progeny (as the most part of men falsely do suppose), but by reason of your office and duty, which is to vindicate and deliver your subjects and brethren from all violence and oppression, to the uttermost of your power. Advise diligently, I beseech you, with the points of that letter, which I directed to the whole Nobility, and let every man *That letter lost by negligence and troubles* apply the matter and case to himself ; for your conscience shall one day be compelled to acknowledge that the reformation of religion, and of public enormities, doth appertain to more than to the Clergy, or chief rulers called Kings. The mighty Spirit of the Lord Jesus

God grant that our nobility would yet understand rule and guide your counsels, to his glory, your eternal comfort, and to the consolation of your brethren. Amen.

From Dieppe, the 27 of October 1557.[1]

These letters received and read, together with others directed to the whole Nobility, and some particular gentlemen, as to the Lairds of Dun [2] and Pittarrow,[3] new consultation was had what was best to be done : and in the end it was concluded, that they would follow forward their purpose once intended, and would commit themselves, and whatsoever God had given unto them, in his hands, rather than they would suffer idolatry so manifestly to reign, and the subjects of that realm so to be defrauded, as long they had been, of the only food of their souls, the true preaching of Christ's Evangel. And that every one should be the more assured of other, a common Band [4] was made, and by some subscribed, the tenor whereof follows :

" We, perceiving how Sathan in his members, the Antichrists of our time, cruelly doth rage, seeking to downthring and to destroy the Evangel of Christ, and his Congregation, ought, according to our bounden duty, to strive in our Master's cause, even unto the death, being certain of the victory in Him : The which our duty being well considered, We do promise before the Majesty of God, and his congregation, that we (by his grace) shall with all diligence continually apply our whole power, substance, and our very lives, to maintain, set forward, and establish the most blessed word of God and his Congregation ; and shall labour at our possibility to have faithful Ministers purely and truly to minister Christ's Evangel and Sacraments to his people. We shall maintain them, nourish them, and defend them, the whole Congregation of Christ, and every member thereof, at our whole powers and waring [5] of our lives, against Sathan, and all wicked power that does intend tyranny or trouble against the foresaid Congregation. Unto the which holy word and Congregation we do join us, and also does forsake and renounce the congregation of Sathan, with all the superstitions, abomination and idolatry thereof : And moreover, shall declare ourselves manifestly enemies thereto, by this our faithful promise

---

[1] This letter was followed by a second, dated 1 December 1557 (Laing's *Knox*, iv, 261–275), and by a third, dated 17 December 1557 (*ibid.*, iv, 276–286).

[2] John Erskine of Dun   [3] Sir John Wishart of Pittarrow

[4] A facsimile of this " Common Band " is given in *National Manuscripts of Scotland*, iii, No. XL.   [5] *expense*

before God, testified to his Congregation, by our subscriptions at these presents—at Edinburgh, the third day of December, the year of God 1557 : God called to witness

Sic subscribitur,
A. EARL OF ARGYLL [1]
GLENCAIRN [2]
MORTON [3]
ARCHIBALD LORD OF LORNE [4]
JOHN ERSKINE OF DUN
Et cetera

Before a little that this Band was subscribed by the forewritten and many others, letters were directed again to John Knox from the said Lords, together with their letters to Master CALVIN, craving of him, that by his authority he would command the said John once again to visit them. These letters were delivered by the hands of Master John Gray, in the month of November, the year of God 1558, who at that same time passed to Rome for expedition of the bulls of Ross to Master Henry Sinclair.[5]

The third vocation of John Knox by the Lords and Church of Scotland

Immediately after the subscription of this foresaid Band, the Lords and Barons professing Christ Jesus convened frequently in council ; in the which these heads [6] were concluded :

First, It is thought expedient, devised, and ordained, that in all parishes of this realm the Common Prayers [7] be read weekly on Sunday, and other festival days, publicly in the parish kirks, with the Lessons of the New and Old Testament, conform to the order of the Book of Common Prayers : And if the curates [8] of the

---

[1] Archibald, fourth Earl of Argyll   [2] Alexander, fourth Earl of Glencairn

[3] James, fourth Earl of Morton

[4] Succeeded his father as Archibald, fifth Earl of Argyll, in 1558

[5] That is, to secure the expedition of the Bulls of provision to the See of Ross in favour of Henry Sinclair. David Panter had died in (probably) October 1558 ; but Sinclair was not provided to the See until 2 June 1561. (Dowden, *Bishops*, 228)

[6] These " heads " may be compared with the later " articles " drawn up by the lords and barons, presented by them to the Queen Regent, and sent by her to the Provincial Council of 1558/9. (Patrick, *Statutes of the Scottish Church*, 156–160 ; Robertson, *Concilia Scotiae*, ii, 146–151, 299–301)

[7] The Book of Common Prayer of Edward VI (*cf.* the letter to Percy from Kirkcaldy of Grange in Laing's *Knox*, vi, 34), though this English book was heartily disliked by Knox and was soon replaced by the Book of Common Order (*ibid.*, vi, 12, 227–333), which was approved by the General Assembly in 1562. (*Booke of the Universall Kirk*, i, 30 ; Laing's *Knox*, iv, 155–156)

[8] That is, *curati*, those entrusted with the ' cure of souls ' in the parishes ; *not* assistants, as in the modern usage

parishes be qualified, to cause them to read the same ; and if they be not, or if they refuse, that the most qualified in the parish use and read the same.

Secondly, It is thought necessary, that doctrine, preaching, and interpretation of Scriptures be had and used privately in quiet houses, without great conventions of the people thereto,[1] while afterward that God move the Prince to grant public preaching by faithful and true ministers.

These two heads concerning the religion, and some others concerning the policy,[2] being concluded, the old Earl of Argyll[3] took the maintenance of John Douglas, caused him preach publicly in his house, and reformed many things according to his counsel. The same boldness took divers others, as well within towns as to landward ; which did not a little trouble the Bishops and Queen Regent, as by the letter and credit, committed to Sir David Hamilton from the Bishop of Saint Andrews to the said Earl of Argyll, may be clearly understood.[4]

.   .   .   .

THE answer received [from the Earl of Argyll], the Bishop and his complices found themselves somewhat disappointed [5] ; for the Bishops looked for nothing less than [6] for such answers from the EARL OF ARGYLL ; and therefore they made them for their extreme defence ; that is, to corrupt and by budds [7] to stir up the Queen Regent in our contrary ; as in the Second Book we shall more plainly hear.

Short after this, God called to his mercy the said Earl of Argyll from the miseries of this life ; whereof the Bishops were glad ; for they thought that their great enemy was taken out of the way : but God disappointed them. For as the said Earl departed most constant in the true faith of Jesus Christ, with a plain renunciation of all impiety, superstition, and idolatry ; so left he it to his son in his testament, " That he should study to set forward the public and true preaching of the Evangel of Jesus Christ, and to suppress all superstition and idolatry, to the uttermost of his power." In

---

[1] *Cf. infra*, 147–148   [2] That is, political affairs, *the polity*   [3] Archibald, fourth Earl
[4] Here Knox inserts the letter from John Hamilton, Archbishop of St. Andrews, to Archibald, fourth Earl of Argyll ; followed by the Memorandum to his messenger, Sir David Hamilton ; followed by the Earl of Argyll's replies. These are printed below in Appendix IV.
[5] See *infra*, Appendix IV   [6] That is, they *least expected*   [7] *bribes*

which point small fault can be found with him to this day. God 10 *May*, *Anno* 1566
be merciful to his other offences.[1] Amen.

[2] THE Bishops continued in their Provincial Council even unto
that day that JOHN KNOX arrived in Scotland.[3] And that they might
give some show to the people that they minded Reformation, they
sparsed abroad a rumour thereof and set forth somewhat in print,
which of the people was called " The Two-penny Faith." [4]

1. Amongst their Acts, there was much ado for caps, shaven
crowns, tippets, long gowns, and such other trifles.

2. *Item*, That none should enjoy office or benefice ecclesiastical,
except a priest.

3. *Item*, That no kirk-man should nourish his own bairns in *Brotherly*
his own company : but that everyone should hold the children of *charity*
others.

4. That none should put his own son in his own benefice.

5. That if any were found in open adultery, for the first fault,
he should lose the third of his benefice ; for the second crime, the
half ; and for the third, the whole benefice.[5]

---

[1] Knox is here alluding to the favour which Archibald, fifth Earl of Argyll, enjoyed
at this time (10 May 1566) from Mary. The marginal note is in the hand of the text.

[2] In the manuscript (folio 101 *recto*) a marginal note, in Knox's own hand, and scored
through, reads, " Heir intak in the beggars summonds warning the freres.' This " Beggars'
Summonds " occurs at the end of the manuscript (folio 388) as a single leaf. It is printed
below as Appendix V.

[3] Knox gives the date of his arrival in Scotland as 2 May 1559 (*infra*, 161), but the
statutes of the Provincial Council of 1559 say that it began on 1 March 1559 and concluded on 10 April 1559 (Robertson, *Concilia Scotiae*, ii, 151, 176). On the other hand
the anonymous writer of the " Historie of the Estate of Scotland " says that " the Councell
being well sett downe in the Blackfryers of Edenburgh, one ranne in and assured them
that John Knox [who] wes new come out of France, had beine all that night in the towne :
at the which newes, they being all astonished, leaving the Councell, rose suddenly from
the board where they satt, and passing forth to the yeard, altogether abashed, fearing
the thing which came suddenly to pass." (*Wodrow Miscellany*, i, 56–57.) To reconcile
the apparent discrepancy, M'Crie suggests that although the Acts of the Council were
concluded on 10 April, the Council was still sitting (*Life of John Knox*, 1831, i, 256 *note*),

[4] Printed in facsimile in *Bannatyne Club Miscellany*, iii, 313–320. A facsimile is also
appended by A. F. Mitchell to his facsimile edition of Archbishop Hamilton's *Catechism*
(Edinburgh 1882). In the manuscript (folio 101 *recto*) originally *three-penny*, but *three* has
been scored through and *twa* added above the line, possibly in Knox's own hand.

[5] Lord Hailes has heavily criticized Knox's account of the statutes passed at this
Council (*Annals of Scotland*, 1819, iii, 260–262) ; and certainly no statute similar to that
given by Knox as No. 5 (and also reported in slightly different terms by Pitscottie in
Chronicles, Scot. Text Soc., ii, 141) can be traced. For the statutes passed in Council,
and referred to by Knox, reference can be made to Patrick, *Statutes of the Scottish Church*,
Scot. Hist. Soc., 163–167.

But herefrom appealed the Bishop of Moray,[1] and other Prelates, saying, "That they would abide at the canon law."[2]   And so might they well enough do, so long as they remained interpreters, dispensators, makers, and disannullers of that law.   But let the same law have the true interpretation and just execution, and the Devil shall as soon be proved a true and obedient servant unto God, as any of that sort shall be proved a Bishop, or yet to have any just authority within the Church of Christ Jesus.   But we return to our History.

The persecution was decreed, as well by the Queen Regent as by the prelates ; but there rested a point, which the Queen Regent and France had not at that time obtained ; to wit, That the Crown Matrimonial should be granted to Francis, husband to our Sovereign, and so should France and Scotland be but one kingdom, the subjects of both realms to have equal liberty, Scotsmen in France, and Frenchmen in Scotland.   The glister of the profit that was judged hereof to have ensued to Scottishmen, at the first sight blinded many men's eyes.   But a small wind caused that mist suddenly to vanish away ; for the greatest offices and benefices within the realm were appointed for Frenchmen.   Monsieur Ruby kept the Great Seal.   Villemore[3] was Comptroller.   Melrose and Kelso should have been a Commend to the poor Cardinal of Lorraine.[4]   The freedoms of Scottish merchants were restrained in Rouen, and they compelled to pay toll and taxations other than their ancient liberties did bear.   To bring this head to pass, to wit, to get the matrimonial crown, the Queen Regent left no point of the compass unsailed.   With the bishops *The Queen Regent, her practices* and priests, she practised on this manner : " Ye may clearly see, that I can not do what I would within this realm ; for these heretics and confederates of England are so banded together, that they stop all good order.   But will ye be favourable unto me in this suit of the matrimonial crown to be granted to my daughter's husband, then shall ye see how I shall handle these heretics and traitors ere it be long."   And in very deed, in these her promises, she meant no deceit in that behalf.   Unto the Protestants she said, " I am not unmindful how oft ye have suited me for reformation in religion

---

[1] Patrick Hepburn

[2] Pitscottie has a like story (*Chronicles*, Scot. Text Soc., ii, 141)

[3] Bartholomew de Villemore

[4] See Pollen, *Papal Negotiations with Mary Queen of Scots*, Scot. Hist. Soc., 28, 30, 40, 42.   The monasteries of Melrose and Kelso had been held *in commendam* by James Stewart, a natural son of James V, but he had died in 1558.   The " poor " Cardinal of Lorraine, however, was disappointed of this intended gift.

and gladly would I consent thereunto ; but ye see the power and craft of the Bishop of Saint Andrews, together with the power of the Duke,[1] and of the kirk-men, ever to be bent against me in all my proceedings : So that I may do nothing, unless the full authority of this realm be devolved to the King of France, which cannot be but by donation of the crown matrimonial ; which thing if ye will bring to pass, then devise ye what ye please in matters of religion, and they shall be granted."

With this commission and credit was Lord James,[2] then Prior of Saint Andrews, directed to the Earl of Argyll, with more other promises than we list to rehearse. By such dissimulation to those that were simple and true of heart, inflamed she them to be more fervent in her petition, than herself appeared to be. And so at the Parliament, held at Edinburgh in the month of October, the year of God 1558,[3] it was clearly voted, no man reclaiming (except the Duke for his interest [4]) ; and yet for it there was no better law produced, except that there was a solemn Mass appointed for that purpose in the Pontifical.

This head obtained, whereat France and she principally shot, what faith she kept unto the Protestants, in this our Second Book shall be declared : In the beginning whereof, we must more amply rehearse some things that in this our First are summarily touched.[5]

[1] James, second Earl of Arran, Duke of Châtelherault

[2] Lord James Stewart, a natural son of James V, later Earl of Moray and Regent of Scotland

[3] 29 November 1558 (*Acts Parl. Scot.*, ii, 505–506)

[4] Châtelherault entered a protest that should Mary die without issue his right of succession should not be prejudiced by the coronation of Francis. (*Ibid.*, ii, 507–508)

[5] *touched upon*

THE END OF THE FIRST BOOK

Τέλος

THE SECOND BOOK
OF THE HISTORY OF THINGS DONE IN SCOTLAND
IN THE REFORMATION OF RELIGION
BEGINNING IN THE YEAR OF GOD
1558

OUR purpose was to have made the beginning of our History from the things that were done from the year of God 1558, to the Reformation of Religion, which of God's mercy we once possessed ; and yet, in doctrine and in the right use of administration of Sacraments, do possess. But because divers of the godly (as before is said) earnestly required that such persons as God raised up in the midst of darkness, to oppose themselves to the same, should not be omitted ; we obeyed their request, and have made a short rehearsal of all such matters as concern Religion, from the death of that notable servant of God, Master Patrick Hamilton, unto the foresaid year, when that it pleased God to look upon us more mercifully than we deserved, and to give unto us greater boldness and better (albeit not without hazard and trouble) success in all our enterprises than we looked for, as the true narration this Second Book shall of witness : The Preface whereof follows —

PREFATIO

LEST that Sathan by our long silence shall take occasion to blaspheme, and to slander us THE PROTESTANTS OF THE REALM OF SCOTLAND, as that our fact tended rather to sedition and rebellion, than to reformation of manners and abuses in religion, we have thought expedient, so truly and briefly as we can, to commit to writing the causes moving us (us, we say, a great part of the Nobility and Barons of the realm), to take the sword of just defence against those that most unjustly seek our destruction. And in this our Confession we shall faithfully declare what moved us to put our hands to the Reformation of Religion ; how we have proceeded in the same ; what we have asked, and what presently we require of the sacred authority [1] ; to the end that, our cause being known, as well our enemies as our brethren in all realms may understand how falsely we are accused of tumult and rebellion, and how unjustly we are persecuted by France and by their faction : as also, that our brethren, natural Scotsmen, of what religion so ever they be, may have occasion to examine themselves, if they may with safe conscience oppose themselves to us, who seek nothing but Christ Jesus his glorious Evangel to be preached, his holy Sacraments to be truly ministered, superstition, tyranny, and idolatry to be suppressed in this realm ; and, finally, the liberty of this our native country to remain free from the bondage and tyranny of strangers.

[1] Here, and elsewhere, " sacred authority " seems to mean the authority safeguarded by religion ; that is, the authority of the State.

WHILE that the QUEEN REGENT practised with the Prelates how that Christ Jesus his blessed Evangel might utterly be suppressed within Scotland, God so blessed the labours of his weak servants, that no small part of the Barons of this Realm began to abhor the tyranny of the Bishops : God did so open their eyes by the light of his word, that they could clearly discern betwix idolatry and the true honouring of God. Yea, men almost universally began to doubt *The first doubt* whether that they might (God not offended) give their bodily presence to the Mass, or yet offer their children to the papistical baptism. To the which doubts, when the most godly and the most learned in Europe had answered, both by word and writ, affirming, " That neither of both we might do, without the extreme peril of our souls," we began to be more troubled ; for then also began men of estimation, and that bare rule among us, to examine themselves concerning their duties, as well towards Reformation of Religion, as towards the just defence of their brethren most cruelly persecuted. And so began divers questions to be moved, to wit, " If that with safe conscience such as were judges, lords, and *The second* rulers of the people, might serve the upper powers in maintaining idolatry, in persecuting their brethren, and in suppressing Christ's truth ? " Or, " Whether they, to whom God in some cases had committed the sword of justice, might suffer the blood of their brethren to be shed in their presence, without any declaration that such tyranny displeased them ? " By the plain Scriptures it was found, " That a lively faith required a plain confession, when *Scriptures answering the doubts* Christ's truth is oppugned ; that not only are they guilty that do evil, but also they that assent to evil." And plain it is, that they assent to evil who, seeing iniquity openly committed, by their silence seem to justify and allow whatsoever is done.

These things being resolved, and sufficiently proved by evident Scriptures of God, we began every man to look more diligently to his salvation : for the idolatry and tyranny of the clergy (called the Churchmen) was and is so manifest, that whosoever doth deny it, declares himself ignorant of God, and enemy to Christ Jesus. We therefore, with humble confession of our former offences, with fasting and supplication unto God, began to seek some remedy in so present a danger. And first, it was concluded, " That the

Brethren in every town at certain times should assemble together, to Common Prayers, to exercise and reading of the Scriptures,[1] till it should please God to give the sermon of exhortation to some, for comfort and instruction of the rest."

And this our weak beginning God did so bless, that within few months the hearts of many were so strengthened, that we sought to have the face of a Church amongst us, and open crimes to be punished without respect of person. And for that purpose, by common election, were elders appointed, to whom the whole brethren promised obedience : for at that time we had no public *This was* ministers of the word ; only did certain zealous men (amongst *called the* whom were the Laird of Dun,[2] David Forrest, Master Robert *Privy* *Kirk* Lockhart, Master Robert Hamilton, William Harlaw, and others) exhort their brethren, according to the gifts and graces granted unto them. But short after did God stir up his servant, Paul Methven (his later fall [3] ought not to deface the work of God in him), who, in boldness of spirit began openly to preach Christ Jesus in Dundee, in divers parts of Angus, and in Fife ; and so did God work with him, that many began openly to abrenounce their old idolatry and to submit themselves to Christ Jesus, and unto his blessed ordinances ; insomuch that the town of Dundee began to erect the face of a public church reformed, in the which the Word was openly preached, and Christ's Sacraments truly ministered.

In this meantime did God send to us our dear brother, John Willock,[4] a man godly, learned, and grave who, after his short abode at Dundee, repaired to Edinburgh, and there (notwithstanding his long and dangerous sickness) did so encourage the brethren by godly exhortations, that we began to deliberate upon some public Reformation ; for the corruption in religion was such, that with safe conscience we could no longer sustain it. Yet because we would attempt nothing without the knowledge of the sacred authority,[5] with one consent, after the deliberation of many days, it was concluded, that by our public and common Supplication, we should attempt the favours, support and assistance of the Queen, then Regent, to a godly Reformation. And for that purpose, after we had drawn our orison and petitions, as followeth, we appointed *The laird* from amongst us a man whose age and years deserved reverence, *of Calder* whose honesty and worship might have craved audience of any *Elder* magistrate on earth, and whose faithful service to the authority

---

[1] *Cf. supra*, 138   [2] John Erskine of Dun
[3] See *infra*, ii, 66–67   [4] *Cf. supra*, 125   [5] See the note, *supra*, 146

at all times had been such, that in him could fall no suspicion of unlawful disobedience. This orator was that ancient and honourable father, Sir James Sandilands of Calder, knight, to whom we gave commission and power in all our names then present, before the Queen Regent thus to speak :

THE FIRST ORATION, AND PETITION, OF THE PROTESTANTS OF SCOTLAND TO THE QUEEN REGENT

ALBEIT we have of long time contained ourselves in that modesty (Most Noble Princess), that neither the exile of body, tynsall [1] of goods, nor perishing of this mortal life, were able to convene us to ask at your Grace reformation and redress of those wrongs, and of that sore grief, patiently borne of us in bodies and minds of so long time ; yet are we now, of very conscience and by the fear of our God, compelled to crave at your Grace's feet, remedy against the most unjust tyranny used against your Grace's most obedient subjects, by those that be called the Estate Ecclesiastical. Your Grace cannot be ignorant what controversy hath been, and yet is, con- *Controversy in religion* cerning the true religion, and right worshipping of God, and how the Clergy (as they will be termed) usurp to themselves such empire above the consciences of men, that whatsoever they command must be obeyed, and whatsoever they forbid must be avoided, without further respect had to God's pleasure, commandment, or will, revealed to us in his most holy word ; or else there abideth *The tyranny of the clergy* nothing for us but faggot, fire, and sword ; by the which many of our brethren, most cruelly and most unjustly, have been stricken of late years within this realm : which now we find to trouble and wound our consciences ; for we acknowledge it to have been our bound duty before God, either to have defended our brethren from those cruel murderers (seeing we are part of that power which God hath established in this realm), or else to have given open testification of our faith with them, which now we offer ourselves to do, lest that by our continual silence we shall seem to justify their cruel tyranny ; which doth not only displease us, but your Grace's wisdom most prudently doth foresee, that for the quieting of this intestine dissension, a public reformation, as well in the religion as in the temporal government, were most necessary ; and to the performance thereof, most gravely and most godly (as we are informed), ye have exhorted as well the Clergy as the Nobility,

---

[1] *loss*

to employ their study, diligence, and care. We therefore of conscience dare no longer dissemble in so weighty a matter, which concerneth the glory of God and our salvation : Neither now dare we withdraw our presence, nor conceal our petitions, lest that the adversaries hereafter shall object to us, that place was granted to Reformation, and yet no man suited [1] for the same ; and so shall our silence be prejudicial unto us in time to come. And therefore we, knowing no other order placed in this realm, but your Grace, in your grave Council, set to amend, as well the disorder ecclesiastical, as the defaults in the temporal regiment, [2] most humbly prostrate ourselves before your feet, asking your justice, and your gracious help, against them that falsely traduce and accuse us, as that we were heretics and schismatics, under that colour seeking our destruction ; for that we seek the amendment of their corrupted lives, and Christ's religion to be restored to the original purity.

The petition Further, we crave of your Grace, with open and patent ears, to hear these our subsequent requests ; and to the joy and satisfaction of our troubled consciences, mercifully to grant the same, unless by God's plain word any be able to prove that justly they ought to be denied.

THE FIRST PETITION

First, humbly we ask, that as we have, of the laws of this realm, after long debate, obtained to read the holy books of the Old and New Testaments in our common tongue, [3] as spiritual food to our souls, so from henceforth it may be lawful that we may convene, publicly or privately, to our Common Prayers, in our vulgar tongue ; to the end that we may increase and grow in knowledge, and be induced, in fervent and oft prayer, to commend to God the holy church universal, the Queen our Sovereign, her honourable and gracious husband, [4] the ability [5] of their succession, your Grace Regent, the Nobility, and whole Estate of this Realm.

Secondly, if it shall happen in our said conventions any hard place of Scripture to be read, of the which no profit ariseth to the conveners, that it shall be lawful to any qualified persons in knowledge, being present, to interpret and open up the said hard places, to God's glory and to the profit of the auditure. And if any think that this liberty should be occasion of confusion, debate, or heresy ;

---

[1] *petitioned*   [2] *government*   [3] *Cf. supra*, 44–45
[4] Mary was married to the Dauphin, Francis, on 24 April 1558.
[5] *ability*, in the sense of effectiveness

we are content that it be provided, that the said interpretation shall underly the judgment of the most godly and most learned within the realm at this time.

Thirdly, That the holy sacrament of baptism may be used in the vulgar tongue ; that the godfathers and witnesses may not only understand the points of the league and contract made betwix God and the infant, but also that the Church then assembled, more gravely may be informed and instructed of their duties, which at all times they owe to God, according to that promise made unto Him, when they were received in his household by the lavachre [1] of spiritual regeneration.

Fourthly, We desire, that the holy sacrament of the Lord's Supper, or of his most blessed body and blood, may likewise be ministered unto us in the vulgar tongue ; and in both kinds, [2] according to the plain institution of our Saviour Christ Jesus.

And last, We most humbly require, that the wicked, slanderous, and detestable life of prelates, and of the State Ecclesiastical, may be so reformed, that the people by them have not occasion (as of many days they have had) to contemn their ministry, and the preaching whereof they should be messengers. And if they suspect that we, rather envying their honours, or coveting their riches and possessions, than zealously desiring their amendment and salvation, do travail and labour for this reformation ; we are content not only that the rules and precepts of the New Testament, but also *The offer* the writings of the ancient Fathers, and the godly approved laws of Justinian the Emperor, decide the controversy betwix us and them : And if it shall be found, that either malevolently or ignorantly we ask more than these three forenamed have required, and continually do require of able and true ministers in Christ's Church, we refuse not correction, as your Grace, with right judgment, shall think meet. But and if all the forenamed shall damn that which we damn, and approve that which we require, then we most earnestly beseech your Grace, that notwithstanding the long consuetude which they have had to live as they list, that they be compelled either to desist from ecclesiastical administration, or to discharge their duties as becometh true ministers : So that the grave and godly face of the primitive Church reduced, [3] ignorance may be expelled, true doctrine

---

[1] *purification* or *baptism* (from Med. Lat. *lavacrum*)

[2] That is, that they should be allowed to partake of both the bread and the wine— the Roman Church having long denied the cup to laymen

[3] *brought back*, that is, restored

and good manners may once again appear in the Church of this Realm. These things we, as most obedient subjects, require of your Grace, in the name of the Eternal God, and of his Son, Christ Jesus ; in presence of whose throne judicial, ye and all others that here in earth bear authority, shall give accounts of your temporal regiment. The Spirit of the Lord Jesus move your Grace's heart to justice and equity. Amen.[1]

These our Petitions being proponed, the Estate Ecclesiastical *The practice of Sathan* began to storm, and to devise all manner of lies to deface the equity of our cause. They bragged as that they would have public disputation, which also we most earnestly required, two things being provided : the former, that the plain and written Scriptures of God *Disputation with conditions* should decide all controversy ; secondly, that our brethren, of whom some were then exiled, and by them unjustly damned, might have free access to the said disputation, and safe conduct to return to their dwelling places, notwithstanding any process which before had been led against them in matters concerning religion. But these being by them utterly denied (for no judge would they admit but *The offer of the Papists* themselves, their Councils,[2] and Canon Law), they and their faction began to draw certain Articles of reconciliation, promising unto us, if we would admit the Mass to stand in her former reverence and estimation, grant Purgatory after this life, confess Prayer to Saints and for the dead, and suffer them to enjoy their accustomed rents, possession, and honour, that then they would grant unto us to pray and baptize in the vulgar tongue, so that it were done secretly, and not in the open assembly. But the grossness of these Articles was such, that with one voice we refused them ; and constantly craved justice of the Queen Regent, and a reasonable answer of our former Petitions. The Queen, then Regent, a woman crafty, dissimulate, *The grant of the Queen Regent* and false, thinking to make her profit of both parties, gave to us permission to use ourselves godly according to our desires, provided that we should not make public assemblies in Edinburgh nor Leith ; and did promise her assistance to our Preachers, until some uniform order might be established by a Parliament. To them (we mean to the Clergy) she quietly gave signification of her mind, promising that how soon any opportunity should serve, she should so put order in their matters, that after they should not be troubled ; for some say they gave her a large purse—40,000 pounds, says the Chronicle

---

[1] This petition is dated 20 November 1558 in *Foreign Calendar, Elizabeth,* i, No. 15 ; but no authority for the date is given.

[2] That is, the decrees of General Councils of the Church

gathered by the Laird of Earlshall.[1] We, nothing suspecting her doubleness nor falsehood, departed, fully contented with her answer ; and did use ourselves so quietly, that for her pleasure we put silence to John Douglas, who publicly would have preached in the town of Leith ; for in all things we sought the contentment of her mind, so far forth as God should not be offended against us for obeying her in things unlawful.

Shortly after [2] these things, that cruel tyrant and unmerciful hypocrite, falsely called Bishop of Saint Andrews, apprehended that blessed martyr of Christ Jesus WALTER MYLN ; a man of decrepit *The apprehension of Walter Myln* age, whom most cruelly and most unjustly he put to death by fire in Saint Andrews, the twenty eighth day of April, the year of God 1558 : Which thing did so highly offend the hearts of all godly, that immediately after his death began a new fervency amongst the whole people ; yea, even in the town of Saint Andrews began the people plainly to damn such unjust cruelty ; and in testification that they would his death should abide in recent memory, there was cast together a great heap of stones in the place where he was burned. The Bishop and priests thereat offended, caused once or twice to remove the same, with denunciation of cursing [3] if any man should there lay any stone. But in vain was that wind blown ; for still was the heap made, till that priests and Papists did steal away by night the stones to big [4] their walls, and to other their private uses.

We suspecting nothing that the Queen Regent was consenting to the forenamed murder, most humbly did complain of such unjust cruelty, requiring that justice in such cases should be ministered with greater indifference.[5] She, as a woman born to dissemble and *The hypocrisy of the Queen Regent* deceive, began with us to lament the cruelty of the Bishop, excusing herself as innocent in that cause ; for that the sentence was given without her knowledge, because the man sometimes had been a priest ; therefore the Bishop's Officer [6] did proceed upon him

---

[1] This Chronicle is not known to be extant. Lindsay of Pitscottie acknowledges his indebtedness to that " nobill man of recent memorie schir william bruce of erleshall knicht quha hes wrettin werrie justlie all the deidis sen flowdane feild." (*Chronicles*, Scot. Text Soc., i, 2). According to the tombstone in Leuchars Church, Sir William Bruce of Earlshall died 28 January 1584 [1585], aged 98. (*Roy. Comm. on Ancient and Historical Monuments, Fife*, 191). According to the " Historie of the Estate of Scotland," the sum to be paid to the Queen Regent " wes within 15,000 lib." (*Wodrow Misc.*, i, 55–56)

[2] Definitely *before*. Myln was martyred in April 1558 and the Petition was presented towards the end of 1558. The false chronology affects the argument.

[3] *excommunication*   [4] *build*   [5] *impartiality*   [6] *Official*

without any commission of the civil authority *ex officio*, as they term it.

We yet nothing suspecting her falsehood, required some order to be taken against such enormities, which she promised as oft before. But because short after there was a Parliament to be held, for certain affairs pertaining rather to the Queen's profit particular nor to the commodity of the commonwealth, we thought good to expone our matter unto the whole Parliament, and by them to seek some redress. We therefore, with one consent, did offer to the Queen and Parliament a Letter in this tenor : [1]

THE FORM OF THE LETTER GIVEN IN PARLIAMENT

" UNTO your Grace, and unto you, Right Honourable Lords of this present Parliament, humbly meanes [2] and shows your Grace's faithful and obedient subjects : That where we are daily molested, slandered, and injured by wicked and ignorant persons, place-holders of the ministers of the Church, who most untruly cease not to infame [3] us as heretics, and under that name they most cruelly have persecuted divers of our brethren ; and further intend to execute their malice against us, unless by some godly order their fury and rage be bridled and stayed ; and yet in us they are able to prove no crime worthy of punishment, unless that to read the Holy Scriptures in our assemblies, to invocate the name of God in public prayers, with all sobriety to interpret and open the places of Scripture that be read, to the further edification of the brethren assembled, and truly according to Christ Jesus his holy institution to minister the Sacraments, be crimes worthy of punishment. Other crimes (we say) in us they are not able to convict. And to the premises are we compelled ; for that the said place-holders discharge no part of their duties rightly unto us, neither yet to the people subject to us ; and therefore, unless we should declare ourselves altogether unmindful of our own salvation, we are compelled, of very conscience, to seek how that we and our brethren may be delivered from the thraldom of Sathan. For now it hath pleased God to open our eyes, that manifestly we see, that without extreme danger of our souls,

---

[1] No record of this Letter or of the Protestation has been preserved in the proceedings of the Parliament of 29 November and 5 December 1558 which, in view of the reference to the Crown Matrimonial (*infra*, 156), must have been the Parliament to which it was presented. (*Cf.* Calderwood, *History*, i, 416–417.) Knox adds that insertion " in the Common Register " was denied (*infra*, 158).

[2] *complains*   [3] *defame*

we may in no wise communicate with the damnable idolatry, and *Protesta-*
intolerable abuses of the Papistical Church ; and therefore most *tion*
humbly require we of your Grace, and of you Right Honourable
Lords, Barons, and Burgesses assembled in this present Parliament,
prudently to weigh, and as it becometh just judges, to grant these
our most just and reasonable Petitions :

" First, Seeing that the controversy in religion, which long hath
continued betwix the Protestants of Almany,[1] Helvetia,[2] and other
provinces, and the Papistical Church, is not yet decided by a lawful
and General Council ; and seeing that our consciences are likewise
touched with the fear of God, as was theirs in the beginning of their
controversy, we most humbly desire, that all such Acts of Parliament,
as in the time of darkness gave power to the Church men to execute
their tyranny against us, by reason that we to them were delated as
heretics, may be suspended and abrogated, till a General Council
lawfully assembled have decided all controversies in religion.

" And lest that this mutation should seem to set all men at liberty
to live as them list, We Secondly require, That it be enacted by this
present Parliament, that the prelates and their officers [3] be removed
from place of judgment ; only granting unto them, nevertheless, the
place of accusers in the presence of a temporal judge, before whom
the Church men accusers shall be bound to call any by them
accused of heresy, to whom also they shall be bound to deliver
an authentic copy of all depositions, accusations, and process led
against the person accused ; the judge likewise delivering the same
to the party accused, assigning unto him a competent term to answer
to the same, after he hath taken sufficient caution *de judicio sisti.*[4]

" Thirdly, We require, that all lawful defences be granted to the
persons accused ; as if they be able to prove, that the witnesses be
persons unable by law to testify against them, that then their accusations and depositions be null according to justice.

" *Item,* That place be granted to the party accused, to explain
and interpret his own mind and meaning ; which confession we
require be inserted in public Acts, and be preferred to the depositions
of any witnesses, seeing that none ought to suffer for religion that is
not found obstinate in his damnable opinion.

" Last, We require, that our brethren be not damned for heretics,
unless, by the manifest word of God, they be convicted to have erred

---

[1] Germany [2] Switzerland [3] *officials*
[4] That is, after he has found a sufficient pledge that he will appear to stand his trial

from that faith which the Holy Spirit witnesseth to be necessary to salvation ; and if so they be, we refuse not but that they be punished according to justice, unless by wholesome admonition they can be reduced to a better mind.

" These things require we to be considered of you, who occupy the place of the Eternal God (who is God of order and truth), even in such sort as ye will answer in the presence of his throne judicial : Requiring further, that favourably ye will have respect to the tenderness of our consciences, and to the trouble which appeareth to follow in this commonwealth, if the tyranny of the prelates, and of their adherents, be not bridled by God and just laws. God move your hearts deeply to consider your own duties and our present troubles."

These our Petitions did we first present to the Queen Regent, because that we were determined to enterprise nothing without her knowledge, most humbly requiring her favourable assistance in our just action. She spared not amiable looks, and good words in abundance ; but always she kept our Bill [1] close in her pocket. When we required secretly of her Grace, that our Petitions should be proponed to the whole Assembly, she answered, " That she thought not that expedient ; for then would the whole Ecclesiastical Estate be contrary to her proceedings, which at that time were great " ; for the matrimonial crown was asked, and in that Parliament granted. " But (said she), how soon order can be taken with these things, which now may be hindered by the Kirk men, ye shall know my good mind ; and, in the meantime, whatsoever I may grant unto you, shall gladly be granted."

We yet nothing suspecting her faslehood, were content to give place for a time to her pleasure, and pretended reason ; and yet thought we expedient somewhat to protest before the dissolution of the Parliament ; for our Petitions were manifestly known to the whole Assembly, as also how, for the Queen's pleasure, we ceased to pursue the uttermost.[2] Our Protestation was formed in manner following :

FORM OF THE PROTESTATION MADE IN PARLIAMENT [3]

" IT is not unknown to this honourable Parliament, what controversy is now lately risen betwix those that will be called the Prelates and rulers of the Church, and a great number of us, the

---

[1] A *bill* is a paper or *writing* of any kind   [2] *to push the matter to the extreme*
[3] Dated 5 December 1558 in *Foreign Calendar, Elizabeth*, i, No. 66 ; but the authority for the date is not given.

Nobility and commonalty of this Realm, for the true worshipping of God, for the duty of Ministers, for the right administration of Christ Jesus his holy Sacraments ; how that we have complained by our public supplications to the Queen Regent, that our consciences are burdened with unprofitable ceremonies, and are compelled to adhere to idolatry ; that such as take upon them the office Ecclesiastical, discharge no part thereof, as becometh true ministers to do ; and finally, that we and our brethren are most unjustly oppressed by their usurped authority. And also we suppose it is a thing sufficiently known, that we were of mind at this present Parliament to seek redress of such enormities ; but, considering that the troubles of the time do not suffer such reformation as we, by God's plain word, do require, we are enforced to delay that which most earnestly we desire ; and yet, lest that our silence should give occasion to our adversaries to think that we repent our former enterprise, we cannot cease to protest for remedy against that most unjust tyranny, which we heretofore most patiently have sustained.

" And, First, We protest, that seeing we cannot obtain a just reformation, according to God's word, that it be lawful to us to use ourselves in matters of religion and conscience, as we must answer unto God, unto such time as our adversaries be able to prove themselves the true ministers of Christ's Church, and to purge themselves of such crimes as we have already laid to their charge, offering ourselves to prove the same whensoever the sacred Authority [1] please to give us audience.

" Secondly, We protest, that neither we, nor yet any other that godly list to join with us in the true faith, which is grounded upon the invincible word of God, shall incur any danger in life or lands, or other political pains, for not observing such Acts as heretofore have passed in favour of our adversaries, neither yet for violating of such rites as man without God's commandment or word hath commanded.

" We, Thirdly, protest, that if any tumult or uproar shall arise amongst the members of this realm for the diversity of religion, and if it shall chance that abuses be violently reformed, that the crime thereof be not imputed to us, who most humbly do now seek all things to be reformed by an order : But rather whatsoever incon- *Let the* venience shall happen to follow for lack of order taken, that may be *Papists* imputed to those that do refuse the same. *observe*

" And last, We protest, that these our requests, proceeding from

---

[1] See the note, *supra*, 146

conscience, do tend to none other end, but to the reformation of abuses in religion only : Most humbly beseeching the sacred Authority to take us, faithful and obedient subjects, in protection against our adversaries ; and to show unto us such indifference [1] in our most just Petitions, as it becometh God's Lieutenants to do to those that in his name do call for defence against cruel oppressors and bloodthirsty tyrants."

These our Protestations publicly read, we desired them to have been inserted in the common Register ; but that by labours of enemies was denied unto us.[2] None the less, the Queen Regent said, " Me will remember what is protested ; and me shall put good order after this to all things that now be in controversy." And thus, after that she by craft had obtained her purpose, we departed in good esperance of her favours, praising God in our hearts that she was so well inclined towards godliness. The good opinion that we had of her sincerity, caused us not only to spend our goods and hazard our bodies at her pleasure, but also, by our public letters *Letters to John Calvin* written to that excellent servant of God JOHN CALVIN, we did praise and commend her for excellent knowledge in God's word and goodwill towards the advancement of his glory ; requiring of him, that by his grave counsel and godly exhortation he would animate her Grace constantly to follow that which godly she had begun. We did further sharply rebuke, both by word and writing, all such as appeared to suspect in her any venom of hypocrisy, or that were contrary to that opinion which we had conceived of her godly mind. But how far we were deceived in our opinion, and abused by her craft, did suddenly appear : for how soon that all things pertaining to the commodity of France were granted by us, and that peace was contracted betwix King Philip and France, and England and us,[3] she began to spew forth and disclose the latent venom of her double heart. Then began she to frown, and to look frowardly to all such as she knew did favour the Evangel of Jesus Christ. She commanded her household to use all abominations at Pasche [4] ; and she herself, to give example to others, did com-

---

[1] *impartiality*   [2] *Cf. supra*, 154, *note* 1
[3] Although the Treaty of Cateau Cambrésis was not concluded until 2 April 1559 (*Foreign Calendar, Elizabeth*, i, Nos. 475–483), the preliminary treaty was concluded on 12 March preceding. (*Foreign Calendar, Elizabeth*, i, No. 405.) In 1559 Easter fell on 26 March. This largely answers M'Crie's difficulties in *Life of John Knox*, 1831, i, 444–446.
[4] *Easter*

municate with that idol in open audience : She controlled her household, and would know where that every one received their Sacrament.   And it is supposed that after that day the Devil took more
violent and strong possession in her than he had before ; for, from
that day forward, she appeared altogether altered, insomuch that
her countenance and facts[1] did declare the venom of her heart.
For incontinent she caused our preachers to be summoned ; for
whom, when we made intercession, beseeching her Grace not to
molest them in their ministry, unless any man were able to convict
them of false doctrine, she could not bridle her tongue from open
blasphemy, but proudly she said, " In despite of you and of your *She had*
ministers both, they shall be banished out of Scotland, albeit they *got her
lesson*
preached as truly as ever did Saint Paul."   Which proud and *from the
Cardinal*
blasphemous answer did greatly astonish us ; and yet ceased we
not most humbly to seek her favours, and by great diligence at
last obtained that the summons at that time was delayed.   For to
her were sent Alexander Earl of Glencairn, and Sir Hew Campbell
of Loudoun knight, Sheriff of Ayr, to reason with her, and to crave
some performance of her manifold promises.   To whom she answered, *Queen*
" It became not subjects to burden their Princes with promises, *Regent's
answer*
further than it pleaseth them to keep the same."   Both those Noble
men faithfully and boldly discharged their duty, and plainly forewarned her of the inconvenients that were to follow ; wherewith
she somewhat astonished said, " She would advise." [2]

In this meantime did the town of Perth, called Saint Johnston, *Saint
Johnston*
embrace the truth, which did provoke her to a new fury ; in which *embraced*
she willed the Lord Ruthven, Provost of that town, to suppress all *the evangel*
such religion there.   To the which, when he answered, " That he
could make their bodies to come to her Grace, and to prostrate *Lord ·
Ruthven's*
themselves before her, till that she were fully satiate of their blood, *answer*
but to cause them do against their conscience, he could not promise" :
She in fury did answer, " That he was too malapert to give her such
answer," affirming, " that both he and they should repent it."
She solicited Master James Haliburton, Provost of Dundee, to
apprehend Paul Methven who, fearing God, gave secret advertisement to the man to avoid the town for a time.   She sent forth such
as she thought most able to persuade at Pasche, to cause Montrose,

---

[1] *deeds* (Fr. *faits*)

[2] In the margin of the manuscript (folio 111 *recto*) there is a note in Knox's own hand,
' luk quhether it be best to tak in heir the beggars warning or in the place befoir
appointed '.   (*Cf. supra*, 139, *note* 2)

Dundee, Saint Johnston, and other such places as had received the Evangel, to communicate with the idol of the Mass; but they could profit nothing [1]: the hearts of many were bent to follow the truth revealed, and did abhor superstition and idolatry. Whereat she more highly commoved, did summon again all the preachers to compear at Stirling, the tenth day of May, the year of God 1559. Which understood by us, we, with all humble obedience, sought the means how she might be appeased, and our preachers not molested: but when we could nothing prevail, it was concluded by the whole brethren, that the gentlemen of every country should accompany their preachers to the day and place appointed. Whereto all men *The first* were most willing; and for that purpose the town of Dundee, the *Assembly* gentlemen of Angus and Mearns, passed forward with their preachers *at Saint* *Johnston* to Saint Johnston, without armour, as peaceable men, minding only to give confession with their preachers. And lest that such a multitude should have given fear to the Queen Regent, the Laird of Dun, a zealous, prudent, and godly man, passed before to the Queen, then being in Stirling, to declare to her, that the cause of their convocation was only to give confession with their preachers, and to assist them in their just defence.[2] She understanding the fervency of the people, began to craft with him, soliciting him to stay the multitude, and the preachers also, with promise that she would take some better order. He, a man most gentle of nature, and *The* most addicted to please her in all things not repugnant to God, wrote *Laird of* *Dun* to those that then were assembled at Saint Johnston, to stay, and *stayed the* not to come forward; showing what promise and esperance he *congrega-* *tion and* had of the Queen's Grace's favours. At the reading of his letters, *the* some did smell the craft and deceit, and persuaded to pass forward, *preachers* unto the time a discharge of the former summons should be had, alleging, that otherwise their process of horning, or rebellion, should be executed against the preachers; and so should not only they, but also all such as did accompany them, be involved in a crime. Others did reason, that the Queen's promises were not to be suspected, neither yet the Laird of Dun's request to be

---

[1] *achieve nothing.* Probably the Queen Regent was more concerned about the danger of civil disturbances. Whitsun fell on 14 May, and that was the day threatened in the Beggars' Summonds. (*Infra,* Appendix V; and see the interesting entries in *Extracts from the Council Registers of Aberdeen,* Spalding Club, i, 315, 316, 321, 322–323)

[2] See "Ane letter wrettin to the Queinis Grace and Regent be the Professouris of Christis Ewangell in the Realme of Scotland," 6 May 1559. (*Spalding Club Miscellany,* iv, 88–92)

contemned ; and so did the whole multitude with their preachers stay.[1]

In this meantime that the Preachers were summoned, to wit, the second of May 1559, arrived JOHN KNOX from France,[2] who lodging two nights only in Edinburgh, hearing the day appointed to his brethren, repaired to Dundee, where he earnestly required them, " That he might be permitted to assist his brethren, and to give confession of his faith with them " : which granted unto him [he] departed unto Saint Johnston with them ; where he began to exhort, according to the grace of God granted unto him. The Queen, perceiving that the preachers did not compear, began to utter her malice ; and notwithstanding any request made in the contrary, gave commandment to put them to the horn,[3] inhibiting all men under pain of their rebellion [4] to assist, comfort, receive, or maintain them in any sort. Which extremity perceived by the said Laird of Dun, he prudently withdrew himself (for otherwise by all appearance he had not escaped imprisonment) ; for the Master of Maxwell,[5] a man zealous and stout in God's cause (as then appeared), under the cloak of another small crime was that same day committed to ward, because he did boldly affirm, " That to the uttermost of his power he would assist the preachers and the congregation ; notwithstanding any sentence which unjustly was, or should be, pronounced against them." The Laird of Dun, coming to Saint Johnston, expounded the case even as it was, and did conceal nothing of the Queen's craft and falsehood.[6] Which understood, the multitude was so inflamed, that neither could the exhortation of the preacher, nor the commandment of the magistrate, stay them from destroying of the places of idolatry.[7]

The manner whereof ·was this : The preachers before had declared how odious was idolatry in God's presence ; what com-

---

[1] This account should be compared with that in Spottiswoode (*History*, i, 271), and with the account given by Knox in his letter of 23 June 1559 to Mrs. Anna Locke. (Laing's *Knox*, vi, 21–27)

[2] In answer to the invitation which had reached him in November 1558 (*supra*, 137)

[3] That is, to declare them rebels and " at the horn." Paul Methven, John Christison, William Harlaw, and John Willock were denounced rebels and put to the horn on 10 May 1559. (Pitcairn, *Criminal Trials*, i, 406*–407*)

[4] Under pain of being themselves denounced as rebels and put to the horn

[5] John Maxwell, second son of Robert, fifth Lord Maxwell, and presumptive heir to his nephew John, eighth Lord Maxwell. (*Scots Peerage*, vi, 481–482)

[6] The " Historie of the Estate of Scotland " does not support Knox's charge of " craft and falsehood." (*Wodrow Miscellany*, i, 56–57) ; the two accounts are compared by Andrew Lang in *John Knox and the Reformation*, Appendix A.   [7] *Cf. supra*, xcviii

mandment he had given for the destruction of the monuments thereof; what idolatry and what abomination was in the Mass. It chanced, that the next day, which was the eleventh of May,[1] after that the Preachers were exiled,[2] that after the sermon which was vehement against idolatry,[3] that a priest in contempt would go to the Mass; and to declare his malapert presumption he would open up a glorious tabernacle which stood upon the high altar.[4] There stood beside certain godly men and, amongst others, a young boy who cried with a loud voice, " This is intolerable, that when God by his Word hath plainly damned idolatry, we shall stand and see it used in despite." The priest hereat offended, gave the child a great blow; who in anger took up a stone, and casting at the priest, did hit the tabernacle and broke down an image; and immediately the whole multitude that were about cast stones, and put hands to the said tabernacle and to all other monuments of idolatry; which they despatched before the tenth man in the town was

The down-casting of the friaries in Saint Johnston

advertised (for the most part were gone to dinner). Which, noised abroad, the whole multitude convened, not of the gentlemen, neither of them that were earnest professors, but of the rascal multitude[5] who, finding nothing to do in that Church, did run without deliberation to the Grey and Black Friars; and notwithstanding that they had within them very strong guards kept for their defence, yet were their gates incontinent burst open. The first invasion was upon the idolatry; and thereafter the common people began to seek some spoil; and in very deed the Grey Friars was a place so well provided, that unless honest men had seen the same, we would have feared to have reported what provision they had. Their sheets, blankets, beds, and coverlets were such as no Earl in Scotland hath the better : their napery was fine. They were but eight persons

---

[1] Thursday

[2] They had been exiled on Wednesday the 10th. (*Supra*, 161, *note* 3)

[3] The preacher was Knox. (Aikman's *Buchanan*, ii, 404 ; Spottiswoode's *History*, i, 271–272). The church was the parish church of the Holy Cross of St. John the Baptist.

[4] This is an interesting statement. Usually the " tabernacle," containing the monstrance or eucharist in which the reserved host was kept, was canopied and was suspended above the high altar.

[5] " The *rascal multitude* " here in the *History*; but in his letter to Mrs. Anna Locke, of 23 June 1559, Knox writes that " *the brethren* . . . put to their hands to reformation in Saint Johnston, where the places of idolatry of Grey and Black Friars, and of Charterhouse monks, were made equal with the ground." (Laing's *Knox*, vi, 23.) The " Historie of the Estate of Scotland " also seems to imply that the " purging " of the monuments of idolatry was the work of " the brethren." (*Wodrow Miscellany*, i, 57)

in convent, and yet had viij puncheons of salt beef (consider the *Their* time of the year, the eleventh day of May [1]) wine, beer, and ale, *provision* besides store of victuals effeiring [2] thereto.   The like abundance was not in the Black Friars ; and yet there was more than became men professing poverty.   The spoil was permitted to the poor (for so had the preachers before threatened all men, that for covetousness sake none should put their hand to such a reformation), that no honest man was enriched thereby the value of a groat.   Their consciences so moved them, that they suffered those hypocrites to take away what they could, of that which was in their places.   The Prior of Charterhouse was permitted to take away with him even so much gold and silver as he was well able to carry.   So were men's consciences before beaten with the word, that they had no respect to their own particular profit, but only to abolish idolatry, the places and monuments thereof : in which they were so busy, and so laborious, that within two days, these three great places, monuments of idolatry, to wit, the Grey and Black thieves, and Charterhouse monks (a building of a wondrous cost and greatness) were so destroyed that the walls only did remain of all those great edifications.

[3] Which, reported to the Queen, she was so enraged that she *A godly* did avow, " Utterly to destroy Saint Johnston, man, woman, and *vow* child, and to consume the same by fire, and thereafter to salt it, in sign of a perpetual desolation."   We suspecting nothing such cruelty, but thinking that such words might escape her in choler, without purpose determinate, because she was a woman set afire by the complaints of those hypocrites who flocked unto her, as ravens to a carrion ; We (we say), suspecting nothing such beastly cruelty, returned to our own houses, leaving in Saint Johnston John Knox to instruct, because they were young and rude in Christ. But she, set afire, partly by her own malice, partly by commandment of her friends in France, and not a little by bribes, which she and Monsieur d'Oysel [4] received from the bishops and the priests here at home, did continue in her rage.   And first, she sent for all the *The com-* Nobility, to whom she complained, " That we meant nothing but *plaint of the Queen* a rebellion."   She did grievously aggreage [5] the destruction of the *Regent*

---

[1] That is, when the winter store of salted meat would normally have been exhausted ; therefore what a store they must have had at the *beginning* of the winter ! See the interesting figures in G. G. Coulton, *Scottish Abbeys and Social Life* (1933), 142–145.

[2] *pertaining* or *proportionate*

[3] A critical analysis of Knox's narrative subsequent to the destruction of the monasteries in Perth has been attempted by Andrew Lang in *Scottish Historical Review*, ii, 118ff.

[4] Henri Cleutin, Seigneur d'Oysel   [5] *lay stress upon*

Charterhouse, because it was a King's foundation [1] ; and there was the tomb of King James the First [2] ; and by such other persuasions she made the most part of them grant to pursue us. And then incontinent sent she for her Frenchmen ; for that was and hath ever been her joy to see Scottishmen dip one with another's blood. No man was at that time more frack against us than was the Duke,[3] led by the cruel beast, the Bishop of Saint Andrews,[4] and by those that yet abuse him, the Abbot of Kilwinning,[5] and Matthew Hamilton of Milburn, two chief enemies to Christ Jesus ; yea, and enemies to the Duke and to his whole house, but in so far as thereby they may procure their own particular profit. These and such other pestilent Papists ceased not to cast faggots on the fire, continually crying, " Forward upon these heretics ; we shall once [6] rid this realm of them."

The certainty hereof coming to our knowledge, some of us repaired to the town [7] again, about the 22 day of May, and there did abide for the comfort of our brethren. Where, after invocation of the name of God, we began to put the town and ourselves in such strength, as we thought might best [serve] for our just defence. And, because we were not utterly despaired of the Queen's favours, we caused to form a letter to her Grace, as followeth :

" TO THE QUEEN'S GRACE REGENT, ALL HUMBLE OBEDIENCE AND DUTY PREMISED

" As heretofore, with jeopardy of our lives, and yet with willing hearts, we have served the Authority of Scotland, and your Grace, now Regent in this Realm, in service to our bodies dangerous and painful ; so now, with most dolorous minds we are constrained, by unjust tyranny purposed against us, to declare unto your Grace, That except this cruelty be stayed by your wisdom, we will be compelled to take the sword of just defence against all that shall pursue us for the matter of religion, and for our conscience sake ; which ought not, nor may not be subject to mortal creatures, further than by God's word man be able to prove that he hath power to command us. We signify moreover unto your Grace, That if by rigour we be compelled to seek the extreme defence, that we will not only notify our innocence and petitions to the King of France,

---

[1] Founded and endowed by James I, it was the only house of the Carthusians in Scotland.   [2] James I was buried there, 22 February 1437.

[3] James, Earl of Arran and Duke of Châtelherault   [4] John Hamilton

[5] Gavin Hamilton   [6] *once and for all*   [7] Perth

to our Mistress and to her husband,[1] but also to the Princes and
Council of every Christian Realm, declaring unto them, that this
cruel, unjust, and most tyrannical murder, intended against towns
and multitudes, was, and is the only cause of our revolt from our
accustomed obedience, which, in God's presence, we faithfully
promise to our Sovereign Mistress, to her husband, and unto your
Grace Regent ; provided, that our consciences may live in that
peace and liberty which Christ Jesus hath purchased unto us by
his blood ; and that we may have his word truly preached, and
holy Sacraments rightly ministered unto us, without which we
firmly purpose never to be subject to mortal man. For better, we *O where is this*
think, to expose our bodies to a thousand deaths, than to hazard *fervency*
our souls to perpetual condemnation by denying Christ Jesus and *now !*
his manifest verity, which thing not only do they that commit open
idolatry, but also all such as seeing their brethren unjustly pursued
for the cause of religion, and having sufficient means to comfort *O would God*
and assist them, do none the less withdraw from them their debtful [2] *that the*
support. We would not your Grace should be deceived by the *nobility should yet*
false persuasions of those cruel beasts, the Church men, who affirm, *consider*
That your Grace needeth not greatly to regard the loss of us that
profess Christ Jesus in this realm. If (as God forbid) ye give ear
to their pestilent counsel, and so use against us this extremity pretended, it is to be feared that neither ye, neither yet your posterity,
shall at any time after this find that obedience and faithful service
within this realm which at all times you have found in us. We
declare our judgments freely, as true and faithful subjects. God
move your Grace's heart favourably to interpret our faithful
meaning. Further advertising your Grace, that the selfsame thing,
together with all things that we have done, or yet intend to do, we
will notify by our letters to the King of France ; asking of you,
in the name of the eternal God, and as your Grace tenders [3] the
peace and quietness of this realm, that ye invade us not with violence,
till we receive answer from our Mistress, her husband, and from their
advised council there. And thus we commit your Grace to the
protection of the Omnipotent.

" From Saint Johnston the 22 of May 1559.
        (*Sic subscribitur*)
Your Grace's obedient subjects in all things not repugnant to God
        " THE FAITHFUL CONGREGATION OF CHRIST JESUS IN
            SCOTLAND."

[1] Mary Queen of Scots and her husband Francis   [2] *due*   [3] *safeguards*

In the same tenor we wrote to Monsieur d'Oysel in French, requiring of him, that by his wisdom he would mitigate the Queen's rage, and the rage of the priests ; otherwise that flame, which then began to burn, would so kindle that when some men would, it could not be slakened ; adding further, that he declared himself no faithful servant to his master the King of France, if for the pleasure of the priests he would persecute us, and so compel us to take the sword of just defence.   In like manner we wrote to Captain Serra la Burse,[1] and to all other Captains and French soldiers, in general, admonishing them that their vocation was not to fight against us natural Scottish men ; neither yet that they had any such commandment of their master.   We besought them therefore not to provoke us to enmity against them, considering that they had found us favourable in their most extreme necessities.   We declared further unto them, that if they entered in hostility and bloody war against us, that the same should remain longer than their and our lives, to wit, even in all posterity to come, so long as natural Scottish men should have power to revenge such cruelty, and most horrible ingratitude.

These letters were caused [to] be spread abroad in great abundance, to the end that some might come to the knowledge of men. The Queen Regent's letter was laid upon her cushion in the Chapel Royal at Stirling, where she accustomed to sit at Mass.   She looked upon it, and put it in the pocket of her gown.   Monsieur d'Oysel and the Captains received theirs delivered even by their own soldiers (for some amongst them were favourers of the truth), who after the reading of them, began to rive their own beards ; for that was the modest behaviour of Monsieur d'Oysel, when truth was told unto him, so that it repugned to his fantasy.   These our letters were suppressed to the uttermost of their power, and yet they came to the knowledge of many.   But the rage of the Queen and priests could not be stayed ; but forward they move against us, who then were but a very few and mean number of gentlemen in Saint Johnston. We perceiving the extremity to approach, did write to all brethren, to repair towards us for our relief ; to the which we found all men so ready bent, that the work of God was evidently to be espied. And because that we would omit no diligence to declare our innocence to all men, we formed a letter to those of the Nobility who then persecuted us, as after followeth :

[1] Corbeyran de Sarlabous

" TO THE NOBILITY OF SCOTLAND, THE CONGREGATION OF
CHRIST JESUS WITHIN THE SAME, DESIRES THE SPIRIT OF
RIGHTEOUS JUDGMENT.

" BECAUSE we are not ignorant that the Nobility of this realm who
now persecute us, employing their whole study and force to maintain
the kingdom of Sathan, of superstition and idolatry, are yet none
the less divided in opinion ; WE, the Congregation of Christ Jesus
by you unjustly persecuted, have thought good, in one letter, to
write unto you severally. Ye are divided, we say, in opinion ; for
some of you think that we who have taken upon us this enterprise
to remove idolatry, and the monuments of the same, to erect the
true preaching of Christ Jesus in the bounds committed to our
charges, are heretics, seditious men, and troublers of this common
wealth ; and therefore that no punishment is sufficient for us :
and so, blinded with this rage, and under pretence to serve the
Authority, ye proclaim war, and threaten destruction without all
order of law against us. To you, we say, that neither your blind
zeal, neither yet the colour of authority, shall excuse you in God's
presence, who commandeth ' None to suffer death, till that he be
openly convicted in judgment to have offended against God, and
against his law written,' which no mortal creature is able to prove
against us : for whatsoever we have done, the same we have done
at God's commandment, who plainly commands idolatry, and
all monuments of the same to be destroyed and abolished. Our *The per-*
petual re-
earnest and long request hath been, and is, that in open assembly *quest of*
it may be disputed in presence of indifferent auditors, ' Whether *the Pro-*
testants of
that these abominations, named by the pestilent Papists religion, *Scotland*
which they by fire and sword defend, be the true religion of Christ
Jesus or not ? ' Now, this our humble request denied unto us, our
lives are sought in most cruel manner. And ye, the Nobility (whose
duty is to defend innocents, and to bridle the fury and rage of
wicked men, were it of Princes or Emperors) do, notwithstanding,
follow their appetites, and arm yourselves against us, your brethren,
and natural countrymen ; yea, against us that be innocent and just,
as concerning all such crimes as be laid to our charges. If ye think
that we be criminal because that we dissent from your opinion,
consider, we beseech you, that the Prophets under the law, the
Apostles of Christ Jesus after his Ascension, his primitive Church,
and holy Martyrs, did dissent from the whole world in their
days ; and will ye deny but that their action was just, and that all

those that persecuted them were murderers before God ? May not the like be true this day ? What assurance have ye this day of your religion, which the world that day had not of theirs ? Ye have a multitude that agree with you, and so had they. Ye have antiquity of time, and that they lacked not. Ye have councils, laws, and men of reputation that have established all things, as ye suppose : But none of all these can make any religion acceptable unto God, which only dependeth upon his own will, revealed to man in his most sacred word. Is it not then a wonder that ye sleep in so deadly a security, in the matter of your own salvation, considering that God giveth unto you so manifest tokens, that ye and your leaders are both declined from God ? For if ' the tree shall be judged by the

Probation against the Papists fruit ' (as Christ Jesus affirmeth that it must be) then of necessity it is that your Prelates, and the whole rabble of their clergy, be evil trees. For if adultery, pride, ambition, drunkenness, covetousness, incest, unthankfulness, oppression, murder, idolatry, and blasphemy be evil fruits, there can none of that generation, which claim to themselves the title of Churchmen, be judged good trees ; for all these pestilent and wicked fruits do they bring forth in greatest abundance : And if they be evil trees (as ye yourselves must be compelled to confess they are), advise prudently with what consciences ye can maintain them to occupy the roume and place [1] in the Lord's vineyard. Do ye not consider, that in so doing ye labour to maintain the servants of sin in their filthy corruption ; and so consequently ye labour that the Devil may reign, and still abuse this realm by all iniquity and tyranny, and that Christ Jesus and his blessed Evangel be suppressed and extinguished ?

Against such as under colour of authority persecute their brethren " The name and the cloak of the authority, which ye pretend, will nothing excuse you in God's presence ; but rather shall ye bear double condemnation ; for that ye burden God, as that his good ordinance were the cause of your iniquity. All authority which God hath established, is good and perfect, and is to be obeyed of all men, yea under the pain of damnation. But do ye not under-

Difference betwix the person and the authority stand, that there is a great difference betwix the authority which is God's ordinance, and the persons of those which are placed in authority ? The authority and God's ordinance can never do wrong ; for it commandeth, That vice and wicked men be punished, and virtue, with virtuous men and just, be maintained. But the corrupt person placed in this authority may offend, and most commonly doth the contrary hereof ; and is then the corruption

[1] *the appointed place*

of the person to be followed, by reason that he is clad with the name of the authority ? Or, shall those that obey the wicked commandment of those that are placed in authority be excusable before God ? Not so ; not so. But the plagues and vengeances of God taken upon kings, their servants, and subjects, do witness to us the plain contrary. Pharaoh was a king, and had his authority of God, who commanded his subjects to murder and torment the Israelites, and at last most cruelly to persecute their lives. But was their obedience (blind rage it should be called) excusable before God ? The universal plague doth plainly declare that the wicked commander, and those that obeyed, were alike guilty before God. And if the example of Pharaoh shall be rejected, because he was an ethnik,[1] then let us consider the facts of Saul : He was a king *The fact of King Saul* anointed of God, appointed to reign over his people ; he commanded to persecute David, because (as he alleged) David was a traitor and usurper of the crown ; and likewise commanded Abimelech the High Priest and his fellows to be slain : But did God approve any part of this obedience ? Evident it is that he did not. And think ye, that God will approve in you that which he did damn in others ? Be not deceived : with God there is no such partiality. If ye obey the unjust commandments of wicked rulers, ye shall suffer God's vengeance and just punishment with them.[2] And therefore as ye tender your own salvation, we most earnestly require of you moderation, and that ye stay yourselves, and the fury of others, from persecuting of us, till our cause be tried in lawful and open judgment.

" And now, to you that are persuaded of the justice of our cause, that sometime have professed Christ Jesus with us, and that also have exhorted us to this enterprise, and yet have left us in our extreme necessity, or at the least look through your fingers in this our trouble, as that the matter appertained not unto you ; we say, that unless (all fear and worldly respects set aside) ye join yourselves with us, that as of God ye are reputed traitors, so shall ye be excommunicated from our society, and from all participation with us in the administration of Sacraments. The glory of this victory, which God shall give to his Church, yea even in the eyes of men, shall not appertain to you ; but the fearful judgment which apprehended Ananias and his wife Sapphira, shall apprehend you and

---

[1] a *Gentile*, that is a *heathen*

[2] The whole of this argument was later developed by Knox more fully in his " reasoning " with Lethington (*infra*, ii, 114 ff).

Let both the one part and the other judge if God have not justified the cause of the innocents

your posterity. Ye may perchance contemn, and despise the excommunication of the Church now by God's mighty power erected amongst us, as a thing of no force ; but yet doubt we nothing, but that our Church, and the true ministers of the same, have the same power which our Master, Christ Jesus, granted to his Apostles in these words, ' Whose sins ye shall forgive, shall be forgiven ; and whose sins ye shall retain, shall be retained ' ; and that, because they preach and we believe the same doctrine which is contained in his most blessed word. And therefore except that ye will contemn Christ Jesus, ye neither can despise our threatening, neither yet refuse us calling for your just defence.[1] By your fainting, and by

From whence this courage did proceed the issue declared

extracting of your support, the enemies are encouraged, thinking that they shall find no resistance : In which point, God willing, they shall be deceived. For if they were ten thousand, and we but one thousand, they shall not murder the least of our brethren, but we (God assisting us) shall first commit our lives in the hands of God for their defence. But this shall aggravate your damnation ; for ye declare yourselves both traitors to the truth once professed, and murderers of us, and of your brethren, from whom ye draw your debtful and promised support, whom your only presence [2] (to man's judgment) might preserve from this danger. For our enemies look not to the power of God, but to the force and strength of man. When the number is mean to resist them, then rage they as bloody wolves ; but a party equal or able to resist them in appearance, doth bridle their fury. Examine your own consciences, and weigh that sentence of our Master, Christ Jesus, saying, ' Whosoever denieth me, or is ashamed of me before men, I shall deny him before my Father.' Now is the day of his battle in this realm : If ye deny us, your brethren, suffering for his name's sake, ye do also deny Him, as himself doth witness in these words, ' Whatsoever ye did to any of these little ones, that ye did to me ; and what ye did not to one of those little ones, that ye did not to me.' If these sentences be true, as concerning meat, drink, clothing, and such things as appertain to the body, shall they not be likewise true in these things that appertain to the preservation of the lives of thousands, whose blood is now sought, for profession of Christ Jesus ? And thus shortly leave we you, who sometimes have professed Christ Jesus with us, to the examination of your own consciences. And yet once again, of you, who, blinded by superstition, persecute us, we require moderation till our cause may be tried, which if ye will not grant unto us for

[1] That is, appealing to you for your just defence of us   [2] *your presence alone*

God's cause, yet we desire you to have respect to the preservation of our common country, which we cannot sooner betray in the hands of strangers, than that one of us destroy and murder another. Consider our petitions, and call for the spirit of righteous judgment."[1]

These our Letters being divulged, some men began to reason whether of conscience they might invade us or not, considering that we offered due obedience to the Authority ; requiring nothing but the liberty of conscience, and our religion and fact to be tried by the word of God. Our Letters came with convenient expedition to the hands of the brethren in Cunningham and Kyle, who convened at the Kirk of Craigie,[2] where, after some contrarious reasons, Alexander, Earl of Glencairn, in zeal burst forth in these words, "Let every man serve his conscience. I will, by God's grace, see my brethren in Saint Johnston : yea, albeit never man should accompany me, I will go, and if it were but with a pike upon my shoulder ; for I had rather die with that company, nor live after them." These words so encouraged the rest, that all decreed to go forward, as that they did so stoutly, that when Lyon Herald,[3] in his coat armour, commanded all men under the pain of treason to return to their houses, by public sound of trumpet in Glasgow, never man obeyed that charge, but all went forward, as we will after hear. When it was clearly understood that the Prelates and their adherents, suppressing our petitions so far as in them lay, did kindle the fury of all men against us, it was thought expedient to write unto them some declaration of our minds, which we did in this form following :

> " To the generation of Antichrist, the pestilent Prelates and their Shavelings within Scotland, the Congregation of Christ Jesus within the same, sayeth,

" To the end that ye shall not be abused, thinking to escape just punishment, after that ye in your blind fury have caused the blood of many to be shed, this we notify and declare unto you, that if ye proceed in this your malicious cruelty, ye shall be entreated, wheresoever ye shall be apprehended, as murderers and open enemies to

---

[1] In *Foreign Cal. Elizabeth*, i, No. 724, this letter is dated 22 May 1559 ; that is, the same date as the letter to the Queen Regent and, if the date is correct, leaving no interval in which " the rage of the Queen and the priests " might be " stayed " (*supra*, 166).

[2] Craigie, near Ayr   [3] Sir Robert Forman of Luthrie

God and unto mankind ; and therefore, betimes cease from this blind rage. Remove first from yourselves your bands of bloody men of war, and reform yourselves to a more quiet life ; and thereafter mitigate ye the authority which, without crime committed upon our part, ye have inflamed against us ; or else be ye assured, that with the same measure that ye have measured against us, and yet intend to measure to others, it shall be measured unto you : That is, as ye by tyranny intend not only to destroy our bodies, but also by the same to hold our souls in bondage of the Devil, subject to idolatry, so shall we with all force and power, which God shall grant unto us, execute just vengeance and punishment upon you. Yea, we shall begin that same war which God commanded Israel to execute against the Canaanites ; that is, contract of peace shall never be made till ye desist from your open idolatry and cruel persecution of God's children. And this we signify unto you in the name of the eternal God, and of his Son Christ Jesus, whose verity we profess, and Evangel we will have preached, and holy Sacraments rightly ministered, so long as God will assist us to gainstand your idolatry. Take this for advertisement, and be not deceived." [1]

These our requests and advertisements notwithstanding, Monsieur d'Oysel and his Frenchmen, with the priests and their bands, marched forward against Saint Johnston, and approached within ten miles to the town. Then repaired the brethren from all quarters for our relief. The gentlemen of Fife, Angus, and Mearns, with the town of Dundee, were they that first hazarded to resist the enemy ; and for that purpose was chosen a platt of ground, a mile and more distant from the town. In this meantime the Lord Ruthven,[2] Provost of the town of Saint Johnston, and a man whom many judged godly and stout in that action (as in very deed he was even unto his last breath), left the town, and departed first to his own place, and after to the Queen : whose defection and revolt was a great discouragement to the hearts of many ; and yet did God so comfort [them], that within the space of twelve hours after, the hearts of all men were erected again ; for those that were then assembled did not so much hope victory by their own strength, as by the power of Him whose verity they professed ; and began one to comfort another, till the whole multitude was erected in a reason-

---

[1] Again, in *Foreign Cal. Elizabeth*, i, No. 726, this letter is dated 22 May 1559, which, if correct, leaves no interval for the suppression of the former petitions.
[2] Patrick, third Lord Ruthven

able esperance. The day after that the Lord Ruthven departed, which was the 24 of May,[1] came the Earl of Argyll,[2] Lord James,[3] Prior of Saint Andrews, and the Lord Sempill,[4] directed from the Queen Regent to inquire the cause of that convocation of lieges there. To whom, when it was answered, that it was only to resist that cruel tyranny devised against that poor town, and the inhabitants of the same, they asked, ' If we minded not to hold that town against the authority, and against the Queen Regent ? ' To the which question answered the Lairds of Dun [5] and Pittarrow,[6] with the Congregation of Angus and Mearns, the Master of Lindsay,[7] the Lairds of Lundy,[8] Balvaird,[9] and other Barons of Fife, ' That if the Queen's Grace would suffer the religion there begun to proceed, and not trouble their brethren and sisters that had professed Christ Jesus with them, that the town, they themselves, and whatsoever to them pertained, should be at the Queen's commandment.' Which answer understood, the Earl of Argyll and the Prior (who both were then Protestants) began to muse, and said plainly that they were far otherwise informed by the Queen, to wit, ' That we meant no religion, but a plain rebellion.' To the which when we had answered simply, and as the truth was, to wit, ' That we convened for none other purpose, but only to assist our brethren, who then were most unjustly persecuted ; and therefore we desired them faithfully to report our answer, and to be intercessors to the Queen Regent, that such cruelty should not be used against us, considering that we had offered in our former letters, as well to the Queen's Grace as to the Nobility, our matter to be tried in lawful judgment,' they promised fidelity in that behalf, which also they kept.

Speakers sent by the Queen to Saint Johnston

The false suggestion of the Queen Regent

The day after, which was the 25 day of May, before that the said Lords departed, in the morning John Knox desired to speak with the same Lords ; which granted unto him, he was conveyed to their lodging by the Laird of Balvaird, and thus he began :

" The present troubles, Honourable Lords, ought to move the hearts, not only of the true servants of God, but also of all such as bear any favour to their country, and natural countrymen, to descend within themselves and deeply to consider what shall be

The oration of John Knox to the Lords

---

[1] This date, given by Knox, shows that little or no interval could have elapsed between the letters to the Queen Regent, to the Nobility, and to the " pestilent Prelates."

[2] Archibald, fifth Earl of Argyll

[3] Lord James Stewart, Prior of St Andrews, subsequently Earl of Moray and Regent

[4] Robert, third Lord Sempill   [5] John Erskine of Dun

[6] Sir John Wishart of Pittarrow   [7] Patrick, later sixth Lord Lindsay of the Byres

[8] Walter Lundy of that Ilk   [9] Sir Andrew Murray of Balvaird

the end of this pretended tyranny. The rage of Sathan seeketh the destruction of all those that within this realm profess Christ Jesus ; and they that inflame the Queen's Grace, and you the Nobles against us, regard not who prevail, provided that they may abuse the world, and live at their pleasure, as heretofore they have done. Yea, I fear that some seek nothing more than the effusion of Scottish blood, to the end that their possessions [1] may be more patent [2] to others. But, because that this is not the principal which I have to speak, omitting the same to be considered by the wisdom of those to whom the care of the commonwealth appertaineth—

"1st. I most humbly require of you, my Lords, in my name, to say to the Queen's Grace Regent, that we, whom she in her blind rage doth persecute, are God's servants, faithful and obedient subjects to the authority of this realm ; that that religion, which she pretendeth to maintain by fire and sword, is not the true religion of Christ Jesus, but is express contrary to the same ; a superstition devised by the brain of man ; which I offer myself to prove against all that within Scotland will maintain the contrary, liberty of tongue being granted unto me, and God's written word being admitted for judge.

"2nd. I further require your Honours, in my name, to say unto her Grace, that as of before I have written, so now I say, that this her enterprise shall not prosperously succeed in the end, albeit for *Let the* a time she trouble the saints of God ; for she fighteth not against *Papists,* *rather* man only, but against the eternal God and his invincible verity. *ambitious* And therefore, the end shall be her confusion, unless betimes she *Romanists,* *judge* repent and desist.

"These things I require of you, in the name of the eternal God, as from my mouth, to say unto her Grace ; adding that I have been and am, a more assured friend to her Grace than they that, either flattering her are servants to her corrupt appetites, or else inflame her against us, who seek nothing but God's glory to be advanced, vice to be suppressed, and verity to be maintained in this poor realm."

They all three did promise to report his words so far as they could, which afterwards we understood they did. Yea, the Lord Sempill himself, a man sold under sin, enemy to God and to all godliness, did yet make such report, that the Queen was somewhat offended, that any man should use such liberty in her presence.

---

[1] That is, the possessions of the sufferers   [2] *open*

She still proceeded in her malice ; for immediately thereafter she sent her Lyon Herald [1] with letters straitly charging all men to avoid the town under the pain of treason. Which letters, after he had declared them to the chief men of the Congregation, he publicly proclaimed the same, upon Sunday, the 27 [28] of May. In this meantime, came sure knowledge to the Queen, to the Duke,[2] and to Monsieur d'Oysel, that the Earl of Glencairn,[3] the Lords Ochiltree [4] and Boyd,[5] the young Sheriff of Ayr,[6] the Lairds of Craigie Wallace,[7] Cessnock,[8] Carnell,[9] Barr,[10] Gadgirth,[11] and the whole Congregation of Kyle and Cunningham, approached for our relief ; and in very deed they came in such diligence, and such a number that as the enemy had just cause to fear, so have all that profess Christ Jesus just matter to praise God for their fidelity and stout courage in that need ; for by their presence was the tyranny of the enemy bridled. Their diligence was such, that albeit the passage *The dili-* by Stirling, and six miles above, was stopped (for there lay the *gence of the Earl* Queen with her bands, and gart cut the brigs upon the waters of *of Glen-cairn, and* Forth, Goodie and Teith,[12] above Stirling), yet made they such *of the* expedition through desert and mountain,[13] that they prevented [14] *brethren of the West,* the enemy, and approached within six miles to our camp, which *for the* then lay without the town, awaiting upon the enemy, before that *relief of St. John-* any assured knowledge came to us of their coming. Their number *ston* was judged to twenty-five hundred men, whereof there were twelve hundred horsemen. The Queen understanding how the said Earl and Lords, with their company, approached, caused to beset all ways, that no advertisement should come to us, to the end that we, despaired of support, might condescend to such appointment as she required ; and sent first to require, that some discreet men of our number would come and speak the Duke and Monsieur d'Oysel (who then with their army did lie at Auchterarder,[15] ten miles from Saint Johnston) to the end that some reasonable appointment might be had. She had persuaded the Earl of Argyll,[16] and all others,

[1] Sir Robert Forman of Luthrie   [2] The Duke of Châtelherault
[3] Alexander, fourth Earl of Glencairn   [4] Andrew Stewart, second Lord Ochiltree
[5] Robert, fifth Lord Boyd   [6] Matthew Campbell of Loudoun, Sheriff of Ayr
[7] John Wallace of Craigie   [8] William Campbell of Cessnock
[9] Hugh Wallace of Carnell   [10] John Lockhart of Barr
[11] James Chalmers of Gadgirth
[12] The Goodie and the Teith flow into the Forth about nine miles and two miles west and north-west of Stirling respectively.
[13] " by verie evill wayes and passages " (*Wodrow Misc.*, i, 58)   [14] *forestalled*
[15] Auchterarder is about fourteen miles south-west of Perth on the road to Stirling.
[16] Archibald, fifth Earl of Argyll

that we meant nothing but rebellion ; and therefore had he promised unto her, that in case we should not stand content with a reasonable appointment, he should declare himself plain enemy unto us, notwithstanding that he professed the same religion with us. From us were sent the Laird of Dun, the Laird of Inverquharity,[1] and Thomas Scott of Abbotshall, to hear what appointment the Queen would offer. The Duke and Monsieur d'Oysel required, " That the town should be made patent,[2] and that all things should be referred to the Queen's pleasure." To the which they answered, " That neither had they commission so to promise, neither durst they of conscience so to persuade their brethren. But if that the

The petition of the Protestants for rendering of Saint Johnston

Queen's Grace would promise, that no inhabitant of the town should be troubled for any such crimes as might be alleged against them for the late mutation of religion, and abolishment of idolatry, and for downcasting the places of the same ; if she would suffer the religion begun to go forward, and leave the town at her departing free from the garrisons of French soldiers, that they would labour at the hands of their brethren that the Queen should be obeyed in all things." [3] Monsieur d'Oysel perceiving the danger to be great, if that a sudden appointment should not be made ; and that they were not able to execute their tyranny against us, after that the Congregation of Kyle (of whose coming we had no advertisement) should be joined with us, with good words dismissed the said Lairds to persuade the brethren to quiet concord. To the which all men were so well minded, that with one voice they cried, " Cursed be they that seek effusion of blood, war, or dissension. Let us possess Christ Jesus, and the benefit of his Evangel, and none within Scotland shall be more obedient subjects than we shall be." With all expedition were sent from Stirling again (after that the coming of the Earl of Glencairn was known, for the enemy for fear quaked), the Earl of Argyll and Lord James foresaid, and in their company a crafty man, Master Gavin Hamilton, Abbot of Kilwinning, who were sent by the Queen to finish the appointment foresaid. But before that they came, was the Earl of Glencairn and his honourable company arrived in the town ; and then began all men to praise God, for that he had so mercifully heard them in their most extreme necessity, and had sent unto them such relief as was able, without

---

[1] John Ogilvy of Inverquharity   [2] That is, open to the Queen Regent's forces
[3] In his letter to Mrs. Anna Locke of 23 June 1559, Knox gives the " petitions " of the Protestants in Perth as simply " that the Evangel might have free passage, and that our consciences should not be thralled to men's traditions." (Laing's *Knox*, vi, 24)

effusion of blood, to stay the rage of the enemy. The Earl of Argyll and Lord James did earnestly [per]suade the agreement, to the which all men were willing. But some did smell the craft of the adversary, to wit, that they were minded to keep no point of the promise longer than they had obtained their intent.

With the Earl of Glencairn came our loving brother John Willock ; John Knox was in the town before. These two went to the Earl of Argyll and [the] Prior,[1] accusing them of infidelity, in so far as they had defrauded their brethren of their debtful support and comfort in their greatest necessity. They answered both, " That their heart was constant with their brethren, and that they would defend that cause to the uttermost of their power. But because they had promised to labour for concord, and to assist the Queen, in case we refused reasonable offers, of conscience and honour, they could do no less than be faithful in their promise made. And therefore they required that the brethren might be persuaded to consent to that reasonable appointment ; promising, in God's presence, that if the Queen did break in any jot thereof, that they, with their whole power, would assist and concur with their brethren in all times to come." This promise made, the Preachers appeased the multitude, and obtained in the end that all men did consent to the appointment foresaid, which they obtained not without great labours. And no wonder, for many foresaw the danger to follow ; yea, the Preachers themselves, in open sermon, did affirm plainly, " That they were assuredly persuaded that the Queen meant no truth. But to stop the mouth of the adversary, who unjustly did burden us with rebellion, they most earnestly required all men to approve the appointment, and so to suffer hypocrisy to disclose the self."

The answer of the Earl of Argyll and Prior of Saint Andrews

The promise of the foresaid

This appointment was concluded the 28 [29] of May,[2] and the day following, at two [in the] afternoon, departed the Congregation

---

[1] The Lord James Stewart, Prior of St. Andrews, later Earl of Moray and Regent

[2] Monday, 29 May 1559 : Knox is strangely one day out in his dates for May and June 1559. (*Cf. supra*, 175.) Keith (*History*, i, 200) gives the terms of the appointment as : (i) That both the armies should be disbanded and the town left open to the Queen. (ii) That none of the inhabitants should be molested on account of the late alteration in religion. (iii) That no Frenchman should enter the town, nor come within three miles of it ; and that when the Queen retires, no French garrison shall be left in the town. (iv) That all other controversies be referred to the next Parliament. Spottiswoode (*History*, i, 274) and Buchanan (Aikman's edn., ii, 406), give similar terms. The terms as given in Knox's letter to Mrs. Anna Locke (Laing's *Knox*, vi, 24) and in the " Historie of the Estate of Scotland " (*Wodrow Misc.*, i, 58) are much vaguer. The agreement about the Regent's French soldiers was one of the " petitions " of the Reformers (*supra*, 176).

from Saint Johnston, after that John Knox had, in his sermon, exhorted all men to constancy, and unfeignedly to thank God for that it had pleased his mercy to stay the rage of the enemy, without effusion of blood ; also, that no brother should weary nor faint to support such as should after be likewise persecuted, " For (said he) I am assured, that no part of this promise made shall be longer kept than the Queen and her Frenchmen have the upper hand." Many of the enemies were at the same sermon ; for after that the appointment was made, they had free entry in the town to provide lodgings.

Before the Lords departed,[1] was this Band made, whose tenor follows, as it was written and subscribed :

"AT PERTH, the last day of May, the year of God 1559, the Congregations of the West country, with the Congregations of Fife, Perth, Dundee, Angus, Mearns, and Montrose, being convened in the town of Perth, in the name of Jesus Christ, for forthsetting of his glory, understanding nothing more necessary for the same than to keep a constant amity, unity, and fellowship together, according as they are commanded by God, are confederate, and become bundin and oblist [2] in the presence of God, to concur and assist together in doing all things required of God in his Scripture, that may be to his glory ; and at their whole power to destroy, and away put, all things that do dishonour to his name, so that God may be truly and purely worshipped. And in case that any trouble be intended against the said Congregations, or any part, or member thereof, the whole Congregation shall concur, assist, and convene together, to the defence of the same Congregation, or person troubled, and shall not spare labours, goods, substance, bodies, and lives, in maintaining the liberty of the whole Congregation, and every member thereof, against whatsoever power that shall intend the said trouble, for cause of religion, or any other cause dependant thereupon, or lay to their charge under pretence thereof, although it happen to be coloured with any other outward cause. In witnessing and testimony of the which, the whole Congregations foresaid has ordained and appointed the Noblemen and persons underwritten to subscribe these presents

[1] The Lords had presumably departed with the Congregation at two o'clock in the afternoon of 30 May 1559 (*supra*, 177), and yet all the copies of this Band, subscribed by them, are dated 31 May. (*Foreign Calendar, Elizabeth*, i, Nos. 799, 800)

[2] *bound and obliged*

(*Sic subscribitur*),

ARCH. ARGYLL [1]   GLENCAIRN
JAMES STEWART [1]   R. LORD BOYD
MATTHEW CAMPBELL OF TERINGLAND [2] OCHILTREE

The twenty-nine day of May [3] entered the Queen, the Duke, Monsieur d'Oysel, and the Frenchmen,[4] who, in discharging their volley of hackbuts, did well mark the house of Patrick Murray,[5] a man fervent in religion, and that boldly had sustained all dangers in that trouble ; against whose stair they directed vi or vii shots, even against the faces of those that were there lying. All men escaped, except the son of the said Patrick, a boy of ten or twelve years of age, who being slain,[6] was had to the Queen's presence. *The first slaughter of the Frenchmen* But she, understanding whose son he was, said in mockage, "It is a pity it chanced on the son, and not on the father ; but seeing that so is chanced, me can not be against fortune." This was her happy entry to Saint Johnston, and the great zeal she tendeth to justice. The swarm of Papists that entered with her began straight to make provision for their Mass ; and because the altars were not so easy to be repaired again, they provided tables, whereof some *Idolatry erected against the appointment* before used to serve for drunkards, dicers, and carters [7] ; but they were holy enough for the Priest and his padgean.[8] The Queen began to rage against all godly and honest men ; their houses were oppressed by the Frenchmen ; the lawful Magistrates, as well Provost as Bailies, were unjustly, and without all order, deposed from their authority. A wicked man, void of God's fear, and destitute of all virtue, the Laird of Kinfauns,[9] was intruded by her Provost above the town, whereat all honest men were offended. They left their own houses, and with their wives and children sought *Against the appointment the second time* amongst their brethren some resting place for a time. She took order that four ensigns of the soldiers [10] should abide in the town

---

[1] Now apparently on the side of the Reformers, and yet only two or three days previously they had been on the side of the Queen Regent (*supra*, 176–177).

[2] That is, Matthew Campbell of Loudoun, who held the lands of Terrinzean in Kyle

[3] Presumably, 30 May (see *supra*, 177, *note* 2 ; 178, *note* 1)

[4] This was apparently contrary to the terms of the appointment (*supra*, 177, *note* 2). See also " Historie of the Estate of Scotland " (*Wodrow Misc.*, i, 59).

[5] Presumably Patrick Murray of Tibbermore

[6] In his letter of 23 June 1559 to Mrs. Anna Locke this incident becomes, "when children were slain." (Laing's *Knox*, vi, 24)

[7] *card players*   [8] *pageant*, used here in the sense of *mummery*

[9] John Charteris of Kinfauns ; but there is no evidence that he ever exercised office.

[10] The "Historie of the Estate of Scotland" says "fower ensignes of Scotts men" (*Wodrow Misc.*, i, 61). " Ensign " is here used for a *company*.

to maintain idolatry, and to resist the Congregation. Honest and indifferent men asked, Why she did so manifestly violate her promise ?

She answered, " That she was bound to keep no promise to heretics : and moreover, that she promised only to leave the town free of French soldiers, which (said she), she did, because that those that therein were left were Scottish men." [1]   But when it was reasoned in her contrary, That all those that took wages of France were

counted French soldiers : she answered, " Princes must not so straitly be bound to keep their promises. [2]   Myself (said she) would make little conscience to take from all that sort their lives and inheritance, if I might do it with as honest an excuse." And then she left the town in extreme bondage, after that her ungodly Frenchmen had most cruelly entreated the most part of those that remained

in the same. The Earl of Argyll, and Lord James foresaid, perceiving in the Queen nothing but mere tyranny and falsehood, mindful of their former promises made to their brethren, did secretly convey themselves and their companies [out] of the town [3] ; and with them departed the Lord Ruthven [4] (of whom before mention is made), the Earl of Menteith, [5] and the Laird of Tullibardine [6] ; who, in God's presence, did confederate, and bind themselves together, faithfully promising one to assist and defend another against all persons that would pursue them for religion's sake ; and also that they, with their whole force and power, would defend the brethren persecuted for the same cause. The Queen, highly offended at the sudden departure of the persons foresaid, sent charge to them to return, under the highest pain of her displeasure.

But they answered, " That with safe conscience they could not be partakers of so manifest tyranny as by her was committed, and of so great iniquity as they perceived devised by her and her ungodly Council the Prelates."

This answer was given to her the first day of June, and immediately the Earl of Argyll and Lord James repaired towards

---

[1] *Cf. infra,* 187

[2] *Cf.* " We are not ignorant that princes think it good policy to betray their subjects by breaking of promises, be they never so solemnly made " (*infra,* 241). Mary of Lorraine's breach of promise was later referred to by James VI in the words, " I ken the story of my grandmother, the queen-regent, that after she was inveigled to break her promise made to some mutineers at a Perth meeting, she never saw good day, but from thence, being much loved before, was despised by her people." (Cited Hill Burton, *History of Scotland,* 1873, vi, 61)

[3] *Cf.* The " Historie of the Estate of Scotland " (*Wodrow Misc.,* i, 59), and *Calendar of Scottish Papers,* i, No. 469   [4] Patrick, third Lord Ruthven

[5] John, fourth Earl of Menteith   [6] Sir William Murray of Tullibardine

Saint Andrews, and in their journey gave advertisement, by writing, to the Laird of Dun, to the Laird of Pittarrow,[1] to the Provost of Dundee,[2] and others, professors in Angus, to visit them in Saint Andrews the fourth of June, for reformation to be made there. Which day they kept, and brought in their company John Knox who, the first day after his coming to Fife, did preach in Crail, the next day in Anstruther, minding the third day, which was the Sunday, to preach in Saint Andrews.[3] The Bishop, hearing of reformation to be made in his Cathedral Church, thought [it] time to stir, or else never ; and therefore assembled his colleagues and confederate fellows, besides his other friends, and came to the town upon the Saturday at night, accompanied with a hundred spears, of mind to have stopped John Knox to have preached. The two Lords and gentlemen foresaid were only accompanied with their quiet households, and therefore was the sudden coming of the Bishop the more fearful ; for then was the Queen and her French-men departed from Saint Johnston, and were lying in Falkland, within twelve miles of Saint Andrews [4] ; and the town at that time had not given profession of Christ, and therefore could not the Lords be assured of their friendship. Consultation being had, many were of mind that the preaching should be delayed for that day, and especially that John Knox should not preach ; for that did the Bishop affirm that he would not suffer, considering that by his commandment the picture of the said John was before burnt. He willed, therefore, an honest gentleman, Robert Colville of Cleish, to say to the Lords, " That in case John Knox presented himself to the preaching place, in his town and principal church, he should gar him be saluted with a dozen of culverins, whereof the most part should light upon his nose." After long deliberation had, the said John was called, that his own judgment might be had. When many persuasions were made that he should delay for that time, and great terrors given in case he should enterprise such a thing, as it were in contempt of the Bishop : he answered, " God is witness that I never preached Christ Jesus in contempt of any man, neither mind I at any time to present myself to that place, having either

The Bishop's good mind to-ward John Knox

---

[1] Sir John Wishart of Pittarrow   [2] James Haliburton

[3] The chronology is difficult. Knox *did* preach in St. Andrews on Sunday 11 June (*infra*, 182). Accordingly it would appear that he reached Fife on Thursday 8 June, and preached in Crail on Friday 9 June, and in Anstruther on Saturday 10 June. How then could the others, in whose company he was, have kept the appointed day of 4 June ? But see *infra*, 182, *note* 4

[4] " Eighteen miles " would be more accurate.

respect to my own private commodity, either yet to the worldly hurt of any creature ; but to delay to preach [on] the morrow (unless the body be violently withheld) I cannot of conscience : for in this town and church began God first to call me to the dignity of a preacher,[1] from the which I was reft by the tyranny of France, by procurement of the Bishops, as ye all well enough know.   How long I continued prisoner, what torment I sustained in the galleys, and what were the sobs of my heart, is now no time to recite.   This only I cannot conceal, which more than one have heard me say, when the body was far absent from Scotland, that my assured hope was, in open audience, to preach in Saint Andrews before I departed this life.[2]   And therefore (said he) My Lords, seeing that God, above the expectation of many, hath brought the body to the same place where first I was called to the office of a preacher, and from the which most unjustly I was removed, I beseech your Honours not to stop me to present myself unto my brethren.   And as for the fear of danger that may come to me, let no man be solist[3] ; for my life is in the custody of Him whose glory I seek ; and therefore I cannot so fear their boast nor tyranny, that I will cease from doing my duty, when of his mercy He offereth the occasion.   I desire the hand nor weapon of no man to defend me ; only do I crave audience ; which, if it be denied here unto me at this time, I must seek further where I may have it."

At these his words, the Lords were fully content that he should occupy the place ; which he did upon Sunday, the 10 [11] of June,[4] and did entreat of the ejection of the buyers and the sellers forth of the Temple of Jerusalem, as it is written in the Evangelists Matthew and John ; and so applied the corruption that was there to the corruption that is in the Papistry ; and Christ's fact, to the duty of those to whom God giveth power and zeal thereto ; that as well the *The Re-* magistrates, the Provost[5] and Bailies, as the commonalty for the *formation* most part, within the town, did agree to remove all monuments of *of Saint* *Andrews* idolatry, which also they did with expedition.[6]

---

[1] *Supra*, 83–84   [2] *Supra*, 109   [3] *solicitous*
[4] *10* may possibly be a transcriber's error for *iv*. If so, the chronological difficulty (*supra*, 181, *note* 3) would be partly resolved.   On the other hand, the " Historie of the Estate of Scotland " says the Archbishop of St. Andrews came there on 12 June, and that " on the morrow " (13 June) Knox passed to the Parish Church to preach.   (*Wodrow Misc.*, i, 59.)   In his letter to Mrs. Anna Locke Knox says that he occupied the pulpit on the Sabbath " and three dayes after," and that the purging of the monuments of idolatry began on 14 June.   (Laing's *Knox*, vi, 25)   [5] Patrick Learmonth of Dairsie and Balcomie
[6] Described in *Foreign Calendar, Elizabeth*, i, p. 321 (5)—Sir James Croft to the Lords of Council, 20 June 1559

The Bishop, advertised hereof, departed that same day to the Queen, who lay with her Frenchmen, as said is, in Falkland. The hot fury of the Bishop did so kindle her choler (and yet the love was very cold betwix them), that without further delay conclusion was taken to invade Saint Andrews, and the two young Lords foresaid,[1] who then were there very slenderly accompanied. Posts were sent from the Queen with all diligence to Cupar, distant only six miles from Saint Andrews, to prepare lodgings and victuals for the Queen and her Frenchmen. Lodgings were assigned, and furiors[2] were sent [on] before. Which thing understood, counsel was given to the Lords to march forward, and to prevent[3] them before they came to Cupar ; which they did, giving advertisement to all brethren with possible expedition to repair towards them ; which they also did, with such diligence, that in their assembly the wondrous work of God might have been espied. For when at night the Lords came to Cupar, they were not a hundred horse, and a certain footmen, whom Lord James brought from the coast side ; and yet before the next day at twelve hours (which was Tuesday, the 13 of June) their number passed three thousand men, which by God's providence came unto the Lords. From Lothian [came] the Lairds of Ormiston,[4] Calder,[5] Halton,[6] Restalrig,[7] and Colston,[8] who, albeit they understood at their departing from their own houses no such trouble, yet were they by their good council very comfortable that day. The Lord Ruthven came from Saint Johnston, with some horsemen with him.[9] The Earl of Rothes,[10] Sheriff of Fife, came with an honest company. The towns of Dundee and Saint Andrews declared themselves both stout and faithful. Cupar, because it stood in greatest danger, assisted with the whole force. Finally, God did so multiply our number, that it appeared as [if] men had rained from the clouds. The enemy understanding nothing of our force, assured themselves of victory. Who had been in Falkland the night before, might have seen embracing and kissing betwix the Queen, the Duke, and the Bishop. But Master Gavin Hamilton, gaper[11] for the Bishopric of Saint Andrews, above all other was lovingly embraced of the Queen ; for he made his solemn vow, " That he would fight, and that he

Cupar Muir

Master Gavin Hamilton's vow

---

[1] That is, the Lord James Stewart and the Earl of Argyll
[2] *billeting officers* (see Littré, s.v. *fourrier* ; *Oxford Dictionary*, s.v. furrier)
[3] *forestall*
[4] John Cockburn of Ormiston
[5] John Sandilands of Calder
[6] William Lauder of Halton
[7] Robert Logan of Restalrig
[8] George Broun of Colston
[9] That is, he once more joined the Reformers (*Cf. supra*, 172)
[10] Andrew, fifth Earl of Rothes
[11] *aspirant*

should never return till he had brought those traitors to her Grace, either quick or dead." And thus, before midnight, did they send forward their ordnance ; themselves did follow before three hours in the morning.

The Lords hereof advertised, assembled their company early in the morning upon Cupar Muir ; where by the advice of Master James Haliburton, Provost of Dundee, was chosen a place of ground convenient for our defence ; for it was so chosen, that upon all sides our ordnance might have beat the enemy, and yet we have stood in safety, if we had been pursued, till we had come to hand strokes. The Lord Ruthven took the charge of the horsemen, and ordered them so, that the enemy was never permitted to espy our number : the day was dark, which helped thereto. The enemy (as before is said) thinking to have found no resistance, after that they had twice or thrice practised with us, as that they would retire, marched forward with great expedition, and approached within a mile before that ever their horsemen stayed ; and yet they kept betwix us and them a water [1] for their strength. It appeared to us that either they marched for Cupar or Saint Andrews ; and therefore our horsemen in their troop, and a part of the footmen, with the ordnance, marched somewhat always before them for safety of the town. The Lords, with the gentlemen of Fife, and so many of Angus and Mearns as were present, kept themselves close in a knot, nigh to the number of a thousand spears.

The towns of Dundee and Saint Andrews were arrayed in another battle, who came not to the sight of the enemy till that after twelve hours the mist began to evanish. And then passed some of their horsemen to a mountain, from the height whereof they might discern our number. Which perceived by them, their horsemen and footmen stayed incontinent. Posts ran to the Duke and Monsieur d'Oysel, to declare our number, and what order we kept ; and then were mediators sent to make appointment. But they were not suffered to approach nigh to the Lords, neither yet to the view of our camp ; which put them in greater fear. Answer was given unto them, " That as we had offended no man, so would we seek appointment of no man ; but if any would seek our lives (as we were informed they did), they should find us, if they pleased to make diligence." This answer received, were sent again the Lord Lindsay [2] and Laird of Wauchton,[3] who earnestly requested us to concord

First answer at Cupar Muir

---

[1] The river Eden   [2] John, fifth Lord Lindsay of the Byres
[3] Patrick Hepburn of Wauchton

and that we would not be the occasion that innocent blood should be shed. We answered, " That neither had we quarrel against any man neither yet sought we any man's blood ; only we were con- vened for defence of our own lives unjustly sought by others." We added further, " That if they could find the means that we and our brethren might be free from the tyranny devised against us, that they should reasonably desire nothing which should be denied for our part." *The second answer*

This answer received, the Duke and Monsieur d'Oysel, having commission of the Queen Regent, required that Assurance might be taken for eight days, to the end that indifferent men in the mean-time might commune upon some final agreement of those things which then were in controversy.[1] Hereto did we fully consent, albeit that in number and force we were far superior ; and for testification hereof, we sent unto them our hand-writs, and we likewise received theirs,[2] with promise that within two or three days some discreet men should be sent unto us, to Saint Andrews, with further know-ledge of the Queen's mind. The tenor of the Assurance was this :

THE ASSURANCE

" WE, JAMES, DUKE OF CHATELERAULT, Earl of Arran, Lord Hamilton, &c., and MY LORD D'OYSEL, Lieutenant for the King in these parts, for ourselves, our assisters and partakers, being presently with us in company, by the tenor hereof promises faithfully of honour to My Lords ARCHIBALD EARL OF ARGYLL, and JAMES COMMENDATOR OF THE PRIORY OF SAINT ANDREWS, to their assisters and partakers, being presently with them in company ; That we, and our company foresaid, shall retire incontinent to Falkland, and shall, with diligence, transport the Frenchmen and our other folks now presently with us ; and that no Frenchman, or other soldiers of ours, shall remain within the bounds of Fife, but so many as before the raising of the last army lay in Dysart, Kirkcaldy, and Kinghorn, and the same to lie in the same places only, if we shall think good : And this to have effect for the space of eight days following the date hereof *exclusive*, that in the meantime certain noble men, by the advice of the Queen's Grace, and rest of the Council, may convene

---

[1] This is confirmed in *Foreign Calendar, Elizabeth*, i, p. 321 (5)—Sir James Croft to the Lords of Council, 20 June 1559. See also Knox's account in his letter of 23 June 1559 to Mrs. Anna Locke (Laing's *Knox*, vi, 26). Pitscottie gives a fuller and more circumstantial account (*Chronicles*, Scot. Text Soc., ii, 152–158).

[2] Sir James Croft reports that the assurance was " granted of either party " (*loc. cit.*).

to talk of such things as may make good order and quietness amongst the Queen's lieges. And further, we, nor none of our assisters, being present with us, shall invade, trouble, or inquiet the said Lords, nor their assisters, during the said space : And this we bind and oblige us, upon our loyalty, fidelity, and honour, to observe and keep in every point above written, but fraud or guile. In witness whereof we have subscribed these presents with our hands. At Gartabank,[1] the xiii day of June 1559.

Subscribed

JAMES

[2] *The other subscription we could not read, but the simile is this,—*   ∏enenk [3]

And, this received, we departed first, because we were thereto requested by the Duke, and so we returned to Cupar, lauding and praising God for his mercy shown ; and thereafter every man departed to his dwelling place. The Lords, and a great part of the gentlemen, passed to Saint Andrews, who there abode certain days, still looking for those that were promised to come from the Queen, for appointment to be made. But we, perceiving her craft and deceit,[4] (for under that assurance she meant nothing else but to convey herself, her ordnance, and French men, over the water of Forth), took consultation what should be done for delivering of

---

[1] The writer in the *Old Statistical Account* (xvii, 160–161) says the place was then known (1796) as Garlie Bank, and that the truce was signed at a spot called the Howlet or Owl Hill.

[2] This note is in the same hand as the text. It shows that the writer had before him the original document.

[3] This was undoubtedly d'Oysel's signature as *Cleutin*. (He was Henri Cleutin d'Oysel, Seigneur de Villeparisis.) Spottiswoode (*History*, i, 278) says the truce was signed by the Duke and d'Oysel.

[4] Even if the Queen Regent had been simply seeking a respite it is still possible that the Reformers themselves broke the assurance. Knox prints the assurance given by Châtelherault and d'Oysel, but not that given by the Congregation (probably he had no access to it). We are told by Sir James Croft, however, that assurance was " granted of either party " (*supra*, 185, *note*), and the " Historie of the Estate of Scotland " says that the Congregation were to " enterprise nothing, nor make no invasion for the space of six dayes following " (*Wodrow Misc.*, i, 60). Yet, writing to Mrs. Anna Locke on 23 June 1559 Knox reports the assurance for eight days and then continues " In the whilk, the Abbay of Lundores, a place of blacke monkes . . . was reformed, their altars overthrowne, their idols, vestments of idolatire, and masse bookes were burnt in their owne presence, and they commaunded to cast away their monkish [habits]". (Laing's *Knox*, vi, 26.) A truce of eight days from 13 June *exclusive* would expire with 21 June, one of six days with 19 June. Lindores may have been purged between 19 (or 21) June and 23 June ; but Knox's words " In the whilk " seem clearly to apply to the truce period.

Saint Johnston from these ungodly soldiers, and how our brethren, exiled from their own houses, might be restored again.

It was concluded, that the brethren of Fife, Angus, Mearns, and *The deliverance of Saint Johnston* Strathearn, should convene at Saint Johnston, the 24 day of June for that purpose ; and in the meantime were these letters written by the Earl of Argyll and Lord James to the Queen then Regent :

"MADAM,—After our hearty commendations of service, this *Letters to the Queen Regent* shall be to show your Grace that upon the 13 day of June, we were informed by them that were communers betwix my Lord Duke, Monsieur d'Oysel, and us, that we should have spoken irreverently of your Grace, which we beseech your Grace, for the true service that we have made, and are ready to make at all times to your Grace, that of your goodness ye will let us know the sayers thereof, and we shall do the duty of true subjects to defend our own innocence ; as we take God to witness of the good zeal and love we bear towards you, to serve you with true hearts and all that we have, as well lands as goods, desiring no other thing for our service but the liberty of our conscience, to serve our Lord God as we will answer to him, which your Grace ought and should give to us freely unrequired.[1] Moreover, please your Grace, that my Lord Duke, and the Noble men being in Stirling for the time, by your Grace's advice, solicited us to pass to the Congregation convened at the town of Perth, to commune of concord, where we did our exact diligence, and brought it to pass, as your Grace knows.[2] And there is a point that we plain [3] is not observed to us, which is, that no soldier should remain in the town after your Grace's departing. And suppose it may be inferred, that it was spoken of French soldiers only, yet we took it otherwise, like as we do yet, that Scottish men, or any other nation taking the King of France's wages, are repute and held French soldiers.[4] Therefore, since we of good will and mind brought that matter to your Grace's contentment, it will please your Grace, of your goodness, to remove the soldiers and their Captains, with others that have got charge of the town, that the same may be guided and ruled freely, as it was before, by the Bailies and Council, conform to their infeftments given to them by the ancient and most excellent Kings of this realm, to elect and choose their officers at Michaelmas, and they to endure for the space of one year, conform to the old rite and

[1] Sir William Kirkcaldy of Grange, writing to Sir Henry Percy [? 24 May 1559] reports an earlier instance of this same promise by the Reformers (*Foreign Calendar, Elizabeth*, i, No. 743).

[2] *Supra*, 176–177   [3] *complain*   [4] *Cf. supra*, 180

consuetude of this realm ; which being done by your Grace, we trust the better success shall follow thereupon to your Grace's contentation,[1] as the bearer will declare at more length to your Grace ; whom God preserve." [2]

To Saint Johnston, with the Gentlemen before expressed, did convene the Earl of Menteith,[3] the Laird of Glenorchy,[4] and divers others who before had not presented themselves for defence of their brethren. When the whole multitude was convened, a trumpet was *The summoning of Saint Johnston* sent by the Lords, commanding the Captains and their bands to avoid the town, and to leave it to the ancient liberty and just inhabitants of the same ; also commanding the Laird of Kinfauns,[5] inset Provost by the Queen, with the Captains foresaid, to cast up the ports of the town, and make the same patent to all our Sovereign's lieges, to the effect, that as well true religion now once begun therein might be maintained, and idolatry utterly suppressed, as also the said town might joise and brook [6] their ancient laws and liberties unoppressed by men of war, according to their old privileges granted to them by the ancient Princes of this realm, and conform to the provision contained in the Contract of Marriage made by the Nobility and Parliament of this realm with the King of France, bearing that none of our old laws nor liberties should be altered : adding thereto, if they foolishly resisted, and therein happened to commit murder, that they should be entreated as murderers. To the which they answered proudly, "That they would keep and defend that town, according to their promise made to the Queen Regent."

This answer received, preparation was made for the siege and assault ; for amongst all it was concluded that the town should be set at liberty, to what dangers soever their bodies should be exposed. While preparation was in making, came the Earl of Huntly, the Lord Erskine, and Master John Bannatyne,[7] Justice-Clerk, requiring that the pursuit of the town should be delayed. *Communing at Saint Johnston* To speak them were appointed the Earl of Argyll, Lord James, and Lord Ruthven who, perceiving in them nothing but a drift of time, without any assurance that the former wrongs should be redressed, gave unto them short and plain answer, "That they would not delay their purpose an hour ; and therefore willed them to certify

---

[1] *contentment*
[2] Printed in *Foreign Calendar, Elizabeth*, i, No. 852, where the editor dates the letter 15 June 1559. [3] John, fourth Earl of Menteith
[4] Sir Colin Campbell of Glenorchy [5] John Charteris of Kinfauns (see *supra*, 179)
[6] *enjoy and possess* [7] Better known as John Bellenden

the Captains in the town, that if by pride and foolishness they would keep the town, and in so doing slay any of their brethren, that they should every one die as murderers." The Earl of Huntly displeased at this answer, departed, as highly offended that he could not dress such appointment as should have contented the Queen and the priests. After their departing, the town was again summoned ; but the Captains, supposing that no sudden pursuit should be made, and looking for relief to have been sent from the Queen, abode in their former opinion. And so upon Saturday, the 25 [24] of June, at ten hours at night, commanded the Lord Ruthven, who besieged the west quarter, to shoot the first volley ; which being done, the town of Dundee did the like, whose ordnance lay upon the east side of the brig. The Captains and soldiers within the town, perceiving that they were unable long to resist, required assurance till twelve hours upon the morn, promising, "That if, ere that hour, there came unto them no relief from the Queen Regent, that they would render the town, provided that they should be suffered to depart the town with ensigns displayed." We, thirsting the blood of no man, and seeking only the liberty of our brethren, condescended to their desires, albeit that we might have executed against them judgment without mercy, for that they had refused our former favours, and had slain one of our brethren, and hurt two in their resistance ; and yet we suffered them freely to depart without any further molestation.

The town being delivered from their thraldom, upon Sunday the 26 [25] of June, thanks were given unto God for his great benefit received, and consultation was taken what was further to be done. In this meantime, zealous men, considering how obstinate, proud, and despiteful the Bishop of Moray [1] had been before ; how *The Bishop of Moray* he had threatened the town by his soldiers and friends, who lay in Scone,[2] thought good that some order should be taken with him and with that place, which lay near to the town end. The Lords wrote unto him (for he lay within two miles to Saint Johnston) "That unless he would come and assist them, they neither could spare nor save his place." He answered by his writing, "That he would come, and would do as they thought expedient ; that he would assist them with his force, and would vote with them against the rest of the Clergy in Parliament." But because this answer was slow in coming, the town of Dundee, partly offended for the

---

[1] Patrick Hepburn, Prior of St. Andrews, was provided to the See of Moray in 1538.
[2] Patrick Hepburn held the Monastery of Scone *in commendam*.

slaughter of their man, and especially bearing no good favour to the said Bishop, for that he was and is chief enemy to Christ Jesus, and that by his council alone was Walter Myln our brother put to death,[1] they marched forward. To stay them was first sent the Provost of Dundee,[2] and his brother Alexander Haliburton, Captain, who, little prevailing, was sent unto them John Knox; but before his coming, they were entered to the pulling down of the idols and dortour.[3] And albeit the said Master James Haliburton, Alexander his brother, and the said John, did what in them lay to have stayed the fury of the multitude, yet were they not able to put order universally; and therefore they sent for the Lords, Earl of Argyll, and Lord James, who, coming with all diligence, laboured to have saved the Palace and the Kirk. But because the multitude had found, buried in the Kirk, a great number of idols, hid of purpose to have preserved them to a better day (as the Papists speak), the towns of Dundee and Saint Johnston could not be satisfied, till that the whole reparation and ornaments of the Church (as they term it),

The destruction of Scone were destroyed. And yet did the Lords so travail, that they saved the Bishop's Palace, with the Church and place, for that night: for the two Lords did not depart till they brought with them the whole number of those that most sought the Bishop's displeasure. The Bishop, greatly offended that any thing should have been enterprised in reformation of his place, asked of[4] the Lords his band and hand-writing, which not two hours before he had sent to them. Which delivered to his messenger, sir Adam Brown,[5] advertisement was given, that if any further displeasure chanced unto him, that he should not blame them. The Bishop's servants, that same night, began to fortify the place again, and began to do violence to some that were carrying away such baggage as they could come by. The Bishop's girnell[6] was kept the first night by the labours of John Knox, who, by exhortation, removed such as violently would have made irruption. That same night departed from Saint Johnston the Earl of Argyll and Lord James, as after shall be declared.

The cause of the burning of Scone The morrow following, some of the poor, in hope of spoil, and some of Dundee, to consider what was done, passed up to the said Abbey of Scone; whereat the Bishop's servants offended, began to

---

[1] *Supra*, 153, where, however, Knox lays the charge against John Hamilton, Archbishop of St. Andrews.   [2] James Haliburton   [3] *dormitory*   [4] *asked back from*
[5] The title *sir* here indicates that he was in priest's orders. (See *supra*, 18, *note* 3.)
[6] *granary*

threaten and speak proudly : and, as it was constantly affirmed, one of the Bishop's sons stogged [1] through with a rapier one of Dundee, for because he was looking in at the girnell door. This bruit noised abroad, the town of Dundee was more enraged than before, who, putting themselves in armour, sent word to the inhabitants of Saint Johnston, " That unless they should support them to avenge that injury, that they should never after that day concur with them in any action." The multitude easily enflamed, gave the alarm, and so was that Abbey and Palace appointed to sackage ; in doing whereof they took no long deliberation, but committed the whole to the merciment [2] of fire ; whereat no small number of us were offended, that patiently we could not speak to any that were of Dundee or Saint Johnston. A poor aged matron, seeing *Speaking* the flame of fire pass up so mightily, and perceiving that many were *of an* *ancient* thereat offended, in plain and sober manner of speaking, said, *matron* " Now I see and understand that God's judgments are just, and that *when* *Scone was* no man is able to save where He will punish. Since my remembrance, *burning* this place hath been nothing else but a den of whoremongers. It is incredible to believe how many wives hath been adulterated, and virgins deflowered, by the filthy beasts which hath been fostered in this den ; but especially by that wicked man who is called the Bishop. If all men knew as much as I, they would praise God ; and no man would be offended." This woman dwelt into the town, nigh unto the Abbey ; at whose words were many pacified ; affirming with her, that it was God's just judgment. And assuredly, if the labours or travail of any man could have saved that place, it had not been at that time destroyed ; for men of greatest estimation laboured with all diligence for the safety of it.

While these things were done at Saint Johnston, the Queen, fearing what should follow, determined to send certain bands of French soldiers to Stirling, for purpose to stop the passage to us that then were upon the north side of Forth. Which understood, the Earl of Argyll and Lord James departed secretly upon the night, and with great expedition, preventing the Frenchmen, they *The* *taking of* took the town (before whose coming the rascal multitude [3] put *Stirling*

---

[1] stabbed   [2] mercy

[3] Again Knox blames " the rascal multitude " (*cf. supra*, 162, *note* 5), but Spottiswoode (*History*, i, 280) and Buchanan (*ed.* Aikman, ii, 412) leave it to be understood that the work was the work of the brethren. Knox had clearly endeavoured to save the Abbey of Scone ; equally clearly, the leaders of the movement had temporarily lost control and the mob was out for " sackage," and for " carrying away such baggage as they could come by " (*supra*, 190). In the breakdown of law and order, and in the " purging of idols," the opportunity for loot was too good to be missed.

hands in the thieves', I should say, friars' places and utterly destroyed them) ; whereat the Queen and her faction, not a little effrayed, with all diligence departed from Edinburgh to Dunbar. And so we with reasonable diligence marched forward to Edinburgh, for reformation to be made there, where we arrived the 29 of June.[1]

Lord Seton The Provost for that time, the Lord Seton,[2] a man without God, without honesty, and oftentimes without reason, had before greatly troubled and molested the brethren ; for he had taken upon him the protection and defence of the Black and Grey Friars ; and for that purpose did not only lie himself in the one every night, but also constrained the most honest of the town to watch those monsters,[3]

The coming of the Congregation to Edinburgh to their great grief and trouble. But hearing of our sudden coming, he abandoned his charge, and left the spoil to the poor, who had made havoc of all such things as were movable in those places before our coming,[4] and had left nothing but bare walls, yea, not so much as door or window ; wherethrough we were the less troubled in putting order to such places.

After that certain days we had deliberated what was to be done, and that order was taken for suppressing of all monuments of idolatry within that town and the places next adjacent, determination was taken, to send some message to the Queen, then Regent ; for she had bruited (as her accustomed manner was, and yet her daughter's is, ever to forge lies), that we sought nothing but her life, and a plain

---

[1] Knox dated a letter to Cecil " From Sanct Johnston, the 28 of June 1559 " (Laing's *Knox*, vi, 32) ; and one to Mrs. Anna Locke, " From Edinburgh, the 29th of June." (*Foreign Calendar, Elizabeth*, i, No. 893 ; Calderwood's *History*, i, 475–476.) The date " 25th June," in Laing's *Knox*, vi, 30, is clearly a mistake, and the Queen Regent was then still holding Edinburgh—*Foreign Calendar, Elizabeth*, i, No. 880. On 29 June the Burgh of Edinburgh sent " honest men " to meet the Congregation at Linlithgow. (*Edinburgh Burgh Records*, iii, 44)

[2] George, fifth Lord Seton

[3] On 3 June 1559 one of the " watch " was before the burgh court " for casting of stanis at the Blak and Gray Freiris wyndowis the last nycht that he was upon the waiche." (*Edinburgh Burgh Records*, iii, 40)

[4] That is, before 29 June. The *Diurnal of Occurrents* gives two different dates— 28 June and 14 June (53, 269)—but in both entries the writer states that the purge was carried out by the Earls of Argyll and Glencairn, the Lord James Stewart, and Lord Ruthven " quha was callit the congregatioun." The " Historie of the Estate of Scotland " says that before the Congregation reached Edinburgh the Friars began to disperse the best of their possessions among their acquaintances, " which thing the rascall people perceaving, went in, finding the yates open, and suddenly fell to work and saked all." (*Wodrow Misc.*, i, 61) The first part of this statement is partially borne out by entries in the burgh records (*Edinburgh Burgh Records*, iii, 40–45), and it is clear that in many places the Churchmen endeavoured to save their more valuable possessions by placing them in the custody of the local burgh officers and of prominent burgesses. (*Cf. Family of Rose of Kilravock*, 226–227)

revoltment from the lawful obedience due to our Sovereign's authority, as by the tenor of these Letters may be seen :

" FRANCIS AND MARIE, by the Grace of God, King and Queen of Scots, Daulphin and Daulphiness of Viennois, to our loved Lyon King of Arms, &c., our Sheriffs in that part, conjunctly and severally, specially constitute, greeting : For sa mekle as [1] our dearest mother Marie, Queen Dowager, Regent of our Realm, and Lords of our Secret Council, perceiving the seditious tumult raised by one part of our lieges, naming themselves THE CONGREGATION, who, under pretence of religion, have put themselves in arms ; and that her Grace, for satisfying of every man's conscience, and pacifying of the said troubles, had offered unto them to affix a Parliament to be held in January next to come (this was a manifest lie, for this was neither offered, nor by her once thought upon, till we required it) [2] or sooner, if they had pleased, for establishing of a universal order in matters of religion, by our advice and Estates of our Realm ; and, in the meantime, to suffer every man to live at liberty of conscience, without trouble, unto the time the said order was taken by advice of our foresaid [Estates]. And at last, because it appeared mekle to stand upon [3] our burgh of Edinburgh, offered in like manner to let the inhabitants thereof choose what manner of religion they would set up and use for that time ; so that no man might allege that he was forced to do against his conscience : which offer the Queen's Grace, our said dearest Mother, was at all times, and yet is, ready to fulfil. None the less, the said Congregation being of mind to receive no reasonable offers, has sensyne,[4] by open deed, declared, that it is no religion, nor any thing thereto pertaining that they seek, but only the subversion of our authority, and usurpation of our Crown ; in manifest witnessing whereof, they daily receive Englishmen with messages unto them, and sends siclyke in England ; and last of all, have violently intrometted with, taken, and yet withholds the irons of our Cunzie house,[5] which is one of the chief points that concerns our Crown ; and siclyke has intrometted with our Palace of Holyroodhouse. Our will is herefore, &c., that ye pass to the Market Cross of our said burgh of Edinburgh,

---

[1] *inasmuch as* [2] See *infra*, 202. The parenthesis is an interpolation by Knox.
[3] *greatly to affect* [4] *since*
[5] *the coining-irons of the Mint.* D'Oysel, writing to Noailles on 22 July, says that the report of Henry II's wound (noted by Knox, *infra*, 198) had encouraged the Protestants to seize the irons of the Mint and to do all they could to overthrow the authority of the Prince. (Teulet, *Papiers d'État*, i, 326)

or any other public place within the same, and there, by open proclamation in our name and authority, command and charge all and sundry persons of the said Congregation, or yet being presently within our said burgh other than the inhabitants thereof, that they, within six hours next after our said charge, depart forth of the same under the pain of treason ; and also, that ye command and charge all and sundry persons to leave their company, and adhere to our authority ; with certification to such as do the contrary [that they] shall be reputed and held as manifest traitors to our Crown, &c." [1]

These letters did not a little grieve us, who most unjustly were accused ; for there is never a sentence of the narrative true,[2] except that we stayed the irons, and that for most just causes, to wit, because daily there was such number of Hard-heads [3] printed, that the baseness thereof made all things exceeding dear [4] ; and therefore we were counselled by the wisest to stay the irons,[5] while [6] further order might be taken. She, with all possible diligence, posted for her faction. Master James Balfour was not idle in the meantime. The Lords, to purge them of these odious crimes, wrote unto her a letter, in form as after followeth :

The third letter to the Queen Regent

" PLEASE YOUR GRACE, be advertised, it is come to our knowledge, that your Grace hath set forth, by your letters openly proclaimed, that we, called by name THE CONGREGATION, under pretence and colour of religion, convene together to no other purpose but to usurp our Sovereign's authority, and to invade your person representing theirs at this present : Which things appear to have proceeded of sinister information, made to your Grace by our enemies, considering that we never minded such thing, but only our mind and purpose was and is to promote and set forth the glory of God, maintain and defend the true preachers of his word ; and according to the same, abolish and put away idolatry and false abuses, which may not stand with the said word of God : Beseeching your Grace to bear patiently therewith, and interpose your authority to the furtherance of the same, as is the duty of every Christian Prince

---

[1] Dated 1 July 1559 in *Foreign Calendar, Elizabeth*, i, No. 905

[2] But the Reformers *were* in communication with England, even Knox himself having written to Cecil as recently as 28 June (see *Calendar of Scottish Papers*, i, Nos. 471, 474, 475), while both Knox and Kirkcaldy wrote to Percy on 1 July (*Ibid.*, i, Nos. 480, 481). Or is Knox taking a casuistical refuge in the use of the word " daily " ?

[3] A small coin of base metal, with the royal cypher, crowned, on one side and a lion rampant on the other. Sometimes called a *Lion*.

[4] *Infra*, 198   [5] *prevent further minting of coins*   [6] *until*

and good magistrate. For as to the obedience of our Sovereigns' authority in all civil and politic matters, we are and shall be as obedient as any other your Grace's subjects within the realm ; and that our Convention is for no other purpose but to save our preachers and their auditors from the injury and violence of our enemies, which should be more amply declared by some of us in your Grace's presence, if you were not accompanied with such as have pursued our lives and sought our blood. Thus, we pray Almighty God to have your Highness in his eternal tuition.[1]

" At Edinburgh, the second of July 1559."

And for further purgation hereof, it was thought necessary that we should simply expone,[2] as well to her Grace as to the whole people, what were our requests and just petitions. And for that purpose, after that safe conduct was purchased and granted, we directed unto her two grave men of our council, to wit, the Lairds of Pittarrow and Cunninghamhead,[3] to whom we gave commission and power, First, To expone our whole purpose and intent, which was none other than before at all times we had required, to wit, That we might enjoy the liberty of conscience. Secondly, [That] Christ Jesus might be truly preached, and his holy sacraments rightly ministered unto us. [Thirdly,] That unable ministers might be removed from ecclesiastical administration ; and that our preachers might be relaxed from the horn, and permitted to execute their charges without molestation, unto such time as either by a General Council, lawfully convened, or by a Parliament within the realm, the controversies in religion were decided. And, for declaration that her Grace was hereto willing, that the bands of French men, who then were a burden intolerable to the country, and to us so fearful that we durst not in peaceable and quiet manner hant[4] the places where they did lie, should be sent to France, their native country : Which things granted, her Grace should have experience of our accustomed obedience.

To these heads she did answer at the first so pleasantly, that she put both our Commissioners in full esperance that all should be granted ; and for that purpose, she desired to speak with some of greater authority, promising, that if they would assure her of their debtful obedience, that she would deny nothing of that which was required. For satisfaction of her mind, we sent again the Earl of Glencairn, the Lord Ruthven, the Lord Ochiltree, and the said

---

[1] *protection* [2] *represent; explain*
[3] Sir John Wishart of Pittarrow and William Cunningham of Cunninghamhead
[4] *haunt*, that is, *frequent*

The craftiness of the Queen Regent may yet be espied

Laird of Pittarrow, with the same commission as of before. But then she began to handle the matter more craftily, complaining that she was not sought in a gentle manner ; and that they in whom she had put most singular confidence, had left her in her greatest need ; and such other things, pertaining nothing to their commission, proposed she, to spend and drive the time. They answered, " That, by unjust tyranny devised against them and their brethren (as her Grace did well know), they were compelled to seek the extreme remedy ; and therefore, that her Grace ought not to wonder though godly men left the company where they neither found fidelity nor truth." In the end of this communing, which was the 12 day of July 1559, she desired to have talked privily with the Earl of Argyll, and Lord James, Prior of Saint Andrews, " For else (as she alleged), she could not but suspect that they pretended to some other higher purpose nor religion." She and her crafty Council had abused the Duke, persuading unto him, and unto his friends, that the said

Accusations

Earl and Prior had conspired, first to deprive our Sovereign her daughter of her authority, and thereafter the Duke and his succession of their title to the Crown of Scotland.[1] By these invented lies she inflamed the hearts of many against us, in so much that some of our own number began to murmur ; which perceived, as well the preachers in their public sermons, as we ourselves by our public proclamations, gave purgation and satisfaction to the people, plainly and simply declaring what was our purpose, taking God to witness that no such crimes ever entered in our hearts as most unjustly was laid to our charge. The Council, after consultation, thought not expedient that the said Earl and Prior should talk with the Queen in any sort ; for her former practices put all men in suspicion, that some deceit lurked under such coloured communing.[2] She had before said, That if she could by any means sunder those two from the rest, she was assured shortly to come by her whole purpose ; and one of her chief Council in those days (and we fear but over inward with her yet), said, " That ere Michaelmas day, they two should leave their heads " ; and therefore all men feared to commit two such young plants to her mercy and fidelity. It was, therefore, finally denied that they should talk [with] the Queen, or any to her appertaining, but[3] in places void of all suspicion, where

---

[1] The House of Hamilton was next in succession to the Crown, always assuming that the divorce of the first Earl of Arran had been valid ; if that divorce had not been valid, then the Lennox-Stewarts were next in succession. (See *supra*, 49, *note* 1)

[2] *pretended conferences*   [3] *except ; save*

they should be equal in number with those that should talk [with] them.

The Queen, perceiving that her craft could not prevail, was content that the Duke's Grace, and the Earl of Huntly, with others by her appointed, should convene at Preston,[1] to commune [with] the said Earl and Prior, and such others as the Lords of the Congregation would appoint, to the number of one hundred on the side, of the which number eight persons only should meet for conference. The *The communing at Preston* principals for their party were, the Duke, the Earl Huntly, the Lords Erskine and Somerville,[2] Master Gavin Hamilton, and the Justice-Clerk.[3] From us were directed the Earls of Argyll and Glencairn, the Lords Ruthven, Lord James, Boyd, and Ochiltree, the Lairds Dun and Pittarrow, who, convening at Preston, spake the whole day without any certain conclusion : For this was the practice of the Queen, and of her faction, by drift of time to weary our company who, for the most part, had been upon the fields from the tenth day of May, that we, being dispersed, she might come to her purpose. In which she was not altogether deceived ; for our commons were compelled to skaill [4] for lack of expenses, and our gentlemen, partly constrained by lack of furnishing,[5] and partly hoping some small appointment, after so many communings, returned for the most part to their dwelling places, for reposing of themselves.

The Queen, in all these conventions, seemed that she would give *The demand of [the] Queen Regent, and answer of the Protestants* liberty to religion, provided, "That wheresoever she was, our Preachers should cease, and the Mass should be maintained." We perceiving her malicious craft answered, "That as we would compel her Grace to no religion, so could we not of conscience, for the pleasure of any earthly creature, put silence to God's true messengers ; neither could we suffer that the right administration of Christ's true sacraments should give place to manifest idolatry ; for in so doing, we should declare ourselves enemies to God, to Christ Jesus his Son, to his eternal verity, and to the liberty and establishment of his Church within this realm ; for your request being granted, there can no Kirk within the same be so established but at your pleasure, and by your residence and remaining there ye might overthrow the same." This our last answer we sent unto her with the Lord Ruthven

---

[1] Preston, East Lothian, adjacent to Prestonpans
[2] John, sixth Lord Erskine, and James, fifth Lord Somerville
[3] Sir John Bellenden or Bannatyne
[4] *the common people on our side were compelled to disperse*
[5] That is, of victuals and other necessities

and Laird of Pittarrow ; requiring of her Grace, in plain words, to signify unto us what hope we might have of her favours toward the outsetting of religion. We also required that she would remove her Frenchmen, who were a fear to us, and a burden most grievous to our country : And that she would promise to us, in the word of a Prince, that she would procure no more to be sent in ; and then should we not only support, to the uttermost of our powers, to furnish

The last offers of the Prot- estants to the Queen Regent

ships and victuals for their transporting, but also, upon our honour, should we take her body in our protection ; and should promise, in the presence of God and the whole realm, to serve our Sovereign her daughter, and her Grace Regent, as faithfully and as obediently as ever we did kings within Scotland : That, moreover, we should cause our preachers give reason of their doctrine, in her audience, to any that pleased to impugn any thing that they did or taught : Finally that we should submit ourselves to a lawful Parliament, provided that the bishops, as the party accused and our plain enemies, should be removed from judgment.

To no point would she answer directly ; but in all things she was so general and so ambiguous, that her craft appeared to all men. She had got assured knowledge that our company was skailled (for her Frenchmen were daily amongst us, without molestation or hurt done unto them), and therefore she began to disclose her mind, and

The scoffing of the Queen Regent

said, " The Congregation has roung [1] these two months bypast : me myself would ring now other two." The malice of her heart being plainly perceived, deliberation was had what was to be done. It was concluded that the Lords, Barons, and gentlemen, with their substantial households, should remain in Edinburgh that whole winter, for establishing of the Church there. And because it was found, that by the corrupting of our money, the Queen made to herself immoderate gains for maintaining of her soldiers, to the

The cause why the irons [were] stayed

destruction of our whole common weal, it was thought necessary that the printing irons, and all things to them pertaining, should be stayed, for fear that she should privily cause transport them to Dunbar.

The death of Harry, King of France

In this meantime came the assured word, first, that the King of France was hurt, and after, that he was dead [2] : which, albeit it ought to have put her in mind of her own estate and wicked enter-

---

[1] *reigned*, or *ruled*

[2] Henry II was wounded in a tournament and died 10 July 1559, whereby Francis, the husband of Mary Queen of Scots, became King of France as Francis II. This was bound to worsen the position of the Congregation, for with the death of Henry II the Guises acquired control in France ; and in Scotland the Queen Regent was a Guise.

prise : for he that same time, in the fulness of his glory (as she herself useth to speak), had determined most cruel persecution against the saints of God in France, even as she herself was here persecuting in Scotland : and yet he so perished in his pride, that all men might see that God's just vengeance did strike him, even when his iniquity was come to full ripeness. Albeit (we say) that this wondrous work of God in his sudden death, ought to have dantoned [1] her fury, and given unto her admonition that the same God could not suffer her obstinate malice against his truth long to be unpunished ; yet could her indurate heart nothing be moved to repentance : for hearing the staying of the printing irons, she raged more outrageously than of before, and sending for all such as were of her faction, exponed her grievous complaint, aggredging [2] the same with many lies, to wit, " That we had declared that which before she suspected ; for what could we mean else but usurpation of the Crown, when we durst put hands to the Cunzie-house which was a portion of the patrimony of the Crown." [3] She further alleged, " That we had spoiled the Cunzie-house of great sums of money." To the which we answered, both by our letters sent to her and her Council, and by public proclamation to the people, that we, without usurpation of any thing justly pertaining to the Crown of Scotland, did stay the printing irons, in consideration that the commonwealth was greatly hurt by corrupting of our money ; and because that we were born councillors of this realm, sworn to procure the profit of the same, we could do no less of duty and of conscience than to stay that for a time which we saw so abused that unless remedy were found should turn to the detriment of the whole body of this realm. And as to her false accusation of spuilzie,[4] we did remit us to the conscience of Master Robert Richardson, Master of the Cunzie-house, who from our hands received silver, gold, and metal, as well cunzeit as uncunzeit [5] ; so that with us there did not remain the valour of a bawbie.[6]

This our declaration and purgation notwithstanding, she, partly by her craft and policy, and partly by the labours of the Bishops of Saint Andrews [7] and Glasgow,[8] procured the whole number that

---

[1] *daunted*, that is, *subdued*   [2] *aggravating*

[3] But this had already been charged against the Congregation before 2 July 1559 (*supra*, 193), though the wording of their reply from Edinburgh—" it is come to our knowledge "—may perhaps mean that they had not then seen or heard the proclamation itself (*supra*, 194).   [4] *spoliation*   [5] *coined and uncoined*

[6] In vulgar parlance, a *halfpenny*   [7] John Hamilton

[8] James Beaton, son of an elder brother of Cardinal Beaton

were with her to consent to pursue us with all cruelty and expedition, before that we could have our company (which then was dispersed for new furnishing) assembled again.[1] The certainty hereof coming to our knowledge, the Saturday at night, the 25 [22] of July,[2] we did in what us lay to give advertisement to our brethren ; but impossible it was that those of the West, Angus, Mearns, Strathearn, or Fife, in any number could come to us ; for the enemy marched from Dunbar upon the Sunday, and approached within two miles of us before the sun rising upon Monday ; for they verily supposed to have found no resistance, being assured that the Lords only with certain gentlemen remained, with their private houses.[3] Calling upon God for counsel in that strait, we sought what was the next defence. We might have left the town, and might have retired ourselves without any danger ; but then we should have abandoned our brethren of Edinburgh, and suffered the ministry thereof to have decayed, which to our hearts was so dolorous that we thought better to hazard the extremity than so to do. For then the most part of the town appeared rather to favour us than the Queen's faction ; and did offer unto us the uttermost of their support, which for the most part they did faithfully keep. The same did the town of Leith, but they kept not the like fidelity ; for when we were upon the field, marching forward for their support (for the French marched nigh *Leith left the Con-gregation* to them), they rendered themselves, without further resistance. And this they did, as was supposed, by the treason of some within themselves, and by the persuasion of the Laird of Restalrig,[4] who of before declared himself to have been one of us and, notwithstanding, that day rendered himself undesired to Monsieur d'Oysel. Their un-provided and sudden defection astonished many ; and yet we retired quietly to the side of Craigingatt,[5] which place we took for resisting the enemy.

In the meantime, divers mediators passed betwix, amongst whom the Lord Ruthven,[6] for our part, was principal. Alexander

---

[1] *Supra*, 197

[2] Saturday fell on the 22 July. According to the " Historie of the Estate of Scotland " the Queen Regent's decision to attack the Congregation in Edinburgh was taken at a Council held at Dunbar on 22 July (*Wodrow Misc.*, i, 63).

[3] The "Historie of the Estate of Scotland" says "the whole number of the Congregation exceeded not 1,500 men " (*Wodrow Misc.*, i, 64).

[4] Sir Robert Logan of Restalrig. The " Historie of the Estate of Scotland " says that Leith surrendered when it saw the numbers of the Regent's forces, "which were about 3,000 men." (*Wodrow Misc.*, i, 64)

[5] ' Craigingalt ' was the name given to the entire Calton Hill. (But see the whole question examined in *Book of the Old Edinburgh Club*, xviii, 33–44).

[6] Patrick, third Lord Ruthven

Erskine [1] did much travail to stay us and our soldiers, that we should not join with them of Leith, till that they, as said is, had rendered themselves to the French. The said Alexander did oft promise, That the French would stay, provided that we would not join with those of Leith. But after that they were rendered, we heard nothing of him but threatening and discomfortable words. Before it was eight hours in the morning, God had given unto us both courage, and a reasonable number to withstand their fury. [2] The town of Edinburgh, so many as had subjected themselves to discipline, and divers others besides them, behaved themselves both faithfully and stoutly. The gentlemen of Lothian, especially Calder, [3] Halton, [4] and Ormiston, [5] were very comfortable as well for their counsel as for their whole assistance. Some gentlemen of Fife prevented the French men; others were stopped by reason that the French had possessed Leith. Always the enemy took such a fear that they determined not to invade us where we stood, but took purpose to have passed to Edinburgh by the other side of the Water of Leith, and that because they had the Castle to their friend, which was to us unknown; for we supposed the Lord Erskine, [6] Captain of the same, either to have been our friend, or at the least to have been indifferent. But when we had determined to fight, he sent word to the Earl of Argyll, to Lord James, his sister's son, [7] and to the other Noble men, that he would declare himself both enemy to them and to the town, and would shoot at both, if they made any resistance to the French men to enter in the town. This his treasonable defiance, [8] sent unto us by the Laird of Riccarton, [9] did abate the courage of many; for we could not fight nor stop the enemy, but under the mercy of the Castle and whole ordnance thereof.

The Lord Erskine and his fact

---

[1] Sir Alexander Erskine of Gogar, second surviving son of John, fifth Lord Erskine

[2] In a letter to Sir James Croft, the Lords of the Congregation say that at this time their " enemies war in nomber thrise more then we." (Laing's *Knox*, vi, 62)

[3] John Sandilands of Calder   [4] William Lauder of Halton

[5] John Cockburn of Ormiston

[6] John, sixth Lord Erskine, later first Earl of Mar. The previous Governor, a Hamilton—Sir William Hamilton of Sanquhar—was apparently removed from office with the advent of the regency of Mary of Guise (*cf. Accounts Lord High Treas.*, x, 212).

[7] The Lord James Stewart (later the Regent Moray) was the natural son of James V by Margaret Erskine, sister to John, sixth Lord Erskine. Archibald, fifth Earl of Argyll, was also married to a natural child of James V, namely, to Jane, or Janet, the King's daughter by Elizabeth Beaton of Creich.

[8] According to d'Oysel, writing to Noailles on 22 July, the Lord Erskine, in the Council at Dunbar, on the morning of the 22nd (*supra*, 200, *note* 2) had promised and sworn to uphold the royal authority. (Teulet, *Papiers d'État*, i, 326)

[9] Henry Drummond of Riccarton

Hereupon was consultation taken ; and in conclusion, it was found less domage [1] to take an Appointment, albeit the conditions were not such as we desired, than to hazard battle betwix two such enemies. After long talking, certain Heads were drawn [up] by us, which we desired to be granted :

" First, That no member of the Congregation should be troubled in life, lands, goods, or possessions by the Queen, her Authority, nor any other Justice within the realm, for anything done in the late innovation, till a Parliament (which should begin the tenth of January next) [2] had decided things in controversy.

" 2. That idolatry should not be erected where it was at that day suppressed.

" 3. That the preachers and ministers should not be troubled in their ministry, where they were already established, neither yet stopped to preach, wheresoever they should chance to come.

" 4. That no bands of men of war should be laid in garneshing [3] within the town of Edinburgh.

" 5. That the French men should be sent away at a reasonable day, and that none other should be brought in the country without consent of the whole Nobility and Parliament." [4]

But these our Articles were altered, and another form disposed, as after followeth :

" AT THE LINKS OF LEITH, THE 24 OF JULY 1559, IT IS APPOINTED IN MANNER FOLLOWING :

" IN the first, the Congregation and their company, other than the inhabitants of the said town,[5] shall remove themselves forth of the said town, the morn at ten hours before noon, the 25 of July, and leave the same void and red [6] of them and their said company, conform to the Queen's Grace's pleasure and desire.

" Item, The said Congregation shall cause the irons of the Cunzie-

---

[1] Probably used in the French sense as meaning less grievous
[2] Supra, 193   [3] garrison
[4] In a letter, in Knox's holograph, to Sir James Croft, and dated at Edinburgh, 24 July 1559, these are the terms which are reported to have been agreed upon on Monday 23 [24] July (Foreign Calendar, Elizabeth, i, No. 1056). In the talks at Preston the Congregation had demanded the withdrawal of the French from Scotland (supra, 198) ; and it is possible that at the Links of Leith a verbal promise to that effect was given, was regarded by the negotiators for the Congregation as a definite pledge, and was represented to Knox, and accepted by Knox, as such a pledge (cf. infra, 204, note 4)
[5] Edinburgh   [6] and leave the same empty and free

house, taken away by them, [to] be rendered and delivered to Master Robert Richardson ; and in likewise the Queen's Grace's Palace of Holyroodhouse to be left and rendered again to Master John Balfour, or any other having her Grace's sufficient power, in the same manner as it was received, and that betwix the making of these Articles and the morn at ten hours.—(For observing and keeping of these two Articles abovewritten, the Lord Ruthven and the Laird of Pittarrow have entered themselves pledges.)

" *Item*, The said Lords of Congregation, and all the members thereof, shall remain obedient subjects to our Sovereign Lord's and Lady's authority, and to the Queen's Grace's Regent in their place ; and shall obey all laws and lovable consuetudes of this realm, as they were used of before the moving of this tumult and controversy, excepting the cause of religion, which shall be hereafter specified.

" *Item*, The said Congregation, nor none of them, shall not trouble nor molest a Kirkman by way of deed,[1] nor yet shall make them any impediment in the peaceable bruiking,[2] joising,[3] and uptaking of their rents, profits, and duties [4] of their benefices, but that they may freely use and dispone upon the same, according to the laws and consuetude of this realm, to the tenth day of January next to come.

In contemplation of these articles arose this proverb— " Gud day sir John, whill Januar. Welcome sir John, whill Januar," &c.

" *Item*, The said Congregation, nor none of them, shall in no ways from henceforth use any force or violence in casting down of kirks, religious places, or reparelling [5] thereof, but the same shall stand skaithless [6] of them, unto the said tenth day of January.

" *Item*, The town of Edinburgh shall, without compulsion, use and choose what religion and manner thereof they please to the said day ; so that every man may have freedom to use his own conscience to the day foresaid.[7]

" *Item*, The Queen's Grace shall not interpose her authority to molest or trouble the preachers of the Congregation, nor their ministry (to them that pleases to use the same) nor no other of the said Congregation, in their bodies, lands, goods, or possessions, pensions, or whatsomever other kind of goods they possess ; nor yet thoill [8] the Clergy, or any others having spiritual or temporal jurisdiction, to trouble them in any manner of sort, privately or openly, for the cause of religion, or other action depending there-

---

[1] *by any deed*   [2] *possession*   [3] *enjoyment*   [4] *dues*
[5] *furnishings*. (Calderwood, *History*, i, 486, has *apparrell*.)   [6] *unharmed*
[7] This is later referred to in the Burgh Records, but the date of the Appointment is left blank. (*Edinburgh Burgh Records*, iii, 46)   [8] *allow*

upon, to the said tenth day of January within written ; and that every man in particular live in the meantime according to his own conscience.[1]

" *Item,* That no man of war, French nor Scots,[2] be laid in daily garrison within the town of Edinburgh, but to repair thereto to do their lawful business, and thereafter to retire them to their garrisons."[3]

This alteration in words and order was made without knowledge and consent of those whose counsel we had used in all such cases before.[4] For some of them perceiving we began to faint, and that we would appoint with unequal conditions, said, " God hath wonderfully assisted us in our greatest dangers : He hath stricken fear in the hearts of our enemies, when they supposed themselves most assured of victory : our case is not yet so desperate that we need to grant to things unreasonable and ungodly ; which, if we do, it is to be feared that things shall not so prosperously succeed as they have done heretofore."

When all things were communed and agreed upon by mid persons,[5] the Duke and Earl of Huntly, who that day were against us, desired to speak the Earls of Argyll and Glencairn, the Lord James, and others of our party : who, obeying their requests, met them at the Querrell Holes,[6] betwix Leith and Edinburgh, who in *The promise of the Duke and Earl of Huntly* conclusion promised to our Lords, " That if the Queen broke to us any one jot of the Appointment then made, that they should declare themselves plain enemies unto her, and friends to us." As much promised the Duke that he would do, in case that she

---

[1] Up to this point these Articles are exactly the same as those reported in Teulet (*Papiers d'État relatifs à l'Histoire de l'Écosse,* i, 327–28, dated 24 July), and in the summary, from a French document, in *Foreign Calendar, Elizabeth,* i, No. 1052 (dated 23 July).

[2] Scots soldiers in French pay had already proved a vexed question (*supra,* 180, 187)

[3] This concluding article does not appear in Teulet (*loc. cit.*), although in the original articles drawn up by the Congregation (and which Knox says were *agreed*) all Frenchmen were to be sent away, and no more brought into Scotland save with the consent of the Nobility and Parliament.   (*Supra,* 202, and *note* 4)

[4] Knox had already referred to " alteration " of the Articles (*supra,* 202) ; and it is possible that the negotiators for the Congregation had agreed to other articles (which did *not* include a clause relating to the French soldiers) without reporting back for further instructions. Comparing these later terms with what was asked for, and what was possibly at first agreed, the Congregation, in their Proclamation of 26 July (*infra,* 205), went back to their original demands as first drawn up, and, according to Knox's letter to Croft, first agreed.   (But see *supra,* 202, *note* 4)   [5] negotiators

[6] The Quarry Holes to the east of Calton Hill, between the present Easter Road and Leith Walk.

would not remove her French men at a reasonable day [1]; for the oppression which they did was manifest to all men.

This Appointment made and subscribed by the Duke, Monsieur d'Oysel, and the Earl of Huntly, the 25 of July, we returned to the town of Edinburgh, where we remained till the next day at noon ; when, after sermon, dinner, and a proclamation made at the Market Cross in form as followeth, we departed.

FORM OF THE PROCLAMATION

" FORASMUCH as it hath pleased God that Appointment is made betwix the Queen Regent and us the Lords [and] whole Protestants of this Realm, we have thought good to signify unto you the chief Heads of the same, which be these [2] :

" 1. First, That no member of the Congregation shall be troubled in life, lands, goods, or possessions, by the Queen, by her Authority, nor by any other Justice within this realm, for anything done in this late innovation, till that a Parliament hath decided things that be in controversy.

" 2. That idolatry shall not be erected, where it is now at this day suppressed.

" 3. That the preachers and ministers shall not be troubled in the ministration, where they are already established, neither yet stopped to preach wheresoever they shall happen to travail within this realm.

" 4. That no bands of men of war shall be laid in garrison within the town of Edinburgh.

" These chief heads of Appointment concerning the liberty of religion and conservation of our brethren, we thought good to notify unto you, by this our Proclamation, that in case wrong or injury be done, by any of the contrary faction, to any member of our body, complaint may be made unto us, to whom we promise, as we will answer to God, our faithful support to the uttermost of our powers."

At this proclamation, made with sound of trumpet, were offended all the Papists. For, first, they alleged it was done in contempt of

[1] This looks like a private promise by Châtelherault, and quite apart from any clause in the Appointment.

[2] Here, in this Proclamation, the Reformers disregard (or repudiate) the " altered " Appointment made by their negotiators at the Links of Leith, and go back to the first four Heads drawn up by them, and which Knox, in his letter to Sir James Croft, says were agreed (*supra*, 202, and *note* 4).

the Authority ; secondly, that we had proclaimed more than was contained in the Appointment ; and last, that we, in our proclamation, had made no mention of anything promised unto them.

To such mummers [1] we answered, " That no just Authority could think itself contemned, because that the truth was by us made manifest unto all, who otherwise might have pretended ignorance. Secondly, That we had proclaimed nothing which [was] not finally agreed upon in word and promise betwix us and them with whom the Appointment was made, whatsoever their scribes had after written, who in very deed had altered, both in words and sentences, our Articles, as they were first conceived [2] ; and yet, if their own writings were diligently examined, the selfsame thing shall be found in substance. And last, To proclaim anything in their favour, we thought it not necessary, knowing that in that behalf they themselves should be diligent enough." And in this we were not deceived ; for within fifteen days after there was not a shaveling in Scotland, to whom teinds, or any other rents pertained, but he had that Article of the Appointment by heart, " That the Kirk men should be answered of teinds, rents, and all other duties, and that no man should trouble nor molest them." [3]

We departing from Edinburgh, the 26 of July, came first to Linlithgow, and after to Stirling ; where, after consultation, the band of defence, and maintenance of religion, and for mutual defence, every one of other, was subscribed of all that were there present. The tenor of the Band was this :

" We foreseeing the craft and sleight of our adversaries, tending all manner of ways to circumvent us, and by privy means intends to assail every one of us particularly by fair hechts [4] and promises, therethrough to separate one of us from another, to our utter ruin and destruction : for remedy hereof, we faithfully and truly bind us, in the presence of God, and as we tender the maintenance of true Religion, that none of us shall in times coming pass to the Queen's Grace Dowager, to talk or commune with her for any letter [or] message sent by her unto us, or yet to be sent, without consent of the rest, and common consultation thereupon. And how soon that either

---

[1] *mutterers*

[2] This seems hardly fair ; certainly it is very special pleading. Even if Knox's letter to Sir James Croft is to be trusted (*supra*, 202, *note* 4), it is clear that the terms of the first agreement had been superseded by the terms of the agreement at the Links of Leith when, it would appear, the negotiators on behalf of the Congregation exceeded their commission.

[3] Here Knox clearly shows that the Appointment at the Links of Leith *had* been accepted, for this reference is to Article 4 of that Appointment.   [4] *engagements*

message or writ shall come from her unto us, with utter diligence we shall notify the same one to another ; so that nothing shall proceed herein without common consent of us all.[1]

" At Stirling, the first day of August 1559."

This Band subscribed, and we, foreseeing that the Queen and Bishops meant nothing but deceit, thought good to seek aid and support of all Christian Princes against her and her tyranny, in case we should be more sharply pursued. And because that England was of the same religion, and lay next unto us, it was judged expedient first to prove them ; which we did by one or two messengers, as hereafter, in its own place, more amply shall be declared.[2]

After we had abided certain days in Stirling, the Earl of Argyll departed to Glasgow ; and because he was to depart to his own country (with whom also passed Lord James), to pacify some trouble which, by the craft of the Queen, was raised in his absence, he required the Earl of Glencairn, Lord Boyd, Lord Ochiltree, and others of Kyle, to meet there, for some order to be taken, that the brethren should not be oppressed ; which with one consent they did, and appointed the tenth of September for the next Convention at Stirling.

While these things were in doing at Glasgow, letters and a servant came from the Earl of Arran to the Duke his father, signifying unto him, that by the providence of God, he had escaped the French King's hands, who most treasonably and most cruelly had sought his life, or at least to have committed him to perpetual prison [3] : *The first knowledge of the escaping of the Earl of Arran out of France*

---

[1] In other words, precaution will henceforth be taken not so much against the "craft" of the Queen Regent as against the possibility of negotiators exceeding their commission and not reporting back for further instructions.

[2] Elizabeth had ascended the English throne on 17 November 1558. At the beginning of Book III (*infra*, 282*ff*), Knox describes more fully the negotiations with England ; but, as we have already seen, the Reformers had been in correspondence with England as early as 23 June 1559 (*Calendar of Scottish Papers*, i, No. 471, and *supra*, 194, *note* 2). Knox himself was one of these " messengers " here referred to. His " instructions " are dated 30 July (Laing's *Knox*, vi, 56) ; he reached Holy Island on 1 August, and thence was secretly conveyed to Berwick Castle, where he explained his instructions to Sir James Croft, his explanation including a request for aid from England. (*Foreign Calendar, Elizabeth*, i, No. 1119 ; *Calendar of Scottish Papers*, i, No. 511)

[3] James, Lord Hamilton, Earl of Arran, eldest son of the Duke of Châtelherault, had set up a Protestant Congregation at Châtelherault ; but, with the renewal of religious persecution in France, and for political reasons also, he was compelled to flee. His escape was facilitated with English connivance and, having made his way to Geneva, he returned, through Germany, to England, where he was received by Cecil and promptly sent north to Scotland—Elizabeth being as fully alive as the French to the importance of the Hamilton claim to be next in succession to the Scottish Crown. In Scotland, Arran's safe arrival, 10 September 1559 (*infra*, 229, *note* 1), was an important and immediate factor in influencing his father definitely to throw in his lot with the Reformers.

for the same time, the said French King, seeing he could [not] have the Earl himself, gart put [1] his younger brother,[2] a bairn of such age as could not offend, in strait prison, where he yet remains, to wit, in the month of October, the year of God 1559 : which things were done by the craft and policy of the Queen Dowager, *Let this be noted* what time the Duke and his friends were most frack [3] to set forward her cause. These letters received, and the estate of his two sons known, of whom the one was escaped and the other in vile prison cast, the Duke desired communing of the Earl of Argyll, who, partly against the will of some that loved him, rode unto the Duke from Glasgow to Hamilton ; where, abiding one night, he declared his judgment to the Duke and to his friends, especially to Master Gavin Hamilton. The Duke required him and the Lord James to write their friendly and comfortable letters to his son, which they both most willingly did, and thereafter addressed them to their journey. But the very day of their departing, came one, Bowtencourt,[4] from the Queen Regent, with letters, as was alleged, from the King and Queen of France to Lord James, which he delivered with a bragging countenance and many threatening words. The tenor of his letters was this :

" *Le Roy.*

" My Cousin, I have been gretumly marvellit,[5] having understood the troubles that are happened in those parts ; and yet more marvel that ye, of whom I had a whole confidence, and also has the honour to be so near the Queen's Grace, my wife, and has received of umquhile [6] the King's Grace my father, her Grace, and me, such graces and favours, that ye should be so forgetful as to make yourself the head, and one of the principal beginners and nourishers of the tumults and seditions there are seen there. The which, because it is so strange as it is, and syne [7] against the profession that ye at all

---

[1] *made to be put*

[2] Lord David Hamilton. Cecil, writing to the Congregation on 28 July 1559, reports that Lord David was " cruelly imprisoned by Monsieur Chevigny, one chosen to oppress the Scots " (*Calendar Scottish Papers*, i, No. 506) ; Randolph, writing to Cecil on 27 August 1560, reports that he had by then been set free (*ibid.*, i, No. 893).   [3] *active*

[4] Jean de Béthencourt, Sieur de Boscasselin, had apparently left Paris before 29 July 1559, Throckmorton reporting that his mission was to charge the Queen Regent to " dissemble " with the Reformers. (*Foreign Calendar, Elizabeth*, i, No. 1094). His instructions (printed in L. Paris, *Négotiations sous François II*) were that the Queen Regent was to make peace ' doulcement et par moyens, s'il est possible.'   [5] *greatly astonished*

[6] *late*   [7] here used in the sense of *moreover*, that is, *after all that*

times have made, I can not goodly believe it ; and if it be so, I can not think but ye have been enticed and led thereto by some persons that have seduced and caused you commit such a fault, as I am assured ye repent of already, which will be a great emplesour [1] to me, to the effect I might lose a part of the occasion I have to be miscontent with you, as I will you to understand I am, seeing so far ye have deceived the esperance I had of you, and your affection towards God, and the weal of our service, unto the which ye know ye are as mekill and mair obleist nor any other of the Lords there. For this cause, desiring that the matters might be dutily [2] amended, and knowing what ye may hereinto, I thought good on this manner to write unto you, and pray you to take heed to return to the good way from which ye are declined, and cause me know the same by the effects that ye have another intention nor this which those follies bypast makes me now to believe ; doing all that ever ye can to reduce all things to their first estate, and put the same to the right and good obedience that ye know to be due unto God and unto me : otherwise, ye may be well assured that I will put to my hand, and that in good earnest, *Brags now* that ye and all they [that] have done, and does as ye, shall feel (through their own fault) that which they have deserved and merited ; even as I have given charge to this Gentleman, present bearer, to make you know more largely of my part ; for which cause, I pray you credit him, even as ye would do myself. Praying God, my Cousin, to have you in his holy and worthy protection.

" Written at Paris, the 17 day of July 1559."

The same messenger brought also letters from the Queen our Sovereign, more sharp and threatening than the former ; for her conclusion was, " *Vous senteras la poincture a jamais.*" [3]

This credit was, " That the King would spend the Crown of France, ere that he were not revenged upon such seditious persons. [4] That he would never have suspected such inobedience and such defection from his own sister in him." To the which the said Lord James answered, first by word, and then by writing, as follows :

---

[1] *pleasure*   [2] *duly*

[3] That is, " You shall feel the prick of it for ever." The letter from Mary has been reprinted by Pollen (*Papal Negotiations with Mary Queen of Scots*, Scot. Hist. Soc., 432) ; the phrase referred to by Knox is : " duquel autrement vous estes asseuré de sentir la poincture, telle quil vous en *souviendra* a jamais."

[4] That is, he would be revenged on such sedition even if he had to expend the whole resources of the Crown of France. Knox reports the ' credit ' of the letters in similar terms to Cecil (*Foreign Calendar, Elizabeth*, i, Nos. 1134, 1200). But see the comment in Pollen, *op. cit.*, xxxii–xxxiv.

" SIR,   " My duty remembered. Your Majesty's letter I received from Paris, the 17 of July last, proporting in effect, that your Majesty should marvel that I, being forgetful of the graces and favours shown me by the King, of blessed memory, your Majesty's father, and the Queen's Grace, my Sovereign, should declare myself head, and one of the principal beginners of the alleged tumults and sedition in these parts, deceiving thereby your Majesty's expectation at all times heard of me ; with assurance, that if I did not declare by contrary effects my repentance, I, with the rest that had put, or yet puts hands to that work, should receive the reward which we had deserved and merited.

" Sir, it grieves me heavily that the crime of ingratitude should be laid to my charge by your Highness, and the rather that I perceive the same to have proceeded of sinister information of them whose part it was not so to have reported, if true service bigane [1] had been regarded. And as touching the repentance and declaration of the same by contrary effects, that your Majesty desires I show, my conscience persuades me in these proceedings to have done nothing against God, nor the debtful obedience towards your Highness and the Queen's Grace my Sovereign, otherwise it should have been to repent, and also amended already, according to your Majesty's expectation of me. But your Highness being truly informed and persuaded that the thing which we have done makes for the advancement of God's glory (as it does indeed), without any manner [of] derogation to your Majesty's due obedience, we doubt not but your Majesty shall be well contented with our proceedings, which being grounded upon the commandment of the eternal God, we dare [not] leave the same unaccomplished ; only wishing and desiring your Majesty did know the same, and truth thereof, as it is persuaded to our conscience, and all them that are truly instructed in the eternal word of our God, upon whom we cast our care for all dangers that may follow the accomplishment of his eternal will ; and to whom we commend your Highness, beseeching Him to illuminate your heart with the evangel of his eternal truth, to know your Majesty's duty towards your poor subjects, God's chosen people, and what ye ought to crave justly of them again ; for then we should have no occasion to fear your Majesty's wrath and indignation, nor your Highness's suspicion in our inobedience. The same God mot [2] have your Majesty in his eternal safeguard.

" At Dumbarton, the 12 of August 1559."

[1] *in the past*   [2] *may* : that is, " May the same God have your Majesty, etc."

This answer directed to the Queen our Sovereign,[1] and to Francis her husband, the Queen Dowager received, and was bold upon it, as she might well enough ; for it was supposed that the former letters were forged here at home in Scotland. The answer read by her, she said, " That so proud an answer was never given to King, Prince, or Princess." And yet indifferent men thought that he might have answered more sharply, and not have transgressed modesty nor truth. For where they burden him with the great benefits which of them he had received, if in plain words he had purged himself, affirming that the greatest benefit that ever he received of them was to spend in their service that which God by others had provided for him, no honest man would have accused him, and no man would have been able to have convicted him of a lie. But Princes must be pardoned to speak what they please.

For comfort of the brethren, and continuance of the Kirk in Edinburgh, was left there our dear brother John Willock who, for his faithful labours and bold courage in that battle, deserves immortal praise. For when it was found dangerous that John Knox, who before was elected Minister [2] to that Kirk, should continue there, the brethren requested the said John Willock to abide with them, lest that, for lack of ministers, idolatry should be erected up again. To the which he so gladly consented, that it might evidently appear that he preferred the comfort of his brethren, and the continuance of the Kirk there, to his own life.[3] One part of the French men were appointed to lie in garrison at Leith (that was the first benefit they got for their confederacy with them),[4] the other part were appointed to lie in the Canongate ; the Queen and her train abiding in the Abbey. Our brother John Willock, the day after our departure, preached in Saint Giles' Kirk, and fervently exhorted the brethren to stand constant in the truth which they had professed. At this, and some other sermons, were the Duke and divers others of the Queen's faction. This liberty and preaching, with resort of all people thereto, did highly offend the Queen and the other Papists. And first they

The residence of John Willock in Edinburgh

---

[1] But the answer printed by Knox was apparently to Francis II. The answer of the Lord James to Mary can be read in Pollen, *op. cit.*, 433–434.

[2] The " Historie of the Estate of Scotland " says that the Congregation of Edinburgh " elected and chose John Knox publiquely in the Tolbooth of Edenburgh for their minister, the 7th of July." (*Wodrow Misc.*, i, 63)

[3] The " Historie of the Estate of Scotland " later records " In the end of the same moneth of August, there arrived at Leith fower ensignes of Frenchmen. About the same tyme the communion wes publiquely administred in St. Giles Church, John Willox being minister, whereat the Queene wes highly offended " (*ibid.*, i, 67).   [4] *Supra*, 200

began to give terrors to the Duke ; affirming that he would be
reputed as one of the Congregation if he gave his presence to the sermons. Thereafter they begould [1] to require that Mass should be
set up again in Saint Giles' kirk, and that the people should be set
at liberty to choose what religion they would ; for that, say they,
was contained in the Appointment, that the town of Edinburgh
should choose what religion they list. For obtaining hereof, was sent
to the Tolbooth, the Duke, the Earl of Huntly, and the Lord Seton, [2]
to solist [3] all men to condescend to the Queen's mind ; wherein the
two last did labour that they could, the Duke not so, but as a be-
holder, of whom the brethren had good esperance. And after many
persuasions and threatenings made by the said Earl and Lord, [4]
the brethren, stoutly and valiantly in the Lord Jesus, gainsaid their
most unjust petitions, reasoning, " That as of conscience they might
not suffer idolatry to be erected where Christ Jesus was truly preached,
so could not the Queen nor they require any such thing, unless
she and they would plainly violate their faith and chief article of the
Appointment ; for it is plainly appointed, That no member of the
Congregation shall be molested in anything that, the day of the
Appointment, he peaceably possessed. But so it was that we, the
Brethren and Protestants of the town of Edinburgh, with our
ministers, the day of the Appointment, did peaceably possess
Saint Giles' Kirk, appointed for us for preaching of Christ's
true Evangel, and right ministration of his holy Sacraments. Therefore, without manifest violation of the Appointment, ye cannot
remove us therefrom, while a Parliament have decided the
controversy." [5]

This answer given, the whole brethren departed, and left the
foresaid Earl and Lord Seton, the Provost of Edinburgh, still in the
Tolbooth. Who, perceiving that they could not prevail in that
manner, began to entreat that they would be quiet, and that they

---

[1] began

[2] According to the Burgh Records, the Duke of Châtelherault, the Earl of Huntly,
and Lord Erskine compeared " in presens of the provest ballies ane pairt of the counsall
dekynnis and ane greit number of the communite," on 29 July 1559. (*Edinburgh Burgh
Records*, iii, 46) George, fifth Lord Seton, was at the time Provost of Edinburgh. The
" Historie of the Estate of Scotland " mentions only Châtelherault and Huntly. (*Wodrow
Misc.*, i, 65)   [3] solicit

[4] This is not supported by the Burgh Records, where the " lordis declarit that thei
wald compell na man to do by [contrary to] his conscience, nor do ony thing that mycht
contravene the said appontment." (*Edinburgh Burgh Records*, iii, 48)

[5] According to the Burgh Records the spokesman for the Congregation of Edinburgh
was Adam Fullarton, whose " supplication " is registered in full in the court books. (*Ibid.*,
iii, 47–48)

would so far condescend to the Queen's pleasure as that they would choose them another Kirk within the town, or at the least be content that Mass should be said either after or before their sermons. To the which, answer was given, " That to give place to the Devil (who was the chief inventor of the Mass), for the pleasure of any creature, they could not. They were in possession of that Kirk, which they could not abandon ; neither could they suffer idolatry [to] be erected in the same, unless by violence they should be constrained so to do ; and then they were determined to seek the next remedy." Which answer received, the Earl of Huntly did lovingly entreat them to quietness ; faithfully promising that in no sort they should be molested, so that they would be quiet, and make no further uproar.[1] To the which they were most willing ; for they sought only to serve God as he had commanded, and to keep their possession, according to the Appointment ; which by God's grace they did till the month of November,[2] notwithstanding the great boasting of the enemy. For they did not only convene to the preaching, daily supplications, and administration of Baptism, but also the Lord's Table was ministered, even in the eyes of the very enemy, to the great comfort of many [an] afflicted conscience. And as God did potently work with his true Minister, and with his troubled Kirk, so did not the Devil cease to inflame the malice of the Queen, and of the Papists with her. For short after her coming to the Abbey of Holyroodhouse, she caused Mass to be said, first in her own Chapel, and after in the Abbey, where the altars before were cast down. She discharged the Common Prayers, and forbade to give any portion to such as were the principal young men who read them. Her malice extended in like manner to Cambuskenneth ; for there she discharged the portions of as many of the Canons as had forsaken Papistry.[3] She gave command and inhibition that the Abbot of Lindores [4] should be answered of any part of his living in the North, because he had submitted himself to the Congregation, and had put some reformation to his place. By her consent and retrahibition [5] were the preaching stools broken in the Kirk of Leith, and idolatry was erected in the same, where it was before suppressed. Her French Captains, with their soldiers in great companies, in time of preaching and prayers,

The Queen Regent's malice against poor men

---

[1] These proceedings are also fully reported in the " Historie of the Estate of Scotland." (*Wodrow Misc.*, i, 65–67)

[2] When the Congregation retreated to Stirling (*infra*, 264–265)

[3] Cambuskenneth, about one mile north-east of Stirling, was an Augustinian Abbey of Canons-Regular.

[4] John Philp, Abbot of Lindores (Fife)   [5] *countermand*

resorted to Saint Giles' Kirk in Edinburgh, and made their common deambulatour [1] therein, with such loud talking, as no perfect audience [2] could be had ; and although the Minister was ofttimes therethrough compelled to cry out on them, praying to God to rid them of such locusts, they nevertheless continued still in their wicked purpose, devised and ordained by the Queen, to have drawn our brethren of Edinburgh and them in cummer [3] ; so that she might have had any coloured occasion to have broken the league with them.[4] Yet, by God's grace, they behaved themselves so, that she could find no fault with them ; albeit in all these things before named, and in every one of them, she is worthily accounted to have contravened the said Appointment. We pass over the oppressing done of our brethren in particular, which had been sufficient to have proven the Appointment to have been plain violated ; for the Lord Seton, without any occasion offered unto him, broke a chaise [5] upon Alexander Whitelaw,[6] as he came from Preston, accompanied with William Knox,[7] towards Edinburgh, and ceased not to pursue him till he came to the town of Ormiston. And this he did, supposing that the said Alexander Whitelaw had been John Knox. In all this meantime, and while that more French men arrived, they are not able to prove that we broke the Appointment in any jot,[8] except that a horned cap was taken off a proud priest's head, and cut in four quarters, because he said he would wear it in despite of the Congregation.

In this meantime, the Queen, then Regent, knowing assuredly what force was shortly to come unto her, ceased not, by all means possible, to cloak the incoming of the French, and to inflame the hearts of our countrymen against us. And for that purpose, she first wrote to my Lord Duke, in form as follows :

[1] *place for a stroll*

[2] *hearing*

[3] *into conflict*

[4] That is, some feigned excuse to break the Appointment

[5] That is, *broke into pursuit of.* Andrew Lang says " broke a chair " on him (*John Knox and the Reformation*, 151). It is difficult to visualize Lord Seton carrying a chair about with him as a weapon of assault and, with it, pursuing his intended victim for some three miles ! (See *Foreign Calendar, Elizabeth*, i, No. 1132)

[6] Alexander Whitelaw of New Grange, Arbroath

[7] Brother to John Knox. He was apparently a merchant in Preston, East Lothian. An account of him is given in Laing's *Knox*, vi, lxxiii–lxxvi.

[8] But Knox is careful to omit that he and Whitelaw had been negotiating with the English at Holy Island and Berwick, and that their presence there, and their departure, were well known to their opponents. (*Foreign Calendar, Elizabeth*, i, Nos. 1097, 1119, 1123, 1124, 1132)

" My Lord and Cousin,

"After heartly commendation ; We are informed that the Lords of the Westland Congregation intend to make a convention and assembly of their kin and friends upon Govan Muir, beside Glasgow,[1] on Monday come eight days, the [21] day of August instant, for some high purpose against us, which we can not scantly [2] believe, considering they have no occasion upon our part so to do. And albeit ye know the Appointment was made by [3] our advice, yet we accepted the same at your desire, and has sensyne [4] made no cause whereby they might be moved to come in the contrary thereof. Like as we are yet minded to keep firm and stable all things promised by you in our behalf. We think, on the other part, it is your duty to require them, that they contravene not their part thereof in no wise ; and in case they mean any evil towards us, and so will break their promise, we believe ye will, at the uttermost of your power, convene with us and compel them to do that thing which they ought, if they will not. Praying you to have yourself, your kin and friends, in readiness to come to us as ye shall be advertised by proclamation in case the Congregation assemble themselves for any purpose against us, or the tenor of the said Appointment : assuring you, without they gather and make first occasion, we shall not put you to any pains in that behalf ; and that ye advertise us, in writing, what we may lippin to [5] herein with this bearer, who will show you the fervent mind we bear to have concord with the said Congregation, what offers we have made to them, and how desirous we are to draw them to the obedience of our Sovereign's authority, to whom ye shall give credit ; and God keep you.

"At Edinburgh, the tenth day of August 1559."

The like letter she wrote to every Lord, Baron, and Gentleman,[6] of this tenor :

" Trust Friend,

"After heartly commendation ; We doubt not but ye have heard of the Appointment made beside Leith, betwix my Lord Duke, the Earl of Huntly, and Monsieur d'Oysel, on the one part, and the Lords of the Congregation, on the other side ; which Appointment

Margin notes: The Queen Regent's false flattering letter to the Duke

The Regent's letter to the Barons

---

[1] Govan Muir is now within Glasgow   [2] scarcely
[3] without   [4] since   [5] confidently expect
[6] The letter sent to Rose of Kilravock, together with a draft of a reply, have been preserved. (Family of Rose of Kilravock, 228-229)

we have approved in all points, albeit it was taken by [1] our advice ; and is minded to observe and keep all the contents thereof for our part. None the less, we are informed the said Lords of the Congregation intend shortly to convene all such persons as will assist to them, for enterprising of some high purpose against us, our authority, and tenor of the said Appointment ; which we cannot believe, seeing they neither have, nor shall have, any occasion given thereto on our part, and yet thinks not reasonable, in case they mean any such thing : and therefore have thought it good to give warning to our special friends of the advertisement we have got, and amongst the rest, to you, whom we esteem of that number. Praying you to have yourself, your kin, and folks in readiness to come to us."— And so forth, as in the other letter above sent to the Duke, word after word.

After that by these letters, and by the deceitful furnishing of her solisters,[2] she had had somewhat stirred up the hearts of the people against us, then she began openly to complain, " That we were of mind to invade her person ; that we would keep no part of the Appointment ; and therefore she was compelled to crave the assistance of all men against our unjust pursuit." And this practice she used, as before is said, to abuse the simplicity of the people, that they should not suddenly espy for what purpose she brought in her new bands of men of war, who did arrive about the midst of August to the number of one thousand men. The rest were appointed to come after, with Monsieur de la Brosse,[3] and with the Bishop of Amiens,[4] who arrived the nineteenth day of September following,[5] as if they had been Ambassadors : but what was their negotiation, the effect did declare, and they themselves could not long conceal ; for both by tongue and pen they uttered, " That they were sent for the utter extermination of all them that would not profess the Papistical religion in all points." The Queen's practice nor craft could not blind the eyes of all men ; neither yet could her subtlety hide her own shame, but that many did espy her

The practice of Queen Regent

The arrival of the French

---

[1] *without*
[2] That is, by the deceitful procurement of those acting on her behalf
[3] Jacques de la Brosse
[4] Nicolas Pellevé, Bishop of Amiens
[5] The *Diurnal of Occurrents* (270) reports their arrival at Leith, with eight hundred men of war, on 24 September 1559. Sadler and Croft, writing to Cecil from Berwick on 27 September, report the arrival at Leith of three ships, "wherein is the Bishop of Amiens and 300 soldiers ; but they have no certainty of La Brosse" (*Foreign Calendar, Elizabeth*, i, No. 1377).

deceit : and some spared not to speak their judgment liberally ; who foreseeing the danger gave advertisement, requiring that provision might be found, before that the evil should exceed our wisdom and strength to put remedy to the same ; for prudent men foresaw that she pretended a plain conquest. But to the end that the people should not suddenly stir, she would not bring in her full force at once (as before is said), but by continual traffic purposed to augment her army so that in the end we should not be able to resist. But the greatest part of the Nobility, and many of the people, were so enchanted by her treasonable solisters, that they could not hear nor credit the truth plainly spoken. The French then, after the arrival of their new men, began to brag : then began they to divide the lands and lordships according to their own fantasies ; for one was styled Monsieur de Argyll ; another, Monsieur le Prior ; the third, Monsieur de Ruthven. Yea, they were assured, in their own opinion, to possess whatsoever they list, that some asked the rentals and revenue of divers men's lands, to the end that [they] might choose the best. And yet in this meantime, she ashamed not to set out a Proclamation, in this form : *The division of the Lords' lands by the French*

" FORSAMEKLE [1] as we understand that certain seditious persons have invented and blown abroad divers rumours and evil bruits, tending thereby to stir up the hearts of the people, and so to stop all reconciliations betwix us and our subjects, being of the number of the Congregation, and consequently to kindle and nourish continual strife and division in this realm to the manifest subversion of the whole Estates thereof ; and amongst other purposes, have maliciously devised for that effect, and have persuaded too many, that we have violated the Appointment lately tane,[2] in so far as any more Frenchmen sensyne [3] are come in : and that we are minded to draw in great forces of men of war forth of France, to suppress the liberty of this realm, oppress the inhabitants thereof, and make up strangers with their lands and goods. Which reports are all (God knows) most vain, fenzeit,[4] and untrue. For it is of truth, that nothing has been done on our part since the said Appointment whereby it may be alleged that any point thereof has been contravened : nor yet was at that time anything communed or concluded to stop the sending in of French men ; as may clearly *A proclamation set out by the Queen Regent, to blind the vulgar people*

---

[1] *Inasmuch* [2] *taken, that is, made*
[3] *since* [4] *feigned*

appear by inspection of the said Appointment,[1] which the bearer hereof has presently to show. What[ever] number of men of war be arrived, we [have] such regard to our honour and quietness of this realm, that in case in the room of every one French man that is in Scotland there were one hundred at our command, yet should

Let the Bishop of Amiens' and Monsieur de la Brosse's letters written to France witness that

not for that any jot that is promised be broken, or any alteration be made by our provocation ; but the said Appointment truly and surely observed in every point, if the said Congregation will in like manner faithfully keep their part thereof. Nor yet mean we to trouble any man in the peaceable possession of their goods and rowmes,[2] nor yet to enrich the Crown, and far less any stranger, with your substance [3] ; for our dearest son and daughter, the King and Queen, are by God's provision placed in the rowme,[4] where all men of judgment may well consider they have no need of any man's goods. And for ourself, we seek nothing but debtful obedience unto them, such as good subjects ought to give to their Sovereigns, without diminution of your liberties and privileges, or alteration of your laws. Therefore, we thought good to notify unto you our good mind foresaid, and desires you not to give ear nor credit to such vain imaginations, whereof, before God, no part ever entered in our conceit [5] ; nor suffer yourselves [to] be thereby led from your due

Few days after declared the truth of this

obedience ; assuring you, ye shall ever find with us truth in promises, and a motherly love towards all ; you behaving yourselves [as] our obedient subjects. But of one thing we give you warning, that whereas some preachers of the Congregation, in their public sermons, speak irreverently and slanderously, as well of Princes in general, as of ourself in particular, and of the obedience to the higher powers ; inducing the people, by that part of their doctrine, to defection from their duty, which pertains nothing to religion, but rather to sedition

---

[1] The heads of the Appointment drawn up by the Congregation had included a fifth, that no more Frenchmen should be brought into the country without the consent of the whole Nobility and Parliament (*supra*, 202) ; but no such clause appeared in the " altered " Appointment concluded at the Links of Leith (*supra*, 202–204) nor in Knox's copy of the Proclamation issued by the Congregation, and based on their original demands (*supra*, 205)—though certain manuscript copies of the Proclamation do contain the fifth head (*cf. Foreign Calendar, Elizabeth*, i, Nos. 1063, 1064). But already the Lords of the Congregation and the preachers, including Knox, had seen that reinforcements from France might well turn the scales against them ; and Cecil had hinted as much in his letters to them (Laing's *Knox*, vi, 53 ; *Foreign Calendar, Elizabeth*, i, No. 1086). Hence their insistence that the arrival of French troops was a breach of the Appointment, and hence Knox's wording that the Regent " ashamed not " to issue such a proclamation as this.

[2] *plots of land* ; here used in the sense of their *inheritance*   [3] *Cf. supra*, 217
[4] *position* ; again with the sense of *inheritance*   [5] *conception*

and tumult, things direct contrary to religion : therefore we desire
you to take order in your town and bounds, that when the preachers
repair there, they use themselves more modestly in that behalf
and in their preaching not to mell sa mekle [1] with civil policy and
public governance, nor yet name us, or other Princes, but with *Jezebel
would be*
honour and reverence, otherwise it will not be suffered.   Attour, [2] *honoured
but Elijah*
since ye have presently [3] the declaration of our intention, we desire to *would not*
know likewise what shall be your part to us, that we may under-
stand what to lippin for [4] at your hands ; whereof we desire a plain
declaration in writing, with this bearer, without excuse or delay.

" At Edinburgh, the twenty-eighth of August 1559."

This proclamation she sent by her messengers through all the
country, and had her solisters [5] in all parts, who painfully travailed
to bring men to her opinion ; amongst whom these were the
principals, Sir John Bellenden, Justice-Clerk ; Master James Balfour,
Official of Lothian, Master Thomas and Master William Scott, sons
to the Laird of Balwearie, [6] Sir Robert Carnegie, and Master Gavin
Hamilton ; who for fainting of the brethren's hearts, and drawing
many to the Queen's faction against their native country, have
declared themselves enemies to God, and traitors to their commonwealth.   But, above all others Master James Balfour, Official for the
time, ought to be abhorred; for he, of an old professor,[7] is become a
new denier of Christ Jesus, and manifest blasphemer of his eternal
verity, against his knowledge and conscience ; seeking to betray his
brethren and native country in the hands of a cruel and unfaithful
nation.

The answer to this former proclamation was made in form as
follows :

" To the Nobility, Burghs, and Community of this Realm
    of   Scotland,   the   Lords,   Barons,   and   others,
    Brethren   of   the   Christian   Congregation,   wishes
    increase   of   wisdom,   with   the   advancement   of   the
    Glory   of   God,   and   of   the   Commonwealth,   &c.   &c.

" The love of our native country craves, the defence of our
honour requires, and the sincerity of our consciences compels us

---

[1] *meddle so much*   [2] *moreover*
[3] That is, " by these presents," hence *now* or *herewith*   [4] *confidently expect*
[5] those acting on her behalf   [6] Sir William Scott of Balwearie
[7] from being a former professor of the reformed faith

(dearest Brethren), to answer some part to the last writings and proclamations set forth by the Queen's Grace Regent, no less to make us and our cause odious, than to abuse your simplicity to your final destruction, conspired of old, and now already put to work. And first, where she alleges certain seditious persons have of malice invented and blown abroad divers rumours [tending] thereby (as she alleges) to stir up the hearts of the people to sedition, by reason that the Frenchmen are croppin in [1] of late in our country ; true it is (dear Brethren), that all such as bear natural love to their country, to you, their brethren, inhabitants thereof, to our houses, wives, bairns, the esperance of your posterity and, shortly, to your commonwealth, and the ancient laws and liberties thereof, cannot but in heart lament, with mouth and tears complain, the most crafty assaults devised and practised, to the utter ruin of all these things forenamed ; and that so manifestly is gone to work, that even in our eyes our dearest brethren, true members of our common-wealth, are most cruelly oppressed by strangers ; in so far that some are banished their own houses, some robbed and spuilzeit [2] of their substance, conqueist [3] by their just labours in the sweat of their brows ; some cruelly murdered at the pleasure of these inhuman soldiers ; and altogether have their lives in such fear and dreddour, as if the enemy were in the midst of them ; so that nothing can seem pleasing unto them, which they possess in the bowels of their native country ; so near judges every man (and not but [4] just cause), the practice used upon their brethren to approach next unto them their selves, wives, bairns, houses, and substances, which altogether are cast at the feet of strangers, men of war, to be by them thus abused at their unbridled lust's desire. Now, if it be sedition (dear Brethren), to complain, lament, and pour forth before God the sorrows [and] sobs of our dolorous hearts, crying to him for redress of these enormities (which elsewhere is not to be found) ; and these altogether do [proceed] of [5] the unlawful holding of strange soldiers over the heads of our brethren ; if thus to complain be sedition, then indeed (dear Brethren), can none of us be purged of that crime ; for as in very heart we damn such inhuman cruelty, with the wicked and crafty pretence thereof, so can we, nor dare we not, neither by mouth's speaking, nor yet by keeping of silence, justify the same. Neither do we here aggrege [6] the breaking of the

---

[1] *have crept in*	[2] *despoiled*	[3] *acquired*	[4] *without*
[5] *from*	[6] *lay stress upon*		

appointment made at Leith (which always has manifestly been done)[1];
but when we remember what oath we have made to our commonwealth, and how the duty we owe to the same compels us to cry out,
that her Grace, by wicked and ungodly counsel, goes most craftily
about utterly to oppress the same, and ancient laws and liberties
thereof, as well against the King of France's promise, [as] her own
duty, in respect of the high promotions that she received thereby,
which justly should have caused her to have been indeed that which
she would be called (and is nothing less in verity), to wit, a careful
mother over this commonwealth ; but what motherly care she has
used towards you, ye cannot be ignorant. Have ye not been even *Let the*
from the first entres [2] of her reign, ever smited and oppressed with *Nobility judge*
unaccustomed and exorbitant taxations, [more] than ever were *hereof*
used within this realm ? Yea, and how far was it sought here to
have been brought in upon you and your posterity, under colour
to have been laid up in store for the wars ? The inquisition taken
of all your goods, movable and immovable, by way of testament ;
the seeking of the whole coal and salt of this realm, to have been
laid up in store and gernal, [3] and she alone to have been merchant thereof, does teach you by experience some of her motherly
care.

" Again, what care over your commonwealth does her Grace
instantly bear, when even now presently, and of a long time bygone,
by the ministry of some (who better deserve the gallows than ever
did Cochrane [4]), she does so corrupt the layit money, [5] and has
brought it in such baseness, and such quantity of scruiff, [6] that all
men that has their eyes open may perceive an extreme beggary
to be brought therethrough upon the whole realm, so that the whole
exchange and traffic to be had with foreign nations (a thing most
necessary in all commonwealths), shall thereby be utterly extinguished ; and all the gains received thereby are that she therewith
entertains strangers upon our heads. For, Brethren, ye know that
her money has served for no other purpose in our commonwealth
this long time bygone ; and the impunity of these wicked ministers

---

[1] The argument here looks like an admission that the actual Appointment with the
Queen Regent did *not* include an article that the French troops should be sent away and
no more French troops brought in save with the consent of the Nobility and Parliament.
(See *supra*, 218, *note* 1)   [2] *entry*, that is, *beginning*   [3] *granary*

[4] A favourite of James III, hanged by the nobles at Lauder Bridge, 1482.

[5] money made of *alloy*

[6] The idea is a coin of base metal with only a thin covering (a *scroof* or *scruff*) of precious
metal.

(whom lately we spake of), has brought the matter to such a licentious enormity, and plain contempt of the commonwealth, that now they spare not plainly to break down and convert the good and stark money, cunzeit in our Sovereign's less age,[1] into this their corrupted scruiff and baggage [2] of Hard-heads [3] and Non Sunts,[4] most like that she and they had conspired to destroy all the whole good cunzie [5] of this realm,[6] and consequently that part of the commonwealth. Besides all this, their clipped and rownged sous [7] which had no passage these three years past in the realm of France, are commanded to have course in this realm, to gratify thereby her new come soldiers. And all these things together are done without the advice or consent of the Nobility and Council of this realm, and manifestly therethrough against our ancient laws and liberties.

Let Sir Robert Richardson, and others, answer to this

"Thirdly, Her last and most weighty proceeding, more fully declares her motherly care her Grace bears to our commonwealth and us, when in time of peace, but any occasion of foreign wars, thousands of strangers are laid here and there upon the necks of our poor members of this commonwealth; their idle bellies fed upon the poor substance of the community, conqueist [8] by their just labours in the painful sweat of their brows. Which, to be true, Dunbar, North Berwick, Tranent, Prestonpans, Musselburgh, Leith, Canongate, Kinghorn, Kirkcaldy, Dysart, with the depauperate souls [9] that this day dwell therein, can testify; whose oppression, as doubtless it is entered in before the justice seat of God, so ought it justly to move our hearts to have ruth [10] and compassion upon these our poor brethren, and at our power to provide remedy for the same. And albeit her strangers had been garneissit [11] with money (as ye know well they were not), yet can their here lying be no ways but most hurtful to our commonwealth, seeing that the fertility of

---

[1] *minority*   [2] That is, this money of weak alloy, this rubbish

[3] *Hard-heads* were small coins of base metal with the royal cypher, crowned, on one side, and a lion rampant on the other side.

[4] *Non Sunts* were coins of base metal, bearing the arms of Francis and Mary, and so called from the legend, on the obverse, "IAM NON SUNT DUO SED UNA CARO."

[5] *coinage*

[6] In 1567 the non sunt was declared to be worth 6d., the bawbee 3d., the plack 2d., and the hard-head a half-penny (*Acts Parl. Scot.*, iii, 43, c. 72), and an Act of 1575 speaks of the dearth of victual and other merchandise through the great quantity of false money, placks and lions called hard-heads struck in the time of the government of the Queen Dowager and Regent. (*Ibid.*, iii, 92b)

[7] *clipped and filed (or worn away)* [*French*] *sous*   [8] *acquired*

[9] *impoverished souls*   [10] *pity*   [11] *furnished*

this realm has never been so plenteous that it was able of any continuance to sustain the self, and inhabitants thereof, without support of foreign countries ; far less able, besides the same, to sustain thousands of strangers wherewith it is burdened to the dearthing of all vivers,[1] as the murmur and complaint of Edinburgh this day does testify. But to what effect the commonwealth is this way burdened, the end does declare ; for shortly were there brought to the fields [these strangers] against our Sovereign's true lieges, even [against] us your Brethren, who (God knows) sought nought else but peace of conscience, under protection of our Sovereign, and reformation of these enormities, for no other cause but that we would not renounce the Evangel of Jesus Christ, and subdue our necks under the tyranny of that man of sin, the Roman Antichrist, and his forsworn shavelings, who at all times most tyranically oppressed our souls with hunger of God's true word, and reft our goods and substance, to waste the same upon their foul lusts and stinking harlots.

" But (O dear Brethren), this was not the chief pretence and final scope of her proceedings (as these days do well declare) ; for had not God given in our hearts to withstand that oppression with weapons of most just defence, thou, O Saint Johnston and Dundee, had been in no better estate nor your sister of Leith is this day. For though we in very deed (God is witness) meant then nothing but, in the simplicity of our hearts, the maintenance of true religion, and safety of our brethren professors of the same, yet lay there another serpent lurking in the breast of our adversaries, as this day (praise to God), is plainly opened to all that list behold, to wit, to bring you and us both under the perpetual servitude of strangers ; for we being appointed,[2] as ye know, touching religion to be reasoned in the Council [3] at the day affixed, and no occasion made to break the same on our side (as is well known), yet came there forth writings and complaints that this day and that day we were prepared to invade her Grace's person [4] (when in very truth there was never such thing thought, as the very deed has declared). But because she was before deliberate [5] to bring in French men to both our destructions, that ye should not stir therewith, she made you to understand that those bands came only for the safety of her own

---

[1] *resulting in the dearth of all victuals*
[2] That is, an Appointment having been made with us
[3] Probably one to be held on 10 January (*supra*, 193, 202, 203–204)
[4] *Supra*, 215–216   [5] That is, *she had already determined*

person. O craft, Brethren ! O subtlety ! But behold the end.
They are come, (yet not so many, no, not the sixth part that she
desired and looked for), and how ?   Not only with weapons to
defend her Grace's person, but with wives and bairns, to plant in
your native rowmes,[1] as they have already begun in the town of
Leith, the principal port and staple of all this realm, the gernall and
furnitour [2] of the Council and Seat of Justice [3] : and here will they
dwell, while they may reinforce them with greater number of their
fellow soldiers, to subdue then the rest, if God withstand not.   And
yet her Grace feared nor ashamed not to write, ' If they were an
hundred French men for every one of them that is in Scotland, yet
they should harm no man.'   Tell thou now, Leith, if that be true !
If this be not a crafty entry to a manifest conquest, forethought
of old, judge you, dear Brethren !   Thus to fortify our towns, and
even the principal port of our realm, and to lay so strong garrisons
of strangers therein, without any consent of the Nobility and Council
of this realm, but express against their mind (as our writings sent to
her Grace bear record), if this be not to oppress the ancient laws
and liberties of our realm, let all wise men say to it.   And further,
to take the barn-yards new gathered, the gernalls replenished, the
houses garnished, and to sit down therein, and by force to put the
just possessors and ancient inhabitants therefrom, with their wives,
bairns, and servants, to shift [for] themselves in begging, if there
be no other means, they being true Scotsmen, members of our commonwealth, and our dear brethren and sisters, born, fostered, and
brought up in the bowels of our common and native country : if
this be not the manifest declaration of their old pretence and mind
to the whole Scots nation, let your own conscience (Brethren), be
judge herein.   Was all Leith of the Congregation ? No, I think not ;
yet were all alike served.

" Let this motherly care then be tried by the fruits thereof :
First, By the great and exorbitant taxations used upon you, and yet
ten times greater pressed at,[4] as ye know.   Secondly, The utter
depravation of our cunzie, to conqueiss [5] thereby money to entertain
strangers, French soldiers, upon you, to make them strongholds,
lest ye should some time expel them out of your native rowmes.
Thirdly, By the daily reinforcing of the said French soldiers, in
strength and number, with wives and bairns, planting in your
brethren's houses and possessions.   Indeed, her Grace is, and has

*The
cause of
the
French
men's
coming
with
wives and
bairns*

---

[1] *places*   [2] *granary and supplier*   [3] Edinburgh
[4] *intended*   [5] *acquire*

been at all times careful to procure by her craft of fair words, fair promises, and sometimes budds,[1] to allure your simplicity to that point, to join yourself to her soldiers to danton[2] and oppress us, that ye the remanent[3] (we being cut off), may be an easy prey to her sleights, which God, of infinite goodness, has now discovered to the eyes of all that list to behold. But credit the works (dear Brethren) if ye will not credit us ; and lay the example of foreign nations, yea, of your own brethren, before your eyes, and procure not your own ruin willingly. If ye tender true religion, ye see how her Grace bears her[self] plain enemy thereto, and maintains the tyranny of their idle bellies, the Bishops, against God's Kirk. If religion be not persuaded unto you, yet cast ye not away the care ye ought to have over your commonwealth, which ye see manifestly and violently ruined before your eyes. If this will not move you, remember your dear wives, children, and posterity, your ancient heritages and houses ; and think well these strangers will regard no more your right thereunto than they have done your brethren's of Leith, whenever occasion shall serve. But if ye purpose, as we doubt not but that all they that either have wit or manhood will declare and prove indeed, to bruik[4] your ancient rowmes and heritages, conquered most valiantly, and defended by your most noble progenitors against all strangers, invaders of the same, as the French pretends plainly this day ; if ye will not be slaves unto them, and to have your lives, your wives, your bairns, your substance, and whatsoever is dear unto you, cast at their feet, to be used and abused at the pleasure of strange soldiers, as ye see your brethren's at this day before your eyes ; if ye will not have experience some day hereof in your own persons (as we suppose the least of you would not gladly have, but rather would choose with honour to die in defence of his own native rowme, than live and serve so shameful a servitude) ; then, Brethren, let us join our forces, and both with wit and manhood resist these beginnings, or else our liberties hereafter shall be dearer bought. Let us surely be persuaded, ' When our neighbour's house A Proverb be on fire, that we dwell not without danger.' Let no man withdraw himself herefrom : and if any will be so unhappy and mischievous (as we suppose none to be), let us altogether repute, hold, and use him (as he is indeed), for an enemy to us, and to himself, and to his commonweal. The eternal and omnipotent God, the true and only revenger of the oppressed, be our comfort and our protector against

---

[1] *bribes*   [2] *daunt*   [3] *remainder, rest*   [4] *possess*

the fury and rage of the tyrants of this world ; and especially from the insatiable covetousness of the Guisian's generation.[1]   AMEN."

Besides this our public letter, some men answered certain heads of her proclamation on this manner :

" If it be seditious [for men] to speak the truth in all sobriety, and to complain when they are wounded, or to call for help against unjust tyranny before that their throats be cut, then can we not deny but we are criminal and guilty of tumult and sedition.   For we have said that our commonwealth is oppressed, that we and our brethren are hurt by the tyranny of strangers, and that we fear bondage and slavery, seeing that multitudes of cruel murderers are daily brought in our country, without our counsel, or knowledge and consent.   We dispute not so mekill whether the bringing in of more Frenchmen be violating of the Appointment [2] (which the Queen nor her faction cannot deny to be manifestly broken by them, in more cases than one), as that we would know if the heaping of strangers upon strangers above us, without our counsel or consent, be a thing that may stand with the liberty of our realm, and with the profit of our commonwealth.   It is not unknown to all men of judgment, that the fruits of our country, in the most common years, be no more than sufficient[ly] reasonable to nourish the born inhabitants of the same.   But now, seeing that we have been vexed with wars, taken upon us at the pleasure of France, by the which the most fruitful portion of our country in corns has been wasted ; what man is so blind but that he may see, that such bands of ungodly and idle soldiers can be nothing else but an occasion to famish our poor brethren?   And in this point (which is the chief) we refuse not the judgment of all natural Scotsmen.

" The Queen Regent alleged, ' That although there were an hundred French men for one in Scotland, yet she is not minded to trouble any in his just possession.'   Whereto we answer, That we dispute not what she intends (which none the less, by probable conjectures, is to be suspected), but always we affirm, that such a multitude of French men is a burden, not only unprofitable, but also intolerable to this poor realm, especially being entreated as they are by her and Monsieur d'Oysel ; for if their wages be paid out of France, then are they both (the Queen, we say, and Monsieur d'Oysel) traitors to the King and Council ; for the poor commons of this

---

[1] *of the House of Guise*

[2] Again looking like an admission that the actual Appointment with the Queen Regent had *not* contained an Article relating to the French troops (*supra*, 221, and *note* 1).

realm have sustained them with the sweat of their brows, since the contracting of the peace, and somewhat before.

" What motherly affection she has declared to this realm, and to the inhabitants of the same, her works have evidently declared, even since the first hour that she has borne authority ; and albeit men will not this day see what danger hangs over their heads, yet fear we, that ere it be long, experience shall teach some that we fear not without cause. The cruel murder and oppression used by them whom now she fosters, is to us a sufficient argument what is to be looked for when her number is so multiplied that our force shall not be able to gainstand their tyranny.

" Where she complains of our Preachers, affirming that irreverently they speak of Princes in general, and of her in particular, inducing the people thereby to defection from their duty, &c.,[1] and therefore that such thing cannot be suffered : Because this occasion is had against God's true Ministers, we cannot but witness what tred [2] and order of doctrine they have kept and yet keep in *The doctrine of our preachers concerning obedience to be given to magistrates* that point. In public prayers they commend to God all Princes in general, and the Magistrates of this our native realm in particular. In open audience they declare the authority of Princes and Magistrates to be of God ; and therefore they affirm that they ought to be honoured, feared, obeyed, even for conscience sake ; provided that they command nor require nothing expressly repugning to God's commandment and plain will, revealed in his holy word. Moreover, they affirm, that if wicked persons, abusing the authority established by God, command things manifestly wicked, that such as may and do bridle their inordinate appetites of Princes, cannot be accused as resisters of the authority, which is God's good ordinance. To bridle the fury and rage of Princes in free kingdoms and realms, they affirm it appertains to the Nobility, sworn and born Councillors of the same, and also to the Barons and People, whose votes and consent are to be required in all great and weighty matters of the commonwealth. Which if they do not, they declare themselves criminal with their Princes, and so subject to the same vengeance of God, which they deserve, for that they pollute the seat of justice, and do, as it were, make God author of iniquity. They proclaim and they cry, that the same God who plagued Pharaoh, repulsed Sennacherib, struck Herod with worms, and made the bellies of dogs the grave and sepulchre of despiteful Jezebel, will not spare the cruel Princes,

---

[1] *Supra*, 218–219
(643)

[2] *path*, that is, *line [of argument]*

murderers of Christ's members in this our time. On this manner they speak of Princes in general, and of your Grace in particular. This only we have heard one of our Preachers say, rebuking the vain excuse of such as flatter themselves, by reason of the authority ; 'Many nowadays (said he) will have no other religion nor faith than the Queen and the authority have. But is it [not] possible, that the Queen be so far blinded that she will have no religion, nor no other faith, than may content to the Cardinal of Lorraine ? [1] And may it not likewise be able, that the Cardinal be so corrupt, that he will admit no religion which does not establish the Pope in his kingdom ? But plain it is that the Pope is lieutenant to Sathan, and enemy to Christ Jesus, and to his perfect religion.' Let men therefore consider what danger they stand in, if their salvation shall depend upon the Queen's faith and religion.' Further we have never heard any of our preachers speak of the Queen Regent, neither publicly nor privately. Where her Grace declares, ' It will not be suffered that our preachers mell [2] with policy, nor speak of her nor of other Princes but with reverence,' we answer, ' That as we will justify and defend nothing in our preachers, which we find not God to have justified and allowed in his messengers before them ; so dare we not forbid them openly to reprehend that which the Spirit of God, speaking in the Prophets and Apostles, has reprehended before them. Elijah did personally reprove Ahab and Jezebel of idolatry, of avarice, of murder ; and siclike [3] Isaiah the Prophet called the magistrates of Jerusalem in his times companions to thieves, princes of Sodom, bribe-takers, and murderers : He complained that their silver was turned into dross, that their wine was mingled with water, and that justice was bought and sold. Jeremiah said, ' That the bones of King Jehoiakim should wither with the sun.' Christ Jesus called Herod a fox ; and Paul called the High Priest a painted wall, and prayed unto God that he should strike him, because that against justice he commanded him to be smitten. Now if the like or greater corruptions be in the world this day, who dare enterprise to put silence to the Spirit of God, which [will] not be subject to the appetites of wicked Princes ? "

We have before said, that the tenth day of September was appointed for a Convention to be held at Stirling, to the which repaired the most part of the Lords of the Congregation. At that

Let such as this day live witness what God has wrought since the writing and publication hereof

The prophets have meddled with policy, and have reproved the corruption thereof

---

[1] Charles de Guise, Cardinal of Lorraine, brother to the Queen Regent
[2] *meddle*   [3] *likewise*

same time arrived the Earl of Arran,[1] who after that he had saluted his father, came with the Earl of Argyll and Lord James to Stirling to the said Convention. In which divers godly men complained upon the tyranny used against their brethren, and especially that more French men were brought in to oppress their country. After the consultation of certain days, the principal Lords, with my Lord of Arran and Earl of Argyll, passed to Hamilton, for consultation to be taken with my Lord Duke's Grace. And in this meantime came assured word that the French men were begun to fortify Leith ; which thing, as it did more evidently discover the Queen's craft, so did [it] deeply grieve the hearts of the whole Nobility there, who, with one consent, agreed to write unto the Queen, in form as follows :

The coming of the Earl of Arran to Scotland, and his joining with the Congregation

" At Hamilton, the xix day of September 1559.

" PLEASE YOUR GRACE,
    " We are credibly informed that your army of French men should instantly begin to plant in Leith, to fortify the same, of mind to expel the ancient inhabitants thereof, our brethren of the Congregation ; whereof we marvel not a little, that your Grace should so manifestly break the Appointment made at Leith, but any provocation made by us and our brethren.[2] And seeing the same is done without any manner [of] consent of the Nobility and Council of this realm, we esteem the same not only oppression of our poor brethren, indwellers of the said town, but also very prejudicial to the commonwealth, and plain contrary to our ancient laws and liberties : Herefore desires your Grace to cause the same work enterprised, be stayed ; and not to attempt so rashly and manifestly against your

Letters to the Queen Regent

---

[1] James, Lord Hamilton, Earl of Arran, eldest son of the Duke of Châtelherault, had escaped from France (*supra*, 207, *note* 3). He reached Berwick Castle in the early hours of the morning of Thursday, 7 September ; he was safely handed over to his friends in Teviotdale about two o'clock in the morning of Sunday, 10 September ; a few days later it was known in Berwick that he was safely in the Castle of Hamilton with his father —under the pseudonym of M. de Beaufort ; and Balnaves reports that he was with the Lords of the Congregation at Stirling on Saturday, 16 September 1559. (*Foreign Calendar, Elizabeth*, i, Nos. 1323, 1337, 1351, 1365. The pages on which these documents appear are, 542–544, 551, 556, and 571 ; for it should be noted that in this volume of the *Foreign Calendar* the numbers 1336–1365 have been duplicated *per incuriam*.)

[2] Again this stress on an agreement which did *not* form part of the Appointment concluded at the Links of Leith (*cf. supra*, 217–218, 220–221, 226) ; also the Lords of the Congregation carefully conceal the fact that on 30 July Knox had been given definite instructions to seek a league with England, and in his interview with Sir James Croft at Berwick had asked for aid in " men and money." (*Foreign Calendar, Elizabeth*, i, Nos. 1097, 1119)

Grace's promise, against the commonwealth, the ancient laws and liberties thereof (which things, beside the glory of God, are most dear and tender unto us, and only our pretence [1]) otherwise, assuring your Grace, we will complain to the whole Nobility and Community of this realm, and most earnestly seek for redress thereof. And thus, recommending our humble service unto your Highness, your Grace's answer most earnestly we desire, whom we commit to the eternal protection of God.

" At Hamilton, day and year foresaid. By your Grace's humble and obedient Servitors."

This letter was subscribed with the hands of my Lord Duke,[2] the Earls of Arran, Argyll, Glencairn, and Menteith ; by the Lords Ruthven, Ochiltree, Boyd, and by others divers, Barons and Gentlemen. To this request she would not answer by writing, but with a letter of credit she sent Sir Robert Carnegie [3] and Master David Borthwick,[4] two whom, amongst many others, she abused, and by whom she corrupted the hearts of the simple. They travailed with the Duke, to bring him again to the Queen's faction. La Brosse and the Bishop of Amiens were short before arrived [5] ; and, as it was bruited, were directed as ambassadors ; but they kept close their whole commission : They only made large promises to them that would be theirs, and leave the Congregation. The Queen did *The petition of La Brosse* grievously complain that we had intelligence with England.[6] The conclusion of their commission was to solist my Lord Duke to put all in the Queen's will, and then would she be gracious enough. It *The answer* was answered, " That no honest men durst commit themselves to the mercy of such throat-cutters as she had about her ; whom, if she would remove, and join to her a Council of natural Scotsmen, permitting the religion to have free passage, then should none in Scotland be more willing to serve her Grace than should the Lords and Brethren of the Congregation be."

[1] *intent*

[2] Assured of the safety of his son, Châtelherault joined the Congregation at Hamilton, on 19 September (the date of this letter), and " gladly subscribed all the bands they had made for religion and other affairs of the Commonwealth." (*Foreign Calendar, Elizabeth,* i, No. 1365) But he was also influenced by the proceedings of the French which tended " to the defrauding of us that are the right heirs to the Crown." (Arran to Cecil, 20 Sept. 1559, in *Calendar of Scottish Papers,* i, No. 599, where the date is given erroneously as 20 December)   [3] Sir Robert Carnegie of Kinnaird

[4] David Borthwick of Lochill. See *Scottish Correspondence of Mary of Lorraine* (Scot. Hist. Soc.), No. CCLXXX

[5] *Supra,* 216   [6] As indeed they had. (*Supra,* 194, *note* 2 ; 229, *note* 2)

At the same time, the Duke's Grace and the Lords wrote to my Lord Erskine,[1] Captain of [the] Castle of Edinburgh, in form as follows :

Letter to the Lord Erskine

" My Lord and Cousin,

  " After our heartly commendation, this present is to advertise you that we are credibly informed the army of French men instantly in this realm, but [2] any advice of the Council or Nobility, are fortifying, or else shortly intends to fortify the town of Leith, and expel the ancient inhabitants thereof; whereby they proclaim to all that will open their ears to hear, or ene [3] to see, what is their pretence.[4] And seeing the faithfulness of your antecessors, and especially of your father, of honourable memory, was so recommended and experimented to the Estates and Councillors of this realm, through affection they perceived in him towards the commonwealth thereof, that they doubted not to give in his keeping the key, as it were, of the Council, the Justice, and Policy of this realm, the Castles of Edinburgh and Stirling [5]; we cannot but believe ye will rather augment the honourable favour of your house, by steadfast favour and lawtie [6] to your commonwealth, than through the subtle persuasion of some (which care not what after shall come of you and your house [and] at the present would abuse you, to the performance of their wicked enterprises and pretences against our commonwealth), utterly to destroy the same. And herefore, seeing that we have written to the Queen's Grace, to desist from that enterprise, otherwise that we will complain to the Nobility and Community of the realm, and seek redress thereof ; we likewise beseech you, as our tender friend, brother, and member of the same commonwealth with us, that ye on no wise mell [7] or assent to that ungodly enterprise against the commonwealth ; and likewise, that ye would save your body, and the jewel of this country committed to you and your predecessors, lawtie and fidelity toward your native country and commonwealth, if ye think

---

[1] John, sixth Lord Erskine   [2] *without*   [3] *eyes*   [4] *intent*

[5] John, fifth Lord Erskine, was one of three lords appointed to be the personal guardians of the young King James V. In 1540, when James V sailed on his expedition to the Isles, he appointed Lord Erskine one of the guardians to his infant son James ; and in 1542 the infant Mary Queen of Scots was placed under his charge. He also held the keepership of the Castles of Edinburgh and Stirling. His son, John, sixth Lord Erskine, to whom this letter is addressed, was keeper of Edinburgh Castle, during the conflict between the Queen Regent and the Lords of the Congregation ; he received the Queen Regent into the Castle in her last illness, and she died there. Later, as Earl of Mar, he was entrusted with the care of the young Prince James [VI], and was Regent from 1571 to 1572. (*Scots Peerage*, v, 609–615)   [6] *loyalty*   [7] *meddle*

to be reputed hereafter one of the same, and would rather be brother to us, nor to strangers ; for we do gather by the effects, the secrets of men's hearts, otherwise unsearchable unto us.[1] This we write, not that we are in doubt of you, but rather to warn you of the danger, in case ye thoill [2] yourself to be enchanted with fair promises and crafty counsellors. For let no man flatter himself : We desire all man [to] know, that though he were our father (since God has opened our eyes to see his will), be he enemy to the commonwealth, which now is assailed, and we with it, and all true members thereof, he shall be known (and as he is indeed) enemy to us, to our lives, houses, babes, heritages, and whatsomever is contained within the same. For as the ship perishing, what can be safe that is within ? So the commonwealth being betrayed, what particular member can live in quietness ? And therefore in so far as the said Castles are committed to your credit, we desire you to show your faithfulness and stoutness as ye tender [3] us, and whatsomever appertains to us. And seeing we are assured ye will be assailed both with craft and force, as now by warning we help you against the first, so against the last ye shall not miss in all possible haste to have our assistance. Only show yourself the man. Save your person by wisdom, strengthen yourself against force, and the Almighty God assist you in both the one and the other, and open your eyes [to] understanding, to see and perceive the craft of Sathan and his supposts.[4]

" At Hamilton, the xix day of September 1559. By your Brethren, &c."

The Duke and Lords understanding that the fortification of Leith proceeded, appointed their whole forces to convene at Stirling the xv day of October,[5] that from thence they might march forward to Edinburgh, for the redress of the great enormities which the French *The tyranny of the French* did to the whole country, which by them was so oppressed that the life of all honest man was bitter unto him.[6]

In this meantime the Lords directed their letters to divers parts of the country, making mention what danger did hang over all men, if the French should be suffered to plant in this country at their

---

[1] That is, the issues show what are the secrets of men's hearts that are otherwise unsearchable   [2] *suffer*   [3] *have regard to*

[4] *supporters*. This is the French phrase *suppôts de Satan*, that is *limbs of Satan*.

[5] This is confirmed in *Scottish Correspondence of Mary of Lorraine* (Scot. Hist. Soc.), Nos. CCLXXX, CCLXXXI. The delay was due to bad weather and the lateness of the harvest. (*Calendar of Scottish Papers*, i, No. 549)

[6] So also Balnaves, writing to Sadler and Croft (*Foreign Calendar, Elizabeth*, i, No. 1365). *All* is frequently used by Knox in the sense of *every*.

pleasure. They made mention further, how humbly they had sought the Queen Regent that she would send away to France her French men, who were a burden unprofitable and grievous to their commonwealth ; and how that she notwithstanding did daily augment their number, bringing wives and bairns ; a declaration of a plain conquest, &c.

The Queen, then Regent, perceiving that her craft began to be espied, by all means possible travailed to blind the people.[1] And first, she sent forth her pestilent posts forenamed in all parts of the country, to persuade all men that she offered all things reasonable to the Congregation ; and that they refusing all reason, pretended no religion, but a plain revolt from the Authority. She tempted every man in particular, as well they that were of the Congregation, as them that were neutral. She assaulted every man, as she thought most easily he might have been overcome. To the Lord Ruthven [2] she sent the Justice-Clerk and his wife, who is daughter to the wife of the said Lord.[3] What was their commission and credit, is no further known than the said Lord has confessed, which is, that large promises of profit were offered, if he would leave the Congregation and be the Queen's. To Lord James, Prior of Saint Andrews, was sent Master John Spens of Condie, with a letter and credit, as follows :

"THE MEMORIAL OF MASTER JOHN SPENS OF CONDIE, THE
    THIRTIETH DAY OF SEPTEMBER.

" 1. YE shall say, that her great favour towards you moves her to this.

" 2. That she now knows, that the occasion of your departing from her was the favour of the word and of religion ; with the which albeit she was offended, yet knowing your heart and the hearts of the other Lords firmly fixed thereupon, she will bear with you in that behalf, and at your own sight she will set forward that cause at

---

[1] The Archbishop of St. Andrews had at once striven to persuade his half-brother, Châtelherault, to return to the " grace and pleasure " of the Regent, but in vain ; and he writes to the Regent to avoid delay, to provide for the worst, to make herself " stark in all sorts," and, in a letter of the day following, to cause the people and good folks to " know the verity." (*Scottish Correspondence of Mary of Lorraine*, Scot. Hist. Soc., Nos. CCLXXX, CCLXXXI)   [2] Patrick, third Lord Ruthven

[3] Sir John Bellenden of Auchnoull, the Justice-Clerk, had married, as his second wife, Barbara Kennedy, daughter of Sir Hugh Kennedy of Girvanmains and Janet Stewart, Lady Methven. Patrick, Lord Ruthven, had married, as his second wife, Janet Stewart, Lady Methven, in 1557. (*Scots Peerage*, ii, 65 ; iv, 261)

her power, as may stand with God's word, the common policy of this realm, and the Prince's honour. (Note, good reader, what venom lurks here ; for plain it is, that the policy which she pretended,[1] and the Prince's honour, will never suffer Christ Jesus to ring [2] in this realm.)

" 3. To say, that the occasion of the assembling of these men of war, and fortifying of Leith is, that it was given her to understand by some about her, that it is not the advancement of the word and religion which is sought at this time, but rather a pretence to over-throw, or alter the authority of your sister,[3] of the which she believes still that ye are not participant ; and considering the tenderness betwix you and your sister, she trusts more in you in that behalf than in any living. (But before the Earl of Arran arrived, and that the Duke departed from her faction, she ceased not continually to cry, that the Prior sought to make himself King ; and so not only to deprive his sister to make himself King, but also to defraud the Lord Duke's Grace and his house : but foreseeing a storm, she began to seek a new wind.)

Let this be noted : O crafty flattery !

" She further willed to offer the away-sending of the men of war, if the former suspicion could be removed. She lamented the trouble that appeared to follow if the matter should long stand in debate. She promised her faithful labours for reconciliation, and required the same of him ; requiring further, faith, favour, and kindness, towards his sister ; and to advertise for his part what he desired, with promise that he might obtain what he pleased to desire, &c."

To this letter and credit, the said Lord James answered as follows :

" PLEASE YOUR GRACE,
" I received your Highness's writing, and have heard the credit of the bearer ; and finding the business of such importance, that dangerous it were to give hasty answer, and also your petitions are so, that with my honour I can not answer them privately by myself : I have thought good to delay the same till that I may have the judgment of the whole Council. For this point I will not conceal from your Grace, that amongst us there is a solemn oath, that none of us shall traffic with your Grace secretly [4] ; neither yet that any of

---

[1] *the political policy which she had in mind*   [2] *reign*
[3] Mary Queen of Scots was half-sister to the Lord James Stewart
[4] *Supra*, 206–207.

us shall make an [ad]dress for himself particularly ; which oath, for my part, I purpose to keep inviolate to the end. But when the rest of the Noblemen shall convene, I shall leave nothing that lies in my power undone that may make for the quietness of this poor realm, providing that the glory of Christ Jesus be not hindered by our concord. And if your Grace shall be found so tractable as now ye offer, I doubt not to obtain of the rest of my brethren such favours towards your service, as your Grace shall have just occasion to stand content. For God I take to record, that in this action I have neither sought, neither yet seeks, any other thing than God's glory to increase, and the liberty of this poor realm to be maintained. Further, I have shown to your messenger what things have misliked me in your proceedings, even from such a heart as I would wish to God ye and all men did know. And this with heartly commendation of service to your Grace, I heartly commit your Highness to the eternal protection of the Omnipotent.

" At Saint Andrews, the first of October.

(*Sic subscribitur*),
        " Your Grace's humble and obedient servitor,

                                J. St."

This answer received, she raged as hypocrisy uses, when it is pricked ; and perceiving that she could not work what she would at the hands of men particularly, she set forth a Proclamation,[1] universally to be proclaimed, in the tenor as follows :

" FORSAMEKLE as it is understood to the Queen's Grace, that the Duke of Châtelherault has lately directed his missives in all parts of this realm, making mention that the French men, late arrived with their wives and bairns, are [begun] to plant in Leith, to the ruin of the commonwealth, which he and his partakers will not pass over with patient beholding, desiring to know what will be every man's part ; and that the fortification of Leith is a purpose devised in France, and that therefore Monsieur de La Brosse and the Bishop of Amiens are come in this country ; a thing so vain and untrue, that the contrary thereof is notour [2] to all men of free judgment ; therefore her Grace, willing that the occasions whereby her Grace was moved so to do be made patent, and what has been her

---

[1] Dated 2 October 1559, in *Foreign Calendar, Elizabeth*, ii, No. 9. Presumably in response to the advice of Archbishop Hamilton. (*Scottish Correspondence of Mary of Lorraine*, Scot. Hist. Soc., No. CCLXXXI)   [2] *notorious, well-known*

proceedings since the Appointment last made on the Links beside
Leith, to the effect that the truth of all things being made manifest,
every man may understand how unjustly that will to suppress [1]
the liberty of this realm is laid to her charge, has thought expedient
to make this discourse following :

" First, Although after the said Appointment, divers of the said
Congregation, and that not of the meanest sort, had contravened
violently the points thereof, and made sundry occasions of new
cummer, [2] the same was in a part winked at and overlooked, in hope
that they with time would remember their duty, and abstain from
such evil behaviour, which conversion her Grace ever sought, rather
than any punishment, with such care and solicitude by all means,
while, in the meantime, nothing was provided for her own security.
But, at last, by their frequent messages to and from England, their
intelligence then was perceived : yet her Grace trusts the Queen
of England (let them seek as they please) will do the office of a
Christian Princess in time of a sworn peace ; through which force
was to her Grace [3] (seeing so great defection of great personages)
to have recourse to the law of nature ; and like as a small bird, being
pursued, will provide some nest, so her Grace could do no less, in
case of pursuit, nor provide some sure retreat for herself and her
company ; and to that effect, chose the town of Leith, as place
convenient therefor ; because, first, it was her dearest daughter's
property, and no other person could acclaim title or interest thereto,
and also because in time afore it had been fortified. About the same
time that the seeking support of England was made manifest, arrived
the Earl of Arran, and adjoined himself to the Congregation, upon

False lying tongue, God has confounded thee ! further promises nor [4] the pretended quarrel of religion that was to
be set up by them in authority, and so to pervert the whole obedience. [5]
And as some of the said Congregation at the same time had put
to their hands, and taken the Castle of Broughty, [and] put forth the
keepers thereof [6] : immediately came from the said Duke to her

----

[1] *that determination to suppress*   [2] *trouble*
[3] *was her Grace compelled*   [4] *upon promises over and above*
[5] Sadler and Croft, writing to Cecil on 8 September 1559, after an interview with
Balnaves, report that he said " the principal mark they [the Lords of the Congregation]
shot at is to make an alteration of the state and authority so that they may enter into
open treaty with Elizabeth. This is very secret ; they mean to bestow it [*sc.* the authority]
on the Duke ; or, if he refuse, his son is as much, or rather more meet for the purpose."
(*Foreign Calendar, Elizabeth*, i, No. 1323)

[6] Knox's " instructions " of 30 July had included an announcement of the Congregation's intention to take Broughty Castle (*ibid.*, i, No. 1097) ; and in the Lords,
answering Declaration they admit its capture (*infra*, 240).

Grace unlooked for, a writing, beside many others, complaining of the fortification of the said town of Leith, in hurt of the ancient inhabitants thereof, brethren of the said Congregation, whereof he then professed himself a member [1] ; and albeit that the bearer of the said writing was an unmeet messenger in a matter of such consequence, yet her Grace direc[ted] to him two persons of good credit and reputation with answer,[2] offering, if he would cause amend be made for that which was committed against the laws of the realm, to do further nor could be craved of reason, and to that effect to draw some conference, which, for inlaik [3] of him and his colleagues, took no end.[4] None the less they continually sensyne continue in their doings, usurping the Authority, commanding and charging free Burghs to choose Provosts and officers of their naming, and to assist to them in the purpose they would be at ; and that they will not suffer provision to be brought for sustentation of her Grace's houses ; and great part has so plainly set aside all reverence and humanity, whereby every man may know that it is no matter of religion, but a plain usurpation of authority, and no doubt but simple men, of good zeal in times bygone, therewith falsely have been deceived. But as to the Queen's Grace's part, God, who knows the secrets of all hearts, well kens, and the world shall see by experience, that the fortification of Leith was devised for no other purpose but for recourse to her Highness and her company, in case they were pursued. Wherefore, all good subjects that have the fear of God in their hearts, will not suffer themselves by such vain persuasions to be led away from their due obedience, but will assist in defence of their Sovereigns' quarrel against all such as will pursue the same wrangously. Therefore, her Grace ordains the officers of arms to pass to the Market Crosses of all head Burghs of this realm, and there by open proclamation command and charge all and sundry the lieges thereof, that none of them take upon hand, to put themselves in arms, nor take part with the said Duke or his assisters, under the pain of treason."

God has purged his people of that false accusation

These letters being divulged, the hearts of many were stirred ; for they judged the narration of the Queen Regent to have been true : others understanding the same to be utterly false. But because the Lords desired all men [to] judge in their cause, they set out this Declaration [5] subsequent :

---

[1] *Supra,* 229–230   [2] *Supra,* 230   [3] *lack*   [4] See *infra,* 241
[5] Dated 3 October 1559 in *Foreign Calendar, Elizabeth,* ii, No. 20

*The de-
claration
of the
Lords
against
the former
proclama-
tion*

" WE are compelled unwillingly to answer the grievous accusations most unjustly laid to our charge by the Queen Regent and her
perverse Council, who cease not, by all craft and malice, to make us
odious to our dearest brethren, natural Scotsmen ; as that we
pretended no other thing but the subversion and overthrow of all
just authority, when, God knows, that we thought nothing but that
such authority as God approves by his word, be established, honoured,
and obeyed amongst us. True it is that we have complained (and
continually must complain) till God send redress, that our common
country is oppressed with strangers ; that this inbringing of soldiers,
with their wives and children, and planting of men of war in our free
towns, appears to us a ready way to conquest : And we most earnestly
require all indifferent persons to judge betwix us and [the] Queen
Regent in this cause, to wit, whether that our complaint be just or

*The
avarice of
them of
Lorraine
and Guise*

not ; for, for what other purpose should she thus multiply strangers
upon us, but only in respect of conquest ; which is a thing not of
late devised by her and her avaricious House. We are not ignorant
that six years past the question was demanded of a man of honest
reputation, what number of men was able to danton Scotland, and
to bring it to the full obedience of France. She alleges, that to say
the fortification of Leith was a purpose devised in France, and that
for that purpose were Monsieur de La Brosse and the Bishop [of]
Amiens sent to this country, is a thing so vain and untrue, that the
contrary thereof is notour to all men of free judgment. But evident
it is, whatsoever she alleges, that since their arrival Leith was begun
to be fortified. She alleges, that she, seeing the defection of great
personages, was compelled to have recourse to the law of nature,
and like a small bird pursued, to provide for some sure retreat to
herself and her company. But why does she not answer, for what
purpose did she bring in her new bands of men of war ? Was there
any defection espied before their arrival ? Was not the Congregation
under appointment with her ? Which, whatsoever she alleges, she is
not able to prove that we had contravened in any chief point, before
that her new throat-cutters arrived, yea, before that they began to
fortify Leith ; a place, says she, most convenient for her purpose,
as in very deed it is for the receiving of strangers at her pleasure :
for if she had feared the pursuit of her body, she had the Inch,[1]
Dunbar, Blackness, forts and strengths already made. Yea, but they
could not so well serve her turn as Leith, because it was her daughter's
property, and no other could have title to it, and because it had been

[1] Inchkeith

fortified of before. That all men may know the just title her daughter and she has to the town of Leith, we shall in few words declare the truth.

" It is not unknown to the most part of this realm that there has *The title* been an old haitrent [1] and contention betwix Edinburgh and Leith : *that the* *Queen* Edinburgh seeking continually to possess that liberty which by dona- *[had] or* *has to* tion of kings they have long enjoyed'; and Leith, by the contrary, *Leith* aspiring to a liberty and freedom in prejudice of Edinburgh. The Queen Regent, a woman that could make her profit of all hands, was not ignorant how to compass her own matter ; and therefore secretly she gave advertisement to some of Leith that she would make their town free if that she might do it with any colour of justice. By which promise, the principal men of them did travail with the Laird of Restalrig, [2] a man neither prudent nor fortunate, to whom the *The* *Laird of* superiority of Leith appertained, that he should sell his whole title *Restalrig* and right to our Sovereign, for certain sums of money, which the *superior* *of Leith* inhabitants of Leith paid, with a large taxation more, to the Queen Regent in hope to have been made free in despite and defraud of Edinburgh. [3] Which right and superiority, when she had got, and when the money was paid, the first fruits of their liberty they now eat with bitterness, to wit, that strangers shall possess their town. This is her just title which her daughter and she may claim to that town. And where she alleges that it was fortified before, we ask, if that [was] done without consent of the Nobility and Estates of the realm, as she now, and her crafty Councillors do in despite and contempt of us the lawful heads and born councillors of this realm.

" How far we have sought support of England, or of any other Princes, and how just cause we had, and have so to do, we shall shortly make manifest unto the world, to the praise of God's holy name, and to the confusion of all them that slander us for so doing. For this we fear not to confess, that as in this our enterprise against the Devil, idolatry, and the maintenance of the same, we chiefly and only seek God's glory to be notified unto man, sin to be punished, and virtue to be maintained ; so where power fails of our-

---

[1] *hatred*   [2] Robert Logan of Restalrig
[3] There had long been, and there was long to be, jealousy and strife between Leith and Edinburgh. In January 1556, however, Mary of Lorraine agreed to purchase the superiority of Leith from Robert Logan of Restalrig for £3,000 (Scots) ; and this sum was apparently paid by the inhabitants of Leith, in six half-yearly instalments of £500 each, on a promise from the Queen Regent that she would erect Leith into a burgh of barony, and later into a royal burgh. The latter part of this arrangement did not materialize. (See J. C. Irons, *Leith and its Antiquities* (1897), i, 231 ff)

self, we will seek wheresoever God shall offer the same ; and yet in so doing, we are assured, neither to offend God, neither yet to do any thing repugnant to our duties. We heartly praise God, who moved the heart of the Earl of Arran to join himself with us, his persecuted brethren ; but how malicious a lie it is, that we have promised to set him up in authority, the issue shall declare. God we take to record, that no such thing has to this day entered in our hearts.[1] Neither yet has he, the said Earl, neither any to him appertaining, moved unto us any such matter ; which, if they should do, yet are we not so slender in judgment, that inconsiderately we would promise that which after we might repent. We speak and write to God's glory. The least of us knows better what obedience is due to a lawful authority, than she or her Council does practise the office of such as worthily may sit upon the seat of justice ; for we offer, and we perform, all obedience which God has commanded ; for we neither deny toll, tribute, honour, nor fear to her, nor to her officers. We only bridle her blind rage, in the which she would erect and maintain idolatry, and would murder our brethren who refuse the same. But she does utterly abuse the authority established by God : she profanes the throne of his Majesty in earth, making the seat of justice, which ought to be the sanctuary and refuge of all godly and virtuous persons, unjustly afflicted, to be a den and receptacle to thieves, murderers, idolaters, whore-mongers, adulterers, and blasphemers of God and all godliness. It is more than evident what men they are, and long have been, whom she by her power maintains and defends ; and also what has been our conversation since it has pleased God to call us to his knowledge, whom now in her fury she cruelly persecutes. We deny not the taking of the House of Broughty [2] ; and the cause being considered, we think that no natural Scotsman will be offended at our fact. When the assured knowledge came unto us that the fortification of Leith was begun, every man began to inquire what danger might ensue to the rest of the realm, if the French should plant in divers places, and what were the places that might most annoy us.[3] In conclusion it was found, that the taking of the said house by French men should be destruction to Dundee, and hurtful to Saint Johnston, and to the whole country ; and therefore it was thought expedient to prevent [4] the danger, as that we did for preservation of our brethren and common country. It is not unknown what enemies those two

The wicked-ness of the bishops

---

[1] But see *supra*, 236, *note* 5   [2] See *supra*, 236, and *note* 6
[3] In the manuscript, *neir us*   [4] *forestall*

towns have, and how gladly would some have all good order and *The cause that Broughty Craig was taken*
policy overthrown in them. The conjectures that the French were
of mind shortly to have taken the same, were not obscure. But
whatsoever they pretended, we can not repent that we (as said is)
have prevented the danger ; and would God that our power had
been in the same manner to have foreclosed their entry to Leith ;
for what trouble the poor realm shall endure before that those
murderers and unjust possessors be removed from the same, the *Let all men judge*
issue will declare. If her accusation against my Lord Duke's Grace,
and that we refused conference, be truly and simply spoken, we will
not refuse the judgment of those very men whom she alleges to be of
so honest a reputation. They know that the Duke's Grace did *The Duke's answer*
answer that if the realm might be set at liberty from the bondage of
those men of war which presently did oppress it, and were so fearful
to him and his brethren that they were compelled to absent themselves from the places where she and they made residence, that he
and the whole Congregation should come and give all debtful
obedience to our Sovereign her daughter, and unto her Grace, as
Regent for the time. But to enter in conference, so long as she keeps
above him and his brethren that fearful scourge of cruel strangers,
he thought no wise man would counsel him. And this his answer we
approve, adding further, That she can make us no promise which
she can keep nor we can credit, so long as she is forced [1] with the
strength, and ruled by the council of [the] French. We are not
ignorant that princes think it good policy to betray their subjects
by breaking of promises, be they never so solemnly made. We have
not forgotten what counsel she and Monsieur d'Oysel gave to the
Duke against them that slew the Cardinal, and kept the Castle of
Saint Andrews [2] : And it was this, " That what promise they list to
require should be made unto them ; but how soon that the Castle
was rendered, and things brought to such pass as was expedient, that
he should chop the heads from every one of them." To the which
when the Duke answered, " That he would never consent to so
treasonable an act, but if he promised fidelity, he would faithfully
keep it," Monsieur d'Oysel said, in mockage to the Queen, in
French, " That is a good simple nature, but I know no other prince
that would so do." If this was his judgment in so small a matter, *Nota*
what have we to suspect in this our cause : For now the question is
not of the slaughter of a Cardinal, but of the just abolishing of all
that tyranny which that Roman Antichrist has usurped above us,

---

[1] *reinforced*   [2] *Cf. supra*, 80

of the suppressing of idolatry, and of the reformation of the whole religion by that vermin of shavelings utterly corrupted. Now, if the slaughter of a Cardinal be a sin irremissible,[1] as they themselves affirm, and if faith ought not to be kept to heretics, as their own law speaks, what promise can she that is ruled by the counsel and commandment of a Cardinal make to us, that can be sure?

The quarrel betwix France and the Congregation of Scotland

" Where she accuses us that we usurp authority, to command and charge free Burghs to choose Provosts and officers of our naming, &c., we will that the whole Burghs of Scotland testify in that case, whether that we have used any kind of violence, but lovingly exhorted such as asked support, to choose such in office as had the fear of God before their eyes, loved equity and justice, and were not noted with avarice and bribing. But wonder it is, with what face she can accuse us of that whereof we are innocent, and she so openly criminal, that the whole realm knows her iniquities. In that case, has she not compelled the town of Edinburgh to retain a man to be their Provost, most unworthy of any regiment [2] in a well ruled commonwealth? [3] Has she not enforced them to take Bailies of her appointment, and some of them so meet for their office, in this troublesome time, as a souter [4] is to sail a ship in a stormy day? She complains that we will not suffer provision to be made for her House. In very deed we unfeignedly repent that before this we took not better order that these murderers and oppressors, whom she pretends to nourish, for our destruction, had not been disappointed of that great provision of victuals which she and they have gathered, to the great hurt of the whole country. But as God shall assist us in times coming, we shall do diligence somewhat to frustrate their devilish purpose. What both she and we pretend,[5] we doubt not but God, who can not suffer the abuse of his own name long to be unpunished, shall one day declare, and unto Him we fear not to commit our cause. Neither yet fear we in this present to say, that against us she makes a most

The Lord Seton unworthy of regiment

Optima collatio

Let the Papists judge if God has not given judgment to the displeasure of their hearts

---

[1] *Supra*, 94   [2] *rule*
[3] George, fifth Lord Seton, Provost of Edinburgh, was an open supporter of the Queen Regent, but had alienated the " good men " of the town by his arbitrary actions. In April 1559 he had ordered one of the Bailies, Alexander Barron, and the Common-Clerk, Alexander Guthrie, to enter themselves in ward, and he had threatened to put three of the Bailies in irons ; in May he had imprisoned one of the Bailies, first in Edinburgh Castle and then in Dunbar ; and in September he was at loggerheads with the Bailies and Council. Not unnaturally at the ensuing elections the Queen Regent, despite an attempt to win over the craftsmen and to secure for them a vote at the burgh elections, lost her supporter in office, and Archibald Douglas of Kilspindie was elected Provost in his stead. (*Edinburgh Burgh Records*, iii, 31–34, 37–38, 52–53, 58 ; Maitland, *History of Edinburgh*, 1753, 15–18)   [4] *shoemaker*   [5] *intend*

malicious lie. Where that she says that it is no religion that we go *The lie* about, but a plain usurpation of the Authority, God forbid that *to the Queen* such impiety should enter into our hearts, that we should make his *Regent* holy religion a cloak and coverture of our iniquity. From the beginning of this controversy, it is evidently known what have been our requests, which if the rest of the Nobility and community of Scotland will cause be performed unto us, if then any sign of rebellion appear in us, let us be reputed and punished as traitors. But while strangers are brought in to suppress us, our commonwealth, and posterity, while idolatry is maintained, and Christ Jesus his true religion despised, while idle bellies and bloody tyrants, the bishops, are maintained, and Christ's true messengers persecuted ; while, finally, virtue is contemned, and vice extolled, while that we, a great part of the Nobility and commonalty of this realm, are most unjustly persecuted, what godly man can be offended that we shall seek reformation of these enormities (yea, even by force of arms, seeing that otherways it is denied unto us) ? We are assured that neither God, neither nature, neither any just law, forbids us. God has made us councillors by birth of this realm ; nature binds us to *The cause* love our own country ; and just laws command us to support our *that moved the* brethren unjustly persecuted. Yea, the oath that we have made, *Nobility of this* to be true to this commonwealth, compels us to hazard whatsoever *realm to* God has given us, before that we see the miserable ruin of the same. *oppose them to* If any think this is not religion which now we seek, we answer, That *the Queen* it is nothing else but the zeal of the true religion which moves us to *Regent* this enterprise : For as the enemy does craftily foresee that idolatry cannot be universally maintained, unless that we be utterly sup- *The same* pressed, so do we consider that the true religion (the purity whereof *mind remains to* we only require) cannot be universally erected, unless strangers be *this day* removed, and this poor realm purged of these pestilences which before have infected it.[1] And therefore, in the name of the eternal God, and of his Son Christ Jesus, whose cause we sustain, we require all our brethren, natural Scotsmen, prudently to consider our requests, and with judgment to decern [2] betwix us and the Queen Regent and her faction, and not to suffer themselves to be abused by her craft and deceit, that either they shall lift their weapons against us their brethren, who seek nothing but God's glory, either

---

[1] " And," to be honest, it should have been added, " unless the Queen Regent be removed of all authority." For, by now, as the Reformers had realized, and had admitted in their negotiations with England, religion and the " policy " were so interwoven that separation of the one from the other was wholly impossible.   [2] *determine, judge*

yet that they extract [1] from us their just and debtful support, seeing that we hazard our lives for preservation of them and us, and of our posterity to come : Assuring such as shall declare themselves favourers of her faction, and enemies unto us, that we shall repute them, whensoever God shall put the sword of justice in our hands, worthy of such punishment as is due for such as study to betray their country in the hands of strangers."

This promise was forgot, and therefore has God plagued. What spirit could have hoped for victory in so desperate dangers ?

This our Answer was formed, and divulged in some places, but not universally, by reason of our day appointed to meet at Stirling, as before is declared.[2] In this meantime, the Queen's posts ran with all possible expedition to draw men to her devotion ; and in very deed she found more favourers of her iniquity than we suspected. For a man that of long time had been of our number in profession, offered (as himself did confess) his service to the Queen Regent, to travail betwix her Grace and the Congregation for concord. She refused not his offer ; but knowing his simplicity, she was glad to employ him for her advantage. The man is Master Robert Lockhart,[3] a man of whom many have had and still have good opinion, as touching his religion ; but to enter in the dress of such affairs, not so convenient as godly and wise men would require. He travailed not the less earnestly in the Queen Regent's affairs, and could not be persuaded but that she meant sincerely, and that she would promote the religion to the uttermost of her power. He promised in her name, that she would put away her French men, and would be ruled by the counsel of natural Scotsmen. When it was reasoned in his contrary, " That if she were so minded to do, she could have found mediators a great deal more convenient for that purpose," he feared not to affirm, " That he knew more of her mind than all the French or Scots that were in Scotland, yea more than her own brethren that were in France." He travailed with the Earl of Glencairn, the Lords Ochiltree and Boyd, with the Laird of Dun, and with the Preachers, to whom he had certain secret letters, which he would not deliver unless that they would make a faithful promise that they should never reveal the thing contained in the same. To the which it was answered, " That in no wise they could make such a promise, by reason that they were sworn one to another, and

---

[1] *withdraw*   [2] *Supra*, 232

[3] Mr. Robert Lockhart had early joined the Reformed Church (*supra*, 148), but there may be some significance in the fact that in January 1560 the Treasurer paid him thirty pounds, and in February 1560 forty pounds, by precept of the Queen Regent. (*Accs. Lord High Treasurer*, xi, 5, 12)

altogether in one body, that they should have no secret intelligence nor dress with the Queen Regent, but that they should communicate with the Great Council whatsoever she proposed unto them, or they did answer unto her." [1] As by this Answer, written by John Knox to the Queen Regent, may be understood, the tenor whereof follows :

" [MADAM,]

" MY duty most humbly premised : Your Grace's servant, Master Robert Lockhart, most instantly has required me and others, to whom your Grace's letters, as he alleged, were directed, to receive the same in secret manner, and to give to him answer accordingly. But because some of the number that he required were and are upon the Great Council of this realm, and therefore are solemnly sworn to have nothing to do in secret manner, neither with your Grace, neither yet with any that comes from you, or from your Council [2] ; and so they could not receive your Grace's letters with such conditions as the said Master Robert required ; and therefore thought he good to bring to your Grace again the said letters close. And yet because, as he reports, he has made to your Grace some promise in my name ; at his request, I am content to testify by my letter and subscription, the sum of that which I did communicate with him. In Dundee, after many words betwix him and me, I said that, albeit divers sinister reports had been made of me, yet did I never declare any evident token of haiterent nor enmity against your Grace. For if it be the office of a very friend to give true and faithful counsel to them whom he sees run to destruction for lack of the same, I could not be proven enemy to your Grace, but rather a friend unfeigned. For what counsel I had given to your Grace, my writings, as well my Letters and Addition to the same, now printed,[3] as divers others which I wrote from Saint Johnston, may testify. I further added, that such an enemy was I unto you, that my tongue did both persuade and obtain that your authority and regiment should be obeyed of us in all things lawful, till ye declared yourself open enemy to this commonwealth, as now, alas ! ye have done. This I willed him moreover to say to your Grace, that if ye, following the counsel of flattering men, having no God but this world and their bellies, did proceed in your malice against Christ Jesus his religion and true ministers, that ye should do nothing else but accelerate and haste God's plague and vengeance upon yourself and upon your posterity : and that ye (if ye did not change your purpose hastily), should bring

---

[1] *Supra*, 206–207   [2] *Supra*, 206–207   [3] *Supra*, 123, *note* 2

yourself in such extreme danger, that when ye would seek remedy, it should not be so easy to be found as it had been before. This is the effect and sum of all that I said at that time, and willed him, if he pleased, to communicate the same to your Grace. And the same yet again I notify unto your Grace, by this my letter, written and subscribed at Edinburgh, the 26 of October 1559.[1]

(Sic subscribitur),
" Your Grace's to command in all godliness
" JOHN KNOX.

" <i>Postscriptum.</i>—God move your heart yet in time to consider that ye fight not against man, but against the eternal God, and against his Son Jesus Christ, the only Prince of the kings of the earth."

At which answer, the said Master Robert was so offended, that he would not deliver his letters, saying, " That we were ungodly and injurious to the Queen Regent if we suspected any craft in her." To the which it was answered, by one of the preachers, " That time should declare, whether he or they were deceived. If she should not declare herself enemy to the true religion which they professed, if ever she had the upper hand, then they would be content to confess that they had suspected her sincerity without just cause. But and if she should declare her malice no less in times coming than she had done before, they required that he should be more moderate than to damn them whose conscience he knew not." And this was the end of the travail for that time, after that he had troubled the conscience of many godly and quiet persons. For he and others who were her hired posts, ceased not to blow in the ears of all men, that the Queen was heavily done to ; that she required nothing but obedience to her daughter ; that she was content that the true religion should go forward, and that all abuses should be abolished ; and by these means they brought a grudge and division among ourselves. For many (and our brethren of Lothian especially) began to murmur, that we sought another thing than religion, and so ceased to assist us certain days, after that we were come to Edinburgh, which we did according to the former diet, the 16 day of October.[2] This grudge and trouble amongst ourselves was not raised by the foresaid Master

---

[1] In the manuscript the date is given as 26 October ; the less probable date, 6 October, is given in Laing's <i>Knox</i>, vi, 82.

[2] The 18 October (Wednesday) in <i>Foreign Calendar, Elizabeth</i>, ii, Nos. 102, 116, and in <i>Diurnal of Occurrents</i>, 270

Robert [1] only, but by those pestilents whom before we have expressed, and Master James Balfour especially, whose venomous tongues against God and his true religion, as they deserve punishment of men, so shall they not escape God's vengeance, unless that speedily they repent.

After our coming to Edinburgh the day forenamed, we assembled in council, and determined to give new advertisement to the Queen's Grace's Regent of our Convention, and in such sort; and so with common consent we sent unto her our request as follows :

" [MADAM]

" IT will please your Grace reduce [2] to your remembrance how at our last Convention at Hamilton, we required your Highness, in our most humble manner, to desist from the fortifying of this town of Leith, then enterprised and begun,[3] which appeared to us (and yet does) an entry to a conquest, and overthrow to our liberties, and altogether against the laws and customs of this realm, seeing it was begun, and yet continues, without any advice and consent of the Nobility and Council of this realm. Wherefore now, as of before, according to our duty to our commonwealth, we most humbly require your Grace to cause your strangers and soldiers whatsomever to depart of the said town of Leith, and make the same patent, not only to the inhabitants, but also to all Scottish men, our Sovereign Lady's lieges. Assuring your Highness, that if, refusing the same, ye declare thereby your evil mind toward the commonweal and liberty of this realm, we will (as of before) mene [4] and declare the cause unto the whole Nobility and commonalty of this realm ; and according to the oath which we have sworn for the maintenance of the commonweal, in all manner of things to us possible, we will provide remedy : therefore requiring most humbly your Grace's answer in haste with the bearer, because in our eyes the act continually proceeds, declaring a determination of conquest, which is presumed of all men, and not without cause. And thus, after our humble commendation of service, we pray Almighty God to have your Grace in his eternal tuition.[5] "

The second admonition to the Queen Regent

These our letters received, our messenger was threatened, and withheld a whole day. Thereafter he was dismissed, without any

---

[1] Master Robert Lockhart [2] *bring back* [3] *Supra*, 229–230
[4] *complain*
[5] *protection*. This letter is dated from Edinburgh, 19 October 1559 (*infra*, 249). And see *Foreign Calendar, Elizabeth*, ii, No. 116

other answer but that she would send an answer when she thought expedient.

In this meantime, because the rumour ceased not that the Duke's Grace usurped the Authority, he was compelled, with the sound of trumpet, at the Market Cross of Edinburgh, to make his purgation, in form as follows, the 19 day of October :

THE PURGATION OF THE DUKE

" FORSAMEKLE as my Lord Duke of Châtelherault, understanding the false report made by the Queen Regent against him that he and his son, my Lord of Arran, should pretend usurpation of the Crown and Authority of this realm, when in very deed he nor his said son never once minded such things,[1] but allanerly [2] in simplicity of heart, moved partly by the violent pursuit of the religion and true professors thereof, partly by compassion of the commonwealth and poor community of this realm, oppressed with strangers, he joined himself with the rest of the Nobility, with all hazard, to support the common cause of that one and of that other ; has thought expedient to purge himself and his said son, in presence of you all, as he had done in presence of the Council, of that same crime, of old, even by *The Duke* summonds, laid to his charge the second year of the reign of our *long be-* *fore falsely* Sovereign Lady.[3] Which malice has continued ever against him, *accused of* most innocent of that crime, as your experience bears witness ; *usurpation* and plainly protests, that neither he nor his said son suits nor seeks any pre-eminence, either to the Crown or Authority, but as far as his puissance may extend, is ready, and ever shall be, to concur with the rest of the Nobility his brethren, and all others whose hearts are touched to maintain the common cause of religion and liberty of their native country, plainly invaded by the said Regent and her said soldiers, who only does forge such vain reports to withdraw the hearts of true Scotsmen from the succour they owe of bound duty to their commonweal oppressed. Wherefore [he] exhorts all men that will maintain the true religion of God, or withstand this oppression or plain conquest, enterprised by strangers upon our native Scotsmen, not to credit such false and untrue reports, but rather concur with us and the rest of the Nobility, to set your country at liberty, expelling strangers therefrom ; which doing, ye shall show yourselves obedient to the ordinance of God, which was established for maintenance of the commonweal, and true members of the same."

---

[1] But see *supra*, 236, *note* 5   [2] *only*   [3] See *Acts Parl. Scot.*, ii, 447-448

The 21 day of October, came from the Queen then Regent Master Robert Forman, Lyon King of Arms, who brought unto us a writing in this tenor and [a] credit :

" AFTER commendation : We have received your letter of Edinburgh the xix of this instant, which appeared to us rather to have come from a Prince to his subjects, nor from subjects to them that bears authority : For answer whereof, we have presently directed unto you this bearer, Lyon Herald King of Arms, sufficiently instructed with our mind, to whom ye shall give credence.

" At Leith, the 21 of October 1559.

(*Sic subscribitur*),

" MARIE R."

His Credit is this :

" That she wondered how any durst presume to command *Let this* *be noted* her in that realm, which needed not to be conquest by any force, *and let all* considering that it was already conquest by marriage ; that French *men judge* *of the* men could not be justly called strangers, seeing that they were *purpose of* naturalized ; and therefore that she would neither make that town *the French* patent, neither yet send any man away, but as she thought expedient. She accused the Duke of violating his promise. She made long protestation of her love towards the commonwealth of Scotland ; and in the end commanded that, under pain of treason, all assisters to the Duke and unto us, should depart from the town of Edinburgh."[1]

This answer received, credit heard, preconceived malice sufficiently espied, consultation was taken what was expedient to be done. And for the first it was concluded, that the Herald should be stayed till further determination should be taken.[2]

The whole Nobility, Barons, and Burghs, then present, were *The order* *of the sus-* commanded to convene in the Tolbooth of Edinburgh the same 21 *pension of* day of October for deliberation of these matters. Where the whole *the Queen* *Regent,* cause being exponed by the Lord Ruthven, the question was pro- *from* poned, " Whether she that so contemptuously refused the most *authority* *within* humble request of the born Councillors of the realm, being also *Scotland*

---

[1] Knox here gives merely the substance of her Herald's commission. Fuller accounts of the " credit " are given by Spottiswoode (*History*, i, 298–300), and by Calderwood (*History*, i, 537–539). The latter derives his account from Buchanan (see Aikman's *Buchanan*, ii, 417–418). [2] See *infra*, 255

but a Regent, whose pretences threatened the bondage of the whole commonwealth, ought to be suffered so tyrannously to empire above them?" And because that this question had not been before disputed in open assembly, it was thought expedient that the judgment of the Preachers should be required ; who being called and instructed in the case, John Willock, who before had sustained the burden of the Church in Edinburgh,[1] [being] commanded to speak, made discourse, as followeth, affirming :

The discourse of John Willock   " First, That albeit magistrates be God's ordinance, having of him power and authority, yet is not their power so largely extended but that [it] is bounded and limited by God in his word.

" And Secondly, That as subjects are commanded to obey their magistrates, so are magistrates commanded to give some duty to the subjects ; so that God, by his word, has prescribed the office of the one and of the other.

" Thirdly, That albeit God hath appointed magistrates his lieutenants on earth, and has honoured them with his own title, calling them gods, that yet He did never so establish any but that, for just causes, they might have been deprived.

" Fourthly, That in deposing of Princes, and those that had been in authority, God did not always use his immediate power ; but sometimes He used other means which his wisdom thought good and justice approved, as by Asa He removed Maachah, his own mother, from honour and authority, which before she had brooked [2] ; by Jehu He destroyed Jehoram, and the whole posterity of Ahab ; and by divers others He had deposed from authority those whom before He had established by his own word." And hereupon concluded he, " That since the Queen Regent denied her chief duty to the subjects of this realm, which was to minister justice unto them indifferently,[3] to preserve their liberties from invasion of strangers, and to suffer them have God's word freely and openly preached amongst them ; *The causes* seeing, moreover, that the Queen Regent was an open and obstinate idolatress, a vehement maintainer of all superstition and idolatry ; and, finally, that she utterly despised the counsel and requests of the Nobility, he could see no reason why they, the born Councillors, Nobility and Barons of the realm, might not justly deprive her from all regiment and authority amongst them."

Hereafter was the judgment of John Knox required who, approving the sentence of his Brother, added,

" First, That the iniquity of the Queen Regent and [her] mis-

---

[1] *Supra*, 211   [2] *possessed*   [3] *impartially*

order ought in nowise to withdraw neither our hearts, neither yet the hearts of other subjects, from the obedience due unto our Sovereigns.

" Secondly, That and if we deposed the said Queen Regent rather of malice and private envy than for the preservation of the commonwealth, and for that her sins appeared incurable, that we should not escape God's just punishment, howsoever that she had deserved rejection from honours.

" And Thirdly, He required that no such sentence should be pronounced against her, but that [it should allow], upon her known and open repentance, and upon her conversion to the commonwealth, and submission to the Nobility, place should be granted unto her of regress [1] to the same honours, from the which, for just causes, she justly might be deprived."

The votes of every man particularly by himself required, and every man commanded to speak, as he would answer to God, what his conscience judged in that matter, there was none found, amongst the whole number, who did not, by his own tongue, consent to her deprivation. Thereafter was her process [2] committed to writing, and registered, as followeth :

" At Edinburgh, the twenty-one day of October 1559.[3] The Nobility, Barons, and Burghs convened to advise upon the affairs of the commonweal, and to aid, support, and succour the same, perceiving and lamenting the enterprised destruction of their said commonweal, and overthrow of the liberty of their native country, by the means of the Queen Regent, and certain strangers her Privy Councillors, plain contrary [to] our Sovereign Lord's and Lady's mind, and direct against the counsel of the Nobility, to proceed by little and little even unto the uttermost, so that the urgent necessity of the commonweal may suffer no longer delay, and earnestly craves our support : Seeing herefore that the said Queen Regent (abusing and over passing our Sovereign Lord's and Lady's commission, given and granted to her), has in all her proceedings pursued the Barons and Burghs within this realm, with weapons and armour of strangers, but any process or order of law, they being our Sovereign Lord's and Lady's true lieges, and never called nor convicted in any crime by any judgment lawful ; as first at Saint Johnston, in the month of May, she assembled her army against the town and inhabitants thereof, never called nor convicted in any crime, for that they professed true

---

[1] *return* [2] That is, the legal process against her
[3] The 23 October 1559, in *Calendar of Scottish Papers*, i, No. 566

worship of God, conform to his most sacred word ; and likewise in the month of June last, without any lawful order or calling going before, invaded the persons of sundry Noble men and Barons with force of arms convened at Saint Andrews, only for cause of religion, as is notoriously known, they never being called nor convicted in any crime : Attour [1] laid garrisons the same month upon the inhabitants of the said town of Saint Johnston,[2] oppressing the liberties of the Queen's true lieges ; for fear of which her garrisons, a great part of the inhabitants thereof fled [out] of the town, and durst not resort again unto their houses and heritages, while [3] they were restored by arms, they notwithstanding never being called nor convicted in any crime. And further, that same time did thrust in, upon the heads of the inhabitants of the said town, Provost and Bailies, against all order of election ; as lately, in this last month of September, she had done in the towns of Edinburgh and Jedburgh, and divers others places, in manifest oppression of our liberties. Last of all, declaring her evil mind toward the Nobility, commonty, and whole nation, has brought in strangers, and daily pretends [4] to bring in greater force of the same ; pretending a manifest conquest of our native rowmes and country, as the deed itself declares : in so far as she having brought in the said strangers, but [5] any advice of the said Council and Nobility, and contrary their express mind sent to her Grace in writ, has placed and planted her said strangers in one of the principal towns and ports of the realm, sending continually for greater forces, willing thereby to suppress the commonweal and liberty of our native country, to make us and our posterity slaves to strangers for ever. Which, as it is intolerable in commonwealths and free countries, so is it very prejudicial to our Sovereign Lady, and her heirs whatsomever, in case our Sovereign Lord decease but [5] heirs of her Grace's person ; and to perfurnish [6] her wicked enterprises, conceived (as appears) of inveterate malice against our country and nation, causes (but any consent or advice of the Council and Nobility) cunzie layit-money,[7] so base, and of such quantity, that the whole realm shall be depauperate, and all traffic with foreign nations everted [8] thereby ; And attour, her Grace places and maintains, contrary the pleasure of the Council of this realm, a stranger in one of the greatest offices

---

[1] *Moreover*

[2] In the manuscript (folio 165 *recto*) the words *of Sanct Johnestoun* have been added in the margin, probably in Knox's own hand.

[3] *until*   [4] *intends*   [5] *without*   [6] *carry out*

[7] *causes to be coined money of metal alloy*   [8] *turned away*

of credit within this realm, that is, in keeping of the Great Seal [1] thereof, whereinto great perils may be ingenerate to the common-weal and liberty thereof : And further, lately sent the said Great Seal forth of this realm by the said stranger, contrary the advice of the said Council, to what effect God knows ; and has else by his means altered the old law and consuetude of our realm, ever observed in the graces and pardons granted by our Sovereigns to all their lieges being repentant of their offences committed against their Highness or the lieges of the realm ; and has introduced a new captious style and form of the said pardons and remissions, attending to the practice of France, tending thereby to draw the said lieges of this realm, by process of time, in[to] a deceivable snare ; and further, shall creep in the whole subversion and alteration of the remanent laws [3] of this realm, in contrary the contents of the Appointment of Marriage ; and also peace being accorded amongst the Princes, retains the great army of strangers after command sent by the King of France to retire the same, making excuse that they were retained for suppressing of the attemptats of the lieges of this realm, albeit the whole subjects thereof, of all estates, is and ever has been ready to give all debtful obedience to their Sovereigns, and their lawful ministers, proceeding by God's ordinance : And the said army of strangers not being paid of wages, was laid by her Grace upon the necks of the poor com-munity of our native country, who were compelled by force to defraud themselves, their wives, and bairns, of that poor substance which they might conquest with the sweat of their brows, to satisfy their hunger and necessities, and quit the same to sustain the idle bellies of these strangers. Through the which in all parts rose such heavy lamentation and complaint of the community, accusing the Nobility and Council of their sleuth [4] that, as the same oppression we doubt not has entered in before the justice-seat of God, so has it moved our hearts to ruth and compassion. And for redressing of the same, with other great offences committed against the public weal of this realm, we have convened here, as said is ; and as oft times of before, have most humbly, and with all reverence, desired and required the said Queen Regent to redress the said enormities, and especially to remove her strangers from the necks of the poor community, and to desist from enterprising or fortification of strengths within this realm, against the express will of the Nobility and Council of the same.

Her daughter followed the same : for to Davy was delivered the Great Seal [2]

---

[1] This was Monsieur de Rubay. (See *supra*, 129, *note* 5)
[2] There is no record that David Riccio ever held the Great Seal.
[3] *the rest of the laws*   [4] *sloth* or *neglect*

Yet we being convened the more stark for fear of her strangers, whom we saw presume no other thing but with arms to pursue our lives and possessions, besought her Grace to remove the fear of the same, and make the town patent to all our Sovereign Lord's and Lady's lieges ; the same on nowise would her Grace grant unto ; but when some of our company in peaceable manner went to view the said town, there was both great and small munition shot forth at them. And seeing therefore that neither access was granted to be used, nor yet her Grace would join herself to us, to consult upon the affairs of our commonweal, as we that be born Councillors to the same, by the ancient laws of the realm ; but, fearing the judgment of the Council would reform, as necessity required, the foresaid enormities, she refuses all manner of assistance with us, and by force and violence intends to suppress the liberties of our commonweal, and of us the favourers of the same : WE, therefore, so many of the Nobility, Barons, and Provosts of Burghs, as are touched with the care of the commonweal (unto the which we acknowledge ourselves not only born, but also sworn protectors and defenders, against all and whatsomever invaders of the same), and moved by the foresaid proceedings notorious, and with the lamentable complaint of oppression of our community, our fellow members of the same : perceiving further, that the present necessity of our commonweal may suffer no delay, being convened (as said is) presently in Edinburgh, for support of our commonweal, and ripely consulted and advised, taking the fear of God before our eyes, for the causes foresaid, which are notorious, with one consent and common vote, ilk man in order his judgment being required, In name and authority of our Sovereign Lord and Lady, Suspends the said Commission granted by our said Sovereigns to the said Queen Dowager ; discharging her of all administration or authority she has or may have thereby, unto the next Parliament to be set by our advice and consent ; and that because the said Queen, by the foresaid faults notorious, declares herself enemy to our commonweal, abusing the power of the said authority, to the destruction of the same. And likewise, we discharge all members of her said authority from henceforth ; and that no cunzie be cunzeit [1] from henceforth without express consent of the said Council and Nobility, conform to the laws of this realm, which we maintain : And ordains this to be notified and proclaimed by Officers of Arms, in all head Burghs within the realm of Scotland. In witness of the which, our common consent and free vote, we have

---

[1] *no coin be minted*

subscribed this present Act of Suspension with our hands, day, year, and place foresaid."

[(*Sic subscribitur*),

BY US, THE NOBILITY AND COMMONS OF THE PROTESTANTS
OF THE CHURCH OF SCOTLAND.] [1]

After that this our Act of Suspension was by sound of trumpet divulged at the Market Cross of Edinburgh, we dismissed the Herald with this answer :

" PLEASE YOUR GRACE,

" We received your answer, and heard the Credit of Lyon King of Arms, whereby we gathered sufficiently your perseverance in evil mind towards us, the glory of God, our commonweal, and liberty of our native country. For safety of the which, according to our duty, we have in our Sovereign Lord's and Lady's name suspended your Commission, and all administration of the policy your Grace may pretend thereby, being most assuredly persuaded your proceedings are direct contrary [to] our Sovereign Lord's and Lady's will, which we ever esteem to be for the weal, and not for the hurt of this our commonwealth. And as your Grace will not acknowledge us, our Sovereign Lord's and Lady's lieges, true barons and lieges, for your subjects and Council, no more will we acknowledge you for any Regent or lawful Magistrate unto us ; seeing, if any authority ye have by reason of our Sovereigns' commission granted unto your Grace, the same, of most weighty reasons, is worthily suspended by us, in the name and authority of our Sovereigns, whose council we are of in the affairs of this our commonweal. And forasmekle as we are determined, with hazard of our lives, to set that town [2] at liberty, wherein ye have most wrongously planted your soldiers and strangers, for the reverence we owe to your person, as mother to our Sovereign Lady, we require your Grace to transport your person therefrom, seeing we are constrained, for the necessity of the commonweal, to suit the same by arms, being denied of the

---

[1] In the manuscript (folio 167 *recto*) a blank space of half a page has been left for the purpose of inserting the names of those who subscribed this " process." The concluding words, within square brackets, have been supplied from the Glasgow MS. Keith remarks (*History*, i, 237), " And for this reason [very few persons having been present at the framing of the Act, in comparison of the whole] perhaps they thought fit not to sign the Act man by man, but to wrap it up after this general manner, viz. *By us the Nobility and Commons of the Protestants of the Church of Scotland* "; but the Act must have been signed " man by man," otherwise the scribe would not have left this blank space for the insertion of the names.   [2] *Leith*

liberty thereof, by sundry requisitions made of before. Attour, your Grace would cause depart with you out of the said town, any person having commission in ambassador, if any such be, or in lieutenantship of our Sovereigns, together with all Frenchmen, soldiers, being within the same, (whose blood we thirst not, because of the old amity and friendship betwix the realm of France and us, which amity, by occasion of the marriage of our Sovereign Lady to the King of that realm, should rather increase nor decrease) ; and this we pray your Grace and them both to do within the space of twenty four hours, for the reverence we owe unto your persons. And thus recommending our humble service to your Grace, we commit your Highness to the eternal protection of God.

"At Edinburgh, the xxiii day of October 1559.

"Your Grace's humble Servitors." [1]

The day following, we summoned the town of Leith by the sound of trumpet, in form as followeth :

"I require and charge, in name of our Sovereign Lord and Lady, and of the Council presently in Edinburgh, that all Scots and French men, of whatsomever estate and degree they be, that they depart of this town of Leith within the space of twelve hours, and make the same patent to all and sundry our Sovereign Lady's lieges ; for seeing we have no such haitrent at either the one or the other, that we thirst the blood of any of the two, for that one is our natural brother, born, nourished, and brought up within the bowels of one common country ; and with that other, our nation has continued long amity and alliance, and hopes that so shall do so long as so they list to use us, and not suit to make slaves of friends, which this strengthening of our towns pretends. And therefore most heartily desires that one and that other, to desist from fortifying and maintaining of this town, [and] in our Sovereigns' and their said Council's name, desires them to make the same free within the space of xii hours."

Defiance given, there was skirmishing without great slaughter. Preparation of scales and ladders was made for the assault, which was concluded by common consent of the Nobility and Barons. The scales were appointed to be made in Saint Giles' Church, so that

---

[1] The names of those on the "Council," elected by the Earls, Lords, and Barons then convened in Edinburgh, and to hold authority until the next Parliament, together with the names of the "twenty-nine [thirty] Earls, Lords, and Barons" from whom the "Council" was chosen, are given in *Foreign Calendar, Elizabeth*, ii, No. 120 ; *Calendar of Scottish Papers*, i, No. 551.

preaching was neglected, which did not a little grieve the preachers, and many godly with them. The preachers spared not openly to say, "That they feared the success of that enterprise should not be prosperous, because the beginning appeared to bring with it some contempt of God and of his Word. Other places (said they) had been more apt for such preparations, than where the people convened to common prayers and unto preaching." In very deed the audience was wonderfully troubled all that time, which (and other misorder espied amongst us) gave occasion to the preachers to affirm, "That God could not suffer such contempt of his word, and abuses of his grace, long to be unpunished." The Queen had amongst us her assured espials,[1] who did not only signify unto her what was our estate, but also what was our counsel, purposes, and devices. Some of our own company were vehemently suspected to be the very betrayers of all our secrets ; for a boy of the Official of Lothian, Master James Balfour, was taken carrying a writing, which did open *Treason amongst the Council* the most secret thing was devised in the Council ; yea, those very things which were thought to have been known but to a very few.

By such domestical enemies were not only our purposes frustrated, but also our determinations were ofttimes overthrown and changed. The Duke's friends gave unto him such terrors, that he was greatly *The Duke and his friends fearful* troubled ; and by his fear were troubled many others. The men of war (for the most part were men without God or honesty) made a mutiny, because they lacked a part of their wages : They had done *The ungodly soldiers* the same in Linlithgow before, where they made a proclamation, "That they would serve any man to suppress the Congregation, and set up the Mass again." They made a fray upon the Earl of Argyll's Highland men, and slew one of the principal children of his chamber ; who notwithstanding behaved himself so moderately, and so studious to pacify that tumult, that many wondered as well of his prudent counsel and stoutness, as of the great obedience of his company. The ungodly soldiers notwithstanding, maligned, and continuing in their misorder, they boasted [2] the Laird of Tullibardine [3] and other Noble men, who cohorted [4] them to quietness. All these troubles were practised by the Queen, and put in execution by the *The Queen Regent's practices* traitors amongst ourselves ; who, albeit they then lurked, and yet are not manifestly noted, yet we doubt not but God shall utter them to their confusion, and to the example of others. To pacify the men of war, a collection was devised. But because some were poor, and

---

[1] *spies*   [2] *threatened*   [3] Sir William Murray of Tullibardine
[4] *exhorted*

some were niggards and avaricious, there could no sufficient sum be obtained. It was thought expedient that a cunzie [1] should be erected, that every Noble man should cunzie his silver work to supply the present necessity ; and therethrough David Forrest, John Hart, and others who before had charge of the Cunzie-house, did promise their faithful labours. But when the matter came to the very point, the said John Hart, and others of his faction, stole away, and took with them the instruments apt for their purpose. Whether this was done by the falsehood and feebleness of the said John, or the practising of others, is yet uncertain. Rested then no hope amongst ourselves that any money could be furnished ; and therefore it was concluded by a few of those whom we judged most secret that Sir Raiff Sadler and Sir James Croft,[2] then having charge at Berwick, should be tempted, if they would support us with any reasonable sum in that urgent necessity. And for that purpose, was the Laird of Ormiston [3] directed unto them in so secret manner as we could devise. But yet our counsel was disclosed to the Queen, who appointed the Lord Bothwell [4] (as himself confessed) to wait upon the returning of the said Laird, as that he did with all diligence ; and so being assuredly informed by what way he came, the said Earl Bothwell foreset his way, and coming upon him at unawares, did take him, after that he was evil wounded in the head ; for neither could he get his led horse, nor yet his steel bonnet. With him was taken the sum of four thousand crowns of the sun, which the forenamed Sir Raiff and Sir James most lovingly had sent for our support.[5] The bruit hereof coming to our ears, our dolour was doubled ; not so much for the

The fact of the Council

The treason of John Hart

---

[1] mint

[2] Elizabeth's agents, then at Berwick, On 8 August 1559 Elizabeth had authorized Sadler to treat with any person of Scotland and to make payments out of a sum of £3,000 delivered to him for that purpose, but so secretly as not to impair the treaty of peace between England and " the King and Queen of Scotland." Sadler had also been given instructions—mainly to nourish opposition to the French and to encourage Châtelherault (or even the Lord James Stewart) to keep alive his interest in the succession to the Scottish Crown. (*Calendar of Scottish Papers*, i, Nos. 520, 521)

[3] John Cockburn of Ormiston

[4] James Hepburn, fourth Earl of Bothwell, subsequently Duke of Orkney, and third husband of Mary Queen of Scots

[5] Cockburn reached Berwick on 30 October ; on 31 October he was given £1,000 (and 200 crowns, i.e. £63, 6s. 8d for his own use), but that same night, on his return journey, he was taken, hurt, and despoiled of all he had by Bothwell near Haddington. (*Foreign Calendar, Elizabeth*, ii, Nos. 169, 171, 176, 183) The £1,000 was made up of 3,157 French crowns, each valuing 6s. 4d., and one crown of 5s. 8d. in silver (*ibid.*, ii, No. 171). These equivalents are in sterling (see *infra*, 357, note 4) ; but there were various reports of the total carried by Cockburn and Teulet suggests that Bothwell kept back part of the monies for his own use. (*Papiers d'État*, i, 379, note)

loss of the money, as for the tinsal [1] of the gentleman, whom we suspected to have been slain, or at the least that he should be delivered to the Queen's hands. And so upon the sudden, the Earl of Arran, the Lord James, the Master of Maxwell,[2] with the most part of the horsemen, took purpose to pursue the said Earl Bothwell, if they might apprehend him in Crichton or Morham, whitherto (as they were informed) he had retired himself after his treasonable fact : We call his fact treasonable, because that three days before he had sent his especial servant, Master Michael Balfour, to us to Edinburgh, to purchase [3] of the Lords of the Council licence to come and speak us ; which we granted, after that he had promised that in the meantime he should neither hurt us, neither yet any to us appertaining, till that he should write his answer again, whether that he would join with us or not. He gave us further to understand that he would discharge himself of the Queen, and thereafter would assist us. And yet in this meantime he cruelly and traitorously hurt and spuilzeid [4] the noble man foresaid. Albeit that the departure and counsel of the Earl of Arran and Lord James, with their company foresaid, was very sudden and secret ; yet was the Earl Bothwell, then being in Crichton, advertised, and so escaped with the money, which he took with himself, as the captain of his house, John Somerville (who was taken without long pursuit) confessed and affirmed. Because the Noble men that sought redress, sought rather his safety and reconciliation than destruction and haitrent, they committed his house to the custody of a captain, to wit, Captain Forbes, to whom, and to all soldiers there left, was given a sharp commandment that all things found within the said house of Crichton (which were put in inventory in presence of the Lords) should be kept till that the Earl Bothwell should give answer, whether he would make restitution or not.[5] Time of advertisement was granted unto him the whole day subsequent, till going down of the sun.[6]

In absence of the said Lords and horsemen (we mean the same day that they departed, which was the last of October) the Provost and town of Dundee, together with some soldiers, passed forth of the town of Edinburgh, and carried with them some great ordnance to

The Earl Bothwell false in promise, and his treasonable fact

---

[1] *loss*

[2] John, second son of Robert, fifth Lord Maxwell, called Master of Maxwell as being heir-presumptive ; afterwards became Lord Herries by his marriage with Agnes, Lady Herries.   [3] *procure*   [4] *despoiled*

[5] Crichton Castle was then the property of the Earl of Bothwell.

[6] Again, in this incident which was a serious moment for the Congregation, Knox is singularly restrained in his condemnation of Bothwell (see *supra*, 71) ; but again it must be remembered that he had " a good mind " to the House of Hepburn (*infra*, ii, 38).

shoot at Leith. The Duke's Grace, the Earl of Glencairn, and the rest of the Noble men were gone to the preaching, where they continued to nigh twelve hours. The French being advertised by one named [   ], clerk, (who after was apprehended) that our

The first defeat of the Congregation

horsemen were absent, and that the whole company were at dinner, issued [forth], and with great expedition came to the place where our ordnance was laid. The town of Dundee, with a few others, resisted a while, as well with their ordnance as hackbuts ; but being left of our ungodly and feeble soldiers, who fled without stroke offered or given, they were compelled to give back, and so to leave the ordnance to the enemies, who did further pursue the fugitives, to wit, to the midst of the Canongate, and to the foot of Leith Wynd.

The cruelty of the French

Their cruelty then began to discover itself ; for the decrepit, the aged, the women, and children found no greater favour in their fury, than did the strong man who made resistance.

It was very apparent, that amongst ourselves there was some treason. For when, upon the first alarm, all men made haste for relief of their brethren, whom in very deed we might have saved, and at least we might have saved the ordnance, and have kept the Canongate from danger, for we were once marched forward with bold courage ; but then (we say) was a shout raised amongst ourselves (God will disclose the traitors one day) affirming " That the whole French company were entered in at Leith Wynd upon our backs." What clamour and misorder did then suddenly arise, we list not to express with multiplication of words. The horsemen, and some of those that ought to have put order to others, over-rode their poor brethren at the entry of the Nether Bow. The cry of discomfort arose in the town ; the wicked and malignant blasphemed ; the feeble (amongst whom the Justice-Clerk, Sir John Bannatyne was), fled without mercy. With great difficulty could they be kept in at the West Port. Master Gavin Hamilton cried with a loud voice, " Drink now as ye have brewed." The French, perceiving by the clamour of our fray, followed, as said is, to the midst of the Canongate, to no great number, but a twenty or thirty of their *enfants perdus*. For in that meantime the rest retired themselves with our ordnance.

The Earl of Argyll

The Earl of Argyll and his men were the first that stopped the fleeing of our men, and compelled the Port to be opened after that it was

Lord Robert Stewart

shut. But in very deed, Lord Robert Stewart, Abbot of Holyroodhouse,[1] was the first that issued out. After him followed many upon

---

[1] Lord Robert Stewart, natural son of James V by Euphemia Elphinstone, Commendator of Holyrood

the backs of the French. At last came my Lord Duke, and then was no man more frack nor was Master Gavin Hamilton foresaid. The French burnt a bakehouse, and took some spuilzie [1] from the poor of the Canongate. They slew a Papist and drunken priest, named sir Thomas Slater, an aged man, a woman giving suck and her child, and of our soldiers to the number of ten. Certain were taken, amongst whom Captain Mowat was one [and] Master Charles Geddes, servitor to the Master of Maxwell.

The Castle that day shot one shot at the French, declaring them *The Castle shot one shot* thereby friends to us, and enemy to them ; but he suddenly repented of well-doing. The Queen glad of victory, sat upon the rampart to salute and welcome her victorious soldiers. One brought a kirtle, one other a pettycoat, the third, a pot or pan ; and of envy more *The Queen Regent's rejoicing and unwomanly behaviour* than womanly laughter, she asked, " Where bought ye your ware ? *Je pense que vous l'aves achete sans argent.*" This was the great and motherly care which she took for the trouble of the poor subjects of this realm.

The Earl Bothwell, lifted up in his own conceit, by reason of this our repulse and discomfiture, utterly refused any restitution ; and so within two days after was his house spulzeid, in which were no things of any great importance, his evidents [2] and certain clothing excepted. From that day back, the courage of many was dejected. With great difficulty could men be retained in the town ; yea, some of the greatest estimation determined with themselves to leave the enterprise. Many fled away secretly, and those that did abide (a very few excepted) appeared destitute of counsel and manhood. The Master of Maxwell, a man stout and witty,[3] foreseeing the danger, *The counsel of the Master of Maxwell* desired most gravely either to take such order that they might remain to the terror of the enemy, or else that they should retire themselves with their ordnance and banners displayed in order. But the wits of men being dashed, no counsel could prevail. Thus we continued from the Wednesday, the last of October, till Monday the fifth of November,[4] never two or three abiding firm in one opinion the space of twenty-four hours. The pestilent wits of the Queen's practisers did then exercise themselves (God shall recompense their malicious craft in their own bosom, we doubt not), for they caused two godly and forward young men, the Lairds of Ferniehurst [5] and Cessford,[6] who once had gladly joined themselves with us, to

---

[1] *spoil*   [2] *title deeds*   [3] *wise*
[4] Wednesday was 1 November and Monday was 6 November
[5] This must be Sir Thomas Ker of Ferniehurst   [6] Sir Walter Ker of Cessford

withdraw themselves and their friends. The same they did to the Earl Morton, who promised to be ours, but did never plainly join. They enticed the Captain of the Castle to deny us support, in case we were pursued ; and, finally, the counsel of some was no less pestiferous against us, than was the counsel of Achitophel against David and his discomforted soldiers. " Render, O Lord, to the wicked according to their malice."

Upon Monday, the fifth [sixth] of November, did the French issue out of Leith betimes, for kepping [1] of the victuals which should have come to us. We being troubled amongst ourselves and, as said is, divided in opinions, were neither circumspect when they did issue, neither yet did we follow with such expedition as had been meet for men that would have sought our advantage. Our soldiers could scarcely be dong [2] forth of the town. The Earl of Arran, Lord James, and a certain with them, made haste. Many honest men then followed, and made such diligence, that they caused the French once to retire somewhat effrayedly. The rest that were in Leith, perceiving the danger of their fellows, issued out for their succour.

The last discomfiture upon Monday

The Earl of Arran and Lord James foresaid, being more forward nor prudent and circumspect, did compel the Captains, as is alleged, to bring their men so nigh, that either they must needs have hazarded battle with the whole French men (and that under the mercy of their cannons also), or else they must needs retire in a very narrow cure. [3] For our men were approached nigh to Restalrig. The one part of the French were upon the north towards the sea, the other part marched from Leith to Edinburgh ; and yet they marched so, that we could have fought neither company, before that they should have joined. We took purpose therefore to retire towards the town, and that with expedition, lest that the former company of the French should either have invaded the town, before that we could have come to the rescue thereof, or else have cut us off from the entry at the Abbey of Holyroodhouse, as apparently they had done, if that the Laird of Grange [4] and Alexander Whitelaw, with a few horsemen, had not stayed both their horsemen and their footmen. The company which was next us, perceiving that we retired with speed, sent forth their skirmishers, to the number of three or four hundred, who took us at a disadvantage ; before us having the mire of Restalrig betwix us and them, so that in no wise we could

---

[1] *intercepting.*   [2] *driven*
[3] *passage.* The word is the same as that in Petty (Petit) Cury, Cambridge.
[4] Sir William Kirkcaldy of Grange

charge them ; and we were inclosed by the park dyke, so that in no wise we could avoid their shot. Their horsemen followed upon our tails, and slew divers ; our own horsemen over-rode our footmen ; and so by reason of the narrowness of the place, there was no resistance made. The Earl of Arran, and Lord James, in great danger, lighted amongst the footmen, exhorting them to have some respect to order, and to the safety of their brethren, whom, by their fleeing, they exposed to murder, and so were criminal of their death. Captain Alexander Haliburton, a man that feared God, tarried with certain of his soldiers behind, and made resistance, till that he was first shot and taken. But being known, those cruel murderers wounded him in divers parts to the death. And yet, as it were by the power of God, he was brought in to the town, where in few, but yet most plain words, he gave confession of his faith, testifying, " That he doubted nothing of God's mercy, purchased to him by the blood of Christ Jesus ; neither yet that he repented that it pleased God to make him worthy to shed his blood, and spend his life in the *The death of* defence of so just a cause." And thus, with the dolour of many, *Alexander* he ended his dolour, and did enter (we doubt not) in that blessed *Hali-burton,* immortality within two hours after that we were defeated. There *Captain* were slain to the number of twenty-four or thirty men, the most part poor. There were taken the Laird of Pitmilly,[1] the Laird of Fernie younger,[2] the Master of Buchan,[3] George Lovell of Dundee,[4] and some others of lower estate ; John Dunbar, Lieutenant to Captain Mowet.[5] Captain David Murray had his horse slain, and himself hurt in the leg.[5]

Few days before our first defeat, which was upon All-Hallow Even,[6] William Maitland of Lethington younger,[7] Secretary to the Queen, perceiving himself not only to be suspected as one that favoured our part, but also to stand in danger of his life, if he should remain amongst so ungodly a company ; for whensoever matters came in question, he spared not to speak his conscience ; which liberty of tongue, and gravity of judgment, the French did highly disdain. Which perceived by him, he conveyed himself away in a

---

[1] David Monypenny of Pitmilly   [2] Andrew Fernie of that Ilk

[3] James Stewart, second son of John Stewart, third Earl of Buchan, and Master of Buchan after the death of his elder brother, John, at Pinkie in 1547

[4] George Lovell, burgess of Dundee

[5] A space has been left here in the manuscript as if for the purpose of adding further names.   [6] 31 October

[7] William Maitland, eldest son of Sir Richard Maitland of Lethington, became Secretary of State to the Queen Regent in December 1558.

How and why William Maitland left Leith

morning,[1] and rendered himself to Master Kirkcaldy, Laird of Grange, who coming to us, did exhort us to constancy, assuring us, that in the Queen there was nothing but craft and deceit. He travailed exceedingly to have retained the Lords together, and most prudently laid before their eyes the dangers that might ensue their departing of the town. But fear and dolour had so seized the hearts of all, that they could admit no consolation. The Earl of Arran and Lord James offered to abide if any reasonable company would abide with them.[2] But men did so steal away, that the wit of man could not stay them. Yea, some of the greatest determined plainly that they would not abide. The Captain of the Castle, then Lord

The Lord Erskine declared himself enemy to the Congregation

Erskine, would promise unto us no favours. But said, " He must needs declare himself friend to those that were able to support and defend him." Which answer given to the Lord James, discouraged those that before had determined to have bidden [3] the uttermost, rather than to have abandoned the town, so that the Castle would have stood their friend. But the contrary declared, every man took purpose for himself. The complaints of the brethren within the town of Edinburgh were lamentable and sore. The wicked then began to spew forth the venom which before lurked in their cankered hearts. The godly, as well those that were departed as the inhabitants of the town, were so troubled, that some of them would have preferred death to life, at God's pleasure. For avoiding of danger, it was concluded that they should depart at midnight. The Duke made provision for his ordnance, and caused it to be sent before ; but the rest was left to the care of the Captain of the Castle, who received it, as well that which appertained to Lord James, as that of Dundee. The despiteful tongues of the wicked railed upon us, calling us traitors and heretics : every one provoked other to cast stones at

The despite of the Papists of Edinburgh

us. One cried, " Alas, if I might see " ; another, " Fie, give advertisement to the Frenchmen that they may come, and we shall help them now to cut the throats of these heretics." And thus, as the sword of dolour passed through our hearts, so were the cogitations and former determinations of many hearts then revealed. For we would never have believed that our natural country men and women could have

---

[1] Writing to Sir James Croft on 29 October, Knox says " Young Lethington, Secretary, is delivered from the fearful thraldom of the Frenchmen, and is now with us in Edinburgh " (Laing's *Knox*, vi, 94). But as early as 24 September 1559 he seems to have had authority from the Congregation to " treat and conclude " (secretly) with England. (*Calendar of Scottish Papers*, i, No. 543)

[2] This, and Knox's succeeding account is supported in Randolph's report to Sadler and Croft. (*Foreign Calendar, Elizabeth*, ii, No. 237)   [3] *abided*

wished our destruction so unmercifully, and have so rejoiced in our adversity. God move their hearts to repentance ! for else we fear that He whose cause we sustain shall let them feel the weight of the yoke of cruel strangers, in whose hands they wished us to have been betrayed. We stayed not till that we came to Stirling, which we did the day after that we departed from Edinburgh [1] ; for it was concluded, that there consultation should be taken, what was the next remedy in so desperate a matter. *The worst is not yet come to our enemies*

The next Wednesday, which was the 7 [8] of November, John Knox preached (John Willock was departed to England, as before he had appointed), and entreated the [4,] 5, 6, 7, and 8 verses of the Fourscore Psalm, where David, in the person [2] of the afflicted people of God, speaketh thus : The fourth verse : " O thou the Eternal, the God of Hosts, how long shalt thou be angry against the prayer of thy people ? 5. Thou hast fed us with the bread of tears, and hath given to us tears to drink in great measure. 6. Thou hast made us a strife unto our neighbours, and our enemies laugh us to scorn amongst themselves. 7. O God of Hosts, turn us again : make thy face to shine, and we shall be saved. 8. Thou hast brought a vine out of Egypt : thou hast cast out the heathen, and planted it, &c." *The sermon of John Knox in Stirling in the greatest of our troubles*

This Psalm had the said John begun in Edinburgh, as it were foreseeing our calamity, of which in very deed he did not obscurely speak, but plainly did admonish us, that he was assured of troubles suddenly to come ; and therefore exhorted all men to prayers. He entreated the three first verses in Edinburgh, to the comfort of many. He declared the argument of the Psalm, affirming for his judgment, that it was made by David himself who, in the spirit of prophecy, foresaw the miserable estate of God's people, especially after that the Ten Tribes were divided, and departed from the obedience of Judah ; for it was not (said he) without cause that Joseph, Ephraim, Benjamin, and Manasseh were especially named, and not Judah ; to wit, because that they came first to calamity, and were translated from their own inheritance, while that Judah yet possessed the kingdom. He confessed that justly they were punished for *The argument of the 80 Psalm*

---

[1] The Congregation left Edinburgh at midnight on Monday 6 November and moved to Linlithgow, thence to Stirling. (*Calendar of Scottish Papers*, i, No. 566) " And the said day [6 November] at evin in the nycht, the congregatioun depairtit furth of Edinburgh to Lynlithquo, and left thair artailzerie void upoun the calsay lyand, and the toun desolate." (*Diurnal of Occurrents*, 54)

[2] In the manuscript (folio 174 *verso*) *presence* has been scored through and *persoune* added in the margin, probably in Knox's own hand.

idolatry committed. But he affirmed that amongst them continually there remained some true worshippers of God, for whose comfort were the Prophets sent, as well to call them to repentance, as to assure them of deliverance and of the promise of God to be performed unto them.

The division   He divided the Psalm in three parts, to wit : In a prayer ; 2. In the ground whereupon their prayer was founded ; 3. And in the lamentable complaints, and the vow which they make to God. Their prayer was, " That God should convert and turn them ; that he should make his face to shine upon them ; and that he should restore them to their former dignity." The grounds and foundations of their prayers were : 1. That God himself had become pastor and governor unto them ; 2. That he had taken the protection of them in his own hand ; 3. That he had chosen his habitation amongst them ; 4. That he had delivered them from bondage and thraldom ; 5. That he had multiplied and blessed them with many notable benedictions. Upon those Two parts he gave these notes :

First, That the felicity of God's people may not be measured by any external appearance ; for often it is, that the same people to whom God becomes not only creator, but also pastor and protector, is more severely entreated, than those nations where very ignorance and contempt of God reigneth.

Secondly, That God never made his acquaintance and league with any people by his word, but that there he had some of his elect ; who, albeit they suffered for a time in the midst of the wicked, yet in the end they found comfort, and felt in very experience that God's promises are not in vain.

Thirdly, That these prayers were dited unto the people by the Holy Ghost, before they came to the uttermost of trouble, to assure them that God, by whose Spirit the prayer was dited, would not contemn the same in the midst of their calamities.

The Third part, containing the lamentable complaint, he entreated in Stirling, in presence of my Lord Duke, and of the whole Council. In the exposition whereof, he declared, Wherefore God sometimes suffered his chosen flock to be exposed to mockage, to dangers, and to appearing destruction ; to wit, that they may feel the vehemency of God's indignation ; that they may know how little strength is in their selves ; that they may leave a testimony to the generations following, as well of the malice of the Devil against God's people, as of the marvellous work of God in preserving his little flock by far other means than man can espy. In explaining these words, " How long shalt thou be angry, O Lord, against the prayer of thy people ? " he declared, How dolorous and fearful it was to fight against that temptation, that God turned away his face from our prayers ; for that was nothing else than to comprehend and conceive God to be armed to our destruction : which temptation no flesh can abide nor overcome, unless the mighty Spirit of God interpose the self suddenly.

The example he gave, the impatience of Saul, when God would not hear his prayers. The difference betwix the elect and reprobate in that temptation, he plainly declared to be, that the elect, sustained by the secret power of God's Spirit, did still call upon God, albeit that he appeared to contemn their prayers ; which (said he) is the sacrifice most acceptable to God, and is in a manner even to fight with God, and to overcome him, as Jacob did in warsling [1] with his angel. But the reprobate (said he), being denied of their requests at God's hand, do either cease to pray, and altogether contemn God, who straitly commandeth us to call upon him in the day of adversity ; or else they seek at [2] the Devil that which they see they cannot obtain by God.

In the Second part he declared, how hard it was to this corrupt nature of ours not to rejoice and put confidence in the self, when God giveth victory ; and therefore how necessary it was that man by affliction should be brought to the knowledge of his own infirmity, lest that, puffed up with vain confidence, he make an idol of his own strength, as did King Nebuchadnezzar. He did gravely dispute upon the nature of the blind world which, in all ages, hath insolently rejoiced when God did chasten his own children, whose glory and honour, because the reprobate can never see, therefore they despise them, and the wondrous work of God in them. And yet (said he), the joy and rejoicing of the world is but mere sorrow, because the end of it tendeth to sudden destruction, as the riotous banqueting of Balthazar declareth. Applying these heads to the time and persons (he said), if none of God's children had suffered before us the same injuries that presently we sustain, these our troubles would appear intolerable ; such is our tender delicacy, and self love of our own flesh, that those things which we lightly pass over in others, we can greatly complain of if they touch ourselves. I doubt not but that some of us have ofter than once read this Psalm, as also that we have read and heard the travail and troubles of our ancient fathers. But which of us, either in reading or hearing their dolours

---

[1] *wrestling*   [2] *seek from*

and temptations, did so descend in to ourselves that we felt the bitterness of their passions ? I think none. And therefore has God brought us to some experience in our own persons.

But, yet, because the matter may appear obscure, unless it be more properly applied, I cannot but of conscience use such plainness as God shall grant unto me. Our faces are this day confounded, our enemies triumph, our hearts have quaked for fear, and yet they remain oppressed with sorrow and shame. But what shall we think to be the very cause that God hath thus dejected us ? If I shall say, our sins and former unthankfulness to God, I speak the truth. But yet I spake more generally than necessity required : for when the sins of men are rebuked in general, seldom it is that man descendeth within himself, accusing and damning in himself that which most displeaseth God. But rather he doubts that to be a cause, which before God is no cause indeed. For example, the Israelites, fighting against the tribe of Benjamin, were twice discomfitted, with the loss of forty thousand men. They lamented and bewailed both first and last ; but we find not that they came to the knowledge of their offence and sin, which was the cause that they fell in the edge of the sword ; but rather they doubted that to have been a cause of their misfortune, which God had commanded : for they ask, " Shall we go and fight any more against our brethren, the sons of Benjamin ? " By which question, it is evident, that they supposed that the cause of their overthrow and discomfit was because they had lifted the sword against their brethren and natural countrymen. And yet, the express commandment of God that was given unto them did deliver them from all crime in that case. And yet, no doubt but that there was some cause in the Israelites that God gave them so over in the hands of those wicked men, against whom he sent them, by his own expressed commandment, to execute his judgments. Such as do well mark the history and the estate of that people may easily see the cause why God was offended. All the whole people had declined from God ; idolatry was maintained by the common consent of the multitude ; and as the text sayeth, " Every man did that which appeareth good in his own eyes." In this meantime, the Levite complained of the villainy that was done unto himself, and unto his wife who, oppressed by the Benjamites of Gibeah, died under their filthy lusts. Which horrible fact inflamed the hearts of the whole people to take vengeance upon that abomination : and therein they offended not ; but in this they failed, that they go to execute judgment against the wicked,

"Specialis applicatio"

Let Scotland yet take heed

without any repentance or remorse of conscience of their former offences, and defection from God. And, further, because they were a great multitude, and the other were far inferior unto them, they trusted in their own strength, and thought themselves able enough to do their purpose, without any invocation of the name of God. But after that they had twice proven the vanity of their own strength, they fasted and prayed, and being humbled before God, they received a more favourable answer, an assured promise of the victory.

The like may be amongst us, albeit suddenly we do not espy it. And to the end that every man may the better examine himself, I will divide our whole company in two sorts of men : The one are those that from the beginning of this trouble have sustained the common danger with their brethren ; the other be those which lately be joined to our fellowship. In the one and in the other, I fear, that just cause shall be found that God should thus have humbled us. And albeit that this appear strange at the first hearing, yet if every man shall examine himself, and speak as that his conscience dites unto him, I doubt not but he shall subscribe my sentence. Let us begin at ourselves, who longest has continued in this battle. When we were a few number, in comparison of our enemies, when we had neither Earl nor Lord (a few excepted) to comfort us, we called upon God ; we took him for our protector, defence, and only refuge. Amongst us was heard no bragging of multitude, of our strength, nor policy : we did only sob to God, to have respect to the equity of our cause, and to the cruel pursuit of the tyrantful enemy. But since that our number hath been thus multiplied, and chiefly since my Lord Duke's Grace with his friends have been joined with us, there was nothing heard but " This Lord will bring these many hundred spears ; this man hath the credit to persuade this country ; if this Earl be ours, no man in such a bounds will trouble us." [1] And thus the best of us all, that before felt God's potent hand to be our defence, hath of late days put flesh to be our arm. But wherein yet hath my Lord Duke his Grace and his friends offended ? It may be that, as we have trusted in them, so have they put too much confidence in their own strength. But granting so be not, I see a cause most just why the Duke and his friends should thus be confounded amongst the rest of their brethren. I have not yet forgotten what was the dolour and anguish of my own heart, when at Saint Johnston, Cupar Muir, and

---

[1] See also Knox to Mrs. Anna Locke, 18 November 1559 (Laing's *Knox*, vi, 100)

Edinburgh Crags, those cruel murderers, that now hath put us to this dishonour, threatened our present destruction. My Lord Duke's Grace and his friends, at all the three journeys, was to them a great comfort, and unto us a great discourage ; for his name and authority did more effray and astonish us, than did the force of the other ; yea, without his assistance, they could not have compelled us to appoint with the Queen upon so unequal conditions.[1] I am uncertain if my Lord's Grace hath unfeignedly repented of that his assistance to those murderers unjustly pursuing us. Yea, I am uncertain if he hath repented of that innocent blood of Christ's blessed martyrs, which was shed in his default. But let it be that so he hath done (as I hear that he hath confessed his offence before the Lords and Brethren of the Congregation), yet I am assured that neither he, neither yet his friends, did feel before this time the anguish and grief of hearts which we felt when, in their blind fury, they pursued us. And therefore hath God justly permitted both them and us to fall in this confusion at once : us, for that we put our trust and confidence in man ; and them, because that they should feel in their own hearts how bitter was the cup which they made others to drink before them. Rests [2] that both they and we turn to the Eternal our God (who beats down to death, to the intent that he may raise up again, to leave the remembrance of his wondrous deliverance, to the praise of his own name), which, if we do unfeignedly, I no more doubt but that this our dolour, confusion, and fear shall be turned into joy, honour, and boldness than that I doubt that God gave victory to the Israelites over the Benjamites, after that twice with ignominy they were repulsed and doung back. Yea, whatsoever shall become of us and of our mortal carcasses, I doubt not but that this cause (in despite of Sathan) shall prevail in the realm of Scotland. For, as it is the eternal truth of the eternal God, so shall it once prevail, howsoever for a time it be impugned. It may be that God shall plague some, for that they delight not in the truth, albeit for worldly respects they seem to favour it. Yea, God may take some of his dearest children away before that their eyes see greater troubles. But neither shall the one nor the other so hinder this action, but in the end it shall triumph.

"Conclusio"

Let the Papists and greatest enemies witness

This sermon ended, in the which he did vehemently exhort all men to amendment of life, to prayers, and to the works of charity,

---

[1] Is this an admission that, after all, the Appointment at the Links of Leith was not in their favour, and was that of the "altered conditions"? (*Supra*, 202, *note* 4 ; 204, *note* 4 ; 205, *note* 2 ; 206, *notes* 2 and 3 ; 218, *note* 1 ; 221, *note* 1)   [2] *Remains*

the minds of men began wondrously to be erected.[1] And immediately after dinner, the Lords passed to Council, unto the which the said John Knox was called to make invocation of the name of God (for other preachers were none with us at that time). In the end it was concluded that William Maitland foresaid should pass to London to expone our estate and condition to the Queen and Council,[2] and that the Noblemen should depart to their quiet, to the sixteenth day of December, which time was appointed to the next Convention in Stirling, as in this our Third Book following shall be more amply declared.

[1] This sermon was undoubtedly notable and inspiring. It is referred to by both Buchanan and the author of the *Historie of the Estate of Scotland*. (Aikman's *Buchanan*, ii, 422 ; *Wodrow Misc.*, i, 72)

[2] His " instructions " are printed in *Calendar of Scottish Papers*, i, No. 589

ENDS THE SECOND BOOK OF THE HISTORY OF THE PROGRESS OF RELIGION WITHIN SCOTLAND

Look upon us, O Lord, in the multitude of thy mercies ; for we are brought even to the deep of the dungeon

THE THIRD BOOK
OF THE PROGRESS OF TRUE RELIGION
WITHIN THE REALM OF SCOTLAND

AFTER this our dolorous departing from Edinburgh,[1] the fury and the rage of the French increased ; for then durst neither man nor woman that professed Christ Jesus within that town be seen. The houses of the most honest men were given by the Queen to French men for a part of their reward. The Earl Bothwell, by *Nota Hepburn against the Earl of Arran being innocent* sound of trumpet, proclaimed the Earl of Arran traitor, with other despiteful words : which all was done for the pleasure and by the suggestion of the Queen Regent, who then thought the battle was won without further resistance. Great practising she made for obtaining of the Castle of Edinburgh. The French made their faggots, with other preparations, to assault the said Castle either by force, or else by treason. But God wrought so potently with the Captain, the Lord Erskine, at that time, that neither the Queen by flattery, nor the French by treason prevailed. Advertisements with all diligence passed to the Duke of Guise, who then was King of France (as concerning power to command),[2] requiring him then to make expedition, if he desired the full conquest of Scotland. Who delayed no time, but with a new army sent away his brother, Marquis d'Elbœuf,[3] and in his company the Martikis,[4] promising, that he himself should follow. But the righteous God, who in mercy looketh upon the affliction of those that unfeignedly sob unto him, fought for us by his own outstretched arm ; for, upon one night, upon the *The drowning of the French* coast of Holland, were drowned of them eighteen ensigns,[5] so that only rested [6] the ship in the which were the two principals foresaid, with their Ladies ; who, violently driven back again to Dieppe, were compelled to confess, That God fought for the defence of Scotland.[7]

From England returned Robert Melville,[8] who passed in company

[1] *Supra*, 264–265

[2] That is, Francis II, the young King of France, was wholly under the influence of Francis, Duke of Guise, brother to the Queen Regent.

[3] René de Lorraine, Marquis d'Elbœuf, a younger son of Claude de Lorraine, first Duke of Guise. In the manuscript (folio 179 *verso*), originally *his brother D'Omall* [d'Aumale] ; but *D'Omall* has been scored through and *Marquis Dalbuf* or *Dalbul* added above the line in a different hand. Claude, Duc d'Aumale was an elder brother of René.

[4] Sebastian de Luxemburg, Duc de Penthièvre, Vicomte de Martigues

[5] That is, *companies*   [6] *remained*

[7] See the reports in *Foreign Calendar, Elizabeth*, ii, Nos. 508 (6), 575

[8] Probably Sir Robert Melville of Murdochcairnie, later first Lord Melville, third son of Sir John Melville of Raith (see *supra*, 106)

to London with the Secretary,[1] a little before Christmas,[2] and brought unto us certain Articles to be answered, as by the contract that after was made, more plainly shall appear.[3] Whereupon the Nobility convened at Stirling, and returned answer with diligence. Whereof the French advertised, they marched to Linlithgow, spoiled the Duke's house, and wasted his lands of Kinneil [4] ; and thereafter came to Stirling, where they remained certain days. (The Duke, the Earls of Argyll and Glencairn, with their friends, passed to Glasgow ; the Earl of Arran, and Lord James, passed to St. Andrews ; for charge was given to the whole Nobility, Protestants, to keep their own bodies, till that God should send them further support).

The French took purpose first to assault Fife ; for at it was their great indignation. Their purpose was, to have taken and fortified the town and abbey, with the castle of St. Andrews ; and so they came to Culross, after to Dunfermline, and then to Burntisland, where they began to fortify ; but desisted therefrom, and marched to Kinghorn, upon the occasion as followeth.

When certain knowledge came to the Earl of Arran, and to [the] Lord James, that the French were departed from Stirling, they departed also from St. Andrews, and began to assemble their forces at Cupar, and sent their men of war to Kinghorn ; unto whom there resorted divers of the coast side, of mind to resist rather at the beginning, than when they had destroyed a part of their towns. But the Lords had given an express commandment, that they should hazard nothing while that they themselves were present. And for that purpose was sent unto them the Lord Ruthven,[5] a man of great experience, and inferior to few in stoutness. In his company was the Earl of Sutherland,[6] sent from the Earl of Huntly,[7] as he alleged, to comfort the Lords in their affliction ; but others whispered that his principal commission was unto the Queen Regent. Howsoever it was, he was hurt in the arm by the shot of a hackbut ; for the men of war, and the rascal multitude, perceiving certain boats of Frenchmen landing, which came from Leith, purposed to stop their landing ; and so, not considering the enemies that approached from Burntisland, unadvisedly they rushed down to the Pettycur (so is that brae be-west Kinghorn called), and at the

The Earl of Sutherland shot

---

[1] William Maitland of Lethington   [2] *Supra*, 271   [3] *Infra*, 302ff
[4] Kinneil, Borrowstounness (Bo'ness)   [5] Patrick, third Lord Ruthven
[6] John, tenth Earl of Sutherland
[7] George, fourth Earl of Huntly. He was a " bye-lyer " (*infra*, 309), and clearly " hedged " throughout the whole of this critical period. (See *Scottish Correspondence of Mary of Lorraine*, Scot. Hist. Soc., No. CCLXXXV)

sea-coast began the skirmishing, but never took heed to the enemy that approached by land, till that the horsemen charged them upon their backs, and the whole bands came directly in their faces ; and so were they compelled to give back, with the loss of six or seven of their men, and with the taking of some, amongst whom were two that professed Christ Jesus, one named Paul Lambert, a Dutchman, and a French boy, fervent in religion, and clean of life, whom, in despite, they hanged over the steeple.[1] Thou shalt revenge, O Lord, in thy appointed time ! The cause that in so great a danger there was so small a loss, next unto the merciful providence of God, was the sudden coming of the Lord Ruthven ; for even as our men had given back, he and his company came to the head of the brae, and did not only stay the French footmen, but also some of ours broke upon their horsemen, and so repulsed them that they did no further hurt to our footmen. In that rencontre was the Earl of Sutherland foresaid shot in the arm, and was carried back to Cupar. The French took Kinghorn, where they lay, and wasted the country about, as well Papists as Protestants ; yea, even those that were confederate with them, such as Seafield, Wemyss, Balmuto, Balwearie, and others, enemies to God and traitors to their country.[2] Of those (we say) they spared not the sheep, the oxen, the kine, and horse ; and some say that their wives and daughters got favours of the French soldiers. And so did God recompense the Papists in their own bosoms, for, besides the defouling of their houses, as said is, two of them received more damage than did all the gentlemen that professed the Evangel within Fife, the Laird of Grange only excepted, whose [house] of the Grange the French overthrew by gun powder. *The casting down of the house of the Grange*

The Queen Regent, proud of this victory, burst forth in her blasphemous railing and said, " Where is now John Knox's God ? My God is now stronger than his, yea even in Fife." She posted to her friends in France news that thousands of the heretics were slain, and the rest were fled ; and therefore required that some Nobleman of her friends would come and take the glory of that victory. Upon

[1] This skirmish apparently took place on Sunday, 7 January 1560, and was led by d'Oysel and La Brosse. (*Calendar of Scottish Papers*, i, No. 609 ; Teulet, *Papiers d'État*, i, 404–405)

[2] John Moutray of Seafield ; Sir John Wemyss of that Ilk ; David Boswell of Balmuto ; and Sir William Scott of Balwearie. La Brosse reports that on 19 April 1560 two hundred livres were given by the French to the Laird of Balwearie, Mr. William Scott, to try to put secretly some victuals on to Inchkeith. (*Two Missions of Jacques de la Brosse*, Scot. Hist. Soc., 122–123)

that information was the Martikis,[1] with two ships, and some captains and horse, directed to come to Scotland ; but little to their own advantage, as we shall after hear.[2]

The Lords of the Congregation, offended at the foolishness of the rascal multitude, called to themselves the men of war, and remained certain days at Cupar ; unto whom repaired John Knox and, in our greatest desperation, preached unto us a most com-fortable sermon. His text was, " The danger in which the disciples of Christ Jesus stood when they were in the midst of the sea, and Jesus was upon the mountain." His exhortation was, " That we should not faint, but that we should still row against these contrarious blasts, till that Jesus Christ should come ; for (said he) I am as assuredly persuaded that God shall deliver us from the extreme trouble, as that I am assured that this is the Evangel of Jesus Christ which I preach unto [you] this day. ' The fourth watch is not yet come ' ; abide a little : the boat shall be saved, and Peter, which has left the boat, shall not drown. I am assured, albeit I cannot assure you, by reason of this present rage ; God grant that ye may acknowledge his hand, after that your eyes have seen his deliverance."

John 6

In that sermon he comforted many. And yet he offended the Earl of Arran ; for, in his discourse upon the manifold assaults that the Church of God had sustained, he brought for example the multitude of strangers that pursued Jehoshaphat after that he had reformed religion. He entreated the fear of the people, yea, and of the King himself at the first ; but after, he affirmed, that Jeho-shaphat was stout, and to declare his courage in his God, he comforted his people and his soldiers ; he came forth in the midst of them ; he spake lovingly unto them. He kept not himself (said he) inclosed in his chamber, but frequented the multitude, and rejoiced them with his presence and godly comfort. These, and the like sentences, took the said Earl to be spoken in reproach of him, because he kept himself more close and solitary than many men would have wished.

After these things, determination was taken that the Earl of Arran, and Lord James, with the men of war, and some company of horsemen, should go to Dysart, and there lie to wait upon the French, that they destroyed not the sea-coast, as they intended utterly to have done. The said Earl, and Lord James, did as they were appointed, albeit their company was very small ; and yet they did so valiantly, that it passed all credibility : for twenty and one days they lay in their clothes ; their boots never came off ; they had

---

[1] See *supra*, 275, *note* 4   [2] *Infra*, 280

skirmishing almost every day ; yea, some days, from morn to even. The French were four thousand soldiers, beside their favourers and faction of the country. The Lords were never together five hundred horsemen, with a hundred soldiers ; and yet they held the French so busy, that for every horse they slew to the Congregation, they lost four French soldiers.[1]

William Kirkcaldy of Grange, the day after that his house was cast down, sent in his defiance to Monsieur d'Oysel, and unto the rest, declaring, that to that hour had he used the French favourably : he had saved their lives, when that he might have suffered their throats to have been cut ; but seeing they had used him with that rigour, let them not look for that favour in times to come. And unto Monsieur d'Oysel he said, " He knew that he would not get him in the skirmishing, because he knew he was but a coward [2] ; but it might be that he should quite him a common [3] either in Scotland or else in France." The said William Kirkcaldy, and the Master of Lindsay,[4] escaped many dangers. The Master had his horse slain under him : the said William was almost betrayed in his house, at Hallyards.[5] But yet they never ceased, but night and day they waited upon the French. They laid themselves in a secret place, with some gentlemen, before the day, to await upon the French, who used commonly to issue in companies, to seek their prey ; and so came forth a Captain Battu,[6] with his hundred, and began to spoilzie ; whom the said Master, now Lord of Lindsay, and the said William, suffered, without declaration of themselves, or of their company, till that they had them more than a mile from Kinghorn, and then began the horsemen to break ; which perceived, the French altogether drew to a place called Glennis House,[7] and made

---

[1] These activities are reported in letters from Arran and the Lord James Stewart to Sadler and Croft (*Calendar of Scottish Papers*, i, Nos. 607, 626(2) ; *Foreign Calendar, Elizabeth*, ii, Nos. 565, 593). Their horsemen, given in one place as five hundred (*Foreign Calendar, Elizabeth*, ii, No. 604(5)), are said in a letter from Arran to be reduced from eight hundred to two hundred, but they " are deliberate to remain so long as they can hold twenty horse together " (*Ibid.*, ii, No. 606). Knox provides a second graphic account of this guerilla warfare in a letter of 29 January 1560 to Gregory Railton. (Laing's *Knox*, vi, 105–107)

[2] D'Oysel is extolled by Brantôme and has been called one of the bravest captains of the sixteenth century. (Teulet, *Papiers d'État*, i, Preface, xi)

[3] " To quite [quit] one's common " is " to pay one's debt " ; hence " to settle accounts with somebody," not necessarily financially.

[4] Patrick Lindsay, later (1563) sixth Lord Lindsay of the Byres

[5] In the parish of Auchtertool, Fife

[6] Possibly a corruption of some name such as Labast or Labat

[7] Possibly Gleniston, Lochgelly

for debate : some took the house, and others defended the close and yard. The hazard appeareth very unlikely, for our men had nothing but spears, and were compelled to light upon their feet. The others were within dykes ; and every man had culverins : the shot was fearful to many, and divers were hurt, amongst whom were Robert Hamilton, and David Kirkcaldy, brother to the said Laird,[1] who both were supposed to have been slain. The said Laird perceiving men to faint, and begin to recoil, said, " Fye, let us never live after this day, that we shall recoil for French skybalds " [2] ; and so the Master of Lindsay and he burst in at the yett,[3] and so others followed. The Master struck with his spear at La Battu, and glancing upon his harness, for fierceness stammered [4] almost upon his knees. But recovering suddenly, he fessned [5] his spear, and bore the Captain backward who, because he would not be taken, was slain, and fifty of his company with him.[6] Those that were into the house, with some others, were saved, and [sent] to Dundee to be kept. This mischance to the French men made them to be more circumspect in scattering abroad into the country ; and so the poor creatures got some relief. To furnish them of victuals, was appointed Captain Cullen,[7] with two ships, who travelled betwix the south shore and Kinghorn, for that purpose. For his wages he spoilzied Kinghorn, Kirkcaldy, and so much of Dysart as he might. For remedy whereof were appointed two ships from Dundee : Andrew Sands, a stout and fervent man in the cause of religion, was the principal. This same time arrived the Martikis,[8] who, without delay, landed himself, his coffers, and the principal gentlemen that were with him at Leith,[9] leaving the rest in the ships till better opportunity. But the said Andrew, and his companion, striking sail and making as they would cast anchor hard beside them, boarded them both, and carried them to Dundee. In them were got some horse, and much harness, with some other trifles ; but of money we heard not.[10] Hereat the French offended, avowed the destruction of St. Andrews and Dundee ; and so, upon a Monday in the morning, the 23 day of January,[11] they marched from

The slaughter of a French captain with his band

---

[1] He is called Thomas Kirkcaldy in *Calendar of Scottish Papers*, i, No. 619.
[2] *worthless fellows ; ragamuffins* [3] *gate* [4] *staggered*
[5] *fixed*
[6] This incident apparently took place on 12 January 1560. (*Foreign Calendar, Elizabeth*, ii, No. 584) [7] Captain James Cullen [8] *Supra*, 275, *note* 4
[9] On 11 January 1560, according to the *Diurnal of Occurrents* (55, 272).
[10] This incident apparently took place on 11 or 12 January 1560. (*Diurnal of Occurrents*, 55 ; *Foreign Calendar, Elizabeth*, ii, Nos. 592(2), 605)
[11] Monday was 22 January

Dysart, and passed the water of Leven [1]; ever keeping the sea-coast, by reason of their ships and victuals, as said is. About twelve hours they espied ships (which were seen that morning by us that were upon the land, but were not known). Monsieur d'Oysel affirmed them to be French ships, and so the soldiers triumphed, shot their volley for salutation, and marched forward to Kincraig,[2] fearing no resistance.

But short after, the English ships met with Captain Cullen, and seized him and his ships, which made them a little to muse.[3] But suddenly came Master Alexander Wood, who had been upon the Admiral,[4] and assured Monsieur d'Oysel, that they were English men, and that they were the fore-riders of a greater number that followed, who were sent for the support of the Congregation. There might have been seen the riving of a beard, and might have been heard such despite as cruel men use to spew forth while as [5] God bridles their fury. Weariness and the night constrained them to lodge there.[6] They supped scarcely, because their ships were taken, in the which were their victuals and ordnance, which they intended to have placed in St. Andrews. They themselves durst not stray abroad to seek [supplies] ; and the Laird of Wemyss's carriage, which likewise was coming with furnishing unto them, was stayed. And therefore, betimes in the morning, they retired towards Kinghorn, and made more expedition in one day in returning, than they did in two in marching forward.

The storm, which had continued near the space of a month, broke in the very time of their retiring, whereby many thought they should have been stayed, till that reasonable company might have been assembled to have fought them ; and for that purpose did William Kirkcaldy cut the Brig of Tullibody.[7] But the French, expert enough in such facts,[8] took down the roof of a parish kirk, and made a brig over the same water, called Devon ; and so they

---

[1] The river Leven which issues from the south-east end of Loch Leven and flows into the sea at the town of Leven on the west side of Largo Bay.

[2] A headland on the east side of Largo Bay

[3] On 23 January 1560. (*Foreign Calendar, Elizabeth*, ii, No. 645(3) ; *Two Missions of Jacques de la Brosse*, 58–59). See also Knox to Railton, 29 January 1560. (Laing's *Knox*, vi, 105)

[4] William Winter, Admiral of the English fleet. His " instructions " are printed in *Foreign Calendar, Elizabeth*, ii, Nos. 441, 623.   [5] *when*

[6] According to La Brosse, at Kirkcaldy (*op. cit.*, 58–59)

[7] North-west of Alloa, Clackmannanshire. According to La Brosse (*op. cit.*, 64–65) on 27 January ; according to Pitscottie (*Chronicles*, ii, 166) on 26 January. See also *Diurnal of Occurrents*, 272–273   [8] *matters* (French *faits*)

escaped, and came to Stirling, and syne to Leith. Yet in their
returning they lost divers ; amongst whom there was one whose
miserable end we must rehearse. As the French spoilyied the
country in their returning, one captain or soldier, we cannot tell,
but he had a red cloak and a gilt morion, entered upon a poor
woman, that dwelt in the Whiteside and began to spoil. The poor
woman offered unto him such bread as she had ready prepared.
But he, in no wise therewith content, would have the meal and a
little salt beef which the poor woman had to sustain her own life,
and the lives of her poor children ; neither could tears, nor pitiful
words, mitigate the merciless man, but he would have whatsoever
he might carry. The poor woman perceiving him so bent, and
that he stooped down in her tub, for the taking forth of such
stuff as was within it, first cowped up [1] his heels, so that his head
went down ; and thereafter either by herself, or if any other company
came to help her, but there he ended his unhappy life ; God so
punishing his cruel heart, who could not spare a miserable woman
in that extremity. " Let all such soldiers receive such reward,
O Lord, seeing that thou art the revenger of the oppressed."

And now, because that from this time forward, frequent mention
will be made of the comfortable support that we, in our greatest
extremity received, by God's providence, from our neighbours of
England, we think it expedient simply to declare by what instruments that matter was first moved, and by what means it came to
pass, that the Queen and Council of England showed themselves so
favourable unto us.

As John Knox had forewarned us, by his letters from Geneva,
of all dangers that he foresaw [to] ensue on our enterprise ; so
when he came to Dieppe, mindful of the same, and revolving with
himself what remedy God would please to offer, he took the boldness
to write to Sir William Cecil, Secretary of England, with whom the
said John had been before familiarly acquainted, intending thereby
to renew acquaintance, and so to open further of his mind. The
tenor of his first letter follows :

*John
Knox's
first letter
to Sir
William
Cecil*

" *The Spirit of Judgment, Wisdom, and Sanctification, I wish
unto you, by Jesus Christ*

" As I have no pleasure with long writing to trouble you, Right
Honourable, whose mind I know to be occupied with most grave

[1] *tipped up*

matters, so mind I not greatly to labour by long preface to conciliate your favours, which I suppose I have already (howsomever rumours bruit the contrary), as it becometh one member of Christ's body to have of an other. The contents, therefore, of these my presents shall be absolved in two points. In the former, I purpose to discharge, in brief words, my conscience towards you : and in the other, somewhat must I speak in my own defence, and in defence of that poor flock, of late assembled in the most godly reformed church and city of the world, Geneva. To you, Sir, I say, that as from God ye have received life, wisdom, honour, and this present estate, in the which now ye stand, so ought you wholly to employ the same to the advancement of his glory, who only is the author of life, the fountain of wisdom, and who most assuredly doth, and will honour and glorify those, that, with simple hearts, do glorify him ; which, alas, in times past ye have not done ; but being overcome with common iniquity, ye have followed the world in the way of perdition. For to the suppressing of Christ's true Evangel, to the erecting of idolatry, and to the shedding of the blood of God's most dear children have you, by silence, consented and subscribed.[1] This your most horrible defection from the truth known, and once professed, hath God to this day mercifully spared ; yea, to man's judgment, he hath utterly forgotten and pardoned the same. He hath not entreated you as he hath done others (of like knowledge), whom in his anger (but yet most justly, according to their deserts) he did shortly strike after their defection. But you (guilty in the same offences) he hath fostered and preserved, as it were in his own bosom, during the time of that most miserable thraldom of that professed enemy of God, mischievous Mary [2] : and now hath he set you at such liberty, as the fury of God's enemies cannot hurt you, except that willingly, against his honour, ye take pleasure to conspire with them. As the benefit which ye hath received is great, so must God's justice require of you a thankful heart ; for seeing that his mercy hath spared you, being traitor to his Majesty ; seeing further, that amongst your enemies he hath preserved you ; and, last, seeing, although worthy of hell, he hath promoted you to honours and dignity, of you must he require (because he is just) earnest

---

[1] The argument against consent by silence is stressed by Knox in his *Appellation to the Nobility and Estates of Scotland*. (Laing's *Knox*, iv, 503)

[2] These last eight words do not occur in the original letter. (*Foreign Calendar, Elizabeth*, i, No. 514 ; Laing's *Knox*, vi, 16)

repentance for your former defection,[1] a heart mindful of his merciful providence, and a will so ready to advance his glory, that evidently it may appear that in vain ye have not received these graces of God ; to performance whereof, of necessity it is, that carnal wisdom and worldly policy (to the which both, ye are bruited too much inclined), give place to God's simple and naked truth. Very love compelleth me to say, that except the Spirit of God purge your heart from that venom, which your eyes have seen to have been destruction unto others, that ye shall not long escape the reward of dissemblers. Call to mind what your ears heard proclaimed in the chapel of Saint James,[2] when this verse of the first Psalm was entreated, " Not so, O wicked, not so ; but as the dust which the wind tossed," etc. And consider, that now ye travel in the same way which then they did occupy ; plainly to speak, now are ye in that estate and credit, in the which ye shall either comfort the sorrowful and afflicted for righteousness sake or else ye shall molest and oppugn the Spirit of God speaking in his messengers. The comforters of the afflicted for godliness have promise of comfort in their greatest necessities ; but the troublers of God's servants (how contemned that ever they appear before the world) are threatened to leave their names in execration to the posterities following. The examples of the one and of the other are not only evident in Scriptures, but also have been lately manifested in England. And this is the conclusion of that which to yourself I say, Except that in the cause of Christ's Evangel ye be found simple, sincere, fervent, and unfeigned ye shall taste of the same cup which politic heads[3] have drunk in before you.

" The other point concerning myself, and that poor flock now dispersed, and (as I here say) rudely entreated, is this : By divers messengers I have requested such privileges as Turks commonly do grant to men of every nation ; to wit, that freedom should be granted unto me peaceably to travel through England, to the end that with greater expedition I might repair towards my own country, which now beginneth to thirst for Christ's truth. This request I thought so reasonable, that almost I had entered the realm without licence demanded ; and yet I understand that it has been so rejected,

[1] Sir William Cecil (later Lord Burghley) had been previously associated with the Protestant movement in England, but had " conformed " during the reign of Mary Tudor. (See E. Nares, *Memoirs of William Cecil, Lord Burghley*, i, 673–674)
[2] Probably a reference to a sermon by Knox himself when preaching as one of the chaplains to Edward VI.   [3] *political rulers*

that the solicitors thereof did hardly escape imprisonment.[1] And some of that flock I hear to be so extremely handled, that those that most cruelly have shed the blood of God's most dear children find this day amongst you greater favours than they do. Alas, this appeareth much to repugn to Christian charity ; for whatsoever hath been my offence, this I fear not to affirm in their causes, that if any which have suffered exile in these most dolorous days of persecution, deserve praise and commendation for peace, concord, sober and quiet living, it is they. And as for me, how criminal that ever I be in God's presence, for the multitude of my sins ; yet before his justice-seat I have a testimony of good conscience, that since my first acquaintance with England, willingly I never offended person within it, (except in open chair to reprove that which God condemneth can be judged offence). But I have (say you) written a treasonable [book] against the Regiment and Empire of Women.[2] If that be my offence, the poor flock is innocent (except such as this day do fastest cry treason) : For, Sir, in God's presence I write, with none in that company did I consult before the finishing of the same ; and, therefore, in Christ's name, I require that the blame may lie upon me alone. The writing of that Book I will not deny, but to prove it treasonable I think it shall be hard. For, Sir, no more do I doubt of the truth of my principal proposition, than that I doubt that this was the voice of God which first did pronounce this penalty against woman, " In dolour shalt thou bear thy children." It is bruited, that my Book is or shall be written against. If so be, Sir, I greatly fear that flatterers shall rather hurt nor mend the matter, which they would seem to maintain ; for, except that my error be plainly shown and confuted by better authority than by such laws as from year to year may and do change, I dare not promise silence in so weighty a business, lest that in so doing I shall appear to betray the verity which is not subject to the mutability of time. And if any think me either enemy to the person or yet to the regiment of her whom God hath now promoted, they are utterly deceived of me. For the miraculous work of God, comforting his afflicted by an infirm vessel, I do acknowledge, and the power of his most

---

[1] Elizabeth, highly offended by Knox's *First Blast of the Trumpet against the Monstrous Regiment of Women* which had appeared early in 1558 when Mary Tudor was still on the English throne, regarded him as a person unfit (or unsafe) to land on English soil. As he wrote to Mrs. Anna Locke from Dieppe on 6 April 1559, just before this letter to Cecil, " my FIRST BLAST hath blown from me all my friends in England." (Laing's *Knox*, vi, 14)

[2] *The First Blast of the Trumpet against the Monstrous Regiment of Women*

potent hand (raising up whom [it] best pleaseth his mercy to suppress such as fight against his glory), I will obey, albeit that both nature and God's most perfect ordinance repugn to such regiment. More plainly to speak, if Queen Elizabeth shall confess that the extraordinary dispensation of God's great mercy maketh that lawful unto her, which both nature and God's law do deny to all women, then shall none in England be more willing to maintain her lawful authority than I shall be : But if (God's wondrous work set aside) she ground (as God forbid) the justness of her title upon consuetude, laws, or ordinances of men ; then I am assured, that as such foolish presumption doth highly offend God's supreme majesty, so do I greatly fear that her ingratitude shall not long lack punishment. And this in the name of the eternal God, and of his son Jesus Christ (before whom both you and I shall stand, to make accounts of all counsel we give), I require you to signify unto Her Grace in my name ; adding, that only humility and dejection of herself before God shall be the firmity and stability of her throne, which I know shall be assaulted more ways than one. If this ye conceal from Her Grace, I will make it patent to the world that thus far I have communicated with you, having also further to speak, if my weak judgment may be heard. Alas, Sir, is my offence (although in that time, and in that matter, I had written ten books) so heinous that I can not have licence, by preaching of Christ Jesus, to refresh those thirsty souls which long have lacked the water of life? No man will I presently accuse ; but I greatly fear that the leprous have no pleasure to behold their faces in the clear glass. Let none be afraid that I require to frequent the Court, either yet of any continuance to remain in England ; but only thirst, in passing forth to my own native country, to communicate with you and some others, such things as willingly I list not to commit to paper, neither yet to the knowledge and credit of many ; and then, in the North parts, to offer God's favours to such as I suppose do mourn for their defection. And this I trust shall be no less profitable to Her Grace, and to all godly within England, than it should be pleasing to me in the flesh.

The worst is not yet come

" This is the third time that I have begged licence to visit the hungry and thirsty amongst you ; which, if now be denied, as before God I have a testimony that so much I seek not myself, as the advancement of Christ's Evangel, and the comfort of such as whom I know afflicted, so shall the godly understand that England, in refusing me, refuseth a friend, how small that ever the power be. The mighty Spirit of the Lord Jesus move your heart deeply to consider your duty unto God, and the estate of that realm in which, by his appointment, ye now serve. From Dieppe, the 10th of April 1559.

(*Sic subscribitur*)

" Yours to command in godliness,

" JOHN KNOX."

To this letter [1] was no answer made ; for short thereafter the said John Knox made forward to Scotland by sea, where he landed the third day of May [2] ; and had such success as in the Second Book is declared. The said John being in St. Andrews after Cupar Muir, [3] entered in deep discourse with the Laird of Grange : the dangers were evident, but the support was not easy to be seen. After many words, John Knox burst forth as follows : " If England would foresee their own commodity, yea, if they did consider the danger wherein they themselves stand, they would not suffer us to perish in this quarrel ; for France hath decreed no less the conquest of England than of Scotland." After long reasoning, it was concluded betwix them two, that support should be craved of England [4] ; and for that purpose, the said Laird of Grange first wrote to Sir Harry Percy, [5] and after rode from Edinburgh and spoke with him ; to whom he made so plain demonstration of the danger appearing to England, that he took upon him to write to the Secretary Cecil ; who with expedition returned answer back again, giving him to understand that our enterprise altogether misliked not the Council, albeit that they desired further resolution of the principal Lords. Which thing understood, it was concluded by some to write unto him plainly our whole purpose. The tenor of our letter was this :

[1] The letter was sent in duplicate, on 10 April and on 22 April. (Laing's *Knox*, vi, 20–21 ; *Foreign Calendar, Elizabeth*, i, 210)

[2] But in Book II (*supra*, 161), and in a letter to Mrs. Anna Locke (Laing's *Knox*, vi, 21), he gives the date of his arrival as 2 May. Possibly he " arrived " in the Firth of Forth on 2 May and " landed " on 3 May.

[3] *Supra*, 183 (13 June)

[4] But it is clear that there had been talk of help from England some time *before* Cupar Muir (see *Foreign Calendar, Elizabeth*, i, No. 848 ; *Calendar of Scottish Papers*, i, No. 465) ; and, writing to Cecil on 28 June, Knox refers to a letter he had previously sent from St. Andrews, but which Cecil later said he had never received. (*Foreign Calendar, Elizabeth*, i, Nos. 887, 973 ; Laing's *Knox*, vi, 31–32)

[5] *Cf. Foreign Calendar, Elizabeth*, i, No. 880

THE FIRST LETTER TO [SIR] WILLIAM CECIL, FROM THE LORDS OF THE CONGREGATION

" THE contents of a letter directed by you (right worshipful) to Sir Harry Percy,[1] were notified unto us by Mr. Kirkcaldy of Grange, this Sunday the 15 [16] of July, by the which we perceive that the said Grange, of zeal and faithful heart which he beareth to the furtherance of this our great, and, before the world, dangerous enterprise, hath travailed with you as with an unfeigned favourer of Christ's true religion, and of the liberty of our country, for knowledge of your minds towards us, in case that we be assaulted by any foreign invasion, or greater power than we be well able to resist. Your comfortable answer to this question we have considered, to our joy and comfort, as also your motions, and what ye demand ; to wit, What we, the Protestants within this realm, do purpose ? To what end we mean to direct our actions ? How we will, and how we be able to accomplish the same ? What doubts we have of any adversary power ? And finally, in case that support should be sent from you, what manner of amity might ensue betwix these two realms ? To the which in brief we answer, That our whole and only purpose (as knoweth God) is to advance the glory of Christ Jesus, the true preaching of his [holy] evangel within this realm ; to remove superstition, and all kind of idolatry ; to bridle to our powers the fury of those that heretofore have cruelly shed the blood of our brethren ; and, to our uttermost, to maintain the liberty of this our country from the tyranny and thraldom of strangers, as God shall assist us. How we [shall] be able to accomplish these premises, is to us unknown ; only our hope is good that He that has begun this good work in us, and hath, by his power, to this hour confounded the faces of our adversaries, will perform the same to his glory, which chiefly we seek in this our enterprise. Because we suppose, that neither our present danger, neither yet the warlike preparation which France maketh against us, be hid from you nor from the Council, we omit that part. As touching the assurance of a perpetual amity to stand betwix these two realms ; as no earthly [thing] of us is more desired, so crave we of God to make us instruments by which this unnatural debate, which long hath continued betwix us, may once be composed, to the praise of God's name, and to the comfort of the faithful in both realms. And if

Let the enemy say if their hope be not frustrated

[1] The letter of 4 July 1559 (*Foreign Calendar, Elizabeth*, i, No. 934 ; Laing's *Knox*, vi, 38–40)

your wisdoms can foresee and devise the means and assurances how the same may be brought to pass, persuade yourselves, not only of our consent and assistance, but also of our constancy, as men may promise, to our lives' end ; yea, and further, of a charge and commandment by us to be left to our posterity, that the amity betwix [us], in God contracted and begun, may be by them kept inviolate for ever. And for the revolting from you to France, which ye seem to fear and suspect, at their pleasure, we utterly abhor that infidelity, for now doth the voice of God continually sound in our ears, ' That such as profane the terrible and reverent name of God, shall not escape vengeance.' Our confederacy, amity, and league, shall not be like the pactions made by worldly men for worldly profit ; but as we require it for God's cause, so will we incall his name for the observation of the same. Moreover, if we should lack any thing to temporal commodity, yet should we never have occasion to return to them ; for we now perceive and feel the weight of their yoke, and intend (by God's grace) to cut away such instruments as by whom this realm was before abused. True it is, that as yet we have made no mention of any change in authority, neither yet were we minded to [do] any such thing till extreme necessity compelled us thereto : but seeing it is now more than evident, that France, and the Queen Regent here, with her priests, pretend to nothing but the suppressing of Christ's Evangel, the ruin of us, and the subversion of [this] poor realm ; committing our innocence to God, and unto the judgment of all godly and natural men, we are determined to seek the next remedy, in which we heartily require your counsel and assistance. And this far we have enterprised to make you participant of our purpose ; because, in the said letters, you required of the [said] Mr. Kirkcaldy some further assurance than his own word of writing, which we doubt not but ye shall shortly receive from more than from us. We dare not hastily make the whole assembly, neither of nobles, neither of barons, privy in this cause, for dangers that may ensue by policy and craft of the adversaries [1] ; your Wisdoms, we doubt not, will communicate these only with such as ye know favourers of such a godly conjunction. It should much help in our opinion, if the preachers both in persuasion and in public prayers (as ours do here), would commend the same unto the people. And thus, after our humble commendations to the Queen's Majesty (whose reign we desire to be prosperous and long,

---

[1] Knox makes a like point in the postscript to his letter, of the same date, to Sir William Cecil. (Laing's *Knox*, vi, 47)

to the glory of God and comfort of his Church), we heartily commit you to the protection of the Omnipotent. From Edinburgh, the 17th [19] of July 1559." [1]

With this our letter, John Knox wrote two, one to the said Secretary, and one other to the Queen's Majesty herself, in tenor as after follows :

JOHN KNOX'S SECOND [2] LETTER TO MR. CECIL, FOR DELIVERANCE OF ANOTHER TO THE QUEEN OF ENGLAND

" WITH my humble commendations. Please you, SIR, to deliver this other letter enclosed to the Queen's Grace. It containeth in few and in simple words my confession, what I think of her Authority, how it is just, and what may make it odious in God's presence. I hear that there is a confutation set forth in print against ' The First Blast.' [3] God grant that the writer have no more sought the favours of this present estate, no less the glory of God, and the stable commodity of his country, than did he who enterprised in that ' Blast ' to utter his conscience. When I shall have time (which now is somewhat precious unto me) to peruse that work, I will communicate my judgment with you.

" The time is now, Sir, that all that either thirst Christ Jesus to reign in this isle, or yet the hearts of the inhabitants of the same to be joined together in love unfeigned, ought rather to study how the same might be brought to pass, than vainly to travail for the maintenance of that [4] whereof we have already seen the danger and felt the smart. If the most part of women be wicked, and such as willingly we would not reign over us ; and if the most godly, and such as have rare graces be yet mortal, we ought to take heed, lest in establishing one judged godly and profitable to her country,

[1] The original of this letter, in the handwriting of Knox, is in the Public Record Office, London. (*Foreign Calendar, Elizabeth*, i, No. 1028) A transcript of the original letter is given in Laing's *Knox*, vi, 40–43. It is signed by the Earls of Argyll and Glencairn, the Lord James Stewart, and the Lords Ruthven, Boyd, and Ochiltree. With it also went a letter from the Congregation to Queen Elizabeth, also written by Knox. (See *Foreign Calendar, Elizabeth*, i, No. 1013 ; Laing's *Knox*, vi, 43–44 and facsimile.)

[2] For his " first letter," see *supra*, 282-287

[3] Alluding to " An Harborowe for Faithfull and Trewe Subjectes agaynst the late blowne Blaste, concerninge the Government of Wemen," printed at Geneva, published anonymously at Strassburg, 26 April 1559, but soon known to have been written by John Aylmer, one of the Marian exiles who was later to become Bishop of London.

[4] Presumably the maintenance of the existing political situation which would include the maintenance of the " auld alliance " with France.

we make an entres [1] and title to many ; of whom not only shall the truth be impugned, but also shall the country be brought in bondage. God give you and other favourers of your country eyes to foresee, and wisdom to avoid the dangers appearing.

" By divers [letters], I have required licence to have visited the North parts of England ; but as yet I have received no favourable answer.[2] The longer, Sir, that it be delayed, the less comfort shall the faithful there receive, the weaker shall the Queen's Grace be. If I were not to her Grace an unfeigned friend, I would not instantly beg such liberty, which to me I know shall neither be profitable nor pleasing in the flesh. The estate of things here common, I doubt not ye know. Some things I have (as oft I have written) which gladly I would communicate, which I mind not to commit unto paper and ink : find, therefore, the means that I may speak [to] such one as ye will credit in all things. The grace of the Lord Jesus rest with you.

" I heartily beseech you to have my service humbly commended to the Queen's Grace ; adding, that whosoever maketh me odious to her Grace, seeketh somewhat besides the glory of God and her Grace's prosperity ; and therefore cannot be assured and unfeigned friends. From, &c." [3]

The letter sent by the said John, to the Queen's Majesty of England, being enclosed in the foresaid Mr. Cecil's letter :

" To the virtuous and godly Elizabeth, by the grace of God Queen of England, &c., John Knox desireth the perpetual comfort of the Holy Spirit

" As your Grace's displeasure against me, most unjustly conceived, hath been, and is to my wretched heart a burden grievous, and almost intolerable ; so is the testimony of a clear conscience to me a stay and uphold, that in desperation I sink not, how vehement that ever the temptations appear. For, in God's presence, my conscience beareth me record, that maliciously, nor of purpose, I never offended your Grace, nor your realm ; and, therefore, howsoever I be judged of man, I am assured to be absolved of Him who

---

[1] Probably *entry*, though it may be used in the sense of *interest*

[2] *Cf. supra*, 285, *note* 1

[3] This letter, in Knox's hand, is in the Public Record Office, London (*Foreign Calendar*, *Elizabeth*, i, No. 979). It is dated 12 July 1559. A full transcript, with an additional long postscript, is given in Laing's *Knox*, vi, 45-47.

only knoweth the secrets of hearts. I cannot deny the writing of a book against the usurped Authority and unjust Regiment of Women ; neither [yet] am I minded to retract or call back any principal point, or proposition of the same, till truth and verity do further appear. But why, that either your Grace, either yet any such as unfeignedly favour the liberty of England, be offended at the author of such a work, I can perceive no just occasion. For, first, my book touched not your Grace's person [in special], neither yet is it prejudicial to any liberty of the realm, if the time of my writing be indifferently [1] considered. [2] How could I be enemy to your Grace's person, for deliverance whereof I did more study and enterprise further than any of these that now accuse me ? And, as concerning your regiment, how could or can I envy that which most I have thirsted, and for the which (as oblivion will suffer) I render thanks unfeignedly unto God ? That is, That He hath pleased him, of his eternal goodness, to exalt your head (which sometimes was in danger), to the manifestation of his glory, and extirpation of idolatry. And as for my offence, which I have committed against England, either in writing that, or of any other work, I will not refuse that moderate and indifferent men judge and discern betwix me and those that accuse [me] : to wit, whether of the parties do most hurt to the liberty of England, I that affirm, ' That no woman may be exalted above any realm, to make the liberty of the same thrall to a strange, proud, and cruel nation ' ; or, they that approve whatsoever pleaseth Princes for the time. If I were as well disposed to accuse as some of them (to their own shame) have declared themselves, I nothing doubt but that in few words I should let reasonable men understand, that some that this day lowly crouch to your Grace, and labour to make me odious in your eyes, did, in your adversity, neither show themselves faithful friends to your Grace, neither so loving and careful over their own native country as they would be esteemed. But, omitting the accusation of others, for my own purgation, and your Grace's satisfaction, I say that nothing in my book contained, is, nor can be prejudicial to your Grace's just regiment, provided that ye be not found ingrate unto God : Ingrate ye shall be proven in presence of his throne (howsoever that flatterers justify your faction) if ye transfer the glory of that honour, in which ye now stand, to any other thing than to the dispensation of his mercy, which only maketh that lawful to your Grace, which nature and law denieth to all women. Neither would I that your

---

[1] *impartially*   [2] That is, it was written during the reign of Mary Tudor

Grace should fear that this your humiliation before [God] should, in any case, infirm or weaken your Grace's just and lawful authority before men. Nay, Madam, such unfeigned confession of God's benefits received shall be the establishment of the same, not only to yourself, but also to your seed and posterity ; where, contrariwise, a proud conceit and elevation of yourself shall be the occasion that your reign shall be unstable, troublesome, and short. God is witness, that unfeignedly I both love and reverence your Grace ; yea, I pray that your reign may be long, prosperous, and quiet ; and that, for the quietness which Christ's members, before persecuted, have received under you.

" But yet, if I should flatter your Grace, I were no friend, but a deceivable traitor. And therefore of conscience I am compelled to say, that neither the consent of people, the process of time, nor multitude of men, can establish a law which God shall approve ; but whatsoever He approveth by his eternal word, that shall be approved, and whatsoever He condemneth shall be condemned, though all men in earth would hazard the justification of the same. And, therefore, Madam, the only way to retain and keep those benefits of God, abundantly poured now of late days upon you, and upon your realm, is unfeignedly to render unto God, to his mercy, and undeserved grace, the [whole] glory of this your exaltation. Forget your birth, and all title which thereupon doth hang ; and consider deeply how, for fear of your life, ye did decline from God, and bow to idolatry.[1] Let it not appear a small offence in your eyes that ye have declined from Christ Jesus in the day of his battle. Neither yet would I that ye should esteem that mercy to be vulgar and common which ye have received ; to wit, that God hath covered your former offence, hath preserved you when ye were most unthankful ; and in the end, hath exalted and raised you up, not only from the dust, but also from the ports of death, to rule above his people, for the comfort of his Kirk. It appertaineth to you, therefore, to ground the justice of your authority, not upon that law which from year to year doth change, but upon the eternal providence of Him, who, contrary to nature, and without your deserving, hath thus exalted your head. If thus, in God's presence, ye humble yourself, as in my heart I glorify God for that rest granted to his afflicted flock within England, under you a weak instrument ; so will I with tongue and pen justify your authority and regiment,

---

[1] A reference to Elizabeth's difficulties during the reign of Mary Tudor, and her outward compliance with Rome by presenting herself at Mass.

as the Holy Ghost hath justified the same in Deborah, that blessed mother in Israel. But, if the premises (as God forbid) neglected, ye shall begin to brag of your birth, and to build your authority and regiment upon your own law, flatter you whoso list, your felicity shall be short. Interpret my rude words in the best part, as written by him who is no enemy to your Grace.

" By divers letters I have required licence to visit your realm, not to seek myself, neither yet my own ease nor commodity ; which, if ye now refuse and deny, I must remit my cause to God ; adding this for conclusion, that commonly it is seen, ' That such as refuse the counsel of the faithful (appear it never so sharp) are compelled to follow the deceit of flatterers to their own perdition.' The mighty Spirit of the Lord Jesus move your heart to understand what is said ; give unto you the discretion of spirits, and so rule you in all your actions and enterprises, that in you God may be glorified, his Kirk edified, and ye yourself, as a lively member of the same, may be an example of virtue and godly life to all others. So be it. Of Edinburgh, the [20th [1]] day of July 1559."

These letters were directed by Alexander Whitelaw,[2] a man that oft hath hazarded himself, and all he had, for the cause of God, and for his friends being in danger for the same cause.

Within a day or two after the departing of the said Alexander, there came a letter from Sir Harry Percy to John Knox, requiring him to meet him at Alnwick, the third of August, for such affairs as he would not write, nor yet communicate with any but with the said John himself. While he was preparing himself for the journey (for Secretary Cecil had appointed to have met him at Stamford), the French men furiously came forth of Dunbar, of purpose to have surprised the Lords being in Edinburgh, as in the Second Book before is declared : Which stayed the journey of the said John, till that God had delivered the innocents from that great danger ; and then was he, having in his company Master Robert Hamilton, minister of the Evangel of Jesus Christ, directed from the Lords, with full commission and instructions to expone their whole cause and estate wherein they stood.

Their passage was from Pittenweem, by sea. They arrived at

---

[1] The date is supplied from the original letter. (*Foreign Calendar, Elizabeth*, i, No. 1032 ; Laing's *Knox*, vi, 47–51)

[2] Whitelaw also carried a letter from Henry Balnaves to Cecil. (*Foreign Calendar, Elizabeth*, i, No. 1030)

Holy Island [1] ; and being advertised that Sir Harry Percy was absent from [the North], they addressed themselves to Sir James Croft, then Captain of Berwick and Warden of the East Marches of England. They showed unto him their credit and commission. He received them gently, and comforted them with his faithful counsel, which was : " That they should travel no farther, neither *Sir James Croft's counsel* yet should they be seen in public, and that for divers considerations. First, The Queen Regent had her espials in England. Secondly, The Queen and the Council that favoured our action, would that all things should be secret so long as they might. And last (said he), I think it not expedient, that in such rarity of preachers ye two be any long time absent from the Lords.[2] And therefore (said he) ye shall do best to commit to writing your whole mind and credit, and I shall promise to you, upon my honour, to have answer to you, and at the Lords again, before that ye yourselves can be at London. And where that your letters cannot express all things so fully as your presence could, I shall supply the same, not only by my pen, but also by my own presence, to such as will inform the Council sufficiently of all things."

The said John and Master Robert followed his counsel,[3] for it was faithful, and proceeded of love at that time. They tarried with him very secretly, within the Castle of Berwick, two days. In the which time, returned Alexander Whitelaw foresaid, with answer to the Lords, and to John Knox ; the tenor of whose letter was this :

MASTER CECIL'S LETTER TO JOHN KNOX

" MASTER KNOX,

" *Non est masculus neque fœmina, omnes enim, ut ait Paulus, unum sumus in Christo Jesu. Benedictus vir qui confidit in Domino ; et erit Dominus fiducia ejus.*

" I have received your letters at the same time that I have thought to have seen yourself about Stamford. What is now hitherto the cause of your [let], I know not. I forbear to descend to the bottom of things, until I may confer with such one as ye are ; and, therefore, if your chance shall be hereafter to come hither, I wish

---

[1] Knox arrived at Holy Island on 1 August 1559 ; he left Berwick for Scotland, with Whitelaw, on the night of 3 August. (*Foreign Calendar, Elizabeth*, i, Nos. 1119, 1124)

[2] Sir James Croft, in his letter of 4 August 1559 to Cecil, reports that Knox had said he could in no wise " be long from his flock." (*Foreign Calendar, Elizabeth*, i, No. 1124 ; Laing's *Knox*, vi, 62)

[3] The " instructions " to Knox of 30 July 1559, and his written amplification given to Sir James Croft, are printed in Laing's *Knox*, vi, 56–59.

you furnished with good credit and power to make good resolution. Although my answer to the Lords of Congregation be somewhat obscure, yet upon further understanding ye shall find the matter plain. I need wish to you no more prudence than God's grace, whereof God send you plenty. And so I end. From Oxford, the 28th of July 1559.

(Sic subscribitur,)

Yours as a member of the same body in Christ,

" W. Cecil."

Albeit the said John received this letter at Berwick, yet would he answer nothing till that he had spoken the Lords ; whom he found in Stirling, and unto whom he delivered the answer sent from the Council of England (for Alexander Whitelaw took sickness betwix Berwick and Edinburgh, and was troubled by the Lord Seton, as in the former Book is declared).[1]   The answer sent by Master Cecil was so general that many amongst us were despaired of any comfort to come from that country ; and therefore were determined that they would request no further.   John Knox laboured in the contrary ; but he could prevail no further, but that he should have licence and liberty to write as he thought best.   And so took he upon him to answer for all, in form as follows :

Answer to Mr. Cecil's Letter [2]

" Two causes impeded me, Right Worshipful, to visit you at any part of England.   Former, no signification of your mind and pleasure was made unto me, for only did Sir Harry Percy will me to come and speak [with] him, which conveniently at that time I could not do, by reason that the French men (which was the second cause of my stay) did then most furiously pursue us, while our company was dispersed ; and then durst I not be absent for divers inconvenients. Neither did I think my presence greatly necessary with you, considering that the matter, which I desired most, was opened and proponed. To the which I would have wished that a more plain and especial

---

[1] Supra, 214

[2] See Foreign Calendar, Elizabeth, i, Nos. 1134, 1200 : the one dated from Perth, [6 August] ; the other from St. Andrews, 15 August.   Here, in his History, Knox dates a garbled version of his letter " of St. Johnston " [Perth] ; but the original, in his own handwriting, is dated from St. Andrews, 15 August, and is much fuller.   A transcript of the original letter is given in Laing's Knox, vi, 67–70 where for " fear Duresme nocht " read " from Durham north." (Calendar of Scottish Papers, i, No. 526)

answer should have been made. For, albeit Mr. Whitelaw, by his credit, Mr. Kirkcaldy, by his letter, and I, both by letters, and by that which I had received from Sir James Croft, did persuade your good minds ; yet could not the Council be otherways persuaded, but that this alteration in France [1] had altered your former purpose. It is not unknown what favour we three do bear to England ; and, therefore, I wish that rather your pen than our credit, or any thing written to any of us, should assure the Lords and others, of your good minds (who are but now in number five hundred).[2] Unless that money be furnished without delay to pay the soldiers with, for their service bypast, and to retain another thousand footmen, with three hundred horsemen, till some stay be had in this danger, these gentlemen will be compelled to leave the fields. I am assured, as flesh may be of flesh, that some of them will take a very hard life before that ever they compone either with the Queen Regent, either yet with France ; but this I dare not promise of all, unless in you they see a greater forwardness. To support us will appear excessive, and to break promise with France will appear dangerous. But the loss of expenses, in my opinion, ought not to be esteemed from the first payment ; neither yet the danger from the first appearance. France is most fervent to conquer us, and avoweth that against us they will spend their Crown (so did my own ears hear Buttencourt [3] brag). But most assuredly I know that unless by us they thought to make an entry to you, that they would not buy our poverty at that price. They labour to corrupt some of our great men by money (and some of our number are poor, as before I wrote, and cannot serve without support) ; some they threaten ; and against others they have raised up a party in their own country. In this mean time, if ye lie by as neutrals, what will be the end ye may easily conjecture. And, therefore, Sir, in the bowels of Christ Jesus, I require you to make plain answer : What the gentlemen here may lippen to,[4] and what the Queen's Majesty will do, may without long delay be put in execution. Rest in Christ Jesus. Of Saint Johnston, the &c. day of, &c."

Answer with great expedition was returned to this letter, desiring some men of credit to be sent from the Lords to Berwick, for the receiving of money for the first support, with promise that if the

---

[1] Probably the reference is to the death of Henry II of France on 10 July 1559.

[2] That is, " should assure the Lords and others (who are but now in number five hundred) of your good minds "

[3] The Sieur de Béthencourt. (*Cf. supra*, 208–209)   [4] *confidently expect*

Lords of the Congregation meant no otherwise than before they had written, and if they would enter in league with honest conditions, they should neither lack men nor money to their just cause. Upon this answer, was directed from the Lords to Berwick, Master Henry Balnaves, a man [of] good credit in both the realms, who suddenly returned with such a sum of money as served all the public affairs till November next ; when John Cockburn of Ormiston [being] sent for the second support and, receiving the same, unhappily fell into [the] hands of the Earl Bothwell, was wounded, taken, and despoiled of a great sum.[1] Upon which mischance followed all the rest of our troubles before rehearsed.

In the Second Book preceding, we have declared how Secretary Lethington [2] was directed to England : but one thing we have before passed by. In that, our greatest dejection, this order was taken : That the Duke's Grace, the Earl of Glencairn, Lord Boyd, Lord Ochiltree, and their friends, should remain together at Glasgow, for comfort of the country, and for giving of answers as occasion should require ; and that the Earl of Arran, the Lord James, the Earl of Rothes, the Master of Lindsay, and their adherents, should continue together within Fife, for the same causes, that advertisements might go from the one to the other as need required. In the negotiation of the Secretary Lethington with the Queen and Council of England (in which he travailed with no less wisdom and faithfulness than happy success) many things occurred that required the resolution of the whole Lords, amongst which there was one whereof before no mention is made.

After that the Queen and Council of England had concluded to send their army into Scotland, for expelling of the French, the Duke of Norfolk was sent to Berwick,[3] with full instructions, power, and commission, to do in all things concerning the present affairs of Scotland, as might the Queen and Councillors in their own persons do. Hereupon the said Duke required such a part of the Lords of Scotland, as had power and commission from the whole, to meet him at such day and place as pleased them to appoint. This advertisement came first to Glasgow, by the means of the Master of Maxwell. Which read and considered by the Lords, conclusion was taken that they would meet at Carlisle ; and that was the procurement of the said Master of Maxwell, for his ease. Hereupon were letters

---

[1] See *supra*, 258   [2] William Maitland of Lethington
[3] He had reached Berwick before 20 January 1560. (*Foreign Calendar, Elizabeth*, ii, No. 604)

directed from the Lords, lying in Glasgow, to Lord James, requiring him, with all possible expedition, to repair towards them for the purpose foresaid. Which letters read and advised upon, commandment was given to John Knox to make the answer : For so it was appointed at the division of the Lords, that he should answer for the part of those that were in Fife ; and Master Henry Balnaves for the part of them that abode at Glasgow. The said John answered as follows :

"To the Lord Duke's Grace, and the Lords at Glasgow

"After humble commendation of my service. Albeit I have written oftener than once to Mr. Henry Balnaves what things have misliked me in your slow proceedings, as well in supporting your brethren, who many days have sustained extreme danger in these parts, as in making provision how the enemy might have been annoyed, who lay in few number nigh to your quarters in Stirling ; and in making likewise provision, how the expectation of your friends, who long have awaited for your answer, might have been satisfied ; Albeit (I say) that of those things I have before complained, yet of very conscience I am compelled to signify unto your Honours, that unless of these, and other enormities, I shall espy some redress, I am assured that the end shall be such as godly men shall mourn, that a good cause shall perish for lack of wisdom and diligence. In my last letters to Mr. Henry Balnaves I declared that your especial friends in England wonder that no greater expedition is made, the weight of the matter being considered. If the fault be in the Lord Duke, and his friends, I wrote also, that the greatest loss should be his and theirs in the end. And now, I cannot cease, both to wonder and lament, that your whole Council was so destitute of wisdom and discretion as to charge this poor man, the Prior,[1] to come to you to Glasgow, and thereafter to go to Carlisle, for such affairs as are to be entreated. Was there none amongst you, who did foresee what inconvenients might ensue his absence from these parts ? I cease to speak of the dangers in the enemy. Your friends have lain in the Firth [2] now xv days bypast (what was their former travail is not unknown) ; they have never received comfort of any man (him only excepted), more than [if] they had lain upon the coast of their mortal enemy. Do ye not consider that such a company shall need comfort and provision from

[1] The Lord James Stewart, Prior of St. Andrews
[2] That is, along the Firth of Forth

time to time ? Remove him, and who abideth that carefully will travail in that or any other weighty matters in these parts ? Did ye not further consider, that he had begun to meddle with the gentlemen who had declared themselves unfriends heretofore [1] ; and also that order would have been taken for such as have been neutral ? Now, by reason of his absence, the one shall escape without admonition, and the other shall be at their former liberty. I am assured that the enemy shall not sleep, neither in that nor in other affairs, to undermine you and your whole cause ; and especially to hurt this part of the country to revenge their former folly. If none of these former causes should have moved you to have considered that such a journey (at such a time) was not meet for him, neither yet for them that must accompany him ; yet discreet men would have considered, that the men that have lain in their jacks, and travailed their horse continually the space of a month,[2] requireth some longer rest, both to themselves, but especially to their horses (before they had been charged to such a journey), than yet they have had. The Prior may, for satisfaction of your unreasonable minds, enterprise the purpose ; but I am assured he shall not be able to have six honest men in all Fife to accompany him : And how that either stands with your Honours, or with his safety, judge ye yourselves. But yet, wonder it is, that ye did not consider, to what pain and fashery [3] shall ye put your friends of England, especially the Duke of Norfolk, and his Council, whom ye shall cause travel the most wearisome and fashious gait [4] that is in England. In my opinion, whosoever gave you that counsel either lacked right judgment in things to be done, or else had too much respect to his own ease, and too small regard to the travail and danger of their brethren. A common cause requireth a common concurrence, and that every man bear his burden proportionably. But prudent and indifferent men espy the contrary in this cause, especially of late days ; for the weakest are most grievously charged, and to whom the matter most belongeth, and to whom justly greatest burden is due, are exempted in a manner both from travail and expenses. To speak the matter plainly, wise men do wonder what my Lord Duke's friends do mean, that they are so slack and backward in this cause. In other actions, they have been judged stout and forward ; and in this, which is the greatest that ever he or they had in hand, they appear destitute both of grace and of courage. I am not ignorant that they that are most inward of his counsel are enemies to God, and therefore cannot but be

[1] *Cf. supra*, 277   [2] *Cf. supra*, 278–279   [3] *trouble*   [4] *road*

enemies to his cause. But wonder it is, that he and his other friends should not consider that the tinsall [1] of this godly enterprise shall be the routing of them and their posterity from this realm. Considering, my Lords, that by God's providence ye are joined with the Duke's Grace in this common cause, admonish him plainly of the danger to come : will him to beware of the counsel of those that are plainly infected with superstition, with pride, and with venom of particular profit ; which if he do not at your admonition, he shall smart, before he be ware : and if ye cease to put him in mind of his duty, it may be that, for your silence, ye shall drink some portion of the plague with him. Take my plain speaking as proceeding from him that is not your enemy, being also uncertain when I shall have occasion to write hereafter. God, the Father of our Lord Jesus Christ, assist you with the spirit of wisdom and fortitude that, to his glory, and to your Lordships' and our common comfort, ye may perform that thing which godly was once begun. Amen. From Saint Andrews, the 6 of February, in haste, 1560. [2]

(Sic subscribitur,)

" Your Lordships' to command in godliness,

" J.K."

Upon the receipt of this letter, and consultation had thereupon, new conclusion was taken : to wit, that they would visit the said Duke of Norfolk at Berwick,[3] where he was.

Thus far have we digressed from the style of the History, to let the posterity that shall follow understand by what instruments God wrought the familiarity and friendship that after we found in England. Now we return to our former History.

The parts of Fife set at freedom from the bondage of those bloody worms, solemn thanks were given, in Saint Andrews, unto God for his mighty deliverance. Short after the Earl of Arran and Lord James apprehended the Lairds of Wemyss, Seafield, Balgony, and Durie,[4] and others that assisted the French ; but they were set shortly at freedom, upon such conditions as they minded never to keep : for such men have neither faith nor honesty. Mr. James Balfour,[5] who was the greatest practiser, and had drawn the band

---

[1] *loss*

[2] In the manuscript, 1559 ; that is, 6 February 1560, for at this time the new year did not begin until 25 March.

[3] See *Foreign Calendar, Elizabeth*, ii, No. 710

[4] *Supra*, 277. Andrew Lundy of Balgony and Robert Durie of that Ilk

[5] Afterwards Sir James Balfour of Pittendreich

of the Balfours, escaped. The English ships daily multiplied, till that they were able to keep the whole Firth : whereat the French and Queen Regent, enraged, began to execute their tyranny upon the parts of Lothian that lay nigh to Edinburgh. Let Mr. David Borthwick [1] witness what favours his wife and place of Addiston [2] found of the French, [3] for all the service that he had made to the Queen Regent.

In the midst of February were directed to England, from the Duke's Grace and the Congregation, the Lord James, Lord Ruthven, the Master of Maxwell, the Master of Lindsay, Master Henry Balnaves, and the Laird of Pittarrow ; who, with their honest companies and commission, departed by sea, all, except the Master of Maxwell, to Berwick, [4] where there met them the Duke of Norfolk, lieutenant to the Queen's Majesty of England, and with him a great company of the gentlemen of the north, with some also of the south, having full power to contract with the nobility of Scotland, as that they did, upon such conditions as in the same contract are specified. And because we have heard the malicious tongues of wicked men make false report of that our fact, we have faithfully and truly inserted in this our History the said contract, as well that which was made at Leith, during the siege, as that which first was made at Berwick, that the memory thereof may bide to our posterity ; to the end that they may judge with indifference, whether that we have done anything prejudicial to our commonwealth, or yet contrarious unto that debtful obedience which true subjects owe to their superiors whose authority ought to defend and maintain the liberty and freedom of the realms committed to their charge ; and not to oppress and betray the same to strangers. The tenor of our contract follows :

The Contract at Berwick

" James Duke of Châtelherault, Earl of Arran, Lord Hamilton, second person of the realm of Scotland, and apparent [heir] [5] to the Crown, the Council, Nobility, and principal Estates of the same : To all and sundry [to] whose knowledge these presents shall come, greeting. We have well considered, and be fully persuaded in what

[1] David Borthwick of Lochill, later Lord Advocate (1573)
[2] In the parish of Ratho, Midlothian
[3] Presumably by the " defouling " referred to, *supra* 277
[4] *Cf. Foreign Calendar, Elizabeth*, ii, Nos. 727, 765, 774
[5] Châtelherault was heir-presumptive to the Crown until the birth of James [VI] in 1566.

danger, desolation, and misery, the long enmity with the kingdom of England hath brought our country heretofore : how weighty and flourishing it shall become if those two kingdoms, as they be joined in one island by creation of the world, so may be knit in a constant and assured friendship. These considerations, grounded upon a most infallible truth, ought no less to have moved our progenitors and forefathers than us ; but the present danger hanging over our heads, by the unjust dealing of those of whom we have always best deserved, hath caused us to weigh them more earnestly than they did. The misbehaviour of the French ministers here hath of late years been so great ; the oppression and cruelty of the soldiers, the tyranny and ambition of their superiors and rulers so grievous to the people ; the violent subversion of our liberty, and conquest of the land, whereat they have by most crafty and subtle means continually pressed so intolerably to us all, that at last, when we could not obtain the redress by humble suits and earnest supplications presented to the Queen Dowager, who both for duty's sake and [the] place she did occupy, ought to have been most careful of our estate ; we have been, by very necessity, constrained not only to assay our own forces, but also to implore the Queen's Majesty of England aid and support, which her Majesty has most gently granted upon certain covenants, specified in a Treaty, passed at Berwick, betwix the Duke of Norfolk's good Grace, Lieutenant for her Majesty, on that one part, and certain our Commissioners, on that other part : Whereof the tenor followeth : [1]

AT BERWICK, the twenty seventh day of February, the year of our Lord God 1559.[2]. It is appointed and finally contracted betwix the noble and mighty Prince, THOMAS DUKE OF NORFOLK, Earl Marshal of England, and lieutenant to the Queen's most excellent Majesty of the said realm, in the name and behalf of her Highness, on the one part, and the right honourable Lord James Stewart,[3] Patrick Lord Ruthven, Sir John Maxwell of Terregles knight, William Maitland of Lethington younger, John Wishart of Pittarrow, and Master Henry Balnaves of Halhill, in the name and behalf of the noble and mighty Prince, James Duke of Châtelherault, second person of the realm of Scotland, and the remaining

---

[1] See *Foreign Calendar, Elizabeth*, ii, No. 781 ; Keith, *History of Affairs of Church and State in Scotland*, i, 258–262   [2] That is, 27 February 1560

[3] Here Knox's scribe has inserted, in brackets, *now erle of Mwray* ; thus this part of the manuscript was transcribed before 21 January 1570 (when the Regent Moray was assassinated).

Lords of his part, joined with him in this cause, for the maintenance and defence of the ancient rights and liberties of their country, on the other part, in form as hereafter followeth :

That is to say, That the Queen's Majesty, having sufficiently understood, as well by information sent from the Nobility of Scotland, as by the [manifest] proceedings of the French, that they intend to conquer the realm of Scotland, suppress the liberties thereof, and unite the same unto the Crown of France perpetually, contrary to the laws of the same realm, and to the pacts, oaths, and promises of France ; and being thereto most humbly and earnestly required by the said Nobility, for and in name of the whole realm, shall accept the said realm of Scotland, the said Duke of Châtelherault, being declared by Act of Parliament in Scotland to be heir apparent to the Crown thereof, and the Nobility and Subjects thereof, unto her Majesty's protection and maintenance, only for preservation of the same in their old freedoms and liberties, and from conquest, during the time that the marriage shall continue betwix the Queen of Scots and the French King, and one year after : And for expelling out of the same realm of such as presently and apparently goeth about to practise the said conquest, her Majesty shall with all speed send unto Scotland a convenient aid of men of war, on horse and foot, to join with the power of Scotsmen, with artillery, munition, and all other instruments of war meet for the purpose, as well by sea as by land, not only to expel the present power of French within that realm, oppressing the same, but also to stop, as far as conveniently may be, all greater forces of French to enter therein for the like purpose ; and shall continue her Majesty's aid to the said Realm, Nobility, and Subjects of the same, unto the time the French (being enemies to the said realm) be utterly expelled hence : And shall never transact, compone, nor agree with the French, nor conclude any league with them, except the Scots and the French shall be agreed that the realm of Scotland may be left in due freedom by the French : Nor shall leave the maintenance of the said Nobility and Subjects, whereby they might fall as a prey unto their enemy's hands, as long as they shall acknowledge their Sovereign Lady and Queen, and shall indure themselves to maintain the liberty of their country, and the estate of the Crown of Scotland : And if in case any forts or strengths within the realm be won out of the hands of the French at this present, or at any time hereafter, by her Majesty's aid, the same shall be immediately demolished by the Scotsmen, or delivered to the said Duke and his party foresaid, at their option and choice ; neither shall the power of England fortify within the ground of Scotland, being out of the bounds of England, but by the advice of the said Duke, Nobility, and Estates of Scotland.

For the which causes, and in respect of her Majesty's most gentle clemency and liberal support, the said Duke and all the Nobility, as well such as be now joined, as such as shall hereafter join with him for defence of the liberty of that realm, shall, to the uttermost of their power, aid and support her Majesty's arm against the French, and their partakers, with horse-men, and foot-men, and with victuals, by land and by sea, and with all manner of other aids to the best of their power, and so shall continue during the time that her Majesty's army shall remain in Scotland.

Item, They shall be enemies to all such Scotsmen and French as shall in anywise show themselves enemies to the realm of England, for the aiding and supporting the said Duke and Nobility, to the delivery of the realm of Scotland from conquest.

Item, They shall never assent nor permit, that the realm of Scotland shall be conquered, or otherwise knit to the Crown of France, than it is at this present only by marriage of the Queen their Sovereign to the French King, and by the laws and liberties of the realm, as it ought to be.

Item, In case the Frenchmen shall, at any time hereafter, invade or cause to be invaded, the realm of England, they shall furnish the number of two thousand horse-men and one thousand foot-men, at the least, or such part of either of them, at the choice of the Queen's Majesty of England ; and shall conduct the same to pass from the Borders of Scotland next England, upon her Majesty's charges, to any part upon the realm of England, for the defence of the same. And in case the invasion be upon the north parts of England, on the north part of the water of Tyne, towards Scotland, or against Berwick, on the north side of the water of Tweed, they shall convene and gather their whole forces upon their own charges, and shall join with the English power, and shall continue in good and earnest prosecution of the quarrel of England, during the space of thirty days, or so much longer as they were accustomed to tarry in the fields for defence of Scotland, at the commandment of their Sovereign, at any time bypast.

And also, the Earl of Argyll, Lord Justice of Scotland, being presently joined with the said Duke, shall employ his force and goodwill, where he shall be required by the Queen's Majesty, to reduce the north parts of Ireland to the perfect obedience of England, conform to a mutual and reciprocal contract, to be made betwix her Majesty's lieutenant or depute of Ireland being for the time, and the said Earl ; wherein shall be contained what he shall do for his part, and what the said lieutenant, or depute, shall do for his support, in case he shall have to do with James Macdonnel,[1] or any others of the Isles of Scotland, or realm of Ireland. For performance and sure keeping whereof, they shall for their part enter to the aforesaid Duke of Norfolk the pledges presently named by him, before the entry of her Majesty's army in Scots ground, to remain in England for the space of six months, and to be exchanged upon deliverance of new hostages, of like or as good condition as the former ; or being the lawful sons, brethren, or heirs of any of the Earls or Barons of Parliament, that have, or hereinafter show themselves and persist open enemies to the French in this quarrel ; and so forth, from six months to six months, or four months to four months, as shall best please the party of Scotland ; and the time of continuance of the hostages shall be during the marriage of the Queen of Scots to the French King, and one year after the dissolution of the said marriage, until further order may be had betwix both the realms for peace and concord.

And, furthermore, the said Duke, and all the Nobility, being Earls and Barons of Parliament, joined with him, shall subscribe and seal these Articles and accounts within the space of twenty or thirty days, at the uttermost, next following the day of the deliverance of the said hostages ; and shall also procure and persuade all others of the Nobility that shall join themselves hereafter with the said Duke, for the causes above specified, likewise to subscribe and seal these Articles at any time after the space of twenty days after their conjunction, upon requisition made to them on the part of the Queen's Majesty of England.

And, finally, the said Duke, and the Nobility joined with him, certainly perceiving that the Queen's Majesty of England is thereunto moved only upon respect of princely honour and neighbourhood, for the defence of the freedom of Scotland from conquest, and not of any other sinister intent, doth by these presents testify and declare that [neither] they, nor any of them, mean by this account to withdraw any due obedience to their Sovereign Lady the Queen, nor in

---

[1] Sir James Macdonnel of Antrim, son of Alexander Macdonnel, chief of the Clan Donnel, Lord of Dunyveg and the Glens. He had married Agnes, daughter of Colin, third Earl of Argyll, and had laid claim to the old Lordship of the Isles. For many of his activities at this time, see *Calendar of State Papers, Ireland* (1509–1573), 133ff, and Index, *s.v.*

any lawful thing to withstand the French King, her husband and head, that during the marriage shall not tend to the subversion and oppression of the just and ancient liberties of the said kingdom of Scotland ; for preservation whereof, both for their Sovereign's honour, and for the continuance of the kingdom in ancient estate, they acknowledge themselves bound to spend their goods, lands, and lives. And for performance of this present Contract for the part of England, the Queen's Majesty shall confirm the same, and all clauses thereinto contained, by her letters patent, under the Great Seal of England, to be delivered to the Nobility of Scotland, upon the entry of the pledges aforesaid within the ground of England.

[In witness whereof, the Commissioners for the Duke of Châtelherault and Nobility of Scotland before named have subscribed these presents, and thereunto affixed their seals, the day, year, and place aforesaid :

> JAMES STEWART
> PATRICK L. RUTHVEN
> JOHN MAXWELL
> W. MAITLAND
> JOHN WISHART
> HENRICUS BALNAVES]

In witness whereof, the said Duke's Grace of Norfolk hath subscribed these presents, and thereunto affixed his seal, the day, year, and place foresaid.

> [THO. NORFOLK]

Which Contract we find honest, reasonable, and that our said Commissioners there hath considerately respected to the commonwealth of this realm, of us, and our posterity ; and therefore do ratify, allow, confirm, and approve the same, with all clauses and articles therein contained, by these presents.

In witness hereof, to the same subscribed with our hands, our seals of arms, in such cases accustomed, are appended. At the camp foiranent [1] Leith, the tenth day of May, the year of God 1560.

(Follow the Subscriptions)

THE DUKE OF CHÂTEL-HERAULT	EARL OF HUNTLY	
EARL OF ARRAN	EARL OF GLENCAIRN	*The subscriptions*
	EARL OF MORTON [2]	

[1] *directly opposite*
(643)

[2] James, fourth Earl of Morton, later Regent of Scotland

27

EARL OF ROTHES [1]	LORD OF SAINT JOHN [8]
EARL OF MENTEITH [2]	ALEXANDER GORDON [9]
LORD OGILVY [3]	LORD JOHN OF ABER-
LORD OCHILTREE [4]	BROTHOC [10]
LORD ROBERT STEWART [5]	LORD BOYD [11]
GAVIN HAMILTON OF	LORD SOMERVILLE [12]
KILWINNING [6]	ABBOT OF KINLOSS [13]
EARL OF ARGYLL	ABBOT OF CULROSS [14]
LORD BORTHWICK [7]	JAMES STEWART OF SAINT
LORD JAMES STEWART	COLME'S INCH [15]

THE INSTRUCTIONS GIVEN, SUBSCRIBED TO THE SAID COMMISSIONERS THAT WENT TO BERWICK, ARE THESE THAT FOLLOW :

AND for the first, If it shall be asked of you by the said Duke of Norfolk's Grace, and others [by] the Queen's Majesty's appointment, appointed Commissioners, if our pledges be in readiness? Ye shall answer, that they are, and in Saint Andrews, the xxiv of this instant, and shall be ready to deliver in hostages for security of our promises, and part of contract, they offering and making security for their part by the Queen's Majesty's subscription and great seal, and delivering the same unto you ; providing that they choose and make their election of the pledges as is convenient.

Secondly, If the said Commissioners shall demand of you, what enterprise the army of England shall take upon hand at their first incoming ? Ye shall answer, in general the expulsion of the French soldiers forth of this realm : and first and in special forth of the town of Leith, seeing their great forces are there.

3. *Item*, If it shall be asked of you, at what place our friends and brethren of England shall be met, and what day, what number, and what noblemen in company ? Ye shall refer all those things to their election and choice.

[1] Andrew, fifth Earl of Rothes   [2] John, fourth Earl of Menteith
[3] James, fifth Lord Ogilvy of Airlie   [4] Andrew Stewart, second Lord Ochiltree
[5] Lord Robert Stewart, natural son of James V, later Earl of Orkney
[6] Gavin Hamilton, Commendator of Kilwinning
[7] John, sixth Lord Borthwick   [8] James Sandilands, later Lord Torphichen
[9] Formerly Bishop of Glasgow ; Bishop-elect of Galloway, and Archbishop of Athens *in partibus*
[10] Lord John Hamilton, third son of Châtelherault, Commendator of Arbroath, and later first Marquess of Hamilton   [11] Robert, fifth Lord Boyd
[12] James, fifth Lord Somerville   [13] Walter Reid   [14] William Colville
[15] Sir James Stewart of Doune, Commendator of Inchcolm, later Lord Doune

4. *Item*, If it shall be asked of you how the armies shall be furnished with victuals, and especially the horse-men ? Ye shall answer, that with their advice a sufficient order shall be taken therein.

5. *Item*, If it be required, how the munition shall be carried, and oxen furnished to that effect ? Ye shall answer, as we have given in commission to Lethington, which we ratify.

6. *Item*, If it be asked, who shall be Lieutenant to the army of Scotland ? Ye shall answer, my Lord Duke's Grace.

7. *Item*, If it shall be inquired, what number our whole army extends to ? Ye shall answer, they will, God willing, be five thousand men.

8. *Item*, If it shall be asked, what manner of way Leith shall be assaulted ? Ye shall desire all preparations to be in readiness, and the advice to be taken after the placing of the armies and view of the strength shortly.

9. *Item*, If it shall be asked of the Castle of Edinburgh, if they will stand friends or not ? Ye shall declare our diligence made, and to be made shortly hereinto ; but for the present can assure them of nothing.

10. *Item*, If it be asked, in case the Castle be unfriendly, where the army shall be placed ? Ye shall answer, for the first in Mussel-burgh and Tranent, and those parts, till the battery and all preparations be in readiness.

11. *Item*, In case it be inquired of all bye-lyers,[1] and in special of my Lord Huntly in the North ? Ye shall answer in general, a good hope is had of the most part thereof ; and touching my Lord of Huntly in special, ye shall show how he has sent writings to my Lord of Arran, with a servant in credit, to assure him of his assistance ; and for that cause has desired letters of suspension of the Queen Dowager's commission to be sent to him, to be used by him in those parts, and other letters to arrest the clergy's rents and her's both in those parts, with proclamations to cause all men to be in readiness to pass forward, for maintaining of the religion and expulsion of strangers. My Lord has written to him that he may come to him in proper person, whereof the answer is not returned as yet.

12. *Item*, If it shall be asked, the place and manner of meeting of our folks, or of us and them, in case Stirling be kept ? We refer the answer hereof to your discretion.

13. *Item*, If it shall be asked that their layed [2] money shall have

---

[1] " *sitters on the fence* "   [2] *alloyed*

passage for their vivers? Ye shall reason the commodity and incommodity thereof with the Council.

14. *Item*, If it shall be asked, what pioneers shall be had? Ye shall answer, the number being expressed, and money be in readiness to pay them, they shall have sufficiency.

15. *Item*, If they shall desire that we declare our cause unto the Princes of Alamagne,[1] and the King of Denmark, desiring their assistance? Ye shall answer, that we think the same good, and shall speedily take order therewith.

16. *Item*, If it shall be asked of you to confirm for us, and in our name, the things passed and granted by our former Commissioner the young Laird of Lethington? Ye shall in all points for us, and in our name, confirm the same, so far as it shall make either for the weal and conjunction of the two realms, or this present cause, or yet for the security of our part for fulfilling of the same : and also, ye shall accept their offers, tending to the same end, and such security on that part as ye may purchase, and especially such as we heretofore expressed. Given at Glasgow, the tenth of February 1559.[2]

Item, We give and grant you full power to augment, or diminish these said heads and Articles, as ye think the weal of the cause shall require in all points.

JOHN OF MENTEITH	JAMES HAMILTON
ANDREW OF ROTHES	ALEX[R]. GORDON
R. BOYD	AR[D]. ARGYLL
WILLIAM MURRAY *of Tulli-bardine*	GLENCAIRN
	OCHILTREE
JOHN ERSKINE *of Dun*	JAMES HALIBURTON [3]

Shortly after this Contract, were our pledges delivered to Master Winter, Admiral of the Navy, that came to Scotland, a man of great honesty, so far as ever we could espy of him, who were safely convoyed to Newcastle. And so the English army began to assemble towards the Border ; whereof the French and Queen Regent assured, they began to destroy what they could in the towns and country about : for the whole victuals they carried to Leith ; the mills they broke ; the sheep, oxen, and kine, yea, the horses of poor

---

[1] *Germany*

[2] That is, 10 February 1560.   In the manuscript, folio 203 *recto* ends with the words " the tent of," and the *verso* is blank.   The folio has then been re-numbered 203–204, and folio 205 *recto* begins, with a new hand, with the words " tent of februar 1559."

[3] James Haliburton, Provost of Dundee

labourers, they made all to serve their tyranny. And, finally, they left nothing which the very enemies could have devised, except that they demolished not gentlemen's houses, and burnt not the town of Edinburgh : in which point, God bridled their fury, to let his afflicted understand that he took care for them.

Before the coming of the land army, the French passed to Glasgow, and destroyed the country there about.[1] What tyranny the Martigues [2] used upon a poor Scots soldier, it is fearful to hear, *The cruel fact of Martigues* and yet his fact may not be omitted. Silver would they give none to the poor men, and so were they slow to depart of the town ; for albeit the drum struck, the ensign could not be got.[3] There was a poor crafts-man, who had bought for his victuals a grey loaf, and was eating a morsel of it, and was putting the rest of it in his bosom. The tyrant came to him, and with the poor caitiff's own whinger first struck him in the breast, and after cast it at him, and so the poor man, staggering and falling, the merciless tyrant ran him through with his rapier, and thereafter commanded him to be hanged over the stair. Lord, thou wilt yet look, and recompense such tyranny ; how contemptible that ever the person was !

The second of April, the year of God 1560, the army by land entered in Scotland,[4] the conducting whereof was committed to the Lord Grey,[5] who had in his company the Lord Scrope,[6] Sir James Croft, Sir Harry Percy, Sir Francis Leek, with many other captains and gentlemen having charge, some of foot-men, some of horse-men. The army by land was esteemed to ten thousand men.[7] The Queen Regent passed to the Castle of Edinburgh,[8] and some others of her faction.[9] At Preston met them the Duke's Grace, the Earl of Argyll (Huntly came not till that the siege was con-

---

[1] On 15 March 1560. (*Diurnal of Occurrents*, 56 ; *Two Missions of Jacques de la Brosse*, 82–83)   [2] *Supra*, 275, note 4

[3] That is, although the drum beat the muster, the men of the company (ensign) did not answer and could not be gathered together.

[4] The *Diurnal of Occurrents* (56) says " Upoun the penult day of March." La Brosse says that on the first day of April " the English came to Preston, where they slept." (*Op. cit.*, 88–89)   [5] William, Lord Grey of Wilton   [6] Henry, Lord Scrope

[7] An ensign, Drummond, reported on 29 March that he had seen the English army at Coldingham and Eyemouth and that he estimated its strength at eight or nine thousand men. (*Two Missions of Jacques de la Brosse*, 88–89. For other estimates, see *ibid.*, 88, note 2)

[8] On 1 April 1560, according to the *Diurnal of Occurrents* (56) and La Brosse (*op. cit.*, 88–89)

[9] The names of those " of her faction " who remained with the Queen Regent in the Castle of Edinburgh are given in the *Diurnal of Occurrents* (56, 274), and in Lesley's *Historie* (Bannatyne Club), 284.

firmed), Lord James, the Earls of Glencairn and Menteith, Lords Ruthven, Boyd, Ochiltree, with all the Protestant gentlemen of the West Fife, Angus, and Mearns. So that for [a] few days the army was great.[1]

After the deliberation of two days had at Inveresk, the whole camp marched forward with ordnance, and all preparation necessary for the siege, and came to Restalrig upon the Palm Sunday Even.[2] The French had put themselves in battle array upon the Links without Leith, and had sent forth their skirmishers who, beginning before ten hours, continued skirmishing till after four hours at after noon, when there was given upon them a charge by some horse-men of Scotland, and some of England. But because the principal Captain of the horse-men of England was not present, the whole troop durst not charge ; and so was not the overthrow and slaughter of the French so great as it once appeared to have been ; for the great battle was once at the trot, but when they perceived that the great force of the horsemen stood still, and charged not, they returned and gave some recourse to their fellows that fled ; and so there fell only in that defeat about three hundred Frenchmen.[3] God would not give the victory so suddenly lest that man should glory in his own strength. The small victory that was got, put both the English and Scots in over great security, as the issue declared. The French inclosed within the town, the English army began to plant their palyeans[4] betwix Leith and Restalrig. The ordnance of the town, and especially that which lay upon Saint Anthony's steeple,[5] did them great annoyance : against which place were bent eight cannons,[6] which shot so continually and so just that, within [a] few

---

[1] Details of the siege of Leith (which now follows), written from the French and the English sides may be read in *Two Missions of Jacques de la Brosse* (Scot. Hist. Soc.), 56–179, and Hayward's *Annals of Queen Elizabeth* (Camden Soc.), 55–67.

[2] The Eve of Palm Sunday was Saturday, 6 April. This is confirmed by La Brosse (*op. cit.*, 98–99). Holinshed speaks of a Council " in the house of one William Atkinson neere to Innereske Church." (*Ibid.*, 93, *note* 3)

[3] This seems to be an exaggeration. (See *Two Missions of Jacques de la Brosse*, 98–101, and 100, *note* 1)   [4] *pavilions*

[5] The French had placed some cannon on St. Anthony's steeple as early as the 11 April. (*Two Missions of Jacques de la Brosse*, 112–113)

[6] According to La Brosse the English artillery was put into a new trench on the night of the 21 April and began to fire on the churches of St. Christopher and St. Anthony (*op. cit.*, 124–125) ; but there was no church of St. Christopher in Leith, and Hayward, correctly, says that the French artillery was mounted on the steeples of the churches of St. Anthony and St. Nicholas. (*Annals of Queen Elizabeth*, Camden Soc., 60) Grey, Croft and Sadler, writing to Norfolk on the evening of the 22 April add a postscript that the steeple [of St. Anthony] has been " put out of all order to do any further annoyance." (*Foreign Calendar, Elizabeth*, ii, No. 1054)

days, that steeple was condemned, and all the ordnance that was on it dismounted, which made the Englishmen somewhat more negligent than it became good men of war to have been. For perceiving that the French made no pursuit without their walls, they took opinion that they would never issue more, and that made some of the Captains, for pastime, go to the town [1]; the soldiers, for their ease, did lay their armour beside them and, as men without danger, fell to the dice and cards. And so, upon the Pasche Monday,[2] at the very hour of noon, the French issued both on horse and foot, and with great violence entered in to the English trenches [and] slew and put to flight all that was found therein. The watch was negligently kept, and so was the succour slow, and long in coming ; for the French, before that any resistance was made unto them, approached hard to the great ordnance. But then the horse-men trooped together, and the foot-men got themselves in array, and so repulsed the French back again to the town.[3] But the slaughter was great : some say it double exceeded that which the French received the first day. And this was the fruit of their security ánd ours, which after was remedied ; for the Englishmen most wisely considering themselves not able to besiege the town round about, devised to make mounts at divers quarters of it, in the which they and their ordnance lay in as good strength as they did within the town. The common soldiers kept the trenches, and had the said mounts for their safeguard and refuge, in case of any greater pursuit than they were able to sustain. The patience and stout courage of the Englishmen, but principally of the horse-men, is worthy of all praise : for, where was it ever heard that eight thousand (they never exceeded that number that lay in camp) should besiege four thousand of the most desperate throat-cutters that were to be found in Europe, and lie so near unto them in daily skirmishing, the space of three months and more ? [4] The horse-men night and day kept watch, and did so valiantly behave themselves, that the French got no advantage from that day back to the day of the assault, whereof we shall shortly hear.

In this meantime was this other Band made of all the Nobility, Barons, and Gentlemen professing Christ Jesus in Scotland, and of

---

[1] That is, Edinburgh

[2] Easter Monday was 15 April. Knox appears to have confused somewhat the order of events, but he is correct in relation to this sortie on 15 April, which is fully described by La Brosse (*op. cit.*, 116–119, and 118, *note* 1).   [3] That is, Leith

[4] Maitland of Lethington was of opinion that 20,000 men would be too few for the task. (*Calendar of Scottish Papers*, i, No. 731, enclosure)

divers others that joined with us for expelling of the French army [1];
amongst whom, the Earl of Huntly was principal.[2]   The Band
follows :

THE LAST BAND AT LEITH

AT EDINBURGH, the xxvii day of April, the year of God one
thousand five hundred and threescore : We, whose names are
underwritten, have promised and oblist [3] ourselves faithfully, in the
presence of our God, and by these presents promise, that we altogether in general, and every one of us in special, by himself, with
our bodies, goods, friends, and all that we may do, shall set forward
the Reformation of Religion, according to God's word ; and procure, by all means possible, that the truth of God's word may have
free passage within this realm, with due administration of the
sacraments, and all things depending upon the said word :   And
siclike, deeply weighing with ourselves the misbehaviour of the
French Ministers here ; the intolerable oppressions committed by
the French men of war upon the poor subjects of this realm, by
maintenance of the Queen Dowager, under colour and pretence of
authority ; the tyranny of their captains and leaders ; and manifest
danger of conquest, in which this country presently stands, by reason
of divers fortifications upon the sea-coast ; and other novelties of
late attempted by them ; promise, that We shall, as well every one
with other, as altogether, with the Queen of England's army, presently come in for our deliverance, effectually concur and join
together, taking aefald [4] [and] plain part, for expulsion of the said
strangers, oppressors of our liberty, forth of this realm, and recovery
of our ancient freedoms and liberties ; to the end that, in time
coming, we may, under the obedience of the King and Queen our
Sovereigns, be only ruled by the laws and customs of the country,
and born men of the land :   And that never one of us shall have
privy intelligence by writing, message, or communication with any
of our said enemies or adversaries in this cause, but by the advice of

[1] An attempt to come to terms during the period 22–26 April had been " broken off
on both parts " ; and naturally so, in view of the terms offered by the Queen Regent.
(*Calendar of Scottish Papers*, i, No. 750)

[2] But, according to Randolph, Huntly did not sign the Band until 28 April ;
he " found many delays and would fain have shifted [shisted] himself . . . he was notwithstanding at last content secretly to do it in the sight only of Lord Ruthven, the Laird
of Lethington, and Randolph, requesting them to keep it secret for two or three days."
(*Foreign Calendar, Elizabeth*, ii, No. 1087(3) ; *Calendar of Scottish Papers*, i, No. 756)

[3] *bound* ; in the sense of *become obliged* (from the French *obliger*)

[4] *honest* ; *without duplicity* ; literally, *one-fold*

the rest (at least of five) of the Council.[1] Attour,[2] that we shall tender the common cause, as if it were the cause of every one of us in particular ; and that the causes of every one of us now joined together, being lawful and honest, shall be all our causes in general. And he that is enemy to the causes foresaid, shall be enemy to us all : in so far that whatsoever person will plainly resist these our godly enterprises, and will not concur as a good and true member of this Common-weal, we shall fortify the authority of the Council to reduce them [3] to their duty. Like as we shall fortify the authority foresaid *Nota* of the Council, in all things tending to the furtherance of the said *—here-upon* causes : And if any particular debate, quarrel, or controversy shall *came the pursuit* arise, for whatsoever cause, bygone, present, or to come, betwix any of us (as God forbid), in that case we shall submit ourselves and our said questions to the decision of the Council, or to arbitrators to be named by them. And providing always, that this be not prejudicial to the ordinary jurisdiction of judges, but that men may pursue their actions by order of law civilly or criminally, [before the Judges Ordinary] [4] if they please.

[In witness of the which we have subscribed this present Band with our hands, day, year, and place above written :

JAMES [5]	JAMES STEWART [13]
JAMES HAMILTON [6]	JOHN MENTEITH [14]
HUNTLY [7]	RUTHVEN [15]
AR[D]. ARGYLL [8]	R. BOYD [16]
GLENCAIRN [9]	OGILVY [17]
ROTHES [10]	OCHILTREE [18]
MORTON [11]	JOHN MAXWELL [19]
A. GORDON [12]	PATRICK LINDSAY [20]

---

[1] Cf. *supra*, 206–207, 234–235   [2] *Moreover*   [3] *bring them back*
[4] These words are omitted in the manuscript.   [5] James, Duke of Châtelherault
[6] James, Lord Hamilton, Earl of Arran, eldest son of Châtelherault
[7] George, fourth Earl of Huntly. He did not sign until 28 April (*supra*, 314, *note* 2)
[8] Archibald, fifth Earl of Argyll   [9] Alexander, fourth Earl of Glencairn
[10] Andrew, fifth Earl of Rothes
[11] James, fourth Earl of Morton. He did not sign until 6 May (*Calendar of Scottish Papers*, i, No. 776)   [12] Alexander Gordon, bishop-elect of Galloway (*cf. infra*, 335)
[13] The Lord James Stewart, Prior of St. Andrews, later Regent of Scotland
[14] John, fourth Earl of Menteith   [15] Patrick, third Lord Ruthven
[16] Robert, fifth Lord Boyd   [17] James, fifth Lord Ogilvy of Airlie
[18] Andrew Stewart, second Lord Ochiltree
[19] John Maxwell, second son of Robert, fifth Lord Maxwell. He was John, Lord Herries, as husband of Agnes, Lady Herries.
[20] Eldest son of John, fifth Lord Lindsay of the Byres ; later Patrick, sixth Lord Lindsay of the Byres

JOHN MASTER [OF] FORBES [1]

LORD SOMERVILLE [2]

JAMES JOHNSTONE, *Apparent of Elphinstone*

PATRICK DOUGLAS [3]

ROBERT CAMPBELL [4]

ANDREW JOHNSTONE

ROBIN CAR [5]

JAMES HALIBURTON [6]

ALEX[R]. DUNBAR *of Cumnock*

GRAYTLY [7]

W[M]. DOUGLAS *of Whittinghame*

GEORGE HOME *of Spott*

JOHN GORDON, *of Findlater* [8]

ALEX[R]. SETON, *Younger of Meldrum*

HENRY GRAHAM, *Younger of Morphie*

ALEX[R]. GORDON *of Abergeldie*

DRUMLANRIG [9]

FERNIEHURST [10]

CRANSTOUN *of that Ilk* [11]

WEDDERBURN [12]

ALEX[R]. HUME

JOHNSON

GEORGE NISBET, *with my hand at the pen* [13]

CUNNINGHAMHEAD [14]

LESLIE *of Balquhain* [15]

JOHN INNES *of that Ilk*

ARTHUR FORBES [16]

W[M]. LESLIE *Younger of Wardis*

JOHN WISHART [17]

DRUMLOYGHIE [18]

CESSFORD [19]

HUNTHILL [20]

MARK KER [21]][22]

[1] Son of William, seventh Lord Forbes ; later (1593), John, eighth Lord Forbes. He can only have been about eighteen years old at this time.

[2] James, fifth Lord Somerville

[3] Probably Patrick Douglas, illegitimate son of Sir James Douglas of Drumlanrig

[4] Robert Campbell of Kinzeancleuch

[5] Probably Robert Ker of Kersland, who signed the Band of 1562 (*infra*, ii, 56) ; or he may be Robert Ker, third son of Sir Andrew Ker of Ferniehurst.

[6] James Haliburton, Tutor of Pitcur, Provost of Dundee

[7] Possibly Barclay of Gartly (Aberdeenshire), first name unknown, who married Catherine, daughter of William, seventh Lord Forbes.

[8] Third son of George, fourth Earl of Huntly

[9] Sir James Douglas of Drumlanrig. He did not sign until 6 May (*Calendar of Scottish Papers*, i, No. 776)

[10] Sir John Ker of Ferniehurst. He did not sign until 6 May, when Randolph describes him as " Farnehirst the father." (*Ibid.*, i, No. 776)

[11] Sir John Cranstoun of Cranstoun   [12] Probably David Home of Wedderburn

[13] That is, he could not write and his signature was written for him in his presence, probably by a notary.   [14] Probably William Cunningham of Cunninghamhead

[15] William Leslie of Balquhain

[16] Possibly Arthur Forbes, fourth son of Alexander Forbes of Pitsligo

[17] Probably Sir John Wishart of Pittarrow

[18] Possibly Drumlochy, Kincardineshire

[19] Sir Walter Ker of Cessford. He did not sign until 6 May (*Calendar of Scottish Papers*, i, No. 776)   [20] Possibly John Rutherford of Hunthill

[21] Commendator of Newbattle, and second son of Sir Andrew Ker of Cessford

[22] The names of those who subscribed this Band are not given by Knox. The signatories have been supplied from a contemporary copy in Harleian MSS. (British Museum), No. 289, folio 7a. (See *Calendar of Scottish Papers*, i, No. 751 ; Laing's *Knox*, ii, 61, *note* 1, where folio 70 should read folio 7a)

This Contract and Band came not only to the ears, but also to the sight of the Queen Dowager ; whereat she stormed not a little, and said, " The malediction of God I give unto them that counselled me to persecute the preachers, and to refuse the petitions of the best part of the true subjects of this realm. It was said to me, That the English army could not lie in Scotland ten days ; but now they [have] lain near a month, and are more like to remain than the first day they came." They that gave such information to the Queen, spake as worldly wise men, and as things appeared to have been ; for the country being almost in all the parts thereof wasted, the victuals next adjacent to Leith either brought in to their provision, or else destroyed [and] the mills and other places, as before is said, being cast down, it appeared that the camp could not have been furnished (except it had been by their own ships, and as that could not have been of any long continuance, so should it have been nothing comfortable). But God confounded all worldly wisdom, and made his own benediction as evidently to appear as if in a manner he had fed the army from above. For [of] all kind of victuals there was more abundance, and of more easy prices, in the camp all the time that it lay, after that eight days were passed, than either there had been in Edinburgh any of the two years of before, or yet has been in that town to this day. The people of Scotland sa mekill abhorred the tyranny of the French, that they would have given the substance that they had, to have been rid of that chargeable burden, which our sins had provoked God to lay upon us, in giving us in the hands of a woman, whom our Nobility in their foolishness sold unto strangers, and with her the liberty of the realm. " God, for his great mercy's sake, preserve us yet from further bondage, in the which we are like to fall if he provide not remedy ; for our Nobility will yet remain blind still, and will follow her affections, come after what so may." But to return to our History.

The daughter will not take example by the mother

The 20 of May, Anno 1566 [1]

The camp abounding in all necessary provision, order was taken for confirmation of the siege ; and so the trenches were drawn as near the town, as they goodly might. The great camp [was] removed from Restalrig to the west side of the Water of Leith ; and so were the cannons planted for the battery, and did shoot at the south-west wall. But by reason all was eird,[2] the break was not made so great upon the day but that it was sufficiently repaired upon the night.

---

[1] This marginal note is in the same hand as the text and appears to have been written at the same time.   [2] That is, because the wall was made of *earth*

Whereof the Englishmen beginning to weary, determined to give the brush and assault ; as that they did upon the seventh day of May, beginning before the daylight, and continuing till it was near

The assault of Leith, the 7 of May 1560

seven hours. And albeit that the English and Scots, with great slaughter of the soldiers of both, were repulsed, yet was there never a sharper assault given of so few hands ; for they exceeded not one thousand men that assaulted the whole two quarters of the town, and yet they damned [1] the whole block-houses ; yea, they once put the French clean off their walls, and were upon both the west and east block-houses. But they wanted backing ; for their ladders wanted six quarters of the just height [2] ; and so while the former were compelled to fight upon the top of [the] wall, their fellows could not win to support them, and so were they by multitude dung [3] back again, when it was once thought the Town was won.

Sir James Croft was blamed of many for not doing his duty that day [4] ; for he was appointed, with a sufficient number of the most able men, to have assaulted the north-west quarter upon the sea side where at a low-water (as at the time of the assault) [the passage] was easy : but neither he, nor his, approached to their quarter appointed. He had before, at their first coming in, spoken with the Queen Regent at the fore block-house of the Castle of Edinburgh.[5] Whether she had enchanted him we knew not, but by suspicion of that day, in the which he deceived the expectation of many, he [was] so far as man could judge, the cause of that great repulse ; for some ascribed the shortness of the ladders to him : but that omitted which might have proceeded of negligence, his absence from the pursuit of his quarter was the cause that such French as were appointed there to defend, seeing no pursuer, came to the relief of their fellows, and so the two, joining together, with great slaughter gave the repulse to our company. The French men's harlots, of whom the most part were Scots whores, did no less cruelty than did the soldiers ; for besides that they charged their pieces, and ministered

---

[1] *rendered useless*

[2] This is confirmed in the letter from Sir George Howard to Norfolk. (*Calendar of Scottish Papers*, i, No. 777)   [3] *driven*

[4] Cecil writing to Elizabeth from Edinburgh on 19 June says that Croft's neglect of duty was the principal cause of the loss of the town—" so evidently as it cannot be denyed." (*Ibid.*, i, No. 821)

[5] For this interview between Croft and Howard and the Queen Regent, see the full account given by La Brosse (*op. cit.*, 100–105). The articles desired by them from the Regent—the removal of the French, and place to make suit to Mary and Francis for pacification and perfect government—are given in *Foreign Calendar, Elizabeth*, ii, No. 978.

unto them other weapons, some continually cast stones,[1] some carried chimneys of burning fire, some brought timber and other impediments of weight, which with great violence they threw over the wall upon our men, but especially when they began to turn backs. Now, albeit in all this we acknowledge the secret work of God, who by such means would beat down as well the pride of England as of Scotland, yet neither ought the feebleness nor falsett [2] of man to be excused, neither yet the cruelty of the adversaries be concealed. The Queen Regent sat all the time of the assault (which was both terrible and long) upon the fore-wall of the Castle of Edinburgh ; and when she perceived the overthrow of us, and that the ensigns of the French were again displayed upon the walls, she gave a gawfe [3] of laughter, and said, " Now will I go to the Mass, and praise God for that which my eyes have seen ! " And so was Friar Black ready for that purpose, whom she herself a little of before had deprehended [4] with his harlot in the chapel : But whoredom and idolatry agree well together, and that our Court can witness this day, 16 May 1566.[5]

The French, proud of the victory, stripped naked all the slain, *The inhumanity of the merciless French* and laid their dead carcasses before the hot sun along their wall, where they suffered them to lie more days nor one : unto the which, when the Queen Regent looked, for mirth she happit [6] and said, " Yonder are the fairest tapestry that ever I saw : I would that the whole fields that is betwix this place and yon, were strewn with the *The Queen Regent's cruel heart* same stuff." This fact was seen of all, and her words were heard of some, and misliked of many. Against the which John Knox spake openly in pulpit, and boldly affirmed, " That God should revenge that contumely done to his image, not only in the furious and godless soldiers, but even in such as rejoiced thereat." And the very experience declared that he was not deceived ; for within few days thereafter (yea some say that same day) began her belly and loathsome legs to swell,[7] and so continued, till that God did execute his judgments upon her, as after we shall hear.

---

[1] This is confirmed by La Brosse (*op. cit.*, 144–145) who also gives details of the losses of the English and Scots. Other details are given in *Calendar of Scottish Papers*, i, Nos. 777, 778.   [2] *falseness*   [3] *guffaw*   [4] *apprehended*, that is, *caught*

[5] This date is given in the text hand and forms part of the text, thus giving the date when this part of the manuscript was transcribed.

[6] *skipped*. But it may be questioned whether it was physically possible for the Queen Regent to see, from the walls of Edinburgh Castle, the dead on the walls of Leith.

[7] In a letter of 29 April the Queen Regent had written " I have a leg that assuageth not from swelling. If any lay his finger upon it, it goeth in as into butter. You know there are but three days for the dropsy in this country." (*Foreign Calendar, Elizabeth*, ii, No. 1093)

The defeat received, it was fully persuaded to the Queen Regent and her faction that the siege would rise, and that the English army would depart. And so began the Papists wondrously to brag; and yet God did frustrate their expectation; for the army concluded to remain till new advertisement came from the Queen in Council.[1]

The comfortable letter of the Duke of Norfolk

The Duke of Norfolk, who then lay at Berwick, commanded the Lord Grey to continue the siege, and promised " That he should not lack men so long as any were to be had betwix Trent and Tweed, for so far was he lieutenant." He further promised his own presence, in case he should be required; and for assurance thereof, he sent his own palzeouns,[2] such as seldom before had been seen in Scotland, with his officers and provision. And with expedition were sent two thousand fresh men, whereby the camp, greatly comforted, began to forget the former discomfiture, and to sustain the daily skirmishing as they did before; in the which the French, after the day of the assault, did ever receive the hurt and the repulse, as the slaughter of many that came to the cockle-raik[3] did witness. The greatest damage that either English or Scots received after that day, was the slaughter of two gentlemen, the one Master of Household to my Lord James, Robert Colville of Cleish, a man stout, modest, and wise; who was shot in the thigh with a falcon or hackbut of crock,[4] and departed the misery of this life within two hours after. The other was Alexander Lockhart, brother to the Laird of Barr, who rashly discovering[5] himself in the trenches, was shot in the head, and immediately thereafter departed this life.

While the siege thus continued, a sudden fire chanced in Leith, which devoured many houses and mekill victual[6]; and so began God to fight for us, as the Lord Erskine in plain words said to the

---

[1] Queen Elizabeth [2] *pavilions*

[3] *raik* may be used here in the sense of *track* (" cockle-track "—the road along which the cockles are carried—like the " mussel-track " by the seventeenth hole at St. Andrews), or in the sense of the actual *carrying* of the cockles. Grey and others in a letter to Norfolk, of 13 May, report, " Yesterday morning some soldiers, &c., issued from Leith to gather cockles and periwinkles on the shore, when I ordered Thome Clarck with my light horse and Fardenando, to set on them, who slew 40 or 50." (*Calendar of Scottish Papers*, i, No. 792)

[4] A *falcon* was a cannon of three-inches calibre. The *hackbut of crock* (or *croche*) was the *arquebus-à-croc*, an arquebus with a hook running along it so that it could be fixed to a tripod or carriage. It varied in size from a small cannon to a musket.

[5] *exposing*

[6] " A very terrible fire " broke out among the houses in the south-west part of Leith on the night of 30 April. (*Calendar of Scottish Papers*, i, No. 766) La Brosse says the fire broke out near the curtain-wall on the west (*op. cit.*, 134-135). The *of Diurnal Occurrents* (58) says the fire started " throw chanceing of fyre in ane certane powder being in ane gairdhous."

Queen Regent : " Madam (quoth he), I can see no more, but seeing that men may not expel unjust possessors forth of this land, God himself will do it ; for yon fire is not kindled by man." Which words offended the Queen Regent not a little ; whose sickness daily increasing, great craft she used that Monsieur d'Oysel might have been permitted to have spoken with her ; belike she would have bidden him farewell (for old familiarity was great [1]) ; but that denied, she wrote as it [had] been to her chyrurgian and apothecary, showing her sickness, and requiring some drugs. The letter being presented to the Lord Grey, he espied the craft ; for few lines being written above and sa mekill white paper left,[2] he said, " Drugs are abundant and fresher in Edinburgh than they can be in Leith : there lurks here some other mystery." And so he began to try ; and by holding the paper to the fire, he perceived some writing [to] appear, and so began he to read. But what it was, no other man can tell ; for immediately he burnt the bill, and said to the messenger, " Albeit I have been her Secretary, yet tell her I shall keep her counsel. But say to her, Such wares will not sell to a new market."

The answer received, she was nothing content : and then travailed she earnestly that she might speak with the Earls Argyll, Glencairn, Marischal, and with the Lord James.[3] After deliberation it was thought expedient that they should speak her, but not altogether, lest that some part of the Guisians' practice had lurked under the colour of [such] friendship. Her regret was unto them all, " That she had behaved herself so foolishly that she had compelled them to seek the support of others than of their own Sovereign ; and said, that she sore repented that ever it came to that extremity. But she was not the wite,[4] but the wicked counsel of her friends on the one part, and the Earl of Huntly upon the other ; for if he had not been [opposed to it], she would have fully agreed with them at their communing at Preston." [5] They gave unto her both the counsel and the comfort which they could in that extremity, and willed her to send for some godly learned man, of whom she might receive instruction ; for those ignorant Papists that were about her, understood nothing of the mystery of our Redemption. Upon their motive was John Willock sent for, with whom she talked a reasonable space,[6] and

---

[1] Cf. the innuendo, supra, 94

[2] Cf. the account given by La Brosse (op. cit., 140–143). Deciphered letters from the Queen Regent to d'Oysel are printed in Foreign Calendar, Elizabeth, iii, Nos. 37, 104.

[3] Cf. Calendar of Scottish Papers, i, No. 812   [4] to blame   [5] Supra, 197

[6] Randolph reports on 8 June that " she is also well content to speake with Mr. Wyllockes, whoe is presently with her." (Calendar of Scottish Papers, i, No. 812)

who did plainly show unto her, as well the virtue and strength of the death of Jesus Christ, as the vanity and abomination of that idol the Mass. She did openly confess " That there was no salvation, but in and by the death of Jesus Christ." But of the Mass we heard not her confession. Some said she was anointed of the Papistical manner, which was a sign of small knowledge of the truth, and of less repentance of her former superstition. Yet howsoever it was, Christ Jesus got no small victory over such an enemy. For albeit before she had avowed, that in despite of all Scotland, the preachers of Jesus Christ should either die or be banished the realm ; yet was she compelled not only to hear that Christ Jesus was preached, and all idolatry openly rebuked, and in many places suppressed, but also she was constrained to hear one of the principal ministers within the realm, and to approve [1] the chief head of our religion, wherein we dissent from all Papists and Papistry. Short thereafter she finished

The death of the Queen Regent

her unhappy life ; unhappy, we say, to Scotland, from the first day she entered into it, unto the day she departed this life, which was the ninth of June, the year of God 1560.[2] " God, for his great mercy's sake, red us [3] from the rest of the Guisian blood.[4] Amen, Amen." For of the tyranny of the Guisian blood in her that for our unthankfulness now reigns above us, we have had sufficient experience. But of any virtue that ever was espied in King James the Fifth (whose daughter she is called) [5] to this hour we have never seen any sparkle to appear.

Upon the sixteenth day of June,[6] after the death of the Queen Regent, came in Scotland Monsieur Randan,[7] and with him the Bishop of Valence,[8] in commission from France, to entreat of peace. From England there came Sir William Cecil, chief Secretary, and Doctor Wotton.[9] Their negotiation was langsum ; for both England

---

[1] She may have been constrained to hear John Willock, but that she " approved " the chief head of the Protestant religion (namely, the idolatry of the Mass and salvation only through the blood of Christ—*cf. supra*, 85 ; *infra*, ii, 18) is highly improbable.

[2] She died during the night of 10–11 June (*Foreign Calendar, Elizabeth*, iii, No. 206 ; *Diurnal of Occurrents*, 59, 276–277 ; La Brosse, *op. cit.*, 176–177). Dr. William Angus has called my attention to an entry in the MS. Household Books, 1560—" Mardy unziesme jour de Juing la royne trespassa dedans le chasteau dedinburg a lheurre de une heure apres mynuict."   [3] *free us*

[4] Mary of Lorraine was the daughter of Claude of Lorraine, Duke of Guise.

[5] Knox here descends to the worst of his innuendos, making a double attack on Mary Queen of Scots and on her mother.

[6] La Brosse (*op. cit.*, 178–179); *Diurnal of Occurrents*, 59, 277

[7] Charles de la Rochefoucault, Sieur de Randan

[8] Jean de Monluc, Bishop of Valence

[9] Nicolas Wotton, Dean of Canterbury and York

and we, fearing deceit, sought by all means that the contract should be sure. And they upon the other part, meaning to gratify such as had sent them (who meant nothing but mere falsett[1]), protracted time to the uttermost ; yea, while them of Leith were very scarce of victuals, and they of the Inch had perished, had [it] not been that by policy they got a ship with victuals, and some munition, which was upon Midsummer Even, whereof they made no small triumph (which also for a season stayed the Appointment). Yet in the end peace was concluded, in form as follows :

THE ARTICLES TRANSACTED AND AGREED BY THE REVEREND
FATHER IN GOD, JOHN BISHOP OF VALENCE, AND MONSIEUR
RANDAN, DEPUTES TO THE KING AND QUEEN OF SCOTLAND,
UPON THE MATTERS PRESENTED TO THEM, BY WAY OF PETITION,
FOR THE PART OF THE NOBILITY AND PEOPLE OF SCOTLAND [2]

In the first, Upon the complaint and petition of the said nobility and people of this country, anent the number of men of war sustained by their Majesties in these parts in time of peace ; It is humbly requested to the said Deputes, that they would provide opportune remedy thereupon, to the solace and relief of the country. The said Deputes considering the said desire to be just and conform to reason, concluded, concorded, and affirmed, That the King and Queen shall procure no French men of war, nor no other nation to come to these parts in time coming, but if strangers would pretend to enter in this realm with a navy or army to occupy the same ; in the which case provision shall be made by their Majesties, the judgment and counsel of the Estates of the realm [to] be had thereto. And that the French men of war, being now in the town of Leith, shall be

---

[1] *deceit*

[2] These " articles " are sometimes called the " Concessions " granted to the Scottish " Propositions " (see Keith, *History of the Affairs of Church and State in Scotland*, i, 296–306). They are not to be confused with the Treaty of Edinburgh, virtually a triangular treaty between France, Scotland, and England (although subscribed only by the English and the French commissioners, for it was deemed too derogatory from the majesty of sovereigns for Francis and Mary to enter into treaty with their own subjects), which confirmed the Treaty of Cambrésis, agreed to the cessation of all warlike operations, and acknowledged Elizabeth's title to the English throne. (*Ibid.*, i, 291–295) One of the articles in the Treaty of Edinburgh, however, did grant the assent of Francis and Mary, through their commissioners, to certain supplicatory petitions presented by the nobility and people of Scotland ; thus the " Concessions " to the Scottish " Propositions " may be regarded as an annex to the Treaty of Edinburgh, and are here given by Knox as being of peculiar importance to Scotland and as representing the fruits of the victory of the Army of the Congregation.

sent to France the same time that the navy and army of Englishmen and Scotsmen has scailled [1] and departed both by sea and land ; the which shall be done in the best manner may be, as at more length consideration shall be had thereupon. As to the bands of Scotsmen of war being at the said place, they shall be broken, and the men of war licentiate [2] to depart. Moreover, as to the forts of Dunbar and Inchkeith, there shall remain in them one hundred and twenty French men of war allanerlie, [3] which shall be parted and distributed in those two places ; and there shall remain no more in Dunbar but threescore men of war, so [long as] it be not affirmed by the Captains chosen to that effect by both the parties that for the keeping of the same a greater number is not needful. Also [these men] to depart when the Estates of the realm can find a good and sure remedy, upon the expenses made in the said places, to keep the same from peril of invasion, or deprivation thereof from them that would pretend to occupy the same ; [and then] they shall show the same to their Majesties as hastily as may be done : and in the meantime, the number of the said men of war shall not be augmented. And in like manner it shall not be lawful to the said men of war to do any injuries to any persons, or yet to maintain or defend any Scotsmen, of what quality so ever they be of, against the will and authority of the magistrates of the realm, nor to receive them in the said places that the minister of justice may not put hands in them ; nor yet shall intromett [4] with them, any manner of way, with the quarrels and discords of the Lords, or other particular men of this realm ; but they themselves shall be obliged, in case of any quarrel, to be punished after the laws and consuetude of this Realm, and to answer for themselves before the Judges Ordinary of the same. Last of all, that from this [time] forth they be not compelled to take any credit, [but] they shall be every month satisfied of their wages ; so that two Scots Lords chosen by the Council may present it at weapon-schawing [5] and musters of the said men of war ; and also to visit the said forts to see if the number of them be eikit [6] ; and it shall not be lesum [7] to the said men of war to take any victuals for their sustentation, to the munition of the said places, but by payment of ready money, numerate, [8] and with the pleasure of them that delivers the same to them : And therefore, the said Lords

---

[1] *dispersed*   [2] *given leave*   [3] *only*
[4] *interfere*, but here used in the sense of *take part with them*
[5] *musters-in-arms*
[6] *increased*   [7] *lawful*   [8] *counted out*

oblisses [1] them to give them sa mekill as is needful to them, they having to pay therefor. [2]

Item, Upon the petition presented to the said Lords Deputes, anent the demolition of the fortifications, the said Deputes consented, concorded, and affirmed, That the fortification of Leith shall be demolished, and that two, three, or four captains shall be chosen by both of the parties, to visit the Castle of Dunbar ; and if it be found by them, that [with] the reparation, amplification, and fortifying made thereof now after the peace greater number of men to the keeping thereof is required, the reparation and fortification thereof shall be demolished, so soon as may be done [3] ; and shall remain only untouched that which may make the said Castle more sure and [in] least danger from invasion ; providing none the less that no greater number of men therein be required for keeping of the same. Moreover, in times coming the King and Queen shall make no more new forts within this realm, and shall not augment them that are else [4] made, nor shall repair them that are demolished, without counsel and consent of the Estates ; nor yet shall transport to [? from] other parts any artillery, munition of war, powder, or victuals, but sa mekill as may gain for [5] keeping of the said places [6] by the space of six months or one year.

Item, Anent the petition made anent the debts contracted by the French men of war in this country, the said [Deputes] concorded, That the King and Queen shall cause restore all that which happens to be found given and granted to the King's Lieutenant and his Captains, and other Officers, for the nourishment, sustentation, and maintenance of the said Frenchmen, or that which is found aucht [7] by the lieutenant for service of his Majesty, that may appear by writ, or confession of parties.

Item, Upon the petition made anent the Convention of Estates of this Realm, the said Deputes consented, concorded, &c., That the Estates of the Realm may convene and hold Parliament, the twentieth day [8] of the month of July next to come ; upon the which day the Parliament shall be continued, as use is, unto the first day of the month of August following. Providing always, that before or they begin to treat any thing in the said Parliament, all tumult of war be discharged and cease, that they that are present may be free without

[1] *binds* ; put themselves *under the obligation to*
[2] That is, provided *they have the money to do it*   [3] See Laing's *Knox*, vi, 113, 129
[4] *already*   [5] That is, *be necessary for*   [6] That is, Leith and Dunbar   [7] *owed*
[8] The articles printed in Keith (*op. cit.*, i, 300) give the correct date, 10 July. (See *Acts Parl. Scot.*, ii, 534*b*) Knox makes a similar error *infra*, 332.

fear of men of war or others; and that in the meantime a messenger be sent by the said Deputes to the King and Queen, to certify them of those things agreed, treated, and concorded,[1] requesting their Majesties humbly to be contented with the same : And the said Convention shall be as lawful in all respects, as [if] the same had been ordained and done by express commandment of their Majesties [2]; providing that no matter be treated therein before the said first day of August.

Item, Upon the article presented anent War and Peace, the said Deputes consented, concorded, etc., That the King and Queen [shall] neither make peace nor war in these parts, but by counsel, judgment, and consent of the Three Estates, according to the ordinance and consuetudes of the country ; and as was observed by their predecessors.

Item, Upon the petition presented to the said Deputes, anent the government and regiment of the Policy,[3] they have consented, etc. That twenty-four worthy men of this realm be chosen by the Three Estates, of whom the King and the Queen shall choose seven, and the Estates seventeen [4]; which in their Majesties' absence shall take order, and make an ordinary council for administration foresaid, so that no man, of whatsoever quality he be, shall have the power to order any thing to be done touching the said business without the mediation, authority and consent of them : so that the said councillors shall convene together as oft as they may, but they shall convene no less nor six together. And when any matter of importance occurs, they shall be all called to council, and take order by them, or the most part of them, if need be. And if it happens any of the said seven chosen by the King and Queen to decease, their Majesties shall choose another forth of the said number of xxiv in place of him that deceased ; and if any of the said xvii [5] chosen by the Estates dies, the remanent [6] forechosen by them shall name another of the said number of twenty-four. Moreover, if it be thought expedient by the said Estates, that other two be augmented to the said number of twelve,[7] then and in that case the King and Queen

---

[1] That is, in these Concessions

[2] But it is to be noted that later in the Concessions all religious questions were to be remitted for decision by their Majesties. (*Infra*, 330)

[3] That is, anent the political government and affairs of state of Scotland ; the *polity*

[4] In the articles printed by Keith, correctly (*op. cit.*, i, 301), the Estates were to choose five persons from the leet of twenty-four, and the King and Queen seven persons, to form a Council of twelve. Unless Knox's figure of seventeen is altered to the correct figure of five, the whole of this particular concession becomes unworkable and almost unintelligible.

[5] Five. (See the preceding note)

[6] That is, another shall be chosen by the remaining *four*

[7] Here Knox gives the correct number.

shall choose one, and the Estates another. And so was this Article agreed under condition, that is to say, That the same be no prejudice in time coming to the King and Queen, and rights of the Crown : And the said Deputes offered their labours to make mediation to the King and Queen, for maintaining pensions and expenses of the said Councillors, and ordinary officers of the said Council, to be provided of the rents and provents [1] of the Crown.

Item, Upon the petition made to the said Deputes anent the Officers of this realm, they consented and concorded, &c., That in time coming the King and Queen shall not depute any stranger in the administration of the civil and criminal Justice ; and in likewise in the office of Chancellory, Keeper of Seal, Treasurer, Comptroller, and other like offices, and shall not use them but shall be content with their own subjects born in this realm. Moreover, it shall not be lawful to put the offices of Treasury [and] Comptrollary in the hands of any kirk man, or others who are not able to exercise the said offices ; the which Treasurer and Comptroller shall be provided of sufficient commission to use the said offices. But it shall not be lawful to them to dispose or sell wards of marriages, or other casualties, or any other things, whatsomever they be, pertaining to their offices, without counsel or consent of the said Council, to that effect that the Council may know that all things be done to the profit of the King and Queen ; and yet they will not bind, or astrict the King and Queen by this article, that they may not give when they think expedient.

Item, They concorded, That in the first convention of the Estates of this Realm, there shall be constitute, ordained, and established a law of oblivion, which afterward shall be confirmed by the King's and Queen's Majesties ; by the which all remembrance of bearing of armour, and other things which has been done, shall be eirdit [2] and forgot, from the sixth day of the month of March, in the year of God, 1558 [3] : And by the same law, those who have contravened the laws of the realm, shall be exempted and free of all pain contained therein, siclike as if it never had been contravened ; providing that the privileges of the said law be not extended to them whom the Estates of the Realm shall judge unworthy thereof.[4]

[1] *issues* (Lat. *proventus*)   [2] *buried*

[3] That is, 6 March 1559. It is difficult to account for this date as that of the beginning of the troubles, though an entry in the Aberdeen Council Register under the date 11 March 1559 records that the whole community " grantit and consentit to support the congregatioun " provided it did not "interpryss ony purpos aganis the authorite." (*Extracts from the Council Register of Aberdeen*, Spalding Club, i, 322)

[4] As Keith observes, this was a one-sided privilege, leaving those who had fought on the side of the Queen Regent at the mercy of the Estates.

Item, It is agreed and concluded, That in the said Convention or Parliament, the Estates of the Realm, as use is, and of the manner is required, shall be called ; in the which all they that have used to convene, and be present, may come without all fear or force done, or to be done to them by any person, so that the said [Estates] shall oblisse [1] them, that where in time coming any sedition, or convention of men of war shall happen to be, without command of the Council, being of the number of twelve,[2] the realm and country shall repute [3] the causers thereof, and them that convenes, as rebels, and shall pursue them as siclike, that they may be punished by the laws of the Realm, so that the King and Queen shall not be compelled in time coming to send any men of war, or strangers in these parts, for obtaining of due obedience of their subjects.

Item, They offered, concorded, and agreed, That there shall be general peace and reconciliation among all Lords and subjects of this Realm ; so that they that are called of the Congregation, and they which are not of the same, shall put no reproach to others of the things which are done from the said sixth day of March 1558.[4]

Item, They offered, concorded, and affirmed, That the King and Queen shall not pursue, revenge, nor make any persecution of [5] the things that have been done, nor yet shall they suffer the same to be done by their subjects, French men, but shall have all things in oblivion, as [if] the same had never been done. And siclike, the Lords of this realm of Scotland shall do of all business betwix them and the French men in these parts. And if by sinister information, or any other occasion, their Majesties have conceived any evil opinion against their subjects, they shall allutterly [6] forget and change the same ; nor they shall not deprive any of them, nor denude any of them, or of their subjects, of the offices, benefices, or estates, which they have bruikit [7] in the said realm before, by reason of any things they have meddled with, from the said sixth day of March 1558.[8] And further, shall make no occasion of deprivation, or deposing of them by any other colour without cause ; but rather they shall esteem and treat them in time coming as good and obedient subjects, providing that the said Lords and other subjects, on their part, make to their Majesties whole obedience, siclike as other faithful and natural subjects owe to their Sovereigns.

Item, It is concorded and agreed, That it shall be lawful to none

---

[1] bind   [2] Here Knox gives the correct number.   [3] hold ; look upon
[4] 6 March 1559   [5] for   [6] entirely   [7] held
[8] 1559

of the Lords of the Nobility of Scotland, or any others, to make convocation of men of war, but in the ordinary causes approved by the laws and consuetude of the realm ; and that none of them shall cause any men of war, strangers, to come in these parts, and mekill less shall attempt to do any thing against the King and Queen, or against the authority of the Council, and other magistrates of the realm ; and they who have presented the said petition shall be oblist thereunto. And in case any of them, or others, find occasion to invade, or take armour against any man, as he [or they] pretends, after that he have communicated the matter with the Council of the realm, he shall present his complaint to their Majesties : and generally, they shall obliss them, under the said pains, to do the things which pertain to good and faithful subjects, for the quietness and tranquillity of the realm, and rights of their Sovereigns.

Item, It is agreed, &c., That if any Bishops, Abbots, or other kirk men shall plaint, or allege them to have received any injuries, either in their persons or goods, the plaint shall be seen and considered by the Estates in the said Convention and Parliament ; and there shall be made redress, as they shall find according to reason. And in the meantime, no man shall stop [1] them, but they shall bruik [2] their goods ; nor shall do any scathe, injury, or violence to them : and if any do contravene to this article, he shall be pursued by the Lords as a perturber of a good commonwealth.

Item, It is concorded, &c., That the said Lords shall obliss them to observe, and cause be observed, all and sundry points and articles agreed in this Treaty : and if it happens that any of them, or any other, would contravene the same, the remanent [3] Lords and residue of the whole people shall be enemies to him, and shall pursue him till he be chastised and punished according to his demerits.

Item, It is concorded, &c., That all the whole Realm may know that the King and Queen are not willing to keep any remembrance of the troubles and differences bygone ; and so far as concerns the Nobility and other subjects of the realm, that their Majesties desire to treat them humanely, and to be favourable to them ; the said Deputes has promised and concorded that the Duke of Châtelherault, and all other Noblemen of Scotland, shall be remitted,[4] and put again in all their goods and benefices, which they had and joysed [5] in France, that they may bruik and joyse [6] the same in the same manner as they did of before those differences, the said sixth day of

---

[1] *interfere with*   [2] *hold ; possess*   [3] *rest of the*   [4] *reinstated*
[5] *enjoyed*   [6] *hold and enjoy*

March, and year foresaid, even as [if] the said controversies had never chanced. And also, that all capitulations and articles agreed upon in times bygone, and specially they that were appointed in the King's and Queen's contract,[1] shall be observed and kept, as well for the part of their Majesties as for the part of the Nobility and people of Scotland. And as concerning David, son to the said Duke of Châtelherault, now being in Bois de Vincent, liberty shall be granted to him to return to Scotland, and to do as he please.[2]

Moreover, when the said Deputes exponed, that some time it might chance that the King might mister of[3] his great guns and artillery in France, the said Lords having consideration thereof, concorded, That no other artillery be translated out of this realm, but those which were sent and brought in from the day and decease of Francis, King of France, of good memory,[4] to these parts ; and that all other artillery and munition be reponed in[5] places where they were taken forth, and specially [those] that have the arms of Scotland shall be put in the places where they were taken forth of ; and there shall be Noble men of Scotland [appointed] therefor, and two for the part of the King's Majesty are to be depute to recognosce the same before the shipping thereof.[6]

And, moreover, that where for the part of the Nobility and people of Scotland, certain Articles concerning the Religion and other points were presented, which the said Deputes would not touch,[7] but considering the weight and importance of them, remitted the same to be recognosced and decided by their Majesties ; the said Lords and Nobility promised, that a certain number of Noble men shall be chosen in the next Convention and Parliament, to be sent

[1] That is, the safeguarding clauses of the marriage-contract
[2] Lord David Hamilton, fourth son of the Duke of Châtelherault, had been taken and imprisoned in France in 1559 (*Calendar of Scottish Papers*, i, No. 506). Randolph, writing on 27 August 1560, reports his release (*ibid.*, i, No. 893).
[3] *have need of*   [4] Francis I, died 31 March 1547   [5] *restored to*
[6] Keith gives the form " and for the distinguishing of these several pieces of artillery, four Commissioners shall be appointed before the embarkation of the troops, viz. two Scottish and two French gentlemen " (*op. cit.*, i, 305–306).
[7] Bishop Lesley states that the postponement of the articles concerning religion was due to the fact that the " Commissioners of Ingland wald haif wished the Congregatione of Scotland to haif ressavit the discipline and ceremonies conforme to the order establishit laitly befoir in thair parliament of Ingland, so that boith the realmes micht haif ben uniforme in religione and ceremonies ; bot the ministers and congregatione of Scotland, thinking thair awin profession eftir the order and discipline of Geneva, to be moir puir, as conteyning no uther ceremonies nor is expressely mentioned in the scriptour, thairfore wald not ressave or admitt any uther ; and the commissioners for France walde not appreve nane of the tua ; and thairfoir that mater was delayit."—(*Historie*, Bannatyne Club, 292)

to their Majesties, who shall expone to their Highness the things which shall be thought needful for the estate of their business, and for the forementioned and other articles and points undecided with the said Deputes, to the effect that they may know their Majesties' intention and benevolence upon the things which shall be exponed for the part of the country ; the which also shall have with them a confirmation and ratification by the Estates of the Realm of the Articles which are concorded and agreed by the said Deputes, to whom also the same time, or of before, shall be given and delivered a like confirmation and ratification made by their Majesties, so being that the said Estates send their ratification foresaid.

[In witness whereof, &c.]

THE PROCLAMATION OF THE THINGS ABOVE WRITTEN, MADE THE EIGHTH DAY OF JULY, THE YEAR OF GOD 1560

TO THE LOVING OF THE MOST PUISSANT LORD, AND COMFORT OF ALL CHRISTIANS : The most puissant Prince and Princess, and most Christian King and Queen Francis and Mary, by the grace of God King and Queen of France and Scotland, and the most puissant Princess Elizabeth, by the same grace Queen of England, Ireland, &c. : It is concorded, and reconciliation of peace and amity made, which is to be observed, inviolably amongst them, their subjects, realms, and countries : Forsamekle in name of the said Prince and Princesses, it is commanded and straitly charged, to all manner of persons under their obedience, or being in their service, from this [time] forth, to desist from all hostility, both by sea and land, and to keep a good peace the one with the other ; and with charge to the breakers under their great peril, &c.

These things transacted, and the peace proclaimed, as said is, sudden provision was made for the transporting of the French to France, of whom the most part were put into the English ships, who also carried with them the whole spulzie [1] of Leith [2] ; and that was the second benefit which they received of their late promised *The profit that Leith got of their promised liberty*

---

[1] *spoil*

[2] According to the *Diurnal* (60–61) " Upoun the xv day of Julij 1560, the Inglis army reteirit to Mussilburgh, and the Frenchemen imbarkit ; and als certane pionaris enterit to labour for the demolitioun of the forth of Leith." A letter from Cecil to the Council (15 July) gives fuller details and reports that there is goodwill all round—the French being glad to be gone, the English glad to carry them, and the Scots glad to curse them hence. (*Calendar of Scottish Papers*, i, No. 864)

liberty, the end whereof is not yet come. The English army by land departed the sixteenth day of July, the year of God 1560. The most part of our Nobility, Protestants, honourably convoyed them (as in very deed they had well deserved). But the Lord James would not leave the Lord Grey, with the other noble men of England, till that they entered in Berwick. After whose returning, the Council began to look, as well upon the affairs of the commonwealth, as upon the matters that might concern the stability of Religion.

As before we have heard, the Parliament [was] concluded to begin the 20th [10th] of July, and to be continued to the first of August next [1] ; and therefore the Lords made the greater expedition that all things might be put in convenient order. But before all things the Preachers exhorted them (for then in Edinburgh were the most part of the chief Ministers of the Realm) to be thankful unto God, and next to provide that the ministers might be distributed as the necessity of the country required. A day was statute, when the whole Nobility, and the greatest part of the Congregation assembled in Saint Giles' Kirk in Edinburgh where, after the sermon made for that purpose, public thanks were given unto God for his merciful deliverance, in form as follows :

Thanksgiving for our deliverance, with Prayers

O Eternal and Everlasting God, Father of our Lord Jesus Christ, who has not only commanded us to pray, and promised to hear us, but also wills us to magnify thy mercies, and to glorify thy name when thou showest thyself pitiful and favourable unto us, especially when thou deliverest us from desperate dangers : for so did thy servants Abraham, David, Jehoshaphat, and Hezekiah ; yea, the whole people of Israel omitted not the same when thou by thy mighty hand did confound their enemies, and deliver them from fear and danger of death intended. We ought not, nor cannot forget, O Lord, in how miserable estate stood this poor country, and we the just inhabitants of the same, not many days past, when idolatry was maintained, when cruel strangers did empire, when virgins were deflowered, matrons corrupted, men's wives violently and villainously oppressed, the blood of innocents shed without mercy ; and finally, when the unjust commandments of proud tyrants were obeyed as a law. Out of these miseries, O Lord, could neither our

---

[1] See *supra*, 325, *note* 8

wit, policy, nor strength deliver us ; yea [they] did show unto us how vain was the help of man, where thy blessing gives not victory. In these our anguishes, O Lord, we suited unto thee, we cried for thy help, and we reclaimed [1] thy name, as thy troubled flock, persecuted for thy truth's sake. Mercifully has thou heard us, O Lord, mercifully, we say, because that neither in us, neither yet in our confederates was there any cause why thou shouldest have given unto us so joyful and sudden a deliverance : for neither of us both ceased to do wickedly, even in the midst of our greatest troubles. And yet has thou looked upon us so pitifully as that we had given unto thee most perfect obedience, for thou has disappointed the counsels of the crafty, thou has bridled the rage of the cruel ; and thou has of thy mercy set this our perishing Realm at a reasonable liberty. Oh, give us hearts (thou, Lord, that only gives all good gift), with reverence and fear, to meditate thy wondrous works late wrought in our eyes. Let not the remembrance of the same unthankfully to slip from our wavering minds. We grant and acknowledge, O Lord, that whatsoever we have received shall fall in oblivion with us, and so turn to our condemnation, unless thou, by the power of thy Holy Spirit, keep and retain us in recent and perpetual memory of the same. We beseech thee therefore, O Father of mercies, that as of thy undeserved grace thou has partly removed our darkness, suppressed idolatry, and taken from above our heads the devouring sword of merciless strangers, that so it would please thee to proceed with us in this thy grace begun. And albeit that in us there is nothing that may move thy Majesty to show us thy favour, O yet for Christ Jesus, thy only well beloved Son's sake, whose name we bear, and whose doctrine we profess, we beseech thee never to suffer us to forsake or deny this thy verity which now we profess. But seeing that thou has mercifully heard us, and has caused thy verity to triumph in us, so we crave of thee continuance unto the end, that thy godly name may be glorified in us thy creatures. And seeing that nothing is more odious in thy presence, O Lord, than is ingratitude and violation of an oath and covenant made in thy name ; and seeing that thou hast made our confederates of England the instruments by whom we are now set at this liberty, to whom we in thy name have promised mutual faith again ; let us never fall to that unkindness, O Lord, that either we declare ourselves unthankful unto them, or profaners of thy holy name. Confound thou the counsels of them that go about to break that most godly league

[1] *called upon*

contracted in thy name, and retain thou us so firmly together by the power of thy Holy Spirit, that Sathan have never power to set us again at variance nor discord. Give us thy grace to live in that Christian charity which thy Son, our Lord Jesus, has so earnestly commanded to all the members of his body ; that other nations, provoked by our example, may set aside all ungodly war, contention, and strife, and study to live in tranquillity and peace, as it becomes the sheep of thy pasture, and the people that daily looks for our final deliverance, by the coming again of our Lord Jesus ; to whom with Thee, and the Holy Spirit, be all honour, glory, and praise, now and ever. AMEN.

Hereafter were the Commissioners of Burghs, with some of the Nobility and Barons, appointed to see the equal distribution of Ministers, to change and transport as the most part should think expedient. And so was John Knox appointed to Edinburgh [1] ; Christopher Goodman (who the most part of the troubles had remained in Ayr) was appointed to Saint Andrews : Adam Heriot to Aberdeen ; Master John Row to Saint Johnston ; Paul Methven (to whom was no infamy then known [2]) to Jedburgh ; William Christison to Dundee ; and David Ferguson to Dunfermline, and Master David Lindsay to Leith. There were nominated for Superintendents, Master John Spottiswoode for Lothian ; Master John Winram for Fife ; Master John Willock for Glasgow ; the Laird of Dun for Angus and Mearns ; Master John Carswell for Argyll and the Isles. These to be elected at the days appointed, unless that the countries whereto they were to be appointed could in the meantime find out men more able and sufficient, or else show such causes as might inable them from that dignity.

The Parliament approaching,[3] due advertisement was made, by the Council, to all such as by law and ancient custom had or might claim to have vote therein.[4] The assembly was great, notwithstanding that some, as well of them that be called Spiritual as

---

[1] The Congregation of Edinburgh, publicly in the Tolbooth, had elected and chosen John Knox to be their minister on 7 July 1559. (Historie of the Estate of Scotland, Wodrow Misc., i, 63 ; supra, 211, note 2)   [2] See infra, ii, 66-67

[3] In the Diurnal of Occurrents (61) it is stated that " Upoun the first day of August, the Parliament tuke begyning, and few or na Lordis come to the samyn, quhill the aucht day of the samyn moneth." See also Maitland to Cecil, 15 August 1560 (Calendar of Scottish Papers, i, No. 880)

[4] For the attendance of about one hundred small barons and lairds, and their claim " to have vote therein," see Rait, Parliaments of Scotland, 199-203. An incomplete list of those who attended the Parliament is printed (from Cotton MSS., Caligula, ix, 144, British Museum) in Acts Parl. Scot., ii, 525-526.

Temporal Lords, contemptuously did absent themselves. And yet
the chief pillars of the Papistical Kirk gave their presence, such as
the Bishops of Saint Andrews,[1] Dunblane,[2] and Dunkeld,[3] with
others of the inferior sort ; besides them that had renounced Papistry,
and openly professed Jesus Christ with us, such as the Bishop of
Galloway,[4] the Abbots of Lindores,[5] Culross,[6] Saint Colme's Inch,[7]
Newbattle,[8] Holyroodhouse,[9] the Prior of Saint Andrews,[10] Coldingham,[11] and Saint-Mary Isle,[12] the Subprior of Saint Andrews,[13] and
divers others whom we observed not.

At the same time of Parliament, John Knox taught publicly the
prophet Haggai. The doctrine was proper for the time ; in application whereof he was so special and so vehement, that some (having
greater respect to the world than to God's glory), feeling themselves
pricked, said in mockage, " We must now forget our selves, and
bear the barrow to build the houses of God." God be merciful
to the speaker [14] ; for we fear that he shall have experience that the
building of his own house (the house of God being despised), shall
not be so prosperous, and of such firmity, as we desire it were.[15]
And albeit some mocked, yet others were godly moved, who did
assemble themselves together to consult what things were to be
proponed to that present Parliament ; and after deliberation, was
this subsequent Supplication offered :

William Maitland's mockage of God

THE BARONS, GENTLEMEN, BURGESSES, AND OTHERS, TRUE
SUBJECTS OF THIS REALM, PROFESSING THE LORD JESUS CHRIST
WITHIN THE SAME : TO THE NOBILITY AND ESTATES OF PARLIA-
MENT, PRESENTLY ASSEMBLED WITHIN THE SAID REALM, DESIRE
GRACE, MERCY, AND PEACE, FROM GOD THE FATHER OF OUR
LORD JESUS CHRIST, WITH THE INCREASE OF HIS HOLY SPIRIT :

---

[1] John Hamilton, Archbishop of St. Andrews   [2] William Chisholm
[3] Robert Crichton   [4] Alexander Gordon   [5] John Philp, or Philips
[6] Probably William Colville, Commendator of Culross
[7] James Stewart, later Lord Doune   [8] Mark Ker
[9] Lord Robert Stewart, natural son of James V, later Earl of Orkney
[10] Lord James Stewart, natural son of James V, later Earl of Moray and Regent of
Scotland
[11] Lord John Stewart, natural son of James V
[12] Robert Richardson, Prior of St. Mary's Isle, Kirkcudbright   [13] John Winram
[14] Calderwood (*History*, ii, 12) supports the marginal note that the speaker was William
Maitland of Lethington. For his " oration " at the Parliament, see *Calendar of Scottish
Papers*, i, No. 879.
[15] The death of his only son in poverty and exile was believed by many to be the
fulfilment of Knox's prophecy. (Robertson, *Inventaires de la Royne Descosse*, Bannatyne
Club, Preface, l, *note*)

PLEASE your Honours to reduce [1] to remembrance, how divers and sundry times we (with some of yourselves) most humbly suited at the feet of the late Queen Regent freedom and liberty of conscience, with a godly reformation of abuses, which by the malice of Sathan and negligence of men, are crept in Religion of God, and are maintained by such as take upon them the name of Clergy. And albeit that our godly and most reasonable suit was then disdainfully rejected, whereof no small troubles have ensued, as your Honours well know ; yet seeing that the same necessity yet remains that then moved us, and, moreover, that God of his mercy has now put into your hands to take such order as God thereby may be glorified, this commonwealth quieted, and the policy thereof established : We cannot cease to crave of your hands the redress of such enormities as manifestly are (and of long time have been) committed by the place-holders of the ministry, and others of the clergy within this realm.

And *First*, Seeing that God of his great mercy by the light of his word, has manifested to no small number of this realm, that the doctrine of the Roman Kirk, received by the said Clergy, and maintained through their tyranny by fire and sword, contained in the self many pestiferous errors, which cannot but bring damnation to the souls of such as therewith shall be infected ; such as are the doctrine of Transubstantiation ; of the Adoration of Christ his body under the form of bread, as they term it ; of the merits of Works, and Justification that they allege comes thereby ; together with the doctrine of the Papistical Indulgences, Purgatory, Pilgrim-age, and Praying to Saints departed ; which all either repugn to the plain Scriptures, or else have no ground of the doctrine of our Master Jesus Christ, his Prophets, nor Apostles. We humbly therefore crave of your Honours, that such doctrine and idolatry as by God's word are condemned, so may they be abolished by Act of this present Parliament, and punishment appointed for the transgressors.

Secondly, Seeing that the Sacraments of Jesus Christ are most shamefully abused and profaned by that Roman harlot and her sworn vassals ; and also because that the true discipline of the ancient Kirk is utterly now amongst that sect extinguished : for who within the realm are more corrupt of life and manners than are they that are called the Clergy, living in whoredom, adultery, deflowering virgins, corrupting matrons, and doing all abomination, without fear of punishment ; We humbly therefore desire your Honours to find remedy against the one and the other.

[1] *bring back*

Thirdly, Because that Man of Sin often most falsely claims to himself the titles of " The Vicar of Christ ; the Successor of Peter ; the Head of the Kirk ; that he cannot err ; that all power is granted unto him," &c., by the which usurped authority, he takes upon him the distribution and possession of the whole patrimony of the Kirk, whereby the true ministers of the word of God long time have been altogether neglected, the godly learning despised, the schools not provided, and the poor not only defrauded of their portion, but also tyrannously oppressed ; We likewise hereof desire remedy.[1]

And lest that your Honours should doubt any of these premises, we offer ourselves evidently to prove that in all the [rabble of the] clergy there is not one lawful minister, if God's word, the practice of the Apostles and their own ancient Laws shall judge of lawful election. We further offer ourselves to prove them all thieves and murderers, yea, rebels and traitors to the lawful authority of Emperors, Kings, and Princes ; and therefore unworthy to be suffered in any Reformed Commonwealth. How maliciously they have murdered our brethren, for no other cause but for that they offered to us the light of God's word, your Honours cannot be ignorant ; and in what hazard their tyranny has brought this whole realm, the ages after will consider. If ye look of them any other fruit in times coming, than ye have seen in them whom we accuse, we are assured ye shall be deceived. Now has God, beyond all expectation of man, made yourselves who some times were suppliants with us for Reformation, judges, as it were, in the cause of God. At least he has subdued your enemies unto you, that by violence they are not able to suppress the verity, as heretofore they have done.

We therefore, in the bowels of Jesus Christ, crave of your Honours, that either they be compelled to answer to our former accusations, and to such others as we justly have to lay to their charge, or else that, all affection laid aside, ye pronounce them by censement [2] of this Parliament such, and cause them to be so reputed, as by us most justly they are accused ; especially, that they be decerned [3] unworthy of honour, authority, charge, or cure within the Kirk of God, and so from henceforth never to joy [4] vote in Parliament. Which if ye do not, then in the fear of God, and by the assurance of his word, We forewarn you, that as ye have [maintained] a grievous yoke, and a burden intolerable upon the kirk of God within this realm, so shall they be thorns in your eyes, and pricks in your sides,

[1] And remedy for all these needs was set forth in the *Book of Discipline* (*infra*, Appendix VIII).　　[2] *judgment*　　　[3] *adjudged*　　　[4] *enjoy*

whom after, when ye would, ye shall have no power to remove. God the Father of our Lord Jesus Christ give you upright hearts, seeking his glory ; and true understanding what this day He who delivered you from bondage, both spiritual and temporal, craves of you by his servants : And your Honours' Answer most humbly we require.

This our Supplication being read in audience of the whole assembly, divers men were of divers judgments ; for as some there were that uprightly favoured the cause of God, so were there many that for worldly respects abhorred a perfect Reformation (for how many within Scotland that have the name of Nobility are not unjust possessors of the patrimony of the Kirk ?). And yet were the Barons and Ministers called, and commandment given unto them, to draw, in plain and several heads, the sum of that Doctrine which they would maintain, and would desire that present parliament to establish as wholesome, true, and only necessary to be believed, and to be received within that Realm : which they willingly accepted, and within four days presented their [1] CONFESSION [OF FAITH].[2]

.   .   .   .

OUR CONFESSION [3] was publicly read, first in audience of the Lords of Articles, and after in audience of the whole Parliament ; where were present, not only such as professed Christ Jesus, but also a great number of the adversaries of our religion, such as the fore-named Bishops, and some others of the Temporal Estate, who were commanded in God's name to object, if they could, any thing against that doctrine. Some of our Ministers were present, standing upon their feet,[4] ready to have answered, in case any would have defended the Papistry, and impugned our affirmatives : but while that no objection was made, there was a day appointed to voting in that and other heads. Our Confession was read, every article by itself, over again, as they were written in order, and the votes of every man were required accordingly. Of the Temporal Estate, only voted in the contrary the Earl of Atholl,[5] the Lords Somerville [6] and

---

[1] The original wording is *this*

[2] The concluding words " as it follows without alteration of any one sentence "— have here been omitted from the text, since the *Confession of Faith*, included by Knox in the body of his *History*, has been removed to an Appendix (*infra*, Appendix VI).

[3] In the manuscript the wording is *This our Confession*

[4] That is, they were not *sitting* as were the members of the Parliament

[5] John, fourth Earl of Atholl   [6] James, fifth Lord Somerville

Borthwick [1]; and yet for their dissenting they produced no better reason, but, " We will believe as our fathers believed." [2] The Bishops (papistical, we mean) spake nothing. The rest of the whole three Estates by their public votes affirmed the doctrine ; and many, the rather, because that the Bishops would nor durst say nothing in the contrary ; for this was the vote of the Earl Marischal [3]—" It is long since I have had some favour unto the truth, and since that I have had a suspicion of the Papistical religion ; but, I praise my God, this day has fully resolved me in the one and the other. For seeing that my Lords Bishops who, for their learning can, and for the zeal that they should bear to the verity would, as I suppose, gainsay anything that directly repugns to the verity of God ; seeing, I say, my Lords Bishops here present speak nothing in the contrary of the doctrine proponed, I cannot but hold it to be the very truth of God, and the contrary to be deceivable doctrine. And therefore, so far as in me lieth, I approve the one and damn the other : And do further ask of God that not only I, but also all my posterity, may enjoy the comfort of the doctrine that this day our ears have heard. And yet more, I must vote, as it were, by way of protestation, that if any persons ecclesiastical shall after this oppose themselves to this our Confession, that they have no place nor credit, considering that they, having long advisement and full knowledge of this our Confession, none is now found in lawful, free, and quiet Parliament to oppose themselves to that which we profess : And therefore, if any of this generation pretend to do it after this, I protest he be reputed rather one that loveth his own commodity and the glory of the world than the truth of God and the salvation of men's souls." [4]

The Earl Marischal's vote in Parliament

After the voting and ratification of this our Confession by the whole body of the Parliament, there were also pronounced two Acts,[5] the one against the Mass and the abuse of the Sacraments, and the other against the Supremacy of the Pope ; the tenor whereof follows :

---

[1] John, sixth Lord Borthwick

[2] Knox's account (which is followed by Spottiswoode, *History*, i, 327) here differs considerably from that given by Randolph who, writing to Cecil on 19 August, says " Of the temporall lords, Cassillis and Caithness said ' Nae ' ! The rest, with common consent and as glad will as ever I heard men speak, allowed it " (*Calendar of Scottish Papers*, i, No. 886). Somerville, it should be noted, had subscribed the Band of April 1560 (*supra*, 316)

[3] William Keith, fourth Earl Marischal

[4] See also Randolph's version of this and other speeches. (*Calendar of Scottish Papers*, i, No. 886)

[5] This in despite of the Concessions at Edinburgh, under which all religious questions were to be remitted for decision by their Majesties. (*Supra*, 330)

THE ACT AGAINST THE MASS [1]

IN the Parliament held at Edinburgh, the tenth of July, the year of God 1560, the said Parliament being continued to the first of August next thereafter following, with continuation of days, upon the twenty-fourth day of the said month of August, the Three Estates then being present : The which day, forsamekle as [2] Almighty God by his most true and blessed word has declared the reverence and honour which should be given to him : and, by his Son Jesus Christ, has declared the true use of the Sacraments, willing the same to be used according to his will and word : By the which it is notour and perfectly known that the Sacraments of Baptism and of the body and blood of Jesus Christ, have been in all times bygone corrupted by the Papistical Kirk, and by their usurped ministers ; and presently, notwithstanding the Reformation already made according to God's word, yet none the less there are some of the same Pope's Kirk that stubbornly persevere in their wicked idolatry, saying Mass, and Baptizing conform to the Pope's Kirk, profaning therethrough the Sacraments foresaid, in quiet and secret places, regarding therethrough neither God nor his [holy] word : Therefore it is statute and ordained in this present Parliament, that no manner of person nor persons, in any time coming, administer any of the Sacraments foresaid secretly, or any other manner of way, but they that are admitted and having power to that effect, nor say Mass, nor yet hear Mass, nor be present thereat, under the pain of confiscation of all their goods [movable and unmovable] and punishing of their bodies at the discretion of the Magistrates, within whose jurisdiction such persons happen to be apprehended, for the first fault ; banishing of the Realm for the second fault ; and justifying to the death for the third fault. And ordains all Sheriffs, Stewards, Bailies, and their deputes, Provosts, and Bailies of Burghs, and other judges whatsomever, within this Realm, to take diligent suit and inquisition within their bounds where any such usurped ministry is used, Mass saying, or they that be present at the doing thereof, ratifying and approving the same ; and take and apprehend them, to the effect that the pains above written may be executed upon them.

  Extractum de libro Parliamenti, per me, etc.

          (Sic subscribitur,)

             JACOBUS McGILL. [3]

[1] *Acts Parl. Scot.*, ii, 535, c. 4   [2] *forasmuch as*
[3] Sir James McGill, Clerk-Register

THE ACT FOR ABOLISHING THE JURISDICTION OF THE POPE [1]

IN the Parliament held at Edinburgh, the tenth day of July, the year of God 1560, and thereafter continued to the first day of August next thereafter following, with continuation of days, upon the twenty-fourth [day] of the said month of August : The three Estates, then being present, understanding that the jurisdiction and authority of the Bishop of Rome, called the Pope, used [with]in this Realm in times bypast, has been very hurtful and prejudicial to our Sovereign's authority, and common weal of this Realm : Therefore has statute and ordained, that the Bishop of Rome have no jurisdiction nor authority [with]in this Realm in times coming ; and that none of our said Sovereign's subjects [of this Realm] suit or desire, in any time hereafter, title or right, by the said Bishop of Rome, or his seat,[2] to any thing within this Realm, under the pains of Barratry,[3] that is to say, proscription, banishment, and never to bruik [4] honour, office, nor dignity within this Realm : And the contraveners hereof, to be called before the Justice or his deputes, or before the Lords of the Session, and punished therefor according to the laws of this Realm : And the furnishers of them with finance of money, and purchasers of their title of right, or maintainers and defenders of them, shall incur the same pains : And that no Bishop, nor other Prelate of this Realm, use any jurisdiction in times to come, by the said Bishop of Rome's authority under the pain foresaid.

Extractum, etc.

These and other things [5] ordinarily done in lawful and free Parliament, we directed to France, to our Sovereigns, Sir James

---

[1] *Acts Parl. Scot.*, ii, 534, c. 2   [2] That is, the Roman See

[3] Barratry was the purchase of a benefice, or of a pension drawn from a benefice. It could thus be equated with simony, though the term was used principally for purchases made *at Rome*, whereby good Scots money was lost to the realm. Banishment and loss of the benefice [or pension] so acquired was prescribed by the Act of 1496. (*Acts Parl. Scot.*, ii, 237, c. 2)   [4] *enjoy*

[5] The " Reformation Parliament " of 1560 also passed a third Act annulling all previous Acts of Parliament " not agreeing with God's Word, and now contrary to the Confession of our Faith according to the said Word published in this Parliament." (*Acts Parl. Scot.*, ii, 535, c. 3)   Such previous Acts were those against " heresy " and those passed to maintain " Haly Kirk." Keith (*History of Affairs of Church and State in Scotland*, i, 324–326), also prints the " Heads of Acts made in the Pretended Parliament in August 1560," which were supplied to him by Thomas Innes from Archbishop Beaton's papers in the Scots College in Paris. These " Heads " embrace a number of other " Acts " over and above those printed in *Acts Parl. Scot.*, ii, 534–535.

Sandilands, Lord of Saint John,[1] with the Acts of the said Parliament, that by them they might be ratified according to the promise of their Highnesses' Commissioners made to us, as by the Contract of Peace most evidently may appear. But how the said Lord of Saint John was entreated we list not rehearse ; but always no ratification brought he unto us.[2] But that we little regarded, or yet do regard ; for all that we did was rather to show our debtful obedience than to beg of them any strength to our Religion which from God has full power, and needeth not the suffrage of man, but in so far as man hath need to believe it, if that ever he shall have participation of the life everlasting. But somewhat must we answer to such as since has whispered that it was but a pretended Parliament and a privy convention, and no lawful Parliament. Their reasons are, the King and Queen were in France ; there was neither sceptre, sword, nor crown borne, &c., and some principal Lords were absent. We answer, That we rather wish the Papists to be quiet, nor too curiously to travail in that head ; for it may be, that while they think to hurt us, they make the Queen and her authority a great blow, and yet amend themselves nothing. For in whose default, we pray you, was the Queen absent from this realm ? We think they will not be so shameless as that they will blame the Protestants thereof. Her person was absent, and [that] to no small grief of our hearts. But were not the Estates of her realm assembled in her name ? Yea, had they not her full power and commission, yea, the commission and commandment of her head the King of France, to convocate that Parliament, and to do all things that may be done in lawful Parliament, even as if our Sovereigns had been there in proper persons?[3] If they will limit the power of princes to the places only where their bodily presence is, it will be thought strange ; for so not only shall kings be compelled to content them with one realm, but also with one city ; for the bodily presence of kings can no more be in divers cities in one instant, than that they can be in divers realms. Hitherto we have understood that wheresoever the Councillors of

---

[1] James Sandilands of Calder succeeded Sir Walter Lyndsay in the office of Preceptor of Torphichen and head of the Order of St. John of Jerusalem in Scotland. In 1564 the possessions of the Order of St. John in Scotland were erected into a temporal lordship, and through this erection Sir James Sandilands became the first Lord Torphichen.

[2] The *Diurnal of Occurrents* reports (281) " Upoun the 19 day of December foirsaid [1560], James lord Sanctjohne come furth of France to Edinburgh, and obtenit litill or nathing of his errands expeid."

[3] Yes; but the final article in the Concessions had expressly excluded religious questions. (*Supra*, 330)

the King, with his power and commission, are assembled to do any thing at his commandment, that there is the King's sufficient presence and authority, wheresoever his own body be living at freedom and liberty. Which, if the Papists deny, we will find fault with them, and with the princes whom they have abused, that more will annoy them than anything that we can lose by the insufficiency of that Parliament ; which, not the less, we are bold to affirm to have been more lawful and more free than any Parliament that they are able to produce these hundred years before it, or yet any that hath ensued since it was ; for in it, the votes of men were free, and given of conscience : in others they were bought or given at the devotion of the prince. All things in it concluded are able to abide the trial, and not to be consumed at the proof of the fire. Of others the godly may justly call in doubt [the] things determined.

To the sword and sceptre, nor yet to the absence of some Lords, we answer nothing ; for our adversaries know well enough that the one is rather a pomp and glorious vain ceremony, than a substantial point of necessity required to a lawful Parliament ; and the absence of some prejudges not the powers of the present, provided that due advertisement be made unto them. But now we return to our History.[1]

The Parliament dissolved, consultation was had how the Kirk might be established in a good and godly Policy, which by the Papists was altogether defaced. Commission and charge was given to Mr. John Winram,[2] Subprior of Saint Andrews, Master John Spottiswoode, John Willock, Mr. John Douglas,[2] Rector of Saint Andrews, Master John Row, and John Knox, to draw in a volume the Policy and Discipline of the Kirk,[3] as well as they had done the Doctrine ; which they did and presented to the Nobility, who did peruse it many days. Some approved it, and willed the same [to] have been set forth by a law. Others, perceiving their carnal liberty and worldly commodity somewhat to be impaired thereby, grudged,

[1] For an analysis of the constitutional authority of the " Reformation Parliament " of 1560, see Rait, *Parliaments of Scotland*, 199–203, 315.

[2] In the manuscript (folio 242 *recto*) the names of Winram and Douglas are supplied in the margin in Knox's hand. The text had originally " the subprior of Saint Andrews " and " the Rector of Saint Andrews " respectively ; the two words " the " were scored through when the marginal names were supplied.

[3] That is, *The Book of Discipline*, printed below as Appendix VIII. But charge had been given them to draw up the heads of Discipline and Policy as early as 29 April 1560 (*infra*, ii, 280), and they had completed their task by 20 May 1560 (*infra*, ii, 323)— that is, long before the meeting of the Parliament, and even before the victory of the Congregation was assured.

insomuch that the name of the Book of Discipline became odious unto them. Everything that repugned to their corrupt affections, was termed in their mockage, " devout imaginations." The cause we have before declared : some were licentious ; some had greedily gripped to the possessions of the Kirk ; and others thought that they would not lack their part of Christ's coat, yea, and that before that ever he was hanged, as by the Preachers they were oft rebuked. The chief great man that had professed Christ Jesus, and refused to sub- scribe the Book of Discipline, was the Lord Erskine [1] ; and no wonder, for besides that he has a very Jezebel to his wife,[2] if the poor, the schools, and the ministry of the Kirk had their own, his kitchen would lack two parts, and more, of that which he unjustly now possesses.[3] Assuredly some of us have wondered how men that profess godliness could of so long continuance hear the threatenings of God against thieves and against their houses and, knowing them- selves guilty in such things as were openly rebuked, that they never had remorse of conscience, neither yet intended to restore any thing of that which long they had stolen and reft. There was none within the Realm more unmerciful to the poor Ministers than were they which had greatest rents of the Churches. But in that we have perceived the old proverb to be true, " Nothing can suffice a wrech " ; [4] and again, " The belly has no ears." Yet the same Book of Discipline was subscribed by a great part of the Nobility [5] : to wit,[6] the Duke's

---

[1] John, sixth Lord Erskine, and later Earl of Mar and Regent of Scotland. While Knox here calls him " the chief great man that had professed Christ Jesus," he had hardly supported the Congregation during the fighting of 1559–60 (*supra*, 201, 264) and he had received the Queen Regent into the Castle of Edinburgh in her last illness. If, however, the words attributed to him during the siege of Leith are to be trusted, then he had by that time begun to favour the Protestant cause. (*Supra*, 320–321)

[2] His wife was Annabella, daughter of William Murray of Tullibardine. Knox later calls her " a sweet morsel for the devil's mouth " (*infra*, ii, 77), but James Melville spoke well of her ; James VI appointed her to be governess to Prince Henry ; and her " true, thankful, worthy and good service " is recorded in the Acts of Parliament. (See Robertson, *Inventaires de la Royne Descosse*, xlii, *note*)

[3] Dr. Donaldson's work on the " Thirds of the Benefices " shows that Erskine had secured a remission of the payment of the " Thirds " from the revenues of Dryburgh, Cambuskenneth and Inchmahome of which he was commendator.

[4] *Wrech* or *wretch*—usually a *niggardly* or *parsimonious* person, but here probably with the stronger sense of *avaricious*. " As the carle riches he wretches." (*Fergusson's Scottish Proverbs*, Scot. Text Soc., 10)

[5] The *Diurnal of Occurrents* (63, 281–282) says that Knox desired the Lords to subscribe *The Book of Discipline* and that, while some subscribed, the Lords Erskine, Crawford, Cassillis, Somerville and others refused.

[6] It is to be noted that this list omits some names contained in the list of signatures given at the end of *The Book of Discipline*, and contains other names not to be found among the signatories (*infra*, ii, 324–325).

Grace,[1] the Earl of Arran,[2] the Earls Argyll,[3] Glencairn,[4] Marischal,[5] Menteith,[6] Morton,[7] Rothes,[8] Lord James, now Earl of Moray [9] ; Lords Yester,[10] Boyd,[11] Ochiltree [12] ; Master of Maxwell,[13] Lord Lindsay elder,[14] and the Master now Lord [15] ; Barons Drumlanrig,[16] Lochinvar,[17] Garlies,[18] Bargany [19] ; Mr. Alexander Gordon, Bishop [20] of Galloway, Alexander Campbell, Dean of Moray, with a great number more, [who] subscribed and approved the said Book of Discipline, in the Tolbooth of Edinburgh, the twenty-seventh day of January, the year of God 1560 [21] by their approbation, in these words :

" WE who have subscribed these presents, having advised with the Articles herein specified and, as is above mentioned, from the beginning of this Book think the same good, and conform to God's word in all points, conform to the notes and additions thereto eiked [22] ; and promises to set the same forward at the uttermost of our powers, providing that the Bishops, Abbots, Priors, and other Prelates and beneficed men, who else [23] have adjoined themselves to us, bruik [24] the revenues of their benefices during their lifetimes, they sustaining and upholding the Ministry and Ministers, as is herein specified, for preaching of the word, and ministering of the sacraments [of God]." [25]

What be the contents of the whole Book, and how that this promise was eluded from time to time, we will after hear.[26]

Short after the said Parliament,[27] were sent from the Council ambassadors to England, the Earls Morton and Glencairn, together

---

[1] James Hamilton, Duke of Châtelherault
[2] James Hamilton, third Earl of Arran   [3] Archibald, fifth Earl of Argyll
[4] Alexander, fourth Earl of Glencairn   [5] William, fourth Earl Marischal
[6] John, fourth Earl of Menteith   [7] James, fourth Earl of Morton
[8] Andrew, fifth Earl of Rothes
[9] The Lord James Stewart, later Earl of Moray and Regent of Scotland
[10] William, fifth Lord Hay of Yester   [11] Robert, fifth Lord Boyd
[12] Andrew Stewart, second Lord Ochiltree
[13] Sir John Maxwell, later fourth Lord Herries
[14] John, fifth Lord Lindsay of the Byres
[15] Patrick, sixth Lord Lindsay of the Byres
[16] Sir James Douglas of Drumlanrig   [17] Sir John Gordon of Lochinvar
[18] Sir Alexander Stewart of Garlies   [19] Thomas Kennedy, younger, of Bargany
[20] In the manuscript (folio 243 *recto*) the word *byschop* has been added in the margin in what looks like Knox's hand.   [21] That is, 27 January 1561
[22] *added*   [23] Here used in the sense of *already*   [24] *possess*
[25] See *infra*, Appendix VIII
[26] *The Book of Discipline* is printed in Appendix VIII
[27] That is, the " Reformation Parliament " of 1560

with William Maitland of Lethington younger. The chief point of their commission was earnestly to crave the constant assistance of the Queen's Majesty of England, against all foreign invasion, and to propose the Earl of Arran (who then was in no small estimation with us) to the Queen of England in marriage.[1]

That same time was the Castle of Sempill [2] besieged and taken, because the Lord thereof [3] disobeyed the laws and ordinances of the Council in many things, and especially in that he would maintain the idolatry of the Mass, and also that he beset the way to the Earl of Arran with a great gathering, as he was riding with his accustomed company.

The Papists were proud, for they looked for a new army from France at the next spring,[4] and thereof was there no small appearance, if God had not otherwise provided. For France utterly refused the confirmation of the peace contracted at Leith, would ratify no part of our Parliament, dismissed the Lord of Saint John without any resolute answer,[5] began to gather new bands of throat-cutters, and to make great preparation for ships. They further sent before them certain practisers (amongst whom the Lord Seton,[6] who had departed with the French out of Leith, was one) to rouse up new troubles within this realm. And all this came partly of the malice of the house of Guise, who had avowed to revenge the displeasure of their sister, both upon England and Scotland, and partly by instigation of proud Beaton, falsely called Bishop of Glasgow,[7] of

[1] The " Commissioun of the Estats to move Queene Elisabeth of England to tak the Erle of Arran to hir husband " is printed, with its signatures, in *Acts Parl. Scot.*, ii, 605–606. It is to be noted that the commission lays stress upon the fact that the Hamiltons were heirs-apparent to the Crown of Scotland ; and the " representations " of the ambassadors laid stress upon the marriage as the safest course for both England and Scotland. (*Calendar of Scottish Papers*, i, No. 926). According to the *Diurnal of Occurrents* (62) the ambassadors, with fifty-four horse, left Edinburgh on 11 and 12 October. Their request was met with the answer that Elizabeth was " not at present disposed to marriage " (*Calendar of Scottish Papers*, i, No. 927) ; and they were back in Edinburgh on 3 January 1561. (*Diurnal*, 63 ; *Calendar of Scottish Papers*, i, No. 945)

[2] Castle Sempill, Renfrewshire. Descriptions of the siege are given in Randolph's letters in *Calendar of Scottish Papers*, i, Nos. 915, 916.

[3] Robert, third Lord Sempill, whom Knox elsewhere describes as " a man sold under sin." (*Supra*, 174)

[4] This is partly confirmed by Randolph's letter to Cecil of 23 December 1560. (*Calendar of Scottish Papers*, i, No. 934)

[5] *Supra*, 241–342. Francis II informed the Estates of Scotland that he was greatly displeased by their proceedings and hoped they would soon return to the good road from which they had deviated. (*Calendar of Scottish Papers*, i, No. 919)

[6] George, fifth Lord Seton

[7] James Beaton. He had abandoned his See and had fled to France in 1560.

Durie, Abbot of Dunfermline [1] and Sauls Seaton,[2] and Mr. John Sinclair, Dean of Restalrig,[3] with such others of the French faction, who had openly spoken that they had refused all portion of Scotland unless that it were under the government of a French man. " Recompense them, O Lord, as thou knowest most expedient for thy own glory, and for the perpetual shame of all traitors to their commonwealth."

The certain knowledge of all these things came to our ears, whereat many were afraid ; for divers suspected that England would not be so forward in times to come, considering that their former expenses were so great. The principal comfort remained with the preachers ; for they assured us in God's name that God should perform in all perfection that work in our hands, the beginning whereof he had so mightily maintained because it was not ours, but his own ; and therefore exhorted us that we should constantly proceed to reform all abuses, and to plant the ministry of the Church, as by God's word we might justify it, and then commit the success of all to our God in whose power the disposition of kingdoms stands. And so we began to do, for troubles appearing made us give ear to the admonitions of God's servants. And while that we had scarcely begun again to implore the help of our God, and to show some signs of our obedience unto his messengers and holy word, lo ! the potent hand of God from above sent unto us a wonderful and most joyful deliverance : For unhappy Francis, husband to our Sovereign, suddenly perisheth of a rotten ear.[4] But because the death of that child was not only the cause of joy to us in Scotland, but also by it were the faithful in France delivered, as it were, from the present death,[5] we think [it] expedient to entreat the same somewhat more largely.

The death of the young King of France, husband to our Jezebel

Those cruel and conjured enemies of God, and of all godliness, the Duke of Guise,[6] the Cardinal of Lorraine,[7] and their faction, who then at their own appetite played the tyrants in France, had determined the destruction of all that professed the true knowledge of Jesus Christ within that realm. What tyranny late before they

[1] George Durie. He too had fled to France in 1560.
[2] Probably Sauls Seat, or Souls Seat, Wigtownshire
[3] In the manuscript (folio 244 recto), Mr. John Sinklar dene of restarick is added in the margin in Knox's hand.
[4] Francis II, King of France, and husband of Mary Queen of Scots, died, after a brief illness, on 5 December 1560, aged sixteen years.
[5] This is partly confirmed in a letter from Throckmorton to Lord Grey, of 4 May 1561. (Foreign Calendar, Elizabeth, iv, No. 169)
[6] Francis, Duke of Guise   [7] Charles de Guise, Cardinal of Lorraine

had used at Amboise, the history of France doth witness.[1] Now, in Orleans, in the month of November, convened the King, unhappy Francis, the Queen our Sovereign, and the Queen Mother, the Duke of Guise, with all his faction, the King of Navarre,[2] and the Prince his brother.[3] So that great was the confluence of the Nobility ; but greater was the assembly of the murderers ; for there was not a hangman in all France which was not there. The prisons were full of the true servants of God : the King of Navarre and the Prince were constituted prisoners.[4] The Sheriff of Orleans, a man fearing God, was taken, and so were many others of the town. Briefly, there was none that professed God or godliness within that town, that looked not for the extremity ; for the walls and yetts [5] were night and day kept with those garrisons of the Guisians : miserable men were daily brought in to suffer judgment, but none was suffered to depart forth but at the devotion of the tyrants. And so they proceeded till the tenth or twelfth of December,[6] when that they thought time to put their bloody counsel in execution, and for that purpose conclusion was taken that the King should depart of the town, and lie at a certain place ; which was done to this intent, that there should no suit be made to the King for the safety of any man's life, whom they thought worthy of death. And so was the King's house in Orleans broken up, his beds, coffers, and tapestry sent away ; his own boots put on, he sitting at the Mass, immediately thereafter to have departed, and so their tyranny to have begun,— when all things, we say, were into this readiness to shed the blood of innocents, the Eternal our God, who ever watches for the pre-

Corrected by Mr. George [7]

servation of his own, began to work, and suddenly did put his own work in execution. For as the said King sat at Mass, he was suddenly

[1] In the " Tumult of Amboise," of February–March 1560, a Protestant plot to seize the Guises had been anticipated and barbarously suppressed.

[2] Antoine de Bourbon, titular King of Navarre

[3] Louis de Bourbon, Prince of Condé. In the manuscript (folio 244 *verso*) an immediately following blank space of about two lines has been left here as if for the addition of further names.

[4] Condé was arrested, but Navarre was apparently left at liberty though under close surveillance.   [5] *gates*

[6] This date is clearly incorrect, for Francis II had died on 5 December.

[7] This marginal note is probably in Knox's own hand. In the manuscript (folio 245 *recto*) an extended marginal bracket embraces the lines from " For as the said King . . ." down to " . . . evanished in smoke." The " Mr. George " was undoubtedly George Buchanan who was in France at the time of the King's death. No alterations have been made in the manuscript, and so if any correction was made, it was made on loose papers or on an earlier manuscript.

stricken with an aposthume [1] in that deaf ear that never would hear the truth of God ; and so was he carried to a void house, laid upon a palliase unto such time as a cannabie [2] was set up unto him ; where he lay till the fifteenth day of December, in the year of God 1560,[3] when his glory perished, and the pride of the stubborn heart evanished in smoke. And so was the snare broken, the tyrants disappointed of their cruelty ; those that were appointed to death raised, as it were, out of their graves ; and we, who by our foolishness had made ourselves slaves to strangers, were restored again to freedom and liberty of a free realm.

" Oh ! that we had hearts deeply to consider what are thy wondrous works, O Lord, that we might praise Thee in the midst of this most obstinate and wicked generation, and leave the memorial of the same to our posterities, which, alas, we fear shall forget thy inestimable benefits." The godly in France upon this sudden death set forth in these verses an admonition to Kings :

AD HUJUS TEMPORIS MONARCHAS PROTREPTICON CARMEN.[4]

> Consiliis Christum oppugnans et fraudibus, ingens
>> Regum ille terror Carolus :
> Ipsis ridiculus pueris, furiosus, et excors,
>> Totus repente corruit.
> Tuque Henrice, malis dum consultoribus utens,
>> Sitis piorum sanguinem :
> Ipse tuo vecors, inopina, cæde peremptus
>> Terram imbuisti sanguine.
> Henrici deinceps, sectans vestigia patris
>> Franciscus infœlix puer,
> Clamantem Christum surda dum negligit aure,
>> Aure putrefacta corruit.
> Versuti, fatui, surdi, hæc spectacula, Reges,
>> Vos sapere vel mori jubent.

[1] That is, a gathering of purulent matter. (*Oxford English Dict.*, s.v. *aposteme*)

[2] *canopy*   [3] But see *supra*, 347, *note* 4

[4] The writer of these verses is unknown. Laing traced them in an anonymous work entitled " Commentaires de l'Estat de la Religion et Republique soubs les Rois Henry et Francois seconds, et Charles neufieme " (1565), where they are introduced (folio 100) with the note " Non long temps apres furent divulguez quelques vers Latins faicts sur la mort dudict Roy François, du Roy Henry son pere, et de l'Empereur Charles cinquieme, qui m'ont semblé estre dignes de memoire, et d'estre conservez a la posterité : lesquels pourtant i'ay voulu icy adiouster, la superscription estant telle qu'il s'ensuit cy apres

AD HVIVS TEMPORIS

Monarchas προτρεπτικὸν Carmen."

The author of the " Commentaires " was Pierre de la Place (1520–1572).

The meaning whereof is, that Charles—

> KYNGE CHARLES that tyrane terrible,
>   Withstanding Christ with witt and craft,
> As mocking stock most miserable,
>   Endit at ones ragine and daft.[1]
> Then Henrie through evill cumpany,
>   Thristing [2] the blood of godlie men,
> With his awin blood, schedd suddantlie,
>   Was maid to wait the end ye ken.[3]
> Last, Francis, that unhappie child,
>   His Father's footsteps following plane,
> To Christ crying, deafe eares did yeild,
>   Ane rotten eare then was his baine.
> O craftie, deif, and foolische Kyngs,
>   These fearfull judgments gone befoir you,
> Biddeth you be wyser in your reignes,
>   Or schamefull death will sone devoir you.

The death of this King made great alteration in France, England, and Scotland. France was erected in some esperance that the tyranny of the Guisians should no longer ring [4] above them, because that God at unawares had broken the staff whereupon they leaned. But, alas, they were deceived : for the simplicity of some was so abused that, against the laws of the realm, to the Queen Mother [5] was committed [the] regiment : which lifted up as well the Duke of Guise as the cruel Cardinal for a season.

The Queen of England and the Council remitted [6] our Ambassadors with answer, " That she would not marry hastily and therefore willed the Council of Scotland, and the Earl of Arran foresaid, not to depend upon any hope thereof." [7] What motives she had, we omit.[8]

The pride of the Papists of Scotland began to be abated, and

---

[1] After his abdication the Emperor Charles V retired to the monastery at Yuste where he died in 1558. But it would appear to be an exaggeration to say that he ended his life " raging and daft."   [2] *Thirsting*

[3] Henry II, King of France, died 10 July 1559 (see *supra*, 198)   [4] *reign*

[5] Catherine de Medici   [6] *sent back*   [7] See *supra*, 346, *note* 1

[8] But Elizabeth clearly saw that with the death of Francis II the influence of the Guises had gone. The influence in the French court was now that of the Queen-Mother, Catherine de Medici. Accordingly, why should not Mary, now a widow, and without support at the French court, herself marry Arran ? That might neutralize in Scotland both the Roman Church and the French party.

some that ever had shown themselves enemies unto us began to think, and plainly to speak (amongst whom the old Sheriff of Ayr [1] was one), that they perceived God to fight for us. The Earl of Arran himself did more patiently abide the repulse of the Queen of England because that he was not altogether without hope that the Queen of Scotland bare unto him some favour. And so he wrote unto her, and sent for credit a ring which the said Queen our Sovereign knew well enough. The letter and ring were both presented to the Queen, and of her received. Answer was returned to the said Earl, after the which he made no further pursuit in that matter : and yet, none the less, he bare it heavily in heart, and more heavily than many would have wished.

The certainty of the death foresaid was signified unto us both by sea and land. By sea received John Knox (who then had great intelligence both with the churches and [with] some of the Court of France [2]) letters that the King was mortally sick and could not well escape the death. Which letters received, that same day, at afternoon, he passed to the Duke's Grace, to his own lodging at the Kirk of Field, [3] [with] whom he found the Lord James in conference together (the Earl of Arran was in Jedburgh), to whom he opened such news as he had received, and willed them to be of good comfort ; for, said he, the advertiser never has yet abused me [4] : it is the same gentleman that first gave us knowledge of the slaughter of Harry King of France ; and showed unto them the letter, but would not express the man's name. While they were reasoning in divers purposes ; and he upon the one part comforting them, and they upon the other part comforting him (for he was in no small heaviness by reason of the late death of his dear bedfellow, Marjory Bowes [5]), while (we say) they three were familiarly communing together, there came a messenger from the Lord Grey, [6] forth of Berwick, with letters assuring him of the death of the King of France. Which divulged and noised abroad, a general Convention of the whole Nobility was appointed to be held at Edinburgh the fifteenth day of January following, in the which the Book of Discipline was perused

---

[1] Sir Hugh Campbell of Loudoun   [2] Cf. infra, ii, 43
[3] Hamilton House, Kirk o' Field, stood roughly on the present site of the Old College of the University of Edinburgh.   [4] " let me down "
[5] Marjory Bowes, Knox's first wife, must therefore have died early in December 1560.
[6] William, Lord Grey of Wilton

newly over again, for some pretended ignorance by reason they had not heard it.[1]

In that assembly was Master Alexander Anderson, sub-principal of Aberdeen, a man more subtle and crafty than either learned or godly,[2] called, who refused to dispute in his faith, abusing a place of Tertullian to cloak his ignorance. It was answered unto him, that Tertullian should not prejudge the authority of the Holy Ghost who, by the mouth of Peter, commands us to give reason for our faith to every one that requires the same of us. It was further answered, That we neither required him, neither yet any man, to dispute in any point concerning our faith, which was grounded upon God's word, and fully expressed within his holy Scriptures ; for all that we believed without controversy. But we required of him, as of the rest of [the] Papists, that they would suffer their doctrine, constitutions, and ceremonies to come to trial ; and principally that the Mass, and the opinion thereof by them taught unto the people, might be laid to the square-rule of God's word, and unto the right institution of Jesus Christ, that they might understand whether that their preachers offended or not, in that, they affirmed, " The action of the Mass to be expressedly repugning unto the last Supper of the Lord Jesus ; the sayer of it to commit horrible blasphemy in usurping upon him the office of Christ ; the hearers to commit damnable idolatry, and the opinion of it conceived to be derogation, and, as it were, disannulling of Christ's death." While that the said Master Alexander denied that the priest took upon him Christ's office to offer for sin, as was alleged, a Mass book was produced, and in the beginning of the Canon were these words read : *Suscipe, Sancta Trinitas, hanc oblationem, quam ego indignus peccator offero tibi vivo Deo et vero, pro peccatis meis, pro peccatis totius Ecclesiæ vivorum et mortuorum, &c.*[3] " Now (said the reasoner), if to offer for the sins of the whole Kirk was not the office of Christ Jesus, yea, that

---

[1] See also *Diurnal of Occurrents*, 63 ; and *Calendar of Scottish Papers*, i, Nos. 948, 958. Knox has already referred to the presentation of *The Book of Discipline* to the nobility in the Tolbooth of Edinburgh on 27 January 1561. (*Supra*, 344–345)

[2] Lesley, who was at the time Official of Aberdeen, and took part in the disputation, calls him " Principal " of the College of Aberdeen (*Historie of Scotland*, Bannatyne Club, 293). In 1569 with the Sub-Principal and three regents he was denounced as an " obstinate papist " and deprived of his office (*Booke of the Universall Kirk*, Bannatyne Club, i, 141–143 ; Calderwood, *History*, ii, 491–492). See also *Collections for a History of the Shires of Aberdeen and Banff*, Spalding Club, 320, *note* 1.

[3] " Holy Trinity accept this oblation, which I, an unworthy sinner, present to thee the living and true God for my own sins, and for the sins of the whole Church of the quick and the dead," &c.

office that to him only might and may appertain, let the Scripture
judge. And if a vile knave, whom ye call the priest, proudly takes
the same upon him, let your own book witness." The said Master
Alexander answered, " Christ offered the propitiatory, and that could
none do but he ; but we offer the remembrance." Whereto it was
answered, " We praise God, that ye have denied a sacrifice propitiatory to be in the Mass ; and yet we offer to prove that, in more
than a hundred places of your Papistical Doctors, this proposition
is affirmed, ' The Mass is a sacrifice propitiatory.' But, to the
second part, where ye allege that ye offer Christ in remembrance,
we ask, first, Unto whom do ye offer him? And next, By what
authority are ye assured of well-doing ? In God the Father, there
falls no oblivion : and if ye will yet shift and say, That ye offer it
not as God were forgetful, but as willing to apply Christ's merits
to his Church ; we demand of you, What power and commandment
ye have so to do ? We know that our Master, Christ Jesus, commanded his Apostles to do that which he did ' in remembrance of
him ' ; but plain it is, that Christ took bread, gave thanks, broke
bread, and gave it to his disciples, saying, ' Take ye, eat ye ; this
is my body which is broken for you. Do this in remembrance of me,
&c.' Here we find a commandment to take, to eat, to take and to
drink ; but to offer Christ's body either for remembrance or application, we find not : and therefore we say, to take upon you an office
which is not given unto you is unjust usurpation and no lawful
power." The said Master Alexander being more than astonished,
would have shifted ; but then the Lords willed him to answer
directly. Whereto he answered, " That he was better seen in
philosophy, than in theology." Then was commanded Master
John Leslie (who then was Parson of Oyne, and now Lord Abbot
of Lindores), to answer to the former argument : and he with *And after*
great gravity began to answer, " If our Master have nothing to *was made*
Bishop of
say to it, I have nothing ; for I know nothing but the Canon Law : *Ross* [1]
and the greatest reason that ever I could find there, is *Nolumus* and
Volumus." [2] And yet we understand that now he is the only patron
of the Mass. But it is no marvel, for he understood that he is a
priest's gett [3] ; and therefore we should not wonder albeit that the
old trowan [4] verse be true, *Patrem sequitur sua proles*. The Nobility
hearing that neither the one nor the other would answer directly,

---

[1] In the manuscript (folio 248 *recto*) there is a caret after *Londoris*, and the marginal
note is probably in Knox's own hand.

[2] *Cf. infra*, 373   [3] *brat ; child. Cf. supra*, 113, *note* 2   [4] *trusted*

said, " We have been miserably deceived heretofore ; for if the Mass may not obtain remission of sins to the quick and to the dead, wherefore were all the Abbacies so richly doted [1] with our temporal lands ? "

The lying Dean of Restalrig called Sinclair [2] Thus much we thought good to insert here, because that some Papists are not ashamed now to affirm, That they with their reasons could never be heard, but that all that we did, we did by fine force ; when that the whole realm knows that we ever required them to speak their judgments freely, not only promising unto them protection and defence, but also that we should subscribe with them, if they by God's Scriptures could confute us, and by the same word establish their assertions. " But who can correct the leasings [3] of such as in all things show themselves the sons of the Father of all lies. Preserve us, Lord, from that perverse and malicious generation. AMEN."

At this same Assembly was the Lord James appointed to go to France to the Queen our Sovereign [4] ; and a Parliament was appointed to begin the twenty of May next following ; for at that time was the return of the said Lord James looked for.[5] And so was that Convention dissolved without any other thing of importance concluded. The said Lord James prepared him for his journey ; (for albeit he passed in the public affairs, he sustained the charge of his own expenses ; and yet there never passed from this Realm in the company of one man so many, and so honest, through England to France). Before he departed, he was forewarned as well of the danger in France, as of the Queen's craft (not that we then suspected her nature, but that we understood the malice of her friends) : he was plainly premonished, that if ever he condescended that she should have Mass publicly or privately within the Realm of Scotland, that then betrayed he the cause of God, and exposed the religion

---

[1] *endowed*

[2] This marginal note seems to govern the words " some Papists are not ashamed now to affirm." For Knox's comments on John Sinclair, see also *supra*, 112–113, 131.

[3] *falsehoods*

[4] But although " appointed " to go to France in January 1561, the Lord James was apparently anxious to stay in Edinburgh until the Parliament to " see what is then done." It was thought advisable, however, that he should take his journey " out of hand " rather than wait for the end of the Parliament ; he left Edinburgh on 18 March, and reached Diziers, where Mary was then residing, on 15 April. (*Calendar of Scottish Papers*, i, Nos. 958, 960, 964, 972, 983 ; Lesley, *Historie of Scotland*, Bannatyne Club, 294)

[5] So also in Randolph's letter to Cecil of 14 March 1561. (*Calendar of Scottish Papers*, i, No. 972)

even to the uttermost danger that he could do. That she should have Mass publicly, he affirmed that he should never consent : but to have it secretly in her chamber, who could stop her ? The danger was shown ; and so he departed.[1]

. . . .[2]

As the servants of God uprightly travailed to have vice punished and virtue planted, so did the Devil ever stir up some in the contrary of both. There was a law made against fornicators and adulterers,[3] that the one and the other should be carted through the towns, and so banished, till that their repentance was offered and received. And albeit this was not the severity of God's law, especially against adulterers, yet was it a great bridle to malefactors; whereat the wicked did wondrously storm. It chanced that one [John] Sanderson, a flesher, was deprehended to have put away his lawful wife (under colour that he was lawfully parted after the manner of the Papistical religion), and had taken to him another in [his] house. The complaint and slander [being] proponed to the Kirk, and trial taken that he was not married with the second woman, neither that he was able to prove that he was divorced by any order of law from the first, he was committed in the hands of the Magistrates who, according to the laws, commanded him to be carted.[4] But the rascal multitude, inflamed by some ungodly craftsmen, made

[1] This passage seems to have been written in the light of subsequent events. It should be compared with Maitland of Lethington's comments in his letter to Cecil of 6 February 1561 (Calendar of Scottish Papers, i, No. 958), and with the Lord James Stewart's letter to Mary of 10 June 1561 (Scot. Hist. Rev., ii, 157–162)—particularly the sentence, ' Above all things, Madam, for the love of God press no matters of religion, not for any man's advice on the earth.'

[2] Here Knox continues " The election of the superintendents hereafter followed in this manner." Most of that folio (249 recto) is then left blank and is succeeded by seven blank pages in the manuscript. " The Form and Order of the Election of Superintendents," together with " The Order of the Election of Elders and Deacons," are given below in Appendix VII as supplied by Laing from the Glasgow MS. of the History and from the printed copies. (See Laing's Knox, ii, 143, note.) Randolph, writing to Cecil on 5 March 1561, says " On Sunday next they choose in divers places for all the shires, superintendents, known and learned men." (Calendar of Scottish Papers, i, No. 967)

[3] See Edinburgh Burgh Records (Burgh Rec. Soc.), iii, 65. (10 June 1560)

[4] By this act of the town, proclaimed on 10 June 1560, the provost, bailies, council and a part of the deacons of crafts of the burgh of Edinburgh ordained that " bordelars, whoremasters and harlots " not giving testimony of their conversion were to be defamed, set on the market cross for six hours, and carted through the town for their first fault ; burned on the cheek and banished for the second fault ; and put to death for the third fault. (Ibid.) The official details relating to Sanderson's case are given, ibid., iii, 89–95.

insurrection, broke the cart, boisted[1] the officers, and took away the malefactor. This was the beginning of further evils, as we will after hear.

In the meantime, while Lord James (we say) was in France, there came an Ambassador from France,[2] suborned, no doubt, with all craft that might trouble the Estate of the Religion. His demands were 1, That the league betwix us and England should be broken : 2, That the ancient league betwix France and Scotland should be renewed : And, 3, That the Bishops and Kirkmen should be reponed[3] in their former places, and be suffered to intromet[4] with their livings. The Council delayed answer to the Parliament appointed in May. In the meantime the Papists of Scotland practised with him. The Earls of Huntly,[5] Atholl,[6] Bothwell,[7] and others, intended to have taken Edinburgh before the said Parliament. The whole Bishops assembled and held council in Stirling. Some whispering there was, that the Duke[8] and the Bishop of Saint Andrews[9] were too familiar ; and some feared that the authority of the Queen should have been usurped, by reason of her absence, and that the Duke was second person,[10] for thereat had some of his pressed immediately after the death of the King of France. The Protestants thereof advertised, prevented[11] them, and came to Edinburgh. The Earl of Arran[12] stood constant with his brethren. There were some that carefully and painfully travailed that nothing prejudicial to the Queen's authority should be done in absence of the Lord James ; to whom the Queen has recompensed evil for good service. Master James McGill,[13] in that point did both stoutly and truly ; for John Knox and he were then fallen in familiarity, in which they yet continue, 20 October 1567,[14] by reason that the

Ambassador from France and his demands

---

[1] *threatened*

[2] Gilles de Noailles. He arrived on 11 March 1561 (*Calendar of Scottish Papers*, i, No. 972), and is said to have left on 7 June 1561 (*Diurnal of Occurrents*, 64, 283). Lethington's reports, made at this time, refer only to the second of the "demands" stated by Knox. (*Calendar of Scottish Papers*, i, Nos. 970, 971)

[3] *replaced in ;* that is, *restored to*   [4] *intermeddle*

[5] George, fourth Earl of Huntly   [6] John, fourth Earl of Atholl

[7] James Hepburn, fourth Earl of Bothwell   [8] The Duke of Châtelherault

[9] John Hamilton, Archbishop of St. Andrews, half-brother to the Duke

[10] James, second Earl of Arran, and Duke of Châtelherault was next in succession to the Crown, always assuming his father's divorce had been valid. (See *supra*, 49, *note* 1)

[11] *forestalled*

[12] James, Lord Hamilton, Earl of Arran, eldest son of the Duke of Châtelherault

[13] He was then Clerk-Register

[14] This date occurs in the body of the text (folio 253 *verso*), providing evidence as to the time of the transcribing of this part of the *History*.

said Master James had embraced the Religion, and professed it publicly.

The Papists and Bishops, disappointed of their principal purpose and enterprise, did yet make broil for trouble ; for the rascal multitude were stirred up to make a Robin Hood, which enormity was of many years left and damned by statute and act of Parliament.[1] Yet would they not be forbidden, but would disobey and trouble the town, especially upon the night. Whereat the Bailies offended, took from them some swords and an ensign,[2] which was occasion that they that same night made a mutiny, kept the ports of the town, and intended to have pursued some men within their own houses ; but that, upon the restitution of their swords and ensign, was stayed. But yet they ceased not to molest, as well the inhabitants of Edinburgh as divers country men, taking from them money, and threatening some with further injuries. Wherewith the Magistrates of the town, highly offended, took more diligent heed to such as resorted to the town, and so apprehended one of the principal of that misorder, named [James] Gillone,[3] a cordiner, whom they put to an assize ; *Some says his name is Kyllone* [and being convicted, for he could not be absolved] for he was the chief man that spoiled John Mowbray of ten crowns of the sun,[4] they thought to have executed judgment upon him, and so erected a gibbet beneath the Cross. But, whether it came by paction with the Provost[5] and some others, or by instigation of the Craftsmen, who ever have been bent too much to maintain such vanity and riotousness, we fully know not, but suddenly there did rise a tumult ; the Tolbooth was broken up, and not only the said Gillone, who before was [con]demned, was violently taken forth, but also all other malefactors were set at freedom ; the gibbet was pulled down, and despitefully broken ; and thereafter, as the Provost and some of the Council assembled to the Clerk's chamber for consultation, the whole rascal [multitude] banded together, with some known unhonest craftsmen, and intended invasion of the said chamber. Which perceived, the Provost, and such as were in his company, passed to the Tolbooth, suspecting nothing[6] that they would have been so

---

[1] Because of the disorderly licence that had come to accompany the festivities of the month of May, an Act of 1555 forbade any person to be chosen as Robin Hood, Little John, Abbot of Unreason, or Queen of May. (*Acts Parl. Scot.*, ii, 500, c. 40)

[2] *banner*

[3] In the *Diurnal of Occurrents* he is called Killone and Kellone (65) ; and Gilloun and Gillone (283)

[4] A crown of the sun was worth at this time about 26s. Scots. (*Cf. Acts of the Lords of Council in Public Affairs*, 634)   [5] Archibald Douglas of Kilspindie

[6] That is, " *not suspecting* that the rascal multitude . . ."

enraged that they would make new pursuit, after that they had obtained their intent. But they were suddenly deceived, for from the Castlehill they came with violence, and with stones, guns, and such other weapons as they had, began to assault the said Tolbooth, ran at the door of it, where, partly by stones cast from above, and partly by a pistol shot by Robert Norwell, which hurt one Tweedy, they were repulsed [from the door] ; but yet ceased not they to cast [stones] and shoot in at the windows, threatening death to all that were within. And in very deed the malice of the craftsmen, who were suspected to be the occasion of that tumult, bore no good will to divers of them that were with the Provost.

The arguments that the Crafts were the cause of that uproar, besides their first misorder that they had used before in taking Sanderson from the execution of punishment,[1] are two. The former, Archibald Dewar, [and] Patrick Schang,[2] with other five deacons [of the crafts] came to John Knox, and willed him to solist[3] the Provost and the town to delay the execution : who did answer, " That he had so oft solisted in their favour that his own conscience accused him that they used his labours for no other end but to be a patron to their impiety." For he had before made intercession for William Harlaw, James Frissall, and others, that were convicted of the former tumult. They proudly said, " That if it was not stayed, both he and the Bailies should repent it." Whereto he answered, " He would not hurt his conscience for any fear of man." And so they departed ; and the tumult (as said is) immediately thereafter did arise. The second argument is, the tumult continued from two at afternoon till after eight at night. The Craftsmen were required to assemble themselves together for deliverance of their Provost [and Bailies] ; but they passed to their four hour's penny,[4] and in their jesting said, " They will be Magistrates alone, let them rule the multitude alone." And so, contrary to the oath[5] that they had made, they denied their assistance, counsel, and comfort to their Provost and Bailies ; which are arguments very probable, that the said tumult rose by their procurement. The end hereof was, that the Provost and Bailies were compelled to give their handwrits that they should never pursue any of them that were of that tumult for any crime that was done in that behalf. And this was proclaimed at the

---

[1] *Supra*, 355–356

[2] Archibald Dewar had been Visitor for the Tailors in 1556, and Patrick Schang was at this time Deacon of the Wrights. (*Edinburgh Burgh Records*, ii, 239, 242 ; iii, 112)

[3] *solicit*   [4] their penny-ale at four o'clock

[5] That is, contrary to the burgess-oath

Cross after nine hours at night ; and so that trouble quieted.[1] But the Nobility avowed that they should not spare it ; and so a great number of that faction were absent from the town, till the arrival of the Queen. The whole multitude were held excommunicate, and were admitted to no participation of the sacraments, unto such time as they satisfied the Magistrates, and made humble suit unto the Kirk.

Of the death of the Queen Regent, we have before spoken,[2] but of her burial was nothing heard ; and it may appear that such matters are unworthy of remembrance. But and if all things shall be rightly weighed, we shall perceive God's just judgments, how secret that ever they be. Before, we heard the barbarous inhumanity that was used at Leith by the French, who exposed the naked carcasses of the slain, as it were in a spectacle, despiting God. We heard that this Queen Regent rejoiced at the sight [3] ; but her joy was suddenly turned in sorrow, as we have heard. The question was moved of her burial. The Preachers boldly gainstood that any superstitious rites should be used within that realm which God of his mercy had begun to purge. And so conclusion was taken that her burial should be deferred till further advisement ; and so she was lapped in a cope of lead,[4] and kept in the Castle from the ninth of June,[5] unto the nineteenth of October, when she by pynours [6] was carried to a ship and so carried to France. What pomp was used there we neither heard nor yet regard.[7] But in it we see that she that delighted that others lay without burial, got it neither so soon as she herself (if she had been on the council in her life) would have required it, neither yet so honourably in this realm, as sometimes she looked for. It may chance be a prognostication that the Guisians' blood cannot have long rest within this realm.

Of the Queen Regent's burial

The Papists, a little before the Parliament, resorted in divers

---

[1] For further details of this tumult on 11 May 1561, and subsequently, see *Edinburgh Burgh Records*, iii, 112–113, 117–118 ; *Diurnal of Occurrents*, 65–66, 283–285 ; Pitcairn, *Criminal Trials* (Bannatyne Club), i, 409 * (where the date is wrongly given as ' Sunday the xij day of May '), 410 *   [2] *Supra*, 322   [3] *Supra*, 319

[4] The cost of the " wobe of leid " to be " ane sepulture " for the Queen's Grace, and of the hangings in the chapel of the Castle are given in *Accounts of the Lord High Treasurer*, xi, 24.   [5] She died on the night of 10–11 June (*supra*, 322, *note* 2)

[6] *labourers*

[7] Apparently the body of the Queen Regent was moved from the Castle of Edinburgh on the night of 16 March 1561 and conveyed to Fécamp. Thence, after funeral ceremonies, the body was taken to Rheims and there interred in the Convent of St. Peter. (Laing's *Knox*, ii, 590–592)

bands to the town, and began to brag, as that they would have defaced the Protestants. Which thing perceived, the brethren assembled together, and yeid [1] in such companies, and that in peaceable manner, that the Bishops and their bands forsook the calsay. [2] The brethren understanding what the Papists meant, convened in council in the Tolbooth of Edinburgh, the xxvii of May, the year of God 1561 ; and after consultation, concluded that an humble Supplication should be presented unto the Lords of Secret Council, and unto the whole assembly, that then was convened, in the which should these subsequent heads be required, and a law to pass thereupon [3] :

First, That Idolatry, and all monuments thereof, should be suppressed throughout the whole realm ; that the sayers, hearers, maintainers, and users of the Mass should be punished according to the Act of Parliament, as said is.

2. That special and certain provision be made for the sustentation of the Superintendents, Ministers, Exhorters, and Readers. That Superintendents and Ministers should be planted where none were. That punishment should be appointed for such as disobeyed or contemned the Superintendents in their function.

3. That punishment should be appointed for the abusers of the sacraments, and for the contemners of the same.

4. That no letters of the Session be given to answer or pay to any person their teinds, [4] without especial provision that the parishioners retain sa mekle in their own hands as is appointed to the ministry ; and that all such as are else [5] given be called in, and discharged ; and likewise that no Sheriffs give precepts to that effect.

5. That neither the Lords of Session, nor any other judges, proceed upon such precepts or warnings, passed at the instance of them that of late have obtained feus of vicarages and parsonages, manses, and kirkyards ; and that six acres (if so much there be) of the glebe, be always reserved to the minister, according to the appointment of the Book of Discipline [6] ; and that every minister may have letters thereupon.

6. That no letters of the Session, nor [any] others take place, while [7] the stipends contained in the Book of Discipline for sustenta-

---

[1] *went*   [2] *causeway, street*

[3] For these articles and the supplication, see also *Booke of the Universall Kirk* (Bannatyne Club), i, 8–10. There the date of the Convention in the Tolbooth is given as 26 May.   [4] *tithes*   [5] *already*   [6] See *infra*, ii, 305

[7] *until*

tion of the ministers be first consigned in the hands, at the least, of the principal of the parishioners.

7. That punishment be appointed against such as purchase, bring home, or execute within this Realm, the Pope's Bulls.

The tenor of the Supplication was this :

PLEASE your Honours, and the wisdoms of such as are here presently convened with you in Council, to understand that by many arguments we perceive what the pestilent generation of that Roman Antichrist within this realm pretends : to wit, that they would of new erect their idolatry, take upon them to empire above our conscience, and so to command us, the true subjects of this realm, and such as God of his mercy has (under our Sovereign) subjected unto us, in all things to obey their appetites. Honesty craves, and conscience moves us, to make the very secrets of our hearts patent to your Honours in that behalf : which is this, " That before that ever those tyrants and dumb dogs empire above us, and above such as God has subjected unto us, that we the Barons and Gentlemen professing Christ Jesus within this realm, are fully determined to hazard life, and whatsoever we have received of our God in temporal things." Most humbly therefore beseeching your Honours that such order may be taken that we have not occasion to take again the sword of just defence into our hands, which we have willingly (after that God has given victory, both to your Honours and us) resigned over in your hands : to the end that God's Evangel may be publicly within this realm preached ; the true Ministers thereof reasonably sustained ; Idolatry suppressed, and the committers thereof punished, according to the laws of God and man. In doing whereof, your Honours shall find us not only obedient unto you in all things lawful, but also ready at all times to bring under order and obedience such as would rebel against your just authority which, in absence of our Sovereign, we acknowledge to be in your hands. Beseeching your Honours, with upright judgment and indifferency, to look upon these our few Articles, and, by these our brethren, to signify unto us such answer again, as may declare your Honours worthy of that place whereunto God (after some dangers sustained) in his mercy has called you. And let these enemies of God assure themselves, that if your Honours put not order unto them, that we shall shortly take such order, that they shall be neither able to do what they list, neither yet to live upon the sweat of the brows of such as are no debtors unto them. Let your Honours conceive nothing of us, but all humble obedience in God. But let the Papists be yet once again assured that their pride and idolatry we will not suffer.

(Directed from the Assembly of the Kirk, the 28th of May 1561, and sent by these brethren, the Master of Lindsay,[1] the Laird of Lochinvar,[2] the Laird of Ferniehurst,[3] the Laird of Whittinghame,[4] Thomas Menzies, Provost of Aberdeen, and George Lovell, burgess of Dundee.)

Upon the which request and Articles, the Lords of Council foresaid made an act and ordinance answering to every head of the foresaid Articles,[5] and commanded letters to be answered thereupon, which divers ministers raised, as in the books of Secret Council is yet to be found. And thus got Sathan the second fall, after that he had begun to trouble the estate of the religion once established by law. His first assault was by the rascal multitude, opposing themselves to the punishment of vice : The second was by the Bishops and their bands, in which he thought utterly to have triumphed ; and yet he in the end prospered worse than ye have heard.

For in this meantime, returned from France the Lord James,[6] who, besides his great expenses, and the loss of a box wherein was his secret poise,[7] escaped a desperate danger in Paris : for, his returning from our Sovereign (who then lay with the Cardinal of Lorraine at Rheims) [being] understood of the Papists at Paris, they had conspired some treasonable act against him ; for they intended either to beset his house by night or else to have assaulted him and his company as they walked upon the streets. Whereof the said Lord James advertised by the Rhinegrave,[8] by reason of old familiarity which was betwix them in Scotland, he took purpose suddenly and in good order to depart from Paris ; as that he did,

[1] Patrick, son of John, fifth Lord Lindsay of the Byres ; later (1563) Patrick, sixth Lord Lindsay of the Byres

[2] John Gordon of Lochinvar, Kirkcudbrightshire

[3] Sir John Ker of Ferniehurst

[4] William Douglas of Whittinghame, East Lothian

[5] See *Booke of the Universall Kirk*, i, 10. Unfortunately, there is a gap in the records of the Privy Council from 22 January 1554 to 4 September 1561.

[6] See *supra*, 354. The Lord James was back in Edinburgh before 5 June 1561. (*Calendar of Scottish Papers*, i, No. 988)   [7] *treasure*, or *hoard of money*

[8] Jean Philippe, comte de Salm, called the Rhinegrave. He had been in Scotland in 1548 in command of German mercenaries in the French army under d'Essé, and had taken part in the sieges of Haddington and Dundee. (See Lesley's *Historie*, Bannatyne Club, 206, 207, 219, 223)

the second day after that he arrived there. And yet could he not depart so secretly, but that the Papists had their privy ambushes ; for upon the Pont of Change [1] they had prepared a procession, which met the said Lord and his company even in the teeth ; and knowing that they would not do the accustomed reverence unto them and their idols, they thought thereupon to have picked a quarrel ; and so as one part passed by, without moving of hat to any thing that was there, they had suborned some to cry " Huguenots," and to cast stones. But God disappointed their enterprise ; for the said Rhinegrave, with other gentlemen, being with the Lord James, rebuked the foolish multitude, and overrode some of the foremost ; and so the rest were dispersed ; and he and his company safely escaped, and came with expedition to Edinburgh, while that yet the Lords and Assembly were together, to the great comfort of many godly hearts, and to no little astonishment of the wicked. For, from the Queen our Sovereign he brought letters to the Lords, praying them to entertain quietness, and to suffer nothing to be attempted against the contract of peace which was made at Leith, till her own home-coming, and to suffer the religion publicly established to go forward, &c. Whereupon the said Lords gave answer to the French Ambassador, a negative to every one of his petitions. [2]

And First, That France had not deserved at their hands, that either they or their posterity should enter with them again in any league or confederacy, offensive or defensive, seeing that so traitorously and cruelly they had persecuted them, their realm and liberties, under pretence of amity and marriage.

Secondly, That besides [3] their conscience, they could not take such a worldly scheme as, without offence committed, to break the league, which in God's name they had made with them whom he had made instruments to set Scotland at freedom from the tyranny of the French, at the least of the Guisians and their faction.

And last, That such as they called Bishops and Kirkmen they knew neither for pastors of the Kirk, neither yet for any just possessors of the patrimony thereof ; but understood them perfectly to be wolves, thieves, murderers, and idle-bellies : And therefore, as

[1] The Pont-au-Change was then the principal bridge in Paris across the Seine.

[2] See *supra*, 356. The reply of the Scottish Council to the French ambassador was apparently given on 1 June 1561 (*Calendar of Scottish Papers*, i, No. 987), which would mean that the Lord James had returned to Edinburgh before that date. (*Cf. supra*, 362, *note* 6)

[3] *out of*

Scotland had forsaken the Pope and Papistry, so could they not be debtors to his forsworn vassals.

With these answers departed the said Ambassador.[1] And the Lords of Secret Council made an act, that all places and monuments of idolatry should be destroyed.[2] And for that purpose was directed to the West the Earl of Arran, having joined with him the Earls of Argyll and Glencairn, together with the Protestants of the West : who burnt Paisley (the Bishop [of Saint Andrews, who was Abbot thereof[3]], narrowly escaped), cast down Failford,[4] Kilwinning, and a part of Crossraguel. The Lord James was appointed to the North, where he made such reformation as nothing contented the Earl of Huntly, and yet seemed he to approve all things. And thus God so potently wrought with us, so long as we depended upon him, that all the world might see his potent hand to maintain us, and to fight against our enemies ; yea, most to confound them, when that they promised to themselves victory without resistance. " Oh ! that we should rightly consider the wondrous works of the Lord our God."

In the Treaty of Peace contracted at Leith, there were contained certain heads that required the ratification of both the Queens. The Queen of England, according to her promise, subscription, and seal, without any delay performed the same,[5] and sent it to our Sovereign by her appointed officers. But our Sovereign (whether because her own crafty nature thereto moved her, or that her Uncles' chief councillors so would, we know not) with many dilatours [6] frustrated the expectation of the Queen of England ; as by the copy of a Letter, sent from the Ambassador of England to his Sovereign, we may understand.[7]

---

[1] De Noailles apparently left Edinburgh on 7 June 1561. (*Diurnal of Occurrents*, 64)

[2] *Supra*, 360 ; 362, *note* 5

[3] John Hamilton. He had received the Abbey of Paisley in 1525 *in commendam* till his twenty-fifth year, and thereafter *in titulum*. (Herkless and Hannay, *Archbishops of St. Andrews*, v, 5)

[4] St. Mary's of Fail, Ayrshire. A house of Trinitarian or Red Friars. According to a satirical ballad the friars of Fail " never wanted gear enough as long as their neighbours' lasted."

[5] The Treaty of Edinburgh was ratified by Elizabeth, 20 September 1560. See also *infra*, 370

[6] A legal term : a dilatory defence or exception, as opposed to a peremptory one

[7] Elizabeth, writing to Randolph on 1 July 1561, enclosed a copy of the answer made of late by the Scottish Queen to the English ambassador so that he might show it " to those he thinks meet." (*Calendar of Scottish Papers*, i, No. 992) It is probable that Knox saw this copy and is here quoting from it.

At Paris, the xxiii of June 1561.[1]

" THE xviii of this present June, I sent Sommer [2] to the Queen of Scots for audience, who appointed me to come to her the same day after dinner ; which I did. To her I did [remember] your Majesty's heartly recommendations, and declared unto her your Majesty's like gladsomeness of her recovery of her late sickness, whose want of health, as it was grievous unto your Majesty, so did you congratulate and greatly rejoice of the good terms of health she was presently in. After these offices, I put her in remembrance again what had passed from the beginning in the matter of your Majesty's demand of her ratification, according to the proport [3] of the said Treaty, as well by me at the first, as afterwards by my Lord of Bedford [4] at his being here, and also followed since again by me in audience, and by my letter to her being in Lorraine : adding hereto your Majesty's further commandment and recharge to me again, presently to renew the same demand, as before had been done."

The said Queen made answer : " Monsieur l'Ambassador, I *Answer* thank the Queen, my good-sister, for this gentle visitation and congratulation of this my recovery ; and though I be not yet in perfect health, yet I thank God I feel myself in very good in the coming to. And for answer to your demand (quoth she), of my ratification, I do remember all those things that you have recited unto me ; and I would the Queen, my good-sister, should think *Crafty* that I do respect [5] the resolute answer in this matter, and per- *dealer ;* *thou* forming thereof, until such time as I may have the advices of the *never re-* *spected* Nobles and Estates of my own realm, which I trust shall not be long *them* adoing ; for I intend to make my voyage thither shortly. And *further* *than they* though this matter (quoth she) does touch me principally, yet does *might* it also touch the Nobles and Estates of my realm too ; and there- *serve to* *thy cor-* fore it shall be meet, that I use their advices therein. Heretofore *rupt* *affections* they have seemed to be grieved that I should do any thing without them ; and now they would be more offended if I should proceed in this matter of myself, without their advices. I do intend (quoth she) to send Monsieur d'Oysel to the Queen your Mistress, my

---

[1] See *Foreign Calendar, Elizabeth*, iv, No. 265, and the comments in Hay Fleming, *Mary Queen of Scots*, 239, *note* 45

[2] John Somer, an English agent in France   [3] *purport*

[4] Francis Russell, Earl of Bedford, and Throckmorton had had interviews with Mary on 18 and 19 February 1561, when they had asked her to ratify the Treaty of Leith (Edinburgh). See their long report to the English Privy Council in *Foreign Calendar, Elizabeth*, iii, No. 1030.   [5] *respite*, that is, *postpone*

This was
secret
lardon ¹
good-sister, who shall declare that unto her from me, that, I trust, shall satisfy her ; by whom I will give her to understand of my journey into Scotland. I mean to embark at Calais.² The King

She meant
she would
seek a safe
conduct
has lent me certain galleys and ships, to convoy me home ; and I intend to require of my good-sister those favours that princes uses to do in those cases. And though the terms wherein we have here-

*Ever
while that
she may
show her
evil will.
If France
would
have sus-
tained
them,
they had
not yet
departed
†The
second
secret
lardon
tofore [been] have been somewhat hard,* yet I trust that from henceforth we shall accord together as cousins and good neighbours. I mean (quoth she) to retire all the French men forth of Scotland, who have given jealousy to the Queen, my good-sister, and mis-contentment to my subjects ; so as I will leave nothing undone to satisfy all parties, trusting the Queen, my good-sister, will do the like, and that from henceforth none of my disobedient subjects (if there be any such) shall find aid or support at her hands.† ''

I answered, '' That I was not desirous to fall in the discourse how those hard terms first began, nor by what means they were nourished ; because therein I must charge some party with injury, and peril offered to the Queen my mistress, which was the very ground of

The
arms of
England
were
usurped
those matters : But I was well assured there could be no better occasion offered to put the former unkindness in forgetfulness, than by ratifying the Treaty of Peace, for that should repay all injuries past. And Madam (quoth I), where it pleases you to suspend the Ratification, until you have the advices of the Nobles and Estates

Your
Papists
and ours
have
practised,
and still
practises
division.
So that
she might
have
England
and the
Pope's
religion,
I think
she lied not
of your realm, the Queen my mistress does nothing doubt of their conformity in this matter, because the Treaty was made by their consent.''

The Queen answered, '' Yea, by some of them, but not by all. It will appear, when I come amongst them, whether they be of the same mind that you say they were then of [or no] : But of this I assure you, Monsieur l'Ambassador [quoth she], I, for my part, am very desirous to have the perfect and the assured amity of the Queen, my good-sister, and will use all the means I can to give her occasion to think that I mean it indeed.''

I answered, '' Madam, the Queen my mistress, you may be

---

¹ Here used in the sense of *sarcasm*, or (because it was ' secret ') in the sense of a *double entendre*. (See Littré, *Dictionnaire de la Langue Française*, s.v. *lardon*.) These marginal notes, and the later notes in square brackets, form a kind of running commentary by Knox.

² ' When d'Oysel reached the English Court he was promptly, if not angrily, informed by Elizabeth that she would not grant Mary a safe-conduct unless she ratified the Treaty of Edinburgh ; and he was requested—instead of proceeding to Scotland—to go back to France with this message.' (Hay Fleming, *op. cit.*, 39, 240, *notes* 46, 47, 49)

assured, will use the like towards you, to move you to be of the same opinion towards her."

"Then (said she) I trust the Queen, your mistress, will not support nor encourage none of my subjects to continue in their disobedience, nor to take upon them things that appertain not to subjects."—[This we must answer here : It appertains to subjects to worship God as he has commanded, and to suppress idolatry, by whomsoever it be erected or maintained.] [1] *The fear of God in the heart of Elijah was disobedience to cursed Jezebel*

"You know (quoth she), there is much ado in my realm about matters of religion ; and though there be a greater number of a contrary religion unto me than I would there were, yet there is no reason that subjects should give a law to their Sovereign, and specially in matters of religion, which, I fear (quoth she), my subjects shall take in hand."—[Answer for the part of Scotland : and if so they had done, they had escaped God's indignation, which has been felt, and still hangs over this realm, for the idolatry and other abominations committed in the same, which shall not cease till that it be suppressed.] *God gives his law as well to the Prince as to the the subject*

I answered, "Madam, your realm is in no other case at this day, than all other realms of Christendom are ; the proof whereof you see verified in this realm : and you see what great difficulty it is to give order in this matter, though the King and all his Council be very desirous thereunto. Religion is of the greatest force that may be. You have been long out of your own realm, so as the contrary religion to yours has won the upper hand, and the greatest part of your realm. Your Mother was a woman of great experience, of deep dissimulation, and kept that realm in quietness, till she began to constrain men's consciences ; and as you think it unmeet to be constrained by your subjects, so it may like you to consider the matter is also intolerable to them to be constrained by you in matters of conscience ; for the duty due to God cannot be given to any other without offence of his Majesty." "Why (said she), God does command subjects to be obedient to their Princes, and commands Princes to read his law, and govern thereby themselves and the people committed to their charges." Answer, "Yea, Madam (quoth I), in those things that be not against his commandments." "Well (quoth she), I will be plain with you : the Religion that I profess, I take to be most acceptable to God : and, indeed, neither do I know nor desire to know any other. Constancy does become all *The consecration of the Cardinal will not suffer you*

[1] This, and the later notes in square brackets, being part of the running commentary by Knox.

folks well, but none better than Princes, and such as have rule over realms, and specially in matters of Religion." [The Turk is as constant in his Alcoram,[1] as the Pope and his sect are in his constitutions.] " I have been brought up (quoth she) in this Religion ; and who might credit me in any thing if I should show myself light in this case ; and though I be young and not well learned, yet have I heard this matter oft disputed by my Uncle my Lord Cardinal, with some that thought they could say somewhat in the matter ; and I found therein no great reason to change my opinion." [Neither yet did Caiaphas, when Christ Jesus did reason in his presence. But what was the Cardinal compelled to confess at Poissy ? [2]]

" Madam (quoth I) if you will judge well in that matter, you must be conversant in the Scriptures, which are the touchstone to try the right from the wrong. Peradventure, you are so partially affected to your Uncle's argument, that you could not indifferently consider the other party. Yet this I assure you, Madam (quoth I), your Uncle my Lord Cardinal, in conference with me about these matters, has confessed that there be great errors and abuses come into the *But the devil would put order to himself* Kirk, and great disorder in the ministers and clergy ; insomuch that he desired and wished that there might be a reformation of the one and of the other." " I have often times heard him say the like " (quoth she). Then I said, " Well, I trust God will inspire all you that be Princes, that there be some good order taken in this matter, so as there may be one unity in Religion through all Christendom."

Change it not before you have it ; for dancing and her sister is the ground of that which yet ye have professed " God grant (quoth she), but for my part, you may perceive I am none of those that will change my religion every year. And, as I told you in the beginning, I mean to constrain none of my subjects; but would wish that they were all as I am ; and I trust they should have no support to constrain me. I will send Monsieur d'Oysel (quoth she) to you before he go, to know whether you will any thing into England. I pray you, so order yourself in his matter betwix the Queen my good-sister and me, that there may be perfect and sure amity betwix us ; for I know (quoth she) ministers may do much good and harm."

I told her, " I would faithfully and truly make declaration of all that she had said unto me, unto your Majesty ; and trusted that she would so satisfy your Majesty by Monsieur d'Oysel in all things, as I should hereafter have no more occasions to treaty with her of any

---

[1] Alcoran, or Koran
[2] That is, at the Colloquy of Poissy (September 1561)

things but of the increase of amity." She said, "There should be no want therein on her behalf."

"This is the effect of the Queen of Scotland's answer to your Majesty's demand of her said Ratification, and of my negotiation with her at this time."

These advertisements somewhat exasperated the Queen of England, and not altogether without cause ; for the arms of England were before usurped by our Sovereign, and by her husband Francis ; and Elizabeth, Queen of England, was of the Guisians reputed little better than a bastard. It was appointed that this title should be renounced. But hereof had our proud and vainglorious Queen no pleasure, and especially after that her husband was dead ; for, thought she, the to-look [1] of England shall allure many wooers to me. The Guisians and the Papists of both the realms did not a little animate her in that pursuit ; the effect whereof will sooner appear than the godly of England would desire. And yet is she that now reigneth over them neither good Protestant nor yet resolute Papist : Let the world judge which is the third.

Queen Elizabeth, we say, offended with the former answers, wrote unto the Nobility and Estates of Scotland in form as follows :

THE QUEEN OF ENGLAND'S LETTER TO THE ESTATES OF SCOTLAND [2]

RIGHT trusty and right entirely beloved Cousins, we greet you. We doubt not, but as our meaning is, and has been always since our reign, in the sight of Almighty God straight and direct toward the advancement of his honour and truth in religion, and consequently to procure peace and maintain concord betwix both these realms of England and Scotland ; so also our outward acts have well declared the same to the world, and specially to you, being our neighbours, who have tasted and proved in these our friendship and earnest good will, more than we think any of your antecessors have ever received from hence ; yea, more than a great number of yourselves could well hope of us, all former examples being well weighed and considered. And this we have to rejoice of, and so may ye be glad, that where, in the beginning of the troubles in that country, and of our succours meant for you, the jealousy, or rather the malice

---

[1] prospect   [2] 1 July 1561. (Calendar of Scottish Papers, i, No. 993)

of divers, both in that realm and in other countries, was such, both to deprave [1] both us in the yielding, and you in requiring our aid, that we were noted to have meant the surprise of that realm, by depriving of your Sovereign the Queen of her crown, and you or the greater part of you to have intended by our succour the like; and either to prefer some other to the crown, or else to make of that monarchy a common-weal : matters very slanderous and false. But the end and determination, yea, the whole course and process of the action on both our parts have manifested, both to the slanderers, and to all others, that nothing was more meant and prosecuted than to establish your Sovereign the Queen, our cousin and sister, in her estate and crown, the possession whereof was in the hands of strangers. And although no words could then well satisfy the malicious, yet our deeds do declare that no other thing was sought, but the restitution of that realm to the ancient liberty, and, as it were, to redeem it from captivity. Of these our purposes and deeds there remains, amongst other arguments, good testimony by a solemn treaty and

The peace contracted at Leith

accord, made the last year at Edinburgh, by Commissioners sent both from us and from your Queen, with full authority in writing, under both our hands and the Great Seals of both our realms, in such manner as other Princes, our progenitors, have always used. By which treaty and accord, either of us fully accorded with other, to keep good peace and amity betwix ourselves, our countries, and subjects. And in the same also a good accord is made, not only of certain quarrels happened betwix us, but also of some differences betwix the Ministers of the late French King, your Sovereign's husband, and you the Estates of that realm, for the alteration of laws and customs of that country attempted by them. Upon which accord there made and concluded, has hitherto followed, as you know, surety to your Sovereign's estate, quietness to yourselves, and a better peace betwix both realms, than ever was heard of in any time past. Nevertheless, how it happeneth we know not, [—We can : for she [2] in her conceit thinks herself Queen of both], that your Sovereign either not knowing in this part her own felicity, or else dangerously seduced by perverse counsel, whereof we would be most sorry ; being of late at sundry times required by us, according to her Band remaining with us, signed with her own hand, and sealed

Princes little re-gard that

with the Great Seal of that realm, and allowed by you being the Estates of the same, to ratify her said Treaty, in like manner as we by writing have done, and are ready to deliver it to her, [yet she]

---

[1] *defame*   [2] That is, Mary Stewart. An interpolation by Knox.

maketh such dilatory answers thereinto [that] as what we shall judge *I think this sentence manck,[2] but I will alter no word* thereof we perceive by her answer that it is meet to require of you.[1] For although she has always answered, since the death of her husband, that in this matter she would first understand the minds of certain of you, before she would make answer ; and so having now of long time suspended our expectation, in the end, notwithstanding that she has had conference both by messengers, and by some of yourselves being with her, yet she still delays it, alleging to our Ambassador in France (who said that this Treaty was made by your consent) it was not by consent of you all ; and so would have us forbear, until she shall return in that her country. And now seeing that her answer depends, as it should seem, by her words, upon your opinions, we cannot but plainly let you all understand that this manner of answer, without some more fruit, cannot long content us. We have meant well to our sister your Queen in time of offence given to us by her. We did plainly, without dissimulation, charge[3] her in her own doubtful estate : whilst strangers possessed her realm, we stayed it from danger. And now, having promised to keep good peace with her, and you her subjects, we have hitherto observed it ; and shall be sorry if either she or you shall give us contrary cause. In a matter so profitable to both the realms, we think it strange that your Queen has no better advice : and therefore we do require you all, being the Estates of that realm upon whom the burden resteth, to consider this matter deeply, and to make us answer whereunto we may trust. And if you shall think meet she shall thus leave the peace imperfect, by breaking of her solemn promise, contrary to the order of all princes, we shall be well content to accept your answer, and shall be as careless to see the peace kept as ye shall give us cause ; and doubt not, by the grace of God, but whosoever of you shall first incline thereto shall soonest repent. You must be content with our plain writing. And, on the other side, if you continue all of one mind to have the peace inviolably kept, and shall so by your advice procure the Queen to ratify it, we also plainly promise you that we will also continue our good disposition to keep the same in such good terms

---

[1] Knox was not unnaturally puzzled by the syntax of this sentence ; hence his marginal note. The copy in the Public Record Office, London, was examined only to find that it agrees exactly with Knox's version. Originally the closing phrase ran " We have thought that it is meet to require of you " ; but the words " have thought " have been scored through, and the words " perceive by her answer " written above the line. The original version makes the meaning clear ; the amended version would have been clearer if the word " that " had also been scored through.

[2] *deficient*   [3] *maintain*

as now it is : and in so doing the honour of Almighty God shall be duly sought and promoted in both realms ; the Queen your Sovereign shall enjoy her state with surety ; and yourselves possess that which you have with tranquillity, to the increase of your families and posterities which by the frequent wars heretofore your ancestors never had long in one estate.

To conclude, We require you to advertise us of what mind you be, specially if you all continue in that mind that you mean to have the peace betwix both the realms perpetually kept. And if you shall forbear any long time to advertise us, ye shall give to us some occasion of doubt, whereof more hurt may grow than good.

From, &c.

These letters received and persused, albeit the Estates could not be convened, yet did the Council, and some others also in particular, return answers with reasonable diligence. The tenor of our [1] Letters was this :

PLEASE YOUR MAJESTY,

That with judgment we have advised [2] your Majesty's letters ; and, albeit the whole Estates could not suddenly be assembled, yet we thought expedient to signify somewhat of our minds unto your Majesty. Far be it from us that either we take upon us that infamy before the world or grudge of conscience before our God that we should lightly esteem the observation of that peace lately contracted betwix these two realms. By what motives our Sovereign delayeth the ratification thereof we cannot tell : but of us (of us, we say, Madam, that have in God's presence protested fidelity in our promises) her Grace has none. Your Majesty cannot be ignorant that in this realm there are many enemies ; and, further, that our Sovereign has Councillors whose judgments she in all such cases preferreth to ours. Our allegiance bindeth us not only reverently to speak and write of our Sovereign but also so to judge and think. And yet your Majesty may be well assured that in us shall be noted no blame if that peace be not ratified to your Majesty's contentment. For God is witness that our chief care in this earth, next the glory of our God, is that constant peace may remain betwix these two realms ; whereof your Majesty and realm shall have sure experience so long as our counsel or votes may stay the contrary. The benefit

[1] The use of the word " our " seems to indicate that Knox was one of the " some others in particular." [2] *considered*

that we have received is so recent that we cannot suddenly bury it in forgetfulness. We would desire your Majesty rather to be persuaded of us that we to our powers will study to leave it in remembrance to our posterity. And thus, with lawful and humble commendation of our service, we commit your Majesty to the protection of the Omnipotent.

Of Edinburgh, the 16 of July 1561.

There were some others that answered some of the ministers of England somewhat more sharply, and willed them not to accuse nor threaten so sharply till that they were able to convict such as had promised fidelity of some evident crime ; which, although they were able to lay to the charge of some, yet respect would be had to such as long had declared themselves constant procurers of quietness and peace.

The sudden arrival of the Queen [1] made great alteration even in the Council, as after we will hear. In this meantime the Papists, by surmising, troubled what they might. Their posts, letters, and complaints were from day to day directed, some to the Pope, some to the Cardinal of Lorraine, and some to our Queen. The principal of these couriers were, Master Steven Wilson,[2] Master John Leslie, called *Nolumus* and *Volumus*,[3] Master James Thornton,[4] and others such as lived, and still live, by the traffic of that Roman harlot.

The Preachers vehemently exhorted us [5] to establish THE BOOK OF DISCIPLINE by an Act and public law ; affirming, that and if they suffered things to hang in suspense, when God had given unto them sufficient power in their hands, they should after sob for it, but should not get it.

And now, because that divers times heretofore we have made mention of the said Book, we have thought expedient to insert the

[1] Queen Mary arrived in Leith harbour early in the morning of Tuesday, 19 August 1561, and landed later in the forenoon, resting for a short time in " Andro Lambis hous." (Hay Fleming, *Mary Queen of Scots*, 44. See also *infra*, ii, 7–8)

[2] Probably the same Wilson whom the Queen Regent described as a kinsman of William Chisholm [I], Bishop of Dunblane (*Calendar of Scottish Papers*, i, No. 797). He was for long an active partisan of Queen Mary (Laing's *Knox*, ii, 180, *note* 1 ; vi, 687) ; for certain of his activities, see Pollen, *Papal Negotiations with Mary Queen of Scots*, Scot. Hist. Soc., Index, *s.v.* Wilson, Stephen. [3] *Cf. supra*, 353.

[4] He appears to have become secretary to James Beaton, Archbishop of Glasgow, who fled to France at the time of the Reformation and became Mary's ambassador there. (Laing's *Knox*, ii, 180, *note* 3 ; vi, 687)

[5] The use of the word " us " again seems to indicate that Knox was " of the Council " (*cf. supra*, 372, *note* 1).

whole in this part of our HISTORY to the end that the posterities to come may judge as well what the worldlings refused, as what Policy the godly Ministers required ; that they (if God grant unto them occasion and liberty) may either establish a more perfect, or else imitate that which avariciousness would not suffer this corrupt generation to approve.[1]

[1] Here Knox inserts in full the Book of Discipline *ad perpetuam rei memoriam*. His text of the Book is printed *infra*, Appendix VIII.

END OF VOLUME ONE